MW00826500

BILLY WILDER

FILM AND CULTURE

FILM AND CULTURE

A series of Columbia University Press

Edited by John Belton

For a complete list of titles, see page 659.

ALSO BY JOSEPH McBRIDE

Frankly: Unmasking Frank Capra

How Did Lubitsch Do It?

Two Cheers for Hollywood: Joseph McBride on Movies

The Broken Places: A Memoir

Hawks on Hawks

*Into the Nightmare: My Search for the Killers of
President John F. Kennedy and Officer J. D. Tippit*

Steven Spielberg: A Biography

Writing in Pictures: Screenwriting Made (Mostly) Painless

*What Ever Happened to Orson Welles?: A Portrait of
an Independent Career*

Frank Capra: The Catastrophe of Success

Searching for John Ford

*The Book of Movie Lists: An Offbeat, Provocative Collection of
the Best and Worst of Everything in Movies*

High and Inside: An A-to-Z Guide to the Language of Baseball

Orson Welles

*Filmmakers on Filmmaking: The American Film Institute Seminars on
Motion Pictures and Television, Vols. 1 and 2* (editor)

Orson Welles: Actor and Director

Kirk Douglas

John Ford (with Michael Wilmington)

Focus on Howard Hawks (editor)

Persistence of Vision: A Collection of Film Criticism (editor)

To Joe McBride

Billy Wilder

Hollywood 78

BILLY WILDER

DANCING
ON THE
EDGE

JOSEPH McBRIDE

COLUMBIA UNIVERSITY PRESS
NEW YORK

Columbia University Press
Publishers Since 1893
New York   Chichester, West Sussex
cup.columbia.edu
Copyright © 2021 Joseph McBride
All rights reserved

Library of Congress Cataloging-in-Publication Data

Names: McBride, Joseph, 1947– author.
Title: Billy Wilder : Dancing on the edge / Joseph McBride.
Description: New York : Columbia University Press, [2021] | Includes bibliographical
    references, filmography, and index.
Identifiers: LCCN 2021004923 (print) | LCCN 2021004924 (ebook) |
    ISBN 9780231201469 (hardback) | ISBN 9780231554114 (ebook)
Subjects: LCSH: Wilder, Billy, 1906–2002. | Motion picture producers and
    directors—United States—Biography. | Austrians—United States—Biography. |
    Jews—United States—Biography. | Motion pictures—United States—
    History—20th century.
Classification: LCC PN1998.3.W56 M33 2021 (print) | LCC PN1998.3.W56 (ebook) |
    DDC 791.4302/32092 [B]—dc23
LC record available at https://lccn.loc.gov/2021004923
LC ebook record available at https://lccn.loc.gov/2021004924

Columbia University Press books are printed
on permanent and durable acid-free paper.
Printed in the United States of America

Cover and book design: Lisa Hamm

Cover image: Billy Wilder rehearsing a tango with Jack Lemmon
as "Daphne" in the cross-dressing comedy *Some Like It Hot* (1959).
United Artists/Photofest

Frontispiece: Billy Wilder in a studio publicity photo from the 1950s.

Do you remember my telling you earlier about that rooming house I lived in when I first was trying to get into the movies in Berlin? Well, next to my room was the can, and in it was a toilet that was on the blink. The water kept running all night long. I would lie there and listen to it, and since I was young and romantic, I'd imagine it was a beautiful waterfall—just to get my mind off the monotony of it and the thought of its being a can. Now we dissolve to 25 years later and I am finally rich enough to take a cure at Badgastein [now Bad Gastein], *the Austrian spa, where there is the most beautiful waterfall in the whole world. There I am in bed, listening to the waterfall. And after all I have been through, all the trouble and all the money I've made, all the awards and everything else, there I am in that resort, and all I can think of is that goddamned toilet. That, like the man says, is the story of my life.*

✳ *Billy Wilder, 1963*

For Ann

CONTENTS

BILLY WILDER

1.0 A caricature of the young "Racing Reporter" Billie Wilder from a February 1926 issue of Vienna's *Die Bühne* (*The Stage*). Wilder's Austrian biographers Andreas Hutter and Klaus Kamolz suspect he drew the portrait himself.

THE PHANTOMS
OF THE PAST

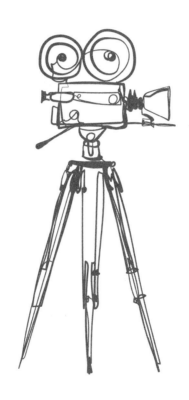

1.1 (top) Billie Wilder (*second from right*) and portly American bandleader Paul Whiteman when Wilder was brought to Berlin in 1926 as a publicist for his idol, an early sign of the young reporter's love for American culture.

1.2 (bottom) Wilder, as Billy the director, returns to the ruins of Berlin in 1947 while making his mordant romantic comedy-drama about postwar corruption, *A Foreign Affair* (a 1948 release). (Paramount/Photofest.)

1

AUSLÄNDISCH

A joke is an epitaph on an emotion.

—Friedrich Nietzsche

HAT FLYING OFF, overcoat billowing behind him, curly red hair blown back, the bespectacled young reporter grinned as he went about his work with a long, forward-leaning stride. Taking notes on the run as he dashed around for stories, Billy Wilder was caricatured in 1926 in a drawing for a Vienna magazine capturing the cocky, hyperactive spirit he displayed as a reporter there and, later, in Berlin, where he was called "Der rasende Reporter" (the Racing Reporter). Born Samuel Wilder, he went under the nickname of Billie but would change it to Billy after escaping Nazism for Hollywood and realizing that Billie was a female name in America. Wilder had a round, slyly impish face, often described as "cherubic." People who knew him only from photographs supposed that meant he was elfin in stature. They did not realize he stood an inch below six feet, an imposing figure who liked to swing a cane or a walking stick. His hunched-forward posture in the drawing came because he was so peripatetic, always going somewhere in a hurry.

Wilder's perpetually restless nature was the result of an early life in constant motion. Much of his childhood in the Austro-Hungarian Empire was spent in trains and hotel—his father, Max, ran cafés in railroad stations before settling into managing a Kraków hotel—and Billy's existence encompassed no fewer than five separate moves into exile. Or six if you count his later years in internal exile as a much-honored filmmaker who eventually found himself unable to work in Hollywood. His films are replete with hotel and train settings as his characters race from place to place, attempting to find their bearings. It doesn't take Sigmund Freud (his longtime bête noire) to recognize that Wilder's bustling energy and impatience were a symptom of enduring anxiety over his rootless condition, his unconscious need to keep moving in order to avoid being trapped. After his insecure upbringing—even if he professed to find it rather enjoyable to be a boy who, in his own words, "never could stand still"—and far more deeply after he fled Hitler in 1933 and emigrated to the United States, Wilder experienced the exile's essential feeling of never quite belonging or knowing a firm identity, always having to be ready to move again, no matter how safe you might feel at the moment.

That feeling never left him. In a rare moment of letting down his guard, he confessed to his German biographer Hellmuth Karasek in the 1970s, "I'm an old man now and have my special fears. I watch the daily obituaries in the newspapers and particularly note the age of the deceased. Most now are younger than me. I am frightened and think: Maybe I was just forgotten. After the obituaries I read the articles in which violent crimes and murders are reported. I find myself constantly having fearful thoughts as to whether the victim was a Jew."

Wilder was a compulsive entertainer. His work seems so accessible and easily intelligible, so beguiling and ostensibly transparent, yet there are troubling and obscure currents moving under its surface that have remained largely unexplored, and its overall shape, development, and raison d'être have remained somewhat mysterious. Beneath what seem the shadowy realms of his artistic personality are "the phantoms of the past," in the words of the mordant cabaret song by Frederick Holländer performed by Marlene Dietrich in Wilder's film *A Foreign Affair* (1948), set in the post–World War II ruins of his former haunt, Berlin. Those phantoms and the way they underlie his body of work as both a reporter and a filmmaker became the objects of my exploration in attempting to bring Wilder into sharper focus.

Even after settling into his more secure life in Hollywood, Wilder was rarely caught sitting. On the set, as Jack Lemmon put it, Wilder "was a live wire, he was a foot and a half off the ground and he had everybody else a foot and a half off the ground all day long with his energy level. He never sat down! I think if there's a picture of him sitting down it must be in the Smithsonian, I don't know—I've never seen one." His habit while writing scripts was to pace back and forth in the office, flicking a riding crop or cane or some other kind of stick, while his more sedate collaborator—there was almost always a collaborator—lay on a couch or sat at a typewriter reshaping the words that poured from Wilder's brain and mouth while the two men argued over how to improve them.* "Billy is too restless to sit at a typewriter," explained his longtime collaborator I. A. L. Diamond. Diamond's screenwriter son, Paul, said of Wilder, "Sharks don't sleep; they have to keep moving." One reason Wilder was such a live wire was that he would take uppers to maintain his energy level while shooting movies, something his second wife, Audrey, deplored.

Whether I was watching Wilder direct a film on a sound stage at Universal, interviewing him in his office in Beverly Hills, or presenting him with the Los Angeles Film Critics Association's career achievement award in a West Hollywood hotel in 1995, it was striking to see what a perpetual motion machine he was even in his old age. Wilder would prowl as he talked, waving his stick, chewing gum, and speaking briskly, spewing out quotable, well-crafted quips. During one of our interviews, he took a phone call and quickly turned down a pitch from a prominent but disreputable producer to remake one of his early screenplays, responding decisively but barely giving it a moment's thought. On the set, he roamed among the actors and crew, making nonstop wisecracks and pithy suggestions and enjoying repartee with visiting reporters and friends he always welcomed to kibitz. Wilder's restless nature also sprang from the psychological source blamed by his alter ego Sherlock Holmes in Wilder's film about the detective: "How I envy your mind, Watson. It's placid, imperturbable, prosaic. But my mind rebels against stagnation. It is like a racing engine tearing itself to pieces, because it's not connected up with the work for which it was built."

Wilder's habitual feeling of being *ausländisch* (foreign or alien) deeply influenced his work as a filmmaker. As a Jew who lived successively in several countries before finding refuge in Hollywood, he often resembled a cabaret artist darkly amusing his audience by dancing on the edge of an abyss. Even

---

* Wilder had solo screenplay credit only on the German films *The Devil's Reporter* (1929), *Emil and the Detectives* (1931), and *Once There Was a Waltz* (1932).

after becoming more secure in his success, he remained a perpetual outsider at heart, always conscious of his marginality. When a character in *Fiddler on the Roof* says, "Our forefathers have been forced out of many, many places at a moment's notice," Tevye makes a joke like Billy Wilder: "Maybe that's why we always wear our hats." Wilder's characters cross boundaries of every kind, physical, social, and psychological. They challenge and violate social mores, operate on the edges of the law, transgress what is considered proper behavior.

The conflicts in his stories are often motivated by class distinctions and dig deeply into the most dangerous realms of psychological disintegration and loss of identity. This often leads Wilder's characters into masquerading, hiding behind assumed identities for the sake of self-preservation or reinvention. The masquerade is a necessary state of being for an exile. It is a fluid state he obsessively replicates onscreen. Exiles by necessity find themselves having to create new identities, learn new languages and customs, and assume disguises of one kind or another for legitimate or quasi-legitimate reasons. For most Wilder characters, masquerading—or another variation, trying to pull off a fraud or scam—is a way of life, as the preoccupation with deception was for the filmmaker himself. But though his characters' shifting sense of identity is a source of peril, a temptation to self-annihilation, it is also a potential source of strength. His films often revolve around a character's need to maintain a personal core of integrity in the most compromising and seamiest of situations. He often expresses this risky condition ironically, with a wry amusement or a cutting edge of satire, a survival mechanism for an outsider accustomed to trying to fit into society without losing himself in the process.

That lifelong insecurity and restlessness extended to Wilder's often idiosyncratic choice of settings and subject matter. Although he enjoyed working in the comfort of Hollywood studio sets, he frequently went on location, including going to Europe to make films, especially in his later years. Thematically, too, Wilder resisted being pinned down, not wanting to be pigeonholed to one kind of film like Alfred Hitchcock or some other major directors. Though Wilder was best known as a satirist, he often made starkly dramatic films as well. He worked in a wide range of genres, including film noir, mysteries, social exposés, war movies, newspaper movies, romantic comedies, and even a musical. His restless enjoyment of jumping from one kind of story to another is also a legacy of his work as a racing reporter.

Within a Wilder film there is a considerable variety of modes, from comic to tragic and everything in between; the films often change tone from moment to moment. They resemble their maker in their brisk pacing and fast talking, though Wilder avoided trendy visual jumpiness, always striving for a visual elegance that resonated with a feeling of the Old World, not only that of Golden Age Hollywood but also the Europe of his youth. Wilder was a cosmopolitan sophisticate, an internationalist who maintained a sharp awareness and sense of perspective about the places where he lived. His work is extremely lucid, never obscure, always clear and direct in its communication with the audience, even while its themes and moods are complex. Its subtexts are often subtle and sometimes surprisingly elusive and allusive.

If Hollywood became in a real sense his home, as it did for his fellow émigré Ernst Lubitsch, Wilder fittingly chose to spend his final years not in a lavish Hollywood mansion but in an apartment, as if he still had his bags packed for a hasty departure. The maker of *The Apartment* lived with Audrey in posh but crowded digs, surrounded by works of modern art overflowing their high-rise condo on Wilshire Boulevard in Westwood. It was far more upscale than the modest and somewhat shabby one-bedroom Manhattan apartment, with only a few art posters for decoration, inhabited by Lemmon's Bud Baxter in that film, but both Wilder and his alter ego always had to worry about their jobs in a heartless, corrupt system.

"ONE OF THE TALENTED ONES"

Wilder reflected in 1970, "If I look back and if I say, 'Well, who would I like to be were I not myself?' I would have to say, naturally, Lubitsch."

Of the famous sign on the wall of his modest working writer's office on Little Santa Monica Boulevard in Beverly Hills, "How would Lubitsch do it?," I write in the introduction to my critical study *How Did Lubitsch Do It?* (2018):

Saul Steinberg, the *New Yorker* cartoonist, designed the sign expressly for Wilder. The lettering was elegant old-fashioned cursive, slanted to the right and shaded at its left edge with baroque curlicue. The rectangular gilt frame, with its suggestion of faded elegance, had a modernist shape of roughly Panavision proportions, like the splendid later films Wilder directed while emulating his mentor, including works of varied public reception such as *The Apartment, Avanti!,* and *The Private Life of Sherlock Holmes.* Lighting a cigar—in another homage to Lubitsch, who was rarely found without his Upmann—Wilder told an interviewer in 1989, "I made that sign. That I way I never allow myself to write one sentence that I would be ashamed to show to my great friend, Ernst Lubitsch."

The motto on Wilder's wall demonstrated his career-long aspiration to emulate the Lubitschean blend of comedy and drama, simultaneously mordant and romantic. Wilder admitted that Lubitsch set a nearly impossible standard: "Oh, if we were lucky, we sometimes managed a few feet of film here and there in our work that momentarily sparkled like Lubitsch. *Like* Lubitsch, not *real* Lubitsch." The German American director's films, such as *Trouble in Paradise, The Shop Around the Corner,* and *Ninotchka* (the latter of which Wilder helped write), explore with great subtlety how men and women should treat each other. Lubitsch's urbane, generous sensibility was honed over many years of adventuresome, precisely executed filmmaking in both Germany and the United States. As Jean Renoir wrote of Lubitsch, "He invented the modern Hollywood." With his tolerant, cosmopolitan attitude toward human behavior and sexuality in particular, Lubitsch brought a sophisticated flavor to the American cinema that, along with the other European filmmakers who followed him, helped transform the industry in their image.

But despite Wilder's considerable debt to Lubitsch, with whom critics often compare him, the differences in tone between their artistic signatures are as pronounced as their similarities. Wilder outlived his time, hanging on until the age of ninety-five, dying in 2002, so his lifespan was forty years longer than that of his mentor. Lubitsch was fourteen when Wilder was born, began directing films in Berlin when Wilder was eight, and died prematurely at fifty-five in 1947, five years after Wilder made his American directing debut. Lubitsch led the way to Hollywood for émigré filmmakers when he was brought over by Mary Pickford in 1922, and Wilder, with his dark sense of humor, described him as "one of the talented ones" who were called by Hollywood rather than having to flee the Nazis, as Wilder did in 1933. Émigré filmmakers, following Lubitsch's path, brought a worldlier and more sophisticated flavor to American filmmaking that helped transform the industry in their image.

Wilder earned his first two important Hollywood screenwriting credits in his formative experiences working with Lubitsch on *Bluebeard's Eighth Wife* (1938) and on the following year's *Ninotchka*. They became such close friends that Wilder moved in with Lubitsch in 1943 to care for him after one of his heart attacks. Who knows how Lubitsch would have fared if he had lived longer, into the period after the studio system collapsed, as it was beginning to do just when he died, or if he had been more of Wilder's directorial contemporary? Wilder knew. In his own waning days of bankability (in 1975), he remarked, "Ernst Lubitsch, who could do more with a closed door than most of today's directors can do with an open fly, would have had big problems in this market."

Wilder was always more ambivalent than Lubitsch, less nostalgic, about the world they had left behind. Although Lubitsch's Hollywood films to some extent romanticize the pageantry of the Austro-Hungarian Empire in which Wilder was born, they share a blend of bittersweet nostalgia and satirical mockery toward that society, in which neither of them, as Jews, would have been fully accepted. In Wilder's case the mockery of Vienna and his mentor's native Berlin has a far sharper edge than Lubitsch's more affectionate viewpoint toward the past. For a long time, nostalgia was regarded as a neurotic affliction, not as it is viewed today as the basking in a warm and fuzzy, often distorted past. Lubitsch's yearning for a place and time when he would not have been socially accepted was something of a neurosis, a stubborn refusal to face facts, and a form of wish-fulfillment.

In Wilder's case, after World War II there always remained not so much nostalgia as the very real temptation of going back to Europe to work, to revisit the scene of the crime, if not to live. Wilder was clearly conflicted about postwar Europe. He satirized contemporary Berlin scathingly in *A Foreign Affair* and *One, Two, Three*. But he romanticized Paris, where he had taken refuge for a year after leaving Germany, in such films as *Sabrina* and *Love in the Afternoon*. "Billy Wilder knew Paris inside out," his German director friend Volker Schlöndorff noted: "He knew the bars. He knew the best places to go. And he loved strolling around the city. It was heaven for Billy Wilder. It was the epitome of *savoir vivre* and of having succeeded. Berlin, that was the hardship, the adolescent phase, climbing the ladder, the struggle to make it. Hollywood was his job. And Paris—that was what life was about."

Wilder remembered discussing the question of returning to live in Europe when he was working with the U.S. Army in Germany after the war and talking with fellow filmmaker Emeric Pressburger, a Hungarian Jew who, like Wilder, worked on the script of *Emil and the Detectives* in their Berlin days. "We wondered where we should go now that the war was over," Wilder said. "None of us—I mean the émigrés—really knew where we stood. Should we go home? Where was home?" But that question answered itself for Wilder. Although he expressed admiration for the French classic *Madame de . . .* (*The Earrings of Madame de . . .*, 1953), directed by a fellow Jewish director, Max Ophüls, born Maximillian Oppenheimer in Germany, Wilder felt ambivalent about Ophüls's return home: "I would like to have made that film. One of the greats, Ophüls. But how could he go back to live in Germany after the war? He did that, you know."

And yet Wilder was drawn back to make films repeatedly in Germany (as late as *Fedora*, 1978), despite the fact that the world he knew had been destroyed in the war and members of his own family had been exterminated in the Holocaust. Unlike Lubitsch, Wilder had left Europe for Hollywood with little or no nostalgia for the pre–World War I imperial era in which he grew up. Although he and Lubitsch both lived through the Great War, Wilder's youth was considerably harsher. He had to help clean the streets of Vienna and stood in long lines for many hours for potatoes; at least Lubitsch, who was exempted from military service because, thanks to his father, he was a Russian citizen, was employed as an actor and director in the Berlin theater and films. Wilder's unsentimental education in his father's hotels, his dodgy pursuits as a street kid rebelling against his family, and his raffish work as a reporter ensured that he saw more of the seamy side of life at an early age.

Wilder's style is far more blunt and more jaundiced, in the style of a journalistic exposé, and Lubitsch's mellower, more delicate and distanced, although Wilder as he aged increasingly came around to the overtly romantic Lubitschean style. Wilder was always, in a sense, a reporter, eager to reveal unpleasant truths, however engagingly, and Lubitsch always remained a man of the theater, eager to please as well as enlighten.

Both Lubitsch and Wilder not only went to Hollywood to continue exercising their craft in relative creative freedom and luxury, but they also fully embraced their new country by becoming American citizens. Wilder was granted citizenship in 1940, four years after Lubitsch. They regarded that status with relief and gratitude. Both deeply loved their adopted homeland of the United States for giving them a haven, for its civil liberties, and for ensuring their greatest periods of success. And yet they both always remained partly European in their personalities, as would be expected of exiles, whether of the more (Lubitsch) or less (Wilder) voluntary kind. They both made films that are simultaneously American and European in their sensibilities.

WISE GUY

It was on a trip by Maximilian (Max) Hersch Mendel Wilder to one of his railway cafés, in the small Galician market town of Sucha (renamed Sucha Beskidzka in 1964, referring to the Beskidy Mountains), that Samuel Wilder was born to Eugenia Dittler Wilder on June 22, 1906. Later part of Poland, Galicia was then part of the Austro-Hungarian Empire. The choice of the name Samuel was in honor of his mother's grandfather. The family name was pronounced "Vill-duh" in the old country. In German, the name means "wild man," an apt connotation for a filmmaker who would become a mischievous social critic, an inveterate troublemaker.*

His mother, Genia (later Gitla), born in 1882 in Nowy Targ, Poland, loved American culture. She had lived in New York for several years, from 1896 onward, with an uncle who had a jewelry store before she returned home and married Max in 1903. She nicknamed Samuel "Billie" after the celebrated soldier, bison hunter, and showman Buffalo Bill Cody, whose *Buffalo Bill's Wild West* touring show she had watched with wonderment in Madison Square Garden, and after the fabled Western gunfighter Wild Bill Hickok. She called her boy "Wild Billie" in the Western games they played. (She did not, as Schlöndorff claims in his documentary on Wilder, nickname him after the psychopathic outlaw Billy the Kid.) Many Germans in Wilder's youth were fascinated by Western and Native American culture—novelist Karl May's Western fiction was hugely popular, including with young Billie—and one

---

* Ernst Lubitsch played a character named Wilder in a play directed by Max Reinhardt in Berlin, *Die Schäferinnen* (*The Shepherdesses*), aka *Ballet Nach Rameau* (*Ballet After Rameau*, 1916).

of the adolescent gang members in his German screenplay *Emil and the Detectives* (1931) is so obsessed with Americana that he dresses as an Indian, speaks only quasi–Native American lingo, and is called "The Flying Deer."

Since Wilder as a young man in Europe developed an intense fondness for American popular culture, especially jazz and movies, his American-sounding nickname was fitting. "Billie Wilder" was his byline as a reporter in Austria and Germany and his credit on German screenplays as well as on his first Hollywood film, the musical *Adorable* (1933, based without his involvement on a film he had written before his emigration from Europe to the United States in January 1934). After he came to Hollywood, he realized that his nickname was a feminine form, so he changed it in 1936. "Billy" proved to be a jaunty, unpretentious name for a filmmaker, and its American-ness was especially fitting for such a quintessentially American artist. Since he came from another country, it served as one of his many forms of protective coloration. But that breezy nickname, coupled with his penchant for comedy, perhaps gave some people an excuse to treat Wilder with less than the seriousness he deserved. Nevertheless, it fits the irreverent nature of his work and his straddling of American and European cultures. (This book will refer to him mostly as Billy Wilder but will call him Billie when relevant in context.)

Billie had an older brother, Wilhelm, or Willie, born in 1904, who left home as a teenager to live with relatives in London and preceded him to America in the early 1920s. Willie manufactured women's purses in New York before beginning a new career in 1945 as an undistinguished director and producer of Hollywood B movies. Billy rarely spoke about Willie beyond saying that "my brother is a dull son of a bitch." It sounds like a joke, but he wasn't kidding, for he told biographer Charlotte Chandler, "My brother and I never talked much. We were never close in anything except age. . . . We didn't share memories. We shared experiences. Then, we each remembered the experiences differently."

Billy Wilder inherited his roaming nature from both parents. His mother's family also ran hotels. She "had a hotel mentality, because she had always lived in hotels, and she had to leave places," he recalled. She met her husband when Max was working as the headwaiter at a Kraków hotel. Billy described his father as a somewhat feckless dreamer, a Don Quixote who could never quite succeed in business, especially after the family was forced to leave Galicia for Vienna. After selling his hotel, Max had to make do by running a trout farm or importing Swiss watches or selling leather goods. Nevertheless, Billy remembered a "wonderful childhood" spent largely on trains as they shuttled around while Max supervised his railroad cafés. It's not coincidental that trains and their romantic promise of freedom and adventure also feature prominently in a number of Billy's films, including his first feature as a director in America, *The Major and the Minor*, as well as *Some Like It Hot* and *The Private Life of Sherlock Holmes*. More sinister doings take place on trains in some Wilder films, notably in *Emil and the Detectives* and *Double Indemnity*.

Since Wilder spent most of his first ten years in Kraków, the ancient Polish capital that at the time was part of the Austro-Hungarian Empire, he hardly remembered his birthplace, the small town of Sucha, twenty-seven miles to the south. Now it is primarily a tourist center for the Beskidy Mountains, part of the Carpathians, where the vampire Court Orlok lives in F. W. Murnau's classic German silent film *Nosferatu*. Billy remembered that area only for the summer visits he would pay to his anxious grandmother Balbina Dittler Baldinger, a hotelier in Nowy Targ, who was always afraid of thieves. He fondly recalled, "I got a Rosebud sleigh from my grandmother. She gave me something." She was murdered by the Germans during World War II.

When Sucha finally got around to honoring its native son in 1996, naming a small street after Wilder that suitably leads to the train station, he was grateful but too old (ninety) and ill to make a return visit. At least that was his excuse. A film historian doing research into Wilder's roots in Sucha, Andreas Hutter, reported that even after the modest commemoration, there seemed to be little awareness of him among the townsfolk there, perhaps in part because the records of the local Jewish community had been lost in the war. The five hundred Jews living in Sucha had been sent to the Auschwitz-Birkenau death camp, only thirty-six miles away. "The town where I was born is still there, but the country is gone," Wilder commented. He also suggested, "If I had stayed there, I wouldn't be here to tell the tale, and they wouldn't have been naming a street after me."

After the family's move to Kraków in his early childhood, his father wanted a more stable existence, so he ran the four-story hotel at the foot of Wawel Castle. Max called his enterprise Hotel City (in English, which he thought made it seem more modern), and it included an outdoor terrace with band concerts, a restaurant, and a billiard room. Billie, who wised up early in life, became a prodigy as a billiard hustler. His biographer Maurice Zolotow would write in 1977, "A large hotel for transients and a gaming room, Billy believes, is a good school for a growing boy. 'I learned many things about human nature—none of them favorable,' he says."

His fascination with this transient and often amoral milieu would become another staple of his work. A number of Wilder's films—including *Five Graves to Cairo, Love in the Afternoon, Some Like It Hot, Irma la Douce,* and *Avanti!*, and two of the best films he wrote but did not direct, *Ninotchka* and *Hold Back the Dawn*—take place largely in hotels, whether raffish or luxurious (and even Bud Baxter's apartment in the film of that name functions as a hot-bed hotel). Hotel life, with its transience and colorful ambience, always seemed to Wilder a suitably unsentimental metaphor for the uncertainty of human existence and the vagaries of social transactions.

"TOO MUCH APPLE PIE"

When the Great War came, Poland was no haven for the Wilders or their fellow Jews. The family ultimately fled to Vienna, 206 miles from Kraków, because the Polish capital was endangered by advancing Russian troops. Just as Lubitsch's father had left Russia to escape pogroms, so too did the Wilders regard Russia as the more imminent threat to their safety.

The Austro-Hungarian Empire of Wilder's youth was an unwieldy conglomeration of states whose already tenuous ties were badly fraying in the early years of the twentieth century, before the Great War broke it asunder. Emperor Franz Josef I had ruled the sprawling monarchy since 1848. The bewhiskered old man was made melancholy by a series of personal tragedies, including the assassination of his wife and the mysterious death of his son and heir-apparent. The German Reich, ruled by the more vital Kaiser Wilhelm II, was growing in strength and ambition as its rival imperial power weakened. In Lubitsch's films, as in the Viennese operettas on which some were based, those waning days of the Austro-Hungarian Empire are the sunset of a world of old-fashioned grace and charm. That legend persists despite the reality of a hidebound aristocratic snobbery increasingly irrelevant and absurd in the industrialized modern age. Lubitsch's films gently mock that archaic world even while expressing a yearning for its illusory forms of elaborate civility.

The seductive trappings that disguised the backward, exclusionary policies of the empire were hardly to Wilder's taste. One of his most anomalous films is the musical *The Emperor Waltz* (1948). Set at the turn of the twentieth century, it revolves around the cultural conflicts that arise when a bumptious American gramophone salesman, Virgil Smith (Bing Crosby), travels to Austria to peddle his wares. Virgil aims to persuade Emperor Franz Josef I (Richard Haydn) to give him a license to sell his newfangled gadget. A pompous imperial courtier in Vienna tells him, "I protect His Majesty from that object just as I protect him from a bomb." Virgil swears he will put his machine over in that country, but the courtier replies, "Not in Austria, I assure you—we do not take to cheap, blatant innovations." Virgil sneers, "You're a bunch of dusty old aunties. You're scared of anything new. You wouldn't have put in the electric light only the emperor did. And you wouldn't have bought an automobile only the emperor did. Well, he's gonna buy the first one of these, do you hear me, and he's gonna endorse it." When Virgil later confronts the emperor about the snobbish disdain he has encountered, Franz Josef admits, "I don't say we are better. As a matter of fact, I think you are better. You are simpler; you are stronger. Ultimately, the world will be yours." "You bet it will!" declares Virgil, one of Wilder's many specimens of what would become known as the "Ugly American."

Though Franz Josef had long prided himself on treating his subjects equally, and Jews supposedly had equal rights under the 1867 constitution, the emperor privately harbored his own feelings of anti-Semitism, and anti-Semitic parties and politicians were a strong force in Austrian politics in the early 1900s. That poisonous mood in the capital, Vienna, played a major role in forming the character of Adolf Hitler, who lived there as an impoverished, failed art student from 1905 to 1913, leaving before the Wilders arrived.

"I remember the attitudes," Wilder said of Austria to his biographer Kevin Lally in 1993. His use of the present tense to describe those attitudes reflects just how strong his memories and feelings still were:

> I think that in the provinces, Nazism is strong, has been stronger than the German Nazism. Let us not forget that Mr. Hitler was Austrian. As they say now, the Austrians are absolute magicians—they have now convinced

the world that Beethoven was an Austrian and Hitler was a German. . . .
The most famous Austrians, whether it be Schnitzler or Mahler or Schoenberg, they were Jewish. The source of anti-Semitism, the bloodline, is the
lack of education. It is impossible to eradicate, it was impossible to do it
two thousand or four thousand years ago. They were always on the march.

Wilder's Vienna schoolmate Fred Zinnemann, the future director who
would work with him in Berlin as a crew member on the avant-garde silent
film *Menschen am Sonntag, ein Film ohne Schauspieler* (*People on Sunday, a Film
Without Actors*, 1930), wrote in his autobiography, "In Austria, discrimination
had been part of life since time immemorial. It was always there—oppressive,
often snide, sometimes hostile, seldom violent. It was in the air and one sensed
it at all levels, in school, at work and in society. A Jew was an outsider, a threat
to the country's culture." Zinnemann remembered Vienna as "a somber place"
because "the Allied blockade had done its work: there had been sawdust in
our bread, hardly any milk, and many kids were growing up with rickets and
soft bones. It was only after the Armistice in 1918 that food relief had been
brought from America by a large group of Quakers headed by Herbert Hoover.
For years afterwards we regarded all American visitors as our saviors, looking upon them in awe and fascination."

The Wilders, according to authoritative research by Andreas Hutter and
Klaus Kamolz for their biography *Billie Wilder: Eine europäische Karriere* (*Billie Wilder: A European Career*, 1998), probably did not move to Vienna until
the spring of 1916, considerably later than Billy often claimed. Wilder lived
in Vienna until 1926 and also found the Austrian capital much more anti-
Semitic than Berlin, at least until the final days leading up to the Third Reich.
Anti-Semitism was a familiar experience for him. His native province of
Galicia was considered a low-class, disreputable, rustic outback in the far
northeastern part of the empire. Jews from Galicia, about a tenth of the population, were held in particular contempt. Many had already come there
fleeing persecution in Russia, which bordered on Galicia, only to find virulent anti-Semitism there as well. At school in Vienna, Wilder was scorned as
a "dirty Polack." And during World War II about half of the six million Jews
killed in the Holocaust were exterminated in his native Poland. So the wan-
derings of the Wilders were part of a much wider pattern of their people's
rootlessness and search for something resembling a haven.

By the time Wilder made it to Berlin, he was a somewhat hardened, self-protective young man of twenty. He remembered his adolescent years in Vienna as a more vulnerable youngster who lived mostly in the streets rather than in his own home, where his mother often beat him and his father was a relatively weak figurehead. Wilder's writing partner Charles Brackett commented in his diary in 1946 about "Billy's feelings for his mother. She was a shrew and he never cared for her, so he says." As film scholar Nancy Steffen-Fluhr puts it, "Wilder was *ausländisch* even in his home."

Wilder was one of about two hundred thousand Jews living in Vienna; Jews also made up about a tenth of the total population of that city, which amounted to about two million in 1910. The postwar emigration of Jews from Russia and other areas increased the degree of anti-Semitism always latent in Vienna, and the inflationary cycle caused by the Great War and its aftermath only exacerbated the problem, causing Austrians to look for scapegoats, a role often assigned to Jews in times of historical crisis and change. When the empire crumbled, its sprawling, tenuous connections not surviving the war, Jews found themselves more vulnerable than they had been under the relatively protective old order of Franz Josef.

The strongest measure of the rejection the Wilder family had to face in Austria came in 1920, when Billie was fourteen. After the war, citizens of the former empire could apply for citizenship in Austria or in the state where their former homeland was located. In the Wilders' case, that would have been Poland, but his father opted to apply for Austrian citizenship. Max Wilder's claim was rejected in August 1920. To quote the official response: "The claim of acknowledgment of Austrian nationality is dismissed because Mr. Max Wilder was not able to bring proof that he belongs to the German majority of the population of Austria according to race and language" (i.e., because he was a Jew). When Hitler made his triumphant entry into Vienna in 1938 during the *Anschluss*, not only did he face little organized opposition, but what appeared to be a sizable majority of Austrians welcomed him and the Nazi takeover of their country. The last time before then that Billie visited Vienna, in 1935, and filled out a residence registration form, he declared, "Citizenship: Pole."

In his youth in Vienna, since Billie was considered something of a street punk, he was sent to Juranek, a gymnasium (secondary school) for problem youth. One reason he wound up there was that he was caught in class with what was considered a piece of pornography, a copy of an Egon Schiele nude drawing, "rather pornographic for its day. . . . I started inquiring about Schiele and he began my undying interest in art" as well as remaining one of his favorite artists. In Billie's later years at Juranek, he realized that the Hotel Stadion opposite his school was a hot-bed joint for prostitution. So he spent much of his time staring out the window and observing the action, research that would come in handy when he directed *Irma la Douce* (1963), his comedy hit about a good-hearted, matter-of-fact Parisian hooker (Shirley MacLaine) and an uptight but romantic policeman (Jack Lemmon) who becomes her pimp. In that ironically wholesome, pastel-colored romance about prostitution, an exotic array of amusingly named prostitutes (Amazon Annie, Lolita, Kiki the Cossack, the Zebra Twins, Mimi the MauMau, Suzette Wong) inhabit Alexander Trauner's gorgeous studio set of a seedy back street and its hot-bed hotel. Wilder drew from his own background in conjuring up this indulgent vision of rambunctious sleaziness, claiming that when he was old enough he purchased the services of a particularly comely prostitute at the Hotel Stadion who was called "Red Fritzi." He said they registered as Mr. and Mrs. Finsterbusch, the name of his professor of French.

Although Billie risked catching venereal disease on that occasion, his forays into delinquency came when he allegedly stole a motorcycle and cars. That might help explain why the protagonist of the first film he directed, the lively comedy-drama *Mauvaise graine* (*Bad Seed*, 1934), made in France and codirected by Alexandre Esway, is a young man from a respectable family who falls in with a gang of car thieves. No record exists, however, of Wilder getting into trouble with the law.

Chafing at what he called the "iron discipline" in schools of that era and probably hampered in his concentration on studies by his restless nature, Billie ignored his father's urging that he attend the University of Vienna law school. Although Jews made up a third of the student body, and Billie passed the entrance exam, he decided he did not want to become a lawyer. One of his schoolmates would have been another future director, Otto Preminger, the son of an attorney general in the empire; Preminger would play a memorable role in Wilder's World War II film *Stalag 17*, the sarcastic commandant of the German POW camp. But like Lubitsch before him, Billie was rebelling against the strong Jewish tradition of higher education, and after his apprenticeship as a reporter in Vienna and from 1926 onward in Berlin, he gradually turned to the outré, modernist art of motion pictures.

The year after Wilder left Vienna, Zinnemann, who also turned his back on a career in the law, went off to Paris to attend film school. Zinnemann remembered that in the 1920s, "an Austrian brand of Fascism had now begun to flourish; the Nazis were but a cloud on the horizon, but people no longer laughed at Hitler. His book, *Mein Kampf*, became obsessive reading, a gospel for millions. Boys came to school with swastikas in their lapels. 'Aren't you ashamed?' I asked one. 'I'm proud of it,' he said."

Wilder wrote sarcastically in a 1927 newspaper review of a Viennese show staged in Berlin, "Oh, we love Vienna. But not too much. Too sweet, too much apple pie, and too much whipped cream." That article making fun of "Viennese optimists" provided a further litany of clichéd local specialties and attractions the young wise-guy reporter could not help mocking, including pastries, waltzes, the Blue Danube, the Prater amusement park, and psychoanalysis. Wilder's bitterness toward the superficial sweetness of that society is understandable, as is his inability under the circumstances to directly express it; he was already learning how to encode his deepest feelings, a trait that would become a crucial protective device throughout his film career.

THE WILDERS AND THE HOLOCAUST

Part of the Wilder family saga was long thought to have ended in Auschwitz-Birkenau near Kraków. But that is not entirely true.

Although Billie's father died in 1928 while visiting his son in Berlin, Billie's mother, stepfather, and grandmother all died at the hands of the Nazis. After settling in America, Wilder traveled to Vienna in November 1935 in a desperate attempt to persuade his mother to flee to America, but she did not want to do so. Like many other Jews in endangered parts of Europe, she felt too rooted to leave, despite her earlier fondness for living in America. After returning as a widow to Kraków, she had married Bernard (Berl) Siedlisker, who ran a bottle stopper factory, in 1931. She did not share her son's awareness of the peril Austria faced from its native son, Hitler. After the end of the war, when Billy Wilder participated in the de-Nazification of the German film industry as a civilian attached to the U.S. Army, he tried to find out what had happened to his family members. Finally the Red Cross told him they apparently had died in Auschwitz, probably in 1941. That was what he usually said, although he sometimes thought that she may have died in the Kraków ghetto. Late in his life he also told his friend Fernando Trueba, the Spanish film director, "I am not sure, but I think they died in Terezin."* Wilder seldom spoke about his mother's death, but in 1996 he confessed to feeling "fury, tears, reproaches" over not taking her to America with him. "What is done is done, and cannot be undone."

Later a document, a Page of Testimony, turned up in the archives of Yad Vashem, the World Holocaust Remembrance Center in Israel, telling a different story of his mother's fate. Her half-brother Mikhael (Michael) Baldinger reported her as "murdered/perished" in 1943 in the Plaszów slave-labor camp, which was commanded by the notoriously psychopathic SS officer Amon Göth. Many of the inhabitants of Kraków's Jewish ghetto had been taken there in Nazi *Aktionen* (actions), culminating in the liquidation of the ghetto on March 13–14, 1943. In that cataclysmic event, two thousand Jews were killed and eight thousand others, those the Nazis considered able to work, were taken to the nearby Plaszów camp. From there, most were eventually sent to die in Auschwitz. But Genia/Gitla never made it there. Billy evidently never knew that she died in 1943 at the Plaszów camp. Her husband Berl had died in 1942 after being deported from Kraków the year before to the Belzec death camp in Poland, along with his son, Moritz David Siedlisker. Billy's grandmother and Genia's mother, Balbina Dittler Baldinger, was killed in Kraków in 1943, as Michael Baldinger also reported.

The liquidation of the Kraków ghetto is the harrowing centerpiece of Steven Spielberg's 1993 film *Schindler's List*, a sustained sequence of graphic violence that is shown helping turn the film's protagonist, businessman Oskar Schindler (Liam Neeson), to his mission of rescuing his Jewish workers from the control of Göth (Ralph Fiennes). Spielberg also depicts, with gruesome authenticity, scenes of terror and murder in the Plaszów camp under Göth, a sadist who killed inmates for sport, and the film contains harrowing scenes

---

* Also called Theresienstadt, Terezin was a concentration camp and ghetto near Prague where Jews from Vienna and elsewhere were sent. The Nazis cynically used it as a propaganda showcase, but it caused the deaths of about thirty-three thousand people and served as a waystation to extermination camps.

at Auschwitz. Wilder tried to buy the rights to Thomas Keneally's "nonfiction novel" about an unlikely hero during the Holocaust when it was published in 1982 as *Schindler's Ark*, but Universal's Sidney Sheinberg had already purchased Keneally's book. Wilder approached Universal but learned that Sheinberg hoped his protégé Spielberg would direct the film. Spielberg temporized for many years before going into production in 1992.

Spielberg's decision to commit to *Schindler's List* was delayed by his lingering anxiety and ambivalence about his Jewish heritage, along with his concern that he was not mature enough or emotionally ready to tackle such a demanding and painful subject. He tried to pass off the project to other directors, including Roman Polanski (who as a child had been part of the liquidation of the Kraków ghetto) and Martin Scorsese. Along the way, Wilder approached Spielberg about working on the film together, with Wilder directing and Spielberg producing or the other way around. But Spielberg was still in his long phase of rebelling against father figures in his life and work, and he seemed to exhibit an oedipal block when the possibility arose of working in the 1980s with celebrated older directors, including David Lean, Orson Welles, and Wilder.

Finally, in the early 1990s Wilder became determined to make *Schindler's List* as his final film, "as a memorial to most of my family, who went to Auschwitz." Knowing that his mother had died in the Plaszów camp might have shaken Wilder even more. He told Cameron Crowe that *Schindler's List* would have been his most personal picture. But ironically, Spielberg said Wilder helped convince him to finally activate the project: "He made me look very deeply inside myself when he was so passionate to do this. In a way he tested my resolve." Spielberg decided he had to make the film himself. The last time Wilder called to ask about collaborating, Spielberg had to tell him he was in active preproduction on *Schindler's List*, just a few months from shooting. Spielberg described that phone call as the most difficult conversation of his life.

Wilder told Crowe, "He was a gentleman, of course, and we acknowledged each other's strong desires. In the end, he could not give it up. He had to do it. I would have done it differently—not necessarily better." However devastated Wilder may have been by the news, he was gracious in his response. When he saw the film, "I was so moved afterwards that for an hour I couldn't utter a single word." He considered *Schindler's List* "the best movie ever" and

said that "they couldn't have gotten a better man. The movie is absolutely perfection." He wrote Spielberg a long letter of appreciation.

After his third viewing, Wilder wrote an article in German about the film,
pointedly choosing to print it in a liberal publication in Munich, where Hitler began his political career. His article for the Bavarian *Süddeutesche Zeitung Magazin* (*South German Newspaper Magazine*) was titled "Everywhere
Around You Could Only See Tissues." Wilder reported:

> Even after the first ten minutes I had forgotten it was a movie. I didn't care
> about camera angles and all that technical stuff—I was only enthralled with
> the total realism. It starts like a newsreel from the period—very difficult
> to stage, to make real. And believe me, these scenes are so authentic it
> makes you shiver. . . . the whole agony came up again. I sat there and saw
> on the screen how the Jews were driven together into the trains on which
> they were deported to the gas chambers, and I looked at the line of people,
> thinking—my mother has to be somewhere in that crowd. But I couldn't
> find her. . . .
>
> The most important feature of this film is: It proclaims for all time that
> these incredible atrocities really happened. We must not forget that. Over
> the years, dust settles on the history, it will be displaced, people will
> forget—young people grow up today without awareness of it, already doubt-
> ing that something horrible was really happening in cultured-Goethe-
> country. The Auschwitz Lie. Oh, say more and more people, concentration
> camps, gassing exist only in the imagination of the Jews. Allow me each
> time to ask the question: If the concentration camps and the gas chambers
> were all imagination, then please tell me, Where is my mother? Where can
> I find her?

The Holocaust shadowed Wilder's life and work in America. His failure
to do enough to get his mother and other relatives out of Europe in time, or
to ever see them again after 1935, tore at him in ways he seldom discussed.
As he often did, he kept his deepest feelings to himself or made jokes about
Hitler and Nazism in his films and elsewhere. When I visited Wilder's Beverly Hills office in 1978, he had a photograph of Hitler on his bulletin board,
with a newspaper clipping strategically attached by a tack in Der Führer's
groin area. The clipping was headed, "European Fare with a Jewish Flavor,"

and listed kosher restaurants in the Fairfax Avenue area of Los Angeles. Wilder's characteristically irreverent way of keeping the image of his mother's murderer always before his eyes as he worked on film projects served, like his films, to demonstrate the truth of Nietzsche's observation about the function of gallows humor.

Wilder may have tried long and hard to cauterize the emotions he felt about the Holocaust, but he could never bury them. Oblique echoes of the Holocaust can be discerned in some of his films, often slipping out in the most unexpected ways. One film that seems to confront the moral issues involved in the Holocaust directly is his newspaper film *Ace in the Hole* (1951), the story of an unscrupulous reporter who keeps a man trapped in a cave to prolong a scoop, with disastrous consequences. It was not coincidental that the uncompromisingly corrosive *Ace* was one of Wilder's biggest flops, partly since it indicts the American public that serves not only as the reporter's audience but also as his callous enablers. And it does so in ways that directly echo the indictment of the German public in *Die Todesmühlen* (*Death Mills*, 1945), a concentration-camp documentary that Wilder helped make, under the auspices of the American army, for German audiences. That two-reel film, assembled from Allied footage of death camps, was principally written as well as directed by a Czech filmmaker, Hans Burger, but Wilder helped edit the film while working with the army as a civilian. The trenchant English narration also seems to bear his imprint; Oskar Seidlin contributed to the narration as well. *Death Mills* was shown to mostly unwilling German civilian audiences; Wilder said he had the idea of withholding their ration allotments unless they sat through it.*

Steffen-Fluhr's provocative essay "Palimpsest: The Double Vision of Exile" (2011) analyzes Wilder films for disguised signs of Holocaust themes, finding them hidden in many nooks and crannies of his work. Gerd Gemünden, author of the critical study *A Foreign Affair: Billy Wilder's American Films* (2008), offers similar readings of Wilder's subtle double meanings, finding

---

* A few shots from *Death Mills* are shown in Orson Welles's *The Stranger* (1946), making that the first commercial film release to include actual Holocaust footage. In it a war crimes investigator for the Allies (Edward G. Robinson) is on the trail of an escaped Nazi (Welles) who "conceived the theory of genocide, mass depopulation of conquered countries." The investigator shows the footage from death camps to the naive American wife (Loretta Young) of the fugitive, who is masquerading as a teacher in a New England boys' school, to make her realize what kind of man her husband actually is.

them even in the first American film he directed, the romantic comedy *The Major and the Minor* (1942). Disarmingly frivolous in tone, this film actually deals with pedophilia, somehow getting it past the Hollywood censors. The film's sly introductory title card reads, "The Dutch bought New York from the Indians in 1626 and by May 1941 there wasn't an Indian left who regretted it." Although the ambiguous wording could be taken to mean that contemporary Indians would disapprove of what had become of their former land after it was turned into a concrete metropolis, it could also be read more literally, "there wasn't an Indian left."

A FILM AGAINST NOSTALGIA

The Emperor Waltz was long interpreted by critics as a failed Lubitsch homage. It is a sour and dispirited musical whose jokes fall unusually flat for Wilder and whose sumptuous Technicolor surface re-creating the Austro-Hungarian Empire has all the artifice of a Lubitsch musical but little of the charm or wit. And yet there seems to have been a hidden agenda to this strange (and excessively lavish) exercise in antinostalgia. Along with Wilder's very dark final film, *Buddy Buddy* (1981), a black comedy about hired killing and suicide, *The Emperor Waltz* shares the distinction of being one of only two films he directed that present themselves as comedies but are almost entirely devoid of actual humor; as such they leave critics searching for explanations of possible ulterior motives for their making.*

An original screenplay by Wilder with his longtime collaborator Brackett, *The Emperor Waltz* deals with the attempt by the brash American gramophone salesman, Crosby's Virgil, to woo a stylish but stuffy and secretly impoverished aristocrat (Joan Fontaine), mockingly named Countess Johanna Augusta Franziska von Stoltzenberg-Stoltzenberg. In what amounts to an extended traveling salesman joke, the boorish American relentlessly pursues the countess over the objections of her ultrasnobbish father, Baron Holenia (Roland Culver), that the marriage is unsuitable for reasons of class. That causes some bite, but the film's tiresome romantic complications (Crosby and

---

* A film that Wilder cowrote but did not direct, *What a Life* (1939), a "comedy" about teenagers, is also unfunny and depressing, probably reflecting his lack of affinity for such material.

Fontaine have remarkably little chemistry, underscoring how little that love story really matters) are paralleled more earnestly with a peculiar subplot, Virgil's attempt to mate his white fox terrier, Buttons, with the countess's black poodle, Scheherazade. Wilder gave his own mother that nickname for her storytelling abilities, her legacy to him. And in *Irma la Douce*, the title character quotes from Rimsky-Korsakov's symphonic suite *Scheherazade* while spinning erotic tales.

Since the mating of dogs in *The Emperor Waltz* is forbidden by the customs if not the laws of the empire, a deranged-looking veterinarian/Freudian dog psychiatrist, Dr. Zweiback (Sig Ruman), tries to drown the dogs on the order of Baron Holenia, supposedly to hide the awful truth from the emperor. It's not coincidental that for the role of the proto-Nazi doctor, Wilder cast the comic actor who was so memorable as Nazi Colonel "Concentration Camp" Ehrhardt in Lubitsch's black comedy, *To Be or Not to Be* (1942). The egalitarian American Virgil angrily prevents this canine extermination, in what Steffen-Fluhr, like some Wilder biographers, considers a thinly coded allusion to the Nazi genocide. Although Brackett, in a 1946 interview, said, "This time we're just having fun," Wilder slipped in a darker subtext, comparing the film to another work by Johann Strauss II, the opera *Die Fledermaus* (*The Bat*), which happened to be Hitler's favorite opera. Also alluding to the nightmarish sequence of the protagonist having the d.t.'s (delirium tremens) in his and Brackett's film *The Lost Weekend* (1945), Wilder slyly told the perennially clueless Hollywood columnist Louella Parsons that "instead of the bat and mouse, we're having Bing Crosby and Joan Fontaine."

Just how intentional the Holocaust theme was for Wilder or whether it emanated to some extent from his subconscious is not fully answerable by means of the director's stated intentions, and Brackett admitted on another occasion, "I don't suppose I ever understood it very well. I was sure Billy would know. After all, Vienna." Wilder told Crowe, "I was not up to making a musical. I don't know, I should have gone to a hospital or something, after being in Germany and cutting an hour-and-a-half [*sic*] documentary about the concentration camps in London." He also suggested that some form of psychological denial was involved, telling Charlotte Chandler, "The picture didn't come out [as] what I wanted, but that wasn't Crosby's fault. It was mine. I was looking back to my childhood in Austria—waltzes, Tyrolean hats, cream puffs—*shutting out what came later* [italics added]. I would like to have done the picture as a tribute to Lubitsch. A tribute to Lubitsch, it was not." Lubitsch, for his part, was not amused. He became angry when Wilder showed him the film, claiming Wilder had ripped off the comic parallelism of human and canine romances—not, in any case, the cleverest or most original of comic conceits—from one of his own projects. This is the only recorded instance of friction between Wilder and Lubitsch.

To allow the musical genre's requisite happy ending in *The Emperor Waltz*, and perhaps as a nod to the emperor's relative liberalism toward his Jewish subjects, Franz Josef eventually countermands the order to exterminate the dogs. Although the notion that this seemingly frivolous musical is a disguised Holocaust allegory may appear far-fetched, it is amply supported by the text and provides a viable explanation for why this otherwise inexplicable film was made shortly after World War II. Given that Wilder felt the need to make a film about the bygone empire and considered it a way of trying to clear his head after the troubling experience of returning to postwar Germany, he still could have chosen many different avenues of approach to the setting. In 1935 he had written an unfilmed screenplay, *The Austrian Mystery*, about the apparent double suicide, or murder-suicide, of the Austro-Hungarian crown prince, Rudolf, and his teenage mistress, Baroness Mary Vetsera, at Mayerling in 1889 (Erich von Stroheim's director-turned-servant in *Sunset Blvd.* is named Max von Mayerling).* Wilder's sardonic comment in later years on the Mayerling tragedy was, "It's always better to go to a hunting lodge and die with a prince than go to the Riviera with some schmuck" (that fate befalls Claudette Colbert with Gary Cooper in *Bluebeard's Eighth Wife*).

But of all the possibilities available for his Viennese musical, Wilder chose the fraught topic of forbidden mating amid class conflicts. Coming immediately after the Nazi Holocaust, such a choice, with its blatant echoes of the Nuremberg Laws forbidding intermarriage between Jews and "Aryans," could hardly have been coincidental. That Wilder made the film as a musical seems a form of canny subterfuge as well as a heavy form of irony, contrasting its schmaltzy Viennese waltzes and luxurious but decadent trappings with the underlying ghastliness of that now-vanished society. When you watch *The*

---

* A French film, *Mayerling*, released the year after Wilder wrote his script, cast Charles Boyer and Danielle Darrieux as the lovers and was directed by Anatole Litvak. It made a star of the young Darrieux, who had appeared in Wilder's directorial debut film, *Mauvaise graine* (1934).

Emperor Waltz with the Holocaust analogy in mind, the film's subtext seems to become increasingly overt as it goes along, hardly coded at all, accounting for its surprising grimness of tone.

The film's ambivalently satirical yet gracious portrait of the ancient, mustachioed emperor, who ruled for nearly sixty-eight years, including the first ten years of Wilder's life, expresses the filmmaker's conflicts over the land he once called home. Wilder often told the story of witnessing the emperor's grand funeral procession with his father on November 30, 1916, from the second floor of the Café Edison on Franz-Josef-Kai. Ten-year-old Billie stood on a marble table to watch the spectacle. As he recalled for Karasek, "Only later I heard that people watched the funeral—right during the horrors of the war, in all the misery and hunger—with silent indifference; at that time I was deeply impressed by its size and solemnity."

What most impressed him was the sight of the four-year-old Crown Prince Otto in his white hussar uniform: "I admired him, I envied him. He seemed to me the future of the world. . . . I dreamed myself into the white prince in the white uniform." Wilder never omitted the bitterly ironic twist to the story: About twenty-five years later, Otto von Habsburg, now making a living giving lectures on his family history to college students, came to visit Wilder at Paramount to pitch a film project about the old dynasty (not *The Emperor Waltz*). Wilder pointedly spent most of the hour-long meeting recalling for the former crown prince how he and his brother Willie had stood in lines for as long as sixteen hours for a handful of potatoes. The former crown prince's reaction to this account is not recorded, but Wilder recalled, "He wanted to know everything about Nelson Eddy and Jeanette MacDonald."

The character actor who plays the bewhiskered Franz Josef in Wilder's film, Richard Hayden, had a memorable role in Lubitsch's final completed film, *Cluny Brown* (1946), and he does his best as the emperor to put some quietly droll inflections on his lines, but his character is essentially melancholic. The very title of *The Emperor Waltz* in context is deeply ironic in light of the Nazi *Anschluss*, since it is borrowed from the "Kaiser-Walzer" (Emperor Waltz) composed by the part-Jewish "Waltz King" Johann Strauss II in 1889, in tribute to both Franz Josef and Kaiser Wilhelm and as a "toast of friendship" from Austria to Germany on the occasion of a visit to the kaiser. *The Emperor Waltz* begins by sarcastically listing some of the emperor's many hereditary titles, including King of Wilder's native Galicia, but conspicuously leaves out

"Duke of Auschwitz," which might have made the film's subtext too obvious to Hollywood.

By setting the film at the emperor's court and conspicuously involving Franz Josef himself in the issue of canine extinction or survival, however, Wilder's film insists on being read as more than a shaggy-dog comedy but as a political allegory. It is a pointed commentary, however oblique, on the so-called racial policies of the empire in which Wilder had been a subject, part of a family ostracized because of its lack of "breeding."

AUSLÄNDISCH

Shortly before Wilder's departure from Berlin in early 1933, he had witnessed a group of SS men beating to death an elderly Orthodox Jew near the Kaiser Wilhelm Church on February 26:

> I watched them beating an old Jew on the Zinnstrasse in broad daylight. Nearly thirty SS men. Strong guys. Butchers. They were writing *"Judenge-schäft"* [Jewish shop] on a store window when they saw the old man with his hat, long whiskers, and coat. They battered him mercilessly. And I was just standing there, completely helpless, with tears in my eyes and my fists clenched in my pockets. . . . I made a move, and my friends held me back, saying: "They'll kill you as well—you can't help him." That was when I knew how it was going to go, and *I* wasn't going to be there. . . . The next day was the Reichstag Fire.

Steffen-Fluhr cites that horrifying story of Wilder as evidence of "the vulnerability, the immense personal pain" that always existed beneath the veneer of his tough, wisecracking surface. She writes of the incident:

> He is in pain. And he is helpless. . . . That pain was inseparable from his Otherness. Wilder was never really *mishpokhe* [one of us]. Not in Poland where he was born into a family of itinerant German-speaking Jews. And not in anti-Semitic Vienna where he was baited as a "dirty Polack" throughout his schooling. . . . Helplessness—the fear of it and the illicit desire for

it—is the emotional pivot point around which Wilder's cinematic world turns. The issue at stake is the paradoxical relationship between *surviving* and *living*. The first rule of survival is "take care of yourself," something Wilder had been doing since he was a little boy. The desire to be "taken care of" was not only unmanly, in Nazi Germany it was deadly, especially for a Jew. And yet, as Wilder's films consistently demonstrate, the walls we build to protect ourselves can entomb us, blocking intimacy; and survival without intimacy is a living death.

Wilder regretfully admitted he failed to take Hitler seriously enough until he came to power, regarding him, as many others did until too late, as a crank, a "ridiculous figure" who would never gain enough support to rule Germany. And he told a story of his final days in Berlin, no doubt somewhat embellished or even perhaps a fantasy, of having come close enough to Hitler to assassinate him. Wilder claimed he happened to find himself not far from Hitler at a film premiere. Karasek writes in *Billy Wilder: A Close-up* (1992) that this close encounter took place (if it did at all) at the UFA-Palast am Zoo on February 2, 1933, less than a month before the Reichstag Fire of February 27. The film was the World War I submarine drama *Morgenrot* (*Dawn*), directed by Gustav Ucicky and Vernon Sewell. Wilder told Karasek that he did "not even nearly" shoot Hitler, explaining, "I lacked two things. Courage and a revolver."

Wilder's slowness to recognize the gravity of the threat of Nazism was an uncharacteristic lapse for the usually prescient young writer and represented a form of denial. "We believed that the nightmare would soon be gone," he told Karasek. "[Hitler's] electoral success was already on the wane." Wilder was on a skiing vacation in Davos, Switzerland, on January 30, 1933, with his girlfriend Hella Hartwig, the daughter of a pharmacist, when they heard the news by radio that Hitler had been named chancellor by President Paul von Hindenburg, the World War I icon whose strength and mental powers were flagging. Wilder surprised but reacted quickly, telling Hella, "I think it's time to go." She said they should first have some coffee and cake. He responded, "Hella, I mean it's time to walk away from Germany. We must return immediately to Berlin and from there possibly abroad." He began frantically selling off as many of his possessions as he could—included his beloved American

Graham-Paige blue sports convertible and Bauhaus furniture—to build up funds for exile. He took what he could get under the fire-sale circumstances, bringing in the equivalent of about a thousand dollars, or about $30,000 in today's money. He was about to become *ausländisch* again.

Even with the growing atmosphere of crisis, Wilder and Hella did not manage to leave for Paris until after the Reichstag Fire. The spectacularly brazen incident most likely was caused by the Nazis, though it was blamed on a Communist scapegoat. The torching of the parliament building would serve as a pretense for the newly appointed chancellor to push through an emergency decree limiting civil liberties, as well as strengthening the Nazi Party's representation in the Reichstag and leading to the Enabling Act of March 23 that gave Hitler dictatorial powers. Billie and Hella saw the fire while sitting in the Café Wien on the Kurfürstendamm, the fashionable street that served as the shopping, hotel, and dining center of Berlin. That conflagration dispelled any remaining illusions of safety.

Wilder told Karasek that they took "the next train" to Paris. But Hutter and Kamolz report that it was actually on March 30 that Billie and Hella finally managed to take a night train to Paris. Although it is understandable that it would have taken some time to get ready for their departure, it seems possible that Wilder exaggerated their speed to make for a more dramatic story (Fritz Lang took even more extreme liberties with his oft-told tale of how he supposedly fled Berlin more abruptly than he actually did). Wilder was among fifty thousand people who fled Germany in 1933, including many of the Jews working in the film industry. He hid his money in his hat band, and Hella had some gold coins provided by her parents that helped them survive over the next few months in Paris. They lived in a hotel filled with fellow refugees, including some people Wilder had known from Vienna and Berlin. Stories that he also departed with valuable rolled-up paintings are untrue, according to biographer Maurice Zolotow, who reports that Wilder did not own any such art at the time.

Wilder's final piece of journalism in Germany was published in *Der Querschnitt* (*The Cross-Section*) on March 3, 1933, four days after the fire, and it reflected the anguished mood of his impending departure. "How I Scrounged Money from Zaharoff" was an account of his brief encounter, not an interview, with the fabulously wealthy, mysterious, and elusive Greek arms dealer

Sir Basil Zaharoff, sometimes known as "The Merchant of Death."* Wilder tells how he once "burned to break the bank of Monte Carlo with my so-very-surefire system. I did not succeed." Kicked out of his hotel, he spent two days walking desperately back and forth between Monte Carlo and Nice, broke and tortured with hunger. He went to the train station and there, in the bookstore, chanced upon a volume featuring a photograph of Zaharoff, described as "the richest man in Europe." From his "hunger walks," he recognized Zaharoff and, knowing the tycoon's daily schedule, schemed to catch him on a park bench in Monte Carlo and pump him for money. Wilder was carrying an empty violin case, given to him by a friend so he could masquerade as a musician looking for work, which legitimized his wearing a tuxedo. After being "paralyzed" with nervousness, Wilder said, "Bonjour, M. Zaharoff," and the tycoon started talking about violin virtuosos. After a short while, Zaharoff complimented Wilder on being a violinist, not a gambler, rose, and walked away. The article suggests that Zaharoff dropped some money in Wilder's violin case.

It appears that the story stemmed from a prior trip Wilder had made to the gambling resort in Monaco with a girlfriend named Kitty Janson. According to biographer Ed Sikov, it was "several years" earlier that Wilder had been sent by *B. Z. am Mittag* (short for *Berlin Zeitung am Mittag*, or *Berlin Newspaper at Noon)* to do a week of travel reporting in Monte Carlo and quickly lost the five thousand marks he had been given to bet. But though the article relates that earlier experience, it has a dark tone that seems to reflect the writer's grim situation at the time of its publication, in the wake of Hitler's takeover. Describing himself as "the wreck without a centime," Wilder writes that he had been haunting the Monte Carlo train station, waiting for the train from Marseilles "for no reason. . . . Maybe I subconsciously wanted to throw myself before the locomotive." That confession of a suicidal impulse in an article printed at this critical juncture in his life, whether genuine or concocted for effect, is a foreshadowing of the opening of Wilder's German-made film *Fedora* (1978), which borrows the scene of a woman's suicide-by-train from Leo Tolstoy's novel *Anna Karenina*.

—

* Lubitsch had made a Hollywood musical titled *Monte Carlo* in 1930. Zaharoff served as a model for the central character in Kenneth Hawks's film *Such Men Are Dangerous* (1930) and for Orson Welles's protagonist in his film *Mr. Arkadin* (1955), who also contains elements of Joseph Stalin.

"CYNICAL?"

Although Wilder was alert and resourceful in fleeing the Nazis before it was too late, the story of his prompt decision to leave in the wake of the Reichstag Fire further accentuates what Steffen-Fluhr points out as his relative helplessness and suppressed rage over his status as a Jew in Berlin, his empty-handedness and inability to do anything in retaliation. Wilder's account of being unable to kill Hitler despite his report of proximity to him is the obverse of Quentin Tarantino's Jewish revenge fantasy in *Inglourious Basterds* (2009), which shows Hitler being assassinated at a film premiere, a spectacle that may be satisfying on one level but seems all the more infuriatingly frustrating precisely because it never happened. Issues of lack of empowerment, frustration, and self-defensiveness, both physical and emotional, would find haunting echoes in many of Wilder's films. However disguised their origins and diverse their expression, these are pervasive obsessions that underlie what is often simplistically described as the "cynical" surface of his work. Wilder's detractors often use that word, even today, to suggest that he somehow overreacted to the world he saw around him, that he should be taken to task for having what they seem to regard as his exaggeratedly bitter view of reality.

When I unthinkingly said to Wilder in 1978 that his romantic streak, more visible in his late work, had been "disguised before under a certain cynicism," he replied, "But if *I'm* cynical, what adjective do you have for Peckinpah pictures?" I said, "'Cynical' is another word in Hollywood for 'realistic.'" He responded, "I don't know. I think every play by Ibsen was cynical, right? Every play by Strindberg was cynical. . . . Now take, for instance, a picture like *The Apartment*. Did you really think that I went out of my way to dramatize things which did not exist? A society where things like this could not happen?"

I apologized to him for glibly using the word "cynical," saying, "I don't mean to stigmatize you with that word." But that word continues to pursue Wilder in the minds of his detractors, however absurdly in light of the social conditions he lived through and brought witness to in his work. I often feel that those who consider Wilder cynical fundamentally misunderstand his work. Some of those detractors must be living a Pollyanna existence, protected by a bodyguard of denial, despite (or more likely because of) the abundant evidence provided by the twentieth century, and beyond, that we do not live in the best of all possible worlds. And the fact that many of Wilder's

characters are cynical, or adopt a mask of cynicism to hide their lost innocence or submerged romanticism, does not mean that the films themselves
are cynical, a common fallacy of misinterpretation.

It can be argued, as I will do in this book, that Wilder explores and satirizes the dangers of cynicism. He shows how some of his characters manage
to transcend or escape that viewpoint, although others fail to do so, whether
tragically or comedically. Wilder's films reveal an anxiety about the despair
associated with modernity and mass culture in the darkening landscape he
lived through in Europe and the United States. His films shine a harsh spotlight on the increasingly jaded societies of both continents.

2.1 (top) In an ironic twist following her loss of sexual innocence, Brigitte Borchert's character finds a pine cone under her derrière in this frame enlargement from *People on Sunday* (1930), an experimental film by Wilder and others. (Filmstudio Berlin / Photofest.)

2.2 (bottom) Inge Landgut as an early Wilder heroine, the spunky and droll Pony Hutchen in *Emil and the Detectives* (1931), with Hans Joachim Schaufuss. Gerhard Lamprecht directed this comedy, which Wilder wrote from Erich Kästner's novel. (UFA / Photofest.)

2

"A KEEN OBSERVER"

OTTO LUDWIG PIFFL (Horst Buchholz): Is everybody in
    this world corrupt?
PERIPETCHIKOFF (Leon Askin): I don't know everybody.

—Wilder's film *One, Two, Three* (1961)

"GET UP! Write anecdotes!," Wilder's mother urged him each morning.
Or so he told his colleagues in his days as a reporter in Vienna. Since
Wilder was grateful to his mother for passing on her gift for storytelling, that
seems a fitting anecdote about his early development as a writer. Genia Wilder,
much of whose own life was spent on the move, seemed more supportive of
her son's fast-paced aspirations than his more conventional, if also peripatetic,
father. If Billie had become a lawyer as his father wished, he would have been
more respectable in those days but never would have been heard of in the
greater world and might not have survived the coming of Hitler.

Wilder often told the suitably salacious story, like a scene in an Arthur
Schnitzler play, of how he broke into journalism when he was only eighteen.
Under the thrall of the glamorously raffish American reporters he had seen
in newsreels, "I was brash, bursting with fury, had a talent for exaggeration,
and was convinced that I would learn in a very short time to ask shameless,
uninhibited questions." Refusing to be deterred after receiving a form letter
of rejection in December 1924 from *The Stage*, a weekly tabloid theater and

cultural magazine in Vienna, he showed up at the office during the lunch hour with a letter of introduction from a high school teacher. Wilder said he caught one of the editors *in flagrante delicto* with his secretary on a couch.* The cocky young man cracked to the editor that he was, "as they say, at the right time at the right place." When the nonplussed editor, buttoning his pants and summoning up a vestige of dignity, demanded to know what experience he had, Wilder cannily replied, "I am a keen observer." The editor told him, "You are hired."

The most authoritative Wilder biographers, Andreas Hutter, Klaus Kamolz, and Ed Sikov, debunk this colorful yarn. They report that Wilder actually was hired on a piecemeal basis by another man, the puzzle editor of *The Stage*, Maximilian Kraemer. Wilder told Hutter, "I made up crossword puzzles. That was the beginning of my career as a journalist." That humble craft accounted for much of Wilder's earliest work in the trade, yet he enjoyed it, since he had inherited a fondness for crossword puzzles from his mother, and it gratified his playful love of words. Wilder's philological bent was displayed incandescently in his career as a screenwriter and never more brilliantly than with his and Charles Brackett's script for the Howard Hawks screwball comedy *Ball of Fire* (1941), about an English professor conducting a raucous field study of slang.

Wilder's first piece of actual reportage in *The Stage*—written after his first puzzle was accepted but before it ran—was a January 22, 1925, profile by Billie S. Wilder of the Hungarian stage actress and operetta prima donna Sári Fedák. She was not only the divorced wife of the great playwright Ferenc Molnár but reportedly also the mistress of the publisher of *The Stage*, a shady Hungarian expatriate named Imré Békessy. Békessy's Kronos Verlag also put out a daily Vienna tabloid, *Die Stunde* (*The Hour*), and Wilder found assignments there as well, writing as a freelancer for both outlets simultaneously. He worked for them regularly until June 1926, when he hurriedly left for Berlin. In the livelier German capital, he gradually cobbled together an increasingly successful but often precarious career as a newspaper and magazine reporter while he continued contributing sporadically to the two Vienna newspapers until 1927. There are two invaluable books in German

---

* When Hellmuth Karasek asked Wilder in 1988 how he wanted to die, Wilder replied, "At 104 years old, healthy, shot by a husband who just caught me with his young wife *in flagrante delicto*."

collecting Wilder's journalism in Vienna and Berlin.* The fact that it took until 2021 for a collection of his journalism to be published in translation in the United States, *Billy Wilder on Assignment: Dispatches from Weimar Berlin and Interwar Vienna*, shows how much more seriously he was regarded for many years in the culture he had to leave behind than in his adopted country. Wilder told students at an American Film Institute seminar in 1976, "I myself started as a writer and still regard myself as a writer." He admitted he became a director largely to protect his scripts from the ham-handed tampering of other directors. So this study, in addition to analyzing Wilder's career as a writer-director, examines in detail his early work as a reporter and as a screenwriter for hire in Europe and the United States. Some of his long-neglected early reportage contains germs of his future films as a screenwriter and director in Berlin and Hollywood. Relatively little commentary has been written on his formative years as a screenwriter before he became a director. The French film he codirected, *Mauvaise graine*, remains little-known. Even some of the films he cowrote in the United States before directing his first Hollywood film in 1942 remain hard to see, so the critical literature on those titles is also scant. This book takes on the challenge of studying the full range of his career on both continents, the only way to get a full sense of his development as an artist.

The kaleidoscopic array of Wilder's reportage sheds light on how the young man who disdained attending college found his true education as a precocious man of the world. His savoir faire was acquired strenuously on the streets of the two great capitals, benefiting from a reporter's license to talk to anyone and everybody. Taking advantage of his energy, inexhaustible curiosity, natural brashness, and quick-witted sense of observation, Wilder's journalism ranges widely in subject matter, presaging the versatility he prized as a filmmaker and providing precursors of his film plots, characters, and obsessions.

His journalism devotes as much attention to obscure people—such as a man who spent his life building a castle out of matchboxes, or a young woman

---

* Rolf Aurich, Andreas Hutter, Wolfgang Jacobsen, and Günter Krenn, ed., *"Billie": Billy Wilders Wiener journalistische Arbeiten* (*"Billie": Billy Wilder's Viennese Journalism*) (2006); and *Der Prinz von Wales geht auf Urlaub: Berliner Reportagen, Feuilletons und Kritiken der zwanziger Jahre* (*The Prince of Wales Is Going on Vacation: Berlin Reports, Features and Reviews of the Twenties*), collected by Klaus Siebenhaar (1996).

encountered outside Christopher Columbus's birthplace in Genoa who didn't know who Columbus was—as to the celebrities he encountered in his jaunts around the continent. He wrote profiles of famous or notorious figures in the worlds of finance and show business (such as the actors Asta Nielsen and Adolphe Menjou, who was "already in peak form" in Ernst Lubitsch's *The Marriage Circle* [1924], and the opera singer Feodor Chaliapin Sr.) and other human interest stories, as well as frequent sports reporting, including profiles of athletes. Wilder also reviewed plays, operettas, and occasional movies. While working on stories in collaboration with press photographers, in the days when photojournalism was an innovation, Wilder acquired what could be considered some early "directing" experience.

Maurice Zolotow writes that when Wilder was a reporter and screenwriter in Berlin, he thought the incongruous look of his "ungainly mane" of red hair

made him look—well, *wrong*, for his boulevardier disguise. That's when he started wearing hats indoors and out-of-doors. If you looked at him more closely and saw the world-weariness in his eyes, you knew that this lad had lived—yes, he had been around the *strasse* a couple of times. As [Paul] Kohner [Wilder's longtime friend, producer, and agent] remarks, "Already in Berlin he was a man who has suffered and knows everything. Yes, he seemed to know everything. Yes, he seemed to know everything about everything. And only twenty-five—it was not be to be believed. As we say, he was *mit allen Wassern gewaschen, und mit allen Hunden gehetzt*. [That means, "He had been washed in all the waters, and pursued by all the dogs."]

FORESHADOWINGS

The pièce de résistance of Wilder's work as a journalist was his four-part 1927 series, "'Herr Ober, bitte einen Tänzer!': Aus dem Leben eines Eintänzers," or "'Waiter, Bring Me a Dancer!': From the Life of an *Eintänzer*."* It was published in both Berlin and Vienna. As that series (to be covered in detail later in

---

* The subtitle to the series would have recalled for German readers Joseph Freiherr von Eichendorff's novella *Aus dem Leben eines Taugenichts* (1826), whose title is rendered in English as *Memoirs of a Good-for-Nothing*. The popular romantic novella is about a low-class son of a miller who rejects his father's trade and falls in love with the adopted daughter of a duke in Vienna.

this chapter) demonstrates, Wilder's early journalism shows an already keen sense of how to grab an audience, illuminate a subject, mix up genres and tones as he does in his film work, and offer wry or sober social commentary.

Journalists in Vienna and Berlin were given considerable license to offer personal comments in "Feuilletons," essayistic pieces containing criticism and literary or even fictional elements. Wilder's journalism shows how he learned to write with such freedom without succumbing to pretension. His stories were often jaunty and jokey but not as sarcastic as one might expect from his later reputation—although one brief vignette in Vienna about a kid getting a toy machine gun for Christmas jumps off the page: "On Christmas Day, little Wotan Wotawa will play with the Christmas gift, and his father will buy him ammunition for New Year's. . . . A sign of the times: the boy gets a machine gun and ventures out on his own." And some other articles, especially a piece about an aging actress, Helene Odilon, show a sense of genuine, understated pathos in Wilder's youthful work that points to his later ability to find emotion in unexpected places and people onscreen.

The haunting February 1926 article in *The Hour* about Odilon, a fifty-three-year old former theater star, seems an uncanny precursor to Wilder's depiction of the plight of the nearly forgotten fifty-year-old silent movie actress Norma Desmond, played by Gloria Swanson in his classic 1950 film *Sunset Blvd.* Wilder offered a candid and compassionate vignette about Odilon's return to Vienna by train on the Salzburg Express while hobbling in poor condition from the long effects of a stroke:

> Yes, this is Helene Odilon. I'm a bit distraught. Well, I knew the lot of the poor woman, but that tragic sight I did not expect. . . . She does not sound sad. Optimism emanates from her words: "I will soon find a sketch I can do sitting. I'll be all right. I would even play a major role. I do not yet know where. I'll be all right." The poor woman is thinking of Sarah Bernhardt. . . . I accompany the ladies [Odilon and her aging female companion] to the tram, help them into the car, put the luggage next to her. She lives in Ottakring [a district of Vienna] with friends.

There the story eloquently trails off like Norma Desmond going out of focus in her final close-up as she addresses "just us and the cameras and those wonderful people out there in the dark."

Another prominent figure Wilder interviewed for *The Hour* was the young American publishing magnate Cornelius Vanderbilt IV. He told Wilder in Berlin that he carried "not much" money, though for Vanderbilt not much meant 250 marks, or about 1,000 euros today. He bummed a meal from the reporter, even though, Wilder claimed, Vanderbilt was "so rich he could buy [the famous Berlin boulevard] Unter den Linden for fun, together with the Brandenburg Gate."

Still, with the notable exception of his unusually long (about five thousand words) and ambitious account of working as an *Eintänzer*, which has the complexity of tone of his mature work as a filmmaker, Wilder's journalism does not show as much supple ability to combine comedy and drama as might be expected, perhaps because most of his short essays or reports had to punch a brief point or two across without too much complication. Or, just as likely, because the difficult combination of comedy and drama would take more time for him to fully master.

Wilder's versatility, curiosity, and facility as a reporter come across in his work in both Vienna and Berlin, but those qualities do not necessarily indicate that he would have become a major journalistic talent if he had not diverted his attention to films. His piece "The Prince of Wales Is Going on Vacation" in the *Berliner Börsen-Courier* (*Berlin Stock Exchange Courier*) in August 1927 is cleverly written and even prescient in its observations, while also showing his journalistic limitations. Wilder characterizes Britain's future ill-fated King Edward VIII, who would reveal himself as a fascist sympathizer during the Nazi era, with some puzzlement as "a funny boy [a phrase the reporter renders in English], a handsome guy" escaping his life of incognito barhopping and sporting events in England while absurdly trying to lead a rugged life on his Canadian ranch. Describing the prince having to change clothes constantly for press interviews and pointless receptions with the locals, Wilder noted, "So how does the world's most popular young man [a phrase also rendered in English] feel, the world's most famous young man? Bored and very unhappy."*

---

* When Jack Lemmon's 1920s Chicago reporter, Hildy Johnson, makes his entrance at his newspaper office in Wilder's film *The Front Page* (1974) wearing fancy clothes and singing to himself because he's planning to get married, another reporter calls out, "Look at him! Prince of Wales!"

Wilder's article, evidently written without the benefit of a meeting with the subject, pales by contrast with a classic piece of journalism to which it bears a distinct resemblance, H. L. Mencken's *Baltimore Evening Sun* column in 1926 on the late film idol Rudolph Valentino. Wilder had the acuity to discern from afar the sadness behind the shallowness of the prince's existence, but Mencken, after meeting Valentino shortly before the actor's unexpected death, wrote with greater eloquence of "the whole grotesque futility of his life . . . the agony of a man of relatively civilized feelings thrown into a situation of intolerable vulgarity" in having to prove his manhood against homophobic attacks in the press. Mencken memorably concluded, "Here was a young man who was living daily the dream of millions of other men. Here was one who was catnip to women. Here was one who had wealth and fame. And here was one who was very unhappy."

Both of these notorious "cynics," Mencken and Wilder, revealed generous streaks of compassion in their portraits of such public figures, the prince and the movie idol. But Mencken went much deeper in his eloquent analysis, because he was already the master of the profession, far more experienced and prominent than a cub reporter fifteen years his junior. And Mencken had the benefit of an intense tête-à-tête with his anguished subject.

Naturally, even in the German collections of Wilder's journalism, there is a fair amount of the run-of-the-mill copy every young reporter has to churn out to earn a paycheck—articles dutifully listing members of high society attending unremarkable gatherings, make-work accounts of such mundane subjects as the mud and the smells of city life, and even stories about the weather, that most crushingly mundane of subjects and the bane of any reporter's apprenticeship. Even so, such duties give a young writer quick adaptability and facility, qualities that would serve Wilder well once he became a screenwriter and director, particularly one who so prized his versatility.

Nevertheless, during his time as a cub reporter, Wilder had to endure some of the most distasteful aspects of the profession. He recalled that in Vienna, "I had to get up, early, at five clock, take the Tramway and go to the parents of a murderer, to ask them for picture of their son, or to visit someone whose entire family had died in a fire. It was very unpleasant." Wilder during his Berlin newspaper days even gained knowledge of female impersonation by offering advice to ladies (tips on beauty, fashion, health, etc.) while posing for *Tempo* as a "female" columnist, a German woman or a Parisienne named

"Raymonde Latour"—shades of Nathanael West's *Miss Lonelyhearts* and Wilder's own cross-dressing romp, *Some Like It Hot.*

But there is much more to Wilder's early journalistic career than mundane or unpleasant make-work. He crafted many clever pieces of essayistic reportage, combining acute observations of the life around him, skillfully arranged to make their dramatic or comedic points, and taking advantage of the chatty approach to offer cogent commentaries on what he was witnessing. Even though the youthful enthusiasm in these stories does not reveal a fully mature talent, it is already free from immature clumsiness and flippancy and shows ample signs of Wilder's later skills and idiosyncratic interests.

If not all of Wilder's stories are gems, they are all fast-paced, professional, and filled with sharply observed atmospheric details. His eye for people is even more acute, as might be expected of a future filmmaker, and the relatively free style of journalism in that age allowed him to put himself into his stories, describing their contexts and settings, making him a direct observer and audience surrogate. He often approaches a subject from an oblique angle before circling around to his central kernel of interest. His interviews with the publicist or the wife of his ostensible subject, or accounts of how he tracked down interview subjects at train stations or in other public places, are as fascinating as their news value, which is sometimes the slightest aspect of the work.

These stories show Wilder rapidly developing a solid sense of storytelling structure, a vivid unfolding of incidents building to a dramatic or ironic climax, as one would see in cinema. Going into screenwriting, as he did in Berlin in the late 1920s, was a natural progression. However wacky or ephemeral some of his journalism was, Wilder later pointed out that his eagerness to keep exploring new forms and material, which persisted throughout his film career, stemmed from his time as a reporter. He went to work each day in a state of excitement, not knowing what would turn up and relishing the challenge.

BELOVED WILDER APOCRYPHA

A storyteller's apocrypha tells as much about him and his self-image as the actuality of his existence. Wilder "printed the legend" in various ways about his newspaper days, most famously with a possibly tall tale about an abortive encounter with none other than Sigmund Freud. Wilder also suggested he was a hard-boiled crime reporter, for which there is little evidence. As might be expected, he tended to focus his attention more on "human interest" stories, the colorful kind that prepared him for a career as a cinematic dramatist.

Wilder's quintessential newspaper yarn was of being sent by *The Hour* in 1925 to interview for a single article four of the most prominent inhabitants of Vienna: Freud and fellow psychoanalyst Alfred Adler, composer Richard Strauss, and playwright and novelist Arthur Schnitzler. Wilder told me that the tabloid sent him out to see them when it was canvassing prominent people for its Christmas edition on what they thought of the new political sensation in Rome, Benito Mussolini, and his Fascist movement. Wilder usually claimed that he went to interview all four luminaries on a single day, although when I asked him, he somewhat sheepishly said it actually took him two days.

Wilder said he managed to interview Adler, best known for his emphasis on the inferiority complex; Strauss, celebrated for such works as the opera *Der Rosenkavalier* and the tone poem *Also sprach Zarathustra*; and Schnitzler, whose works, often breaking ground by dealing frankly with sexuality, include the play *Reigen* (*La Ronde*), filmed by Max Ophüls, and *Traumnovelle* (*Dream Novella*), filmed by Stanley Kubrick. Wilder shared a deep affinity for the work of Schnitzler, although he did not film any of his works. Wilder's longtime screenwriting partner I. A. L. Diamond observed that the director was part of "an old Viennese tradition that comes down from Schnitzler. It is a Middle European attitude, a combination of cynicism and romanticism. The cynicism is sort of disappointed romanticism at heart—someone [critic Andrew Sarris] once described it as whipped cream that's gotten slightly curdled."

The climax of Wilder's journalistic yarn about that fabulous article was always his visit to Freud's apartment, where he saw *"the* couch" and interrupted the doctor at lunch. When Freud appeared, wearing a napkin as a bib, Wilder displayed his card identifying himself as "BILLIE S. WILDER/Reporter der STUNDE." Freud, who was allergic to reporters, supposedly pointed to the door and said one word, *"Raus!"* (Get out)

A great story, but Hutter and Kamolz could not find any evidence that Wilder ever went to interview those four men, and no such interviews appear in the comprehensive collection of his Viennese journalism. Maybe that absence indicates that Wilder struck out with all four subjects, not only with Freud. But in any case, Wilder vividly told the anecdote, whether imaginary or not, and it evidently carried a strong metaphorical truth for him, if the proliferation of absurd and even sinister psychiatrists in his film work is any indication of his need to get back at Freud and his brethren for some obscure offense. With only rare exceptions, psychoanalysis, already fashionable in the 1920s, was a bête noire in his films and interviews to the end of his days. Perhaps Wilder's hostility was a manifestation of what is known as "the anxiety of influence," for as a dramatist himself of acute psychological perception, he had a certain affinity for Freud, a fellow Viennese of Galician Jewish ancestry and the author of *Wit and Its Relation to the Unconscious*. Wilder's work is steeped in psychological insights that often dramatically and comedically echo Freud's. That very affinity may have made Wilder feel resentful of a related discipline that purports to penetrate more deeply into the human psyche than even the best writer-directors can do.

Lubitsch also mocked that period's vogue for psychoanalysis in his influential Hollywood film *The Marriage Circle*, a comedy-drama set in Vienna about a married psychiatrist's frantic attempts to ward off sexual temptation. Among the unsympathetically portrayed psychiatrists, psychologists, or just plain quacks, Viennese or German, in Wilder's films are Sig Ruman's Nazi-like dog psychiatrist Dr. Zweiback in *The Emperor Waltz*, Martin Gabel's frenzied Dr. Max J. Eggelhofer in *The Front Page* (author of *Self-Abuse and Anti-Social Behavior* and *The Joy of Impotence*), and Klaus Kinski's twisted Dr. Hugo Zuckerbrot in *Buddy Buddy* (proprietor of a loony Southern California desert sex clinic whose motto is "Ecstasy Is Our Business"). José Ferrer's ruinously incompetent plastic surgeon Dr. Vando in *Fedora* is not a psychiatrist but might as well be, since he's the deluded Fedora's live-in counselor and enabler. And while pretending to be impotent to seduce Marilyn Monroe's Sugar in *Some Like It Hot*, Tony Curtis's Joe tells her he spent six months in Vienna with Professor Freud, to no avail.

Oskar Homolka's Professor Gurkakoff is an exception to this rule in the benign Wilder and Brackett script for Howard Hawks's *Ball of Fire*; he kindly offers fatherly psychological insights about romance to his colleague Professor Potts (Gary Cooper). And the nonmedical investigators who appear frequently in Wilder's films, from Keyes in *Double Indemnity* to Sherlock Holmes, offer more sympathetic variations on his usual psychiatrist figures, whom they resemble in some ways, but these men too tend to fail in their tasks, with equally disastrous consequences.

There is also no evidence that Wilder interviewed the Hungarian playwright Ferenc Molnár, as is sometimes claimed. Yet the witty Molnár played a significant role in Wilder's artistic development and particularly his theme of masquerading. Wilder told Cameron Crowe that he was strongly influenced by Molnár's dazzlingly ingenious play *The Guardsman* (1910), which also had a major impact on Lubitsch's work. That high comedy about a jealous actor who impersonates a dashing guardsman to see if he can seduce his own actress wife presents a model for the many impersonations and farcical sexual situations in the films of both directors. The jealousy that Jack Benny's insecure actor Josef Tura harbors for his incorrigibly flirtatious actress wife, Maria (Carole Lombard), in Lubitsch's *To Be or Not to Be* is derived from *The Guardsman*. Long after Wilder watched Molnár's machine-gun-speed one-act farce about a fast-talking Parisian bank president, *Egy, kettö, három* (1929), onstage in Berlin, he filmed it as *One, Two, Three*. He transposed the play to divided Berlin in the Cold War climate of 1961 while transforming the protagonist into an American Coca-Cola executive (James Cagney). Wilder had been impressed by seeing the Austrian actor Max Pallenberg, a veteran of Max Reinhardt's Deutsches Theater in Berlin, starring in the play; Pallenberg was celebrated for his ability to rattle off dialogue at an amazing clip, as Wilder made Cagney do in the film, exasperating the veteran star and driving him into a lengthy period of retirement.*

Wilder's ridicule of Vienna during his days as a newspaperman after he migrated from that stuffy setting to the trendier modern city of Berlin was not merely a youthful sophisticate's pose but a symptom of more serious complaints he could not express in print back home, including about Austrian anti-Semitism. And he did not find it easy to write about such subjects in Germany. That such feelings festered for many years helps account for his extraordinary act of "re-making the Holocaust as a Bing Crosby musical," as Nancy Steffen-Fluhr puts it, despite his claim that his motive for making *The Emperor Waltz* was nostalgia for Austrian popular traditions. There is no

---

* A 1930 English adaptation by Sidney Howard was directed onstage by James Whale and starred Arthur Byron and Ruth Gordon; another version, in 1952, was retitled *President*.

doubt that Wilder always harbored a certain ambivalent feeling for Vienna, as is natural to do with one's boyhood haunts and formative experiences, no matter how traumatic they may be. Even late in life, despite it all, Wilder continued to love Austrian cuisine and Viennese operettas, including Franz Lehár's *Die lustige Witwe* (*The Merry Widow*), which his two favorite directors, Erich von Stroheim and Lubitsch, both filmed.

Wilder admitted in the 1940s, "What I hate most about the Austrians is that I cannot hate the Austrians."

"PLAYING THE AMERICAN"

Even when young Billie was dashing around European capitals as a newspaper and magazine reporter, churning out a wide variety of copy, keenly observed, rich with atmosphere, and laced with his characteristically sardonic wit, he always had at least one eye directed squarely at a future in America. The young Wilder consciously modeled himself on the brash, glamorously raffish reporters he saw in American feature films and newsreels. A friend and coworker from the Berlin period, Hans Sohl, described Wilder as a rakish young man "who, with his hat tilted on his head and hands in the pockets of his pants, was already playing the American while we still hadn't discovered America at all." "I had always wanted to go to America, but it took Mr. Hitler to make me leave UFA," Wilder said in later years (UFA was the leading German film studio, Universum-Film Aktiengesellschaft, or Universe-Film Share Company).

Billy's American-ness came virtually from birth, with his nicknaming by his mother after American Western characters. From boyhood he was a devotee of American films, especially those of the dashingly adventurous, brashly humorous Douglas Fairbanks and the astonishingly inventive and acrobatic comedian and director Buster Keaton, whom he preferred to Charlie Chaplin because Keaton was unsentimental. While in Berlin and planning to work in English, Wilder read the works of such American authors as Mark Twain and Bret Harte, both known for, among other things, picaresque tales of life in the far West where Wilder also hoped to go adventuring. He also immersed himself in the American Western tales of the German novelist Karl May and the contemporary work of American authors Ernest Hemingway and F. Scott

Fitzgerald. Wilder in his formative years during the 1920s was rebelling against the staid old culture of his youth in Vienna and turning his creative energies to two strikingly modernist art forms, movies and journalism, fields in which the United States was setting the international standards.

Wilder's greatest passion in his youth was for another thoroughly American art form, jazz. You can see and hear that passion on display throughout *Some Like It Hot*, set in the Roaring Twenties. He has Tony Curtis's female impersonator saxophonist, Josephine, ask Marilyn Monroe's Sugar Cane,* the voluptuous lead singer of Sweet Sue's Society Syncopators, with feigned disdain, "Syncopators—does that mean you play that very fast music— *jazz?*" Sugar replies, "Yeah. Real hot." To which Josephine, trying to pass for a prim and proper lady, disingenuously replies, "I guess some like it hot. I personally prefer classical music." Not Wilder, even though he grew up in Vienna, a city that was synonymous with classical music (Gustav Mahler and Richard Strauss) and operetta (especially Lehár's), and though his use of classical music from various countries in his films is as knowing as his more prominent use of popular music, even if he employs classical music more often in an ironic or sarcastic manner. Unlike the traditional Viennese musical idioms, jazz was new and fresh, a clean break from the past, exotically foreign, and a rage in Europe during his youth. Jazz captured the mood of young people anxious for social upheaval and eager to explore their creative energies. That the reactionary elements of Europe frowned on jazz for its licentiousness (its very name was slang for sex) and its roots in African American culture only accentuated the dangerous appeal of those qualities for a young Americanophile such as Wilder.

Wilder particularly admired the rotund American bandleader Paul Whiteman, known as the "King of Jazz." Though Whiteman was white, and his big-band music was more mainstream than the African American jazz tradition, Duke Ellington wrote in his autobiography that "no one as yet has come near carrying that title with more certainty and dignity." When Whiteman and his band came to Vienna to give concerts in June 1926, the excited young Wilder wrote for *The Hour* about the bandleader's arrival by train from

---

* Although most printed references to *Some Like It Hot* give the character's name as "Kane," the authoritative sources—the screenplay as typed and as published in the 1959 movie tie-in edition—spell it as Cane.

Berlin and whirlwind tour of Vienna. Wilder cited a Chicago *Tribune* poll of the most famous Americans listing Whiteman as second in popularity only to Charlie Chaplin. And Wilder proclaimed the poll as the "People's voice—the voice of God." His tribute includes a detailed ode to Whiteman's "amusing" mustache, a "visual pleasure. . . . This is the mustache of the day after tomorrow. Copyright by Paul Whiteman."* Looking suave in a cocked hat, sport coat, and tie, Wilder managed to stand in admiring profile next to the beaming bandleader as Whiteman posed with fellow musicians for the photo that appeared with the article showing his arrival and reception on the Franz-Josefs-Bahnhof.

In Wilder's anxiety to relocate to Weimar Berlin, the locus of cultural ferment in Europe at the time, he latched onto the bandleader, negotiating a train ticket and lodging in a brief job as his publicity agent, partly in exchange for the promise of a favorable review sent from Berlin to *The Hour*. "Whiteman Celebrates Triumphs in Berlin" was the title of Wilder's unabashed review of a concert on June 27 before four thousand people packed into the Grosses Schauspielhaus. Leading a tuxedo-clad band of what Wilder called twenty-nine "ingenious comedians, ingenious musicians," Whiteman opened with carnival music from New Orleans and played a variety of ragtime, jazz, and Charleston music. The concert was visually arresting, starting with a purple spotlight softly discovering the orchestra in the darkened hall. Another striking effect involved the hall going dark again and Whiteman using a flashlight to single out various musicians as they played and clowned around. The pièce de résistance was a work Whiteman had commissioned and popularized, George Gershwin's innovative classical-cum-jazz composition *Rhapsody in Blue* (1924). Wilder described it as "a big sensation over there in the USA, an attempt to exploit the rhythms of American folk music. When Whiteman plays, it's a great artistic thing."

The bandleader symbolized what Wilder already loved about America as well as providing him with a means of escaping to Berlin, the most Americanized, culturally, of European capitals. In his punchiest and most aroused style, Wilder closed the review with this proclamation: "Für Jazz? Gegen

---

* The sardonic master of ceremonies in Wilder's film *Irma la Douce* (1963), the portly Parisian barkeeper Moustache, perhaps owes something to Whiteman; the part was supposed to have been played by the rotund Charles Laughton before he became fatally ill and had to be replaced by Lou Jacobi.

Jazz? Modernste Musik? Kitsch? Kunst? Bedürfnis! Notwendige Bluterneuerung des verkalkten Europas." Translation: "For Jazz? Against Jazz? Most modern music? Kitsch? Art? Need! Necessary blood renewal of the fossilized Europe." The word *verkalkten* can be translated as either "fossilized" or "calcified." Viewed either way, Wilder's declaration of his fervent need to leap into modernism jumps off the page.

Partly because of his genuine enthusiasm for the American bandleader and the sophisticated pop culture he represented, Wilder displayed no apparent shame over the conflict of interest involved in swapping that review for a train ticket out of Vienna and a job guiding Whiteman around Berlin nightspots. Wilder was no stranger to the sometimes flexible ethics of the journalism world, and he had other reasons for getting out of town, like the jazz musicians in *Some Like It Hot*. The one actual press scandal he found himself embroiled in took place near the end of his time in Vienna. His employer at the two papers, Imré Békessy, was exposed in 1926 as running a shakedown scheme to provide favorable coverage in *The Hour* in exchange for advertising. Banks and cafés were attacked in that paper unless they submitted ads. Although this kind of slippery ethics is rampant in journalism even today, one of Wilder's journalistic rivals accused him in print of involvement in a form of extortion the Viennese press sarcastically called a "café tax." That probably helped motivate Wilder's urgent need to break away to Berlin that summer. No doubt he considered a rave review he would have written anyway a small price to pay for his escape from a stifling past to a cosmopolitan metropolis that represented the stepping-off point to his future.

In those days Wilder, displaying his youthful bravado, fit in with the kind of wisecracking, unabashedly cynical reporters who appear in his film *The Front Page* (1974), based on the play by former Chicago reporters Ben Hecht and Charles MacArthur.* Billie was still a tyro when he left for Berlin and never did much crime reporting either there or in Vienna, despite his later claims; he mostly wrote personality profiles and pieces about cultural

---

* Hecht, who had spent some time reporting on political violence in Weimar Berlin, was the prototypical newspaperman-turned-screenwriter. He and MacArthur would go on to become prolific and celebrated screenwriters. In the Wilder film of *The Front Page*, managing editor Walter Burns, while trying to talk reporter Hildy Johnson (Lemmon) out of quitting their newspaper, says of Hecht, "Look at him now—sitting under those goddam palm trees, writing dialogue for Rin-Tin-Tin. What's the matter with you guys? You're traitors, all of you. If it isn't Hollywood, it's Broadway—or Paris—write the Great American Novel—be Scott Fitzgerald. Christ!"

activities. Even with his raffish demeanor, he was pulling off something of a masquerade in his younger days by acting as hard-boiled as the police reporters in that play. When I asked him on the set of *The Front Page* if he was drawing from some of his own experiences as a reporter in the 1920s, it was with a bravado exaggerated for comic effect to an eager young reporter that he cocked his eyebrow and replied, "Hardly. It would be very censorable even today."

By the time Wilder came to film the play, his attitude toward such callous "Gentlemen of the press!" (a line the furious prostitute character literally spits at them, toward the camera) had become considerably harsher with the wisdom of age. Wilder can still relish the unholy joy Burns shows in beating the competition, but Walter Matthau's Burns in the film, as Neil Sinyard and Adrian Turner point out in their critical study *Journey Down Sunset Boulevard: The Films of Billy Wilder* (1979), plays Mephistopheles to Hildy's Faust. Noting that the Faustian theme recurs frequently in Wilder's work, such as in *Sunset Blvd.*, they write that

> the subject of Wilder's [*Front Page*], if not that of the original play, is damnation. . . . The film is fundamentally concerned with the struggle to save [Lemmon's Hildy] as a mature, responsible human being. . . . Far from imbuing the newspaper profession with "wit and affection," Wilder sees it as the source of his hero's sickness, from which the man (like [Don] Birnam and his bottle [in Wilder's 1945 film about alcoholism, *The Lost Weekend*]) must free himself in order to survive. . . . The impossibility of redemption in *The Front Page* makes it one of Wilder's bleakest works. Wilder cannot accept Burns on the terms in which the play offers him—as a lovable rogue. His callousness and selfishness are too extreme for that. Wider embellishes the harshness of this portrait.

That jaded attitude toward journalism in his later years contributes to making the film less funny than the play, the result not of failure but of intent.

Despite his own unpleasant youthful chores in coaxing photographs of dead people from their families, Wilder never went anywhere near as far to get a story as the ruthlessly ambitious reporter Chuck Tatum (Kirk Douglas) in his film *Ace in the Hole*. Tatum, who has been fired by big-city papers for various forms of insubordination and other irresponsible behavior and is fortunate to have found a job he despises in the backwater city of Albuquerque, New Mexico, is so desperate to get a ticket back to the big time (in his case, New York) that he keeps a man trapped in a cave to prolong an exclusive. Wilder's beginnings as a reporter in two of Europe's biggest cities—including its most corrupt, Berlin—left him with no illusions about human nature.

Those years exposed him to the climate of corruption and casual amorality that bred figures like Tatum, who is nothing more than a racketeer in the guise of a reporter, even if Wilder can't hide a certain admiring glee in the way Tatum hoodwinks everyone with his elaborate hoax. The ambivalence with which Wilder views unscrupulous newspapermen such as Burns and Tatum is what makes these films giddily unsettling exposés, so deliberately appalling in their dark combinations of comedy and drama, the quality that makes Wilder what Joan Didion (in a review of his 1964 film *Kiss Me, Stupid*) called "a moralist, a recorder of human venality." Wilder told biographer Charlotte Chandler of his own newspaper days, "Some of this I remembered for *Ace in the Hole*, which critics called cynical. It was kinder than what I saw, sanitized." Tatum glibly cites an actual Pulitzer Prize–winning reporter as a role model, but Hildy tells Walter in Wilder's *The Front Page* when he suggests pulling an illegal ruse to take a photograph of a hanging, "Walter, you'll either get the Pulitzer Prize or you'll get a year in the clink."*

"BLOOD RENEWAL"

In Berlin, where Wilder stayed after Whiteman and his troupe blitzed out of the German capital, the young reporter found his personal "blood renewal" (a phrase that in hindsight has uncomfortable echoes of Nazi propaganda). After his fast-paced period as a prolific member of the press in Vienna, Wilder found the decadent Berlin a comparative joy to live in, endlessly colorful and stimulating, but a tougher sell for his work as a freelancer. Although there were no fewer than 149 newspapers in Berlin and almost 400 magazines by

---

* The ruse alludes to a photo taken by a Chicago reporter at the execution in 1928 of murderess Ruth Snyder, whose story inspired the James M. Cain novel *Double Indemnity*, which Wilder filmed in 1944 with Barbara Stanwyck.

1930, it still took a while and some aggressive self-marketing for a youngster to succeed. Even though Wilder was always the opposite of a provincial—urbane and streetwise, he affected a hard-boiled veneer that only partially concealed the compassion and romanticism that can be discerned in his reportage—he was still a relative tyro competing with more seasoned pros in the third largest city in Europe (after London and Paris), with a population of four million.

In those days, life was often a struggle between paychecks for Wilder until he entered the film business a few years later. He lived at first in a succession of modest digs, often having trouble paying the rent. He roamed the streets for saleable news and feature angles. He banged out his stories on a portable typewriter at the cavernous Romanisches Café (Romanesque Café) at the end of the Kurfürstendamm, the center of action in the metropolis. Wilder's lively and chic hangout was all the more fashionable because it was funky rather than glamorous, a hub for the intelligentsia and artists and thus perhaps the most celebrated of Berlin's sixteen thousand cafés in the Weimar period. Wilder's illustrious fellow habitués included artist George Grosz; playwright Bertolt Brecht; composer Hanns Eisler; novelists Franz Werfel, Joseph Roth, and Erich Maria Remarque; and Billie's journalistic role model and sometime mentor, the radical leftist political reporter and activist Egon Erwin Kisch. A Jew who was born in Prague, Kisch called himself "Der rasende Reporter" (the Racing Reporter, with a secondary meaning of Raging Reporter), a nickname that influenced the application of the tag "Racing Reporter" to Wilder as well. Kisch was a prominent foe of the Nazis. They burned his books and imprisoned him briefly before expelling him as a trouble-causing alien.

With its bohemian, intellectual clientele and atmosphere, the Romanisches Café provided the newcomer with a playground for the kind of provocative, dishy conversation he cherished and put to good use professionally. He could catch all the latest artistic and political gossip there, while honing his penchant for wit and incisive social commentary against the masters of the game. And since it was a haunt for some prominent screenwriters, the café fed into Wilder's growing ambition to enter the movie business.

Wilder gradually caught on as a journalist and made something of a name for himself with his essayistic, eclectic servings of slices of Berlin life, suffused with the brash and often sarcastic "Berlin style" he fell into so naturally. Jean Renoir defined that style when he wrote of Lubitsch in 1967:

> To maintain the admirable balance of nature, God provides to the defeated nations the gift of Art. It is what happened to Germany after the defeat of 1918. Berlin, before Hitler, was blossoming with talents. In this short Renaissance, the Jews, not only of Germany but also of the surrounding countries, brought to this capital a certain spirit which was probably the best expression of the time. Lubitsch was a great example of this ironic approach to the big problems of life. His films were loaded with a kind of wit which was specifically the essence of the intellectual Berlin in those days. This man was so strong that when he was asked by Hollywood to work there, he not only didn't lose his Berlin style, but he converted the Hollywood industry to his own way of expression.

The same can be said of Wilder. The characteristic irreverence of Berlin's inhabitants in the Weimar era when he was flourishing there was often described as a brash café sensibility, or the *Berliner Schnauze* (lip). It is a quality that can be seen throughout Wilder's films, which benefit from a wise-guy skepticism that makes profound observations about life and is too often mistaken for mere "cynicism." Hannah Arendt in 1946 defined that Berlin sensibility in terms that apply well to Wilder's films, as "extreme skepticism and keenness of mind together with simple kindness and a great fear of sentimentality." Berlin offered a wealth of story potential, far more so than Vienna, but because of the intense competition in Berlin journalism, Wilder had to be creative in seeking out subject matter and aggressive in peddling his stories. He sold them to the *B.Z. am Mittag* (familiarly known as the *B.Z.*), beginning with his profile of Whiteman; the business-oriented newspapers *Berliner Nachtausgabe* (*Berlin Night Edition*) and *Berliner Börsen Courier* (*Berlin Messenger Exchanges*); the *Mittagsblatt* (*Noon Edition*); the tabloid *Tempo*; and the more high-toned literary journal *The Cross-Section*.

Berlin was Europe's liveliest and most artistically fertile city in the period when Wilder lived there, the final years of the Weimar Republic. The ceaseless political turmoil of the postwar period played its part in stimulating social and artistic upheavals and experiments of every kind during the 1920s.

Changes in government, civil war, street violence, and ideological clashes between the incipient Fascist movement and left-wing political parties, accompanied by wild swings in economic conditions, guaranteed that every aspect of German life would be examined and reexamined not only by politicians but also by journalists, sociologists, and artists. The rampant inflation of the early postwar period had led to a period of relative economic stability by the time Wilder migrated there in 1926, but the mood of Berlin was still volatile, a hotbed for daring new approaches to everything from artistic and sexual expression to revolutionary politics, left and right. It was an exciting and stimulating time for the dynamic young reporter to cover the city and mull Berlin's many conflicting facets in print. Although disturbing political and social trends were never far below the surface as Nazism gradually accumulated supporters among the more "respectable" elements of the populace, there was such a riot of diversity on display in in pre-Nazi Berlin's artistic and personal license that young writers such as Wilder or the Englishman Christopher Isherwood could not have found a climate of greater ferment in which to develop their talents.

Times were changing so quickly that the expressionist movement in art, theater, films, and literature—revolutionary in the first decades of the twentieth century and central in importance during the early 1920s as a way of conveying the inner life through distorted exterior settings and actions—had already given way to what was called the *Neue Sachlichkeit* or "New Objectivity," a movement that called for greater realism and a more direct confrontation with the problems of everyday life. The New Objectivity was seen as a further influence of American culture on Berlin life, a blunter and more businesslike, less dreamlike approach than the extravagant, aesthetically flamboyant style explored by the expressionists, who portrayed the world through a subjective eye. Some decried the new trend for abandoning the more daring psychological and artistic exploration of the expressionist period in exchange for a grittier, less experimental, less inward-looking approach. But the advent of the New Objectivity coincided neatly with Wilder's roaming the streets and cafés to report with boundless curiosity on the evolution of social mores. It seemed to fit the hard-boiled attitude he had already developed in Vienna and his disdain for its trendy Freudianism and what he considered pretension in the world of art.

The New Objectivity would manifest itself in Wilder's first major film work, as a writer on the independent film *People on Sunday* (1930), directed by Robert Siodmak and Edgar G. Ulmer. That well-received, still-influential low-budget film, shot vividly on locations in Berlin, qualifies as avant-garde in challenging the conventions of commercial filmmaking, taking a documentary-like approach to a casual narrative about the lives of five ordinary young people who lived in the city at the time, played by nonactors. Wilder's first screen credit, however, came in 1929 with the blatantly commercial UFA comedy *Der Teufelsreporter: Im Nebel der Grosstadt* (*The Devil's Reporter: In the Fog of the Big City*), which drew directly, but facetiously, from his newspaper work.

Even after Wilder found a toehold in the thriving Berlin movie business, he kept supplementing his screenwriting with freelance journalism for a while to keep lodging house proprietors off his back. Those experiences were reflected in black-comic form in a short film to which Wilder reportedly contributed for Siodmak's tryout at UFA in 1930, *Der Kampf mit dem Drachen oder: Die Tragödie des Untermieters* (*The Fight with the Dragon or: The Tenants' Tragedy*). The twelve-minute grotesque comedy—to borrow the phrase Lubitsch used for some of his German farces—starred Felix Bressart (later one of the Soviet commissars in *Ninotchka*) as a harassed tenant who flips his lid and destroys his room. He caused his landlady's death from a heart attack but is exonerated by a jury composed of tenants with similarly oppressive proprietors. But the director and his brother Kurt (who also had worked with Wilder on *People on Sunday*) received the sole screenwriting credits on the short.

Sometimes the struggling Wilder had trouble keeping a roof over his head and had to sleep in the train station for a few nights. But he eventually prospered enough as a screenwriter at UFA to be able to afford a fancy American sports car, his blue Graham-Paige convertible. And as a witty, worldly man-about-town, just as he had been in Vienna, he seldom lacked for female company. The always hyperactive Wilder liked to quip in later years that his chronic bad back had been developed in his youthful days as a reporter: "I think it is all the result of those hot nights in Vienna when I was screwing girls standing up in doorways—and sometimes, alas, no girls—*just doorways*."

DANCING ON THE EDGE

"Waiter, Bring Me a Dancer!: From the Life of an *Eintänzer*," Wilder's career-shaping series dealing with his work as a dancer for hire, has often been cited by biographers and other profilers and appears in all three volumes of his collected journalism, in German and English. That four-part series ("Seeking a Position," "My First Day in the Hotel," "My Colleagues," and "The Daily Service") is the best early demonstration of Wilder's audacity, his combination of *Berliner Schnauze* and tender sensitivity, displaying the full range of his youthful writing talents.

Wry, seriocomic, intimate, unashamed, and precisely detailed in its atmosphere and character observations, the series first appeared in *B. Z. am Mittag* from January 19 through 24, 1927. It caused "a small scandal," Wilder recalled, bringing him some notice in Berlin at a time when clever writers had to work especially hard publishing outré material to distinguish themselves in that self-consciously decadent atmosphere. Wilder subsequently sold the series to *The Stage* in Vienna, which ran it that June with a slightly different subtitle, "Erlebnisse eines Eintänzers" (Experiences of a Tea Dancer).

The partly fictionalized series anticipates central themes of his film work, including his career-long obsession with the intricacies of the masquerade, the conflicts between love and money and sexual exploitation and romance, and the dangers of overly self-protective emotional detachment. The writing and structure of the series is an adroit blend of stylistic approaches, much as his films would blend genres, often in surprising ways. And as Klaus Siebenhaar comments in his collection of Wilder's Berlin journalism, the series already displays his familiar style in "the perfect dramaturgy of the scenes and the skillful structure . . . ostensibly factual, cold and succinct" but revealing "deep in his heart a secret moralist. . . . Because the bottom line is that behind the mask of the self-ironic chronicler is the melancholy of loneliness and the fear of being a loser."

Most strikingly, Wilder's experiences as an *Eintänzer* are reflected in the numerous outright gigolo characters who appear in the films he wrote and/ or directed. They range from the benign portrait of the romantic Leon (Melvyn Douglas) in Lubitsch's *Ninotchka* to the tormented but ultimately redeemed Georges Iscovescu (Charles Boyer) in Mitchell Leisen's *Hold Back the Dawn* (1941) and the tragic Joe Gillis (William Holden) in Wilder's own classic *Sunset Blvd.* Gillis clearly is drawn from Wilder's precise, bitter memories of what he found to be a rather humiliating experience as a paid dancer, for all his bravado in recounting that work at the time. Toward the end of Wilder's career, even the great Sherlock Holmes is offered temporary work as a gigolo, although the detective and the filmmaker treat the offer lightly in *The Private Life of Sherlock Holmes.* All those films, when viewed in conjunction with his 1927 series, indicate that while Wilder's experiences as an *Eintänzer* may not have been as literally degrading as the role of an actual gigolo, the humiliating and ridiculous aspects of the job did have a significant effect on him personally and imaginatively. The series makes a point of maintaining that he kept his distance sexually from his clients. But he gave somewhat differing accounts over the years of what led to writing that remarkable blend of journalism and dramatized, confessional memoir.

The variety of meanings *Eintänzer* has been given in translation, reflecting different social connotations placed on the job, range from "tea dancer" and "dancer for hire" to "taxi dancer" to the translation with the most overtly sexual implications, "gigolo." Wilder's series dramatizes the emotional complexities of the *Eintänzer* role and the way he negotiated intricate exchanges with women as a paid dancer while attempting to maintain his dignity and not sink into the degradation of being a male prostitute. A scholar who studied Wilder's work as an *Eintänzer* against the backdrop of the social role played by such male dancers in Weimar Germany, Mihaela Petrescu, refers to him as an "unreliable narrator" of the kind common in literature or blends of journalism and fiction. Wilder admitted to me that the series "was not all factual." It cannot be taken literally but more as a commentary on that milieu and how he perceived the men and women involved in it; he saw in these people the kinds of characters who later would appear in his films. The series suggests that Wilder's innate romanticism, intelligence, and professional distance as a writer covering the *Eintänzer* scene allowed him to surmount the ambiguities of his role with aplomb, although with considerable difficulty. But his darker portraits of gigolos onscreen can be seen as cautionary tales extrapolated from his brief but vividly felt time working as an *Eintänzer.* His close brush with the most destructive aspects of that ambiguous profession enabled him to create such debased but still sympathetic characters and to portray with acute understanding their compromised situations in degrading conditions.

Wilder worked as an *Eintänzer* for two months in October–December 1926 after losing his job that September as a reporter for the *Berlin Night Edition*. At the same time as he was working as a paid hotel dancer, he was giving dance lessons with an American girlfriend named Margerie. With those jobs he was making a more comfortable living than he had been accustomed to earning as a reporter but was working night and day, doing both late-afternoon and evening shifts at a hotel where he danced and dined with clients. Billie always tried to maintain a dapper image in any case, but he used his advance from a friend who got him the dancing gig to buy new evening clothes, and from his first ten days' pay he bought a portable gramophone for teaching the Charleston with Margerie. She would demonstrate the new American dance craze for the husbands while Billie taught it to their wives.

Wilder told me in 1978 that someone had recently sent him a copy of the series and that he found it

rather well-written reportage, with projections of thoughts, of dreams, it was not all factual. It was serialized in the *B. Z. am Mittag*, which was one of the great German papers—a very classy paper published by a very classy outfit. It was a kudo to be printed in that paper, especially a risqué story, as this was, because it told you about the German bourgeois ladies coming to that hotel for five o'clock tea when people were still dancing there. They still do it in Zurich—between five and seven an orchestra is playing and people are dancing, can you imagine? Ladies are sitting there having their coffee with their *schlag* [whipped cream topping] and their pastry. And the dancers are there, lined up and going up to the ladies, who are almost at their menopause. They get their tips or some basic salary.

I wrote about that series of approaches and dialogues: how to get a better tip, what to do. If you said, "I'm not doing well, actually I'm a writer, but I've got to do anything for a living. Especially—you have no idea—the shoes, the afternoon and the evening shoes, they are very expensive." Then instead of giving you a good tip she'll send you twelve pairs of old shoes from her husband.

When that account is compared with the actual series, it can be seen that Wilder had done some rewriting of the series in his mind, as a good screenwriter will always do. The specific lines of approach he cited don't appear in the series, but "Waiter, Bring Me a Dancer!" reads like a scenario that could be filmed today. It would make an atmospheric, emotionally complex period film musical drama about Weimar Berlin, the Billy Wilder equivalent of *Cabaret*. The series has a classical trajectory taking his character—perhaps as much a semifictionalized surrogate figure as "Christopher Isherwood" is in his *Goodbye to Berlin* stories—from miserable depths in the coldhearted metropolis to illusory and dubious "success" in a tawdry profession before letting him walk away in an enigmatic, downbeat, but soul-revivifying ending.

Although the series does not identify by name the hotel where he worked, Wilder recalled serving as a paid dancing partner for ladies in one or both of two prominent Berlin hotels, the Adlon and the Eden. There are darkly nostalgic references to both locales in *A Foreign Affair*, Wilder's remarkably morbid comedy-drama about postwar Berlin. The Adlon, near the Brandenburg Gate, was virtually destroyed in the war and rebuilt in 1997 as the Hotel Adlon Kempinski Berlin. The prototypical "grand hotel," it was the model for the popular novel *Menschen im Hotel* (*People in a Hotel*, 1929) by Vicki Baum (published in English as *Grand Hotel*).* There is a sardonic reference to the bombed-out Adlon Hotel in *A Foreign Affair* during a tour of the city given to visiting dignitaries by a U.S. Army colonel.

Petrescu's 2013 study for the journal *New German Critique* could find no firm documentation that Wilder worked at both the Adlon and Eden other than his claim in a 1963 *Playboy* interview, "I danced as a gigolo for a while in the Eden Hotel, and at the Adlon I served as a teatime partner for lonely old ladies." In 1992, I heard Wilder deny that he worked at the Adlon. He made the correction at a Los Angeles reception held by the consul general of Germany honoring Curt Siodmak (who had changed his name from Kurt) with the Order of Merit from the Federal Republic of Germany. In his acceptance speech, Siodmak remembered Wilder from his days as an impoverished young reporter in Berlin picking up tips and a story while "dancing with the ladies at—what was it?—the Adlon Hotel." "Eden," Wilder called out, adding jokingly that it was Fred Zinnemann who had danced at the Adlon,

---

* Baum was a Viennese Jew who worked as a journalist in Berlin and later went to Hollywood, where MGM filmed her novel as a multistar extravaganza in 1932. Wilder pays homage to that film by showing Bud trying vainly to get through TV commercials to watch it in *The Apartment*.

with "small women." The slender director of *High Noon* and *A Man for All Seasons,* who stood five feet six and a half inches, had been an assistant cameraman on *People on Sunday.* Wilder, almost half a foot taller, had a longtime propensity to kid Zinnemann in odd ways; an article Wilder wrote in Berlin in 1929 described him as "my dead schoolmate Zinnemann. . . . Terribly pale and thin. . . . They buried him long ago."

A drum being used by the musicians in the underground showcase for the Dietrich character in *A Foreign Affair,* the Lorelei nightclub, identifies their band as the Hotel Eden Syncopators (from whom Wilder borrowed the word "Syncopators" for the girls' band in *Some Like It Hot*). The Eden on Budapester Street, a short walk from the Kurfürstendamm, fits the description in Wilder's series of "a huge hotel" where he worked, located near the Kaiser Wilhelm Memorial Church. The hotel was most notorious as the location where the radical leftists Rosa Luxemburg and Karl Liebknecht were tortured during their interrogation in January 1919 before being executed for their roles in leading the Spartacist uprising. Though large, the Eden was not as "grand" as the Adlon but rather *louche* by comparison. The Eden was a magnet for prostitutes of various kinds, both high-class girls and others who flaunted their specialty in flagellation, but its bar was popular among actors and other figures in the arts and regarded as a sophisticated hangout. The ballroom drew a broader clientele. Wilder wrote of dancing with "ladies who send the waiter for me and savor the tango with eyes closed in ecstasy . . . with embarrassingly inept newcomers for whom a trip to Berlin without five o'clock tea seems pointless . . . with ladies who are there every day and of whom you know not whence and hither; with a thousand types."

Was Wilder merely posing as an *Eintänzer* temporarily at the end of 1926 as a creative way to get material to write about in his struggling days as a reporter, as he sometimes claimed? That's what he once told me when I pressed him on the subject. He seemed slightly embarrassed and defensive. But when I asked him about the series on another occasion, he made a more significant admission: He said he became an *Eintänzer* because he needed a job and *then* decided to write about it. That was also what he admitted to the reader in a 1929 article about a friend who encouraged him to take the job, and the series itself supports that explanation.

Wilder presents his down-and-out protagonist as desperately broke and hungry, a reporter who hasn't sold an article in three weeks. He is reduced to sleeping on a railway station bench because of his fear of "the poisonous face of the landlady, shrieking" ordering him to vacate his room for not paying his rent. Fortuitously, Wilder was tipped off about the job by a dancer he ran into on a street in Berlin, a man named Roberts he knew casually from Vienna, part of the team of Yvette and Roberts.* They specialized in the Charleston, like Wilder, who had brought his passion for hot American jazz from Vienna to Berlin. Roberts floated Wilder enough marks to pay his rent and other needs as well as finding the job at the hotel where he performed. Wilder not only was in no position to refuse the position as *Eintänzer,* it was a godsend.

But to validate the enterprise in a literary (and moral) sense, Wilder begins by quoting a note from his close friend Alfred Henschke, a novelist and poet who wrote erotic songs for cabarets. Henschke went by the pseudonym "Klabund." Klabund had tuberculosis, and Wilder remembered him dismissing the "tiny red dot" he coughed into his handkerchief: "And that tiny red dot was what killed him." Because of his illness, Klabund and could not dance with his wife, actress Carola Neher, so they hired Wilder as an *Eintänzer* one night and struck up a friendship. The note from Klabund: "Dear B.W.—Write your memoirs of an *Eintänzer.* The only thing that interests us today in literature is the raw material from which it is made: Life, reality, actuality. The motto of 'vitalism' is: All life is only a parable.—Yours truly, Klabund." Wilder tells his readers what he takes from this encouragement: "So do not be ashamed of what you did. Not even giving the excuse, as an argument, that 'An occupation is an occupation.' Or that 'Work is no disgrace.' But direct and straightforward."

Klabund also helped Wilder get the series published in the *B. Z.* In 1929, the year after his mentor died, Wilder wrote a tribute to his friend, recalling the three nights it took to write the series: "Then I took everything to Klabund. . . . My memoirs seemed very poor. But Klabund took pleasure in them. He sat there for an hour and corrected them. . . . The *B. Z.* printed these memories of an *Eintänzer.* Klabund wrote me a few lines of introduction. We met in a café, and he gave me these lines with which I should

---

* They may have helped inspire a UFA film based on an idea by Wilder, *Seitensprünge* (*Infidelity,* 1931), about an unhappy married couple and a team of Spanish dancers they meet in a nightclub.

preface the essays. Very fine words: You should write about life as it is." That would remain Wilder's touchstone for the rest of his days.

LESSONS IN LIFE'S VICIOUSNESS

Wilder was schooled in the tricks of the trade by the sleazy, yellow-faced hotel dance director, who assigned each *Eintänzer* to approach specific ladies sitting at tables sipping tea, wine, or Champagne. A man with a boneless handshake, the dance director puts today's reader in mind of the oily Hollywood clothing salesman in *Sunset Blvd.* who whispers in Joe Gillis's ear to take the expensive vicuna coat. Hearing the words "After all, if the lady is paying" and seeing the man's smirk behind his pencil mustache represents one of the lowest stations of the cross for that Wilder gigolo.

The young Billie Wilder's boss trains him in the elaborate hypocrisies involved in approaching clients with a solicitous, "May I ask the lady?" That ritual made Wilder think, "I must look very stupid, bent down to the lady in this weird position with my face scarlet red." The man further instructs him, "Remember this: You are not here for your pleasure. You have to dance. Even with ladies you do not like. Yes, the less you like them, the more honestly and conscientiously you provide your service. The first commandment of *Eintänzers* is: there must be no wallflower. He has to pick them, because that's what he is paid for. Take note of that!"

Wilder goes on, "I earn my living honestly, honest and hard because I dance a lot and conscientiously. Perfectly, listless, without thought, without opinion, without heart, without brain. What counts here are only my legs, they belong to this treadmill, and they have to stomp to the rhythm, relentlessly, eternally one two, one two, one two. I dance with young and old, with little ones and with women two heads taller than me, with pretty ones and sexy ones and ones who aren't so pretty and sexy."

The series starkly portrays the torturous physical and psychological strains of the profession: "The blood beats against my temples, my legs seem paralyzed by a stroke. Everything is blurred. . . . an endless dance. The shirt sticks to my body. I grit my teeth." Along with his concise and biting character touches, Wilder expertly limns the pungent atmosphere: the thin scent of Coty perfume hanging in the air after a lady brushes past him while he is sitting in the hall of the hotel on his first day at work "irritates my nerves"; the "loud and humid" ballroom is filled with "the smell of burnt hair"; the bored musicians are dully going through their paces.

Contrary to what Wilder later recalled about being successful in the job because of his superior conversational skills, the series portrays him as much more in demand for his expert and up-to-date dancing abilities than for his gift of gab. At one point he dances with the two skinny teenage daughters of an indifferent father but a mother who has "prohibited energetic conversation with the gigolo." The series indicates that the verbal talent that made Wilder so special throughout his life was frustratingly and sometimes infuriatingly not desired by his dancing partners, whom he portrays as viewing him as little more than a hired body, a convenient prop and flatterer. The bitterest point of the series comes when Wilder recounts a brief conversation with a woman who says with pitying condescension, "I'm really sorry that you have to work here," but still expects him to praise her dancing and her figure. He dutifully complies but confides to his readers, "The Eternal Feminine—I am only a paid *Eintänzer*."

He follows that observation with a section beginning, "It's hard to believe people can be so vicious."

Wilder illustrates his point by relating an incident in which he misunderstands a table number and approaches a homely lady whose male companion roars at him, "What vulgar impertinence do you allow yourself here? How dare you molest this lady?" The manager forces Wilder to apologize a second time, demonstrating that "The guest is always right." Here we see Wilder in the process of learning in the starkest terms the painful lessons about human cruelty that will be so amply demonstrated in his films.

Petrescu's study reveals the intricacies of the social context Wilder was navigating. Weimar Berlin was filled with thousands of dance halls and other establishments where social dancing took place. It was a craze, like tennis and other forms of physical exercise, and millions of Germans were taking dance lessons of the kind Billie and Margerie gave. But the ambiguous way the *Eintänzer* was regarded in that milieu illuminates the complex attitude Wilder took in the series.

An *Eintänzer* was an actor by necessity, counterfeiting romantic interest, and Wilder was doubly so, since he was something of an imposter as a dancer for hire, as many of his film characters would be in their temporarily adopted professions. But he was playing his role out of desperation and as a means of research and canny self-advancement as a professional journalist. With his acutely humorous observational ability and keen sensitivity toward a slight, the part of him aware of his servile position must have felt like Eliza Doolittle in George Bernard Shaw's satire of class differences, *Pygmalion*, who says, "You see, really and truly, apart from the things anyone can pick up (the dressing and the proper way of speaking, and so on), the difference between a lady and a flower girl is not how she behaves, but how she's treated." Wilder's series minutely chronicles and analyzes the mixture of faux servility and humiliation, preening and pretending, and submission to flirting and condescension that made up his foray into that craft.

The role of an *Eintänzer* was not necessarily, or even primarily, as debased as the oft-used translation "gigolo" or as popular culture then and now about Weimar Berlin would tend to indicate, Petrescu writes. The profession existed in the realm of Weimar's "moral laxity" that allowed for some ambiguity about how sexual in nature paid dancing actually could be. Many of the men who took that position in Berlin hotels during the 1920s were former military officers, who tended to come from the aristocracy. Though temporarily down on their luck and unemployed, they behaved with characteristic gentility and practiced the craft with punctilious discipline, skill, and good manners. Wilder was not from that social class but had a similar self-esteem, poise, and cockiness. He displayed an ability to handle himself with aplomb even in the face of condescension (as he often experienced in his youth as a Jewish outsider in Poland, Austria, and Berlin) and to maintain and convey a sense of social superiority and sophistication despite the relatively humble position he was temporarily inhabiting.

This intense experience interacting with a wide variety of strangers in a Berlin hotel honed Wilder's sense of the uneasy complexities of hotel life, an atmosphere already second nature to him from his youth as the son of a Kraków hotelier. And the emphasis on music in the series, with its knowing references to tangos and pop tunes and its structure as a quasi-musical, is echoed throughout his film work. He always showed an unerring ear for popular music to lend melancholic, ironic, or amusingly atmospheric qualities to films intermingling comedy and drama with music. Jack Lemmon believed Wilder's taste in music was a clue to his essentially romantic nature: "When you go back over his films, *think* about his choice of music. *It* is so lush and romantic—and sentimental—you don't believe it. *More* than necessary. . . . Billy very often is humming. Or singing. (And he's flat as a haddock, incidentally; he's *absolutely* fuckin' tone deaf.) But I know what he's *trying* to sing: it's *always* very romantic. And he's totally unaware of it."*

In the series Wilder goes into considerable detail, largely satirical, about the social rituals involved in a man in his position approaching the ladies for dances and about the elaborate "beautification" preparations he was expected to maintain. In its radical modernizing of traditionally rigid notions of sexual identity, Weimar Berlin, Petrescu relates, fostered a new attitude of "sensitive masculinity" that extended to greater acceptance of male use of cosmetics and other forms of beautification previously associated mostly with women. Wilder describes that process of preparation in considerable detail, cataloging a variety of beauty products "such as one can only guess on a lady's vanity table," and viewing their necessity with ironic humor: "My grooming now lasts a good hour, and it is such a grotesquely complicated process that I begin to be ashamed facing my landlady." Wilder's ironic tone in the series, as Petrescu puts it, serves as a counterbalance to the indignity of that job, and his self-conscious, painstaking immersion in the performative rituals of the *Eintänzer* similarly "asserts his masculinity primarily through humor." He uses that tone "to reflect wittily on his status as a commodity of Weimar culture. . . . Wilder is fully aware of his commodification, to which he alludes in the very title of his series." Such awareness and an emphasis on the role of money in romantic situations would become a hallmark of his film work, the sardonic sense of love and sex turned into impersonal products through prostitution or some other kind of financial transaction, often involving impersonation or acting.

The feminization of the *Eintänzer* and reflection of the blurring of sexual roles in Weimar Berlin point to the radical deconstruction of gender roles in some of Wilder's later work, especially to *Some Like It Hot*, his cross-dressing farce set in that same period. Once Hollywood censorship began loosening

---

* Lemmon could have been thinking of the lushly romantic, insistently sentimental music that plays over the opening credits of *The Apartment* and is heard as a running theme, counterpointing the film's tragic elements. The tune is "Jealous Lover," written for the film *The Romantic Age/Naughty Arlette* (1949) by the prolific film and television composer and orchestra conductor Charles Williams. Wilder remembered the tune and hummed it for the United Artists music department until they identified it and secured the rights to use it (uncredited) with the score by Adolph Deutsch as the "Theme from *The Apartment*."

from the late 1950s onward, *Some Like It Hot* and other Wilder films delved increasingly deeply into issues of sexual identity and how society defines gender. As well as critically examining the nature of masculinity and delving more into the complexities of women's roles vis-à-vis men and sexuality, his films began overtly examining actual or humorously suspected homosexuality in his characters. In that fascination we can see the influence of the freewheeling Weimar Berlin milieu and the *Eintänzer* interlude on Wilder's development as an artist. His films view sexual experimentation and gender confusion as a positive development, an opportunity for growth. Often such tendencies are presented humorously, but sometimes they are more seriously depicted as enhancing characters' lives. Nowhere is this more clearly seen than in the way the callous lady-killer in *Some Like It Hot*, Joe (Curtis), learns to become a more sensitive man. He stops exploiting Sugar's feelings after literally walking around in women's shoes, as "Josephine," along with his friend Jerry/"Daphne" (Lemmon), who actually winds up engaged to a rich old man. Although *Some Like It Hot* is an extreme case in its farcical exaggeration, Wilder films in general are obsessively concerned with this conflict between callousness and empathy in both men and women.

In his *Eintänzer* series, Wilder portrays the demands of his professional role with some distaste as mechanistic and inhuman. He feels like a cog on an assembly line, an example of the modern industrial practice of mass production that in the 1920s was called "Fordism," after Henry Ford's methodology, a term that came to stand for advanced capitalism and modernity itself. The robotic manner Wilder identifies as part of the professional detachment of his role resembles the mechanized kick-line routines of the Tiller Girls, a popular British band and "fancy-dancing" troupe. He celebrated them in a blatantly lubricious article for *The Hour* about their April 1926 arrival by train in Vienna ("thirty-four of the loveliest legs descend from the train. . . . You do not know where to look"). Although the troupe were under the eye of their stern female supervisor, Wilder managed to date one of them anyway, and he later had a romance in Berlin with a troupe member named Olive Victoria.

Wilder later boasted about his success with women even in his days as a struggling reporter. For "The Tiller Girls Are Here!" he turned his roving eye on several dancers he quizzed in turn: "Dorothy has beautiful eyelashes, and she also knows how to flirt. 'Which boarding school were you brought up in?' 'In the monastery of the Holy Virgin.' . . . Hilda II: Keeps her head always askance. 'Do you believe in love at first sight?' 'When I look at you, yes.' . . . Joyce laughs seductively. 'Bernard Shaw?' 'I don't know, I don't know him.'" Wilder was thoroughly besotted by this trainload of vixens, especially Olive, about whom he eventually published a poem. He told Hellmuth Karasek, "That infatuation cost me my job, because one day I was so tired after a sleepless night, the editor caught me sleeping in a phone booth." Before that, Wilder followed up shortly with a second article, a virtual mash note: "A Tiller Girl is pretty, smart, nice, not uneducated, graceful, clever-witted, tactful, calculating, golden; all this makes a Tiller Girl."

In striking contrast to Wilder's erotic attraction to those dancers and the way he characterizes them in print, the style of the Tiller Girls led the Marxist philosopher/critic Siegfried Kracauer to view them as relatively unerotic, mere interchangeable automata. In "The Mass Ornament," an often-quoted cultural analysis first published in a Frankfurt newspaper in 1927, Kracauer wrote, "These products of American 'distraction factories' [although they originated in England, the Tiller Girls had a dance school in New York] are no longer individual girls, but indissoluble female units whose movements are mathematical demonstrations." Kracauer not only dismissed such popular amusements as vapid entertainment, related to the "capitalist production process," but also found sinister political implications in their work, for "the desired effect is to train the greatest number of people in order to create a pattern of unimaginable dimensions." That critic's blindness to those chorus girls' individuality put him in stark contrast to Wilder, a budding artist (and already polished womanizer) who sketched in each dancer's personality in a few deft strokes. Wilder's lack of affinity with the Marxist approach to seeing the world, and what some critics, fairly or not, would call his leering approach to femininity, are on display in his articles on the dance troupe, along with his common humanity, a quality not always valued by theoreticians but indispensable to popular artists.

When, in effect, Wilder was put in the position of one of the Tiller Girls, he regarded the numbingly unemotional aspect of his job as *Eintänzer* with the strongest ambivalence. Although maintaining professional self-control enabled him to keep his self-respect by not succumbing to the degradation of prostitution, it also fostered the dehumanizing sense of emotional distance his films tend to criticize in their characters. The contrast between the quasi-sexual nature of the job and the dancer's resulting but emotionally risky need for detachment, particularly Wilder's need to maintain that attitude since he was working only temporarily at the job and planning to write about it, offers the same dramatic conflict and suspense we see in his films. Petrescu notes that "Wilder is told that the *Eintänzer* has to distance himself from any personal inclinations toward his clients. The ability to rise above personal preferences and engage with a variety of clients resonates with some defining traits of the *Neue Sachlichkeit* [the New Objectivity movement], such as detachment, self-control, and lack of or control of emotions . . . best exemplified in the figure of the *kalte persona* [cold person] . . . a figure who is detached emotionally and whose cool conduct conceals and controls any signs of 'feminine' vulnerability."

This detachment, however chic it may have seemed to many in Weimar Berlin and however much the characteristically brash Wilder leaned further in that direction out of self-protection, is viewed as a double-edged sword in his films, a dangerous tendency toward emotional deadening and callous mistreatment of other people. But the distance Wilder carefully maintains in his role as dancer for hire is salutary in the sense that it distinguishes him from the reckless desperation of the tragic or nearly tragic gigolo characters in his films. His attitude toward those days as a paid dancer gradually darkened in retrospect. An actual part-time *Eintänzer* appears only two years after the series in Wilder's first notable screenplay, *People on Sunday*, but there the profession is treated casually. Wolfgang von Waltershausen, a nonactor like the film's other principals, is identified in a title by his occupations, as an "officer, farmer, antique dealer, *Eintänzer*, and wine trader." Wolfgang is not a gigolo but a ladies' man, a slick and somewhat callous one, even if there seems no social stigma attached to the *Eintänzer* profession in that early Wilder film. The darker aspects of being a gigolo became increasingly evident as Wilder continued projecting his experiences into cinematic fiction, gradually looking back at his past experiences with more jaundiced eyes, or perhaps just viewing them more clearly with age.

The *Eintänzer* series ends on a bitter and sardonic note. Wilder recounts how "a beautiful dark woman in precious ermine, with a gown underneath that looks like silver armor" dined and danced almost silently with him for two hours.* He is unappreciated for his wit or even basic intelligence as they

---

* Wilder wrote "einer schönen schwarzen Frau," an ambiguous phrase that could have been translated then to refer to "a beautiful Black woman" or "a beautiful black-haired woman."

eat their nine-course meal, drink an expensive bottle of dry Veuve Clicquot Champagne, and come and go from the dance floor. All she says to him is, "Do you think the Black Bottom is coming into fashion?" He finds her silence deeply insulting: "It must be imagined that she thinks, I have rented two legs because I feel like dancing, but their owner is an idiot." At the conclusion of the evening, she compounds the insult by commanding him to accompany her home in a taxicab. Although "nervous," he goes along, evidently weighing the risks of taking the momentous step from *Eintänzer* to full-out male prostitute. But he wiggles out of the encounter by feigning ignorance at her home on Kantstrasse when she asks condescendingly, "Do you know who Kant was?"

The article concludes sardonically, "Who Kant was? Poor dear. I do not want to spoil the joke for which she spent seventy-two marks, not including carfare. I answer, 'Of course, ma'am, a Swiss national hero.' She purses her lips, raises her hand, and caresses my cheek, as with a poor, confused child. Then she enters the house and locks the door behind her. I raise my collar and walk down the street."

By playing dumb, he's left with dignity intact, a kind of victory over his reduced circumstances, a demonstration that he is morally superior to this snobbish woman and the social role he refuses to allow to demean him. That dignity was a trait he would give to the prostitutes in his films, whom he does not look down on but treats with warmth and respect. And though he would starkly portray the self-destructive tendencies of gigolos onscreen, he always maintains his and our sympathy with them as well, along with the sense of pity Aristotle defines as our overriding response to tragedy.

Nevertheless, much of Wilder's film work deals with the sordid nature of the transactions involved in such encounters and the toll they take on the human spirit, as well as on his characters' conflicts between the temptation of succumbing to or abandoning the "life." The self-loathing many critics have perceived in Wilder's protagonists is partly a reflection of his experience as an *Eintänzer*, playing on lonely women's need for emotional attention in exchange for his more or less impersonal skills as a depressingly rote role-playing dancer and conversationalist. Self-loathing by Wilder characters is often a cause for criticism by his detractors, who reject this strain in his work as if it represents a flaw rather than his acknowledgment of an uncomfortable truth about how life is lived under conditions of moral compromise.

Wilder drew a great deal of drama out of such conflicts, but he also could treat them with humor. The locus classicus of the theme comes as Betty asks Gillis when they are working on a script together, "Don't you sometimes hate yourself?" With a sardonic grin, Joe shoots back, "Constantly!"

THE RACING REPORTER'S LEGACY

Although "Waiter, Bring Me a Dancer!" did not make Wilder an overnight sensation, the series helped advance his reputation in the competitive world of Weimar Berlin journalism.

What it brought him in the short run was a job as a night editor and feature writer for the *Berlin Messenger Exchanges*. But his features there were published under abbreviations of his name or under various pseudonyms, including "Richard Wiener" and "Julian." It was not until Wilder lost that unglamorous job in April 1928 that he found a full-time post at the more widely read *B. Z.*, which had run the *Eintänzer* series, but he gave up that job by September to concentrate on screenwriting. His rise as a screenwriter was rapid, even if the work he turned out in Germany was highly uneven, and he continued to write an occasional piece of journalism for the next couple of years.

How far Billie might have gone as a reporter is purely conjectural. Who knows what kind of pieces Wilder might have turned out if he had stayed in the profession? His reporting career, bright and witty and cheeky as it was, was too short to allow a definitive evaluation of his abilities in that line of work. But the restlessness evident in his relatively quick move into films—he concentrated on journalism for only a little more than three years before shifting his focus to screenwriting in 1928—suggests he did not feel compelled to pursue journalism with his full intensity and commitment. Although reporting appealed to him with its immediacy and variety and access to fascinating people, the unavoidable superficiality of most newspaper work no doubt left the ambitious young Wilder wanting something more. His writing talents were precocious but still developing in his days as a reporter, and it seems inevitable in retrospect that he soon found his true métier in the relatively fresh medium of motion pictures. But he would not have become the gifted craftsman and social critic he was, or become able to put across his criticism while also entertaining his audiences, without having learned his trade in the popular press.

FILMIC PREMONITIONS

The influence of films is obvious on the young reporter who occasionally interviewed stars and covered film sets. The first such recorded visit Wilder made to one was in August 1925 to the filming in a Vienna studio of *Der Rosenkavalier* (*The Knight of the Rose*), a silent film based on the opera by Richard Strauss and directed by Robert Wiene, who had made *The Cabinet of Dr. Caligari*. And for *The Stage* in February 1926, Wilder wrote an article entitled "The Props of the American Film," a jocular but mostly witless catalogue of clichés from the films of Japan, Spain, France, and the United States: American films largely deal with billionaires, horses, guns, and so forth. Wilder even reviewed films in Vienna and Berlin, but he was rarely a first-rate practitioner of that craft. He tended to recount plots more than offering analysis, but his joyous appreciations of such comic performers as Laurel and Hardy and Charlie Chaplin, in particular, shine through his sketchy reviewing.

And Wilder displayed an acute sense of aesthetic taste, especially discerning for that time, when he wrote about *Greed*, the much-maligned 1924 masterpiece of the Vienna native Erich von Stroheim, whom he would later direct in two films. Under the title *Gier nach Geld (Lust for Money)*, *Greed* played only one day in Berlin in 1928. Wilder briefly reviewed it for *B. Z. am Mittag*, noting, "Of the former outrage over this cruel naturalistic depiction of human depths of depravity, there is now no trace. . . . Even though it is one-sided and with some empty symbols, in places it is a stirring soul painting of a woman [Trina, played by Zasu Pitts], in which the lust for money awakens all ugly passions. It is gripping by the forcefulness of its presentation. Watching it is not a restful experience, yet it is a pleasure, albeit of a different kind."

In a much longer profile of Stroheim in April 1929 for the *Cross-Section*, Wilder quoted Universal chief Carl Laemmle as telling the director, while shaking his head after seeing *Blind Husbands* (1919), "My dear Stroheim, you are ahead of us by five years," a comment Wilder heard repeated in Berlin after *Greed* was shown. Wilder wrote in the profile that he appreciated the director's "George Grosz types" in *Greed* displaying "brutal thoughts" on their faces, as well as Stroheim's morbid irony and ability to make cinematic associations, such as the way he "demasks for this first time: this is what a wedding is in truth, this is what a funeral is in truth" in the famous scene showing a funeral procession seen through an apartment window while, inside, a wedding is taking place in the foreground. When Wilder was making his first film with Stroheim in Hollywood, *Five Graves to Cairo* (1943), he introduced himself to the legendary actor-director ("whom I adored from my high-school days") by saying that he had always been *ten* years ahead of the rest of the film industry. "Twenty," snapped Stroheim. Wilder wrote in the profile that Stroheim's latest film, *Queen Kelly*, was "said to be great." Stroheim eventually was fired from that Gloria Swanson film, which was left unfinished, a major debacle in his career (it was later released after being partly reshot). But Wilder memorably showed Swanson watching *Queen Kelly* with self-admiration in her role as the deranged silent-film diva in *Sunset Blvd*. As Michael Wilmington and I wrote, Wilder's work "emulates [Stroheim's] fatalism, even to the point of having Stroheim personally set up the last shot in *Sunset Blvd*."

With melancholic shrewdness, Wilder pointed out in his profile, "Stroheim is a poor man. DeMille, Griffith, Lubitsch do not know what to do with their money. Murnau has bought a yacht and will be sailing it between Japan and California for a year. Stroheim and his family live in a simple house, and he drives a four-cylinder car. The pure fool of Hollywood." Wilder later said of his own films, "I always think of my style as a curious cross between Lubitsch and Stroheim." Stroheim's acerbic blending of hyperrealism, social commentary, and grotesque expressionism left its imprint on the darker side of Wilder, both stylistically, especially in his work in what became the film noir genre, and more generally in his jaundiced view of humanity. Wilder admired Stroheim for an additional reason, telling Zolotow that Stroheim "succeeded in slyly getting a lot of sex perversion into those films he shot in 1919, 1920. In regard to sex perversion, Mr. von Stroheim was not only twenty years ahead of his time—he was fifty years ahead of his time."

For *The Stage* in 1926, Wilder even published a tantalizingly brief item on Lubitsch (who had left Germany for the United States in 1921), a description of what purports to be a risqué real-life Lubitsch Touch. This sketchy piece indicates a certain level of familiarity with Lubitsch's work, but only glancingly and superficially. It scarcely begins to suggest the degree of the mature

Wilder's fascination with his future mentor. Wilder offers a feeble anecdote about an actress named Daisy going for an audition with Lubitsch ("the Almighty") and being asked to show her legs. Seeing the left leg, the director says, "Not bad! The other leg, please!" Daisy is "ashamed" to show the other leg and replies instead, "Looks just the same!" Whereupon Lubitsch supposedly jokes, "So? You are committed. For my next film: *The Lady with the Two Left Feet!*"

Despite the scattered inklings in his early journalism of the career he soon would begin pursuing, Wilder strikingly complained in one of his 1927 Berlin articles, "Filmterror," about "my film aversion." He explained that "the film terror" he was experiencing stemmed from being photographed by an "offensive" street cameraman taking motion picture shots of people to sell for a mark apiece. At first Wilder thought the cameraman was scouting people to appear in a film and reacted congenially, but when he figured out what was happening he became angry that the man accosted him twice a day for months on his way to and from a restaurant for lunch. Wilder tried hiding from the camera but finally resorted to paying the man and writing on the film strip in thick red ink, "This person wishes not to be filmed anymore." While this article seems ironic in retrospect, it does not have the whimsical tone one might expect. Wilder seems to have been genuinely offended by being captured unwillingly on film.

Although Wilder plays a bit part in his first credited screenplay, *The Devil's Reporter*, as a dapper reporter named "Billie Wilder," wearing a jauntily tilted felt hat, that wacky comedy was directed by someone else (Ernst Laemmle, a nephew of Universal Pictures chief Carl Laemmle), and in the films Wilder directed, he never emulated Alfred Hitchcock's penchant for cameo appearances. He later appeared in numerous documentaries, however, and even played himself in an episode of *The Jack Benny Program* in 1962. Relaxed and adroit in his comic timing while haggling with the former Lubitsch star over money and the size of his role in a proposed comeback film, Wilder exits by telling Benny, "Everybody should do what he's good at. Just I think you should stick to television . . . and I should stick to directing." Although Wilder had been camera-averse in his more insecure early years, perhaps because he didn't consider himself especially good-looking, his 1920s journalism otherwise makes clear that he was already in the thrall of the medium that would soon supplant his first career. So the suggestion in his 1927 article of ambivalence over being photographed for movies is intriguing and enigmatic, perhaps a warning from his subconscious about his future career; it seems the mark of someone sensing his fate seeking him out unwillingly and not being entirely comfortable with where it will lead him. As a character puts it in a film Wilder cowrote, *Ein blonder Traum (A Blonde Dream*, 1932), "Film, that's no profession for adults."

We can find the roots of *The Devil's Reporter* in Wilder's heavy-breathing coverage of the Tiller Girls pulling into Vienna by train. A black-comic piece he had written the day before, entitled "In Vienna Six People a Day Disappear," also may have percolated in his mind when he wrote his first credited screenplay. But the idea for the film came while he was working as a reporter in Berlin in 1928. He read an article in *The Hour* about one of the Tiller Girls reported as kidnapped on another visit by the troupe to Vienna. That turned out to be a publicity stunt but gave him the plot springboard for a newspaper comedy about a group of thirteen American millionaires' daughters visiting Berlin by train with a housekeeper only to be kidnapped by a gang of blackmailers. They are rescued by an intrepid rewrite man ambitious to become a racing reporter (like Wilder himself) for the aptly titled *Rapid Journal*. The aspiring reporter is played by Eddie Polo. A native of Vienna, the actor and stuntman had appeared in Hollywood serials directed by and starring Francis Ford but had been working in Germany since 1926 as both an actor and a director. The character in Wilder's script is named Eddie Polo, and his reporter's job rather absurdly involves doing physical stunts.

More significant for film history than the fact that Wilder pillaged his real-life interactions with the girls' band and dance troupe for his first credited German script is that they provided adumbrations of his mature masterpiece *Some Like It Hot*. That 1920s-set film also borrowed from his covert experience with female impersonating in Berlin as a newspaper columnist offering advice for ladies. And even the roots of Wilder's seemingly most impersonal film as a director, *The Spirit of St. Louis* (1957), his earnestly hero-worshipping account of Charles Lindbergh's landmark flight from Long Island to Paris in 1927, may be found in his journalism from that era. The roving young reporter repeatedly displays a fascination with the growing trend of airplane travel. Wilder's modernistic passion for mechanized speed is also evident in his articles in his love of fast cars, the criminal fixation of the protagonist of his directorial debut film, *Mauvaise graine*.

Wilder's lifelong love of athletics can be seen in his intermittent early sports reporting in Vienna and Berlin, including covering Winter Olympic games or interviewing the heavyweight boxing champion Max Schmeling. Wilder's sports obsessions can be seen in his 1966 film *The Fortune Cookie*, about an insurance scam involving a television cameraman feigning a football injury, and in his habit of naming film characters after athletes, especially college football players. One of his favorite character names, Sheldrake, used for a producer in *Sunset Blvd.* and a dentist in *Kiss Me, Stupid* and most memorably for Fred MacMurray's sleazy insurance executive in *The Apartment*, was taken from a UCLA basketball player, Eddie Sheldrake '51.*

It may well be that the *Eintänzer* series, which reads so strikingly like a film scenario with its smoothly shifting scenes and colorful dialogue and atmosphere, helped bring Wilder to the attention of people in the film business he aspired to enter. Indeed it may have been deliberately designed as an audition piece as his interests turned more in that direction. Sikov lists various people who may have helped Wilder become a screenwriter, noting that he "had met a number of working screenwriters at the Romanisches [Café] as well as the newspapers for which he wrote." He struck up an important acquaintance with the most famous German screenwriter, Carl Mayer, writer of such expressionist classics as *Das Cabinet des Dr. Caligari* (*The Cabinet of Dr. Caligari*) and *Der letzte Mann* (*The Last Laugh*), at the Café Kranzler, where Wilder went each morning to get the papers off the train from Vienna. Wilder claimed to have begun his screenwriting career assisting established screenwriters. Sikov reports, "With his growing list of connections, not to forget his talent and spiny ambition, Billie found his way into the ghostwriting racket. Berliners had an unpleasant term for ghostwriters: they called them *Neger—niggers.* Most of the scripts Wilder wrote as a *Neger* were for

---

* Wilder followed baseball and football obsessively on television. During the Dodgers-Phillies playoffs in October 1978, he told me and Todd McCarthy while we were chatting about sports, "A writer is always looking for an excuse not to write. The Dodgers are the best excuse of all. Show me a writer who enjoys writing and I'll show you a lousy writer. That doesn't mean, however, that if you do not enjoy writing, you are necessarily a good writer." In 1970 Wilmington and I observed in our career profile of Wilder, "Wilder's conception of life as a game, with the swifties on one side and the law on the other, may also account for his fondness for sports. . . . A football game is the perfect stylization of the con-game; it is played out in the open, enforced rigorously by uniformed officials, it is action through grace and strategy—but the underbelly is gambling and commercialism."

Curt Braun, whom Wilder calls a 'walking script factory,' and the writer-director Franz Schulz."

Wilder in later years claimed he contributed to as many as 150 or 200 scripts and treatments without credit, surely a considerable exaggeration, but whatever work he did in that shadowy realm prepared him for a running start once he began getting credited onscreen in 1929. Ghostwriting turns up as a central theme in his film work in the Paramount musical *Rhythm on the River* (1940), from a clever story by Jacques Théry and Wilder (originally titled *Ghost Music)* about a team (Bing Crosby and Mary Martin) who fall in love while writing songs for a famous composer (Basil Rathbone) suffering from writer's block or mere incompetence (the screenplay was by Dwight Taylor). Joe Gillis also works as a ghostwriter in *Sunset Blvd.* to turn Norma's huge pile of yellowing pages of her *Salomé* screenplay project into something more presentable, if not filmable (the choice of *Salomé* is in part a reference to the scandalous opera by Richard Strauss, whom Wilder dubiously claimed to have interviewed in Vienna). Gillis tells the audience when he starts to read Norma's work, "Sometimes it's interesting to see just how bad bad writing can be. This promised to go the limit."

François Truffaut once observed that you can tell a lot about a director from knowing what his occupation was before he began making films. Journalism played a key role in turning Wilder into the incisive, witty social commentator he would become as he moved into the world of screenwriting and directing.

3.1 (top) Lilian Harvey with Willy Fritsch and Willi Forst as she sings her poignant song about the illusory nature of happiness against a historic Berlin backdrop in *A Blonde Dream* (1932), toward the end of the Weimar era. Wilder cowrote this musical comedy directed by Paul Martin. (UFA/Alamy.)

3.2 (bottom) Harvey's Jou-Jou on a studio soundstage in her nightmarish fantasy of going to Hollywood in *A Blonde Dream*, reflecting what Wilder called his early "Filmterror" in Berlin. (UFA/Alamy.)

3

"FILM, THAT'S NO PROFESSION FOR ADULTS"

Back then [in Europe], there was hardly a screenwriter or director who did not say: "I would really like to go to Hollywood!" . . . [And yet] One always asked oneself, "Am I good enough to write in Hollywood? Am I good enough to direct in Hollywood?"

—Billy Wilder, 1980

WHEN I interviewed Wilder with Todd McCarthy in 1978, one of the topics we discussed was his final return as a filmmaker to Germany to make *Fedora*, an even more morbid commentary on the Hollywood star system than *Sunset Blvd.* Shooting a tax-shelter production based in Munich after Hollywood rejected the project was a strange sort of homecoming for a major American filmmaker who had served his apprenticeship in Berlin.

Wilder's willingness to go back to Germany intermittently to make films after World War II was in contrast to Ernst Lubitsch's utter rejection of his former homeland after Hitler's takeover in 1933. On his final visit to Berlin in December 1932, Lubitsch told a Jewish journalist, Bella Fromm, who asked if he might work there again, "That's finished. I'm going to the United States. Nothing good is going to happen here for a long time. The sun shines every day in Hollywood." Lubitsch died not long after the war ended, but given his attitude toward Germany—after the Nazi takeover, he refused to let the language be spoken in his home, according to his daughter, Nicola—it is doubtful he would have succumbed to any such overtures. But even though Wilder lost close relatives in the Holocaust, he was always more pragmatic, returning to Germany after the war to work for the U.S. Army on the de-Nazification effort and for Hollywood studios doing location shooting on *A Foreign Affair* and *One, Two, Three*.

Fedora brought his career full circle from one kind of exile to another, almost fifty years later. Even though that film was shot in English, it was a bittersweet sort of return to his roots in the German cinema. Wilder told us, "I have some kind of a reputation in Germany, why I don't know, because when I left Germany I was just one of the writers at UFA. Since the other ones are dead, suddenly the mantle of [F. W.] Murnau, and of Fritz Lang, and of Erich Pommer, and of Lubitsch falls on my shoulders. I was just a writer of maybe one or two pictures that were of some interest. But now I come to Germany and they gave me a party and, my God, old UFA is going to rise again."

The "one or two pictures that were of some interest" would include, by anyone's measure, *People on Sunday* and *Emil und die Detektive* (*Emil and the Detectives*, 1931). Some of the others have their merits as well, especially the 1932 releases *A Blonde Dream* and *Scampolo, ein Kind der Strasse* (*Scampolo, A Child of the Streets*).* But though Wilder was always justifiably proud of *People on Sunday*, he disparaged most of his journeyman work as a screenwriter in Germany, saying that the films he had to work on were "too sentimental." In a darker mood, he complained to biographer Kevin Lally, "Do I have to talk about them? They were all lousy." But when "pressed" by Lally about *Emil and the Detectives*, Wilder admitted, "That was pretty good."

Wilder was overly dismissive of his other German work, despite its wildly uneven nature and tendency to fall prey to the kind of schmaltz he later disdained in Hollywood. It was no coincidence that he spoke fondly of *Emil* and *People on Sunday*, although superficially they are quite different kinds of films, since *People on Sunday* is a shoestring semidocumentary drama with an amateur cast, and *Emil* is a polished work of professional narrative filmmaking. It is a charmingly comical adaptation, with some dark elements, of a popular children's novel about adolescents banding together in the metropolis to catch

---

* *Scampolo* is also known as *Ein Mädel der Strasse* (*A Girl of the Streets*) and *Um einen Groschen liebe* (*Love for a Penny*).

an adult criminal. But despite their genre differences, both films stand out in the list of Wilder's German credits because of the sustained use and raw authenticity of their street settings and their often grim implications about daily life in Berlin.

They also contrast sharply with the deliberately airy escapism of most of Wilder's assignments at UFA, the country's leading studio, in his brief period as a German screenwriter (1928–1933). As he indicated, those other films tend to suffer from the kind of formulaic, escapist, sentimental plots he would avoid in the films he eventually directed in Hollywood. A number of Wilder's German scripts were for *operettenfilmen*, or cinematic operettas. A popular genre that flourished with the coming of sound, it was one he did not find particularly congenial to his talents or interests (he mocks the genre to some extent in *The Emperor Waltz*). Nevertheless, he worked in that format surprisingly often in both Germany and the United States, if not always by his own wish, but sometimes even in the films he directed. Unlike the operettas Lubitsch was filming in Hollywood, which draw from the Viennese tradition and have luxurious settings and often royal or upper-class characters, many of the operettas being made in Germany while Wilder was toiling there had contemporary settings, with characters from the working class.

Even so, while Lubitsch in *The Love Parade*, *Monte Carlo*, and *The Smiling Lieutenant* cleverly and paradoxically provides biting social satire thinly disguised under frivolous surfaces, the agenda of the German *operettenfilm* genre in Wilder's time at UFA was not social criticism or subversion of the established order (at least overtly). Siegfried Kracauer aptly characterized most films made in Germany during the years directly leading up to the Nazi regime as being part of "a culture of distraction."

THE FILM CONNOISSEUR

Wilder had gone into films with the enthusiasm of a youthful fan and connoisseur, having enjoyed the American comedies of Buster Keaton and Charlie Chaplin and the comical adventure films of Douglas Fairbanks Sr. But Wilder told Hellmuth Karasek that he was inspired to take the filmmaking profession seriously as an occupation by three brilliant and ambitious "art" films in particular:

※ Sergei Eisenstein's landmark Soviet silent drama *Battleship Potemkin* (1925), with its powerful use of montage and images of the kinds of outrages that lead to revolution; Wilder always cited the revealing shot of maggots in the sailors' supposedly healthy meat as his model of a powerful close-up;

※ René Clair's groundbreaking French musical *Sous les toits de Paris* (*Under the Roofs of Paris*, 1930), which experimented with graceful camerawork and a freer use of sound than was usual in the first talkies, as well as combining comedy and stark drama in the unsettling ways Wilder would always relish; and

※ Leontine Sagan's trenchant attack on Prussian education values, *Mädchen in Uniform* (*Girls in Uniform*, 1931), a passionate work of social criticism that served as an antimilitary allegory and dared to explore what it portrays as a potentially liberating but tentative lesbian relationship between a student and a teacher in a girls' school.

Wilder admired *Potemkin* because of "the way the film jumps the audience by the throat as [Eisenstein] overwhelmed his audience"; *Under the Roofs of Paris* because Clair "showed me everything that is beautiful in life. . . . A tribute to optimism"; and *Mädchen* because of "the fact that the camera has no limits! . . . Suddenly, you feel compassion and sympathy for people you classified as 'social outcasts.' . . . The movie makes us compassionate."

But if Wilder thought he could make films like that as a lowly screenwriting apprentice in the German commercial system, he found he was mistaken. The times were against him, and the films to which he was assigned were in large part designed as the antithesis of challenging cinema.

A HELL OF A START

Wilder's screenwriting career (at least after he emerged from the status of ghostwriter) did not begin entirely inauspiciously. However ridiculous, the larkish silent film *The Devil's Reporter* in 1929 (the title could also be translated as *The Daredevil Reporter* or *A Hell of a Reporter*) at least drew on his day job as a Racing Reporter with some tongue-in-cheek wit.

Wilder sold the script to Paul Kohner, a native of Bohemia who ran the Universal Productions office in Berlin with producer Joe Pasternak, a Hungarian. They needed a script pronto for Ernst Laemmle to direct; "Uncle

Carl's" nephew had spent time in Hollywood, where he had been an assistant director for Lubitsch on the silent films *Lady Windermere's Fan* and *So This Is Paris*. Kohner, like Wilder, would flee Hitler and establish himself as an important Hollywood figure. He ran a talent agency representing, among other illustrious directors, Wilder himself. Kohner also helped run a Hollywood fund to support fellow refugees from Nazis, a project crucial to saving many lives and one in which Lubitsch was importantly involved and to which Wilder contributed. Pasternak, who also took credit for giving Wilder his professional start, became a successful Hollywood producer of schmaltzy Deanna Durbin movies—one of which Wilder helped write without credit—and other conventional fare.

As Wilder's agent, Kohner came full circle with the director, arranging the financing for *Fedora* after Universal dropped its option on the project. When I asked Wilder if it was Kohner who set up the deal with a German tax-shelter group, the director said, "Yes, because he's of that origin there and being the—how shall I say this?—Ingmar Bergman man [i.e., the celebrated Swedish director's Hollywood agent], you know, the Big European Celluloid Connection. It was not difficult to set it up, but I just could not get the money here. Look, I can't lose, because if this picture is a big hit [it wasn't], it's my revenge on Hollywood. If it is a total financial disaster, it's my revenge for Auschwitz."

The Devil's Reporter, which runs about an hour, is paced at breakneck speed, as an almost constant chase. The notion of a lowly rewrite man seizing the opportunity to act like a serial hero (or superhero, in today's parlance) to rescue the bevy of comely American heiresses from a gang of kidnappers is amusing, at least in theory if not entirely in execution. Director Laemmle ably stages a variety of wild stunts on the streets of Berlin, giving a rapid tour of the metropolis suitable to someone of Wilder's incorrigibly restless nature or for viewers who need to catch an early train. Eddie Polo spends most of the picture hanging off buildings and jumping in and out of cars and open-air buses. He is accompanied by an amusing copyboy sidekick, Maxe (Fred Grosser), who seems to have wandered in from a casting session for the upcoming production of *Emil and the Detectives*.

Wilder correctly pointed out to me that Polo was too old to make such derring-do more than barely believable. Yet Wilder's disenchantment with the first film to bear his name was so extreme that he grossly exaggerated Polo's actual age when he said of *The Devil's Reporter*, "Oh, it was bullshit, absolute bullshit. The leading man was an old Hungarian-American cowboy actor by the name of Eddie Polo, and he was already, by that time, seventy-five." Polo was actually fifty-four. In addition to his movie background in both the United States and Germany, he was a former circus acrobat, a real-life daredevil, the first man to parachute from the Eiffel Tower. But as game as he is with his stunts in *The Devil's Reporter*, the part should have gone to a man in his twenties.

There are signs that the film recognizes its own absurdities, which is part of its not inconsiderable charm and chutzpah. By the climax, Eddie is calling in the rescue story with a phone in one hand and a gun in the other to hold off the bad guys, and *The Devil's Reporter* becomes positively surreal in its silliness, like a Marx Bros. movie on steroids. The unlikely, suspiciously hasty happy ending showing Eddie, now a star reporter, winning the hand of the maidens' attractive young teacher is a letdown by contrast. It would have been enough to show him as a successful, more confident reporter banging out another story with Maxe's assistance. What seems to have bothered Wilder most about the film, however, is that he thought Polo was having an affair with his girlfriend, Olive Victoria. He wrote a poem about her, "Fifth from the Right," for a Berlin newspaper, and many years later he confessed to Cameron Crowe that he "was just kind of haunted by her," especially because she spoke very good English.

That colored Wilder's recollections of what is, by and large, a piece of unpretentious entertainment that could have led to his continuing to write zany comedies and other idiosyncratic films drawn from the personal storehouse of his highly varied journalistic background. Instead, when he was hired by UFA in 1930, he usually was assigned to operettas and other quasi-Lubitschean comedies that seem like pale imitations of the master. But first he and a group of young colleagues made the cheekily avant-garde classic *People on Sunday*, a film destined to be influential internationally, even though Wilder's subsequent career in Germany went off in a much different direction.

"A FILM WITHOUT ACTORS"

People on Sunday was conceived in June 1929 in a spirit of rebellion of the small group of tyro filmmakers against the commercial system. They challenged the enforced escapism that was the rule in mainstream German cinema, a reactionary tendency that militated against social commentary and realism. Daringly made as part-documentary, part-fiction, shot outside the studios on the streets and in the countryside around Berlin, the low-budget *People on Sunday*, principally written by Wilder, is a fascinating and influential hybrid. Directors Robert Siodmak and Edgar G. Ulmer treat its low-key dramatic elements in the semidocumentary manner later identified with Italian neorealism; the loose, playful style also prefigures the French Nouvelle Vague (New Wave). The cast members (only one of whom had any professional experience) play characters drawn from their own lives, thrown together on a bittersweet weekend excursion.

After the film was finished, no one wanted this offbeat effort until an adventurous UFA executive named Hanns Brodnitz, senior manager for the company's Berlin theaters, picked it up for distribution. The Berlin premiere of *People on Sunday* was held at the prestigious UFA-Theater am Kurfürstendamm on February 4, 1930. It instantly catapulted to fame Wilder and his remarkable group of collaborators on that "experiment," at least within the artistic circles that paid attention to films and within the German industry. Although the public largely neglected *People on Sunday*, it was a critical sensation.

UFA quickly snapped up Siodmak and Wilder, although to make more commercial fare. After Siodmak escaped from Germany in 1933 and spent time in Paris, he had a distinguished career in the United States on moody mystery and horror films and in film noir, a genre strongly influenced by German expressionism. Siodmak returned to work in Europe in the postwar era. Ulmer, a native of Czechoslovakia, went on a more eccentric path as a minimalist B-movie maker that made him a cult figure with his classic low-budget noir *Detour* (1945) and other work on the margins of the industry in Hollywood, New York, and later back in Europe. Their remarkable array of collaborators on *People on Sunday* included cinematographer Eugen Shüfftan and assistant cameraman Fred Zinnemann, who also would go on to major careers in the United States. Before Ulmer worked on *People on Sunday*, he had already worked in Hollywood on Murnau's masterpiece *Sunrise* (1927), assisting the German art director Rochus Gliese. Gliese was the original director of *People on Sunday* but quit a few days into the shooting.

As often happens in filmmaking, but with even more rancor in the case of this landmark film, the principals gave out contradictory stories over the years in staking their various claims to credit. Kurt (later Curt) Siodmak, Robert's brother, is credited for contributing to the writing of *People on Sunday*. As Curt he would become a popular novelist and screenwriter, best known for the classic horror film *The Wolf Man* (1941) and the novel and film *Donovan's Brain*, but he was embittered by what he felt was the slighting by both his brother and Wilder of the extent of his involvement. Like others involved, Curt claimed to have helped finance the production, which was produced by Seymour Nebenzal and Moriz Seeler,* and he never ceased complaining about Wilder getting more prominent writing credit; I even had to listen to a harangue by Curt Siodmak on that subject when I expressed my appreciation for the film during the 1992 Los Angeles reception at which he was honored with Germany's Order of Merit. Today, and with so many conflicting stories from the collaborators, it's virtually impossible to make a definitive judgment on the film's authorship beyond relying on the screen credits: *"Manuskript: Billie Wilder, nach einer Reportage von Kurt Siodmak"* (Script by Billy Wilder based on reportage by Kurt Siodmak).

Wilder staked his share of claim at the time to the screenwriting credit in a pair of promotional newspaper articles published in *Tempo* (July 1929) and *Der Montag Morgen* (*The Monday Morning*, February 1930). "It was a miserable time. It was a great time," he reported of their nine months of filming with "a completely ridiculous sum of money [about 28,000 marks, or $7,000, the equivalent of about $100,000 today] to deal with a few truths that seem important to us." He wrote that the film originated in coffee-house discussions at the Romanisches Café among the young team about making something that would disregard commercial conventions to become "A film of Berlin, of its people, about the everyday things that we know so well." The script, Wilder reported at the time, consisted of "seven typewritten pages." The nonactress around whom the story revolves, Brigitte Borchert, was interviewed for a 2000 documentary film about the production, *Weekend am Wannsee* (*Weekend at the Wannsee*). She recalled witnessing daily story conferences among the collaborators: "They didn't have a script or anything. And that's how it went. . . . We'd sit at a nearby table while they'd decide what to do that day." Ulmer's recollection in 1970, however, was that "Billy Wilder

---

* Seymour Nebenzal's father, Heinrich Nebenzahl (who spelled the family name differently), had helped arrange the funding for the film.

wrote the script on pieces of scratch paper in the Romanisches Café." Adding to the confusion, or legend, Wilder told Cameron Crowe that he had a copy of his script, written at the café, and it ran twenty-five pages.

While drawing inspiration from the New Objectivity that refocused artistic attention from expressionism to ordinary life, *People on Sunday* partly imitated the format of the "city symphony" documentaries that had become fashionable in the late silent period for their panoramic perspectives on urban life. Walther Ruttmann's *Berlin: Die Sinfonie der Grosstadt* (*Berlin, Symphony of a Great City*, 1927), was the obvious prototype, although Dziga Vertov's Soviet film *The Man with the Movie Camera* (1929) is a superior example and was cited by Ulmer as a key influence. But *People on Sunday*, as its title indicates, becomes the diametrical opposite of those relatively impersonal works: a portrait of a city through intimate, anecdotal looks at some representative inhabitants. Like Wilder's *Eintänzer* series, it seems like a documentary report but is fictionalized. It set out to tell what Wilder called in his *Tempo* article "a very, very simple story, quiet and yet full of melodies that sound for all of us daily. Without gags or punchlines. . . . The five people in this film are you and me."

Made at the very end of the silent period, *People on Sunday* was immediately recognized as a daring artistic experiment, a film that with its gritty blend of documentary and a slight narrative tried to reclaim some of the special qualities that had made the German industry the world leader in the 1920s, before many of its top figures, including Lubitsch and Murnau, were lured away by Hollywood. Aside from a few landmark films in the late 1920s, such as Fritz Lang's *Metropolis* (1927) and Georg Wilhelm Pabst's *Die Büchse der Pandora* (*Pandora's Box*, 1929), the German industry had fallen into relative artistic doldrums. The industry was now making mostly undistinguished formula pictures. A cultural malaise seemed to have taken over Berlin from the artistic daring and experimentation that characterized the immediate postwar years, inspired by the violent upheavals and desperation running amok throughout German society. But as relative calm was briefly restored before the Nazi storm, audiences and filmmakers alike indulged themselves in safely complacent, escapist entertainment that broke no dangerous new ground. This tendency owed much to the moderate economic recovery of the mid-1920s, with the stabilization of the German currency and an infusion of foreign capital.

Although the recovery arrested the ruinous course of inflation that had caused the food shortages and exacerbated the political crises of that decade, it did not trickle very far down the economic ladder. *People on Sunday* reflects the caustic exposé approach of Wilder's journalistic background in using a cross-section of Berliners to dramatize this socioeconomic situation from a more critical point of view than most newspapers allowed. The film shows the marginal life that ordinary working people were leading just after the start of the worldwide Great Depression, not much different from Wilder's own as a struggling reporter in terms of lack of economic stability. By implication, *People on Sunday* casts serious and prescient doubt on Germany's future.

Average Berliners, portrayed onscreen by five young people in roles resembling their own lives (the one who had some prior cinematic experience was Christl Ehlers, but only as an extra), are shown to have just enough money to earn a bit of leisure time, one day a week to escape the daily grind. The film initially seems to focus on the rocky relationship of one couple, a rough-looking, coarse-acting cab driver played by Erwin Splettstösser (a round-faced fellow bearing something of a resemblance to Wilder), who quarrels with his girlfriend, a model named Annie Schreyer. In a scene displaying Wilder's cinephilia (often an aspect of his work as a director as well), they vindictively tear apart a wall display of pictures of favorite film stars, destroying Erwin's picture of Greta Garbo and Annie's of Garbo's onscreen and real-life lover John Gilbert. This hostile couple are separated when the depressed Annie chooses to sleep instead of going out on the Sunday jaunt; she winds up snoozing through almost the entire film. Instead, Erwin's rakishly handsome friend Wolfgang von Waltershausen joins him to go hunting among the available girls they encounter, finding a pair of friends played by Ehlers and Borchert.

The title is derived from the characters' outing to the Wannsee, the lake on the outskirts of Berlin that served as a popular working-class weekend resort. The January 1942 meeting that established the implementation of the policies for the Holocaust, the Wannsee Conference, would take place in the same location, retrospectively throwing the shadow of historical catastrophe over the initially heedless but gradually downbeat proceedings onscreen.

The Erwin-Annie domestic narrative scenes, somewhat flat and tedious, teasingly misdirect the viewer by proving not to be the thinly plotted film's main focus. They are less compelling than the documentary-like glimpses of

the characters on the streets of Berlin—especially a prolonged sequence of
Wolfgang stalking Christl and finally picking her up at a trolley stop—and
on their group outing to the Wannsee. The scenes at the resort include a
charming montage of people posing for a still photographer, seen in freeze
frames, one of the film's seemingly impromptu touches that anticipate the
French Nouvelle Vague.

As Noah Isenberg comments,

> While [*People on Sunday*] continues to draw on the once dominant trend
> of Neue Sachlichkeit (New Objectivity), with its visual riffs on popular
> advertising, design, photography, and technology, its main conceit is its
> utter resistance to prevailing modes and industry norms. The film turns
> its back on studio production, instead allowing the city and its many
> inviting locations (its boulevards and cafés, its lakes, boardwalks, beaches,
> and other places of leisure and recreation) to substitute for the standard
> sets, while at the same time allowing amateurs to play the kinds of roles
> otherwise reserved for film stars. . . . It is also very much an exploration,
> in line with Siegfried Kracauer's [1930] study of Weimar Germany's
> white-collar workers, *The Salaried Masses*, of the new cultural habits of
> the petit bourgeoisie.

In the course of their Sunday "frolic," the wholesome-looking, nineteen-
year-old blonde Brigitte becomes the film's central character, the first true
Billy Wilder heroine, a prototype of Shirley MacLaine's Fran Kubelik in *The
Apartment*, another film about sexual exploitation of a young woman by a
heartless man in a big city. Brigitte, a gramophone salesgirl recruited by producer Seeler from an actual record store on the Kurfürstendamm, is the
most appealing performer in *People on Sunday*. Sweet-natured and lissome,
her character has an open, modern attitude about sex that gets her into some
trouble. The primary focus of the ensemble piece is on the seduction of this
naive, warm-hearted young woman by the suave and handsome young man
Brigitte aptly calls "Wolf." Several years older than her, with varied occupations including *Eintänzer*, he manipulates her for sexual purposes. He oppor-
tunistically shifts his attention from her friend Christl after she slaps him
when he tries to kiss her. But Christl nevertheless comes to resent his dalliance in the woods with Brigitte, whom she had introduced as "my best friend."

Brigitte's obliquely portrayed sex scene with Wolf is justly famous for its inversion of the cinema's romantic expectations.

As Wolf rolls on top of her, Shüfftan's camera starts panning away while they loll back on the ground. The camera sweeps up along the trees, mockingly initiating the clichéd shorthand of ecstasy familiar from countless films. But in this wry imitation of a Lubitsch Touch, the camera tilts down sardonically to a pile of discarded cans and other trash (anticipating Lubitsch's mocking intercutting of a lovers' tryst with a garbage gondola at the beginning of his 1932 romantic comedy *Trouble in Paradise*). As the camera resumes panning slowly back along the trees to the couple in the woods, suggesting the passage of time although ambiguously with this unbroken shot, it reveals the narcissistic Wolf standing fully dressed, looking down as Brigitte sprawls on the ground, engaging in a postcoital nap.

She wakes and looks longingly at him, but her mood is disrupted by finding a pine cone under her rear end (Wilder biographer Maurice Zolotow, determined to make him seem crass, inaccurately claims it is "a rusty can of sardines," evidently mixing up the pine cone with the earlier glimpse of discarded cans). The two young lovers laugh over the symbolic impediment to their happiness, and Brigitte straightens out her underwear, leaving little doubt as to what has happened, even if the unbroken shot offers the filmmakers a teasing form of plausible deniability. As the foursome use a pedal-drive boat to return to the big city, with Brigitte unabashedly smitten, Wolf proves himself even more of a cad, already flirting with two other girls they pass on the lake. Christl, though with a gloating look, puts her arm around the disappointed Brigitte in consolation.

Along with that double personal betrayal and the twist back to a chastened form of ambiguous female friendship/rivalry, a complex development of sexual intrigue that provides the first memorable traces of Wilder's personality on film, the concluding scenes of *People on Sunday* are unrelentingly grim in their implications. The five subjects return to their drone-like lives in the city, with the emotionally wounded Brigitte making an unsuccessful attempt to prolong her brief encounter with Wolf, who instead makes plans with Erwin to go to a soccer game the following Sunday. Male bonding takes precedence over romance, as it sometimes does in Wilder, but always with an edge of disenchantment rather than the celebratory tone of so many Hollywood films in which buddy-buddy bromance is depicted.

The characters' final submersion back into the crowd (the film has simi-larities to King Vidor's 1928 MGM masterpiece, *The Crowd*, which Wilder quotes directly in *The Apartment*) demonstrates in socioeconomic terms exactly how pitiful, and cruelly illusory, their brief release into the countryside actu-ally has been. In large, didactic titles, intercut with documentary shots of the characters and masses of other Berliners returning to their jobs and schools, the film spells out its social message:

> *wieder Arbeit* [Back to work].
> *wieder Alltag* [Back to everyday life].
> *wieder Woche* [The week again].
> *4 Millionen* [Four million people]
> *warten* [waiting] *auf* [for] *den nächsten* [next] *Sonntag* [Sunday].
> *Ende.* [The End]

Berliner Tageblatt reviewer Eugen Szatmari, like most of his colleagues, found the guerrilla style of the enterprise a refreshing antidote to the typical German studio production: "Young people got together and, with laughably little means, without sets or ballrooms or opera galas, without stars, with a few human beings they drew from their professions, they shot a film and achieved a total success, for which one has to congratulate them and which hopefully will finally open up the eyes of the film industry." Unfortunately, those hopes were not to be fulfilled, because the contrasting economic and political imper-atives dominating the German film industry were too strong. Wilder also blamed their film's commercial failure on the fact that, because of its low bud-get, it was a silent when the industry was already largely converted to sound.

Ironically, though, it was the critical success of the avant-garde *People on Sunday* that gave Wilder the cachet to enter the commercial industry that the low-budget film was designed to critique and counteract. The production companies were not interested in replicating the kind of experimental *succès d'estime* Wilder and his collaborators had with *People on Sunday*. As Wilder put it, "And so we had to go back to what the studios thought had a chance to make some profit. Our idea of doing pictures on a slightly higher level fell on its face." They were absorbed into it much as their characters were absorbed back into the workaday world of the big city, though without suffering their anonymity and lack of success.

While the commercial films Wilder wrote for UFA rarely attempt the resolutely unconventional, even confrontational art-film tone of *People on Sunday*, and some are little more than hackwork, his overall output at Germany's leading studio is better than he liked to remember. Despite the many obstacles he faced in that system, which militated against originality and social criticism, Wilder did his best to slip his brand of mordant fatalism, harsh realism, and bittersweet poignancy into the cracks of the plots he was handed. As a fledgling screenwriter with little clout, he had no hope of being able to transform the films entirely but managed to score intermittent successes that, especially when seen in the context of the time, are impressive enough achievements.

IN THE "POISON LABORATORY"

UFA in the pre-Nazi period was controlled by the powerful businessman and media mogul Alfred Hugenberg, who acquired a majority interest in the foundering company in 1927 and transferred it to Nazi ownership after the party took power in 1933. Hugenberg said in 1927 that his goal with his newspapers and other media interests was to "bring back to the national cause" wavering elements in the country "or to hold them to the national track." Hugenberg had been chairman of the supervisory board of Krupp Steel, part of the leading German armaments company, Friederich Krupp AG. He was a major far-right supporter of Hitler and when the Nazis took power would become a member of the chancellor's cabinet, although he was quickly forced to resign over his policy disputes with Hitler.

In the period before the Nazi takeover, Hugenberg gave orders to churn out light film entertainments designed to downplay the severity of the country's economic problems and peddle what seems in retrospect an irrational optimism. Those who worked for Hugenberg were viewed with disfavor by activists such as Willi Münzenberg, a labor organizer who declared that the revolutionary workers' movement should focus on Hugenberg's film enterprises more than on his bourgeois press holdings: "Hugenberg's film activity is a hundred times more dangerous than his newspapers. Very few workers read the Hugenberg papers, but millions of workers see the nationalistic and counterrevolutionary films from Hugenberg's poison laboratory."

Operettas from that "poison laboratory" were especially adept in manipulating cinematic formulas to reassure the masses that despite their often miserable social conditions and physical surroundings and the political battles raging in the Reichstag and in the streets, nothing was fundamentally wrong with the system. The films suggested that things were going to turn out fine if the public would just stop worrying so much and indulge instead in blind optimism. Films of "distraction" were made to obfuscate the fact that Germany was in serious trouble during the Depression and to lull the masses into the passivity that would make them willing puppets for their fascistic leaders. Letting the audience see just enough unemployment and poverty on-screen to cause concern was a prelude to sweeping those problems under the cinematic rug. Preparing Germany for even stronger leadership to straighten out social problems was the barely disguised raison d'être for most of UFA's escapist "product."

UFA accordingly developed the kind of generic formulas that Wilder found himself stuck in repeatedly. Besides aiming at sentimental reassurance with some of the traditional nostalgic romances and operettas set in old-world Vienna, UFA cranked out modern operettas featuring unemployed or underpaid characters who somehow managed to show dauntless pluck while laughing and singing their way through the general crisis. Any hints of serious flaws in the system could be dispelled, or at least UFA hoped, with forced happy endings and jolly conformist songs. Under the circumstances, it is remarkable how much undercutting of this formula Wilder managed to achieve in some of the *operettenfilmen* he wrote, as he played with the supposedly reassuring conventions and satirized or slyly subverted them by juxtaposing escapist schmaltz with some harsh elements of the reality under which he and his fellow Berliners lived.

Kracauer in *From Caligari to Hitler* analyzes the "overflowing cheerfulness" of these escapist films from the years of crisis leading up to the Nazi takeover as reflecting "the desire to believe that all was well. It was as if, now that economic depression threatened to upset the existing order of things, people were possessed by the fear of a catastrophe and in consequence cherished all kinds of illusions about the survival of their world. Scores of films—mostly comedies interspersed with songs—fed such hopes. . . . Their surprising preponderance was an infallible sign of widespread despair." Ultimately, as Kracauer put it, "what all these screen opiates tended to demonstrate" was that "everyday life itself is a fairy tale. . . . A favored expedient consisted in pretending that the underprivileged themselves were fully satisfied with their lot." UFA's *operettenfilmen* typically depict happy crowds of German workers marching or riding bicycles while singing idiotically about their joyous conformity and their acceptance of their inadequate economic conditions. These scenes are blithe precursors of the precision mass marching and singing of more belligerent Nazi hymns in Leni Riefenstahl's propaganda documentary about the 1934 Nuremberg rally, *Triumph of the Will*.

One of the UFA films cowritten by Wilder, the 1932 operetta *A Blonde Dream*, begins with a procession of bike-riding window-washers singing this inane, blatantly propagandistic workers' anthem:

> We like the world, with or without money . . .
> We won't despair and we won't complain,
> As long as they leave us hope.
> So march along and don't lose your head,
> Because one thing is certain:
> Everyone will make it sometime,
> Everyone who is capable is a success.

Hugenberg's fascist agenda is distilled succinctly both in the films' plots, with their enforced happy endings and other forms of falsity, and in these musical interludes, which serve as paeans to submission and conformism. Such songs were handed to Wilder and his fellow screenwriters to work their plots and characters around, a task he found both unpleasant and aesthetically difficult, although, thanks to his subversive wit and ingenuity, not entirely futile.

But as a working writer at UFA he could not have failed to recognize the bind he was in artistically. It was inevitable that for a filmmaker and reporter of Wilder's mordant tastes and talents, the kind of fare UFA specialized in and he had to churn out during those anxious years would have struck him as rebarbative. He told Lally,

> It was a shallow time in German pictures. The big companies that were making pictures, they were kind of lost in schmaltz. . . . You had producers saying that you had to find a place for six or eight songs and then, in

conversations with the composers and lyricists, you had to try to fine-tune what the character of those songs should be, whether they helped the story and how the connection with the theme of the story could be established. But you always had to make compromises. And often it was that the songs had not helped the plot, that they only interfered with the development of the story and unnecessarily held it up.

This was not the way Lubitsch worked in his groundbreaking Hollywood musicals of that time, which integrate songs with comedy scenes with what seemed effortless nonchalance. But Lubitsch was a powerful director and producer who controlled every aspect of his films. Wilder in the early 1930s was just another cog in the UFA machine, trying to cope covertly with his daunting challenges while slipping some of his sensibilities into his work.

Ironically, as Kracauer suggests, it was the very unreality and mendacity of UFA's cinematic and political agenda that made it possible for a clever screenwriter such as Wilder to call attention to the contrivances that such escapist films were using to distort the ugly reality on the streets. As can be seen in retrospect, he occasionally did so in almost Brechtian fashion, by ironically foregrounding the contrivances. That limited success was also due, in part, to Erich Pommer, the leading German film producer and former UFA production chief, who made films through his independent unit at the studio in that period. Wilder's jaundiced view of both his Berlin filmmaking period and his early years in Hollywood led him to undervalue Pommer's influence:

When someone in Hollywood later tried to fool me into thinking that American cinema was commercial in contrast with European art cinema, I only had to think of the Willi Forst, Willy Fritsch, and Lilian Harvey films. . . . As the boss of UFA, Erich Pommer desired nothing more than, for example, Samuel Goldwyn did in Hollywood: They both wanted to kidnap the cinema audience for hours from their worries and put them into a beautiful dream world. "No one spends money for a movie ticket to get to know the life of a miner's family"—so had Pommer outlined his program. . . . What is going on there, the viewer knows well enough already—this [also] was Goldwyn's belief.

But Pommer, who had been the patron of Lang and Murnau, believed in trying to blend commercial and artistic demands in his productions, and, with the help of Wilder and others, he occasionally succeeded in doing that, despite the prevailing commercial pressures from Hugenberg and the marketplace. That task prepared Wilder for working under Hollywood censorship, and while working as a screenwriter in Germany, he was not as entirely glum as he later made his experience sound. According to Wilder's longtime friend and collaborator Walter Reisch, a fellow Viennese who also fled Hitler and wound up in Hollywood, Wilder was "Pommer's favorite writer . . . Billie was the life of the party. Pommer adored him, always had him around, always listened to him."

Pommer had already spent some time working in Hollywood before returning to Berlin and shared an affinity for American culture with Wilder himself, yet Wilder later said of the producer, "He was a very sober, very talented man—but there were no laughs there." Nevertheless, Pommer produced two noteworthy German films cowritten by Wilder, *A Blonde Dream* and *Der Mann, der seinen Mörder sucht (The Man Who Searched for His Own Murderer,* 1931). After Pommer fled the Nazis and went back to America, he gave Wilder one of his first American script credits on a musical starring Gloria Swanson, *Music in the Air* (1934).

BURROWING FROM WITHIN

Kracauer's observation about how German "people were possessed by the fear of a catastrophe" in the period before the Nazi takeover helps account for the anxiety one can discern today just below the surface of the seemingly insignificant storylines of Wilder's German films of the early 1930s. Some of the commercial films Wilder wrote—*A Blonde Dream, The Man Who Searched for His Own Murderer, Emil and the Detectives,* and *Scampolo*—are of considerable interest for the subversive inflections on UFA formulas Wilder was able to slyly introduce, more or less between the lines. He was able to do so partly through his own ingenuity but also because he found some collaborators who were trying to make something of value in a system that tended to discourage originality.

Wilder found ways of making artistic use of the widespread social agitation of Berlin, which his reportorial skills helped him discern and place in counterpoint with the escapist elements. This ability is most obviously in evidence in his stories taking place in contemporary settings such as *Emil* and *A Blonde Dream*, but even in such ostensibly frothy romantic fare as *Once There Was a Waltz* (1932) and his most traditional German *operettenfilm, Ihre Hoheit Befiehlt* (*Her Highness Commands*, 1931).

Her Highness Commands, about a princess of a mythical kingdom finding love with a palace guardsman, uses what would become Wilder's familiar narrative strategy of the masquerade to satirize how the duties of monarchy stifle a woman's romantic impulses, also a Lubitschean preoccupation. The period of the story is deliberately left undefined, which cleverly allows it to be viewed either as escapism or as a mockery of a society clinging to outmoded conventions. As such it is a subtle commentary on the Germany of the early 1930s, which was to some degree yearning for the return of the militaristic pageantry of prewar days, a stubborn desire that soon would erupt back onto center stage with the Nazis' deployment of pageantry for chillingly propagandistic effect. *Once There Was a Waltz*, set in contemporary Vienna, adroitly places the conventions of the operetta (including an original score by Franz Lehár) against the straitened circumstances of two young people involved in a plot to deceive each other into thinking they are wealthy. Their actual social conditions are contrasted sharply with the traditional elements of romantic fantasy.

Wilder was able to express his personal preoccupations in modern operettas because of his affinities with their Vienna or Berlin settings and narrative elements representative of widespread economic distress. His nonmusical films also manage to draw to some extent from that atmosphere of crisis. As Wilder commented later, "Writers are not so much affected by bad economic times, because most writers know bad economic times very well."

In films as diverse as the black comedy *The Man Who Searched for His Own Murderer, Emil and the Detectives, A Blonde Dream,* and *Scampolo,* Wilder's scripts are intermittently able to turn their street locations to advantage. That gives the lightest or silliest of plots a semidocumentary quality occasionally reminiscent of the gritty realism he and his collaborators brought to *People on Sunday* before the commercial system enfolded them in 1930. Wilder's work burrowing within the UFA system was almost obsessively focused on the difficulties of earning a living and the financial and social hardships faced by his characters, who often resort to illicit means of survival. Wilder's German work shows a subversive tendency to dwell on and identify with outsiders and marginal characters in Berlin life, including criminals, Bohemians, children, and other "street people." His final film before fleeing Germany, *Was Frauen träumen* (*What Women Dream*, 1933), deals with a female kleptomaniac. Even if the film soft-pedals the threat of the police by making them buffoonish, which seems a combination of UFA's influence and Wilder's attempt to ridicule the threat he and others faced, you can sense just below the surface Wilder's own displaced fears of being pursued and caught as a "criminal" for being Jewish.

Wilder and his *People on Sunday* collaborator Robert Siodmak teamed at UFA for the offbeat film *The Man Who Searched for His Own Murderer*. Wilder wrote the black comedy about a cowardly would-be suicide with Ludwig Hirschfeld and Kurt Siodmak from a play by Ernst Neubach. The film marks Wilder's first collaborations with two composers who would become major contributors to his work, Friedrich (later Frederick) Holländer and Franz Wachsmann (later Waxman). Holländer not only wrote the score but also plays a gangster chief. Best known for his work with Marlene Dietrich on Josef von Sternberg's *Die blaue Engel* (*The Blue Angel*, 1930) and his many other collaborations with the actress/singer, Holländer later wrote songs for her in Wilder's *A Foreign Affair* and plays the piano as she sings in an underground nightclub; he also worked for Wilder on *Sabrina* as well as for Lubitsch on *Angel* and *That Lady in Ermine*. Wachsmann, credited as musical director on *The Man Who Searched for His Own Murderer*, went on to compose the music for several Wilder films, including *Mauvaise graine* and *Sunset Blvd.*

A farcical comedy about suicide represented a different kind of experiment for Wilder and Robert Siodmak, a lurid subject they thought would be more commercial than *People on Sunday*, but it fell on its face with the public, partly because it was "*too* original," as Joe Gillis refers to some of his unsold stories in *Sunset Blvd.* Their UFA concoction is a bizarre proto–film noir that plays cheekily with the conventions of the gangster genre. Although slickly directed and intermittently clever, the film is hard to evaluate conclusively, since it was rendered rather choppy and frantic after its disastrous commercial release by being reedited and drastically shortened from ninety-eight minutes to only fifty-two for its reissue as *Jim, der mann mit der Narbe* (*Jim, the Man with the Scar*) (also the title of Neubach's play).

The premise is intriguingly morbid: a meek Berliner named Hans Herfort (Heinz Rühmann) can't bring himself to blow his brains out, so he hires a hitman (Raimund Janitschek) to kill him but changes his mind after falling in love. The film was a daring attempt to spin a darkly absurdist tale at a time when the public was not ready for such drastic tonal shifts.* Reviewers liked the zany *Man Who Searched for His Own Murderer*, but from what we have left of it, the film seems mechanical and predictable in its twists on the basic "gag," including the farming out of the hit to the Man with the Scar. And since we never learn why Hans is suicidal, other than that he is a hysteric, we feel little emotional connection with him or anyone else in the midst of the mayhem. Some elements of Wilder's streetwise sensibility and disdain for conventional happy endings are on display here: the concluding wedding ceremony has the couple put in handcuffs by Holländer, anticipating the wedding in a jail at the end of Lubitsch's *Merry Widow*. The morbid humor of *The Man Who Searched for His Own Murderer* is characteristic of Wilder as well as a telling comment on the Berlin Zeitgeist. But the net result of this failed experiment seems to have been a chastening lesson for both Wilder and Siodmak about the limits to which they could go in disregarding commercial formulas.

The necessity of having streetwise survival skills in a time of peril becomes the raison d'être of the far more successful and entertaining Wilder film version of *Emil and the Detectives*, directed by Gerhard Lamprecht. The popular 1929 children's novel by Erich Kästner is one of those enduring properties that keeps getting filmed in different eras. The script of the 1931 version is credited only to Wilder, although Imre (later known as Emeric) Pressburger made uncredited contributions to it. Pressburger later teamed with Michael Powell on a series of brilliant British films.[†]

---

* The story evidently was inspired by Jules Verne's novel *Les tribulations d'un Chinois en China* (*The Tribulations of a Chinese Gentleman in China*, 1879), which Philippe de Broca filmed in 1965 (aka *Up to His Ears*). Among the later films the German film resembles are Aki Kaurismäki's *I Hired a Contract Killer* (1990), Warren Beatty's *Bulworth* (1998), and Wilder's *Buddy Buddy*.

† When the novel was filmed again in England in 1935 and by Disney in Germany in 1964, Wilder was not credited. There also were German versions in 1954 and 2001 and a Japanese version in 1956.

A sensitively directed ensemble piece with a breezy sense of space, *Emil* has a quasi-documentary look as it follows a group of Berlin children in pursuit of an adult thief (Fritz Rasp). He has stolen the money of a boy traveling by train from the provinces, Emil Tischbein (engagingly played by Rolf Wenkhaus). Emil has been entrusted with the money to take to his impoverished grandmother in the big city. Wilder's economical, beautifully structured script keeps the action moving smoothly through a series of gritty street locations and effortlessly captures the language of children, whether in wise-guy or sweet mode. The boy known as "The Flying Deer," who lives as a pseudo-Indian, is another sign of Wilder's affinity for American life.

Although its tone is mostly lighthearted, *Emil* has an underlying seriousness in its visuals and social implications. Like many of Wilder's German films, it revolves around economic problems, the theft and recovery of Emil's money and his mother's attempt to relieve the grandmother's impoverished circumstances. The portrait of the city is not flattering, since the thief who preys on the provincial boy is a Berliner, and the social system is portrayed as dysfunctional, since the children don't trust the police and have to band together to catch the criminal. The scene of the newly arrived Emil having his suit revamped into more suitable urban attire by a streetwise Berlin kid, Gustav—a miniature Billie Wilder, played by Hans Joachim Schaufuss—is cute but a telling sign of the wising-up necessary for urban survival. The film's endorsement of what amounts to a comical form of mob action is not entirely benign in its implications, even if *Emil* stirs admiration for the children's pluck and self-reliance. The fact that Wenkhaus, Schaufuss, and other boys who appear in the film were killed in World War II is another sobering aspect of *Emil and the Detectives*; all the early 1930s Wilder films set in Berlin, like Lubitsch's silent films, are shadowed by the awareness that their settings would eventually become the rubble of *A Foreign Affair*.

Kästner criticized Wilder on the grounds that he not only "embellished" his story but also "vulgarized it," not the last time that word would be applied to Wilder. Kästner's objection seemed to stem mostly from one scene, the theft of the money on a train, which Wilder intensified from the book to make the thief seem even creepier (he is played with a sinister smile by Rasp, a former Reinhardt actor known for his appearances in films by Lang and Pabst). In the novel, the man, who is not vividly characterized, gives Emil chocolate; Emil eventually falls asleep and has an elaborate dream from which he wakes to find his money gone. It's suggested but not entirely clear that he may have been drugged. The film makes that explicit: the thief gives drugged candy to Emil, whose hallucinatory reaction provides the excuse for an impressively expressionistic sequence in the distorted train car and the boy's flying over Berlin with an umbrella, like a proto–Mary Poppins. The thief's resemblance to a child molester is unmistakable. But it's hard to agree with Kästner that such a serious undertone is harmful to a film that deals with an adult criminal menacing a child and a group of children banding together for their own protection. Like some other viewers then and later, Kästner was not sympathetic to realistically dark elements being mixed with comedy in Wilder's works (Kästner, an anti-Nazi pacifist, soon faced another kind of darkness in his own life when the Nazis burned his books in 1933).

Kästner's anger over that one sequence evidently blinded him to the considerable charms of *Emil and the Detectives*, including the naturalistic performances Lamprecht draws from his large cast of youngsters. Wenkhaus makes an intelligent young hero who adapts quickly to his metropolitan surroundings, as did Wilder, the youth from the provinces who did not take long to become thoroughly cosmopolitan. Inge Landgut gives an indelible performance as Emil's delightfully named cousin, Pony Hütchen. One of the first true Wilder heroines, she is a spunky and independent girl who helps provide leadership for the otherwise all-boy gang and eventually is confronted with a choice of two youthful suitors, Emil and Gustav. Before putting her arms around both in the ending, Pony Hütchen cleverly resolves the problem by saying, "I'll maybe tell you in ten years. But as long as you're still rascals, I'll take you both." That mischievously suggestive ending prefigures the joyous ménage-a-trois final shot of Lubitsch's *Design for Living* (1933), based on the 1932 play by Noël Coward.*

"SOMEWHERE IN THE WORLD"

Another intriguing early Wilder film, *A Blonde Dream*, followed the prototype of the UFA *operettenfilm*, Pommer's production *Die Drei von der Tankstelle (Three from the Filling Station)*. That popular 1930 musical, written by

---

*   Earlier in the year in which *Emil* was released, Inge Landgut played the unforgettable role of the child murder victim of Peter Lorre's character in Fritz Lang's *M—Eine Stadt sucht einen Mörder (M—A City Is Looking for a Murderer)*. She went on to a long career in films and television and was known for dubbing actresses in English-language films and TV shows into German.

Franz Schulz and Paul Frank and directed by Wilhelm Thiele, deals with three friends who go bankrupt but are still able to buy a business. They spend much of their time courting a pretty young blonde played by Lilian Harvey. She and one of her male leads, Willy Fritsch, were the predominant romantic team in German films from 1926 through 1939. The "dream couple," as they were known, made twelve films together. *A Blonde Dream* is a 1932 vehicle for them along with Willi Forst as impoverished young Berliners in a bohemian love triangle who eke out a manic-depressive existence while the woman harbors futile dreams of going to Hollywood.

The influence of the *Three from the Filling Station* prototype and *A Blonde Dream* can be seen as far into Wilder's future as his 1964 American comedy *Kiss Me, Stupid*. That dark comedy deals with two songwriters, one of whom runs a filling station, trying to escape their miserable surroundings by achieving the unlikely dream of success in show business. Wilder directly lifts a sight gag for *Kiss Me, Stupid* from *Three from the Filling Station*: the first customer in the German film pulls up to fill only his cigarette lighter with gas. The joke is repeated with a truck driver in the scene that establishes the dismal small town of Climax, Nevada, in *Kiss Me, Stupid*. Not for Wilder the mindlessly sunny optimism of the filling station proprietors in the proto-Nazi UFA film proclaiming that friendship is sufficient "even when the whole world collapses"; in Wilder's later variation, the sight gag with the lighter validates the songwriters' desperation to get out of town. Wilder adds a topper in having his American trucker neglecting to pay for that tiny amount of gas.

A Blonde Dream, directed by Paul Martin, contains Wilder's most impressive, yet also most problematical, work in the *operettenfilm* genre. The film was shot simultaneously in German, English, and French versions to take advantage of Harvey's multilingual talents and international appeal; making such alternate versions was a common practice for UFA in the early sound era. It was a plum assignment for the young writer to be assigned to such a major commercial vehicle along with Walter Reisch, who would collaborate with Wilder and Charles Brackett in 1939 on the screenplay of *Ninotchka*. The unresolved ideological conflicts of *A Blonde Dream* and its eloquent incoherence are among its most compelling elements today.

Amid UFA's imposed we're-so-happy-to-be-poor agenda, this operetta, highly popular at the time, captures some of the melancholic, foreboding atmosphere of 1932 Berlin. It can be read in a contrary way as a wistful plea for a better life in a country that, from our privileged hindsight, is teetering on the edge of catastrophe. As biographer Ed Sikov writes, "Of all the operettas Billie Wilder wrote in Germany, *Ein blonder Traum* is by far the edgiest and most politically conscious—a brittle, cynical comment on what Berlin audiences knew to be their own grim social reality in 1932." The main characters are two window-washers (Fritsch, known as Willy I, and Forst, Willy II) and a former small-time acrobat and full-time dreamer named Jou-Jou (Harvey), who desperately wants to go to Hollywood. They share life in three abandoned railway cars in the countryside outside Berlin, trying to make the best of a decidedly tenuous situation. On the surface they seem contented enough living in the countryside on little money—Jou-Jou and her male companions sing, "We don't pay any rent anymore . . . / If our nest was even smaller, we simply couldn't care less." But their effort to convince themselves that they are living an idyll is obviously strained, such as in the sign Jou-Jou paints over her dwelling with unconscious irony, "Villa Hollywood." She admits in a moment of rare lucidity, "It's difficult for artists these days."

Lilian Harvey was the London-born daughter of an English mother and a German father; the saucy actress-singer became a major German star in that period, and she was Pommer's mistress at the time of *A Blonde Dream*. She represented wistful charm and buoyant optimism in the face of seemingly impossible odds that captivated many German filmgoers. That Wilder and Reisch were able to bring some intermittent social sting and emotional complexity to the plot about the two marginally employed young men's courtship of the distracted Jou-Jou was a tribute to the writers' considerable ingenuity and ability to find ways of working around their restrictions. The sly, not-so-covert political subversion of *A Blonde Dream* can be heard, if you listen, in the very names of the characters. "Willy" was the irreverent popular nickname of the deposed Kaiser Wilhelm I, and modern, post–World War II audiences, at least, could hardly fail to find a double meaning in the name Jou-Jou (even if in German, the word for Jew, *jude*, is pronounced *you-da*). The name Jou-Jou sounds more French than German (in French, the word for Jew is *juif*, pronounced *zjuif*), and to extend the metaphor, as an aspiring actress with dreams of going to Hollywood, Jou-Jou represents the international nature of artists; as such she is a challenge to fervent nationalism, a female version of the Wandering Jew. But she surrenders her symbolic role as itinerant artist for that of an enforced Nazi ideal, the German hausfrau, when the film makes her give up her artistic dream and settle down with one of the two men.

The two window-washers (one of whom almost kills the other out of jealousy) and the talented but seriously deluded would-be actress (who's duped by an unscrupulous imposter into thinking she has a place waiting for her in Hollywood) ultimately are pathetic figures, victims of what Sikov aptly terms the film's "cruel ironies." *A Blonde Dream*'s convoluted, ideologically mandated "happy ending" is unbelievable and unsatisfactory, existing in conflict with other elements of the story. The film's view of Hollywood is also conflicted and seems to represent Wilder's own misgivings about his own career dreams.

In the film's most remarkable sequence, Jou-Jou has an expressionistically filmed nightmare about what might happen if she actually made it all the way to Hollywood. America, in Wilder's fantasy imagination, is initially depicted as benign. The Statue of Liberty bends down, waving her torch to welcome Jou-Jou's arrival by train over the water in New York harbor (that patriotic American landmark being treated as a sympathetic symbolic figure is a startling moment in a 1932 German movie). At the train station in Hollywood, the German starlet is greeted as a celebrity, but the director and crewmen waiting at the film studio for her audition turn out to be monstrously lecherous. They make her do a humiliating dance that ends with her collapsing in despair in oversized, Chaplinesque shoes, like giant bricks, as her lovely singing voice becomes mockingly distorted into a deep growl. They force her to strip and walk a tightrope in artificial rain, a grotesque twist on the balancing act she performed back in Germany. The Hollywood "director" is the same crudely caricatured German porter who treated her rudely at the American consulate in Berlin when she applied for a visa; it's as if she can't escape Germany even in the "land of freedom" (the humiliating process of trying to get a visa to America will become the subject of one of Wilder's best Hollywood scripts, *Hold Back the Dawn*).

The "upbeat" resolution of the putatively "escapist" *A Blonde Dream* by having Jou-Jou renounce her dreams and settle for her window-washer boyfriend seems depressing today, yet UFA obviously intended it as a positive, practical exhortation to the audience to forget their idle fantasies of genuine escape from their bleak circumstances. But even in Jou-Jou's studio-imposed submission to conservative values, an element of subversion creeps in. She is allowed moments of sadness and ambivalence over her decision, and her hesitancy speaks volumes: "I . . . I've been to Hollywood . . . I've dreamed enough now." Her desperation becomes frenzied as she sings and dances for a visiting Hollywood producer impassively watching her routine in an office in the American Embassy. Looking chagrined as she exits the building, Jou-Jou finally rejects her dream with relief and a big smile, and her friends joyfully endorse her choice while she parades on a bicycle with Willy I and other window-washers. The ending's sexist, proto-Nazi propaganda agenda is so blatant that it is clear Wilder could hardly have supported such a conclusion, even if his view of Hollywood in this film is as bleak as it will be in *Sunset Blvd.*

Between the cracks of the plot and in the face of its propagandistic intent, *A Blonde Dream* not only manages to cast a cold eye on the characters' consolatory attempts to make their marginal lives seem bearable but also expresses sympathy for the impossibility of Jou-Jou's thwarted dreams. The film most movingly wears its complex heart on its sleeve in her wistful song on a rooftop shortly after she meets the two men, "Irgendwo auf der Welt gibt's ein kleines bisschen Glück" (Somewhere in the World There's a Little Bit of Happiness) (lyrics by Robert Gilbert and Werner R. Heymann, with music by Heymann, who later worked for Lubitsch on *Ninotchka* and four other American films and always regarded this song as his favorite work):

> Somewhere in the world there's a little bit of happiness,
> I dream of it every single moment. . . .
> If I knew where it was, I would go out into the world,
> Because for once I want to be happy
>   with my whole heart.
> Somewhere in the world my road to heaven begins,
> Somewhere, somehow, sometime.

With potent visual symbolism, she sings on the roof of one of Berlin's landmark buildings, the Neuer Marstall (New Royal Stables) in the center of the city. Facing the later-destroyed Berliner Schloss, or royal castle, which is partly visible in the scene, the Marstall in 1932 was the city library and today continues to serve that function as well as housing the Hanns Eisler Academy of Music (named after the composer, who was a victim of the Hollywood blacklist). The building had been not only the stable for the royal horses and carriage but also the place where revolutionaries made plans to overthrow the imperial dynasty in 1918–1919, leading to the formation of the Weimar Republic. Considering the highly charged symbolic resonance of Jou-Jou's surroundings as she bares her heart—with the roof offering a broad view of the crowded Berlin cityscape below and into the distance—and our knowledge of the unlikelihood of the character's chances of escape from the urban meat grinder, this lovely song about hoping for a better future is deeply poignant in its very futility, especially given our retrospective knowledge of what ensued for Germany the following year.

The supposedly romantic happy ending of *A Blonde Dream* was contrary to what Wilder and Reisch wanted, which was for the two rival males to go off together, leaving Jou-Jou alone with her little dog, making it another of Wilder's romantically disenchanted buddy-buddy movies, which range from *People on Sunday* and *Some Like It Hot* to his final film, *Buddy Buddy*. Harvey objected to what she considered an insult, so Wilder and Reisch contrived an improbable but ironic switch. The Hollywood producer offers Jou-Jou a lowly consolation job as a chorus girl, but Willy II persuades him not to inflict that fate on her, declaring, "Film ist kein Beruf für erwachsene Leute" (Film, that's no profession for adults). Ironically, his detailed speech about how awful life is for a woman in Hollywood, a speech that could be given without change today, causes the producer to offer him a job there discouraging actresses from going into the business. The plot gimmick enables Jou-Jou to settle down with Willy I, with her little dog trailing behind the couple in the final shot.

The degrading experience Jou-Jou has in her premonitory nightmare of Hollywood will be echoed in the actual circumstances endured in two Wilder-directed films by characters played by his alter ego William Holden, Joe Gillis and the struggling producer Barry Detweiler in *Fedora*, and, in the end, by Wilder himself in his final years of unemployment in Hollywood. Unlike Jou-Jou, however, Wilder was not deterred from his own dream of Hollywood despite knowing its potential dangers. That awareness perhaps was reflected in his previously admitted "Filmterror" a version of which is on display in Jou-Jou's bad dream, and might have stemmed from his anxiety about whether he was "good enough" to write and direct in Hollywood. Soon enough, Wilder would be forced by historical circumstances to face and surmount his self-doubts.

The tongue-in-cheek, seemingly conformist but covertly satirical "happy ending" of *A Blonde Dream* can be seen as functioning on two levels. The balancing act Wilder had to perform in those perilous years is the kind that Douglas Sirk (another director who would escape Nazi Germany for Hollywood) described to Jon Halliday in *Sirk on Sirk*: "Everything seems to be OK, but you well know it isn't. By just drawing out the characters you certainly could get a story—along the lines of hopelessness, of course. You could just go on. . . . But the point is you don't have to do this. And if you did, you would get a picture that the studio would have abhorred." To help make his point, Sirk cited Euripides's tragedy *Alcestis*: "You see, there is no real solution of the predicament the people in the play are in, just the *deus ex machina*, which is now called 'the happy end,' and which both Hollywood and Athenians and assorted Greeks were also so keen on. But this is what is being called Euripidean irony. It makes the crowd happy. To the few it makes the *aporia* [irresolvable internal contradiction] more transparent."

Harvey went to Hollywood soon after making *A Blonde Dream* and made four films for Fox but failed to become an American star. She returned to Nazi Germany in 1935 but had to flee in 1939 because she kept in contact with Jewish colleagues and had helped a gay choreographer escape the Nazis. In her somewhat confused political odyssey, she settled in Vichy France but was stripped of her German citizenship in 1943 because she had performed for French troops. But by then she had returned to the United States and found work as a volunteer nurse. Before her death in 1968, she wound up running a souvenir shop on the French Riviera, a finale only marginally less grim than Norma Desmond's.

In her prime, though, she was a talented performer who bedazzles *A Blonde Dream* with her lithe beauty and buoyant singing and dancing, contributing greatly to this conflicted film's enduring charms. Wilder's sour memory of the star—claiming that Jou-Jou's dog could "act the pants off Lilian Harvey"—and the shortsightedness of his resulting dismissal of *A Blonde Dream* to later interviewers show that hell hath no fury like a screenwriter whose ending is changed by an actress's diktat.

FAUX LUBITSCH

Several years before he began working with Lubitsch in Hollywood, Wilder evidently started trying to emulate him at UFA by the early 1930s. But while

Wilder was writing such romantic concoctions as *Her Highness Commands*, *Once There Was a Waltz*, and his final German film, *What Women Dream*, his own artistic personality was still embryonic.

While the first two films are entertaining, laced with clever twists, and well-constructed, the style of all three is a diminished echo of Lubitsch. The master's Hollywood work in that period in the same genres of operetta and romantic comedy is much sharper stylistically, deeper emotionally, and more acute in its social satire. Although Wilder was working under considerably less congenial conditions than Lubitsch enjoyed in Hollywood, the apprentice was only gradually learning his craft, and Wilder's Lubitschean side would not begin to fully bloom until he took lessons directly from the master when they worked together on *Bluebeard's Eighth Wife* and *Ninotchka*. As Wilder admitted much later in his career (1975), "Occasionally, I look for an elegant twist and I say to myself, 'How would Lubitsch have done it?,' and I will come up with something and it will be *like* Lubitsch, but it won't *be* Lubitsch." He had learned that lesson back in Germany.

Amid the homages, these German films also display some elements of Wilder's characteristically jaded and sarcastic sensibility. Clever wordplay is one of the appealing characteristics of Wilder's Berlin scripts, as it would be in his Hollywood films as well. *Her Highness Commands*, for instance, puns on the words *Sein* (to be, or what you are) and *Schein* (how you appear), which gets to the heart of Wilder's career-long concern with deception, disguise, and how role-playing expresses the hidden aspects of personality. Much of Wilder's work revolves around such coded meanings, and the jocularity of his wordplay, including his extensive use of double entendre, both masks and conveys his most serious concerns. He learned in his heavily circumscribed German work how to slip in his coded double meanings; his seemingly transparent American films are more layered with subterranean themes than they appear, partly because he was so often pushing the commercial envelope with controversial material and partly because double meanings had become his habitual method of expression as a canny exile and social satirist.

Even for their time, *Her Highness Commands* and *Once There Was a Waltz* were deliberately retro, self-consciously riffing on the operetta genre, like Lubitsch's highly stylized work in that field. Along with its traditional Mittel European fantasy setting, *Her Highness Commands* takes the timeworn approach of having the princess, Marie-Christine (Käthe von Nagy), pretend to be a commoner (a manicurist named "Mizzi")* so she can frequent a work-ers' bar to romance a lieutenant of the palace guard, Karl von Conradi (Willy Fritsch), pretending to be a delicatessen clerk. The princess, just returned from schooling in England and therefore not recognizable to the lieutenant as roy-alty, is hoping to escape an arranged marriage with a weird prince (Paul Heidemann) whose fascination with Egyptology makes him more interested in mummies than in her charms.

Egyptology was a rage in the 1920s, the decade when King Tut's tomb was discovered, and Wilder probably was aware of Lubitsch's flamboyantly melo-dramatic treatments of Egyptian subjects in *The Eyes of the Mummy Ma* and *The Wife of Pharaoh*. The portrayal of the foolishly grinning, bespectacled prince in *Her Highness Commands* as an emotional mummy is droll (he's "only interested in people of the female gender if they've been dead two thousand years") and more than sufficient to galvanize Marie-Christine's need to escape him. The film also has Lubitschean fun with retainers and servants carrying out ridiculously elaborate rituals of court etiquette, and in the process it exten-sively imitates the master's use of doors. The treatment of the king amounts to a prolonged Lubitsch Touch, since he never appears onscreen but issues commands only through a mechanized lightboard; we eventually learn that the king is kept out of sight because he is a child.

The princess's repeated promotions of the baffled Lieutenant Conradi all the way up to general are an amusing serial "touch" that echoes Queen Cath-erine's honoring her lovers with medals in Lubitsch's American-made com-edy set in a mythical kingdom somewhat resembling pre-Soviet Russia, *Forbidden* Paradise (1924).† In *Her Highness Commands*, Conradi's occasional chafing at being under the control of a princess is similar to the way Maurice Chevalier's prince consort has his sense of male sovereignty sorely tested by being under the thumb of his queen (Jeanette MacDonald) in Lubitsch's

---

* Wilder makes a key female character in his romantic comedy *Avanti!* (1972) a manicurist, though she is not seen onscreen, and her daughter briefly impersonates that profession. In *Kiss Me, Stupid*, Polly the Pistol (Kim Novak) worked as a manicurist before turning to prostitution, and the philandering husband tries to convince his wife that Polly is "a manicurist I met—I had my nails done while you were gone."

† Josef von Sternberg, in addition to borrowing some crowd shots from Lubitsch's 1928 film, *The Patriot* (1928), for *The Scarlet Empress* (1934), builds on that Lubitsch Touch for even richer comic/erotic effect with Marlene Dietrich's Catherine the Great, who pins a medal on one of her studs while declaring with a smirk, "For bravery—*in action*."

innovative 1929 musical *The Love Parade*. But Lubitsch explores the gender power imbalance theme with greater satirical complexity and emotional depth.

Although the plot mechanics of *Her Highness Commands* are derivative, the film exercises them with some panache, partly thanks to brisk direction by Hanns Schwarz, making the best of a modest budget, and because Wilder is delving into what would become one of his strongest career preoccupations, that of the masquerade. Even in this temporizing UFA diversion, our sympathy for the two young lovers is largely brought about because of their need to engage in playacting to express their true desires within a repressive system they manage to outwit.

Having characters pretend to be people they are not is not only a fertile comic device but also a reflection of the habitual mindset of the exile, and as such a device that can convey deep emotional conflicts. Wilder's peripatetic childhood and youth had taken him in dizzying succession from Galicia to Poland to Vienna to Berlin and had thoroughly steeped him in such survival strategies; by the early 1930s he was already having to think of another possible relocation. Exiles live in a perpetual state of masquerade, whether they want to or not, and whether they even realize what they are doing or not. It is their survival and defense mechanism, the protective device that keeps them safe in new, strange, and hostile environments. A person fleeing his or her native land, or temporary residence, soon learns to adapt to disguises and false identities while navigating the perilous paths of exile. Even if one is honest, just being a newcomer in a strange land feels like a state of disguise.

Wilder's constantly unsettled existence left indelible marks on his view of the world, intensifying his reflexive need for self-protection, his habit of keeping his emotions close to his vest, and his sense of life as a constant con-game. His endlessly protean adaptability, his cleverness in fending for himself and becoming successful wherever he had to flee, enabled him to endow his characters, even back in Germany, with a powerful degree of ingenuity in the fine art of the masquerade.

Wilder's forced departure in 1933–1934 from Germany to the United States by way of Paris naturally intensified his exilic mode of thinking and behaving. Of necessity, assuming the identity of an American would make the masquerade an even more central and obsessive characteristic of his writing and directing, something far deeper than a mere plot contrivance or an excuse for gags. Although masquerading involves falsifying one's identity out of self-protection or for possible advantage, its downside is self-deception that can lead to self-destruction. The masquerade can be the mark of a fragmented and contradictory personality, a theme Wilder explores with increasing richness and depth in films as diverse as *The Major and the Minor*, *The Lost Weekend*, *Sunset Blvd.*, *Some Like It Hot*, *Kiss Me, Stupid*, and *Fedora*.

A Hollywood remake of *Her Highness Commands*, *Adorable* (1933), gave Billie Wilder his first credit on an American film, but he had no actual involvement in the production since he was still in Europe at the time it was made (the American version was written by George Marion Jr. and Jane Storm). *Adorable* was directed at Fox by Wilhelm Dieterle, a German exile and former Reinhardt actor. Dieterle later changed his first name to William and had a long and distinguished American career before returning to Germany in 1958. *Adorable* was a clumsy cultural transplantation into a vehicle for the fading silent star Janet Gaynor. She plays an overage and childish princess in love with a low-ranking military officer. To ease his discomfort over their class differences as the romance comically intensifies, she keeps promoting him to ridiculous extremes. The ghastly title song keeps recurring throughout, but not ironically as with Robert Altman's use of *his* title song in *The Long Goodbye*. "You're so completely adorable / Is the way to your heart explorable?" are among the many deplorable lyrics in the Gaynor musical, although the song does have one good line: "Everything I can think of to say is censorable."*

Set in 1933 but in a mythical kingdom and lumberingly stagebound, *Adorable* is a justly forgotten piece of stale strudel. It loses the mildly engaging *operettenfilm* charm of *Her Highness Commands* and makes its plot contrivances even harder to swallow. While trying to emulate Lubitsch's groundbreaking *The Love Parade* and his other musicals, *Adorable* is a programmer that lacks their wit or stylistic finesse or the bittersweet nuances Lubitsch brings to romantic relationships and class issues. The guardsman is played by Henri Garat (billed as Henry), a handsome French actor who lacks the brazen charm of Lubitsch musical star Maurice Chevalier.† With its sluggish

---

* Fox frugally recycled the tune for the score of a lurid 1935 programmer to which Wilder contributed anonymously, *Thunder in the Night*.

† Just before *Adorable*, Garay had appeared in *Un rêve blond* (1932), the French version of *A Blonde Dream*. That version also starred Lilian Harvey and was directed by Paul Martin (along with André

pacing, *Adorable* loses the atmospheric charm provided by European studio production values and becomes more schmaltzy and forgettable than the already threadbare original.

Another of Wilder's German films dealing at length with a masquerade is *Der Falsche Ehemann* (*The False Husband*, 1931), a romantic farce about identical twin brothers (Johannes Riemann). A narcoleptic Berlin businessman named Peter and a charming ski resort manager named Paul switch places to help revitalize the Berliner's business and marriage. Peter's trade, fittingly, is selling a sleeping tonic called Somnolin; for excitement, his *zaftig* blonde wife (Maria Paudler) has to turn to a violinist (Tibor Halmay) who entertains the bourgeoisie but may be moonlighting as a gigolo. The jaunty twin instead concocts a popular pep tonic called Energin (an equivalent of Viagra) and flirts with the wife until her real husband is ready to change places with some degree of gusto.

Paul's hyperefficient takeover of the business, comically shocking the employees, resembles James Cagney's rapid-fire running of his Berlin Coca-Cola plant in Wilder's adaptation of a Ferenc Molnár play to the Cold War era, *One, Two, Three*. There may also be a political message in *The False Husband*, smuggled in more subtly, when Paul looks with disdain at Peter's somnolent business operations: "That is *tempo?* That is 1931? People don't need pills to sleep today—people need pills for energy!" Through this farcical façade, former *Tempo* reporter Billie Wilder may have been trying to warn his fellow Berliners that even though they moved briskly on the streets, that tempo was illusory, since most of them were politically asleep and urgently needed to be awakened before it was too late.

Cowritten with Paul Frank and directed by Johannes Guter, *The False Husband* is expertly crafted and fairly amusing until the thin plot becomes laborious in its overly elaborate carryings-on. The film is not substantial enough to do more than riff on the German preoccupation with the doppelgänger, the doubling of personality, a concept that had been exercised more seriously in the landmarks of German expressionist cinema. Both Lubitsch and Wilder were influenced greatly by that psychological and artistic concept, incorporating it in explicit or implicit ways throughout

---

Daven); it brought Wilder a co-screenplay credit with Walter Reisch (the adaptation was by Bernard Zimmer).

their comedies and dramas of deception, misunderstanding, and duality of character. Wilder would incorporate doppelgänger themes in his work as a writer-director most explicitly in such role-playing stories as *The Major and the Minor, Some Like It Hot, Kiss Me, Stupid*, and, in its most extreme form, *Fedora*. That preoccupation increased after he left Germany and explored brisker, more adroit, and deeper ways of working out his preoccupation with the kind of psychosexual game-playing he only lightly touched on in *The False Husband*.

Once There Was a Waltz is set in May 1932 in the Vienna Wilder had left behind without undue nostalgia. The film indulges in the schmaltzy traditions of the Viennese operetta (the German phrasing of the title is derived from the traditional phrase used for fairy tales) but wraps around them a romantic farce that seems almost postmodern in its parodistic approach. The film is explicitly framed as a jaded young Berliner's look at the Austrian capital's moribund traditions. Rudi Moebius (Rolf von Goth) is a financially strapped stockbroker grudgingly pursuing an arranged marriage in Vienna with a young woman, Lucie Welding (Lizzi Natzler), whose family actually is as broke as he is. Lucie's father refers to the marriage as a union between the Rhine and the Danube, and Rudi's elderly business partner ominously pronounces it a "symbol of the union of Austria and Germany" (i.e., a thinly disguised symbolic *Anschluss* ahead of schedule).

But the young "couple" have already met by accident in the company of different partners, so they can't help confessing the truth to each other, and everyone eventually realizes what a greedy sham they are enacting. The farcical plot mechanics wind up with all the characters opening a "Vienna Café" in Berlin near the Brandenburg Gate, using the older people as the serving staff in a more benign melding of cultures than they had envisioned earlier. Wilder would later replay this jolly foreign café-opening finale in *Ninotchka*, another of his many fertile borrowings from his German screenwriting.

Since we know that Wilder largely despised Vienna, regarding it as more anti-Semitic than Berlin and a musty city shamelessly trading off its aristocratic past for the sake of tourist *Kronen*, the film's montage of Viennese landmarks seen from an open-air tour bus comes off as a sarcastic spin on the atmospheric interlude that was de rigueur in such movies. The pace of this cinematic tour is absurdly frenetic, and the singing commentary to the customers, including Japanese tourists, is like a vaudeville routine provided by the unruly father (Paul Hörbiger) of Rudi's blonde flame, Steffi Pirzinger (Mártha Eggerth). The sequence also points forward to the darkly sarcastic guided tour of bombed-out Berlin for members of the U.S. Congress by an army officer in Wilder's 1948 film *A Foreign Affair.*

Rudi's "last night of freedom" before his scheduled meeting with his would-be fiancée and her family takes him to a Franz Lehár waltz show featuring girls dancing to the title song of *Once There Was a Waltz* in regimented patterns with goose-stepping soldiers. This piece, and the rest of Lehár's music in the film, was written especially for it. The stage show's highly militaristic staging seems, at least in retrospect, a sly mockery of Vienna's theatrical and imperial traditions, as well as a commentary on the nostalgia for militaristic pageantry that persisted in the waning days of the Weimar Republic and soon would lead to the Nazis' full-blown employment of such spectacles to regiment the masses. Despite the undercutting of Lehár, it was something of a coup for the film to have a score by the celebrated Hungarian composer best known for *The Merry Widow.* Eggerth was a celebrated soprano, also Hungarian, who combined film work with a long career in stage operettas.

When Rudi unexpectedly encounters the fetching Steffi at the theater, he finds it painless to abandon his mercenary marital scheme and woo her instead. "Are young guys in Berlin always so fast?," she wonders before giving in, even when he insists, "Kiss me today and forget me tomorrow." When he tells her he's about to be "incarcerated" for life, it's understandable that she assumes he's a criminal, not a man about to get married. There's a Lubitschean dissolve from Steffi's view of the bars of a prison window to Rudi entering the gate of the prospective fiancée's house; in much of Wilder's work, the two states are seen as identical. The plot twists here may be entirely predictable but pleasingly so in terms of the film's smoothly ritualistic deployment of genre conventions (as suggested by Rudi's last name, which evokes the circular twists of the Möbius strip). These devices are in keeping with the light tone of the proceedings and another sign of Wilder's already highly polished story construction.

Once There Was a Waltz was directed by Victor Janson, the actor who plays the American millionaire Mr. Quaker in Lubitsch's *The Oyster Princess* and appeared in eleven other films directed by Lubitsch. Janson's visual elaboration of the waltz show—with hat-check girls, footmen, and even coats in the cloakroom dancing along to the music—is imitation Lubitsch. And though *Once There Was a Waltz* takes a mostly tongue-in-cheek approach to the Viennese operetta genre, some genuine poignancy clings to the title song's evocation of an already quaint cultural tradition and way of life that were fast fading and soon to vanish entirely with Hitler's *Anschluss*:

> There once was a waltz;
> there once was a Vienna.
> They were better times,
> but now they are long gone,
> and everything comes to an end.
> Then, with a waltz, the good times return.

Wilder was not entirely immune from such sentimental backward glances, as would be evident from his later work, which had the benefit of much greater psychological and temporal distance from his roots in the Austro-Hungarian Empire. That perspective ultimately enabled his aesthetic to be more fully Lubitschean.*

A WILDER *STRASSENFILM*

Another of Wilder's better efforts in Germany is an October 1932 release that has songs but is not overly bound by the *operettenfilm* formula. *Scampolo, A Child of the Streets* is a blend of the musical and the *Strassenfilm* (street film), a genre with darker overtones dealing with the clash between proletarian and bourgeois life. *Scampolo* draws fruitfully from both genres in which Wilder had been working. Its story of a teenage waif living by her wits on the streets is one of eight film versions of the Italian play of that title by Dario Niccodemi, which already had been filmed there as silents in 1917 and 1928 (the title literally means "cloth remnant" but figuratively refers to a castoff, a nothing). A French version, *Un peu d'amour* (*A Little Love*), starring Magdelaine Ozeray, was made at the same time as the German film by the same

---

* An English-language version of *Once There Was a Waltz*, *Where Is This Lady?*, also starring Eggerth, was released in Great Britain in 1932.

director, Hans Steinhoff. Wilder received screenplay credits on both, along with Max Kolpé and Felix Salten (and Paul Nivoix on the French film).*

The German version, considerably altered in plot from the play, stars the fetching gamine Dolly Haas. She bears a striking resemblance both physically and in acting style to Audrey Hepburn, who later would star for Wilder in *Sabrina* (1954) and *Love in the Afternoon* (1957).† There can be no doubt that Wilder recognized the similarities between the two leading ladies, because *Love in the Afternoon* replicates both the opening and the ending of *Scampolo*. Each begins with a water-spraying truck symbolically cleaning the muck from a street in the early morning and ends with the female character being pulled aboard a vehicle by her previously ambivalent older male lover. In the case of *Scampolo*, Karl Ludwig Diehl's Maximilian lifts her into an airplane bound for England, while in *Love in the Afternoon*, Gary Cooper's Frank Flannagan lifts Hepburn's Ariane into a train headed out of Paris.

Scampolo and *Love in the Afternoon* differ greatly in theme, however. Hepburn's Ariane is a music student and daughter of a Paris detective, although she puts that respectable life in jeopardy by conducting a clandestine affair in a hotel suite with an American millionaire playboy. Scampolo in the Wilder version lives precariously in a telephone kiosk and has no visible family.‡ Scampolo scrapes by with a delivery job for a laundry that regularly takes her to a seedy hotel where she befriends the out-of-work, despondent Maximilian. Cooper is too old for his somewhat corresponding role in *Love in the Afternoon* and dispiriting as a rake involved with a young woman, a role at odds with his by-then usual persona as a man of rectitude. But Diehl has no such problems of image to overcome and is believably glum and unglamorized

---

*   Kolpé, a Jew of Russian descent who founded the Berlin cabaret Anti, was a longtime friend of Wilder's; they also collaborated on *Mauvaise graine*. Felix Salten was a prominent Vienna journalist and a Jew who eventually fled Berlin for Switzerland. In a paradox Wilder must have relished, Salten was the author not only of the children's classic *Bambi, a Life in the Woods* (1923), the source of Disney's animated feature in 1942, but also, anonymously, of *Josefine Mutzenbacher oder Die Geschichte einer Wienerischen Dirne von ihr selbst erzählt* (*Josephine Mutzenbacher or The Story of a Viennese Whore, as Told by Herself*). That fictional autobiography from 1906 is a notorious novel of hard-core lewdness Wilder admitted reading frequently and even mentioned as a film project late in his life.

†   Haas left Germany in 1936 for England. She later had a successful American stage career and an enduring marriage with the fabled caricaturist Al Hirschfeld. She played few American film roles but has a noteworthy small part in Hitchcock's *I Confess*.

‡   This is something of a premonition of Wilder's early months in Hollywood.

as a middle-aged former British bank manager who would watch out for Scampolo if he could only manage to do so for himself.

With her encouragement, Maximilian (the same name as Wilder's hotelier father) eventually sets up a language school at his hotel. Among his lessons: "The most important word in French is *l'amour*; in English it's *the money*; in Spanish it's *el torero*." Scampolo's other good friend is the hotel manager, Gabriel (Paul Hörbiger), an amiable bumbler who longs for her himself but is destined to lose out, gracefully, when Maximilian gets back on his feet with the help of an old friend and business partner and takes her out of Germany (just in time politically, though the film doesn't acknowledge it overtly). Haas is spunky as the resourceful waif and only rarely succumbs to her latent despondency, which is mostly evident in her engagingly wistful song near the beginning, filmed in a long take as she walks through the streets lamenting, "I don't know anybody/Nobody knows me" and longing for "a little bit of love."

Mostly filmed on relatively small studio sets in Berlin, *Scampolo* occasionally ventures onto the actual streets of Vienna and was directed efficiently by Steinhoff. A former actor, he would go on to make propaganda films for the Third Reich, including the UFA feature *Hitlerjunge Quex: Ein Film vom Opfergeist der deutschen Jugend* (*The Hitler Youth Quex: A Film About the Sacrificial Spirit of German Youth*), released in September 1933. Wilder later described Steinhoff as "a man without any talent at all. He was a Nazi, a hundred percent. There were many Nazis who had talent. I would never say that Leni Riefenstahl didn't have talent. That was certainly a great thing she did with *Triumph of the Will*. But I say Steinhoff was an idiot—not because he was a Nazi, but also because he was a terrible director."

Wilder's negative view of the director's politics seems to have affected his view of Steinhoff's work on *Scampolo*, which is actually a charming, often touching film. Though the glimpses of actual street life are limited, they help give it an aura of authenticity, and the studio scenes capture the messy bustle of lower-class life. The emphasis on the grinding poverty of the central characters and the dismal atmosphere of the shadowy hotel, the Pension Royal (a kind of setting Wilder knew well), make *Scampolo* more emotionally compelling than the frothier fare Wilder had to turn out in that period. Scampolo's indomitable nature, which enables her not only to survive but to triumph, is more convincing in a relatively gritty romantic comedy-drama than it would be in a full-blown operetta.

The plot contrivance that enables Maximilian to find a job and escape from Germany, with Scampolo joining him at the last minute, is another of those magical happy endings that, as Sirk pointed out, may gratify the undemanding spectator but, in its arbitrary nature, only serves to emphasize its improbability. And in the hindsight of history, this romantic fantasy carries extra resonance as a nearly impossible wish fulfillment of escape from Berlin, one that nevertheless would be reflected in Wilder's own narrow escape from Hitler. An especially double-edged "Wilder touch" in *Scampolo* is that a blackboard listing hotel guests behind in their rent conspicuously includes the name of Billie Wilder, who falls further behind as the film progresses. As funny as the in-joke may be, that was a situation he had often faced in Berlin, and it helps establish the personal nature of Wilder's empathy for a "nothing" such as Scampolo, whom Haas plays with ingratiating sincerity.

After *Scampolo*, Wilder worked for Steinhoff again, apparently reluctantly, on the comedy *Madame wünscht keine Kinder* (*Madame Wants No Children*), released in January 1933.* Based on a novel by Clément Vautel, it was a remake of a 1926 silent film directed in Germany by Alexander Korda. Wilder received an adaptation credit on *Madame Wants No Children*, along with Kolpé. The screenplay credit went to the prolific Austrian Jewish songwriter Fritz Rotter, who later immigrated to Hollywood. He wrote the original German lyrics for "I Kiss Your Hand, Madame," a song Wilder uses in *The Emperor Waltz*. According to plot synopses, the 1933 sound version of *Madame* (which could not be found for this study) is a comedy about a female physical culture fanatic (Lian Haid) married to an obstetrician (Georg Alexander) who very much wants children. The film contrives to have the athletic wife settle down as a childbearing hausfrau, thereby quelling her futile rebellion against the inevitable role imposed on women in Nazi Germany, which promoted the fascist ideal of Aryan bodily perfection but relegated most women to subservience at home.

The films Wilder worked on in Germany were deteriorating noticeably in quality toward the end of his time there. Perhaps that was a sign that he was distracted by more pressing events in Berlin or was having a harder time functioning in the industry as the political situation worsened. The film that

---

* A French version directed by Steinhoff and Constantin Landau, *Madame ne veut pas d'enfants*, opened that February.

followed *Scampolo* in his oeuvre, *Das Blaue vom Himmel* (*The Blue from the Sky*, 1932), yet another *operettenfilm*, was the least of his efforts in that genre. It is not only a slipshod endeavor but a film of stupefying asininity.

Victor Janson, who worked with Wilder on *Once There Was a Waltz*, again directed, and one can only imagine that this former Lubitsch actor was aiming for surreal silliness and missing the mark, although the slapdash plotting is partly to blame. Another Lubitsch regular, Margarete Kupfer, has a supporting role. The only novelty in *The Blue from the Sky* is that it takes place largely in the U-Bahn, Berlin's subway network ("U" for underground and "Bahn" meaning "railway"). That is a dubious distinction, since it provides an uncomfortably claustrophobic setting for song-and-dance numbers, awkwardly conveying the film's theme of repression versus freedom.

Mártha Eggerth again is on hand with her vibrant soprano to star as ticket-taker Anni Müller, but the score is so thin and repetitious that it mostly consists of her dull chorus, "One day alone with you/I don't need any more than that" but "a piece of sky, a piece of heaven." Anni conveniently gets her wish when courted by a not very dashing airmail pilot, Hans Meier (Hermann Thimig), who warbles on the brink of the apocalypse, "What do I care about the world?/The sky is blue; I have no worries." Even though Hans loses his job when he comes late to work while courting Anni, he quickly finds another, skywriting for Tabu Cigarettes, perhaps a reference to Murnau's valedictory film, *Tabu: A Story of the South Seas* (1931).

The Blue from the Sky ends as Hans appends a heavenly love message to Anni. Before that there is a brief misunderstanding when Hans thinks she is prostituting herself to the head of the cigarette company, though she's only begging him to give her boyfriend a job. In this situation, which anticipates later films Wilder directed, we sense his pen temporarily sharpening. His ambivalent view of women is humorously captured in the reactions of an adolescent boy (Hans Richter, from the cast of *Emil and the Detectives*), who commiserates with the aviator by saying, "Mâdchen sind quatsch" (Girls are nonsense) but declares when all is resolved at the end, "Herr Meier, I'm going to become a pilot too, and girls aren't nonsense."

The technical quality of the film is surprisingly poor: Janson's idea of atmosphere is to intercut jarring stock footage of thunderstorms with hokey, clumsily staged action. The director tries to "open up" *The Blue from the Sky* not only with flying scenes (mostly shot, however, against process screens) but also with a musical parade and country picnic for exuberantly marching and dancing U-Bahn workers that doesn't so much mock the mindlessly propagandistic Hugenberg formula as serve as its apotheosis. When Wilder characterized most of his German films as "lousy," he must have had *The Blue from the Sky* high in his mind.

But the experience, like his other efforts in Germany, was not wasted. The film's "meet-cute" gag is that Meier works nights and Anni works days, giving them only a few minutes at a time for their frantic courtship. That is a device that has been used in other romantic comedies and in a better film would have served as a pointed reflection of the desperation of Berlin working life. It provided Wilder with the germ of a romantic comedy gimmick for the screenplay that Joe and Betty Schaefer (Nancy Olson) in *Sunset Blvd.* are sneaking off at night to write together, about a pair of male and female teachers: "And don't make it too dreary," Joe says. "How about this for a situation: she teaches daytimes. He teaches at night. Right? They don't even know each other, but they share the same room. It's cheaper that way. As a matter of fact, they sleep in the same bed—in shifts, of course." Another element Wilder took away for future refinement was using the U-Bahn for a sharp political gag he and I. A. L. Diamond wrote for *One, Two, Three*. Cagney's exasperated Coca-Cola executive grills his unctuous, heel-clicking German subordinate Schlemmer (Hanns Lothar) about what he did in World War II:

> SCHLEMMER: I was in the *Untergrund*, the Underground.
> MacNAMARA: Resistance fighter?
> SCHLEMMER: No, motorman in the Underground. You know, the subway?
> MacNAMARA: Of course you were anti-Nazi and you never liked Adolf.
> SCHLEMMER: Adolf who? You see, down where I was, I didn't know what was going on up there. Nobody ever told me anything.

A NONPERSON

Because he was a Jew, Wilder was stripped of credit on his last work as a German screenwriter, *What Women Dream*, which was released in Berlin in April 1933, shortly after he had fled the country.

This glossy but depressing would-be romantic comedy deals with a female jewel thief, a kleptomaniac pursued by a would-be sugar daddy. A sour piece of piffle Wilder wrote with Franz Schulz (for whom Wilder claimed to have been a ghostwriter earlier), it was directed by the Hungarian Géza von Bolváry. *What Women Dream* seems to echo Lubitsch's *Trouble in Paradise*, but that apparently is coincidental, since the German film was released only five months later. Lubitsch's romantic comedy masterpiece about a pair of jewel thieves whose lives become intertwined with a rich woman they are robbing offers rich social commentary about how people survived in the Great Depression. There is genuine emotional depth in its portrayal of the intense emotions stirred by that complex love triangle. *What Women Dream* has none of those qualities. Cold and detached, it is almost clinical in its portrayal of kleptomania and the techniques of thievery.

The film's grimness and lack of wit no doubt reflect the increasing desperate climate in which it was made. The lack of genuine romance or eroticism was part of a pattern identified by Klaus Kreimeier in his book *The UFA Story* (1992) as stemming from the time when the German cinema was discarding "the explosive sensuality of its early years and was orienting itself to middle-class 'taste' . . . [and when Germany's film stars] lent their charisma to an inhibited middle-class eroticism that stripped the erotic of its magical qualities." With UFA increasingly under the spell of totalitarianism and a resulting loss of interest in celebrating individualism or exploring psychological depths—characteristics that had given emotional weight to German films in the expressionist period—the studio was fast becoming starkly antithetical to Wilder's characteristic talents, while the world outside the studio was turning actively hostile to him and his people and to artists in general.

The thief in *What Women Dream*, Rina Korff, despite going into an unmistakable orgasmic state whenever she sees a jewel (perhaps a vestige of Wilder's personality surviving the production process), is an unengaging and charmless character. That is only partly due to her being played by Nora Gregor, the icy Austrian actress best known as the leading lady of Jean Renoir's French masterpiece *La règle du jeu* (The Rules of the Game, 1939).*

---

* Gregor, who was Jewish, married the conservative Austrian politician Ernst Rüdiger Starhemberg in 1937. They fled to Switzerland after the *Anschluss* the following year and eventually emigrated to South America, where she committed suicide in 1949.

Rina's pursuer and would-be protector in *What Women Dream* (Kurt Horwitz) is an even less appealing character, a sinister society criminal who runs an illicit Berlin casino and uses the threat of blackmail to try to seduce her. The contrast between these two heartless opportunists and the delightfully elegant, droll, and emotionally engaged characters of Lubitsch's film could not be more dispiriting.

The only genuine humor in *What Women Dream* is an eccentric supporting turn by Wilder's friend Peter Lorre, the Brechtian actor who had become a star in German films with his unnerving performance as the child murderer in Fritz Lang's *M*. Lorre offers a flighty riff in *What Women Dream* as a ridiculously inept, giggling police inspector named Otto Füssli. Unfortunately, this diverting performance marked the only time Lorre and Wilder would work together, even though they remained friends in Hollywood and for a time were roommates there.

Although *What Women Dream* debuted in Hungary on April 4, 1933, as Karasek notes in his Wilder biography, it had its Berlin premiere on Hitler's birthday, April 20, accompanied by singing of the Nazi anthem, "The Horst Wessel Song," and "the writers Fritz Schulz and Billie Wilder were expunged from the opening credits and the program booklets" (Wilder by then was in Paris). This film was suitable for a Nazi premiere because it contains a bizarre song extolling the sexual appeal of policemen, which seems a paean to fascist authority when presented as a straight-faced production number by a chorus line of girls at the casino. And yet it was introduced previously in the film, parodistically, as a duet by Füssli and Rina at a piano, with Rina picking the unsuspecting Füssli's pockets as he bounces on the piano bench, crooning with foolish self-aggrandizement.

So, like most of Wilder's work for UFA, *What Women Dream* comes off as somewhat schizoid, reflecting the unsettled times and the conflicting agendas at play among the collaborators and their bosses. Wilder's writing of the Lorre character and the inspector's equally bumbling partner is clearly an attempt to mock the authorities. The trouble is that presenting German policemen as idiots in early 1933 comes off as a desperate, hopelessly inadequate attempt to deny harsh reality by someone writing with one foot out the door.*

---

* Universal remade this undistinguished film in Hollywood in 1934, again without Wilder's direct input, as *One Exciting Adventure*, starring Binnie Barnes and Neil Hamilton.

There is a more intriguing undertone to *What Women Dream*, however, a sense in which Wilder's farewell to German cinema is a reflection, conscious or not, of his own precarious state. Centering a would-be romantic comedy on criminals constantly in danger of being exposed and sent to jail, while portraying an apparent society woman as a kleptomaniac who makes a vain attempt to escape by train and tries unsuccessfully to shake her addiction to antisocial behavior, gives the film an edgy atmosphere of pervasive social instability. The "respectable" young perfume salesman, Walter Koenig (Gustav Fröhlich), who finds himself drawn to Rina is one of the many otherwise likable Wilder characters unable to resist corruption. Coupled with the film's failed attempt to satirize the police in any meaningful way, these elements make *What Women Dream* a thoroughly depressing piece of nonentertainment.

Wilder's understandably anxious, preoccupied state of mind—the sense he must have felt of himself as a potentially hunted "criminal" because he was Jewish—helped turn a piece of inconsequential fluff into a symptom of the precariousness of life in Berlin in those final days before any dream of democracy and freedom died.

ESCAPE

After fleeing Berlin on March 30, 1933, with his girlfriend, Hella Hartwig, Wilder settled in the Hotel Ansonia in Paris on the rue de Saigon near the Arc de Triomphe. They shared that dingy refugee haven with Lorre, Franz Wachsmann, Holländer, Kolpé, and Wilder's Berlin journalist colleague Hans G. (later Jan) Lustig. From time to time their Berlin colleague Marlene Dietrich, who was in Paris that summer of 1933 doing recordings, looked in to give them moral support. Besides the Ansonia bunch, German refugees in Paris included producer Erich Pommer and directors Lang, Max Ophüls, and Joe May. Wilder's Austrian passport prevented his deportation from France to Germany, but his hotel life was still a precarious existence. He had studied French in school, not English, and his survival instincts made him realize that Vienna or Prague or some other part of the former Austro-Hungarian Empire ultimately would offer no safety.

Although Wilder could take some comfort in being around fellow exiles during his nine months in the French capital, he remembered the "cold and repellent atmosphere in which we lived as emigrants in Paris." Holländer described the Hotel Ansonia with its "small but dirty" rooms as a "nest for the expelled, refuge of the expropriated, holding tank, transition camp, hotbed for all kinds of premature births—of ideas for the future to suicide plans." Holländer also noted that the hotel was hit with a "sleeping epidemic" as the depressed, dispirited German exiles increasingly had trouble getting out of bed.

MAUVAISE GRAINE

Wilder's true refuge was work, but since he did not have a visa or a labor permit, he had to scrape by doing some uncredited script work until he was fortunate enough to make his directing debut. He teamed with Alexandre Esway on the low-budget French-language film about a gang of car thieves, *Mauvaise graine* (*Bad Seed*), filmed in 1933 but released in the summer of 1934. Wilder later said he was not particularly ambitious to be a director at the time but took the job "out of sheer necessity." Esway, a Hungarian who put together the funding, had some directorial experience, but Wilder received first-position credit on the fast-paced crime melodrama/love story, and the star, the teenage Danielle Darrieux, recalled that he was the only one of the pair she ever saw on the set: "He was young, but he knew just what he wanted, and he was totally in control, like the other best directors I worked with."

The credited writers for the "scénario" are Lustig, Wilder, and Kolpé, listed by last names only, "avec la collaboration" of Claude-Andre Puget (his name is in all capitals, unlike those of the other writers; Wilder evidently needed help with his French from Puget, as he would with English from his future collaborator Charles Brackett). The jazzy score by Franz Waxmann (as Wachsmann was spelling his name then) with Allan Gray is one of the film's Americanized elements, along with its long stretches of action accompanied only by music without dialogue and, most prominently, its delirious delight in fast cars and dizzying chase sequences.

Thanks to extensive location shooting on the streets of Paris and the highway, a necessity of the low budget, *Mauvaise graine* also shares the cinéma-vérité approach of *People on Sunday*. Not only do most of the interior scenes take place in the gang's garage, all the other interiors also were shot there on

drab, rudimentary sets. But in its jaunty tone, Wilder's debut film most anticipates the playfulness, off-the-cuff flavor, and jarring jump-cutting of the
French Nouvelle Vague films, especially Jean-Luc Godard's landmark *À bout
de souffle* (*Breathless*, 1959), which it resembles in its blending of genres: crime,
comedy, and love story. Wilder's future work as a director similarly would
often cross genres for unsettling effect, and this debut film daringly intercuts
farcical action with gut-wrenching violence.

The heart and soul of *Mauvaise graine* reflects Wilder's unsettled state of
mind as an exile scraping by in Paris on the edge of desperation. Andrew Sarris observed that its "disturbingly mixed moods" represent "the lyrical tra-
versals of a camera in exile." The film involves constant, frenetic movement
and ends with the romantic couple migrating from their native country under
duress. The young protagonist, Henri Pasquier (Pierre Mingard), the son of
a doctor, is a feckless playboy so fixated on fast cars that when his father, fed
up with his son's irresponsibility, sells the young man's convertible, Henri
turns criminal as a car thief to support his habit. Another character tells
Henri, "You're the prodigal son. Maybe you'd rather go home," but Henri
says, "Go screw yourself! I don't have a home."

The hapless protagonist's loss of his car at the beginning and making his
living in a shady enterprise link Henri to Joe Gillis in *Sunset Blvd*. Joining
the gang of thieves leads to Henri's romance with Darrieux's fetching Jeannette, who lures older men into distracting situations while their cars are stolen. Their eccentric, otherwise all-male accomplices include an African
mechanic who masquerades as a chauffeur (Gaby Héritier) and Jeannette's
brother, Jean-la-Cravate (Raymond Galle), a gay youngster who has a fetish
for stealing ties and an instant attraction to Henri. These diverse strands, not
all fully explored in an often jokey film that seems more interested in wildly
careening shots from moving cars, eventually fall away as the last part of the
film focuses on something deadly serious: Henri and Jeannette deciding to
flee France by boat to Casablanca.

Wilder's identification with criminals stems both from his own alleged episodes of juvenile delinquency as a car and motorcycle thief and on a deeper
level from his sense of himself as a stigmatized outsider whose ethnic background, previously the source of humiliation, now put him on a run for his
life. The film takes a mostly uncritical attitude toward the car thieves, other
than their villainous chief (Michel Duran), who tries to kill the troublesome

Henri. The casual amorality of *Mauvaise graine* reflects Wilder's sense of proportion: Car theft is a relatively minor crime in the scheme of things in the Europe of 1933 as well as a pardonable means of survival. Jeannette has joined the gang only because she lost her job as a secretary—another Wilder commentary on the economic pressures of those times—and wistfully admits she still yearns for the security of a regular job.

After the couple's sabotaged car crashes in a police chase, they head for the port of Marseilles. The film emotionally climaxes in a long, atmospheric early-morning tracking shot, worthy of Jean Renoir, as they walk toward their destiny, bedraggled and exhausted. Jeannette eloquently expresses their sense of reaching the end of the line in her drained look and by telling Henri, "I am dead." Her words and bearing are a stark expression of what Nancy Steffen-Fluhr, in her essay on Wilder's "Double Vision of Exile," calls "this liminal figure—the living deadman—[that] haunts" his body of work. The journey of these two criminal characters metaphorically encapsulates his loss of a homeland and family after the Nazi takeover, his perpetual sense of exile, and "his sense of 'being in-between' cultures." *Mauvaise graine* reflects how Wilder characterized his Parisian exile period: "It was sad. We were sad."

Darrieux was one of the great beauties of the screen and would go on an astonishingly long career reaching into 2016, less than a year before her death at the age of one hundred. She entered films in 1931 and gave her crowning performances in the 1950s Ophüls classics *La Ronde, Le Plaisir,* and *Madame de. . . .* At sixteen in *Mauvaise graine,* lissome and softly pretty rather than the glamorous, finely sculpted, queenly presence she would become, she charmingly incarnates an uninhibited yet still demure character who makes a fittingly gutsy and unconventional Wilder heroine. Jeannette has the emotional complexity of Jou-Jou or Scampolo, with hints of a more tragic potential in her reckless behavior and shifts from gaiety to grimness, mood swings characteristic of future Wilder heroines.

Henri does a "meet-cute" by impersonating Lubitsch regular Maurice Chevalier in order to pick up Jeannette. One of Wilder's most dexterous pieces of direction in this debut film, a true Lubitsch Touch, is a tracking shot of Jeannette strolling down a Paris street, self-possessed and swanky, attracting the attention of an older man in a convertible who clearly thinks she is a prostitute. The man pulls up alongside her. Just then a horse-drawn van drives between them and the camera. As it passes, we see that she is in the car, being driven away. This sophisticated, suggestive use of ellipsis is echoed elsewhere in the film in two other touches influenced by Lubitsch: Wilder does not show the moment when Henri steals his first car but simply shows him driving away; and Henri reveals her brother's death to Jeannette without the audience hearing his words, because a boat whistle is blowing. These skillful pieces of direction are unusually subtle for a director making a first film and show how practiced Wilder had become, through his extensive work as a screenwriter, in the finer points of filmmaking.

Mauvaise graine ends with a fast tracking shot of waves as seen from the boat as it departs Marseilles with the young couple escaping into an uncertain future. As Henri tells Jeannette, "It's our only chance." That ending could not be more expressive of Wilder's own life journey, which saw him departing (alone, since he and Hella had broken up) on a ship for the United States on January 22, 1934. He took a British ship, the *Aquitania*, so he could practice his English, including by reading novels—Ernest Hemingway's *A Farewell to Arms*, Sinclair Lewis's *Babbitt*, and Thomas Wolfe's *Look Homeward, Angel*.

Since Wilder was no longer in France when his directorial debut premiered, *Mauvaise graine* meant almost nothing to his career. After a fairly well-received release in France, it did not resurface until many years later. One Paris reviewer wrote, "Rarely have the different refined methods of car theft been better demonstrated, so I was glad, after the premiere of the film, to find again my car, which I had parked in front of the cinema, safe and sound." The reviewer presciently noted that Darrieux's "youthful charm and porcelain face will never be forgotten." Kolpé, in a November 1933 letter to Dietrich in Hollywood while the film was in postproduction, told her he thought it was "quite good, but I think the script was better. It was really hard to work in France."*

Wilder shared the feeling of having come through an ordeal in making *Mauvaise graine*. "I cannot say that it was fun," he told Karasek, and he explained to Charlotte Chandler,

---

* Gaumont remade *Mauvaise graine* in England in 1936 as *The First Offence*, starring John Mills and Lilli Palmer and directed by Herbert Mason. Wilder was not credited for that version, but he received a cowriting credit on a French remake, *La voyageuse inattendue* (*The Unexpected Voyager*, 1950), directed by Jean Stelli and starring Georges Marchal and Dany Robin.

We were always having to change the script to fit what we had, or didn't have. There was pressure. People depend on you, and you aren't really in control, but you can't show that, or everyone gets nervous. I like to have a script and more or less stick to it. . . . After how hard it was to make, I was surprised how lively and spontaneous people found it. I still didn't think of myself as a director, not exactly. I wasn't certain I *liked* being a director, but I did know I could do it. That was satisfying. . . . I remember *People on Sunday* like I remember the first girl I kissed. Better. *Mauvaise graine* was more like the first girl I ever went to bed with.

THE GOLDEN DOOR

Wilder's passage to the United States resulted from the sale of a film treatment he wrote with Kolpé, "Pam-Pam," to Columbia Pictures. Joe May, the pioneering German producer-director, a Berlin colleague and fellow refugee from UFA and Nazism who had made it to Hollywood earlier, persuaded Columbia to send Wilder a one-way boat ticket. They put him to work for six weeks as a contract writer at $150 a week. He had a three-month visitor's visa. His initial weeks in the United States in 1934 were spent at the Long Island home of his brother, Willie, before he debarked for Hollywood.

Retooling elements from *A Blonde Dream, Scampolo,* and *Mauvaise graine,* "Pam-Pam" dealt with a young runaway actress who holes up in an abandoned Broadway theater and falls in with a gang of criminals putting on a show. The story at least obliquely satirized the criminality that often pervades show business, displacing it from the film industry to the stage. "Pam-Pam" sounds like a precursor to Woody Allen's jovial comedy about a gangster showing an unexpected flair for theatrical showmanship, *Bullets Over Broadway* (1994). But after Wilder turned "Pam-Pam" into a screenplay for Columbia, it vanished into the limbo of unproduced pictures. Kolpé turned it into a stage musical that premiered in Vienna in 1937.

Selling the treatment to Columbia was no panacea. The time went by fast, and after Wilder became unemployed again, he had to leave the United States in the spring of 1934 to try to get another visa to reenter as a resident alien. Driving his beat-up 1928 De Soto coupe—a far cry from the stylish new Graham-Paige (American-made) convertible he had sported in Berlin—he traveled south to San Diego and east to Calexico, where he crossed into Mexico. The border city of Mexicali, the capital of the Mexican state of Baja California, was 190 miles from Los Angeles and had the closest American consulate. Wilder languished in a seedy hotel with other would-be immigrants, some of whom had spent years hoping to get into the United States as part of the quota system.

Foreigners wanting to obtain entry permits had to apply outside the country and wait with their documentation for quota numbers as legal immigrants. They were required to prove that they were not "likely to become a public charge" and to file declarations of intent to become permanent citizens, with seven years allowed to petition for naturalization. After opening its doors to immigrants during the Industrial Revolution, the United States had largely closed them with the Immigration Act of 1924, allowing few to receive quota numbers. The flood of mostly Jewish refugees from Hitler met with especially stern restrictions imposed by anti-Semitic forces in the State Department, especially Assistant Secretary of State Breckenridge Long. Although Wilder had been raised in hotels and frequently used them as settings for his movies, his stay in Mexicali was another of the most depressing times in his life. Before he became a Hollywood director, he would mine that experience (along with his dispiriting period at the Hotel Ansonia in Paris) for the most directly autobiographical script of his life, *Hold Back the Dawn*.

When Wilder received the Irving G. Thalberg Memorial Award for his producing career from the Academy of Motion Picture Arts and Sciences on April 11, 1988, he told one of his favorite stories, a moving account of how he finally was accepted into America, with the suspense and passion of a scene from one of his films: "I would very much like to thank one specific gentleman without whose help I would not be standing here tonight. I have forgotten his name but I have never forgotten his compassion." Recalling his insecurity as one of many exiles in the wake of the Nazi takeover and his unhappy expulsion from Hollywood, Wilder said that as he entered the consulate and met with an American official he thought was the consul,

I was drenched in sweat. It was not the heat. It was just the panic, the fear. I knew that I needed a whole bunch of documents: affidavits, official proof of former residence, sworn testaments that I had never been a criminal or an anarchist. I had nothing, zilch. Just my passport and my birth certificate and some letters from a few American friends vouching that I was harmless. It looked hopeless.

The consul—he looked a little bit like Will Rogers—examined my meager documentation. "Is that all you have?" he asked. And I said, "Yes."

Wilder told the official that after his hasty exit from Berlin, he had tried unsuccessfully to get the necessary papers from Nazi Germany. He said that if he went back to Germany, they would put him on a train and "ship me off to Dachau. So, he just kept staring and staring at me and I was not sure whether I was getting through to him. . . . Finally he asked me, 'What do you do? I mean professionally?' And I said, 'I write movies.'" The official began pacing back and forth behind the anxious young refugee, who was still a Polish citizen. Wilder related, "I felt that he was measuring me. Then he came back to the desk, picked up my passport, opened it, and took a rubber stamp and went [*thumps twice*], handed me back the passport and he said, 'Write some good ones.' That was fifty-four years ago. I've tried ever since. I certainly did not want to disappoint that dear man in Mexicali."

Wilder received many phone calls after his speech, and one caller told him that the consul would have been on holiday at the time. The man who let him into the United States was the vice consul, whose name he was told was Meyer. Actually, his guardian angel was Willys A. Myers. Myers's sympathy with Wilder may have stemmed from the fact that he was also a member of the international family of show business: his lifelong hobby was as an amateur magician. Wilder may have felt that his reentry into the United States, which enabled him to survive against such long odds, was something magical. Even though he had not been able to make a film for more than six years, he told the audience at the Academy Awards ceremony that as he looked back he felt, "I've lived a charmed life."

Wilder called his Hollywood colleagues "without any doubt, the most generous people in the world," and he would always be grateful for being allowed to become an American citizen in 1940, on what he considered "one of the shining days of his life," as Zolotow put it. But it is among the bitter ironies of Wilder's career that after he fled fascism and emigrated to America, the first few film assignments he was given in Hollywood, while struggling to establish himself from 1934 onward as he learned to write in a new language, were inferior to his best work in Berlin. Those early Hollywood films were less suited to his talents and even more banal and compromised than most of the escapist, formulaic fare he had to write at UFA. It was only after his fortuitous teaming by Paramount with the American writer Charles Brackett in 1936 that Wilder was able to start to escape the straitjacket of his first decade in two countries that had very different political systems but remarkably similar film industries.

4.0 Director Mitchell Leisen with Claudette Colbert and the scriptwriting team of Charles Brackett and Wilder making *Arise, My Love* (1940). It was Leisen who caused Wilder to return to directing by cutting a key scene from *Hold Back the Dawn* the following year. (Paramount/Photofest.)

"WRITE SOME GOOD ONES"

4.1 (top) Charles Boyer and Olivia de Havilland in the bittersweet love story *Hold Back the Dawn* (1941). Directed by Leisen from a Brackett and Wilder screenplay, it drew on Wilder's experiences as a gigolo and refugee from Hitler waiting to enter the United States from Mexico. (Paramount/Photofest.)

4.2 (bottom) Brackett and Wilder on a Paramount soundstage, revising the script of the first film Wilder directed in America, the slyly subversive romantic comedy *The Major and the Minor* (1942). (Paramount/Photofest.)

4

"I WAS NOT IN THE RIGHT COUNTRY"

Chased from my country now I have to see
If there's some shop or bar that I can find
Where I can sell the products of my mind.

—Bertolt Brecht

THE YOUNG immigrant screenwriter was, he later recalled, at "the low point of my life." Over the Christmas holidays of 1935, Billie Wilder (as he was still calling himself) was sleeping in the ladies' room of West Hollywood's Chateau Marmont Hotel. Later an iconic landmark, the hotel was an attempt to re-create a European ambience on a hillside just above the Sunset Strip. In time Sunset Boulevard would become a location identified with Wilder himself, but for now he was a miserable, impecunious tenant holed up without a view of that glamorous thoroughfare. Wilder occupied the Chateau's least appealing quarters, where "women were coming in and peeing and looking at me funny."

Or that was what he liked to tell people. Wilder may have been embellishing the yarn; other sources have him sleeping on a cot in a vestibule outside the ladies' room. Perhaps the distinction hardly matters. According to a history of the hotel, Wilder only briefly occupied that little nook until he managed to move to an actual room after the holiday season. For some time before this episode, from August 1934 onward, he had been living in what a manager of the hotel, no doubt giving her own spin, remembered as "our love-liest small suite." That was only a small furnished cubicle, but not the ladies' bathroom, and he had peace and quiet and could write there. The manager, former silent film actress Ann Little, remembered Wilder banging away on his typewriter incessantly: "He stayed in his room and worked till all hours of the night. I can't remember a time when I didn't see a light coming from beneath his door as I would make my evening rounds. That young man was much too hard on himself."

He was, because it was a desperate time. Billie Wilder was a refugee from Nazism struggling to reconstruct his life in a new language and culture, suf-fering guilt pangs for being safe in America while his family and their fellow Jews were imperiled under Hitler. Taking $5,000 scraped together from writ-ing a couple of unproduced scripts for Pioneer Pictures with an older and more experienced screenwriter and former newspaperman from New Eng-land, Oliver H. P. Garrett, Wilder left behind the modest quarters to make a trip to Vienna that November.* He went to try to persuade his mother to leave the country.

But as hard as her son tried, he could not convince her she was in danger from the Nazis in a land he and others considered even more anti-Semitic than Germany. He found that Genia and her husband, Berl, "were so old and accustomed to their surroundings that they no longer wanted to live in a strange new world." To Genia and even to her son, what Hitler ultimately would do to the Jews was "beyond our imagination, nothing that prevented her staying in Austria," Wilder recalled. "What I knew and felt was that Aus-tria would not be for long, regardless." On that same trip, Wilder visited the old flame from Berlin with whom he had fled to Paris, Hella, but realized their moment had passed.

Billie came back to Hollywood in December feeling defeated, "worried about the knowledge that my mother was in danger, and [knowing] that the war was on the way for Europe, [and] suddenly I wasn't sure if I fitted in around here in Hollywood." It was yet another blow to find that his digs at the Chateau Marmont had been taken during the busy holiday season. He had expected the small haven to be held for his return. Begging the manager

---

* The scripts were for a musical called *Encore* and a romance about spies and gambling, *Gibralter*. Wilder and Garrett also were frequent tennis partners.

to be allowed to stay, Wilder volunteered, "I would rather sleep in a bathroom than in another hotel." He was just a few miles from the Paramount studios, but he might as well have been back in Vienna. He felt as utterly demoralized as the out-of-work screenwriter Joe Gillis at the beginning of *Sunset Blvd.*, who tells us he was "grinding out original stories, two a week. Only I seemed to have lost my touch. Maybe they weren't original enough. Maybe they were *too* original."

Wilder remembered of that grim period, "I had the feeling I was not in the right country and I didn't know if there was a right country for me. Right here was the low point of my life."

His early years as a Hollywood screenwriter, 1934 to 1936, as he struggled to acclimate himself to American life and a new film industry before teaming with Charles Brackett, were the most creatively arid of Wilder's career: "I dragged my carcass up and down Hollywood Boulevard, and starved around for a year and a half before I sold two original stories." Eager though the Jewish refugee was to transform himself into an American, he was hampered not only by his initial lack of knowledge of English but also because his Mittel European background caused the Hollywood studios to pigeonhole him as a writer of frothy musicals and silly comedies set in Europe. Despite some bright spots here and there, and elements that look forward to the films he eventually directed, those early American films seldom rise above hackwork.

But he was learning more about his craft and how to succeed in the Hollywood system, and by the end of the decade, Wilder would be nominated for an Academy Award for collaborating on the script of a film classic for the director he would come to regard as his master, Ernst Lubitsch's *Ninotchka*, with Charles Brackett and Walter Reisch (from a story by Melchior Lengyel).

"WEIMAR ON THE PACIFIC"

Lubitsch was followed to Hollywood by F. W. Murnau and some other émigrés in the 1920s, but the German colony in Hollywood grew exponentially after the Nazis took power in 1933. The Austrian screenwriter-actress Salka Viertel presided over the expatriate community at her Sunday salon in her Santa Monica Canyon home. That cultural institution, as she writes in her autobiography, *The Kindness of Strangers*, benefited from "the informality and the haphazard intermingling of the famous with the 'not famous' and the 'not yet famous.'" Although hers was known as a "literary salon," she was a leftist who was later blacklisted, and "political discussions, verging on personal bitterness, were unavoidable among the Europeans and amazed the Americans."

Frequent guests in the eclectic ménage of Salka and her intermittently present writer-director husband, Berthold Viertel, included Murnau (before his untimely death in 1931), Charlie Chaplin, Garrett, Bertolt Brecht, Aldous Huxley, Christopher Isherwood, and Fred Zinnemann, as well as Max Reinhardt and his producer son Gottfried, pianist Arthur Rubinstein, composers Dimitri Tiomkin, Bronislaw Kaper, and Hanns Eisler, conductor Otto Klemperer, and stars such as Greta Garbo, Miriam Hopkins, and Johnny Weismuller.

In a sprawling metropolis without much of a geographic or cultural center, Salka's salon served as an equivalent of Wilder's favorite hangout in Berlin, the Romanisches Café. She provided a haven of refugee culture, a comfortable place for artists and intellectuals to schmooze. Wilder, as a very junior and relatively insignificant member of the salon, made infrequent visits, mostly out of loneliness, and was largely content to listen and learn. The expatriate community was unofficially headed by the Nobel Prize–winning novelist Thomas Mann, an august figure who kept mostly aloof from the Hollywood trenches (he famously declared, "Where I am, is Germany") but was supportive of many of their political causes. His older brother, Heinrich, author of the novel that served as the basis for *The Blue Angel*, was more visible in the salon. The modernist classical composer Arnold Schoenberg was another major figure in Southern California's circle of refugee artists.

As Donna Rifkind writes in her biography of Salka Viertel, *The Sun and Her Stars*, the extraordinary place of refuge she gave her fellow émigrés on the edge of the ocean near Hollywood owed its existence to "the speed with which she has seen houses and homelands snatched away, their inhabitants forced out into different kinds of wilderness, obliged to rebuild what they could with whatever opportunities they managed to seize."

For Viertel and most of the other expatriates who became influential in American culture worked in the popular art form of filmmaking, Hollywood offered a place of safety and a platform. These filmmakers brought a more cosmopolitan and sophisticated flavor to American filmmaking that helped transform the industry in their image. So many European refugees, primarily

Jews escaping Hitler, came to Hollywood in the 1930s and early 1940s that Los Angeles area became known as "Weimar on the Pacific."

Among the approximately ten to fifteen thousand refugees who fled Europe for Southern California between 1933 and 1941 were more than eight hundred film industry people given a new home by the Hollywood studios. They also included such other directors as Fritz Lang, Robert Siodmak, William Dieterle, Zinnemann, Otto Preminger, Joe May, Max Ophüls, Jean Renoir, René Clair, Douglas Sirk, Julien Duvivier, Henry Koster, and Edgar G. Ulmer; producers Erich Pommer, Joe Pasternak, and Sam Spiegel; actors Marlene Dietrich, Hedy Lamarr, Luise Rainer, Paul Henried, Conrad Veidt, Marcel Dalio, Peter Lorre, and many others (some of whom had to make a living playing Nazis); novelist Erich Maria Remarque and novelist-playwrights Franz Werfel and Lion Feuchtwanger; novelist-screenwriters Vicki Baum and Curt Siodmak; composers Erich Wolfgang Korngold, Franz Waxman, and Werner Heymann; and songwriter Frederick Holländer. Some of them had already worked with Wilder in Europe and/or would figure prominently as collaborators on the films he wrote and directed in the United States.

The European Film Fund played a vital role in supporting the refugees during the unsettled years of the 1930s and the war. The fund was primarily run by Liesl Frank and Charlotte Dieterle, whose husbands, writer Bruno Frank and director William Dieterle, also were among its organizers. The prominent Hollywood agent Paul Kohner, the Czech refugee who had produced Wilder's Berlin screenplay *The Devil's Reporter*, was a major figure in the fund's operation. Others important in its work included Lubitsch, Salka Viertel, screenwriter Felix Jackson, and Universal Studios chief Carl Laemmle. The fund drew regular contributions from many people in Hollywood (usually 1 percent of their weekly earnings), including Wilder. It provided financial support and studio jobs for those who fled to the American film mecca, many of whom continued struggling to reestablish themselves in their not-always-welcoming new land.

EXILE CINEMA

That astonishing wave of immigrant talent greatly influenced and enhanced the artistry of Hollywood, much as the Jewish scientists forced to leave Nazi Germany helped lead the way for American scientific prowess. European filmmakers brought a new level of worldliness to what had been a lively but still largely immature and Victorian American film industry. Along with their crucial contributions to the romantic comedy and musical genres, they would have especially strong influences on horror films and film noir. Wilder left his mark on the noir genre strongly with *Double Indemnity* and *Sunset Blvd.*, and the latter has elements of the horror film. More broadly, he dealt with dreadful aspects of life frequently in his work, sometimes bluntly in films of social criticism, made with the clear-eyed perspective of an outsider in a new land, and sometimes sarcastically, while bringing his continental sensibility to both American subject matter and films made in English but set in Europe.

"Exile cinema relies heavily on allegory," Gerd Gemünden writes in *Continental Strangers: German Exile Cinema 1933–1951* (2014). "We need to think of the political in much broader terms than merely the thematic or ideological content of a given film. As Thomas Elsaesser has argued, the illusionary dimension of filmmaking needs to be considered political in itself." Gemünden adds in his critical study of Wilder:

> The loss of political and economic security and of social and personal identity is a fundamental part of being a refugee, and strategies of impersonation, drag, shape shifting, and cultural mimicry are central to the exile's efforts to survive forced displacement, economic hardship, and social ostracism. In order to meet the studios' demand of what German and Austrian culture is all about, exiled filmed professionals had to perform Expressionist angst, Viennese schmaltz, and Prussian militarism whether or not it had any relation to their cultural heritage or aesthetic sensibilities. Thus even when in the service of entertainment, impersonation and masquerade always entail a political dimension, serving as allegory for the price the exile has to pay in his or her quest for assimilation, for blending in, or for mere survival.

Gemünden notes that strategies of shifting and camouflaging identity "are prominent in the comedies of Wilder and Lubitsch and their dark, only seemingly sarcastic, sense of humor." And due to the often taboo, deliberately and self-protectively elusive nature of such exilic strategies, the constant ingenuity of both filmmakers in circumventing and playing with censorship is integral to their form of subversive self-expression through disguised, allegorical means. For in the words of Joel Fineman, "historically, we can note that allegory seems regularly to surface in critical or polemical atmospheres, when for political or metaphysical reasons there is something that cannot be said."

Wilder and the other refugees "driven into Paradise" (in Schoenberg's words) brought with them the adventurous artistic spirit that made the Weimar period so influential. The social and political ferment of that time had led to daring formal experimentation and an often politicized approach to the content of books, films, and plays. In Germany, as Peter Gay observes in *Weimar Culture: The Outsider as Insider* (1968), those artists had been part of "a precarious glory, a dance on the edge of a volcano. Weimar culture was the creation of outsiders, propelled by history into the inside, for a short, dizzying, fragile moment." Despite the fragmentation and scattering of Weimar culture due to the Nazi convulsion in Germany, Ehrhard Bahr writes in *Weimar on the Pacific: German Exile Culture in Los Angeles and the Crisis of Modernism* (2007) that its influence and staying power was largely due to its transplantation to the vibrant exile community of Los Angeles. The exiles "revised and modified Weimar modernism to meet the challenges of the period between 1933 and 1958." Although Los Angeles in those years was often shortsightedly dismissed as an uncultured environment compared with New York, and Hollywood was generally viewed as philistine, Bahr notes that "Los Angeles's lack of a cultural infrastructure provided an opportunity for Weimar culture not only to reestablish its identify in exile, but also to fulfill its promise. In an environment with an established cultural infrastructure, where the influences of competing cultures could have proved overwhelming, this second flourishing of Weimar culture might not have been possible."

What Anthony Heilbut writes in *Exiled in Paradise: German Refugee Artists and Intellectuals in America from the 1930's to the Present* (1983) applies particularly well to Wilder, one of the most prominent and successful among that group:

> In one of many historical ironies, during their [post-1929] emigration the people produced by cities like Berlin and Vienna would become the chroniclers and arbiters of social change in America. Their acuity dated from a time when as outsiders themselves, they had been able to register change with the immediacy of someone absorbing a visual impression. The unique

Berlin skill was to take in all this intellectual and sensory information at once. . . .

The émigrés' political experiences, not to mention the cultural legacy of Berlin, Frankfurt, and Vienna, had made the refugees alert to signals and gifted at interpretation. Their irrepressible curiosity and questioning temperaments proved to be salutary, both psychologically (giving hard lives a bracing edge) and economically (providing a means of employment). For, in one of the more exorbitant occupational demands placed on immigrants, some of them were expected to comprehend a new culture and, with barely any breathing time, make sense of it for the natives. As if theirs were a generation of Tocquevilles, they found themselves employed as professional explainers. And with an exile's combination of craft, cunning, and chutzpah, they set to work. While they were still trying to learn the language, refugees were hired to observe American society at its most idiomatic and to analyze its most inarticulate citizens. . . .

Uncertain about the prospects for high art in so wild a territory, they also arrived with a genuine respect for American movies and jazz. Knowing so much already—no matter how partial or artificial the knowledge—they became in short order professional interpreters of the American temperament. Bertolt Brecht once observed that émigré filmmakers—although the demand was not limited to Hollywood—were expected to decipher the Americans' hidden needs and discover for them a means of fulfilling them: this was called delivering the goods. Within a few years, while their English was still threadbare, the émigrés had achieved a remarkable success. . . . In exile, the fantasists of America would become its shrewd and practical observers. Exile required the special alertness to culture and politics that they had initially cultivated as the German humanist tradition's last, best heirs.

THE DILEMMA OF JEWISH IDENTITY IN HOLLYWOOD

Although Hollywood was enriched with the exiles' presence, many immigrant Jews felt they were treated as second-class citizens and aliens not only by average Americans but even by some of their fellow Jews in the studios.

Hollywood liberal and leftist activists, galvanized by the rise of fascism in Germany and Spain and fearing the inevitable coming of another world war, formed the Hollywood Anti-Nazi League in 1936. Although the organization splintered along with the Popular Front in Hollywood after the signing of the Nazi-Soviet Pact in 1939, its leadership in the antifascist effort and prominent communist members caused it to be viewed as suspect by the House Committee on Un-American Activities (HUAC), which was formed in 1938 ostensibly to combat fascism but soon morphed into a primarily anti-communist force.

Hollywood studios in that era—with some exceptions, such as the then-liberal Warner brothers, New Deal supporters who made *Confessions of a Nazi Spy* in 1939—tended to shy away from depicting the Nazi menace in the 1930s. The Hollywood studios, partly since they were still doing business in Germany (except for Warner Bros., which pulled out in 1934), mostly had been avoiding projects that urged intervention against Germany or valorized the Loyalist cause in the Spanish Civil War. The studios also behaved timidly out of a deeply ingrained sense of self-protection against domestic opposition. Reactionaries in Washington and elsewhere viewed with suspicion any Hollywood film they thought tried to propagandize against fascism, even in relatively subtle ways. As late as 1941, isolationists brought the issue into the open by holding congressional hearings attacking Hollywood and particularly Warners for what they considered, not always incorrectly, films that lobbied against isolationism and Nazism. Hollywood was accused of "war-mongering" and working covertly on behalf of President Franklin D. Roosevelt's interventionist agenda. Anti-Semitic innuendoes crept into the debate, such as when Senator Gerald Nye (R–North Dakota), a prominent isolationist, charged during the hearings that people in Hollywood "responsible for the [anti-Nazi] propaganda pictures are born abroad."

Some filmmakers were pushing in their work for directly supporting the antifascist cause in Europe, such as in producer Walter Wanger's 1938 film for United Artists about the Spanish Civil War, *Blockade*, directed by Dieterle and written by the prominent Hollywood leftist John Howard Lawson. Another of the few American films dealing with that war was Paramount's Brackett-Wilder comedy-drama *Arise, My Love* (1940), a somewhat forced hybrid of love story and anti-Franco propaganda directed by Mitchell Leisen. A schizoid companion piece to the writing team's subtler, more satirical

Ninotchka, *Arise, My Love* was the most propagandistic political film Wilder managed to make in his period as a Hollywood screenwriter before the United States entered World War II, although other scripts of his from that time contain some trenchant reflections on the war in Europe and the refugee crisis.

Before *Arise, My Love* went into production, Wilder and Brackett were writing an original screenplay for Leisen, *La Polonaise*. It would have dealt with an American athlete who goes to Poland after the 1939 German invasion to try to aid his grandmother (Maria Ouspenskaya) but gets pulled into the war after she refuses to escape with him. The title refers to a Warsaw radio station that continually broadcast Chopin's patriotic *Polonaise in A flat Major, Op. 53* (the "Heroic" Polonaise) as German troops captured the city. Clearly drawn from Wilder's painful personal mission to try to save his mother from the Nazis, that project was to have starred William Holden, who much later became one of Wilder's quintessential leading men but was unavailable because Columbia insisted that he star in the Western *Arizona*. So *Arise, My Love* was rushed into production, with shooting beginning on June 24, 1940, two days after the French surrender to Germany.

Other Hollywood filmmakers who dealt with fascism overtly in 1940 included British émigré Alfred Hitchcock in *Foreign Correspondent* (for Wanger and United Artists) and Frank Borzage in his German-set *The Mortal Storm* (MGM). Even a Three Stooges short that year, *You Nazty Spy!*, a Columbia comedy set in a country called Moronika, broadly lampooned Hitler, Mussolini, Goering, and Goebbels. Other films served more obliquely as propaganda. Warners' rousing 1941 film about a World War I hero, Howard Hawks's *Sergeant York*, became a runaway hit while dramatizing how a pacifist Tennessee farmer played by Gary Cooper abandons (or modifies, depending on your point of view) his convictions to become a military hero fighting the earlier German threat in Europe.

But despite these limited and gradual forays into grappling with the reality of Europe at war and what that could mean for the United States, Hollywood generally avoided dealing with the persecution of Jews as Jews or hid their identities onscreen. The very word "Jew" was mostly taboo in Hollywood films; Chaplin had gotten away with using it in his bold 1940 satire on Hitler, *The Great Dictator*. FDR encouraged him to make the film, but it made many in Hollywood and elsewhere in the United States uneasy. Chaplin was a wealthy founder and part-owner of United Artists, so he could afford to break that taboo. Even the German Jew Lubitsch, in his daring and controversial black comedy *To Be or Not to Be* for UA in 1942, had to rewrite Shylock's most celebrated speech from *The Merchant of Venice* ("Hath not a Jew eyes?"), a centerpiece of the film, to avoid using the word "Jew." That taboo was not fully lifted until after the war, when two 1947 films, *Crossfire* and *Gentleman's Agreement*, directly confronted the issue of anti-Semitism.

Many Hollywood Jews in the 1930s also were in personal conflict over just how German they should be regarded in their new land and how open with their Jewishness. Much of the United States during the Depression era was isolationist and xenophobic, and anti-Semitism was still virulent in many quarters, limiting the kinds of professions in which Jews were allowed to enter or prosper. Some of the barriers were rigid against both American-born Jews and immigrant Jews. Politics, the law, business, and academia were openly biased against Jews, a situation that would not improve much until after the war. Even in more sophisticated quarters during the prewar period and the war itself, what was euphemistically called "genteel anti-Semitism" affected many otherwise moderate or even liberal people (Eleanor Roosevelt and her husband among them). That deeply ingrained bias helped account for quota systems in higher education and the legal profession and the pressures placed on Jews to assimilate by adopting more WASP-sounding names, downplaying or deserting their religious practices, or deemphasizing their cultural roots.

Many American Jews were fearful of becoming too prominently identified as Jews because of a perception that it could be dangerous to their lives and careers or that such activism might be seen as not "good for the Jews." Some influential American Jews, such as the Sulzberger family that owned the *New York Times*, did not want to spread the perception that the war in Europe was being fought on behalf of Jews. That unfortunately led the *Times* to downplay reports of the persecution of Jews and not demand more action by the shamefully reluctant U.S. government to help them, a reticence shared by some others in the American Jewish community. Some were worried about causing problems for themselves politically in the United States or for their families back in Europe. In that overall context, Jewish émigrés in Hollywood were often caught in a bind between allegiance to their people under persecution and a sense that they were living on borrowed time in a country that was not particularly sympathetic to them and failed to understand the world crisis until too late.

Although Wilder was always vocal about his family's plight and that of the European Jewish population in general, he did not talk much about his religious beliefs, and though he enjoyed displaying Jewish humor and sometimes used Yiddish words in interviews, he did not otherwise identify himself prominently with his Jewish heritage. Nevertheless, he revealed a religious tendency by putting "Cum Deo" or the initials "C.D." (With God) on the first pages of his screenplays. But he could not resist making a joke about it, explaining, "I got that from a writer whom I worked with in Germany. He said, 'It can't hurt.' Look, this is the cheapest way of bribing that thing in the clouds there." Maurice Zolotow noted, "Without advertising it, he goes to the synagogue often to pray and meditate." When Robert F. Kennedy was shot in Los Angeles in 1968 but still clinging to life, Wilder prayed most of the day at the Sinai Temple in Westwood, near his apartment. And after Steven Spielberg made *Schindler's List*, the project about the Holocaust that Wilder had wanted to direct, Wilder wrote his impassioned article praising the film and decrying the rise of Holocaust denial.

"THE POOR DOPE"

Although even before arriving in his new country, Wilder was awarded his first Hollywood credit on *Adorable*, the feeble musical Fox remake of *Her Highness Commands*, neither it nor his European work meant much to Americans when he arrived by boat from Paris in January 1934. At twenty-seven, he was alone, with eleven dollars to his name.

Despite his considerable experience in Europe as a screenwriter, a journalist, and even briefly a director, Wilder was starting over. *People on Sunday* had been something of a cult success in Germany, but Wilder recalled that his credits in that country "were films that most people here had not heard of. There was no *Last Laugh* behind me as there was behind Murnau. I had none of the accomplishments of a Lubitsch. It is entirely possible that many of us who came to America on our own initiative without any impressive credentials from Europe could have ended up as a head waiter at the Beverly Wilshire Hotel or opened a haberdashery store."

His older brother, Willie, was busy making women's purses (Wm. Wilder Co., Inc., Original Handbags) when Billie stayed with him briefly on Long

Island en route to Hollywood. But Willie eventually followed him there for his own largely subterranean filmmaking career that seemed to piggyback on his brother's success. Accurately described by critic Glenn Erickson as "Billy Wilder's prolific but talent-challenged brother," Willie spent more than two decades producing and directing low-budget movies in various genres (film noir, musical shorts, science fiction), as well as episodic TV shows. He signed his name William Wilder on the first two films he produced, but Billy made him change his credit to W. Lee Wilder when he made his directorial debut on *The Glass Alibi* in 1946. Billy did not want people to confuse them or have his brother mistaken for his distinguished colleague and friend William (Willy) Wyler. Billy criticized his brother's movies harshly, declaring, "They weren't anything that interested me, so I didn't see them. I saw one. I didn't expect much of it, and it didn't let me down. It wasn't even bad, which is worse. He should have stuck with leather purses."

Although Willie mostly toiled in what Erickson identifies as "his groove of incompetence," his producing career began surprisingly auspiciously in 1945 with *The Great Flamarion*, a taut and hauntingly offbeat noir directed by Anthony Mann. Erich von Stroheim stars as a lonely theatrical performer with a trick gunshot act who is lured into committing murder onstage by a femme fatale who then betrays him. But Willie's follow-up film with Mann, *Strange Impersonation* (1946), is lackluster and rather absurd, even if it shows that Willie shared some of Billy's fascination with the masquerade. With their common cultural background and exilic sense of pessimism, it is not surprising that one can find weak echoes of Billy's work in the con-men, murderous couples, gigolos, and aliens of various kinds who populate Willie's films. But it would be idle to draw detailed comparisons between the brothers' work, since Willie's films are so routine and lacking in wit or imagination.

With rare exceptions, they not only tend to have minimal production values, fleshed out with stock footage, but their scripts (which he did not write) are clotted with expository dialogue, hokey narration, silly storylines, and cheap plot twists. Sometimes it even seems that Willie is consciously imitating Billy, and *Double Indemnity* in particular. That must have irked his younger brother and contributed to the disdain he displayed toward Willie. *The Glass Alibi* (1946) and its remake, *The Big Bluff* (1955), deal with con-men who marry wealthy women with fatal illnesses but impatiently plot to murder them. Albert Dekker is mildly compelling in *The Pretender* (1947) as a crooked

business manager whose scheme drives him mad with paranoia. These protagonists are so sleazy that they make Fred MacMurray in *Double Indemnity* almost seem an upstanding member of society. And it's tempting to see
The Glass Alibi as a thinly disguised expression of hostility toward Willie's
talented younger brother, since the central character is an appallingly
unscrupulous reporter and aspiring novelist who "wants to be a big shot . . .
ever since he was a kid."

Most of Willie's work in the 1950s was not in noir, which was falling out
of fashion, but in low-budget sci-fi for the baby boomer Saturday matinee
audience. *Phantom from Space* (1953) at least generates some sympathy for its
trapped, semi-invisible alien, but *Killers from Space* (1954) calls to mind Ed
Wood's *Plan 9 from Outer Space*, with ludicrous-looking aliens kidnapping
Peter Graves (shortly after he played a German traitor for Billy in *Stalag 17*)
as a pawn in their plot to take over Earth. Willie continued cranking out
mind-numbingly mundane programmers until 1968.* He died in 1982, as
obscure as his younger brother is celebrated; Willie is credited on his tombstone as William, the name Billy did not want him to use onscreen.

When Billie finally stepped off the train in Hollywood from New York in
the spring of 1934, the Hollywood romantic comedy genre was undergoing a
radical change. Frank Capra's sleeper hit for Columbia, *It Happened One
Night*, was democratizing and deglamorizing the genre with its newspaper
reporter hero, Clark Gable, bringing snooty heiress Claudette Colbert down to
earth. Lubitsch, on the other hand, was filming his grandest musical, *The
Merry Widow*, for MGM with his romantic team of Maurice Chevalier and
Jeanette MacDonald in their final pairing before Chevalier returned to
France. But that adaptation of the Lehár operetta was an expensive flop,
showing how the times were changing to more proletarian subject matter and
turning Lubitsch to other genres. Colbert, who had starred with Chevalier in
the director's sparkling Paramount musical *The Smiling Lieutenant* (1931), told
me that before *It Happened One Night*, the term "romantic comedy" was rarely
if ever heard in Hollywood; the term used before then was "high comedy,"
which Lubitsch films exemplified. She recalled that while making the Capra

---

* Some of Willie Wilder's films were written by his son Myles, who went on to a busy career
writing episodic television shows, as well as producing the *Dukes of Hazzard* series in the 1980s. Paul
Diamond, I. A. L. Diamond's screenwriter son, reports that Myles "did the best imitation of Billy,
ever."

film, "Clark and I kept wondering, 'What kind of reception can this kind of picture actually get?' This was right in the middle of the Depression. People needed fantasy, they needed a dream of splendor and glamour, and Hollywood gave it to them. And here we were, looking a little seedy, riding our bus."

But while Hollywood's transition from glamour to a certain degree of grit (albeit still-glossy and romantic grit) was underway, it would take Wilder a while to navigate these changing styles in his humble capacity as a junior studio writer with minimal control over his work.

Wilder at first inconspicuously rented a room in the Hollywood Hills home of the Viennese producer-director Joe May and his actress wife, Mia, while writing "Pam-Pam" as part of Joe's deal with Columbia Pictures. Half of Wilder's $150 weekly paycheck during his six-week stint at the studio went to the Mays for his room and board. And one of the more humiliating experiences Wilder underwent as a newcomer to Hollywood was earning a few bucks by jumping fully clothed into a swimming pool at the home of Erich Pommer, who had employed him as a writer in Germany. Even if Wilder was impressed that the Mays also had a pool in their Mediterranean-style home, he later may have been remembering those clownish, undignified days in the midst of Hollywood riches when he had Joe Gillis narrate *Sunset Blvd.* while floating dead in a swimming pool. Joe May, after his Hollywood filmmaking career failed, ran a Hungarian restaurant on Sunset Boulevard called the Blue Danube, with Mia as the cook and the financial backing of Wilder and other fellow émigrés, but it also went under. Ed Sikov's biography of Wilder suggests that the failure of the Blue Danube in 1949 and the ignominious ruination of his old friend and patron helped influence the conception in that period of *Sunset Blvd.*

Living in the apparent paradise of Hollywood "serves the unprosperous, unsuccessful/As hell," the refugee playwright and screenwriter Bertolt Brecht observed. That acidulous piece of wisdom was from one of the most celebrated of his bleakly truthful poems about the film capital. Bahr observes in *Weimar on the Pacific* that even though Los Angeles symbolized "the hope for a better future" in that era, "the most appropriate locale for art that dealt with both the reality of fascism and World War II," the contrast between the brutal reality the émigrés had left behind and the city's paradisiacal setting was "startling. . . . The idyllic landscape functioned like a Hollywood movie set that produced alienation because of its apparent perfection."

While grinding out his early screenplays, Wilder in his desperation and grim determination to succeed against long odds resembled one of the forlorn figures suffering in the hellish hotel of the quintessential Hollywood novel Nathanael West would publish in 1939, *The Day of the Locust*. Wilder could have served as one of the role models for the tormented, hotel-dwelling screenwriter in the Coen Bros.' *Barton Fink* (1991), a literal vision of Hollywood-as-Hell that owes as much to West as it does to Clifford Odets, whom the title character mostly resembles. The stark poverty and outcast state of Joe Gillis while surrounded by Hollywood plenty is Wilder's bitter reflection of his state of mind in the years before he made his name in America.

LEARNING THE LINGO

In retrospect, in light of Wilder's later reputation for acerbic social satire and trenchant drama, it may seem incongruous that a zany musical would be the toehold to survival for that Jewish refugee screenwriter in America. But Wilder had come to be regarded as something of a specialist in musicals in his early years in both Berlin and Hollywood. Although he was a closet romantic beneath his veneer of hard-boiled realism, he had not been particularly happy providing comical interludes for UFA musicals. "Pam-Pam," his abortive transitional project conceived in Europe, and his other early Hollywood scripts such as *Music in the Air*, *Lottery Lover*, *Champagne Waltz*, and *Rhythm on the River* followed similar formulas.

That was more out of necessity than inclination. After "Pam-Pam" fell through, Wilder was hired by fellow refugees May and Pommer to work on another schmaltzy musical, *Music in the Air*. Wilder found himself typecast in Hollywood as an impersonal craftsman hired to provide a gloss of ersatz German atmosphere to recycled schmaltzy material filmed on studio sound stages and back lots. Hollywood has always tended to pigeonhole people, and Wilder was in danger of becoming trapped in peddling sweet, frothy concoctions, albeit with an occasional dash of arsenic he somehow managed to drop into the mix. He must have been dismayed to work as a repackager of European musical escapism for Hollywood studios rather than as a writer of more challenging material directly reflecting the turbulent contemporary world and its sociopolitical conflicts. But initially, no one in Hollywood wanted biting social satire from Wilder, who was still spelling his first name as Billie because he did not yet realize that in English it is a feminine name. His first screen credit as Billy Wilder did not come until 1937, on the story of *Champagne Waltz*.

Wilder underwent a grueling trial to pay his dues while learning a new language and struggling to understand American cultural mores as he honed his craft in an alien studio factory system. Mired on the Hollywood assembly line, often working on uncongenial material or shunted aside in favor of other writers, he had ample reason to worry that he would never amount to much in his new country and film industry: "When you are a writer, when you are deprived of your language, you know, more or less, you are dead." Yet that rocky period, and his eventual success teaming with Brackett and Lubitsch, gradually taught Wilder how to succeed in the byzantine Hollywood system, how to begin expressing his own viewpoint within the American commercial framework, and how to outwit his bosses and the industry censors while smuggling subversive material into outwardly acceptable Hollywood entertainment.

At first, since Wilder knew only German and French, he wrote his screenplays in German and had them surreptitiously translated so the studios didn't realize he could barely speak or write English. "I had no confidence when I was first starting out because I only knew English from going to the movies," he recalled. He added, "I was here because I wanted to stay here. I was landed by emigration in my dream city. . . . As the ancient Romans said, *Ubi bene, ibi patria* [Where life is good, that is your homeland]." And he reflected,

It had become clear to me with the advent of the talkies that Hollywood and its universal language, English, would be the future. . . . My biggest handicap was my English. I was a writer in a language I could not speak. Even so I did not want to talk to German compatriots but with Americans. A language is learned like swimming by jumping into deep water. I often listened to the radio, sports programs and soap operas, such as *Dear John* or *As the World Turns*, mainly because I would hear the fastest slang I could acquire. After three years, I realized suddenly that I had begun to think in English. After five years I had no more problems with my English.

Wilder's urgent need during the 1930s to become fluent in his new language was an essential survival skill for a refugee, particularly since he was a writer by trade. He faced the same problem such great writers as Joseph Conrad and Vladimir Nabokov had to surmount, reconstituting himself in a new culture while simultaneously learning a new language. That daunting cultural acclimation process can be pulled off successfully only by someone with immense skill and social adaptability. Wilder's idiosyncratic style was not hampered but benefited greatly from writing in a new language, although, unlike those literary giants, he always needed a collaborator in English. He gradually evolved his characteristic blend of underlying gravitas with effervescent wit and wordplay. Wilder's journalistic training enabled him to size up situations quickly and take stock of how to solve them. As another German émigré to Los Angeles, the philosopher and sociologist Theodor Adorno, put it, "For a man who no longer has a homeland, writing becomes a place to live."

While listening to the radio, Wilder would write down expressions he didn't know and try to master twenty new words a day. He practiced by spending copious amounts of time chatting with young American women, a task with welcome side benefits he pursued *con molto brio*. A former desk clerk at the Chateau Marmont recalled, "Every once in a while, he would come out for air to pick up a newspaper or magazine and ask if we had any books he could borrow. He read a lot and listened to his radio, not so much for the news but to practice his English. He was so determined to learn. . . . But what I remember most about him was that he had a very busy social life. I doubt if he dated the same girl twice. He was quite the ladies' man."

Wilder's adaptation to his new country and the movie business, as arduous as it felt in the beginning, was relatively quick and eventually hugely successful. That could have been foreseen from his longtime affinity for American culture, especially the popular culture of movies and music, which was no mere expediency but a genuine passion. The dashing young reporter who had talked his way into a job as a publicist for Paul Whiteman's American jazz band in Berlin and made his living as a dancer and Charleston instructor before breaking into screenwriting with an eye toward Hollywood proved a natural for the American film business. Wilder had a knack for adapting to new surroundings, as he had shown with his attunement to the beat of Berlin street and night life and the talent that established his name as an au courant journalist with a gift for cleverly conveying the excitement of popular culture.

Wilder gradually absorbed an encyclopedic knowledge of American song lyrics in his early days in Hollywood listening to the radio obsessively. The pervasive influence of popular music in his work is reflected in his gift for snappy, colloquial dialogue, replete with colorful American slang, delivered in vibrant rhythms. His use of classical music in his films tends to be more ironically pointed or sarcastic. His work as a director has the visual grace and elegance (a word he often used to describe his stylistic ideal) of a polished dancer, drawing instinctively from the kind of flowing, intricate, lively, precisely executed jazz or waltz rhythms he had absorbed while plying that profession.

ACCLIMATION

Writing about European subjects initially was a handy crutch for Wilder, even if his sights were fixed determinedly on acclimating to his new country. Although being an exile again heightened his sense of alienation, it sharpened his perceptions and enhanced his characteristic sense of ironic distance from his surroundings, a dual perspective that already had become second-nature to him in Vienna, Berlin, and Paris. Wilder was part of what fellow Jewish writer Stefan Zweig described as "the ever-recurring—since Egypt—community of expulsion." That perspective increasingly would serve as a key source of Wilder's creativity as a filmmaker and social critic.

As Anthony Heilbut notes of German émigrés in the United States, "Their first impressions were, perforce, visual; the refugees' English was often an inadequate vehicle for instruction, even if the sights around them had not been so amazing. Later they would detect, in language and behavior, clues that remained invisible to the natives, but at first, noticing was something one did with one's eyes." Wilder was always a reporter at heart, and his journalistic training enabled him to size up situations quickly and take stock of them in a sharply knowing way. But the exposés of American life would come later, after he figured out how to function more successfully in the Hollywood system.

Wilder deliberately did not interact much with his fellow European refugees when he first came to Hollywood and after his return from Mexico with the coveted status of a resident alien visa. He scorned the refugees he thought were only marking time with illusory faith in the future of Germany: "Most of the refugees had a secret hope: 'Hitler will be defeated and I will go back home.' I never had such a thought. This was home. Some people have a musical ear; I had a clean-cut vision: 'This is where I'm going to die.'" The French director François Truffaut, who was offered many American projects but turned them down because he always struggled with English, told me in the 1970s that he thought the foreign directors who managed to adapt to Hollywood were the ones from totalitarian regimes where they could not return, such as Milos Forman and Roman Polanski. Truffaut said he and Jean Renoir and other French directors were unable to adapt partly because they had the safety valve of going back to their homeland (except during the war years while France was under German occupation).

"Those of us coming from Germany . . . had no choice but to leave home," Wilder agreed. "For me," he said, "it was a question of fighting it out here and surviving or going back and winding up like most of my family in the ovens of Auschwitz. . . . Although in my case it is also true that even without Hitler I would have dreamed of coming to Hollywood to make pictures." Wilder found most of his fellow European refugees too old or hidebound to adapt to a new country or uncomfortable speaking a nonnative language. Some, like Lubitsch and Fritz Lang, avoided the German language after Hitler took power. That decisive orientation to their adopted country helped both directors become notable successes in America. Wilder likewise wanted to be around Americans speaking English.

Brecht, who considered himself not an "emigrant" but an "exile," constantly fought against fitting into American culture. He hastened back to (East) Germany when he was among the prominent subjects of persecution during the postwar Red Scare. Wilder, by contrast, wholeheartedly embraced his new country, even while fully recognizing and criticizing its flaws. As he said in 1976, "We who had our roots in the European past, I think, brought with us a fresh attitude towards America, a new eye with which to examine this country on film, as opposed to the eye of native-born movie makers who were accustomed to everything around them." Like so many other immigrants, he was passionate about the freedoms he enjoyed in the United States, which in his case crucially included the artistic freedom to express himself as a social critic. But ever alert to fault lines in his adopted culture, he was a liberal who never took American democracy for granted; he said later in life that he felt the most important American institution is the Supreme Court, since (at least theoretically) it is tasked with upholding the Constitution. As newcomers often do, at least the ones who are determined to stay and forge an American identity, he felt the country allowed him to shed the unwelcome trappings of his past and learn new ways of operating while reinventing and expanding his shifting identity. That is a tendency particularly pronounced in California, which the local writer Julia M. Sloane famously called "the land of the second chance, of dreams come true, of freshness and opportunity."

But if Wilder always felt more like a grateful immigrant than an exile, that perhaps also reflected his lifelong sense of pragmatism, his Jewish survivor's ability to adapt to new surroundings out of necessity and to assess where he was most secure and could not only live but prosper. As Thomas Mann put it at a May 1941 gathering in Salka Viertel's salon, "Here in this young land you necessarily feel yourself to be foreign. But ultimately, what today is the meaning of foreign, the meaning of homeland? . . . When the homeland becomes foreign, the foreign becomes the homeland." Wilder was so accustomed to being an exile that it became his habitual way of life. In Berlin, Paris, and now Hollywood, he lived in what were, in many ways, cities of exiles. In those polyglot cities, the unsettled condition of exile was to varying degrees familiar, at times strangely comforting, and often hazardous. The constant role-playing in his films, penchant for themes of masquerade, and precarious blend of comedy and drama are reflections of his ability to cope with such uncertainties. His tendency toward dark humor, including the gallows humor that characterizes Jewish writers' and comedians' view of life, was exacerbated by exile. Wilder's work, with its affinity for danger and breaking boundaries, is always dancing on the edge, his characters poised between self-destruction and redemption.

In his early years in Hollywood, despite the studios' attempt to reduce him to a cultural stereotype, Wilder was determined to assimilate, to Americanize himself, a complex process that gradually enabled him to get work as a chameleon personality who fit in with the studio system. That was why he initially resisted foregrounding his foreignness, even if, and probably especially because, Hollywood was doing just that with his first writing assignments. Not only was the young Wilder determined to master the English language, he wanted to be accepted as a popular filmmaker who could appeal to a mass audience while still making films dealing honestly with his personal preoccupations.

Although Wilder became celebrated as one of Hollywood's greatest wits, and his films revel in dazzling uses of American slang, it was somewhat ironic that he never lost his insecurity about his English, which was one reason he always wanted to work with collaborators. After his initial period foundering on his own or working with ad hoc partners in Hollywood, he gravitated to those for whom the language came more naturally. In his acceptance speech for his 1986 American Film Institute Life Achievement Award, Wilder thanked Charles Brackett, "who desperately tried to help me improve my English."

Wilder eventually spent most of his American career working successively as a writing partner with the native-born Brackett and the Rumanian Jewish immigrant I. A. L. Diamond, whose flawless English reflected the fact that he had come to the United States as a child, not as an adult as Wilder had. But Wilder also viewed writing as a social activity, not as a solo occupation. That was partly because of his restless and talkative nature but also because language for any exile is an essential part of assimilation. A writer-director in a highly collaborative medium such as film must master the means of communication, verbal and otherwise, both with his coworkers and with the audience. Wilder always found it necessary to have an extensive creative interchange testing ideas with a sharp-witted collaborator before he would feel confident to go on the sound stage to make a film. And as a director he would discourage improvisation by actors, believing they could not come up with better lines on the spur of the moment than he and his writing partner could write with painstaking care in their office over a period of several months.

For all his fluency in English, Wilder would always retain his German accent, like Lubitsch, who also came to the United States in his adulthood. People in Hollywood and elsewhere found Wilder's accent delightfully exotic, but that was a double-edged sword; perhaps there was an element of condescension lurking below the surface of their amusement. Salka Viertel caustically observed that most of her American friends, "when I attempted to speak correctly," would tell her not to lose her "charming" and "cute" accent, leading her to think that "this American kindness toward foreigners is one of the reasons for their own bad diction and lazy speech."

Heilbut observes that refugee intellectuals "would discover their 'colorful personality' to be a major asset. This meant that character was diminished to an assortment of tics and cadences, curious accents and funny clothes. 'Personality' signified the dissolution of the concept of 'individual' in a vat of frivolous stylistic assumptions. By misapprehending everything important, the proponents of personality could make out of a bewildered refugee an 'unforgettable character.'" Wilder certainly became a "character," playing up for his own benefit what Heilbut identifies as that clownish side of an immigrant's personality, but he did so in his own supremely witty way, transcending cultural limitations. John Russell Taylor points out in *Strangers in Paradise: The Hollywood Emigres 1933–1950* (1983) that though Wilder "remained foreign enough to be colourful," he also "had observed closely enough to know just how far he could go without becoming unacceptable to American tastes. He had, in other words, become an American filmmaker, though with continental trimmings."

Although he learned how to avoid the pitfalls as well as exploit the strengths of his dual identity, Wilder could not help being made aware of the precarious ambivalence of his position in American culture. "Billy is terribly self-conscious about his accent," Zolotow reports in his 1977 biography of Wilder. "Once, sitting with a group outside his beach house at Trancas, north of Malibu, he mispronounced a slang phrase. His face darkened. He said suddenly, 'I wish I did not have this accent.' . . . When anyone makes fun of his speech—as [Humphrey] Bogart did [during the making of their 1954 film *Sabrina*]—Billy is hurt."* In an even more pointed sign of how Wilder always remained somewhat sensitive about his way of speaking, Zolotow relates that he became upset when

---

* One of the rare filmed interviews in which Wilder does not speak only English is the three-hour documentary of his engagingly casual but in-depth exchange in 1988 in his Beverly Hills office with German director Volker Schlöndorff and biographer Hellmuth Karasek, *Billy Wilder, wie haben Sie's gemacht?* (*Billy, How Did You Do It?*). Wilder veers back and forth between English and German, which is fascinating to hear, but his cultural anxiety over language and his loose, unguarded demeanor helped account for why he was dissatisfied with the documentary and forced Schlöndorff and his codirector, Gisela Grischow, to delay its release until 1992. Wilder claimed he didn't like the way he casually swiveled in his chair and opened his mail or used a back scratcher while talking, but that was an excuse. The informality is part of what makes it an unusually intimate glimpse of the veteran filmmaker.

Barbra Streisand mimicked his accent at a posh Hollywood dinner party. Uncharacteristically, "Billy did not utter a joke all evening. He was morosely silent."

Perhaps that unpleasant encounter reminded him of Louis B. Mayer's infamous diatribe after Paramount's studio preview of *Sunset Blvd.* in 1950. The MGM chief, who had long been the most powerful and tyrannical man in Hollywood, was railing against Paramount to his flunkies for letting Wilder make an exposé of the decadent underbelly of the film industry. Wilder often retold the story with a mixture of pride, relish, and still-palpable anger. According to one version, Mayer was shouting to his stooges, "That Wilder! He bites the hand that feeds him! We should horsewhip this Wilder . . . he should be sent back to Germany." Wilder went over to Mayer and simply replied, "Yes, I directed this picture. Mr. Mayer, why don't you go fuck yourself!" In another Wilder version, Mayer shouted, "You bastard, you have disgraced the industry that made you and fed you. You should be tarred and feathered and run out of Hollywood." And in a more elaborate version, the director made his profane retort after the aging studio mogul, himself an immigrant from Ukraine, told him, "You have dirtied the nest. You should be kicked out of this country, tarred and feathered, you goddamned foreign son-of-a-bitch."

Whatever the exact words Mayer shouted in his intemperate outburst against the iconoclastic director, it took some courage for an immigrant filmmaker to tell one of Hollywood's founding fathers to "go fuck yourself." In any case, by then Mayer's power was on the wane, and Wilder was important enough in the industry to get away with it, as he had with his opposition in 1947 to the Hollywood blacklist that was put in place after that year's HUAC hearings and in 1950 to the Screen Directors Guild (SDG) loyalty oath.* Mayer's ranting that he wanted him "kicked out of the country" or "sent back to Germany" brutally reminded the Jewish director that he was a refugee who was expected to be grateful that the industry had rescued him and so many others from Hitler.

"Although Mr. Wilder always had conflicts with the studio executives, he looks back on the old moguls with affection now," Stephen Farber reported

---

* The SDG did not become the Directors Guild of America until 1960, when it merged with a former rival, the Radio and Television Directors Guild.

in a *New York Times* interview in 1981, at the end of Wilder's career. Wilder is quoted as saying, "There was a certain nobility about them. I remember in 1934 when I arrived in Hollywood, there were a lot of German, Austrian, and Hungarian refugees who came here to escape Hitler. They were all taken in by the studios—actors, composers, writers. Even Brecht got a job." But however much Wilder appreciated the charity he was extended by his fellow Jews and others in the American film industry, such a sense of dependency, owing them his very survival, left him feeling somewhat insecure, as most immigrants are made to feel in America, hitting him in the most sensitive part of his psyche. Mayer's malicious reminder of Wilder's marginal status as an immigrant washed up on the shore of America, coming from a mogul who was also a Jewish immigrant, stung him. So, too, must have the prolonged poisonous atmosphere of thinly veiled anti-Semitism underlying his contentious relationship with Brackett. The posthumously published diaries of Wilder's longtime writing partner reveal that Brackett's problems with Wilder's personality stemmed partly from the fact that he was Jewish, as will be discussed in the next chapter dealing with the intricacies of their working and personal relationship.

Despite the downsides of being an immigrant, the struggles Wilder faced in trying to make smoothly practical use of his complex cultural identity during his years of apprenticeship as a screenwriter eventually paid off. He went on to become, after Lubitsch, Hollywood's foremost interpreter of the interplay between European and American culture. That was the great theme of Henry James's work, and thanks in part to James's magisterial influence, as well as to the changing role of the United States on the world stage in the twentieth century, it was a theme that became central to American attempts to define the country's identity.

Like James, Wilder was ambivalent about American culture. But he was more positive and enthusiastic about some of its aspects, and, unlike James, who after long travels abroad spent his later years living in Europe, Wilder had no desire to go back to settle there after fleeing fascism, although with his later films he was increasingly drawn there to work. In their critical study of Wilder, Neil Sinyard and Adrian Turner write that he

> can be regarded as a sort of Henry James in reverse. Even allowing for the
> considerable difference between their respective artistic temperaments and

cultural eras, both are equally fascinated with innocence and experience and, as a corollary of that, with America and Europe. James is the American who settles in Europe and whose work returns again and again to the theme of the impact of Europe on the American sensibility. Wilder often explores the same theme but from his particular vantage point as the European who has settled in America.

The critical yet still affectionate attitude Wilder displayed toward his adopted land led him to show, increasingly as time went on, brash or naive Americans abroad being exposed to Europe's more salutary cosmopolitan aspects, making most of them more sophisticated and better people. Stephen Farber, in a 1971–1972 essay on Wilder, similarly points to the importance of that recurring cultural encounter in his films but identifies it as a function of "the more general drama that obsesses him—the confrontation of innocence and experience. . . . Wilder does not believe that innocence can survive unscathed." As Farber puts it, Wilder's films are given their immense vitality by their fascination with that confrontation and by his "ambivalence toward innocence," a tendency that leads him to deal knowingly and empathetically with people on both ends of the experiential spectrum. Wilder was in the great tradition of James, Mark Twain, Ernest Hemingway, and other writers who acutely examine and satirize the clash between ingenuous Americans and what those characters consider cynical European culture. Their eye-opening experiences with more worldly foreign values make them wiser, if often sadder, people, a situation that recurs throughout Wilder's body of work. He provided a bridge between the blinkered American culture he satirizes for its culpable innocence of the greater world (as Graham Greene observes in his 1955 novel *The Quiet American*, "Innocence is a form of insanity") and the more broad-minded and aware but often decadent European culture.

Wilder's early years in America, while Europe was undergoing a time of crisis, helped crystallize his thoughts about life in his former homeland(s) and contrast it with the life he was now leading. As novelist Anthony Burgess wrote of another writer whose life and work were shaped by the experience of exile, James Joyce, "Exile was the artist's stepping back to see more clearly and so draw more accurately; it was the only means of objectifying an obsessive subject-matter." By the end of the 1930s, when Wilder had become acclimated to American life and learned to master the treacherous art of surviving and prospering in the Hollywood system, he became more at ease satirizing the cultures of both his old and new countries. The cosmopolitan nature of the films Wilder directed from 1942 until 1981 would enable him to satirize the mores and flaws of his new country with a special acuteness while contrasting them knowingly with the culture of prewar and postwar Europe. Although his home remained in Los Angeles, he became a truly international filmmaker, a representative of Hollywood's worldwide appeal at its best.

JOURNEYMAN

Glimmers of Wilder's personality and style can be discerned, however fleetingly, in the deeply flawed movies he toiled on before his providential teaming with Brackett in 1936. Before we move on to study in detail the best pre-1942 Brackett and Wilder screenplays—the ones written before Wilder launched his Hollywood directing career—it's instructive to focus on some aspects of his earlier journeyman work and what it shows of his struggle to release and develop his latent talent.

Wilder often didn't even know all the Hollywood writers who shared credit with him before he teamed with Brackett; scripts could pass through numerous hands before reaching the screen. That was not uncommon in the studio system, which shuffled writers around like pawns and allocated credit whimsically before the Screen Writers Guild was recognized in 1938, winning the right to determine credits. It's impossible to know exactly what Wilder contributed to some of the early Hollywood films that bear his name among the writing credits. Even now that's often the case with screenwriters, but the biographical evidence indicates that Wilder was largely unhappy with how his work was handled in those days and how, as a hired hand in the factory conveyor belt, he was often rewritten and had to share credit with others. Sometimes he was given only a story credit after working on screenplay drafts, and other times he worked on films with no credit at all, a few of which can be identified. The subject matter of some of those films seems alien to

Wilder's sensibilities, and others resemble weak rehashes of his better work (or Lubitsch's).

So it would be futile and foolish to analyze those 1934–1936 films in too much detail and with too much assurance in attributing certain elements to Wilder. Hollywood was not clamoring for the fresh viewpoint of this brash young refugee, but some parts of these uneven, mostly impersonal hodge-podges do stand out as harbingers of his future, more successful work, conveying unmistakable suggestions of his influence. He would revisit and improve on some of their situations and other elements in his later work as a writer-director who was able to exert much more control over his destiny.

The first film assignment Wilder received from May that reached the screen was 1934's *Music in the Air*. That Pommer production set in Bavaria brought Billie a co–screenplay credit with Howard I. Young. Based on a popular but inferior Oscar Hammerstein II–Jerome Kern stage musical, *Music in the Air* is a cloyingly vapid and sluggish musical comedy about Gloria Swanson's theatrical diva swanning her way through a Munich operetta production while trying to appropriate a callow young songwriter and schoolteacher from the countryside, Karl Roder (Douglass Montgomery).

What's most intriguing about *Music in the Air* from the overall perspective of Wilder's career is the casting of Swanson, the former silent movie queen, as Frieda Hotzfelt, the vain, delusional prima donna. After following it with only two films in the 1940s, Swanson would make her spectacular return to the screen in a not entirely dissimilar but much darker role as the faded, mad silent movie diva Norma Desmond in 1950's *Sunset Blvd*. Nevertheless, she claimed to have forgotten the earlier film on which she and Wilder (however remotely) collaborated. Despite the overall tedium of *Music in the Air*, there are some adumbrations of the later Wilder masterpiece in the way Swanson pursues Karl; he's not jaded like Joe Gillis, but at one point Frieda makes a similar grasping hand gesture in the air toward the young songwriter, which Wilder may have recalled when he made *Sunset Blvd*. That theme of mismatched generational sexual exploitation in *Music in the Air* is echoed in the pursuit of Karl's ingenuous girlfriend (blank-faced June Lang) by Swanson's suave, blasé lover and lyricist (John Boles). And as in many Wilder works, there is self-conscious playacting involved when the older couple construct a fictional story to ensnare the younger pair.

But though occasional flashes of sassy charisma from Swanson perk up some scenes, Wilder must have noted the flaws in her amusing but overly busy, campy performance. It could have shown him how to modulate her flamboyant personality more carefully for the demands of her role as the aging silent movie star adrift in her lonely mansion. "Oh, dear! Everybody deserts me," moans the self-pitying Frieda, pointing forward to Norma's far more meaningful, hushed delivery of "Nobody leaves a star." Unlike Swanson's earlier comical outburst, that later line is chilling and a prelude to a suicide attempt and murder.

The stage version of *Music in the Air* opened in November 1932 and ran through September 1933; the fact that its premiere predated Hitler's takeover of Germany helps account for why the show manages to avoid dealing with Nazism. But the film version, released while Hitler was Führer and persecuting the Jews, seems odd and irresponsible in ignoring recent events while portraying Bavaria as a jolly, care-free fantasyland with clichéd peasants in traditional costumes doing corny musical numbers. The one enduring song that came from this farrago is the charming "I've Told Ev'ry Little Star," which many singers have recorded over the years; it provides an ironically intercut double duet between the younger and older couples at the end of the film. Wilder probably had nothing to do with the decision to evade the issue of the drastic changes in Germany when the show was adapted to the screen after Hitler's takeover, but it must have galled him to see the result. When the play was revived on Broadway in 1951, Hammerstein changed its setting to Switzerland, which had been neutral during World War II. In any event, *Music in the Air* is second-rate Hammerstein and Kern, and its screen incarnation seems plodding, tiresomely predictable, and lifeless as well as hopelessly antiquated. The only amazing thing about this film is the depth of talent it took to bring forth such a feeble trifle, a glaring example of the negative aspects of the 1930s American entertainment assembly line. Brackett aptly called the film an "abortion."

Billie Wilder received a screenplay credit in 1935 on another mediocre Fox musical, *Lottery Lover*, whose even more inane working titles were *Love Can Be Fun* and *Weak in Paris*. The production history of *Lottery Lover* was the kind of "mad goulash" (to use a later Wilder phrase) with screenwriting musical chairs not atypical then—or more recently: as screenwriter Joe Eszterhas

has observed, "One man wrote *War and Peace*. Thirty-five screenwriters wrote *The Flintstones*"—and such a mishmash helps account for how weak the young Wilder's output in Hollywood generally was.

Franz Schulz, his collaborator in Germany on *What Women Dream*, shared screenplay credit on *Lottery Lover*. They were among a dozen writers who toiled on the threadbare project. Another was Lubitsch's former longtime writer, Hans Kräly, who had a falling-out with the director when he learned that the writer was having an affair with his wife. A Viennese writer-director, Hanns Schwarz (now calling himself Howard Shelton), collaborated with Wilder and Schulz on their version of *Lottery Lover*, which was translated by Jerome Lachenbruck. Neither Schwarz nor Lachenbruck received a screen credit, however; and Sam Hellman was awarded the dialogue credit. There were further German connections: Paul Martin and then Schwarz were scheduled to direct the film with Lilian Harvey starring, but those plans fell through when the actress who had played Wilder's Jou-Jou in *A Blonde Dream* walked out on another Fox film, and Schwarz became ill. Eventually, German refugee William (formerly Wilhelm) Thiele, who had directed Harvey in *Three from the Filling Station*, became the director of *Lottery Lover*, with British actress Pat Paterson replacing Harvey as the ingénue.

Set in contemporary Paris, *Lottery Lover* deals with a group of young U.S. Navy bluejackets looking for action. They pool their resources, with the help of a freelance tour guide, into finagling a date for the bashful winner of their lottery, Frank Harrington (the engaging Lew Ayres), with the star of the Folies Parisiennes, the flighty Gaby Aimee (Peggy Fears), so they can all vicariously enjoy the thrill of his conquest. The romantic complication is that Frank is falling in love with another woman of Paris, Paterson's Patty, a more down-to-earth and sincere young Canadian actress he hires to rehearse his seduction of Gaby. With its mocking blend of military regimentation and musical numbers, the film borrowed elements from Lubitsch, who once said, "I've been to Paris, France, and I've been to Paris, Paramount. I think I prefer Paris, Paramount." But it imitates Lubitsch in a dull, watered-down way, even with a few intriguing aspects of voyeurism, quasi-prostitution, and pimpery thrown into the mix.

Those disturbing elements are all that make the picture eventually come fitfully alive, since the way they conflict with the romance between the young leads and the way their playacting turns genuine rouses Wilder's creative interest more than the stupefyingly foolish formulaic aspects of the story. Occasional Wilderian flourishes aside, many a Hollywood hack could have applied the same stale coating of schmaltz to these warmed-over rehashes of European operettas and comedies to which he was assigned in his years of struggle. He also did uncredited work on some other, even less memorable films in that period.

The most wildly incongruous was a Raoul Walsh programmer called *Under Pressure* (1935), with a moronic plot about "sand hogs," men who build underwater tunnels below New York's East River. The film is mostly shot in dark, dank studio sets of tunnels filled with sweaty, semi-naked men doing their harrowing jobs. One of Walsh's lesser efforts, written mostly by Borden Chase, its claustrophobia and emphasis on male agony offers an odd form of entertainment unless it could serve as sadomasochistic beefcake softcore porn. The reliable he-man team of Victor McLaglen (as "Jumbo") and Edmund Lowe (as "Shocker"), who act like cavemen, make the film only marginally watchable (they had earlier starred for Walsh in his 1926 silent hit *What Price Glory* and two early-sound sequels, *The Cock-Eyed World* and *Women of All Nations*, as well as another directed by John Blystone, *Hot Pepper*). But it's mind-boggling that Wilder was saddled with such abysmally derivative material as *Under Pressure*. "OK, kid, let me tell you the story," Walsh told Wilder. "There are two cocksuckers and they are crazy about the same old cunt." Biographer Hellmuth Karasek commented, "Wilder took five minutes before he caught on to some extent what that meant. It was a rough awakening in Hollywood polished vernacular."

Another 1935 film on which Wilder worked without credit was Fox's *Thunder in the Night*, a fairly ludicrous crime thriller based on a play by Ladislas Fodor. Set in Budapest with awkwardly integrated elements of political intrigue and a witless screenplay credited to Frances Hyland and Eugene Solow, it never rises above its B-movie ambience (melodramatic moments actually keep getting punctuated by thunder) but at least has intermittent noirish visual interest (the ace Bert Glennon was the cinematographer) and a competent performance by Lowe as a suave detective.

Even though America had saved Wilder's life, as his work was continually trashed by the studios he could not help realizing that his dream of going to Hollywood was becoming something of a nightmare, like Jou-Jou's vision in *A Blonde Dream* of being stripped by leering technicians on a sound stage who transform her personality grotesquely, making it impossible to sing and dance.

Wilder must have felt the way Brecht did in his trenchant poem comparing the career of a Hollywood screenwriter to the life of a prostitute:

> Every day, to earn my daily bread
> I go to the market where lies are bought.
> Hopefully
> I take up my place among the sellers.

"HOLD THAT TIGER"

The first glimmer of promise of a better career for Wilder in Hollywood did not appear that way to him when it reached the screen. But *Champagne Waltz* (1937), an intermittently brash and breezy musical comedy he helped write before teaming with Brackett, bears Wilder's characteristic stamp more clearly than any of his previous work in the United States. This Paramount film set in Vienna and New York followed the lead of *Music in the Air* by not making any references to Nazism; the *Anschluss* was only a year away at the time of the film's release and already seemed inevitable. *Champagne Waltz* has second-rate musical numbers and looks shabby next to Lubitsch's films and the Astaire-Rogers series from RKO. Yet it has a little more substance than Wilder's earlier American screenwriting efforts. Most important, it marks the first appearance in Hollywood of a recognizable Wilder character type, the wisecracking, hard-edged, but ultimately good-hearted American bandleader Buzzy Belew.

Buzzy is played by Fred MacMurray, who made his name as that kind of amiable wise guy. MacMurray began as a saxophone and clarinet player and vocalist with the Gus Arnheim Orchestra and went on to a long and varied acting career, winding up as an amiable paternal figure in Disney movies and on the TV sitcom *My Three Sons*. But he would be most memorably cast against type in two classics Wilder directed, as the insurance salesman who turns to murder in the film noir *Double Indemnity* (1944) and a sleazy, hypocritical insurance company executive in 1960's *The Apartment*. Wilder gets only a story credit, however, on *Champagne Waltz*, with H. S. (Hy) Kraft. Their script, *Moon Over Vienna*, was rewritten by Frank Butler and Don Hartman, who were awarded the screenplay credits.* *Champagne Waltz* is directed in uninspired fashion by the veteran A. Edward (Eddie) Sutherland. When Brackett saw the film before it opened, he wrote in his diary, "This is the picture on which Billy worked with high hopes. Seeing it shattered him."

It's clear in retrospect, however, that the principal credit for bringing Buzzy to the screen belongs to Wilder. His nascent "touch" was beginning to take hold, however tenuously, and recognized only in the Paramount story department headed by Manny Wolfe, who had his sharp eyes tuned to Wilder's talent and potential. Before the film's release, Wolfe gave Wilder his big break by assigning him to work with Brackett and Lubitsch on *Bluebeard's Eighth Wife*. The brash American character who clashes with European culture in that screwball comedy, millionaire businessman Michael Brandon (Gary Cooper), is akin to Buzzy Belew, although Buzzy is far more likable.

Champagne Waltz is weighed down by tedious interludes featuring the colorless opera singer Gladys Swarthout. The studio was trying unsuccessfully to build her into a rival to operatic soprano-turned-movie-star Grace Moore, whose star was already fading. Swarthout's Elsa Strauss and her father (Fritz Leiber) run the Viennese Waltz Palace, struggling to maintain the viability of the stately family cultural tradition of Strauss waltzes and songs in the face of competition next door from a raucous American jazz band. Elsa's father considers Buzzy's music "noise," and she scorns the American bandleader as "riffraff." But Wilder sees vitality in both forms of music. This clash of semiclassical and modern pop styles, and the question of their relative commercial staying power, serves as shorthand for the conflict between old-fashioned, rather staid European values and the more lively and buoyant American popular culture.

That is a fertile theme to which Wilder often returned with increasing incisiveness as his career developed. The lovely flashback in *Champagne Waltz* to the performance by Johann Strauss II of "On the Beautiful Blue Danube" at the royal court in the presence of Emperor Franz Josef I would be echoed in

---

* Kraft, best known as a playwright, was later blacklisted, like other writers who shared credit with Wilder in this period, Hollywood Ten members Lester Cole and Samuel Ornitz. Butler and Hartman became one of Paramount's most successful teams on Bing Crosby–Bob Hope "Road" comedies. Butler won an Oscar with Frank Cavett for the screenplay of Crosby's best-picture Oscar winner *Going My Way* (1944), directed by Leo McCarey, and Hartman was a songwriter as well.

Wilder's musical *The Emperor Waltz*. Even more evocatively, the sentiment would be epitomized in his tribute to the sweeping, graceful crane shots of classical Hollywood filmmaking with the *Last Waltz* sequence in *Fedora* (1978), which evokes the finest dance numbers of Lubitsch and Ophüls.

Buzzy's invasion of Vienna has particular resonance when you know that Wilder was a jazz fanatic in his youth and attached himself in Vienna and Berlin as a press agent to the "King of Jazz" who incarnated the brassy culture Wilder aspired to join. Wilder's call in his June 1926 Vienna newspaper review for the "necessary blood renewal of the fossilized Europe" by American jazz encapsulates the thematic concerns of *Champagne Waltz*, which two decades later are echoed in the musical elements of *Some Like It Hot*. Jack Oakie is reliably funny in *Champagne Waltz*, evoking the portly Whiteman as well as Wilder himself in the role of a brassy press agent for Buzzy's band. At one point the down-and-out Buzzy even tells Elsa he has changed his name to Paul Whiteman because it "looked better in lights." Before coming to America, the impoverished Wilder, struggling to succeed as a reporter in Berlin, had told his mother he had changed his name to Thornton Wilder and sent her clippings about the great success he was having as a novelist with *The Bridge of San Luis Rey*.

After Buzzy's success sinks the Strauss family enterprise, a sad situation redolent with cultural symbolism, he has a crisis of conscience and gives up his band, going on the skids until a happy ending is contrived with Elsa coming to New York and opening a nightclub with him. They blend their musical styles in a wildly improbable bicultural enterprise. Their Waltz Jazz Palace features what *New York Times* reviewer Frank S. Nugent aptly called a "monster, and rather monstrous" finale of "On the Beautiful Blue Danube" performed side-by-side with Buzzy's band brassing out its signature tune, "Hold That Tiger." Buzzy's budding romance with Elsa is grounded partly in his teaching her to chew gum American-style, an evocative touch that reflects Wilder's personality and inveterate gum-chewing habit, as well as the famous romantic gum-chewing scene between American soldier John Gilbert and a French girl (Renée Adorée) in King Vidor's classic World War I film, *The Big Parade* (1925). Elsa also repeats Buzzy's catch-phrase "E Pluribus Unum," which he invokes to explain the United States, one of numerous heartfelt tributes over the years in Wilder's films to his adopted land.

Buzzy carries enough emotional complexity to make the character's misbehavior a thoughtful commentary on the value and ethics of American cultural appropriation. The clashes and unlikely blending of the two cultures as a result of their eventual romance prefigure, however awkwardly, Wilder's role in his mature work as a sophisticated commentator on and satirist of bicultural influences in American life.

Nugent, who would go on to a stellar career as John Ford's favorite screenwriter, seemed to intuit that the problems with *Champagne Waltz* stemmed from a failure on the studio's part to trust the work of (the still largely unknown) Wilder:

> Paramount is reported to have been so pleased with the first draft of "Champagne Waltz" that it returned the film to the studios for $40,000 worth of embellishments, calculated to make it even more entrancing. It was a generous impulse, but a misguided one; something in the nature of fastening heavy golden buckles to a ballet dancer's slippers. In its final, redecorated state at the Paramount the picture displays a distressing habit of tripping over its own feet. Intermittently it is gay and lighthearted and graceful but it does not sustain the mood too well.

Noting in his diary that Wilder was "depressed" by *Champagne Waltz* and its reception, Brackett wrote, "It didn't help that the reviews echoed his opinion exactly. He had hoped for better things."

5.1 (top) Wilder's mentor Ernst Lubitsch directing Greta Garbo as the Soviet commissar who finds romance in Paris in the witty political satire *Ninotchka* (1939), from an Oscar-nominated screenplay by Brackett and Wilder and Walter Reisch. (MGM / From the Collections of the Margaret Herrick Library, Academy of Motion Picture Arts and Sciences.)

5.2 (bottom) Gloria Swanson in her haunted mansion as faded silent screen star Norma Desmond in the final Brackett-Wilder film, *Sunset Blvd.* (1950), with her gigolo Joe Gillis (William Holden), the patron saint of Hollywood hack screenwriters. (Paramount / Photofest.)

5

BRACKETTANDWILDER
. . . AND LUBITSCH

NINOTCHKA (Greta Garbo): Why should you carry other
    people's bags?
RAILWAY PORTER (George Davis): Well, that's my business,
    Madame.
NINOTCHKA: That's no business. That's social injustice.
PORTER: That depends on the tip.

—*Ninotchka* (1939)

"CHARLIE BRACKETT, meet Billy Wilder. From now on you're a team."
With those words in August 1936, Paramount's canny story editor, Manny
Wolfe, set in motion a quantum jump in Wilder's career. So wedded in Hollywood's consciousness that they sometimes were referred to as "Brackettandwilder," the team in their fourteen years together would go on to write sixteen
screenplays (not counting others to which they contributed without credit as
studio contract writers). Their collaboration encompassed the first eight films
of Wilder's Hollywood directing career, with Brackett also serving as a producer. Although Wilder disingenuously told a *Life* magazine writer in 1944
that they were "The Happiest Couple in Hollywood," the Brackettandwilder
"marriage" was often acrimonious behind the scenes. They were a classic
example of collaborators whose starkly different backgrounds and conflicting
personality traits complemented each other creatively.

Wilder's career gained immeasurably from his involvement with the older (by thirteen years), more socially distinguished American blue blood Brackett. Their teaming came at a time when the émigré writer was foundering and needed not only a leg up in the industry but also, just as important, a collaborator to help refine his developing craft in a new language. It was only when Wilder was fortuitously teamed with Brackett that he was able to escape the straitjacket of his first decades in two countries with very different political systems but depressingly similar film industries. The formative Brackett phase of Wilder's career established him as one of Hollywood's leading filmmakers, although that body of work would be matched later, and arguably surpassed, by his long collaboration with I. A. L. Diamond, with whom he was more compatible. The Writers Guild of America recognized the achievements of both of Wilder's major collaborators by giving them the guild's most prestigious award with him, the Laurel Award for Screenwriting Achievement. Wilder won with Brackett in 1957 and with Diamond in 1980, making him the only writer who has won that prize twice.

The scion of an old-guard wealthy political and banking family from Saratoga Springs, New York, Brackett attended Williams College and earned a law degree from Harvard, like his father, who served in the New York legislature. Brackett's World War I service in the Allied Expeditionary Force earned him the French Medal of Honor. But his wayward creative passions led him to start selling short stories to the popular weekly magazine the *Saturday Evening Post* while still in law school. "Charlie" established his cultural pedigree by landing the job of drama critic of the *New Yorker* in 1925, a position he held until 1929, when he was replaced by Robert Benchley.* Some of Brackett's stories were sold to Hollywood, but the novels he began writing at Harvard and continued turning out until 1934 never caught on as literature. Nor were they made into films, and his screenwriting credits before Wilder were not memorable. Brackett was known in Hollywood for his urbane craftsmanship, genteel demeanor, collegial diplomatic skills, and WASPish emotional reserve. His personality starkly contrasted with that of Wilder, the European Jew from modest origins who restlessly survived several successive exiles to rise to the top in Hollywood through sheer talent and

---

* Benchley is the humorist who filmed a series of popular comic short subjects and memorably plays a married lecher in *The Major and the Minor.*

survival skill. Wilder is generally considered the temperamental member of the team, with the acidic tongue and a harshly unsparing outsider's sense of social satire, stemming from his often bitter life experience and the jaundiced perspective of continual exile.

But the Hollywood studio publicity machine was often obfuscatory, and film histories can be uninformative or deceptive. As Maurice Zolotow notes in his Wilder biography, the celebratory *Life* magazine profile of the team and other glowing publicity accounts were "grossly inaccurate."

> But, like so many unhappily married people, they looked good in public, and so everybody thought it was a euphoric relationship, when it was as rent by fits of temperament and jealousy and spleen as the collaboration of Gilbert and Sullivan. And like the two Englishmen, Brackett and Wilder would have long periods during which they ceased talking to each other and communicated through their secretary. It was rather complicated to proceed with a literary collaboration during these Trappist-like phases, but somehow they managed.

Wilder, for his part, valued Brackett's polished writing skills, his experience in navigating the Hollywood system, and his status in the industry as senior partner. Brackett's somewhat grudging recognition of Wilder's revitalizing infusion of creative energy, imagination, and daring is evidenced by how he continued to work with Wilder for so long despite many complaints in his diary that he wanted to break free of their relationship.

Just as crucial as Wilder's teaming with Brackett on August 17, 1936, was the immigrant screenwriter's first opportunity to work with Ernst Lubitsch, whose work he had admired and tried to imitate while working for UFA in Berlin. Unlike Brackett and Wilder, Lubitsch and Wilder shared many cultural and temperamental characteristics as European Jews who had lived through the collapse of empires in the Great War, as well as the riotous but audaciously modernistic Weimar Republic era in Berlin. They were not blue bloods like Brackett but outsiders by birth, with irreverent, bawdy senses of humor.

The collaboration of Wilder and Brackett with Lubitsch on *Bluebeard's Eighth Wife* (a 1938 release) also rescued and revitalized Brackett's lagging Hollywood career by making him part of a dynamic new team who worked with top directors. Lubitsch made the decision to hire them within about half an hour after Wolfe brought them to the director's office for a getting-acquainted story session. Wilder impressed Lubitsch (whom he already knew slightly) with what became a classic example of the "meet-cute," Hollywood parlance for a clever way to bring a couple together onscreen. Wilder won himself and Brackett the assignment by proposing the celebrated opening with Gary Cooper's American millionaire, Michael Brandon, trying to buy only a pair of pajama tops in a clothing shop in Nice and causing consternation among the shop clerks until Claudette Colbert's Nicole De Loiselle appears and offers to buy the pajama bottoms for a man she knows. Ironically, despite this sparkling opening and the creative potential of this new trio, the film that brought Lubitsch and Wilder together was something of a fiasco.

Lubitsch's final film for Paramount, where his box-office fortunes and dominance in the field were ebbing, *Bluebeard* proved a clumsy, sour, often grating venture into the trendy new realm of screwball comedy. Brandon cavalierly marries women and discards them, but while he is visiting the Riviera, his latest "romantic" target (Colbert) sees through him, turns the tables, and tries to bilk him of his money. Screwball comedy was a genre that was popular then and remains so today largely because it deals with sexual antagonism, with the battle between the sexes sometimes literally erupting into violence, as it does in *Bluebeard*. This alleged comedy abounds in scenes of shoving and slapping and slugging, mostly with the misogynistic male partner wreaking violence on the woman, although she retaliates and eventually manages to get him committed to a mental asylum and put into a straitjacket.

Lubitsch had anticipated that raucous vein of humor, though more genially, in his German farce about an American tycoon and his sex-starved daughter in Berlin, *The Oyster Princess* (1919), and his bawdy sex farce *Kohlhiesel's Daughters* (1920), a loose takeoff on Shakespeare's *The Taming of the Shrew* set in the Bavarian mountains. But *Bluebeard's Eighth Wife* is a coarse and caustic example of post-Code Hollywood comedies revolving less around romance than intemperate sexual conflict. Wilder's brash sensibility, breaking out of the starting gate with unbridled energy stored up from years of frustration, seems dominant, but not in the salutary way he would handle risqué romantic material on the films he later wrote and directed with Diamond, such as *Some Like It Hot*, *Kiss Me, Stupid*, and *Avanti!*

Having worked with Lubitsch once did not exempt Brackett and Wilder from thankless assignments on run-of-the-mill Paramount pictures, such as *Blossoms on Broadway* (1937), an idiotic semi-musical (yet another in that format on which Wilder toiled in his apprenticeship years) about Nevada yokels in New York fleeced by a conman (Edward Arnold) and an aspiring showgirl masquerading as a gold heiress (Shirley Ross). After their work was rewritten, the team took their names off the project, which Brackett aptly described as "terrible." Another inane picture they worked on without credit was *The Big Broadcast of 1938* (1938), the last and most successful of a series of four Paramount musical revues, vaudevillian grab-bags with flimsy and silly plotlines strung around radio shows. This one is distinguished only by Bob Hope (in his feature film debut) and Ross singing "Thanks for the Memory," the Oscar-winning song that became his trademark. But W. C. Fields is tiresome in protracted routines, and director Mitchell Leisen, whose secretary blamed Fields for causing his first heart attack, regarded the film as "embarrassing."

Even a Paramount project with a supposedly higher pedigree, *French Without Tears* (made in 1939, released in 1940)—from a play by the young Terence Rattigan, directed by his longtime collaborator Anthony Asquith in England but set in prewar France—is a vapid time-waster about a flirtatious, emptyheaded American girl (Ellen Drew) frolicking through a men's school for cramming in the French language. The uncredited Brackett and Wilder at least acquired some facility writing dialogue for the Welshman Ray Milland, which would serve them better on *The Lost Weekend* than with his tiresomely blasé performance here as one of the British students. Brackett's diaries refer to other ephemeral projects for which they fortunately escaped blame. At least the time they spent in this Hollywood writers' purgatory helped inform their empathetic portrait of Joe Gillis, the patron saint of hack screenwriters.

It was not long, though, before Brackett and Wilder's awkward experience with Lubitsch on *Bluebeard* led to a far more polished and seamless collaboration by the three men (along with Walter Reisch) on one of the masterworks of the cinema, *Ninotchka*. That 1939 Garbo film was recognized as a classic from its initial release, and Wilder's first Oscar nomination was a remarkable achievement after only five years in Hollywood. Combining romantic comedy with political satire at a time when the international situation made personal relationships especially precarious, *Ninotchka* was filmed on the brink of world war and released shortly after the German invasion of Poland. A masterful blend of Lubitsch's characteristic adroitness in cross-cultural social satire and graceful finesse in subtly exploring the intricate nuances of male-female relationships, the film deals with a stern Soviet commissar on a mission to Paris who finds love in the unlikely person of a seemingly worthless gigolo (Melvyn Douglas), the kept man of a haughty White Russian countess in exile (Ina Claire).

One of the few Hollywood films dealing with the clash of communism versus capitalism that transcends ideological caricaturing, *Ninotchka* is a consummately sophisticated romantic detente between opposite but ultimately complementary characters. In that respect it is not unlike the creative partnership that flourished for a time between the left-liberal Wilder and the conservative Republican Brackett.

During the postwar Red Scare in October 1947, Brackett wrote in his diary that he told Wilder he thought the House Committee on Un-American Activities (HUAC) had a right to ask screenwriter Dalton Trumbo whether he was a Communist, "whereupon Billy had a complete tantrum, saying that if that was so, this wasn't the country he'd been lead [*sic*] to believe it was, and he'd prefer to go back home." Six days later, Brackett reported, "Billy informed me that he wasn't a communist but he gave considerably to the left, which makes him a Fellow Traveler I should think." This was not a completely fresh thought for Brackett, who wrote in a May 1944 diary entry that he was "somewhat infuriated by the political discourse and activities of Billy, the worst citizen I know—typical of all immigrants, who immediately want to improve and oversee the running of the country." In a lighter moment that year, when Wilder complained that Brackett made him play cribbage instead of gin rummy during their work breaks, the director quipped, "Oh, well, what do you expect from a man who voted for Dewey?" Despite all the aggravation, Wilder probably recognized for a while that having a conservative partner served as protective coloration for a liberal opponent of HUAC. But it is clear from Brackett's diary that their increasingly bitter arguments over political issues were what finally made Wilder realize the need to work with more simpatico writing partners.

The political arguments in *Ninotchka*, however, are balanced (arbitrated?) by Lubitsch in a humane, amusing, and generous way. The film makes the romantic couple's mutual liberation from their constricting social roles entirely convincing. Recognizing the extent of Lubitsch's creative influence on *Ninotchka*, the three screenwriters, in an unusual move, petitioned the Screen Writers Guild to let the director share writing credit, which the fledgling guild, highly sensitive to credit issues, denied. Wilder later said of Lubitsch, "If the truth were known, he was the best writer that ever lived." Lubitsch wrote in a summary of his career shortly before his death in 1947, "As to satire, I believe I probably was never sharper than in *Ninotchka*, and I feel that I succeeded in the very difficult task of blending a political satire with a romantic story." That he was able to do so owes much to Wilder's political savvy as a former reporter in Vienna and Berlin and his jaded, yet ultimately romantic, take on sexual politics and the theme of love versus prostitution.

Wilder's momentous teaming with Brackett and Lubitsch in 1936 vaulted him from hack status to a position as one of Hollywood's finest screenwriters. One of the five turning points of the young writer's life, it ranks with the Reichstag fire that caused him to flee Germany; being reduced to sleeping in the ladies' room (as he claimed) at the Chateau Marmont, "the low point of my life"; the generous help of the consular official who gave him refuge in the United States; and the excision of a scene involving a cockroach in his and Brackett's 1941 screenplay *Hold Back the Dawn*. Wilder benefited from remarkably good fortune in getting his foothold in the United States and Hollywood when he most needed it, although he had been paying his dues for a long time to get to that point and was ready when it came. As the baseball guru Branch Rickey put it, "Luck is the residue of design."

But as life would have it, those formative years of Wilder's work with Brackett and Lubitsch on two wildly divergent films, in the midst of other work, came at a time of terrible anxiety for the younger writer. He was wrestling with his anguish and guilt over being unable to persuade his mother to leave Vienna and his helplessness in anticipating and following the outbreak of war from his distant safe outpost in Hollywood. His frequent mood swings—recorded unsympathetically by Brackett in his diary—included what his collaborator observed as a nervous breakdown and one nearly suicidal period. Those lows were balanced with the euphoria of relatively unfettered creativity, Wilder's marriage on December 22, 1936, and his naturalization as an American citizen in Los Angeles on August 9, 1940.

Wilder wed Judith Coppicus Balken,* an elegant twenty-five-year-old woman, a painter who had lived in France. They were introduced by Jacques

---

* Judith's last name is given in other Wilder books as Iribe. Her mother had remarried Hollywood art director and costume designer Paul Iribe, a Frenchman whose most prominent work was with Cecil B. DeMille on *The Ten Commandments* (1923) and other films, as well as directing three silent films himself. He died in 1935.

Théry, a French émigré who was a sometime writing collaborator with Wilder. Like Brackett, Judith had Hollywood connections and came from a higher social class. An uncle had been prominent in California politics, and her father, German immigrant Francis Charles Coppicus, was a theatrical impresario who had managed Enrico Caruso, Feodor Chaliapin, and Nijinsky (and, like Wilder, had promoted Paul Whiteman in the 1920s). Before Judith married Wilder, she had been the wife of a Dallas oil and gas man, (James) Bailey Balken. The Wilders had twins on December 21, 1940, but their boy, Vincent, died on the following March 31, leaving Victoria as Wilder's only child. Judith also had a young daughter who lived with them, Lois Balken. The couple divorced in 1945; Judith later married another Austrian immigrant, Adolf Badner, and died in 2002.

The highs and lows of Wilder's family life may help account for the uneven quality of his writing in the late 1930s and early 1940s. They provide a partial explanation for the emotional and even physical violence onscreen that sometimes conflicted with his romantic impulses, but also for the deep feeling and acute social commentary in some of these films.

In studying the beginnings of the Brackett and Wilder partnership, it's also vital to factor in the lasting influence of Wilder's creative and personal relationship with Lubitsch, the master he had previously tried to emulate from afar in his German works. Lubitsch was reluctant to hire Germans in Hollywood because he did want to seem exclusively a "foreign" director—the most cosmopolitan of directors, he had become Hollywood's foremost mediator between Europe and American culture—but he was aware of Wilder's work in Germany, according to Brackett. That seems to have been a factor in bringing them together creatively, and since Lubitsch was head of production at Paramount in 1935–1936, he was aware of the special talents on the writing staff.

Together he and Brackett played indispensable roles in helping Billie Wilder, the homeless exile yearning to break into the Hollywood system, become Billy Wilder. Through those two collaborators, Wilder learned to smoothly combine an outsider's perspective with an insider's savvy toward the system of production and censorship. He developed even more sharply honed survival skills than he had displayed in Europe and a masterful ability to play by the rules of the Hollywood game while still managing to turn out personal films.

"THAT ABRASIVE PAPER"

Collaborations are always somewhat mysterious, especially in the film world, in which the written record of what actually goes on between people is often scant, and memories are notoriously malleable. Often even the participants can't truly answer questions of who was responsible for what in that back-and-forth process in which one person's idea builds on, modifies, or responds to the other's; the genuine answer to who is responsible is usually "both." So for the author of a critical study of Wilder to attempt to isolate the contributions of Brackett or Diamond or his other important collaborators in too much detail is somewhat quixotic.

Films are works of joint authorship, although usually the most lasting ones are those in which one personality has the dominant vision. But no director can do it on his own, as Wilder freely acknowledged in discussing his writing collaborators with much greater generosity than is common in Hollywood. He worked so closely with Brackett and Diamond that not only the dialogue but also the general visual scheme of the films was established on paper in the office before he took the film on the floor. Here's a striking and characteristic example: Brackett and Wilder wrote a nonverbal scene in their Oscar-winning screenplay for *The Lost Weekend* (1945, based on the novel by Charles Jackson). Alcoholic writer Don Birnam (Milland) is prowling his apartment to hide a liquor bottle before taking a clandestine drink from another:

He crumples the bag and throws it in the fireplace. He takes one bottle, starts towards a bookcase and is about to hide it behind the books when he changes his mind. He looks around the room. His eyes fall on the ceiling. He goes to the table next the couch, pulls it into the middle of the room, brushes some magazines to the floor, takes a small chair, puts it on the table, climbs to the table, from the table to the chair. He is now directly below the ceiling lighting fixture, an inverted metal bowl about two and a half feet in diameter. Don reaches over the edge and deposits the bottle inside the bowl so it can't be seen from the room. He climbs down, readjusts the table, the chair, and puts the magazines back. Don picks up a glass which is over a carafe on the mantelpiece. He puts it next the bottle by the wing chair. He opens the bottle, pours a glass about three quarters full, puts the glass down. He loosens his tie and lets himself fall into the easy chair. He looks through the open window on the lights of New York. His eyes slowly wander to the glass. He smiles. It's a smile of relief, of contentment at being alone with his vice. There's a little pain in his smile, too.

Later, in a famous cinematic touch, Don will enter the apartment as his bender worsens, switch on the light, and with "a half-crazed smile" see the shadow of the bottle he hid revealed in the light fixture and open the bottle "fiercely." This is the kind of carefully prepared payoff Wilder's scripts often contain, and their brilliant dialogue often obscures the degree to which they tell their stories visually.

What, then, was the nature of the seemingly symbiotic collaborative relationship between Brackett and Wilder, who later declared that they "had nothing in common except writing"? How did these opposites attract in creatively combustive ways before their differences gradually drew them apart?

"The anomaly of their relationship is that two more antithetic personalities would be hard to find," Lincoln Barnett wrote in his *Life* profile of the team.

Brackett is a courtly, somewhat rumpled, affable gentleman of 52 who looks as though he might be vice president of a bank in Saratoga Springs, N.Y.— which he is [his father was the president]. Wilder is a loquacious, elegant, sardonic young man of 38 who moves with the lithe grace of a professional dancer—which he once was. . . . Brackett is a congenital Republican with liberal instincts, Wilder is a fervid New Dealer with leftish leanings. Brackett is an agoraphobe who jitters if the office door is left open. Wilder is a claustrophobe who can't stand closed doors. . . .

Wilder is galvanic, facile, prolific with ideas, endowed with visual imagination. Brackett is critical, contemplative, gifted with a graceful literary style and cultivated taste. When Wilder sparks off a salvo of suggestions, Brackett sorts good from bad and imparts to the best of them adroit turns of action and phrase. The exquisite, lambent dialog that is the hallmark of all their pictures is generally ascribed to Brackett although Wilder, despite his accent, has a keen ear for the American idiom and an acute sense of the flexibility of words. . . . Wilder is cynical, taut, acidulous, a realist. Brackett is urbane, gentle, fanciful. Wilder is an instinctive dramatist who envisages story ideas through the camera's mobile eye. "I'm a celluloid maniac," he says. Brackett is primarily a novelist, attuned to niceties of continuity and construction.

Brackett's blue-blooded background and uprooting to Hollywood in the 1930s gave him a solid grounding in the class issues that provide some of the most fruitful tensions in the films he made with Wilder. Wilder felt class differences keenly in both Germany and the United States and was able to analyze them acutely while mocking the vicious pretensions behind them, as Lubitsch does more gently. Although outwardly Brackett appeared to be a consummate insider, he also seemed never to be quite comfortable either back home in New York or in Hollywood. In his own way he was something of a covert outsider, a man of conflicted social impulses with which Wilder could relate on a deep level.

Brackett may have been gay or bisexual. Anthony Slide, who edited Brackett's diaries for publication in 2015, while fairly exhaustively examining the possible evidence about his sexual orientation, leaves it inconclusive. In any case, Brackett seemed to be living in a state of emotional ambivalence toward each of his dual lives—the decadent, if somewhat frayed around the edges, high society of the East Coast and the déclassé, undervalued, yet affluent existence of a Hollywood writer-producer—and when coupled with what may have been sexual ambivalence, those tensions were a valuable source of creative ferment for a writer, even if they seem to have contributed to his depressive personality. The troubled characters Brackett excelled in writing with no small help from his more volatile partner emanated partly from these complexities and from Brackett's own sensitivity to the illusions and hypocrisies of life as a perpetual masquerade. Wilder's profound lifelong obsession with the masquerade came from his restless sense of himself as an incessantly precarious and wary exile. Yet the root causes of both men's fascination with role-playing can be traced to a common need to erect defenses against fundamental insecurities.

Brackett helped give Wilder a vital leg up in Hollywood by being a more known and established quantity in the industry. Although he cultivated a reticent demeanor, he was a sociable man, widely acquainted with other writers on both coasts and respected by people of different political orientations. He served in 1938–1939 as president of the fledgling Screen Writers Guild. For both Wolfe and Lubitsch at Paramount, Brackett no doubt was seen as a reassuringly restraining force on Wilder's rowdy personality, an older and wiser man who could balance his wilder instincts. Brackett's graceful, if somewhat musty and overly ornate, command of English prose in his novels and screenplays was a guarantee that the scripts he turned out with Wilder would be finely polished. But Wilder's flamboyance and energy would make their work together far livelier than the screenplays Brackett cowrote without him.

Brackett's scripts with earlier partners were gabby and lethargic affairs, overly ornate and stagey in their mildly witty dialogue, feeble and unconvincing in their romantic aspects, and often tiresome in their craftsmanlike but predictable plot contrivances. They included two tepid Robert Montgomery vehicles written on loan to MGM, *Piccadilly Jim* (1936, from the 1917 novel by P. G. Wodehouse) and *Live, Love and Learn* (1937). In *Piccadilly Jim*, Montgomery plays a cartoonist who relentlessly stalks a wealthy woman and mocks her obnoxious family in a comic strip; in *Live, Love and Learn*, he is a penniless artist of no great talent who marries a rebellious rich woman (Rosalind Russell) but is corrupted by success. The grim turn of the latter film makes it somewhat more watchable as it explores a situation familiar to self-loathing Hollywood screenwriters—selling out their limited store of creativity for a life of luxury, a situation that foreshadows the downfall of Joe Gillis.

Brackett's pre-Wilder creative personality and his ambivalent attitudes toward class issues are delineated more revealingly in his novels. The first of the five, *The Counsel of the Ungodly* (1920), originally serialized in the *Saturday Evening Post*, is a mild social satire about a sixtyish aristocrat down on his luck who masquerades as a butler. He does so to help a young niece, stuck in a family of louts, escape a loveless marriage to a caddish old fortune hunter. Though the novel is conversant in the ways of the idle rich, it is written more or less like a screenplay, with verbose, would-be witty dialogue and minimal descriptions. Its pallid characterizations are matched by jabs at social pretension that are irreverent but fail to draw blood. Even the indulgent editor of Brackett's diaries, Slide, calls his first four novels "quite frankly difficult to read and appreciate today."

But Brackett's limited literary cachet and his position with the *New Yorker* brought him one of the less prominent seats at the Algonquin Round Table, Manhattan's equivalent of Wilder's Berlin haunt, the Romanisches Café. Brackett's final novel, *Entirely Surrounded* (1934), again laid among the wealthy, languid set hanging around Saratoga Springs, is partly a satire on the boozy pretensions of the Round Table litterateurs. One character aptly describes their interaction as "the dead rattle of good manners," except when it gets bitchy, as it often does. Ambitious and polished, yet oddly inert, the book revolves around a hapless young would-be novelist "suffering from the guilty conviction that he should work," especially since his trust fund is running out. Brackett catches the feeling of being simultaneously an insider and an outsider, but the novel is scattershot and formless, unlike his screenplays with Wilder. Brackett's reductive caricatures of Dorothy Parker, Alexander Woollcott, et al. engage in "an interminable Via Dolorosa" of snide but toothless game-playing that pales in comparison with the rapier wit of the original group. Brackett's swan song as a novelist squanders a potentially good subject by being so suffocatingly genteel that even its fleeting moments of character action are too often interrupted by aimless games of croquet or cribbage.

Brackett's literary efforts, to his frustration, never remotely rivaled those of the more artful and genuinely droll writers he seemed to be consciously emulating with his comedies of manners, such as F. Scott Fitzgerald and Henry James, whose work is less insular and snobbish, more generous and aesthetically daring. Ed Sikov's Wilder biography pinpoints the problem with Brackett's novels: "They aren't Fitzgerald; they're what Fitzgerald's characters would have read."

With his literary career going nowhere, Brackett succumbed to the temptation of Hollywood. He made a false start in 1932 at RKO before returning in disillusionment to New York, but he signed a Paramount contract in 1934. He approached his work in movies with dogged determination and less cynicism than his wildly witty but self-destructive *New Yorker* colleague Herman J. Mankiewicz, whose boozy career was redeemed by cowriting *Citizen Kane* with Orson Welles in 1941. The *New York Times* observed in its obituary of Brackett in 1969 that he "combined the philosophical tolerance of the legal mind with the acerbic wit of the critic" and was generally regarded in Hollywood as having "a scholar's zeal for tracking down basic human foibles."

Despite his literary background and strengths as a screenwriting craftsman, and though he was earning $1,000 a week in 1936, four times as much as Wilder, Brackett had achieved only middling success in the industry and was similarly in need of a strong writer-director with whom to collaborate (by 1939, Wilder himself was making $1,000 a week). Sikov notes, "However unconscious Manny Wolfe's perception may have been, he knew that Brackett needed somebody to toughen him up a little, someone who would make up for the edginess this sophisticated, . . . erudite man lacked." And as Wilder recalled, when Brackett became his partner, the older man "was just kind of hanging around Paramount and did not know what the hell to do."

The unsung hero who made film history by bringing together Brackett and Wilder, Menahem Mandel (Manny) Wolfe, was born in Russia and emigrated at the age of two with his family from there to Minnesota. He had planned to become a rabbi but became sidetracked into newspaper reporting and managing stage shows in New York, where he also worked with Isadora Duncan's dance troupe. Wolfe broke into the film industry in 1928 as a reader for Warner Bros. before moving to Paramount in 1931. So as the studio's story editor at only thirty-two, he had a rich cultural background that gave him a shrewd sense of talent. He first considered sending Brackett to audition for Lubitsch with Frank Partos, a Hungarian immigrant contract writer who had worked on earlier films with Brackett. Partos toiled without credit on MGM's *Grand Hotel* and was one of the founders of the SWG. The reasons Wolfe settled on Wilder instead in 1936—fortuitously for us, though not for Partos—are not known, but it's likely that the Berlin background Wilder shared with Lubitsch was a factor.*

Before being teamed with Wilder, Brackett knew him slightly as "a jaunty young foreigner . . . a young Austrian I've seen about for a year or two and like very much. I accepted the job joyfully. . . . I was enormously impressed with this world-weary man." But on the first day they worked together in August 1936, signs of trouble already were evident: Brackett observed that Wilder "paces constantly, has overextravagant ideas, but is stimulating." That constant pacing—accompanied by the compulsive swinging of canes and other kinds of sticks—would grate more and more on his partner's nerves as

---

* Although Partos is mostly forgotten today, he worked on *The Uninvited* (1944), which Brackett helped produce, and received an Academy Award nomination for the 1948 film *The Snake Pit*, which won Olivia de Havilland the best-actress Oscar for playing a patient in a mental asylum. Partos died at age fifty-five in 1956. Manny Wolfe went from Paramount to RKO and Universal-International and wound up working for the independent low-budget producer Edward Small before dying prematurely in 1952 at the age of forty-eight.

time went by. At first, however, Brackett enjoyed Wilder's "blasé quality . . . a kind of humor that sparks with mine." He verbally sketched Wilder as "a slim young fellow with a merry face, particularly the upper half of it, the lower half of his face had other implications. But from his brisk nose up it was the face of a naughty cupid." Brackett's précis of Wilder's life after his birth "some place in Poland" noted superciliously that he had "just about the education of a bright young American college graduate." Wilder had been "a dancer for hire at fashionable restaurants" before writing "a delightful and successful picture" in Germany, *Emil and the Detectives*. Brackett conceded Wilder's superior visual sense: "One great advantage was his: he had cut the teeth of his mind on motion pictures. He knew the great ones as he knew the classic books."

Brackett's belatedly published diaries reveal in detail the many private tensions that beset Hollywood's "happiest couple" but are frustratingly short on nitty-gritty details of their working methods as well as colored by the senior partner's intemperate biases against Wilder. Brackett's frequent anti-Semitic sneers are distressing—including a May 1941 complaint after a studio luncheon with Wilder and others, "Was never so impressed by the complete absence in the Jewish nature of an instinct like our feeling of patriotism"; a remark in 1949 about a Jewish producer, "I wonder if a Jew has ever been known to acknowledge that he got an idea from anyone"; and a comment in July 1938 that the performers in a musical revue about organized labor sponsored by the Hollywood Anti-Nazi League were "the most insultingly ugly crowd of Jews I ever saw. . . . To me it is very funny that the Anti-Nazi League should have sponsored it. They ought to have paid a couple of thousand dollars to keep it out of town. I prefer Tory humor."

Brackett privately vented other personal animosities toward the volatile temperament of "My little Manic Depressive," his hypochondria, what Brackett considered Wilder's rude manners, and his active love life arranged on the telephone in their office. Brackett in 1946 characterized Wilder as adopting the posture of "The Rebel discriminated against. This comes on him now and then—he craves occasional persecution as animals crave salt. With the passage of years, however, and his great success, it's getting goddamned hard to find any persecution."

Brackett's troubled family life contributed to the frequent strains in their relationship. He went home each night to an alcoholic, invalid wife, perhaps a reason he maintained a wide network of friends among fellow writers and others in the studios while taking an active role in labor issues despite his basic conservatism. His upper-crust background and eminence within the Hollywood hierarchy provided the irreverent newcomer Wilder with a welcome degree of reflected industry status in that transitional period.

The diaries reveal the extent to which the Brackett-Wilder relationship was affected by Brackett's neurotic insecurities about the growing power imbalance in his relationship with Wilder. Those were manifest in Brackett's dependence on his junior partner's endlessly incandescent flow of creative ideas and gradually in Wilder's assumption of more responsibility and prestige as director of their screenplays. Wilder eventually tired of Brackett's emotional neediness and self-pitying, often-melodramatic tendency to bring his personal troubles and complaints to the office. Wilder found the demeanor of his second longtime screenwriting partner, "Iz" Diamond, a refreshing contrast. Their easy rapport for many years was more strictly professional and less personal than Wilder's relationship with Brackett.

Diamond was a Rumanian Jewish émigré with a quiet, reserved, professorial demeanor. His wife, Barbara Bentley Diamond, who had been a novelist, said, "He is withdrawn and certainly anything but gregarious." His son, Paul Diamond, also a screenwriter, agreed with my description of his father as "professorial," adding that he was "reserved and very formal, not aloof but a shade intense, but not emotionally so. I saw him angry a lot, probably more than most people, but quiet anger." Wilder and Diamond had a vigorous give-and-take while working in the office and had a rule that if one didn't like something, they would drop it. As Murray Schumach reported in a 1963 profile of Diamond for the *New York Times*, "Diamond estimates that, for every week of talk about each script, they get one hour of typing. Each of the writers has the capacity for retaining lines and scenes in his head until it is time to type." Their relationship had its strains but was far more congenial than Wilder's with Brackett, which also involved extensive talking through ideas.

Shortly after beginning work with Wilder, Brackett recorded in his diary, "He is a hard, conscientious worker, without a very sensitive ear for dialogue, but a beautiful constructionist. He has the passion for the official joke of a second-rate dialogist. He's extremely stubborn, which makes for trying work sessions, but they're stimulating." The complaint about Wilder being a weak dialogue writer sounds strange today but perhaps reflects Brackett's early disdain for Wilder's admitted problems with what he felt then was his "ridiculous" English, as well as Brackett's impatience with his young partner's compulsive penchant for tossing off facile quips. In time, Wilder would become recognized as Hollywood's master of dialogue writing and personal wit, and his skill with the critical art of screenplay construction also would be peerless.

But within less than a month after their collaboration began, Brackett complained that he was "almost driven mad by [Billy's] niggling passion for changing words without changing the meaning"; a more sympathetic observer might have put that down to his perfectionism or insecurity with English. Brackett wrote that the way he found to work with Wilder was "to suggest an idea, have it torn apart and despised. In a few days it would be apt to turn up, slightly changed, as Wilder's idea. Once I got adjusted to that way of working, our lives were simpler." By the end of their first few weeks working together, in November 1936, the team were insulting each other over their past credits in Hollywood, and Brackett bemoaned, "If I do more on the script than he expects, he becomes very difficult." And at the end of 1937, after more than a year of collaborating, Brackett complained, as he often would in years to come, "Billy playing young genius—my nerves on edge." Then there would come a time in February 1939 when Brackett recorded:

> Arrived at the office at nine. Billy arrived a few minutes later with a small wooden Bulgarian flute which he played all day. Had a pleasant conference with Ted Reed [Jay Theodore Reed, the producer-director of the film they were writing, the dismal *What a Life*]—felt the need of proceeding with more speed and when Billy played his flute I took it and smashed it across my knee. Billy's face turned scarlet, he rushed from the room and came back in a very bitter mood.

Wilder did not leave diaries, but as the more famous partner and a celebrated Hollywood raconteur, he was far more often sought out by the media, and, after his partnership with Brackett ended in 1950, he gave many interviews to biographers and journalists burnishing his legend. Wilder tended to be more laconic and discreet about their collaboration than Brackett was in his diary, although he did admit in 1993, "We fought a lot. Brackett and I were like a box of matches. We kept striking till it lights up. He would sometimes throw a telephone book at me." Wilder complained in his 1999 interview book with Cameron Crowe that Brackett was "a rabid Republican" and "a very loquacious man"—two irritants Wilder did not have to suffer from the liberal, reserved Diamond—but he acknowledged that his many quarrels with Brackett were "difficult, constructive fights." Brackett "didn't think like I did at all, didn't even approve of me. But, by God! When we started out mapping out dialogue, there were sparks!"

Wilder always recognized and was grateful for the key role Brackett played in his artistic development and professional advancement:

> I found that if I had a good collaborator it was very pleasant to talk to somebody and not come into an empty office. . . . I liked working with him. He was a very good man. . . . [Brackett] spoke excellent English. He was a very classy guy, a couple of pegs above the ordinary Hollywood writer. . . . He was patient, and he never laughed when I made mistakes in English, which was most of the time. He understood what I meant, and he showed me the right way. . . . Brackett forced me to *think* in English, especially when I argued with him, which was a lot. . . .
>
> What was good about our collaboration was: Two collaborators who think exactly alike is a waste of time. . . . Unless there are sparks that fly, it is totally unnecessary to have a collaborator. . . . We did not agree on much, but what we agreed on was more important than the long list of what we did not agree on. You have to know what you can argue about, safe argument territory. It's a question of something sacred. [But ultimately,] I wanted to approach different themes, to question things. I didn't quite have a hold on what I wanted to do, but I wanted to explore. We just couldn't agree on what these themes should be.

They remained friends after their breakup in 1950, if distantly. Brackett loyally defended Wilder publicly in one crucial instance—when Wilder was under vitriolic attack for his blackest social satire, *Ace in the Hole* (1951), the first film he made after their collaboration—and Brackett generally refrained from airing his personal and professional grievances in public. Wilder, for his part, came to Brackett's defense when Twentieth Century-Fox terminated his contract in a 1962 wave of belt-tightening. Fox president Darryl F. Zanuck invited Wilder to work for the studio, but Wilder sent him a telegram about the "DISGUST" he and others felt about the "BRUTAL AND CALLOUS DISMISSAL OF PEOPLE. . . . NO SELF-RESPECTING PICTURE MAKER WOULD EVER WANT TO WORK FOR YOUR COMPANY. THE SOONER THE BULLDOZERS RAZE YOUR STUDIO THE BETTER IT WILL BE FOR THE INDUSTRY."

Although Brackett had professed shock when Wilder ended their long working relationship with seeming abruptness, as if he didn't see it coming, that was a sign of self-delusion. His diary is filled with declarations and threats about how badly he wants to get free of Wilder, even if, like many an unhappy spouse, he can't seem to do so the next morning. In September 1938, when Wilder was assigned to a script without him, Brackett wrote that he was "delighted at a respite from Billy and will work hard to see, if I'm a good boy, if it can't be made permanent." In July 1939, while they were working on *Ninotchka*, Brackett wrote about a "violent quarrel" he had with Wilder, "from whom I fear I shall have to part company, much as the thought of working alone now terrifies me—reconciliation—but I doubt the value of any reconciliation with him." And in 1944, Brackett told himself, "I've long felt a parting of the ways was inevitable."

To explain their ultimate breakup, Wilder reverted to his familiar metaphor for their working relationship—the lighting of matches, or the failure to do so. Tellingly, his explanation was also an echo of a celebrated Wilder touch about love and partnership between two men in the film that caused the first serious rupture in his relationship with Brackett. Wilder's senior partner refused to collaborate with him on 1944's *Double Indemnity* because of his distaste for the source material, the hard-boiled James M. Cain novel about insurance fraud, adultery, and murder. Wilder wrote the script instead with another novelist, Raymond Chandler. In that film, the emotional closeness between a team of insurance men—Edward G. Robinson's fatherly Barton Keyes and his wayward "son," Fred MacMurray's Walter Neff—is memorably conveyed in their striking matches for each other to light Keyes's cigars and a cigarette for the dying Neff. Wilder's explanation of why he broke up with Brackett after *Sunset Blvd.* was offered in 1996 to an interviewer for the *Paris Review*: "Twelve years [*sic*] together, but the split had been coming. It's like a box of matches: you pick up the match and strike it against the box, and there's always fire, but then one day there is just one small corner of that abrasive paper left for you to strike the match on. It was not there anymore. The match wasn't striking."

But for a glimpse of Brackett and Wilder working together harmoniously in the midst of their relationship, *Life*'s Barnett gave a valuable contemporaneous description of their working routine while they were writing *The Lost Weekend*, the film that marked their fruitful reunion after *Double Indemnity*:

> Brackett & Wilder consider four months about par for the composition of a screen play. For the first three months they orally resolve such problems as "Who are we rooting for?" "Why do they fall in love?" and "How do we get the dame out of the room?" When they are ready for "paper work" (a generic term commonly understood in Hollywood to mean writing as opposed to talking), they go into The Bedroom [the larger of their two office areas, where they also took naps after lunch] and warn their secretary, Helen Hernandez [whom they began working with in 1939], to exclude all but their best friends. Brackett takes off his shoes, lies down on the sofa with a gross of sharp pencils at his side and props a tablet of legal foolscap on his knees. Wilder paces the floor swinging a cane—a light one when inspiration flows freely, a bludgeon when the going is slow. Every syllable of every line of dialog is exhaustively discussed. No word or bit of business, no fade-in, camera angle or dissolve is recorded until both partners agree fully on its dramatic value.

Wilder's account in later years of how he worked with Brackett was identical. The impeccable craftsmanship of their screenplays, their thematic range and stylistic versatility, and their character insight and wit owed a great deal to Brackett. Even if Wilder, as Brackett himself admitted, was more of a visual thinker, the story always came first in Wilder films, and while he told me his approach to visual style was to be "as subtle and elegant as possible," his camera was at the service of the characters. The films Brackett and Wilder made together are so well-crafted that they appear to be seamless blends of their complementary creative contributions. Their clashes behind the scenes were resolved in their office at Paramount, and though Brackett gradually came to resent Wilder's more dominant status in their partnership, the films themselves did not appreciably suffer from that power imbalance. The partners' professionalism and care for the end result ensured that the work transcended their personal differences and feuds.

But Wilder's career after their breakup was far more successful than Brackett's, demonstrating that he was the central creative force of his work, as he also was with Diamond. During Brackett's partnership with Wilder, he separately wrote (with Théry) and produced *To Each His Own* (1946), for which Olivia de Havilland won an Oscar under Leisen's direction. Though she is affecting as an unwed mother who sublimates her suffering as a lonely workaholic businesswoman, the creaking, often wildly implausible plot mechanics of this lugubrious Madame X tale are off-putting. The highlight of Brackett's post-Wilder films was George Cukor's charming but seldom-recognized human comedy with Thelma Ritter in a rare leading role, *The Model and the Marriage Broker* (1952, written with Reisch and Richard L. Breen). Brackett's other writing credits included the routine Marilyn Monroe melodrama *Niagara* (1953) and the mildly diverting Jules Verne adaptation *Journey to the Center of the Earth* (1959). But his only Oscar in that period came inexplicably for *Titanic* (1953, with Reisch and Breen), which turned the fabled catastrophe into a claustrophobic soap opera about a quarreling married couple aboard the ship. Brackett also produced such uninspired mainstream films as *The King and I*, *Ten North Frederick*, and *State Fair*.

"HOW DID LUBITSCH DO IT?"

Sometimes it's as revealing of a working relationship to study what can go wrong as to analyze how it can work well. The two pivotal films Brackett and Wilder wrote for Lubitsch offer fascinating case studies of the way the three men at first failed to mesh and then brought forth a masterpiece.

Even more so than Wilder's collaboration with Brackett, the influence of Wilder's creative and personal relationship with Lubitsch, the most cosmopolitan of directors and the man David Niven called "the masters' master," was arguably the most important of his career. And though it's remarkable that the same team of writers and director that could make a film as clumsy and abrasive as *Bluebeard's Eighth Wife* would next make a classic of consummate grace and elegance, *Ninotchka*, the roots of the latter's success can be found in some of the same creative differences that made *Bluebeard* fail to coalesce and made it such an anomaly in Lubitsch's career.

Lubitsch was still considered one of the leading Hollywood directors in 1936, but his career was emerging from something of an impasse. Widely regarded by reviewers and his peers as perhaps the most stylish and accomplished director in the business, and something of a household name in the

United States even if only a relatively modest but reliable commercial success, he had revolutionized Hollywood in the 1920s after being imported from Germany. He excelled there in a dizzying variety of genres, including farce, surrealistic fantasy, romantic comedies, and spectacles. His international success with *Madame DuBarry* (1919) and other spectacles—historical sagas with a refreshingly modern sexual frankness, made with gigantic sets and casts of extras thanks to the depressed German currency after the war—caused Hollywood to see him as the new D. W. Griffith, but one without the hindrances of Victorianism.

After coming to America, however, Lubitsch mostly turned his back on the spectacle genre and made a series of intimate comedy-dramas often revolving around marital infidelity and other risqué situations. *The Marriage Circle* (1924) is perhaps his most influential film, an astonishingly subtle study of a marriage straining under temptation; it was a game-changer for a wide array of major filmmakers throughout the world. Lubitsch had singlehandedly created the modern romantic comedy. In the period before strict censorship was imposed on Hollywood, he transformed the industry by subtly but candidly incorporating the loosening sexual morality of the Jazz Age with a European sophistication about male-female relations. With the coming of sound, he helped create the musical genre in films from *The Love Parade* through *The Merry Widow*. His talkies, most notably *Trouble in Paradise* (1932), the consummate romantic comedy, added the dimensions of witty dialogue (Samson Raphaelson was usually his screenwriter) and artfully employed musical scores to enhance the layers of oblique innuendo he could find in love triangles and other unorthodox sexual combinations.

Yet by the mid-1930s Lubitsch's status as a leading director and his commercial viability were in doubt. As the Depression deepened, the comedy-dramas of Frank Capra and other directors made the audience more receptive to stories of everyday life than to musicals about royal shenanigans in mythical kingdoms. Lubitsch's most lavish film, his 1934 of Franz Lehár's *Merry Widow*, lost money, and it was near the ending of shooting in July that the Hays Code became more strictly enforced. Lubitsch took a year off to reassess his career while serving, largely unhappily, as production chief at Paramount, where he had been working since the late 1920s. He returned to directing with *Angel* (1937), a Dietrich vehicle about adultery that, in the face of Code strictures, had to approach its subject with a degree of oblique-ness extreme even by Lubitsch's standards. His previously elaborate, pointedly witty visual style was replaced with the more "invisible" Holly-wood style, a deceptively deadpan method he handled with seemingly effortless adroitness. That enhanced his ability to avoid showing his hand too obviously while conveying his subversive points with even greater sub-tlety than before.

But with the audience waning for his brand of sophisticated comedy about sexuality, Lubitsch succumbed to the new trend of screwball comedy with *Bluebeard's Eighth Wife*, in what appears in retrospect to have been miscon-ceived desperation. Hollywood—and particularly Paramount, his longtime base of operations—was beginning to consider Lubitsch a bit passé and too refined in the changing commercial climate brought about by the tightened Code and the resulting change of tone of screen comedy from sexual sug-gestiveness to sexual aggression. So he responded by reaching out to a newly minted team of writers.

Lubitsch meshed with Wilder partly because of their shared backgrounds as Jewish outsiders in the German capital. The son of a Russian immigrant who fled czarist oppression and ran a women's tailor shop with his German wife, Lubitsch was an incorrigible cutup in school (like Wilder, who grew up in a more unstable environment mostly in hotels and on trains). Ernst failed miserably in his father's attempts to enlist him in the clothing trade, prefer-ring the raffish milieu of theater and film and quickly becoming successful as both an actor and a director. Wilder's work as a reporter in Vienna and Berlin and his early work as a screenwriter made him gravitate to more topi-cal material than Lubitsch generally favored. But Wilder's background as a displaced citizen of the former Austro-Hungarian Empire gave him a per-versely conflicted nostalgia for that vanished era, different yet not far incon-gruent from the ironic romanticism Lubitsch cherished toward its flamboyant rituals. Both men were prone to mocking the pretensions of the German and Viennese high societies that excluded them.

Lubitsch and Wilder carried that slyly subversive streak along with their nostalgic impulses and urbane style as they journeyed to Hollywood. Their immersion in American life, however grateful they were to be welcomed as émigrés in a relatively free country, made them acutely conscious of the absurdities and hypocrisies of American prudery and materialism. Wilder's wise-guy sensibility must have made him seem the perfect man to turn to when Lubitsch needed a fresh young writer to help crank out a rowdy screwball comedy in hopes of reclaiming his commercial viability.

Although Wilder had written his brief 1926 magazine item in Vienna about a Lubitsch Touch, his knowledge of the director's work in Germany actually was spotty, as he rather surprisingly revealed many years later to Crowe. Wilder said of Lubitsch, "He didn't do any comedies in Germany, he did great big expensive historical pictures." Although recalling that Lubitsch acted in farcical comedies, in which he launched his film career, Wilder went on to claim, "It never occurred to him that there was gold to be mined in directing comedy, because he did not make out-and-out elegant comedies in Berlin." This mystifying ignorance about the variety of Lubitsch's directorial output in Germany—which included many kinds of comedies, some of which were indeed "elegant" in style as well as in setting—showed that Wilder was much more familiar with Lubitsch's American films. It is strange that Wilder never felt sufficiently motivated to explore the full range of his mentor's work, but he was a pragmatic filmmaker rather than a scholar and took from it what he wanted. That imperfect understanding, and some fundamental differences in their sensibilities, might help explain why it would take a long time and several attempts of various quality and fidelity before Wilder finally directed a film—*Avanti!* in 1972—that could be considered fully successful in capturing the Lubitschean style.

Wilder recalled that when he first encountered Lubitsch in Hollywood long before their work on *Bluebeard*, they simply shook hands. "He had no interest in me when I arrived. In fact, he was very reluctant to give jobs to Germans; it was only four years later that he hired me. . . . Actually he wanted to have Brackett." When Wolfe first raised the possibility with Brackett in July 1936 of working with Lubitsch on a trial basis with Partos, Brackett confided in his diary, "I don't really know Lubitsch and he makes me uncomfortable." A meeting between those two writers and Lubitsch evidently did not go well. But ironically, after Brackett teamed with Wilder and started working with Lubitsch, the director at first seemed to gravitate more easily toward the more experienced and polished Brackett. He and Lubitsch seemed so compatible that early in the writing process, Wilder "shouted indignantly" at his partner, "For Christ's sake, what is this? He apologizes to you! You and he will be making a baby together before the picture is through!"

"AMERICAN UNDERSTOOD"

Screenwriters in the 1930s tried to outdo themselves by conjuring up "meet-cutes." Wilder's pièce de résistance in that department was the one about the pajamas that he had saved up in the notebook he kept with cinematic ideas (as he did throughout his career) and pulled out when he and Brackett had their audition with Lubitsch. That Wilder "touch"—still one of his most celebrated—won them the job of adapting *Bluebeard's Eighth Wife*.

Samson Raphaelson, Lubitsch's go-to screenwriter, was gone for this project (his excuse was being busy at other studios and on a play), which helps account for its uncharacteristically harsh nature. Raphaelson explained that a key element of Lubitsch's approach always was, "He wouldn't be content unless we got a brilliant opening shot. . . . [He would often say,] 'How do ve get into it? How do ve open? It gotta be brilliant!' . . . He wanted to open with laughter and with style—and style, of course, is the essence of Lubitsch." A Lubitsch opening had to have his characteristic obliqueness and wit, had to find a fresh and ingenious way of answering his perennial question, "How do we do that, without doing that?" And "This scene must be *hilahrious*," he would keep telling his writers.

Brackett and Wilder, in a tribute to Lubitsch after his death, remembered that as a "terrifying statement. . . . Thereupon, all minds involved focused on making the scene *hilahrious* and were held to that task with a kind of pneumatic-drill steadiness until, by George, the scene became *hilahrious*. . . . To write for Ernst Lubitsch was an education, a stimulus, a privilege, but it was no cinch. . . . One had to understand the kind of stylized film he wanted to make, and supply it with material. And always he was there, saying, 'Is this best we can do? Does it ring the bell? When it's right, it rings the bell.'" If that process sounds arduous, it was, according to the evidence in Brackett's diary, and though in *Ninotchka* the end result seems effortless, the effort unfortunately shows throughout most of *Bluebeard*. Only the opening is truly "*hilahrious*."

When Lubitsch mused about how to bring together the American millionaire with the French aristocrat down on her luck on the Riviera, Wilder trotted out his idea for Colbert to offer to buy the bottoms of Cooper's pair of pajamas. That makes his smug millionaire jealous, since he assumes, as do we, that the man must be her husband or lover (he actually turns out to be her father). As Crowe notes, this rather salacious touch allows the audience to "imagine, along with the characters, what they each look like half-dressed." But as one of the Hollywood censors observed of Lubitsch, it was hard to blue-pencil him because even though they knew what he was saying, they didn't know *how* he said it. Wilder pointed out that Lubitsch always wanted a "Superjoke" to top the topper. In this case the director embellished the pajama gag by having the sales clerks run up a flight of stairs to confer with the store manager, who calls the elderly owner (Charles Halton) at home to ask his approval. The owner gets out of bed to take the call, showing a spindly pair of legs as he reveals that he is wearing only pajama tops.

Lubitsch's dawdling on this meet-cute, which takes up almost a reel of film without losing audience interest, shows his already keen appreciation for Wilder's contribution (the one aspect of the film for which Wilder always exercised the most bragging rights; Wilder drew it from his own habit of sleeping only in pajama tops).* Despite Michael's sour, aggressive, stingy personality, which is established from the onset, the sequence is rather sweet, thanks to the jolly sexual conceit with the pajamas and the insouciant charm of Colbert's character. But the film goes sharply downhill from that point on. Although Nicole is sharp enough to outwit Michael and turn the tables, which gives the audience some satisfaction, their relationship is so acrimonious and physically punishing that it becomes extremely unappealing to watch. And the sight of Michael winding up in a straitjacket is not exactly "*hilahrious.*"

There's a marvelous, and subtle, Lubitsch Touch immediately preceding the meet-cute. It's one Wilder remarked on in interviews to illustrate Lubitsch's genius with telling, witty detail. Before Michael stops outside the clothing shop, he studies a sign in the window:

---

* Wilder includes a variation on this gag in *Avanti!* when the illicit lovers Pamela Piggott (Juliet Mills) and Wendell Armbruster Jr. (Jack Lemmon) are surprised in their hotel room by a U.S. State Department official. She wears pajama tops, and he wears the bottoms as they pretend she is the hotel manicurist, the job her late mother used to have in London.

MAN SPRICHT DEUTSCH

SI PARLA ITALIANO

ENGLISH SPOKEN

AMERICAN UNDERSTOOD

Wilder remembered that after they wrote the first three lines, Lubitsch "took a pencil and wrote underneath that 'American understood.' A tiny little joke, but it meant everything."

"RIGHT *IN YOUR FACE*"

Some of the differences between the sensibilities of Lubitsch and Wilder are already visible in the way Wilder's pugnacious sensibility infiltrated itself into the unaccustomed roughhousing of *Bluebeard's Eighth Wife*. Wilder claimed to Crowe, "Lubitsch was never blunt, you know—it was never right *in your face*." Except, notably, in this one instance.

Even when Lubitsch had shown the quarreling Bavarian mountain couple physically brawling in *Kohlhiesel's Daughters*, the humor was not nasty, because the roughhousing comedy was made to seem like foreplay between two people who gradually realize they are suited to each other and form an unlikely match. Emil Jannings's "taming" of Henny Porten as the "ugly" sister (half of her tour-de-force double role) is oddly heartwarming as he gradually melts her fierce defenses. There's a major difference in the way *Bluebeard* makes use of the earlier film's uncredited source material, *The Taming of the Shrew*: Michael consults a copy of Shakespeare's comedy in exasperation while trying to figure out how to deal with Nicole (she studies a book called *Live Alone and Like It*), and the lesson he takes from the play is simply to slap her around.

With mostly unfunny and lamentable results, *Bluebeard* is uncharacteristically harsh for Lubitsch in its treatment of sexual relations, adopting conventions of the screwball genre alien to his better instincts. The film's situation of the wealthy playboy who compulsively marries and discards partners before buying them off with divorce settlements is not only implausible but more disturbing than amusing. Apparently the only reason a film that so flagrantly violates the Hays Code made it past the censors was that its source is a French play, Alfred Savoir's *La huitième femme de Barbe-bleue* (1921), adapted for the Broadway stage that year by Charlton Andrews as *Bluebeard's 8th Wife*, starring Ina Claire.* Lubitsch was known for his general finesse in using foreign locales as settings for the kind of vicariously titillating naughtiness American audiences would have found unacceptable among their own puritanical kind.

Despite its winning and cheeky performance by Colbert as the freewheeling French adventuress, *Bluebeard* often comes off as cruel and misogynistic in showing her being manhandled by Cooper, whose playing of a smug fashion plate, a recklessly wealthy and cavalier skirt-chaser on the prowl in a foreign country, is clumsy and hard to believe. Nicole, the daughter of a penniless marquis (an atypically unfunny Edward Everett Horton), tells Michael, "You buy wives, just like . . . like shirts—and after you've worn them, you toss them away." Cooper's acting utterly lacks charm. Worse than that, his performance lacks the manic verve and crass, sarcastic arrogance Wilder later would evoke from the memorable heels he was fond of daring the audience to like, such as Kirk Douglas in *Ace in the Hole*, William Holden in *Stalag 17*, and Dean Martin in *Kiss Me, Stupid*.

The screwball comedy genre produced some classic films—such as *It Happened One Night*, *My Man Godfrey*, *Easy Living*, *The Awful Truth*, and the classic 1940s comedies written and directed by Preston Sturges, including *Sullivan's Travels*, *The Palm Beach Story*, and *The Miracle of Morgan's Creek*—as well as some that are more painful than funny to watch today because of the highly abrasive degree of their physical and psychological animosities. Into that category I relegate Howard Hawks's *Bringing Up Baby* and most other Hawks "comedies," as well as Sturges's *The Lady Eve* and *Bluebeard's Eighth Wife*.

Bringing Up Baby epitomizes the problem I find with the genre, because it is built on physical and psychological aggression. The film's German psychiatrist (Fritz Feld) declares that "the love impulse in men very frequently reveals itself in terms of conflict." Cary Grant's bashful paleontologist is driven half-mad and his work ruined by Katharine Hepburn's psychotic heiress. As the film gets increasingly grim, the bespectacled scientist winds up crawling

---

* The play was made into a 1923 silent film starring Wilder's future Norma Desmond, Gloria Swanson, and directed by Sam Wood, who was not known for his sense of humor.

around on his hands and knees in a dark wood looking for his missing bone. That kind of sexual hostility in the genre strikes a chord with contemporary audiences, but I find *Bringing Up Baby* more depressing than amusing. I experience most of Hawks's so-called adventure films as being much funnier than his comedies and agree with Jacques Rivette's 1953 assessment in *Cahiers du Cinéma* of the common theme of Hawks's comedies, which also can be seen in other screwball comedies: "Could we be offered a more bitter view of life than this? I have to confess that I'm quite unable to join in the laughter of a packed theatre when I am riveted by the calculated twists of a fable [*Monkey Business*] which sets out—gaily, logically, and with an unholy abandon—to chronicle the fatal stages in the degradation of a superior mind."

In the belligerently unromantic climate of 1938 Hollywood, Paramount's dissatisfaction with Lubitsch's usual style of sophisticated romantic comedy and graceful interchanges between the sexes was evident in the trailer the studio devised for *Bluebeard*. A bizarrely offensive, flagrantly misogynistic sales job, it goes out of its way to demolish audience notions of the once-beloved "Lubitsch Touch." Concentrating on the screwball genre's obsession with violence between the sexes, the trailer is entitled HOW TO HANDLE YOUR EIGHTH WIFE! and begins with what it calls Michael's "superb technique" of dealing with Nicole—he fiercely stomps down a hallway and smashes a vase before pushing open a door and slapping her. A title card proclaims, "COOPER CLUNKS COLBERT." The trailer goes on, "In case you missed the finer points of the Lubitsch touch, WE REPEAT THE LESSON." This time they're shown slapping each other. "You'll learn plenty about handling Sweethearts—when you see . . . ERNST LUBITSCH'S *BLUEBEARD'S EIGHTH WIFE*." The trailer displays further examples of physical violence as well as part of the deliberately repugnant "love scene" of a tipsy Nicole chewing on onions to repel her husband's advances and overcome her own covert attraction to him. When you watch this trailer, it's hard to escape the conclusion that despite Paramount's long creative association with Lubitsch, they were trashing him before ignominiously kicking him out the door because he was slipping commercially. Never known for grace or gratitude, Hollywood outdid itself in that instance.

Brackett's diary shows that Lubitsch was unusually preoccupied during the writing of *Bluebeard,* with the making of *Angel.* Wilder recalled the director telling them, "Go ahead and structure the picture, I'm shooting, but I'll give you an hour here and there." Perhaps his intermittently distracted attitude helps account for why *Bluebeard* seems more a Wilder film than a Lubitsch film; it's so nasty that it fits the often-unfair critical stereotype later developed of Wilder in some critical circles as a heartless "cynic." But as an example of how trying to pinpoint one collaborator's contribution to a film can be surprising or misleading, Brackett reveals in his diary that he was responsible for the scene with the onions, demonstrating that the prevailing industry mood of unromantic hostility infected him as well as Wilder.

Andrew Sarris identified the basic problem I find with *Bluebeard* when he described the genre in 1978 as

> the sex comedy without sex . . . [with a] correlation of slapstick and violence with frustration. . . . I would suggest that this frustration arose inevitably from a situation in which the censors [following the strict enforcement of the Code] removed the sex from sex comedies. Here we have all these beautiful people with nothing to do. Let us invent some substitutes for sex. The wisecracks multiply beyond measure, and when the audiences tire of verbal sublimation, the performers do cartwheels and pratfalls and funny expressions. . . . It does not matter whether a couple is married or not. The act and the fact of sex are verboten from 1934. The nice naughtiness that characterized such early thirties comedies [as Lubitsch's *Trouble in Paradise* and *Design for Living*] . . . has been supplanted by the subterfuges of screwballism.

Sarris analyzed even the popular Fred Astaire–Ginger Rogers musicals from that period as stemming from "the need for a new symbolic language of motion and gesture to circumvent repression." Zolotow put it more bluntly: *Bluebeard* "belonged to a now outmoded genre of Hollywood picture known as the UFF, or Unfinished Fuck."

Film historian John Belton further defined the essence of the screwball comedy as "films in which attractive, romantic leads engage in slapstick (rather than delegating it to their inferiors) in lieu of explicit sexual activity, expressing genuine feelings for one another through physical violence." That overriding aspect of the genre was alien to the bawdy embrace of sexuality characteristic of Lubitsch but somewhat more congenial to Wilder, whose view of sexuality, evolved on the streets of Vienna and Berlin, was much darker in that era, even though Wilder later gravitated back toward the kind of overt romanticism (mixed with sarcastic humor) seen in the better Lubitsch comedies. Lubitsch was not often as overtly caustic as Wilder, but he could be equally scathing in his satire, even if he used a rapier and not a pistol as his weapon of choice. Although Lubitsch's films help define romanticism in cinema, his work is always tinctured with an acidulous dose of irony. But his characteristically oblique approach to sexuality did not imply in other films that his couples were not having sex off-camera, so it was a serious miscalculation for him and Paramount to think he could thrive in a genre that substitutes violence for sex.

When *Bluebeard* ends with Michael in his straitjacket under Nicole's control, she gets off a Wilderian quip that is drolly acerbic, if a disheartening way to summarize the film's attitude toward love and marriage: "Why do you think a woman puts a man into a straitjacket? Because she loves him." Lubitsch seemed to acknowledge misgivings over the direction he had taken by commenting on the ending to the *New York Times*, "Subtlety, ha? Don't tell them there's a sledge-hammer in it." The previous year he had pointed out, "The Lubitsch touch is the direct opposite of the equally famous sledgehammer touch. . . . As befits its name, it carries a terrific sock, a sock, which in fact stuns the audience. . . . I do not think audiences need to have a point driven home with a sledgehammer."

Wilder and Brackett would venture into the screwball realm with happier results with *Midnight* (1939) for director Mitchell Leisen, *Ball of Fire* (1941) for Howard Hawks, and Wilder's own Hollywood directorial debut in 1942, *The Major and the Minor*. And by the 1950s, Belton notes, the Code was eroding to the extent that it allowed "the regeneration of the long-repressed sex comedy," since "the displacement of romantic, sexual heat onto violent, physical slapstick was no longer necessary." That helps account for the genuine eroticism of Wilder's screwball-influenced masterpiece starring Marilyn Monroe and two males in drag, *Some Like It Hot* (1959), although that film too has plenty of violence and physical slapstick mixed with sexual elements that seemed unusually brazen and advanced for its time.

The portrayal of Michael Brandon in *Bluebeard* as a repellently smug tycoon who assumes he can buy anything and anybody in the world is another incarnation of Buzzy Belew from *Champagne Waltz*, one of the "Ugly American" abroad characters Wilder would often feature in his work.* Others, in films he directed, include Bing Crosby's gramophone salesman in *The Emperor Waltz*, Jean Arthur's right-wing member of Congress in *A Foreign Affair*, Cooper's Pepsi-Cola magnate in *Love in the Afternoon*, James Cagney's Coca-Cola executive in *One, Two, Three*, and Jack Lemmon's sexist conglomerate chief in *Avanti!* Wilder's best scripts allow the humanity of his spoiled-capitalist characters to come through and even allow for the possibility of their transformation into genuine romantics. That never happens with Michael, who is simply mocked and humiliated and finally physically and psychologically subjugated by Nicole. As a con-woman who gives him his due, she is more engaging and sympathetic to watch as she goes about exploiting his weaknesses. Today's audiences understandably respond favorably to the element of turnabout in gender relations that the screwball genre represents. But it's a cold, relentless series of mutual attacks in *Bluebeard*, whose very title suggests a literal kind of lady-killer.

Cooper seems egregiously miscast, devoid of humor or charm; this ill-fitting role came after Capra had established the star's enduring screen image by casting him as a shy, small-town romantic who inherits a fortune but gives most of it away to the needy in *Mr. Deeds Goes to Town* (1936). As I wrote in my biography *Frank Capra: The Catastrophe of Success*, that comedy-drama "marked a departure for Cooper, whose previous roles had allowed free rein to his natural sexual swagger. Capra would not acknowledge the extent to which he had transformed the actor in his own image, claiming that he simply was following Cooper's own personality: though the actor was a notorious ladies' man, Capra contended that he seduced women through his apparent shyness ('They came to him')." Pauline Kael argued that "Frank Capra destroyed Gary Cooper's early sex appeal when he made him childish as Mr. Deeds. Cooper, once devastatingly lean and charming, the man Tallulah and Marlene had swooned over, began to act like an old woman and went on to a long sexless career—fumbling, homey, mealymouthed."

---

* The phrase came into common usage long after Wilder began writing such characters. The 1958 novel *The Ugly American* by William Lederer and Eugene Burdick deals with arrogant American diplomats in Southeast Asia; it was filmed in 1963 with Marlon Brando starring. A Burmese journalist in the novel says, "A mysterious change seems to come over Americans when they go to a foreign land. They isolate themselves socially. They live pretentiously. They're loud and ostentatious. Perhaps they're frightened and defensive, or maybe they're not properly trained and make mistakes out of ignorance."

Although Cooper and Dietrich had smoldered together in Josef von Sternberg's 1930 *Morocco*, Lubitsch should have learned from *Desire*, a tepid 1936 romantic comedy he produced, in which Cooper plays awkwardly opposite Dietrich's jewel thief as a rich American on holiday in Spain, that the actor's persona had irrevocably changed. Frank S. Nugent wrote in his *New York Times* review of *Bluebeard*:

> Although it's not a bad comedy by our current depressed standards, it has the dickens of a time trying to pass off Gary Cooper as a multi-marrying millionaire. Put seven divorced wives behind Mr. Deeds, each with a $50,000-a-year settlement, and it becomes pretty hard to believe that he's just a small boy at heart—which is the principal charm of Paramount's gangling hero. In these days it's bad enough to have to admire millionaires in any circumstances; but a millionaire with a harem complex simply can't help starting the bristles on the back of a sensitive neck.

When Brackett watched *Bluebeard's Eighth Wife* with Wilder again five years after its release, he admitted in his diary, "It is terrible! Screwball comedy, long sequences to almost practically no dramatic purpose, climax sequences so brief as to be choppy—a really embarrassing picture, but it brought back a lot of fond memories of Lubitsch."

INTERLUDE

Before their triumph with *Ninotchka* in 1939, Brackett and Wilder paid their dues like most Hollywood contract screenwriters on a potpourri of projects, only one of which had any merit. *Midnight*, a romantic comedy released earlier that year and directed by Leisen, is a frivolous yet delightfully frothy story indulging the team's shared fascination with masquerading and hijinks across class barriers. But Leisen became Wilder's bête noire for trashing a key scene the team wrote for *Hold Back the Dawn*, the 1941 film that is most celebrated in cinematic history for driving the despondent Wilder back to directing in order to protect his material. Leisen is also "credited" with the same function in the career of Preston Sturges, his screenwriter on *Easy Living* and *Remember the Night* (1940).

But that one glaring problem aside, *Hold Back the Dawn* is a gem, a deeply personal work for Wilder with its echoes of his struggle to surmount the roadblocks of the United States immigration system and become an American. A largely unsung classic of romantic comedy-drama, it can stand muster in the hierarchy of Brackettandwilder's achievement with *Ninotchka* and their brilliantly witty script for Hawks's zany 1941 comedy about gangsters and philology, *Ball of Fire*. Leisen also directed their script for *Arise, My Love* (1940), their uneven mélange of romantic comedy and political propaganda. Leisen's work as a director was often sophisticated but was also erratic (even *Easy Living* gets tiresomely protracted and silly), and Wilder regarded him as too fussy about decor and not attentive enough to stories and characterizations. Leisen had begun as an art director and costume designer, and his overt gayness was a fact that Wilder sometimes gratuitously dragged into his attacks on him.

Leisen regarded Wilder with similar distaste. He told David Chierichetti for their oral history, *Mitchell Leisen: Hollywood Director*:

> Writing a script with Charles Brackett and Billy was very hard work, but we got results. We had daily meetings [on *Midnight*] in [producer] Arthur Hornblow [Jr.]'s office, and built the thing up slowly, sequence by sequence, arguing all the way. Billy Wilder was a middle European fresh from the old country [*sic*], and most of my fights were with him. Having done eight years of psychoanalysis, I knew that a character had to follow a certain emotional pattern. I'd say, "Billy, you have this guy doing something that is completely inconsistent. You suddenly introduce a completely different emotional setup for this character, and it can't be. It has to follow a definite emotional pattern."
>
> Well, Billy couldn't figure this one out, but Brackett could. Brackett was sort of a leveling influence. He would referee my quarrels with Billy. As a team they were the greatest. Billy would scream if you changed one line of his dialogue. I used to say, "Listen, this isn't Racine, it's not Shakespeare. If the actors we have can't say it, we must give them something they can say." Later, I went on the set one day when Billy was directing one of his own scripts and it was very funny. He was having to rewrite the whole thing!

In response, Wilder told Zolotow,

> Leisen spent more time with Edith Head worrying about the pleats on a
> skirt than he did with us on the script. He didn't argue over scenes. He
> didn't know shit about construction. And he didn't care. All he did was he
> fucked up the script and our scripts were damn near perfection, let me tell
> you. . . . Charlie hated him as much as I did. Because if we gave in to him
> there would be holes in the script which he shot. Charlie never was a peace-
> maker. That's bullshit. It was Arthur Hornblow who refereed our
> fights. . . . And about this Shakespeare—well, I didn't think our lines were
> the Ten Commandments chiseled with a platinum hammer out of Carr-
> ara marble. It was just—oh hell, there were these voids in most of his films
> where any screenwriter could see Leisen has been chopping. *Midnight* is
> perfect because I fought him every inch of the way.

Wilder was spoiled by having worked with Lubitsch, who had greater respect
for his writers. But even if Leisen was a few notches below Lubitsch in talent
and stature, he had a true sense of style and, when not tempted to mess with
a script, a gift for bringing out vivid performances. Wilder was fortunate to
have Leisen directing some of his work in that transitional period, as he later
grudgingly acknowledged. When he lamented in our 1978 interview the coars-
ening of modern Hollywood filmmaking and the loss of the classic tradition, he said with wistfully graceful alliteration, "All of that is gone: Lubitsch,
Leisen, *Love in the Afternoon*."

The blend of Wilder's cosmopolitan European sensibility and Brackett's
more traditional American nature helps account for the way they mutually
enriched each other's work and careers in 1936–1942. But even as Wilder
became increasingly Americanized, they followed Lubitsch's example by continuing to gravitate to some extent to films with European settings, such as
on *Bluebeard's Eighth Wife*, *Midnight*, *Arise, My Love*, and *Ninotchka*. Wilder
was still feeling his way gradually into the American scene. His occasional
ventures into purely American vehicles before and even during his teaming
with Brackett sometimes were less successful and occasionally found him dis-
mally mismatched with the subject matter. Two films they helped write
about all-American teenagers, *That Certain Age* (1938) and *What a Life* (1939),

are bizarre anomalies in the Wilder filmography. Brackett and Wilder fortunately avoided receiving credit on the Deanna Durbin musical mishmash *That Certain Age* but are the screenwriters of record on the insufferable *What a Life*, based on a 1938 Broadway play by Clifford Goldsmith.

That Certain Age—produced by Joe Pasternak, who had produced Wilder's screenplay *The Devil's Reporter* in Germany—strangely mixes some recognizable Wilder interests (journalism, politics, the coming world war) with a pseudo-romance touching on what later would be called the *Lolita* theme. Durbin was a charming songstress who had become a star in 1936 and went on to star in a string of popular musicals. Just sixteen in *That Certain Age*, she plays a budding singer who lives on a lavish country estate in the eastern United States with a father who is a newspaper tycoon (John Halliday). She has an unrequited crush on a visiting foreign correspondent played by the thirty-seven-year-old Melvyn Douglas. On a break from covering the Spanish Civil War, his Vincent Bullitt is shocked, *shocked* when he very belatedly realizes what's going on in her mind and recoils in the way the Hays Office insisted on even when it let this kind of vaguely improper storyline slip through its grasp. Fortunately for all concerned, Durbin is brought back to her senses and rejoins a troupe of kids putting on a show, led by her jealous adolescent boyfriend (Jackie Cooper), a peevish Boy Scout who rats out her feelings for Vincent.

Brackett and Wilder would handle this touchy theme with far more skill and satirical flair with Ginger Rogers in *The Major and the Minor*, Wilder's Hollywood directing debut. Iowa-born Susan Applegate, fleeing her seamy life in New York, doesn't have enough money to get back to the Midwest by train on an adult ticket, so she disguises herself as a twelve-year-old called "Su-Su." She escapes New York lechers only to land in the world of horny adolescent cadets at a midwestern military school and to fall in love with a conveniently myopic U.S. Army officer, Major Philip Kirby (Ray Milland), who fails to see through her disguise; his attraction to her throughout this slyly outrageous film is a sign of subconscious pedophilia. Perhaps that proto-Nabokovian film's rather astounding ability to outwit the Hollywood censors owes something to the team's experience in struggling unsuccessfully to pull off the peculiar mishmash of *That Certain Age*. They were rewriting a script for Durbin by Bruce Manning and probably were relieved when he took over and redid their work, however incoherently. Durbin has some charming songs, but Douglas's obliviousness to the teenager's feelings and his alarm when she expresses them are hard to believe in such a worldly man. The goofy visual confusion Milland's military officer displays toward the transparently grown-up "Su-Su," a device, along with the later film's overall comic styliza-tion, allows the viewer to willingly suspend disbelief.

Jackie Cooper, the former child star and future television director, not only plays Durbin's callow love interest in *That Certain Age* but also stars in *What a Life* during his gawky adolescent phase. The story of "the worst pupil in this school," bullied by jocks and inept with girls, *What a Life* inexplicably led to a series of popular films revolving around the character of Henry Aldrich.* The stupefyingly banal storyline of *What a Life*—almost unthink-able for Wilder's attention—involves Henry's dilemma in finding a date for a school dance. The film's only interest is that Henry is being pursued by Betty Field, who even in her screen debut at twenty-three possessed a plaintive, spooky screen persona, perpetually on the edge of hysteria; it would reach its full dark flowering when she played a young woman involved in an incestu-ous relationship with her father (Claude Rains) in *Kings Row* (1942).

"Sometimes don't you hate to get up in the morning, Henry?," the assis-tant principal in their small-town high school, Mr. Nelson (John Howard), asks him in *What a Life*. "I mean, don't you dread all the things that can hap-pen to you in one day?" One wonders what possible connection Wilder could have found with the miserable, neurotic loser Henry Aldrich other than per-haps as a distantly distorted all-American echo of his own underachieving, troubled, semidelinquent youth in Vienna, which was reflected more directly in *Mauvaise graine*. Henry is more of a clumsy toady than a genuine rebel, but he is rescued by Mr. Nelson encouraging his talent as a cartoonist, so Wilder was struggling to find a personal connection with his whiny protag-onist. But this film about humiliation and the need for self-respect has an impossible time finding any fun or even acidulous humor in Henry's situa-tion. *What a Life* might have turned out (marginally) better if Paramount had stuck to its original plan of having William Holden make his screen debut as Henry, but Wilder's involvement with Holden would have to wait eleven years.

---

* Jimmy Lydon soon replaced Cooper in the series, and the play also had radio and television spin-offs.

Three exceptions to the rule of Wilder's maladroitness in dealing with American material in his apprenticeship period can be explained by his more clearly personal interest in their complex and sophisticated subject matter. Besides the virtually autobiographical *Hold Back the Dawn*, *Rhythm on the River* and *Ball of Fire* were based on cleverly plotted scripts he helped originate with other writing partners. Those two comedies deal with different forms of the writing profession—as does the comedy-drama *Hold Back the Dawn*, if you factor in its Hollywood studio framing story—and all three draw from Wilder's preoccupation with the masquerade.

Yet another of the numerous semi-musicals Wilder wrote in his apprenticeship period in both Germany and Hollywood, his cowritten story about a songwriting team for *Rhythm on the River* shrewdly draws from his vast fund of knowledge of American pop music. He uses pop songs memorably in his films, from the sultry 1941 jazz hit "Tangerine" to accompany the doomed romance between the murderous couple in *Double Indemnity* (MacMurray's Neff and Stanwyck's Phyllis Dietrichson) to the inane 1960 novelty hit "Itsy Bitsy Teenie Weenie Yellow Polkadot Bikini" as an instrument of East German torture in *One, Two, Three*. *Some Like It Hot*, among its other pleasures, is a joyous romp with Sweet Sue and Her Society Syncopators through the pop music catalogue of the Jazz Age, from "Runnin' Wild" and "Sweet Georgia Brown" to "I Wanna Be Loved by You" and "I'm Thru with Love."

Kiss Me, Stupid, Wilder and Diamond's corrosive farce about a team of hapless songwriters, is prefigured to some extent by the exploited songwriting naif in the Wilder screenplay *Music in the Air* and the more jaded team of ghostwriters in *Rhythm on the River*, for which Wilder wrote the original story with Jacques Théry; Dwight Taylor gets screenplay credit. Bing Crosby's Bob Sommers and Mary Martin's Cherry Lane are tutored in their shabby trade of ghosting for the celebrated songwriter Oliver Courtney (Basil Rathbone) by his jaundiced assistant, Billy Starbuck (Oscar Levant), whose blasé wisecracking and physical appearance evoke Wilder himself. The film was directed by Victor Schertzinger, who was also a composer and songwriter; he and Johnny Mercer wrote "Tangerine." *Rhythm* is a wry, sometimes acerbic satire on the mingled joys and tensions of a writing partnership, although the plot bogs down in rustic courting scenes when the squabbling couple are thrown together in a delayed "meet-cute" before realizing they are collaborating in a songwriting factory for Rathbone's inept and arrogant Courtney.

The film draws extensively from Wilder's keen interest in the phoniness of show business as a form of prostitution and the struggle of love to survive and overcome those obstacles. The frustrations of Crosby's talented but dispirited composer (the actor is almost terminally laid-back in the role) echo Wilder's own *tsouris* in that period and his work as a "ghost" for other screenwriters back in Germany. "I don't want to be a ghost anymore," Bob declares, "I want to be the Real McCoy." Martin's smart, ambitious, genuinely wholesome lyricist (one of the charming singer's too-infrequent film roles) prefigures Betty Schaefer in *Sunset Blvd.*—admirable young female characters who demonstrate the supposedly "cynical" Wilder's recognition that honesty and show business are not necessarily incompatible, even if disillusionment with its seaminess is inevitable.

The gradually darkening vision Wilder was allowed to pursue after turning to directing can be seen in the contrast between the simple pleasure the small-town Bavarian schoolteacher takes at the end of *Music in the Air* while hearing his song on the radio from faraway Munich, a wish-fulfillment fantasy achieved without the need of actual corruption, and the sting of the ending of *Kiss Me, Stupid*. That acidulous film has small-town Southern California songwriter Orville J. Spooner (Ray Walston), the naive partner of scheming Barney Millsap (Cliff Osmond), hearing Dino (Dean Martin) croon one of their songs on television. Dino has obtained it by banging Spooner's wife without his knowledge. One reason the semi-musical *Rhythm on the River* is mostly forgotten is that despite its acerbic aspects, it lacks the real bite of Wilder's later full-throttled take on showbiz corruption. The sappy happy ending Hollywood demanded in those days has Bob and Cherry announcing their upcoming nuptials over the radio at a nightclub and publicly performing their own bland love song, "Only Forever."

EXPLORING "PARIS, PARAMOUNT"

As I write in my critical study of Lubitsch, what he called "Paris, Paramount" was "that fictive place in California, where Lubitsch made some of his most memorable films at various studios . . . part of the artificial but vital world that these dispossessed [European émigré] artists helped invent in their own image and in bittersweet tribute to their bygone culture." As war approached and overtook Europe in 1939–1940, Wilder explored that artificial cityscape with Brackett in three romantic comedies of highly varying tone and quality.

Leisen's *Midnight* is a polished, efficient film of considerable charm, but it's a diversion devoid of the emotional depths reached by *Ninotchka* and intermittently attempted in *Arise, My Love*. The latter is one of the rare Wilder scripts that is poorly structured, as if it doesn't know quite what it is trying to do. The urgency he and his collaborators felt as the war swept through Europe—and perhaps some guilt over making films at such a safe, luxurious distance—unhinged *Arise, My Love* but was perfectly integrated into the bittersweet moments of *Ninotchka*. The Lubitsch film was released in November 1939 but was set just before the war as a farewell to the graceful old-world culture in danger of extinction.

The theme of masquerade—stemming not only from Wilder's lifelong penchant as an exile perpetually in psychological transit but also a tendency that came naturally to a gay director such as Leisen having to lead a double life in Hollywood—is given a thorough and delightful workout in *Midnight*. The adult fairy-tale aspects of this briskly paced comedy are signaled in the title and the admonitory words of chorus girl heroine Eve Peabody (Claudette Colbert), "Don't forget, every Cinderella has her midnight." Eve is on the run from financial ruin in Monte Carlo, meeting cute on a rainy night in Paris as she cajoles a Hungarian émigré taxi driver, Tibor Czerny (Don Ameche), into driving her around to look for work in a decreasingly fashionable string of nightclubs. Tibor is a bohemian who disdains money and in a moment of harsh but not inaccurate judgment calls Eve "an American golddigger." Nevertheless, it is her determination to escape a life of struggle that has given her a hard-boiled veneer resistant to love and a yearning for a life of luxury. The amiable Tibor falls for her anyway, and their class conflicts are treated in far more believable and civilized ways in this jolly romp than the pitched battles Colbert has with Cooper in *Bluebeard's Eighth Wife*.

Eve tries to break into high society that first night in Paris by crashing a swanky, pretentious party presided over by Hedda Hopper (then making her transition from stuffy actress to right-wing gossip columnist). The filmmakers deftly skewer the hostess's ignorant snobbery. The chorine who owns nothing but a gold lamé dress desperately masquerades as "The Baroness Czerny." Her charade continues at a more lavish weekend gathering at the Versailles chateau of a wealthy, unhappily married couple (John Barrymore and Mary Astor). Barrymore steals the show in his droll, self-mocking role as Georges

Flammarion. Roused to a baroque display of the sheer joy of acting, Barry-more was in the latter stages of his career and read all his dialogue off cue cards, which helps account for his quirky mannerisms. Leisen recalled, "It was always funny the ways he could find to stall in a scene while he was try-ing to find the cards with his next speech."

Georges hires Eve to woo away his wife's shallow younger lover, Jacques (Austrian exile Francis Lederer), a playboy whose family, as Georges puts it, "makes a very superior income from a very inferior Champagne." When Tibor shows up unannounced at the chateau to pursue Eve, he instinctively mas-querades as "The Baron Czerny" but ironically fails to convince the socialites when he defiantly tries to reveal his true identity, because the quick-witted Eve has convinced them he's crazy. These parts of *Midnight* bear a superficial resemblance to Jean Renoir's classic from that same year, *The Rules of the Game*. Similarly set in a French country chateau with characters pursuing intricate sexual liaisons, Renoir's is a far more corrosive film in its politically allegori-cal satire of the decadent upper class, while *Midnight* is unabashed escapism.

It's stylish and has a true madcap mood in keeping with the best tradition of screwball comedy and little of the physical or emotional violence that often mars the genre. Reversing audience expectations for a romantic comedy, but in keeping with the film's screwball tendencies, Tibor is the frustrated roman-tic in the relationship. Eve's obsessive pursuit of money leads her to spurn him for what amounts to an innocent form of pretend prostitution as a hired "lover," as Wilder adapts one of his pet themes to the strictures of the Code. Colbert's characteristically icy demeanor hides an emotional vulnerability Leisen and the screenwriters bring out in subtle ways. Yet she and the film seem somewhat mechanical in execution. "She was a good, funny actress, a professional who never missed a line—but on the other hand, there was noth-ing surprising about her," Wilder told Crowe. "She did not like *It Happened One Night*. She liked *Midnight* best. What did she know?"

Eve's moments of softening—such as when she realizes Georges truly loves his wife, which leads her to go along with his con job—help make plausible her gradual caving in to Tibor's emotional sincerity, convincingly captured by Ameche, a gentle, underrated actor who also shines in Lubitsch's *Heaven Can Wait* (1943). But the machinations of the courtroom sequence that finally brings the lovers together are forced and frenetic in the screwball mode and more absurd than the general tone of the film. *Midnight* unfolds, however, in a breezy yet relaxed manner, and the plot and character twists are handled with the adroitness of a highly skilled team of Hollywood pros. It is a superior example of machine-tooled entertainment from the studio era, with all the strengths and limitations that implies. The film's offhand style, however engaging, keeps it from delving deeply into emotional issues. Wilder, quickly rising to professional expertise with Brackett's help, was now ready to graduate to the very pinnacle of the filmmaking world by creating a masterpiece with Lubitsch, Brackett, and Reisch.

But before examining what makes *Ninotchka* such an enduring classic, a film that brings together all the strands of Wilder's evolving talent in concert with those of his collaborators, it's worth seeing how he and Brackett faltered without the strong guiding hand of Lubitsch when they wrote their other lightly politicized romantic comedy from that period set largely in "Paris, Paramount," *Arise, My Love*. Released in November 1940, the film opens by raising the still-touchy subject of the recently concluded Spanish Civil War, with a female reporter (Colbert) pulling off an impersonation to help an American aviator (Milland) escape from imprisonment for fighting with the Loyalists.

"Lookie, Lookie, Lookie, Here Goes Cookie!" are the last words the captive Tom Martin chooses to deliver (in song) to a priest as he's about to be executed by Franco's regime. Tom hits on that mocking note after he rejects more conventional sendoffs, "Death to tyrants!" and "Long live liberty!" That surprising and invigorating moment from the aviator slightly modifies a Mack Gordon hit sung by Gracie Allen in Paramount's *Here Comes Cookie* (1935) and by Cooper in *Bluebeard's Eighth Wife*. It signals that we're going to be in an irreverent Billy Wilder movie with elements of black comedy undercutting patriotic clichés.

If only all of *Arise, My Love* had lived up to that moment.

The intricate Brackett and Wilder screenplay was based on Théry's adaptation of an original story by Benjamin Glazer and Hans Székely, aka John S. Toldy (the story won an Academy Award, probably more because of its topicality than for its quality). Tom is sprung by the ambitious American wire service fashion columnist masquerading as his wife, Augusta "Gusto" Nash. That leads to an hour of mostly light romantic comedy about his attempt to wear down her resistance to emotional commitment while she interviews him in Paris for a feature celebrating (and gilding) his heroism. Single-mindedly devoted to advancing her career, Gusto worries about losing her professional focus if she surrenders to love. Tom is at loose ends, depressed over the failure of the Loyalist cause and vacillating about his future commitment to "the main event" after those "palooka preliminaries."

Gusto has the racing reporter spirit Wilder displayed in Vienna and Berlin, and Tom, the jaded but insouciant idealist, is given Wilder's own birthdate of June 22, 1906. The couple are drawn together but kept at an emotional distance by their common tendency toward reluctant romanticism, a conflict Wilder explores fruitfully throughout his career. Although Tom unfairly scorns Gusto as "Miss Willpower" and complains, "I ran into an iceberg," the best sequence intercuts him waiting at a café with her pacing restlessly in her hotel room across the street, unsure whether to join him. "Oh, That Mitzi!" from Lubitsch's Paris-set Paramount musical *One Hour with You* (codirected with George Cukor, 1932) plays on the soundtrack (other Lubitschean references abound). The coming of the world war gradually overtakes the couple's romance in *Arise, My Love*. That mixture could have been bracing if handled more smoothly, but the film unfortunately comes off as schizoid and heavy-handed as it accelerates the laying-on of rhetorical speechifying.

Wilder was out of his creative element in trying to help craft what turned into a fervent appeal for American engagement in the world conflict. But *Arise, My Love* nevertheless was a somewhat gutsy project for Paramount to make in early 1940. Even with its wrapping inside the soothing commercial format of the romantic comedy genre, it is "the strongest of the anti-isolationist films" made by Hollywood before the attack on Pearl Harbor, Bernard F. Dick writes in his book *The Star-Spangled Screen: The American World War II Film* (1985). Since the studios were mostly avoiding topical films about fascism, antifascist Hollywood filmmakers, even after the outbreak of World War II in September 1939, were confused about how to make use of their talents politically other than donating to antifascist causes and joining the Hollywood Anti-Nazi League. But most of the American public was still strongly isolationist even by the time *Arise, My Love* went into production just after the June 1940 French surrender to Germany. Right-wing, anti-Roosevelt members of Congress were actively trying to discourage the attempts of filmmakers to rouse public opinion against the Axis Powers. Nevertheless, Hollywood's involvement was intensifying as a result of the Nazi invasion of Poland, the fall of France, and the Battle of Britain.

As Larry Ceplair and Steven Englund write in *The Inquisition in Holly-wood: Politics in the Hollywood Film Community, 1930–60* (1980), the studios were "somewhat in advance of their audience in hawkishness," and Hollywood began to make more "films sympathetic to the British, opposed to the Germans, and supportive of war readiness." But the isolationist America First Committee "expressed outrage and opposition to the few features and newsreels which, in Hollywood's tepid fashion, seemed to be promoting American entry into the war." The committee accused the industry of "a violent propaganda campaign" in support of President Roosevelt's interventionist agenda. In mid-1941 the Senate Subcommittee on War Propaganda began investigating Hollywood films about the world situation, including *Confessions of a Nazi Spy, Escape* (1940), Chaplin's *The Great Dictator, Sergeant York,* and *Dive Bomber* (1941). The industry responded with what Ceplair and Englund call "an overwhelming counteroffensive from studio management." Increasing support among the American populace for the Allied cause and revulsion against the anti-Semitic positions of America First and its allies in the Senate helped scuttle the congressional investigation. Shortly before Pearl Harbor in December 1941, "the Subcommittee's case collapsed of its own emptiness." But this shabby episode served as a prelude to the renewed attack by Congress on Hollywood during the Cold War, when the film industry, from fear of being accused of communist sympathies and "premature antifascism" (to use the Orwellian term thrown at the Hollywood left), caved in and instituted the blacklist in 1947. That was the issue that finally ruptured the relationship between Brackett and Wilder.

The interlacing of the political background with the couple's romantic flirtation in *Arise, My Love* works well enough for the first hour before the wartime setting—continuously revised by the screenwriters under the pressure of actual world events—becomes the foreground. The jarring shift to darkly dramatic disruptions of the budding romance, complete with grim newsreel footage of the Germans invading one country after another, drives out most of the comedic elements. The change of tone plausibly reflects the film's thematic concentration on the importance of individual engagement with world events, the same point Humphrey Bogart will make in Warners' *Casablanca* two years later when he tells Ingrid Bergman, "Ilsa, I'm no good at being noble, but it doesn't take much to see that the problems of three little people don't amount to a hill of beans in this crazy world." But that theme is seam-lessly handled in *Casablanca*, and the writers of *Arise, My Love* and Leisen don't know how to control the abrupt shift they clumsily attempt.

The Star-Spangled Screen reports, "Since Paramount still had distribution facilities in Germany when *Arise, My Love* was being filmed (24 June–15 August, 1940), the studio decided to shoot scenes with anti-Nazi dialogue in two versions: one [toned down] for the foreign market, one for the domestic. The decision, however, was unnecessary: two days after *Arise, My Love* was completed, the Nazi government imposed its ban on American films." Among the anti-Nazi references are such Wilderian jokes as Tom's dubbing a rat in his Spanish cell "Adolf" and Gusto replacing a Berlin correspondent who committed the offense of "yelling for gefilte fish" at a reception for Foreign Minister Joachim von Ribbentrop. *Arise, My Love* veers into seriousness with such incidents as a re-creation of the September 3, 1939, torpedoing of the SS *Athenia*, the first British ship sunk by the Germans in the war (more than 110 passengers and crew died; one of the people rescued was Nicola Lubitsch, the director's infant daughter).

That catastrophe is part of the film's prolonged finale, a trial to watch with its succession of temporizing endings, as if it doesn't know how to finish but keeps getting updated with each day's news arriving on the set. According to Chierichetti's book on Leisen, that was literally true: the director "told the press that he was holding off shooting the end of the film until the last day, and the conclusion would be dictated by the newspaper headlines that morn-ing." Tom and Gusto being saved from the sinking is not even the climax, which is reserved for the film's uncharacteristic (for Wilder) flag-waving speechifying about saving the world from fascism. That may have been rous-ing at the time but comes off as trite and corny today, especially in this some-what frivolous context.

As a Jew anguished over the fate of his family in Europe and anxious over his own failure to take direct action against fascism while he stayed in Hol-lywood making movies, Wilder no doubt felt those sentiments urgently at the time—as well as the religious sentiments he rarely allowed to enter his work as they do here—but he and Brackett don't manage to make the rheto-ric sound organic. *Arise, My Love* draws its title from the Old Testament Song of Solomon and works it into an ending oration by Gusto in the Forest of

Compiègne after the bitter low point of the French surrender: "Tom, remember your prayer [every time he takes off in his plane]? This time we have to say it to America—'Arise, my love, arise, be strong!' So you can stand up straight and say to anyone under God's heaven, all right, whose way of life shall it be, yours or ours?" Anticipating the Manichean rhetoric of Capra's wartime *Why We Fight* series, this fade-out is in keeping with the propagandistic God-is-on-our-side exhortations common in American films made during the war.

Wilder privately was not irreligious, but overt religiosity seems jarring in the context of a film that starts out as a jaunty romantic comedy. His European journalism reveals a fascination with flying that he shared by many people in the Roaring Twenties, and Tom's ritualistic invocation of the Bible verses while soaring into the air is echoed in other rare religious gestures by Wilder onscreen in his film about Charles Lindbergh's 1927 transatlantic flight, *The Spirit of St. Louis*. Lindbergh is portrayed as irreligious, but he gets some quasi-supernatural help. After falling asleep in flight, he is saved by sunlight "miraculously" reflecting from a mirror on his instrument panel; it was given to him by a young woman (Patricia Smith) who appears serendipitously just before his takeoff, like an angel, telling him she came all the way from Philadelphia because "I had to. You needed the mirror." And he does not realize until near the end of his flight that he has been accompanied by a medal of St. Christopher (the patron saint of travelers) sent to him by a priest (Marc Connelly, the playwright of *Green Pastures*) who once took lessons from the barnstorming aviator; an anxious colleague surreptitiously slipped the medal into Lindbergh's sandwich bag before his departure. The medal flashes in the sunlight before Lindbergh reverentially hangs it on the instrument panel as if to help guide him to his landing. And the panicky Lindbergh invokes the priest's landing prayer, saying, "O God, help me," as the medal trembles on the panel just before his plane touches ground in Paris. However uncharacteristic of Wilder, that is a potent scene.

While interviewing Tom in *Arise, My Love*, Gusto asks him, "Did you ever meet Lindbergh?" But when he denies her suggestion that Lindbergh's flight inspired him to become an aviator, she concocts a mendacious tale like a reporter from *The Front Page*, that Tom was "in New York, one of the million cheering throats waving flags as [Lindbergh] rolled up the avenue, and right then and there you made your final decision to fly or die, hmm? You don't mind a little embroidery?"*

The patriotic, flag-waving denouement of *Arise, My Love* feels strangely qualified in light of what the two characters actually do. In the throes of their romance, they earlier decided to flee the war and go back home to America, abandoning their posts in Europe. Tom flies one last rescue mission after the ship sinks, and despite declaring that he won't desert the wartime cause, he conveniently shatters his arm and has to return to the States as a flying instructor. Gusto insists she can write patriotic messages more freely in America than in Europe: "We're marching back, both of us!" Those sentiments seem like rationalizations. They may reflect the mixed messages being sent by the still-uncommitted United States in the early stages of the war and some cautious handling on Paramount's part. But they also might reflect Wilder's own reluctance to serve in the war and the guilt he evidently felt, despite his personal obligations to his imperiled family back in Europe.

Brackett's diary records revealing arguments he and Wilder had in October 1947 over Wilder's failure to join the U.S. Army when he was offered a commission in the early stages of the war. As Brackett admits, he advised Wilder he could do more good making films in Hollywood than enlisting or accepting an opportunity for a wartime commission as a civilian making propaganda films, but Wilder complained in retrospect, "You did the one mean thing to me—you kept me out of the Army." Wilder did finally serve with the army, but it was as a civilian (in uniform) from May to September 1945 in Germany and Austria. Officially he went back to Germany as production chief for the Film, Theatre, and Music Control Section of the Army Psychological Warfare Division of the Supreme Headquarters Allied Expeditionary Force (SHAEF). He was supposed to oversee the reconstruction of the German film and theater industries and, as part of the de-Nazification process, help decide who should be allowed to resume work. But other than for his work on *Death Mills*, the documentary about the Holocaust, Wilder's duties were largely fruitless, as were the efforts of the German colleague who

---

*   In Wilder's film *Sunset Blvd.*, when Norma (Swanson) goes back to Paramount to see her former director, Cecil B. DeMille, she says, "Last time I saw you was someplace very gay. I remember waving to you. I was dancing on a table." DeMille replies, "Lots of people were. Lindbergh had just landed in Paris."

succeeded him in the de-Nazification mission, producer Erich Pommer. De-Nazification was soon dampened by the cynically pragmatic American decision to work with former Nazis in government and intelligence because the Cold War with the USSR took precedence.

Wilder's belated decision to join the army and his work back home during the war may have evoked some of the feelings of helplessness he felt watching an old Jewish man being beaten by Nazis in 1933 Berlin and in failing to persuade his mother to leave Vienna. Those conflicted feelings helped color his somewhat muddled approach to *Arise, My Love*. The most tangible result of Wilder's eventual military service was to make his 1948 Hollywood film about postwar Berlin, *A Foreign Affair*, a far more trenchant blend of romantic comedy and political drama than *Arise, My Love*. The protagonist of *A Foreign Affair* is an Army Intelligence officer who, like Wilder, is involved in the de-Nazification effort but has become thoroughly jaded by the corruption surrounding him in the ruined city. The film outgrew its originally stated (and perhaps partly disingenuous) intent to become something far more provocative. Unlike *Arise, My Love*, it avoids the usual propagandistic approach of Hollywood films dealing with the American military and shows how he had learned to put a more personal, idiosyncratic stamp on films with wartime characters.

A Foreign Affair arose out of "Propaganda Through Entertainment," a memo Wilder wrote to the army on August 16, 1945, proposing a feature that would be effective precisely because it would avoid the more obvious kind of propaganda about the situation in Berlin:

> I found the town mad, depraved, starving, fascinating as a background for a movie. My notebooks are filled with hot stuff. . . . As for the GI, I shall not make him a flag-waving hero or a theorizing apostle of democracy. As a matter of fact, in the beginning of the picture I want him not to be too sure of what the hell this war was all about. I want to touch on fraternization, on homesickness, on the black market. Furthermore (although it is a "love story") boy does *not* get girl, He goes back home with his division while the girl [a starving, suicidal German widow of an officer in the Luftwaffe] "sees the light." There shall be no pompous messages. . . . I am conceited enough to say that you will find this "entertainment" film the best propaganda yet."

Rather than humiliating the Germans with the storyline of that project, Wilder wanted to give them a glimmer of hope so they could rehabilitate themselves. The film he made for Paramount in 1947–1948 included aerial footage he shot of the ruins in 1947 and followed the earlier provocative general outline in some but not all respects. The final result onscreen was so irreverent, so psychologically and politically authentic, so daringly unlike the usual Hollywood jingoistic fare, that it caused consternation at Paramount and within the U.S. government.*

The brilliant, audacious way Wilder had of taking the mickey out of potentially schmaltzy situations in *A Foreign Affair* stands in stark contrast to the hollow preachments at the end of *Arise, My Love.* Cloaking that topical film's propaganda in escapist entertainment may have seemed clever or devious in 1940, but Wilder and Brackett did so far less effectively than with the temporal and aesthetic distance they later achieved by making their postwar film set in the ruins of Berlin.

"GARBO LAUGHS"

"Russian girl saturated with Bolshevist ideals goes to fearful, capitalistic, monopolistic Paris. She meets romance and has an uproarious good time. Capitalism not so bad, after all."

That was Melchior Lengyel's story pitch for *Ninotchka.* He was a Hungarian playwright and screenwriter who supplied the story material for three other major Lubitsch films, *Forbidden Paradise, Angel,* and *To Be or Not to Be.* He fully deserved his Academy Award nomination for the original story of *Ninotchka,* which he wrote with Greta Garbo in mind after learning that MGM was looking for a comedy to advertise with the tag line "Garbo Laughs" (an echo of its "Garbo Talks" tag for *Anna Christie* in 1930). Lengyel's outline for *Ninotchka* may have been sketchy but contained the essence of the story. Although the film won no Oscars, it also received nominations for Brackett, Wilder, and Reisch as screenwriters, for Garbo, and for MGM for best

* The screenplay of *A Foreign Affair* is credited to Brackett and Wilder and Richard L. Breen, adapted by Robert Harari from an original story by David Shaw (whose brother, novelist Irwin Shaw, also contributed without credit).

picture, yet not for Lubitsch. That may seem inexplicable for such a masterful work of direction, but comedies usually have been slighted in the Oscars, and *Ninotchka* had unusually stiff competition in 1939, often regarded as the greatest year in Hollywood's history (although the best film of that year was *The Rules of the Game*).

Lubitsch, with his Russian roots, and his screenwriters took the story idea and gave it depths of characterization, emotional weight, contemporary urgency, and a more nuanced political point of view. The film allows the initially stern Soviet commissar, Nina Ivanovna Yakushova, on a trade mission to Paris, and her French playboy lover, "Count" Leon d'Algout (Melvyn Douglas), to parry with intelligent arguments for their respective ideologies while coming together in their incongruous love affair. While *Ninotchka* indeed is slanted toward "capitalism not so bad," it is "one of the rare Hollywood anticommunist films that can be watched today not with embarrassment but delight," as I write in *How Did Lubitsch Do It?*, since its satire is so sophisticated and knowledgeable and its characterizations so memorably rounded. While the film's political acuity was partly due to Wilder's background as a European reporter, Lubitsch also had strong antitotalitarian instincts. *Ninotchka* drew cogently from the director's horrified firsthand observations of Stalinist brutality and conformity and the bleak life of the common people on a visit to Moscow in early 1936; he cut short that honeymoon trip with his second wife, Vivian, who was part Russian.

But getting to the beautifully constructed, seamlessly interwoven blend of romance and political satire in the final screenplay was a long and complicated process. Lubitsch inherited the project after George Cukor departed to direct *Gone With the Wind*, from which, in a notorious example of Hollywood musical chairs, Cukor was fired, leading him to direct another film for MGM in 1939, *The Women*. Writer-producer Gottfried Reinhardt (Max's son and an assistant to Lubitsch on *Design for Living*) since 1937 had been developing with other writers the project that finally was called *Ninotchka* (after a series of other titles were floated, including *A Kiss for the Commissar*, *We Want to Be Alone*, and *A Foreign Affair*). Those who worked on the script included Lengyel himself, Jacques Deval (the French playwright of *Tovaritch*, a comedy about White Russian exiles in Paris filmed in 1937 as *Tovarich*, meaning "comrade"), and S. N. Behrman (the playwright who had contributed to some of Garbo's classics at MGM, including *Queen Christina* and *Anna Karenina*).

Some of the key scenes had been roughed out—including the couple's visit to the Eiffel Tower, trysts in Leon's apartment, and the celebrated restaurant scene in which Ninotchka finally breaks down and laughs—but the script was in disarray when Lubitsch came aboard and won the right from the studio to control its reworking.

Lubitsch had been at loose ends since Paramount, his home base since the late 1920s, had let him go following the successive box office disappointments of *Angel* and *Bluebeard's Eighth Wife*. His pet project was *The Shop Around the Corner*, an adaptation of Miklós László's play *Parfumerie*, but he could not get it financed, even after buying the property to produce independently and paying Samson Raphaelson to write his brilliant screenplay. During that period, Brackett observed in his diary on June 3, 1938: "Worked all day at Billy's [on *Midnight*], having luncheon at Little Hungary with Ernst Lubitsch, who has no studio commitment, a rather terrifying thought, since one would think that he would have been made quantities of irresistible offers." Eventually, Lubitsch figured out how to get *Shop* filmed as a low-budget MGM production by making a two-picture deal contingent on his making the more expensive and glamorous *Ninotchka* first. Both became among his personal favorites and most beloved pictures.

For the script of *Ninotchka*, Lubitsch turned to the Viennese writer-director Reisch—Wilder's friend and colleague from Berlin who became a longtime friend of Lubitsch's as well—before borrowing Brackett and Wilder from Paramount to join the team in March 1939. One of Reisch's crucial contributions was to turn what Ninotchka is trying to sell in Paris—a Siberian nickel mine—into diamonds, the confiscated crown jewels of an exiled White Russian grand duchess. Behrman was not pleased, but Lubitsch explained, "You can photograph them sparkling on the tits of a woman." The combination of talents made magic. Lubitsch's finesse with romantic comedy was not impeded this time by having to follow the roughhousing formulas of the screwball genre but was allowed to play out in gentler, more civilized, droll exchanges between two sophisticated people. Because Lubitsch was operating in familiar and congenial territory, his creative personality is dominant in *Ninotchka*, although Wilder and the other writers helped him navigate the shoals of political satire.

As is often the case in the largely artificial world of Lubitschean comedy, the characters are fully aware of their role-playing. Ninotchka and Leon negotiate the nature of romantic attraction in a sociopolitical situation that does everything, at first, to work against it. The meta aspects of much of the dialogue play out most spectacularly in the seduction scene in Leon's apartment, an elaborately witty debate in which he gives Ninotchka a lengthy, earnestly poetic lecture on love, and she says simply, "You're very talkative." She insists that "Love is a romantic designation for a most ordinary biological, or shall we say chemical, process." But the scene is punctuated by kisses eagerly received and given by the deceptively prudish-seeming commissar, much to Leon's surprise and delight. With the couple poignantly seen from an overhead angle, making them appear more vulnerable, she murmurs that their kiss was "restful" and commands, *"Again!"* After she repeats the kiss, Leon echoes her verbal command, an example of how the film plays with genre and gender conventions. Such affectionate, teasing humor about love and sexual attraction was perfectly attuned to Lubitsch's knowing approach to romantic comedy and the complex relations between the sexes.

Aside from a few choice visual touches—such as the gag about cigarette girls going in and out the door of the commissars' suite as they succumb to off-screen debauchery or the dissolve from the men's Russian hats as they turn into Western luxury items—the film is shot in Lubitsch's recently adopted "invisible" style. It was designed to get around censorship by disguising his post-Code hand even more than before, but this film's concentration on the intricate dialogue of courtship more than on innuendo about off-screen sexual activity evidently helped make it less censorable. Richard J. Anobile, who edited a 1975 photo book of images and dialogue from *Ninotchka*, misleadingly describes Lubitsch's direction as "plain and unobtrusive" and even claims that "one would be hard pressed to consider his style cinematic. Lubitsch's *Ninotchka* could easily have been a stage play." Actually, the camera is frequently making small and subtle, perfectly calibrated but hardly noticeable movements to heighten emotion, provide critical distance, or capture complex moods with Lubitsch's always cinematically expressive blocking. As François Truffaut declared in his 1968 essay on Lubitsch, "If you said to me, 'I have just seen a Lubitsch in which there was one needless shot,' I'd call you a liar. His cinema is the opposite of the vague, the imprecise, the unformulated, the incommunicable. There's not a single shot just for decoration; nothing is included just because it looks good. From beginning to end, we are involved only in what's essential."

The dialogue is less oblique than usual for a Lubitsch film, due to the characters' concentration on political ideas and Wilder's career-long obsession with clarity. Brackett complained in 1941 about what he called "Billy's terrifying neurosis that everything isn't crystal clear to the audience." One of Wilder's wry screenwriting maxims was "Make subtlety obvious," which was written on a plaque above the table reserved for him in his old age at the Beverly Hills restaurant Mr. Chow. But despite that difference in approach between Wilder and Lubitsch, much of the feeling in *Ninotchka* comes between the lines, from evanescent expressions on Garbo's face that qualify or contradict Ninotchka's doctrinaire political views. Wilder tried to hang out on the set to watch Garbo at work, but she thwarted him. He said later, "The face, that face, what was it about that face? You could read into it all the secrets of a woman's soul. You could read Eve, Cleopatra, Mata Hari. She became all women on the screen. Not on the sound stage. *The miracle happened in that film emulsion*. Who knows why? Marilyn Monroe had this same gift." *Ninotchka* also glows with Lubitsch's love of cinematic artifice in MGM's elegant equivalent of "Paris, Paramount," this time photographed by Garbo's favorite cameraman, William H. Daniels. The delicate score by Werner R. Heymann, who worked on five other Lubitsch films and three other films written by Wilder (including *Bluebeard's Eighth Wife*), contributes to making *Ninotchka* one of the screen's most memorable love stories.

Ninotchka is one of the gems of Wilder's career as well as Lubitsch's and equal to any Wilder directed. It is not heavy-handed propaganda like *Arise, My Love* but a shrewd political allegory embedded inextricably and gracefully in the romantic comedy genre. The self-conscious nature of the odd couple's role-playing and the gradual stripping-away of their facades to reveal them as genuine romantics brought out the best in Wilder, who shared the director's propensity for game-playing and lent the story his own fascination with masquerading and revelation. Wilder's own views of romance perhaps had somewhat mellowed since he had married in 1936. But Judith was conservative, and their political differences may have influenced the script of *Ninotchka*. The ideological tensions between Ninotchka, who says on her entrance, "Don't make an issue of my womanhood," and the suave Leon, who earns his living as a kept man for the Grand Duchess Swana, also seem to have drawn fruitfully from the differences in political views and temperament between Brackett and Wilder. Wilder's experiences as an *Eintänzer* and his career-long concentration on the conflicts between money and love, between soulless sex and love, are reflected in the romanticism just under the surface of Leon's professional charm. When he declares a "complete readjustment of my way of living" after falling in love with Ninotchka, Swana cynically comments that has "the ugly sound of regeneration." Her cruelty as a niece of the deposed czar leaves no room for change (she longs for the good old days when peasants could be whipped), but the script also brings out her insecurities and bitterness toward the loss of her homeland, allowing us to see her in Ina Claire's subtly inflected performance as a human being rather than merely a heartless villain.

The film generously gives the best possible arguments it can find for both Ninotchka and Leon to defend the respective systems that control their lives, while simultaneously allowing us to view them and their ideologies from a satirical distance. Douglas was not the first choice for Leon—William Powell was cast but became ill, and Cary Grant, Gary Cooper, and Clark Gable turned down the role—and though Douglas was something of a second-rate star, his less glamorous appearance works to the film's advantage. He was a keenly intelligent actor with a self-aware, self-mocking approach to playing a gigolo that helps make him appealing to Ninotchka as well as to the audience. His amused reaction to her hostility helps break down her reserve. When she asks what he does for mankind, he wryly replies, "For mankind? Yes, uh, not so much. But for womankind, the record is not quite so bleak." Leon's defenses of capitalism tend to be apologias for luxury and appreciation of its aesthetic value, two items Lubitsch always takes seriously in his films. Ninotchka more fervently defends her country's sociopolitical system, often in impassioned close-up, pointing out the technological advances of the USSR following its liberation from czarist rule, although that premise is qualified by her acknowledgment about their need to prevent the people's suffering from hunger and by the script's commentaries on Stalinist repression. Her mission to Paris to sell Swana's crown jewels is undertaken to make up for crop shortages, the sign of a flawed economic system (she speaks with expertise, being an economist by profession). Her final line, even though delivered in exile, is defiant: "No one shall say Ninotchka was a bad Russian!"

But she unconsciously betrays her country when she chillingly declares early in the film, in a matter-of-fact tone, "The last mass trials were a great success. There are going to be fewer but better Russians." Wilder biographer Ed Sikov misattributes the authorship of her remarks, calling them "the first truly offensive line[s] in Billy Wilder's screen career" and evidence of how Wilder "earned a reputation for being the master of mass bad taste." Brackett reported, however, that this macabre but painfully candid joke was written by Lubitsch himself. In 1952, defending the film's political viewpoint during the McCarthy era, Brackett wrote, "This happens to be a line tossed into the script by Ernst Lubitsch, but I spring to its defense with ardor, as would Billy Wilder. Could a single sentence better compress the inhuman Russian point of view? Could that point of view be held up to ridicule in a healthier way?" This touch of dark humor is an unusual acknowledgment in a 1930s Hollywood film of the brutality of the Stalinist purge trials and the Great Terror. *Ninotchka* drew vividly from Lubitsch's observations in Moscow of the people's deprivation, lack of privacy, conformism, and fear.

Lubitsch had become a citizen of Germany before that was stripped away by the Nazis in 1935 because he was Jewish; the following January he became a citizen of the United States. He was under no illusions about Stalinism after having witnessed it in action on his trip to the USSR. Upon his return he resigned from the Hollywood Anti-Nazi League, a Popular Front organization, telling Salka Viertel, "I know it from a reliable source that the Reds are controlling the Anti-Nazi League." Instead, in October 1939 he prominently rejoined the antifascist cause by helping run the European Film Fund with Paul Kohner and others. Lubitsch was a liberal, not a conservative, but he was instinctively antiauthoritarian. He was deeply troubled by the postwar Hollywood Red Scare and infuriated by the 1947 HUAC hearings. His view of the USSR, however, was not clouded by false sentimentality, unlike those in Hollywood who looked the other way at the true nature of Stalinism. Lubitsch was said to have based Ninotchka partly on the actress and writer Ingeborg (Inge) von Wangenheim, whom he visited in Moscow. The wife of an actor in two of his German films, Gustav von Wangenheim, she had been living in Moscow since 1933 as what Lubitsch considered a slavish communist ideologue. When she finally saw *Ninotchka* in the 1970s, she proved him correct by denouncing it in her memoir as a "counterrevolutionary concoction."

Wilder was more of a leftist than Lubitsch, and the *Life* profile of Brackett and Wilder in 1944 reported, "Wilder has mixed feelings about *Ninotchka* because as a Russophile he fears it offended the U.S.S.R. 'I've always wanted to see Odessa,' he mused recently, 'and now I'm afraid we never will.' 'I can last a long time,' said Brackett, 'without seeing Odessa.'" Nevertheless, Zolotow reports that "almost all of the anti-Soviet jibes" came from Wilder; his scripts are full of political gags, even in the most unlikely everyday situations. When the store owner in *Bluebeard's Eighth Wife*'s extended "meet-cute" objects to selling pajama pants and tops separately, he exclaims, "Oh, no, no, never, never! Well, this is Communism!" The harried floor manager explains to Cooper's Michael Brandon, "The consequences might prove disastrous. Now, our president says we've had enough trouble in Europe as it is." Wilder's caustic wit compelled him to needle people on all sides of the political spectrum, and *Ninotchka* works so well partly because it skewers both systems with well-aimed arrows, considerably sharper and more elaborate than the offhand ones in *Bluebeard*.

Among the choice anti-Soviet jibes are Leon's quip when he realizes that Ninotchka is a Russian: "I love Russians. Comrade, I've been fascinated by your Five-Year Plan for the last fifteen years." She retorts, "Your type will soon be extinct." The coldly mercenary nature of capitalism is exposed in Leon's somewhat ashamedly being a kept man, his devious manipulation of the three comical Soviet commissars (Sig Rumann [later Ruman], Felix Bressart, and Alexander Granach) originally sent before Ninotchka to sell the crown jewels, and Leon's suavely executed bargaining over the jewels. This dual vein of satire is combined on Ninotchka's arrival in Paris when she sternly asks the railroad porter why he wants to carry her bags, and he replies with his quip about the importance of tipping. And when a smooth-talking Parisian jeweler tells the commissars he regrets he will have to take a loss on the deal but is undertaking it only for prestige, two of them mutter, "Capitalistic methods.—They accumulate millions by taking loss after loss."

Although Lubitsch sometimes is mistakenly considered an apolitical director, his films, the comedies as well as his historical spectacles, offer many trenchant social observations. Aaron Schuster persuasively links *Ninotchka* with *Trouble in Paradise* (his romantic comedy dealing with the Great Depression) and *To Be or Not to Be* (his black comedy about Nazism): "These three films, the most socially conscious in Lubitsch's oeuvre, form a kind of trilogy which deals with the crisis of capitalism and its two historic solutions: fascism and communism." Lubitsch acknowledged in a 1939 interview, "We can't make pictures in a vacuum now. We must show people living in the real world. No one used to care how characters made their living—if the picture was amusing. Now they do care. They want their stories tied up to life. . . . Now [a character] must have a job, or else the fact that he doesn't work becomes the important thing about him."

Leon's many impassioned tributes to the sensuality and gaiety of Parisian society (such as telling Ninotchka when the clock in his apartment strikes midnight, "One half of Paris is making love to the other half") are shadowed by his own ironic recognition of his uselessness as what she calls "the arrogant male in capitalistic society." As they gaze over the skyline at night from the Eiffel Tower and he tries to divert her attention from its technological achievement to the city's aesthetic appeal, Ninotchka tells him, "Now, don't misunderstand me. I do not hold your frivolity against you. As basic material, you may not be bad. But you are the unfortunate product of a doomed culture. I feel very sorry for you." Unfazed, he replies, "Ah, but you must admit that this doomed old civilization sparkles. Look at it. It glitters!" She replies, "I do not deny its beauty. But it is a waste of electricity." The gradual thawing of Ninotchka's icy demeanor and emotional reserve (after Leon's flirting prompts her to order, "Suppress it") under the warmth of Western freedom and luxury and Leon's devoted, cleverly insightful wooing makes her one of many characters in Wilder films who learn to move from repression to liberation.

From all accounts, the writing process on the final version of *Ninotchka* went far more smoothly than the clash of styles on *Bluebeard*. Wilder deferred to Lubitsch gratefully, since they were more at ease collaborating by then, and Lubitsch was working at full strength. Wilder paid him the screenwriter's ultimate compliment: "I think that all the pictures that he made should have his name as a collaborator, at least on the script. You don't just sit down and write, 'Lubitsch does this.' You come up with twenty suggestions, and he picks the one that makes a Lubitsch touch. . . . What he did was purify, and that was what made him a great writer. . . . If the truth were known, he was the best writer that ever lived. Most of the 'Lubitsch touches' came from him." Brackett felt the same way. He said in 1959, "I feel it is wicked that Billy Wilder and Walter Reisch and I are even mentioned in connection with *Ninotchka*; it was so much Ernst Lubitsch's own baby. He was a director in a creative frenzy at the time, and everything he did was to me wonderful and funny and stimulating. . . . I give him the full credit for the picture."

The example Wilder liked to cite of how Lubitsch worked with his writers is what he called "the famous Lubitsch key scene." It's actually an intricately developed three-step gag. Wilder recalled, "We worked weeks [in Lubitsch's house] wondering how we could show that Garbo, in *Ninotchka*, was becoming bourgeois—that she was starting to become interested in capitalist things. We wrote a bunch of different things." Then one day during a story conference, Lubitsch disappeared into the bathroom. When he came out, he declared, 'Boys, I've got it. I've got the answer. It's the hat.'"

Upon her arrival in the Paris hotel, Ninotchka passes a silly-looking conical women's hat in a lobby display case and says, with a smug shake of her head, "How can such a civilization survive which permits their women to put things like that on their heads? It won't be long now, comrades." Crucially, there is a second stage in the buildup, as Ninotchka simply passes the showcase and shakes her head silently, but a bit less vehemently. Lubitsch finally reveals how she has changed by having her shoo the three commissars out of her suite, lock two doors, kneel in front of a chest, unlock a drawer, and take out that very hat, putting it on and looking at herself in a mirror.

In his interview documentary with Volker Schlöndorff, Wilder comments in German, "And we know this woman has been—," and Schlöndorff interjects, "*beschädigt*," meaning "corrupted" or "damaged." Wilder does not disagree; in another interview he said "she has fallen into the trap of capitalism, and we know where we're going from there." The subtle difference between Wilder's mordant worldview and Lubitsch's perspective is evident in the more ambiguous filming of the scene. There is a bittersweet feeling in the quizzical way Ninotchka studies herself in the mirror, head in hand (the script says she is "aghast at seeing a complete stranger"), but Lubitsch regards the progression of her attitude toward Western frivolity more positively. He approves of her gradual metamorphosis from a woman who is all business to one who also cares about luxury and the sensual side of her nature. The careful preparation for this transformation, the structure of the tripartite gag, is what makes it so persuasive. Wilder said of this Lubitsch Touch, "That's not a screenwriter's idea. It's the idea of a plastic artist." And he recalled, "It's funny, but we noticed that whenever he came up with an idea, I mean a really *great* idea, it was after he came out of the can. I started to suspect that he had a little ghostwriter in the bowl of the toilet there. . . . I guess now I feel he didn't go enough."*

Wilder was quickly learning from Lubitsch how to be more of a plastic artist, how to express feelings in pictures as much as in words. Those lessons he would carry with him throughout the directing career he resumed three years later, in which he tried to emulate Lubitsch's elegant camerawork. And though Wilder was more explicit in his narrative style than Lubitsch—and yet with hidden subtexts coursing beneath the surfaces of his stories—he kept in mind as much as possible, with his sly verbal and visual wit, another key lesson from his mentor. Wilder defined the Lubitsch Touch as "a different way of thinking. Lubitsch is difficult to copy. He is a director who is not afraid that people won't understand him, unlike those who say, Two plus two makes four, and one plus three also makes four, and one plus one plus one plus one also makes four. But Lubitsch says, Two plus two—that's it. The public has to add it up." And if you let the audience add it up, Lubitsch told him, "They'll love you forever."†

MGM publicity to the contrary, Garbo had laughed before onscreen, as she does in Rouben Mamoulian's 1933 *Queen Christina* and Cukor's 1936 *Camille*, but she relished the chance to play her first outright comedy. She said in a 1938 interview, "I am tired of period pictures and I want to do something modern now. My next film is to be a comedy. . . . Will I be allowed to keep my lover in it? Certainly I am hoping so. Don't you think it is high time they let me end a picture happily with a kiss? I do. I seem to have lost so many attractive men in the final scenes." Although Lubitsch

---

*   *Ninotchka* was turned into a Cole Porter stage musical, *Silk Stockings*, in 1955, with a book by George S. Kaufman, Leueen MacGrath, and Abe Burrows, and remade for the screen in 1957 by director Rouben Mamoulian; Cyd Charisse was cast in the Garbo role opposite Fred Astaire. As I write in *How Did Lubitsch Do It?*, "Charisse is able to convey Ninotchka's change of heart with her breathtakingly graceful dancing in an autoerotic equivalent of *Ninotchka*'s key scene, substituting silk stockings for the hat, but her acting otherwise consists mostly of granitic stares." And the character in the musical "*is* fiercely prudish before her transformation, her hardened attitude a reflection of the Cold War era's more rigidly condemnatory attitude toward Communism."

†   Wilder did not work again with Lubitsch after *Ninotchka*, partly because he became a director and because Lubitsch had decisively parted company with Wilder's home studio, Paramount. But they remained close friends and for a while even lived together. When Lubitsch was recuperating from the major heart attack he suffered in 1943, he asked Wilder, who had been living alone after breaking up with Judith, to move in with him. Wilder stayed for several weeks in Lubitsch's Bel Air home but left because he felt he was disturbing him. And he admitted to Hellmuth Karasek, "I remember how sad it all was. Above all, that someone had changed from one day to the other from a great director to a sick old man was deeply depressing."

found her "probably the most inhibited person I have ever worked with" and had to cajole her into playing drunk scenes, he realized after meeting her in 1932 that her shyness was a cover for the "fine sense of humor" he coaxed her into revealing onscreen. Her close friend Mercedes de Acosta, the Spanish poet and dramatist, wrote that during the time Garbo was making *Ninotchka*, "Never since I had known her she had been in such good spirits. She had been shooting the first gay picture she had ever done, and Lubitsch was directing it. '[It is] the first time I have had a great director since I am in Hollywood,' she said. Greta was a changed person; [she] laughed constantly. She would imitate Lubitsch's accent. . . . It was fascinating to see how by playing a gay role rather than a sad one how her whole personality changed."

Even before the climactic mirror shot, Ninotchka's personality begins to soften and flower in the great restaurant sequence, which analyzes and plays with the nature of humor much the way the seduction scene deals with romance. Both sequences rely largely on two-shots to help balance and respect the two characters' emotions. The restaurant set piece is Lubitsch's tribute to the vital importance of comedy in human life, the artistic testament of a comedic director.

Lubitsch and his writers have Leon follow Ninotchka into a humble workers' café and try to wear down her stern facade by telling a series of jokes. As she notes while keeping a deadpan and mechanically downing her meal (her humorlessness here and elsewhere is part of the sly undertone of the humor), Leon's jokes aren't particularly funny, and his increasingly strained, incensed attitude causes him to garble a punchline. Finally, in exasperation, he leans back in his chair and takes a pratfall on the floor. Laughter erupts around him. Lubitsch cuts to a medium close-up of Ninotchka, too, laughing uproariously. The script indicates, "For a split second NINOTCHKA makes an effort to control the irresistible impulse to laugh but loses the battle and herself roars with laughter." But instead, in a thrilling frisson, Lubitsch and his editor, Gene Ruggiero, capture her *already* in the act of laughing, her inhibitions thrown to the winds. Ironically, Leon doesn't think his tumble is funny, but after a pause he "sees the humor of the situation and starts to howl with laughter too. The ice is broken at last!" And the whole place laughs again as the scene fades out, an example of what Wilder called the Lubitschean "Superjoke," the topper of the topper.

The scene encapsulates Lubitsch's explanation an interviewer shortly before his death: "What exactly, you ask me, is the Lubitsch touch? . . . It's naughty and it's gay. It's based on the theory that at least twice a day the most dignified of human beings is ridiculous."*

If *Ninotchka* is more sentimental in spots than Lubitsch's films usually tend to be, that is due largely to its elegiac nature. The film was shot from May 31 to July 27, 1939, when everyone knew the world war was imminent. Its satire of the USSR, which flew in the face of the Popular Front movement, might have been more controversial had it not been for the unexpected signing of the Nazi-Soviet nonaggression pact on August 23, when the film was in postproduction. That event caused a bitter rupture in the tenuous entente between Hollywood's liberals and Communists, which was predicated on Soviet opposition to the Fascist powers. Wilder was one of those who strongly disagreed with the Hollywood Communists on that allegiance with Hitler. The war broke out on September 1 with the German invasion of Poland. Because of those events, an anxiously amusing preliminary title was added to the film over a view of Paris including two famous churches (neither of them Notre-Dame; Lubitsch always avoided the cliché), while setting the story in the just-vanished past: "THIS PICTURE TAKES PLACE IN PARIS IN THOSE WONDERFUL DAYS WHEN A SIREN WAS A BRUNETTE AND NOT AN ALARM—AND IF A FRENCHMAN TURNED OUT THE LIGHT IT WAS NOT ON ACCOUNT OF AN AIR RAID!"

Although *Ninotchka* would be banned in the USSR and censored in some other countries over the years, it was greeted with widespread popular and critical acclaim after premiering on November 3. The praise came from widely differing political viewpoints. Hearst's *New York Daily Mirror* commented, "Garbo does more in one line to debunk Soviet Russia than we have been able to do in a hundred editorials!" Otis Ferguson's review in the liberal *New Republic* observed that the "meeting-of-East-and-West" humor made it "the

---

* The restaurant set piece probably helped inspire the magnificent scene in Preston Sturges's *Sullivan's Travel* (1942) of convicts on a chain gang, including a fugitive director of Hollywood comedies, laughing uproariously at a Disney cartoon. Sturges also includes a humorous tribute to Lubitsch. When the wannabe movie actress played by Veronica Lake meets the director (Joel McCrea) in a diner, she says, "All right, give me a letter of introduction to Lubitsch." He replies with a hint of jealous peevishness, "I might be able to do that too. Who's Lubitsch?"

first movie with any airiness at all to discover that Communists are people and may be treated as such in a story."

That the film has endured as a classic with viewers across the political spectrum is due in part to that intellectual balancing act. William Paul's 1983 critical study *Ernst Lubitsch's American Comedy* points out that "Lubitsch was able to maintain something of a distance in his observation of political paradox in *Ninotchka*" because "in a universe of playful characters, Ninotchka must appear a fool, but the world itself has changed in this film: poised on the brink of chaos, it seems to certify her seriousness." And in their 1979 critical study of Wilder, Neil Sinyard and Adrian Turner make a case that *Ninotchka* "stands up as a clear example of discreet propaganda, advocating solidarity between America and the Soviet Union in the struggle against Hitler. If the ideology of Communism has to be softened a little and the lures of Capitalism informed with a certain sourness, the reconciliation between them is no less moving or meaningful. It is not what each of them represents that is important, but what each of them opposes." Seen in the light of the film's allusions to Nazism, in its preliminary title and the scene of two people ominously but comically exchanging Nazi salutes in the train station just before Ninotchka makes her first appearance, *Ninotchka* could be considered an enduring tribute to and act of faith in the spirit of the Popular Front ideal.

Ninotchka was received as both on-target with its satire and poignant in its nostalgic regret for a conflicted yet gentler period in world history at a demarcation line in epochal change. Commissar Buljanoff—played by Lubitsch's *haimish* surrogate figure, Felix Bressart, a German Jewish refugee who also appears in *The Shop Around the Corner* and *To Be or Not to Be**—tells Ninotchka at a low moment back in Moscow, "They can't censor our memories, can they?" The emotional high point, as Lubitsch and the writers had already intended but the change in circumstances made more profound, is Ninotchka's impassioned and melancholy speech in her hotel suite after she gets drunk on Champagne at a Parisian nightclub. It was foreshadowed in

---

* Bressart, born in East Prussia, was a refugee from Nazism who had appeared in numerous German films, including one Wilder reportedly helped write, *The Fight with the Dragon or: The Tenants' Tragedy*. In a chilling irony, Berlin journalist Bella Fromm, who was Jewish, reported in her March 17, 1933, diary entry: "Hitler is inordinately fond of motion pictures. He spends many hours every night in his private movie room. It takes two or three full-length pictures a night to satisfy him. Once after seeing a picture in which Felix Bressart appeared, the Fuehrer said: 'This fellow is wonderful. A pity he is a Jew.'"

Wilder's work by Lilian Harvey's wistful song on a Berlin rooftop in *A Blonde Dream* just before the Nazi takeover about how she wants to find happiness "somewhere in the world. . . . Somewhere, somehow, sometime." Leon has stopped Ninotchka from declaiming her speech to the other patrons of the posh nightclub, so in her emotionally liberated state she delivers it privately to him, but directly, in effect, to the audience: "Can I make a speech now? Comrades! People of the world! The revolution is on the march! I know— bombs will fall. Civilization will crumble. But *not yet, please*. Wait. What's the hurry? Give us our moment. Let's be happy!"

What made Lubitsch happy? Wilder remembered that on the way back from the Long Beach preview in a studio limousine with the screenwriters and MGM executives, the director was reading aloud the audience preview cards: "'Very good' . . . 'brilliant.' . . . Twenty cards. But when he comes to the twenty-first card, he starts laughing as hard as I ever saw him laugh, and we say, 'What is it?' He keeps the cards to himself; he does not let anybody even look. Then, finally, he calms down a little and starts reading. And what he read was—I have the card—"

It said, "Great picture. Funniest film I ever saw. I laughed so hard, I peed in my girlfriend's hand."

"SHE WAS—SWELL"

When actress-writer Carrie Fisher was asked by *Film Comment* in 2011 to con- tribute a "Guilty Pleasures" column, she began with *Hold Back the Dawn*:

> It was one of Billy Wilder's first [*sic*] writing credits, starring Olivia de Havilland and Charles Boyer, and it's about people who just don't belong. She's a schoolteacher, and he can't get over the [Mexico-United States] bor- der, so he marries her by lying to her because, really, he just wants to get into the States. He's a gigolo, but ultimately he falls in love with her. I went up to Billy Wilder once and said, "I love that movie." And he looked at me like I was insane.

I love that movie too. Wilder undervalued it because of a bitter run-in he had with director Mitchell Leisen and Boyer over the omission of the scene involving a cockroach. That loss convinced him he would have to return to directing to protect his scripts. Even when Wilder and Brackett saw the film in rough cut, they found it "a pretty bad picture—jerky—undistinguished in writing. . . . not a disgrace, but nothing to crow about," Brackett confided to his diary. That seems a bizarre response, but sometimes filmmakers are blind to the quality of their own work, especially if the shooting was problematical. Although *Hold Back the Dawn* was nominated for six Oscars, including best picture, actress, and adapted screenplay, it won none in the year of *Citizen Kane* and *How Green Was My Valley*. That must have rankled not only Brackett and Wilder, but even more so de Havilland, who gives one of the most moving performances of her career as Emmy Brown but notoriously lost to her sister and archenemy, Joan Fontaine, in Alfred Hitchcock's *Suspicion*.*

For a film with such a pedigree as *Hold Back the Dawn*, it is strange that it was so forgotten in recent years that it was not officially released on DVD or Blu-ray until 2019. Wilder's oft-repeated story about his displeasure with the film played a part in unfairly diminishing its reputation. Because it fell into the category of a "women's picture" or "melodrama," it probably was stigmatized for that reason as well, since reviewers and even many film historians long tended to sneer condescendingly at that genre. Even today, some still deride what are now labeled "chick flicks," although more enlightened historians recognize that "women's pictures" from Hollywood's Golden Era are among the richest in dealing frankly with social issues. The film's title, although expressive in context to refer to both characters' awakening (romantic and sexual in her case, romantic and moral in his), seems hackneyed and generic, the kind that could be applied to numerous Hollywood love stories of that period; a film's reputation can be hurt by a weak title.

Nevertheless, *Hold Back the Dawn*, like *Ninotchka*, is a major film that deserves to be regarded as among the best to which Wilder ever contributed. His vitriolic aspersions on Leisen ignore the empathetic and insightful way the director guides the performances and gives the film a believable atmosphere, including an unusual degree of location shooting for that era in Oxnard, San Clemente, and Baja California. Wilder's intense personal involvement with the story of a penniless European desperately trying to get into the United

---

* Wilder and Thomas Monroe were also nominated for the original story of *Ball of Fire* but lost to Harry Segall for *Here Comes Mr. Jordan*.

States while stagnating in a Mexican hotel, "the end of the Earth," draws from his experience in Mexicali waiting anxiously for a visa to reenter California. It also evokes his agonized temporizing as an exile in a Paris hotel and his restless years as a youth growing up in hotels (and on trains; the film describes the couple as "like two trains halted for a moment at the same station"). Boyer's Georges Iscovescu is, like Wilder, a man perpetually in transit.

A Rumanian refugee and professional continental lover, Georges is even a screenwriter of sorts. He is shown successfully pitching the story to a director (Leisen himself) on a soundstage at Paramount while on the lam from the federal police. That metafilm framing device foregrounds the story's personal nature for Wilder as a formerly struggling screenwriter and prefigures the memorable scene at the studio with Swanson and DeMille in *Sunset Blvd.* Before Georges sneaks onto a soundstage while on a tour of the lot with some American rubes, *Hold Back the Dawn* opens with a written prologue, "Perhaps the best way to begin this story is to tell you how it came to us. . . ." Leisen takes a break from the (re-created) shoot of his film *I Wanted Wings* (1941, with Brian Donlevy and Veronica Lake appearing, but not William Holden, another near-miss for Wilder) to listen skeptically, at first, to the fugitive's tale. Selling it earns Georges enough to pay back the savings he fleeced from Emmy and ultimately helps him enter the country legally by reconciling with her. So Hollywood comes to the rescue of this down-and-out exile on the run from the authorities, just as it did for Wilder. The benevolent act of an American consular official in granting Wilder a visa ("Write some good ones") is echoed in the film's depiction of a sharp but benign American immigration inspector, Hammock (Walter Abel), who does a similar favor for Georges.

Georges is a gigolo and dancer, like Wilder while he was struggling in Berlin. This heel who becomes more than "slightly reformed" by the end is one of the most acute and honest depictions of the antiheroes who populate Wilder's work. These characters get their comeuppance and/or "regeneration" often through romantic involvement of women with greater emotional sincerity. While glibly pretending to romance the intelligent but guilelessly trusting, lonely young schoolteacher from the small town of Azusa, California, the jaded, older Georges is hooking up in the hotel with an old partner in sleaze, a ruthless dancer and golddigger named Anita Dixon (Paulette Goddard). Anita may owe something (if not her crooked personality) to the girlfriend who taught the Charleston with Wilder in Berlin. The deceptively glamorous Anita is portrayed as even more heartless and contemptible than Georges, but at least she has the saving grace of self-mocking humor. Their scheme to work as a team seducing and soaking rich people in America is a striking example of Wilder's career-long concentration on the theme of prostitution.

Hold Back the Dawn is set in the summer of 1940, with Georges among a small expatriate community waiting to enter the United States during wartime. The other characters' eloquent expressions of love for American liberty and history are heartfelt statements by Wilder. They convey his deep sense of gratitude for being given a haven in his adopted country. The script makes a telling satirical point when, at a July 4 celebration, a Dutch professor (Victor Francen) writing a book on the founding of the United States while surviving in the Hotel Esperanza (the Spanish word for "hope") recites from the Emma Lazarus poem "The New Colossus," inscribed on a plaque inside the pedestal of the Statue of Liberty:

> Give me your tired, your poor,
> Your huddled masses yearning to breathe free,
> The wretched refuse of your teeming shore.
> Send these, the homeless, tempest-tost to me,
> I lift my lamp beside the golden door!

The capper is that the American immigration inspector at the celebration doesn't know who wrote the poem (and it's fitting that Lazarus was a Jewish woman). Hammock confuses the inscription with Thomas Jefferson's words "Life, Liberty and the pursuit of Happiness" in the Declaration of Independence.

With such fervent sentiments uttered by foreigners trying to enter the United States and its dramatization of actual immigration issues on the border, *Hold Back the Dawn* is not only "ripped from the pages" of 1941 headlines but also more topical today than at any other time since its release. Although the optimism of the love story of two individuals who finally manage to circumvent immigration barriers is qualified to some extent by the film's acknowledgment of the restrictive American policies toward the millions fleeing that war (especially Jews, even if they are not specifically mentioned), its hopeful expressions of belief in America's acceptance of refugees are aspirational on Wilder's part and especially poignant in today's time of rampant xenophobia. "There is a wire fence," Georges bitterly tells Leisen's director character. "You can see right through into [the] United States. If you are an American or have a visa, you just walk in. Yes—a wire fence. Don't let them tell you it's only twelve feet high. It's a thousand miles high." And to explain when he meets Emmy why he has "very little" affection for the United States, Georges says of the fence, "You Americans make a very definite point of it."

Although *Hold Back the Dawn* was adapted from a story by Katherine (Ketti) Frings, it was a substantial departure from its source material. A fan magazine writer, she based her forty-page treatment, "Memo to a Movie Producer," and the novel version published in 1940 (a movie tie-in with the same title as the film) on her involvement with a German boxer named Kurt Frings, whom she married in 1938 and divorced in 1963. They met in France, where he was working as a ski instructor, and lived for a time in the Mexican border town of Tijuana, just across from San Diego, while she commuted from Southern California until he received his entry permit in 1940. The treatment was written in the form of a letter to the film's producer, Arthur Hornblow Jr., but the couple in the story underwent radical changes when Wilder made it autobiographical.

The novel contains the basic situation of a foreigner waiting in a Mexican hotel (in Tijuana, although the town is unnamed in the film) while his American wife tries to get him a visa. The process is ultimately successful but is complicated by perjury he committed in an act of desperation while applying for a visa in Europe. The characters in the novel are one-dimensional figures, too simply and cautiously drawn from the author's own life. The ex-boxer, Klaus, is an upstanding, loyal, and somewhat pathetic fellow, and the fan magazine writer, Jennifer, is not a naif like Emmy but an earnest but creatively frustrated Hollywood hanger-on and aspiring fiction writer. Because the characters are so bland, the novel lacks the emotional drama and complexity of the screenplay, which stems from Georges's caddish, deceitful behavior toward the innocent Emmy and his gradual transformation into a mensch. Frings's novel becomes tedious because the situation has little tension other than the couple's endless waiting and bogs down in interactions with people at the hotel. Any venality is laid off awkwardly on minor characters, including one who is something like Georges, a Hungarian playboy named Tibor, whose unscrupulous behavior toward women might have helped point the screenwriters to enliven their male lead by combining him and Klaus. But Wilder's own experiences as an *Eintänzer* and man about town in Europe made Georges largely a character of his own creation.

According to Zolotow's biography of Wilder, Kurt Frings somehow obtained a copy of the screenplay and was incensed at the way he was portrayed in such an entirely different and unflattering light. Frings complained to Wilder and told Hornblow he would sue but dropped his claim when, ironically in view of the film's themes, Hornblow threatened not only to have him arrested for stealing the script but also deported. Frings eventually became a Hollywood agent, representing de Havilland, Elizabeth Taylor, and such Wilder stars as Audrey Hepburn and Hildegarde Knef.* Ketti Frings's screenwriting credits after *Hold Back the Dawn* included *The Accused* (1949) and *Come Back, Little Sheba* (1952), and she won a Pulitzer Prize in 1958 for her stage adaptation of Thomas Wolfe's novel *Look Homeward, Angel*.

Brackett and Wilder smarted over Kurt Frings's objections and believed they had turned the story into something new, which was mostly accurate, since they had created the all-important conflict between the natures of the two central characters. They managed to get their credit changed from "Screenplay by" to "Written by," the Writers Guild code for an original screenplay, while Ketti Frings received the story credit. Before shooting began, the Mexican government also raised concerns about the depiction of that country, which Paramount assuaged partly by casting Eva Puig, the widow of a former Mexican secretary of state, as the hotel maid, a part that had been assigned to an American; Lupita finds a German refugee named Wechsler hanging from the ceiling in the room that Georges, in a black-comic touch, manages to claim as his own. A comical Mexican garage mechanic was changed to a Russian, another refugee (a hilarious performance by Mikhail Rasumny). The town and hotel were depicted as less shabby than they had been envisioned in the script.

Wilder was not happy with all these pressures being exerted on the production. But it does not hurt the film that Mexico was treated with greater respect than usual in Hollywood films of that era. During a toast to American Independence Day, two of the refugees praise Mexico for giving them a

---

* I was represented briefly as a screenwriter in the early 1970s by the Kurt Frings Agency but never met him.

safe harbor, and a Mexican priest tells the newly married couple, "God bless you, good neighbors," a reference to the Roosevelt administration's Good Neighbor Policy toward Latin America. A religious festival to bless brides and bridegrooms in another small Mexican town becomes a turning point in the story, beautifully filmed with genuine warmth and reverence as the symbolic "wedding ceremony" between the uncomfortable Georges and the radiant Emmy following their perfunctory civil ceremony. Their Mexican honeymoon, although troubling because his guilt over conning her is becoming more acute as he gets to know her and see life through her eyes, helps bring him around to regarding his bride in a genuinely romantic light, abandoning his former mendacity.

His narration is our window into the inner life he conceals with his elaborate Wilderian masquerade. Narration is a device Wilder often uses to convey the inner feelings of his duplicitous, role-playing characters. The eleven tips for screenwriters Wilder gave to Cameron Crowe included, "In doing voice-overs, be careful not to describe what the audience already sees. Add to what they are seeing." Sometimes Wilder's narration substitutes for on-screen dialogue to provide an attitude toward a scene or situation. As Emmy drives Georges back from the honeymoon, he confides to us in voiceover, "She kept talking about the United States, about Boulder Dam and how her brother went to school with a very famous man by the name of Joe DiMaggio and what the FHA [Federal Housing Administration] is and what the word 'swell' means. That's exactly what she was—swell."

The contest between cynicism and romanticism, between money and love, that dominates much of Wilder's work is clearly, almost allegorically dramatized in the relationship between these two characters. Georges is the epitome of a jaded European cynic, a continental lover who has made his living by duping rich women (a mother and daughter are said to have tried to gas themselves as a result, among the many attempted suicides or actual suicides in Wilder films). After an American consular official tells Georges that the small Rumanian quota will force him to wait up to eight years for a visa, he heeds Anita's suggestion to go back to his old tricks and follow her callous example by marrying and quickly dumping a gullible American. He cruelly preys on Emmy only after striking out with another American woman he approaches with suave professionalism during the holiday festivities but learns she is already married. Emmy is in town for a field trip with a bunch of bratty boys in a school station wagon. She and Georges "meet cute" when one of the boys throws firecrackers at him and he angrily rebuffs her attempt to apologize. Then he pulls a dirty trick when the station wagon breaks down and he deliberately makes an engine part disappear so he will have time to put the moves on her. It's a ploy Wilder will reuse in *Kiss Me, Stupid* when Barney's garage mechanic/wannabe songwriter disables Dino's car to trap him overnight in the miserable Nevada desert town so he and his writing partner can peddle their wares.

Wilder characteristically takes the risk with Georges of creating a contemptible cad and daring the audience to care about him. Leisen said, "I did not want to create any sympathy for the heel in the beginning. . . . I didn't intend to make him sympathetic until the very end when it gets down to the nitty-gritty, when she's had the [quasi-suicidal car] accident and he jumps the border to get to her. He goes to the hospital and gives her the will to live. Then you realize this man is really in love with the woman." But we do feel some empathy with Georges along the way, partly because of his nearly hopeless situation in immigration limbo but mostly because Emmy gradually recognizes and brings out his better nature, which we realize he has long repressed because of the squalid circumstances of his career as a gigolo in Europe. By surrounding Georges with émigré characters who have fled intolerable conditions, Wilder and Brackett convey something of the perilous world situation they endure, although Georges unsentimentally admits he fled because he was embroiled in a scandal. The most powerful motivating factor in his relationship with Emmy is her natural goodness and sincerity, a quality that could have become cloying in a movie romance under other hands but de Havilland makes convincing and appealing, as she had done with her celebrated performance two years earlier as the generous, strong-willed Melanie Wilkes in *Gone With the Wind*.

"Anyone who knows me knows the cynicism hides my sentimentality," Wilder "said slowly" to a Los Angeles *Times* interviewer in 1986. He told the interviewer while discussing the autobiographical elements of his films, "Isn't it pieces of yourself, of your life, that you inevitably use? You suck art out of your finger in a way." The interviewer mentioned the gigolo in *Hold Back the Dawn*, and Wilder said, "Or let's take *Sunset Blvd.* Maybe you believe it when William Holden's car is repossessed. Because, yes, it happened to me, it happened here in Hollywood, and it happened to work in that movie."

Emmy's equivalent in *Sunset Blvd.* is Nancy Olson's wholesome story editor, Betty Schaefer. Such female characters are not uncommon in Wilder, who writes them with conviction, although they are seldom discussed or admired by critics, who tend to consider cynical behavior more honest, not realizing (as the saying goes) that "the wicked forget the good can be wise." When de Havilland was asked why she relished the challenge of portraying "good girls" in films, she replied, "I think they're more challenging. Because the general concept is that if you're good, you aren't interesting. And that concept annoys me, frankly. They have the same point of view about girls who are plain. They think that somebody who's intellectual is sexless. Ha. Ha." To borrow what Molly Haskell wrote about Melanie, Emmy Brown has "a moral majesty," and her "utter sincerity was part of her fineness. She captures the inner security of a perfectly loving woman."

With what Georges sneeringly calls "her hungry heart" that led her into his "trap," Emmy ingenuously believes the smooth patter he is peddling about being "perhaps the loneliest man" in the world. His shameless tale full of self-pity nevertheless awakens her loving nature and causes the overly trusting young woman to marry him within a few hours of their meeting. That development might have seemed hard to believe, but the writing, direction, and de Havilland's sensitive acting helps convince us that this guileless woman would fall for such a corrupt man. We see closer and closer shots of Emmy, with pauses and hesitations as she studies Georges's face, revealing her evolving emotions and letting down her guard.

A character perceptively observes of James Stewart's naive senator in Frank Capra's *Mr. Smith Goes to Washington*, "This boy's honest, not stupid." Emmy has the wholesomeness of a Capra heroine; Capra wanted her to star with Stewart in *You Can't Take It with You* and *It's a Wonderful Life*. Emmy is not stupid but unsophisticated—a quality once regarded as a virtue, when "sophisticated" meant devious or deceptive. She has led a sheltered, repressed life, following the patterns laid down for her in small-town America and her school board. She has yearnings for something better; that's why she's saving her money for postgraduate education at a teachers' college and resists an engagement proposal from her kind but dull principal (Charles Arnt). Georges craftily senses the loneliness this radiant young woman must feel; de Havilland's natural beauty and simple but elegant white dress match her emotional forthrightness when she gives herself to Georges. While Emmy sleeps fitfully in the hotel lobby the night they meet, he tells us, "Her heart was beating fast, and her neat, tidy senses were all thrown out of gear." Her initially shy nature is a sign of insecurity and sexual inexperience and a lack of the kind of cunning George uses to seduce her. But while he liberates her dormant romantic passions and sensuality, especially on their honeymoon, during which he feigns an injury to avoid taking sexual advantage of her, his feelings of unworthiness and self-loathing, a condition shared by many Wilder protagonists, become more acute.

As *Hold Back the Dawn* progresses, Georges loses his glib, devilish charm and becomes more solemn while Emmy becomes increasingly exuberant, making plans for their future life. The religious overtones that sometimes peek through in Wilder's world are not mocked; the film's title appears over a painting of the Mexican church where their "wedding" ceremony will take place, and the ritual makes Georges aware of the sacrilegious nature of his act, the enormity of the harm he is planning to do to the woman he has emotionally as well as financially defrauded. He uses the pickup line that seeing her is "like a sudden breeze on a stifling day" but later admits more honestly in his narration that kissing her is "like kissing fresh snow." Her sincerity is what moves and disturbs him and rouses his dormant conscience.

Emmy's girlish gaiety and enthusiasm for America are expressions of Wilder at his most optimistic, his heartfelt way of expressing gratitude for being accepted by his adopted country in a time of world crisis. During the Mexican celebration, Emmy tells George that her mother was "foolish" for suggesting they Americanize their last name: "This is *America*—for the Rockefellers and the Joneses, for the McGonigles and the Frankfurters, for the Jeffersons and the Slovinskis. You see, it's—it's like a, like a lake, clear and fresh, and it'll never be stagnant while new streams are flowing in." Georges retorts, "Well, your people are building pretty high dams to stop those streams." She says, "Just to keep out the scum, Georges, don't you see?" That word suddenly reveals a streak of prejudice, a limitation in her provincial background. But it stings for more than one reason. Georges reacts in close-up with a stricken expression, because he knows that's what he is. He eventually decides "not to behave like a swine for once in my life."

When the truth is revealed about his deceit, Emmy proves "tougher than we thought," as her doctor says near the end of the film. She has the strength of character—"that inner fiber of *steel*," as Robert Mitchum said of Lillian Gish—that de Havilland also finds in Melanie and other characters. It's ironic that one sign of Emmy's goodness is that she is willing to lie—and to the U.S. government—on behalf of Georges, even after she learns what he has done to her. When Anita harshly exposes the truth, Emmy refuses to betray the man she loves or prevent him from entering the country, declaring in a double-edged line, "I learned life from a schoolbook, remember?" She pretends to Hammock that Georges told her all about his past and that *she* asked *him* to marry her. "It's a fine marriage," she tells the flabbergasted immigration inspector. After he departs, she tells Georges that when she first met him, "I shouldn't have been so vain. I should have looked at your face more clearly." She puts on her glasses for the first time in the film, says goodbye, and walks out, leaving her wedding ring behind.

Earlier Georges, while trying to con her with his self-pity, spoke a form of hidden truth she had no way of understanding, because of his deceptive behavior. Echoing Jeannette near the end of *Mauvaise graine*, he says, "I am dead, you see. I've asked myself thousands of times why they shouldn't bury me, why I should go on breathing and talking and walking. I was dead." Nancy Steffen-Fluhr interprets this recurring theme of the protagonist as a "living deadman" or a "dead man walking," a key to Wilder's work, as centered covertly around his feelings of helplessness as a Jew and an exile, with "the vulnerability, the immense personal pain" carefully hidden behind his facade as a jokester and entertainer. Although she barely mentions *Hold Back the Dawn* because Wilder did not direct it, it exemplifies as much as any of his films what she identifies as the "blocking of intimacy. . . . All Wilder protagonists struggle with this conundrum, especially in the films he made from 1943 to 1951, when his survival as a director was contingent on his ability, to mask his identity, keeping his fists in his pockets."

Steffen-Fluhr connects Wilder's obsession with living death as reflections of his hidden anguish over the Holocaust and survivor's guilt stemming from his abandonment of his mother when he tried to save her to no avail. Wilder's lifelong feeling of being a Jewish outsider and exile in various societies made him akin to the Wandering Jew of folklore, and he explores in his films the trauma caused by those feelings of helplessness, rage, and alienation. So it is no coincidence that the theme emerged most strongly during the war and its immediate aftermath. Wilder's protagonists must deal with that guilt and either overcome it (usually through love) or let its consequences devour them; we see the theme over and over in such characters as Walter Neff in *Double Indemnity*, Don Birnam in *The Lost Weekend*, Joe Gillis, and Chuck Tatum in *Ace in the Hole*. Being "the living deadman" is a terminal form of the masquerade, stemming from the need of the exile and the Jew to deal with the threat of oblivion through adaptation and/or disguise, while facing the bitter truth that "to survive is to be buried alive inside the deaths one did not die."

In this sense, *Hold Back the Dawn*, so nakedly autobiographical but not recognized as such because a screenwriter in Hollywood is a covert operative perennially unrecognized as an author by the industry and critics, serves as the template for much of Wilder's later work as a director. It is significant that what he regarded as the mutilation of a key scene in his screenplay by Leisen and Boyer is what drove him to become a director, to overcome the helplessness he felt as a screenwriter lacking the power to protect his work. That traumatic experience was also Wilder's rebirth as a creative artist.

Georges is reborn as a man and as an American through Emmy's love and goodness; it is paradoxical that her goodness perversely attracts a form of evil yet is powerful enough to surmount and transform it. There is suggestive use of crosscutting in the climactic scenes between Anita telling Emmy the truth about Georges and the pregnant Berta Kurz (Rosemary DeCamp), a refugee in the Hotel Esperanza from Wilder's home country (Austria), desperately sneaking across the border to give birth on American soil. She has her baby behind a Lubitschean closed door in the United States Customs and Immigration station—itself an ambiguous symbol of closed and open doors to America. This episode is drawn from Frings's novel, but the film greatly intensifies the passionate feelings the waiting immigrants have toward America as a repository of their hopes and dreams of freedom, a reflection of Wilder's own deeply felt convictions about his adopted country. When I interviewed Katharine Hepburn about Capra, an Italian immigrant for whom she worked in *State of the Union*, she observed, "I think *they* know more about what this country means than those of us who were born here and criticize it. Those of us who were born here, we take it for granted." And as she said of Capra, Wilder had a different attitude: "Pleased to be here."

Anita's revelation of Georges's true nature as a con man could have caused his moral "death" but instead leads to his moral rebirth by making him abandon his old flame and all she represents and throw himself on Emmy's mercy. With the crosscutting, the baby being born as an American citizen—Washington Roosevelt Kurz, whose appearance is heralded on the soundtrack by "California, Here I Come"—is symbolically linked with George's rebirth as a future citizen of the land of freedom.

"La Marseillaise" is also played at the end of *Hold Back the Dawn*, when a French barber (Curt Bois) returns in triumph to Mexico, having become an American citizen since he is a relative of the Marquis de Lafayette, who had been awarded the status of a "natural born" American citizen for his service to the United States during the Revolutionary War. This patriotic finale, while adding a bit of humor, avoids what in a clichéd film would have been a rendition of "The Star-Spangled Banner," but Wilder tends to avoids jingoistic flag-waving (except in *Arise, My Love* and his 1943 war film, *Five Graves to Cairo*). The French national anthem and the parade for the barber instead underscore the cosmopolitan nature of the film's themes and the long kinship between France and the United States, then in jeopardy due to the recent fall of France. The ending of this September 1941 release reminds the still-isolationist audience of what U.S. Army Colonel Charles E. Stanton declared during a ceremony at Lafayette's tomb in Paris in 1917, during World War I: "Lafayette, nous voilà" (Lafayette, we are here).

After Georges has broken through the border in a car, pursued by police, and drives through the night to Emmy's hospital bed in Los Angeles, she also returns from near-death, through his willing her to live (the film even gave him a strange premonition of her auto accident, as it ventured into the realm of mysticism and magic). Finally, through the benevolence of the immigration inspector, Emmy is seen waving Georges's entry papers from the American side of the border, with an American flag flying next to her. From an overhead angle, he is seen pushing toward her through a crowd going in the opposite direction. We can imagine the couple's final clinch, which the film has the discretion not to show (that scene was shot, but Leisen and Hornblow convinced Paramount not to use it); *Hold Back the Dawn* leaves us with the image of Georges still heading toward the border of his new country, suggesting that, like Wilder, he is a man ever in transit. Georges has wryly told the inspector he is advertising his availability as a "slightly reformed character, eager for some decent work—any place on the globe that will have him."

THE COCKROACH

Although Wilder was working with a group of collaborators at the peak of their powers, he clearly was the dominant creative force on this exceptionally personal film. The experience of working with Lubitsch on *Ninotchka*, vaulting him into the top ranks of Hollywood writers, seems to have galvanized Wilder's talents and given him the confidence to write such a soul-baring screenplay. Perhaps one reason he came to disdain *Hold Back the Dawn*, largely irrationally, is that it exposes so much about himself. It is unusual in his work to foreground his life and feelings this nakedly, rather than behind a hard-boiled veneer and through the stream of subtextual signs and references Steffen-Fluhr identifies as his way of conveying his most troubled obsessions via the careful misdirection of his "double vision." She calls *Ace in the Hole* Wilder's most personal film, but though it is a profoundly felt Holocaust allegory with a venal reporter as its "walking deadman" protagonist, and by far Wilder's darkest film, the one that alienated the American audience as much as any he ever made, it is more covertly personal than *Hold Back the Dawn*. Overtly personal works are usually discouraged in Hollywood, but that film draws from a world situation of such urgency that Wilder's own experiences with immigration could be grafted seamlessly onto the original material and mined by Paramount under the protective coloration of romantic entertainment, however deeply the love story conveys Wilder's underlying obsessions.

The intensity of his anger over the removal of a key scene from his and Brackett's screenplay, and the resulting major change in his life and career, can be understood as a reflection of how crucial the script was in directly reflecting what Steffen-Fluhr calls his "immense personal pain." The clash with Leisen and Boyer came over a scene early in the script showing the despondent Georges in his Mexican hotel room. Previously we had seen Georges enter the town jauntily swinging his cane; a cane was an implement Wilder liked to wield while writing (Steffen-Fluhr describes canes and other forms of sticks as the symbolic weapons Wilder, "pacing compulsively," used to overcome his feelings of helplessness, the reason "he can never let go"). The undisguised allegorical scene that went unfilmed helps express the Kafkaesque nature of Georges's situation:

> Interior. Iscovescu's Room. Iscovescu is pacing the floor restlessly, cane in hand. As he passes the washstand, his eyes fall on something. He stops. A cockroach is crawling down the wall on its way to a haven behind the blotchy mirror. Iscovescu raises his stick.
>
> ISCOVESCU (to the cockroach): Where do you think you are going?! You're not a citizen, are you? Where's *your* quota number?!
>
> He smashes the cockroach with his stick.

Wilder often told the story of what happened when he learned that the scene would not be in the picture (instead we see Boyer lying in his bed, wagging his cane nervously up and down, and hear him tell us that his nerves are "in such a state by now that hook in the ceiling seemed to be beckoning"). Paramount did not encourage writers to visit sets while their films were in production, but Wilder managed to get onto the set in anticipation of watching the cockroach scene being filmed. When he found it had been cut, he charged over to Lucey's restaurant on Melrose Avenue next to the studio, his and Brackett's regular luncheon haven, and confronted Boyer, who was wearing his seedy costume. As Wilder remembered it, the actor explained: "I could not speak such lines—to this—this cockroach. One does not talk to cockroaches. One does not ask a cockroach for his passport. You wish me to look *stupide?*"

When Wilder tried to explain why the scene was important, Boyer said, "I do not wish to have these discussions while I am at the table. Go away, Mr. Wilder. You disturb me."

That evidently was a bit rewritten in Wilder's memory, for Brackett's diary reports the incident somewhat differently. It happened on March 6, 1941, the same day they became enraged to learn that Ketti Frings was getting a story credit. They were working at the Samuel Goldwyn Studio on their next project, *Ball of Fire*. When the team lunched back at Lucey's, Wilder saw Boyer eating in his shabby attire and asked what scene they were shooting, "The cockroach scene?" Boyer replied, "I don't like cockroaches. We are not doing the cockroach scene." To which Wilder replied, "It's in the script, isn't it?" The writers then declared to Leisen, "No cockroach scene, no end of the picture, and not just a casual cockroach scene, a well done one." Leisen "fumed" and insisted, "I don't think it's such a charming scene." The writers "yelled" back, "It's not supposed to be charming. You've shot the charming scene . . . this is a lump of black in contrast to that."

Brackett writes that it was the next day they learned the cockroach scene had not been filmed despite their complaint, and they "started to raise more woe." Wilder's account picks up back in the office at Goldwyn after the incident at Lucey's while he exploded to Brackett, whacking the furniture with his cane: "I'll kill him, I'll kill him. I'll beat out his brains. No, he has no brains. He is an actor. I've got a better idea, Charlie. If that bastard ain't talking to cockroaches, he ain't talking to nobody. Let us give the rest of the picture to Olivia de Havilland."

It might seem that refusing to let Boyer say much in the third act would be a self-sabotaging act that would hurt the story, but Brackett and Wilder cunningly work his muteness into the characterization. Georges loses his glibness as guilt and fondness for Emmy take over his personality. When Anita, after trying to destroy the marriage, demands, "What's the matter, Georges, why are you so quiet?," he simply walks out without a word. Sometimes omitting dialogue is more eloquent than anything a character can say. To Emmy after she lies to save him, Georges says, "I've always been full of words—you know, big ones, fancy ones. Just one more—thanks." Despite what Wilder thought of Boyer, he gives a complex performance as the saturnine, self-lacerating Georges, whose darkness and despondency are as believable as his gradual transformation into a mensch. From a conventional Hollywood point of view, it is easy to see why Boyer would not want to play the scene identifying himself with a cockroach, even if he was willing to play a character entertaining thoughts of suicide. Perhaps, like Leisen, he found the cockroach scene uncomfortable because it was so atypical for a Hollywood film in its blatant and indeed disgusting symbolism, an anguished cry from Wilder's wounded heart.

In Chierichetti's oral history, Leisen offers no comment on the excision of the cockroach scene. But Wilder's anger over it and their other battles over scripts was so acute that he succumbed to homophobia in ranting to Zolotow about how the director "fucked up" their scripts:

> Leisen was too goddam fey. I don't knock fairies. Let him be a fairy. Leisen's problem was that he was a stupid fairy. He didn't have the brains to see that if Charlie and me, if we put in a line, we had a goddam reason for putting in that line and not a different line, and you don't just go out and cut a line or a piece of action to please some actress, at least without putting another line or action in its place. I ask you, is that so difficult to understand? . . . Leisen wasn't the only director who didn't know what a script was. He was more arrogant and more ignorant than the average.

Wilder's obsession with making things "crystal clear to the audience" (as noted by Brackett) exists in parallel with the many symbolic elements Wilder brought to his films (although with his lack of sympathy for Wilder personally, Brackett may not have fully understood that), but usually those elements are more disguised than the killing of the cockroach. Wilder tends to hide his symbols or temper them with humor, but in this case the meaning is so obvious, and spelled out in the dialogue to boot, that virtually every spectator would have understood the connection between Georges and the cockroach. There is humor in the scene, but it is very black comedy, a form that much of the audience in 1941 would have found unfamiliar (among the reasons some reacted the following year against Lubitsch's *To Be or Not to Be*).

Wilder could not bear the loss of this scene because the subject matter of exile, exclusion, and immigration was too urgent for him as an exiled Jew in the early days of the war, and Georges's bitterness and reformation were too close to his heart and personal story. The imagery of the cockroach symbolizing the man without a country carries deeper, covert meanings as well, ones that many viewers would not have understood, the kind that give Wilder's films their double layers. The cockroach evokes not only the novella *Metamorphosis* (1915) by his fellow Jewish writer Franz Kafka but also the Nazi propaganda equating Jews with vermin. The unusually raw feelings expressed in *Hold Back the Dawn* may have been so painful for Wilder to deal with that he could never react to the film without strong, even irrational emotion, not only to the loss of this cherished scene but even to the film's considerable strengths.

The cure he found for his helplessness as a screenwriter was to control his own work as a director, to put the stick symbolically back into his hand. "I made myself rather unpopular at Paramount," he recalled, "because I would come on the set and they would chase me off. I was known as The Terror. They would say, 'Keep Wilder away from us, he's always raising hell, he wants everything done his way.'"

When Wilder managed to direct his own scripts again in 1942, he and Brackett found another devious way to take revenge on Boyer. In *The Major and the Minor*, they had a scene in New York's Grand Central Station with Ginger Rogers buying her train ticket. The decor includes a magazine rack. On it is a movie fan magazine. A young girl asks her mother to buy it so she can read an article entitled, "Why I Hate Women: By Charles Boyer."

"THE PEJORATIVE USE OF 'ZIGZAG' "

Wilder continued his love affair with America in 1941 with *Ball of Fire*. He characteristically expresses that passion through a celebration of language. This charming and erudite romantic comedy is a cinematic equivalent of H.

L. Mencken's *The American Language. Ball of Fire* deals with a shy philologist, Professor Bertram Potts (Gary Cooper), writing the entry on slang for an encyclopedia. He and seven fellow professors of mostly advanced years live in a quaint old New York brownstone one calls a "mausoleum," a repository of the world's knowledge that evokes "the phantoms of the past." The trouble begins because they are up to the letter "S." Even though they have ordered statistics on saltpeter, which in those days was used in school lunch programs and elsewhere as a supposed dampener of sexual urges, Prof. Magenbruch (S. Z. "Cuddles" Sakall) sheepishly admits, "Maybe my data on sex is a little outdated." When Potts realizes he has lived such an isolated life that he knows little about actual everyday speech, he recruits a sexy nightclub singer, Katherine (Sugarpuss) O'Shea (Barbara Stanwyck), to wise him up.

The screenplay by Brackett and Wilder for director Howard Hawks, based on a story by Wilder and another Paramount staff writer, Thomas Monroe, is a dazzling display of verbal virtuosity, a showcase for how much Wilder had learned about the language of his new country in seven years. He had conceived the story during his final year in Germany, but he and his writing partners reworked it into a celebration of American popular culture and values. The Wilder-Monroe treatment, "From A to Z," is about a British linguist, Professor Thrush, who at the age of ten wrote his thesis on "The Faults in Shakespeare's English Grammar" and now recruits a burlesque queen named Babe for his field study. The pedant's nationality was changed so Cooper could play the role. Producer Samuel Goldwyn wanted another film for the usually taciturn star, with whom he had made six films, including William Wyler's *The Westerner* (1940). The casting of such an archetypal figure contributed to the thorough Americanness of a film that would have been much different if it had been set in Germany. It presumably was Wilder who worked in a needling connection between Potts and both Brackett and Hawks by having the square professor declare, "In the last election I voted the straight Republican ticket."

The final screenplay Wilder helped write before returning to directing, *Ball of Fire* was directed in snappy but relaxed fashion by Hawks, the Hollywood master who made some of the best films in several genres. Wilder not only received a hefty fee but made it a condition to be able to study Hawks at work. "I spent all the time on the set watching him shoot," Wilder told me, "because I wanted to see a picture from beginning to end before I started directing myself." It's been argued that Wilder's visual style as a director—graceful but unobtrusive camerawork, using close-ups sparingly while emphasizing group behavior—owes as much to Hawks as it does to Lubitsch, whose visual style tended to be more pointed and montage-oriented, as least before the Code was rigorously enforced. When I asked Wilder what he learned from Hawks, I unfortunately preempted his response by asking, "Technique?," and he echoed that word rather than offering a deeper response: "He was an extremely practical, adept, knowing celluloid man. . . . But I would not think he was a model. Maybe Lubitsch much more was, and Stroheim, kind of a strange mixture." Hawks's WASPish sensibility was at odds with Wilder's, so Wilder was perhaps accurate in stressing the "practical" lessons he learned from Hawks over thematic similarities, even if both gravitated toward the intricacies of sexual relationships. Wilder has a more genuine and complex interest in female characters than Hawks, who tended to like a woman if she is "one of the guys," but Wilder also explored buddy-buddy homoerotic relationships, although those are far more prevalent in Hawks.

It is mostly because of the script that *Ball of Fire* stands out among Hawks's comedies by being more genuinely romantic rather than dealing with physical and psychological aggression between the sexes. And as a result, the film is unusual among his comedies by actually being funny, while initiating but then *reversing* the situation of what Rivette calls "the degradation of a superior mind."

Robin Wood notes in his critical study *Howard Hawks* that *Ball of Fire* follows the director's favored concentration on themes of male group cohesion, but with "Hawks's oddest group" lending "an unusual gentleness" to the comedy. Gregg Toland's deep-focus cinematography stresses the cohesion of the group by keeping them together in virtuosic but unobtrusively elaborate compositions. When Potts's repressed emotions and sublimation of his sexual impulses are disrupted by the intrusion of Sugarpuss into his cloistered world, he and his fellow professors use their collective brainpower to vanquish the forces of brutality and chaos. They cleverly outwit gangsters who invade their home to hold them hostage as part of a scheme to marry off Sugarpuss to her gangster boyfriend, a decadent dandy called Joe Lilac (Dana Andrews), so she won't testify against him in a murder trial. The Al Capone–like Lilac sports a facial scar in a joking reference to Hawks's 1932 gangster classic, *Scarface*.

In the context of the brutal world of 1941, the intellectuals' triumph over the thugs has a clear political dimension, making a cogent point about democracy versus barbarism that is atypical of Hawks, a conservative filmmaker whose films generally eschew political issues, but characteristic of Wilder, especially during that wartime period. Potts's character pointedly refers to the "totalitarian," apelike appearance of two gangsters holding machine guns on them: "You see, your inferiority is a function of the bony structure of your skull." The thug called Pastrami (Dan Duryea) gleefully responds by firing his gun at a globe, sneering, "I'll show you what makes the world go round!," and cackling maliciously as his bullets symbolically make the globe spin out of control. The Wilder-Monroe treatment describes the denouement as "the triumph of science and knowledge over brute force, of intellect over iniquity, of Einstein over Capone."

Hawks and the writers play against the farcical aspects of the gangsters by treating their brutality seriously, as they do with Potts's intellect and emotions. Sugarpuss's masquerade as a sweet and smitten young woman leads the naive Potts along romantically, much as Georges does to Emmy in *Hold Back the Dawn*. Sugarpuss similarly experiences remorse over her deceit and succumbs to her naively romantic partner's honesty and sincerity—as well as finding him "pretty." The treatment of this theme is more comedic than in *Hold Back the Dawn*, but Stanwyck's ability to show the bruised heart beneath her hard-boiled facade is entirely convincing.* Her tough/tender playing of a floozie chantoozie ("She jives by night!") has similarities to her own hard life as a chorus girl in mobbed-up nightclubs before she entered movies. Cooper's inherent simplicity, modesty, and emotional directness are equally beguiling as Potts is transformed from a gullible, boyish dupe into a mature lover after being painfully wised up about life by falling for a con-woman.

Much more congenial than Cooper's bizarre role as a callous lady-killer in *Bluebeard's Eighth Wife*, Potts draws from the beguiling but sexually reticent mold of the character Cooper played for Capra in *Mr. Deeds Goes to Town*. Although Pauline Kael's complaint that Capra "destroyed Cooper's early sex appeal when he made him childish as Mr. Deeds" is largely true about the

---

* Ginger Rogers, Jean Arthur, and Carole Lombard declined the role, Rogers because she wanted to play only "ladies," and Lucille Ball wanted it but was rejected, much to Brackett's distress after he saw her warm and boisterous turn as a burlesque performer named Bubbles in Dorothy Arzner's *Dance, Girl, Dance* (1940).

overall development of the actor's career, he and Stanwyck had meshed well together in Capra's comedy-drama, *Meet John Doe*, during the same annus mirabilis when Hawks made *Ball of Fire* and guided the actor to an Academy Award in the title role of *Sergeant York*. Hawks is expert in giving his male characters an unusually low-key, unaggressive sex appeal, as he does with Cooper opposite Stanwyck in *Ball of Fire*. What's most typical of Hawks is the role reversal in the romance between the shy, repressed professor and the brassy, assertive dame who coaxes him out of his intellectual and psychological shell. Hawks's male characters tend to be sexually inadequate or ambivalent, and the aggressiveness of his female characters counters a strain of latent homosexuality running throughout his work. Not only do the eight men live together in *Ball of Fire*, two of them admit they share a bed during electric storms. But the film's quirky yet charming male-female relationship of two wildly different people who find common romantic ground has the sparks and humor both Hawks and Wilder always draw from sexual situations.

As in *Hold Back the Dawn*, the cynical partner gradually loses a self-protective veneer when confronted with an honest, guileless person who expresses sincere emotion. Sikov writes in his biography of Wilder, "'Pottsie' is the first man in her life who respects and covets her soul as well as her body. This revelation of mutual tenderness and affection between two deeply flawed, superficially ridiculous, and radically mismatched people is not unique in Wilder's career. . . . Wilder was still receptive enough to this kind of heartbreakingly ideal love. . . . And he was lucky enough to be working with a director who knew precisely what he meant."

Sugarpuss is the kind of smart, dominant professional woman Hawks adores, at home anywhere and able to take over the most challenging situations. Her liberation of Bertram's latent sexuality while delighting the old professors with her cavorting conveys the joy Hawks and Wilder take throughout their careers in giving the finger to puritanism. The difference between the two filmmakers is that Hawks, for all his raciness, is also sexually repressed, while Wilder is more at ease in bringing out tender emotions between men and women as well as their more destructive sexual impulses. Hawks's influence on Wilder nevertheless is felt strongly in many of the films Wilder directed, especially in the gender-bending *Some Like It Hot*, a male buddy-buddy movie with a strongly feminist theme. That film also contains riffs on *Scarface* and other Hawks films, since Wilder loves throwing movie jokes into his work, as he and Hawks do in *Ball of Fire* by having Duryea imitate Cooper's unusual method of firing a gun in *Sergeant York* by first wetting the sight with his thumb ("I saw me a picture last week").

Wilder's brash, infectious delight in colorful language permeates this extravaganza of pop-culture Americana. The process by which the sheltered intellectual Potts learns to talk like a regular American guy and becomes more voluble than Cooper usually was onscreen was inspired by Wilder's own immersion in the language as a newcomer by listening to the radio and dating American women. Potts's background as an academic prodigy since childhood, unaccustomed to women, makes him behave toward Sugarpuss like a stranger in a strange land. *Ball of Fire*'s erudition also owes a great deal to Brackett's educational background and linguistic elegance, as well as his familiarity with the world of the New York intelligentsia. Potts before making his field study of slang is like the genteel, repressed Ivy Leaguer Brackett; but after he meets Sugarpuss, he becomes more like Wilder, livelier, impulsive, a man of the streets, a roving reporter, a libertine. Potts goes out into the world after an encounter with a jive-talking garbage man (Allen Jenkins) makes him realize he has been an "idiot." Potts tells his colleagues,

> It's catastrophic, gentlemen, catastrophic. I've just finished my article on slang, twenty-three pages compiled from a dozen reference books—eight hundred examples—everything from the idiotic combination "absitively" to the pejorative use of "zigzag." I traced the evolution of "hunky-dory," tracked down "skidoo" from "skedaddle." Eight hundred examples, and I may as well throw it in the wastebasket. Three weeks' work! Outmoded, based on references twenty years old. Take "smooch," take "dish," take, uh . . . "hoytoytoy." Not one of them included. . . . That man talked a living language.

Potts resembles George Bernard Shaw's Professor Henry Higgins in *Pygmalion* as he carries a notebook while eavesdropping on strangers all around New York in a montage sequence resembling *People on Sunday* (he writes down, "The screamin' meemies . . . Plenty Gestanko. Just a Jerk. Two ply Poke. Bop the Apple. Oolie Droolie"). When he finds Sugarpuss, who uses "words so bizarre they made my mouth water—'shove in your clutch,' for instance," and brings her into their bachelor quarters to study, the situation evokes Higgins's use of Eliza Doolittle but without the callous misogyny and class bias of Shaw's professor; *Ball of Fire* differs from that play in showing the professor being radically transformed by his subject. As both in Shaw and in Wilder's Arthur Conan Doyle adaptation, *The Private Life of Sherlock Holmes* (1970), there's a disapproving old housekeeper, a foil for the screenwriters to mock in *Ball of Fire* as she scolds Potts for his impropriety. According to Zolotow, Wilder spent several days hanging out for research purposes in a drugstore near Hollywood High School, listening to teenagers talk and "treating his respondents, especially the ones who were nubile and tight-sweatered, to sundaes and banana splits. He almost got arrested on suspicion of molesting minors." That experience helped inspire his and Brackett's next screenplay, *The Major and the Minor.*

The Runyonesque linguistic frolicking in *Ball of Fire* found a perfect director in Hawks, whose mastery of directing slangy, elaborate, overlapping dialogue helps enliven this story centered around a group of idiosyncratic academics talking obsessively about their research specialties (although often with sexual connotations). But while the film is masterfully directed with ensemble dialogue, it does not have the fast pace typical of Hawks films, because, as he said, it "was about pedantic people. Whenever you've got professors saying lines, they can't speak 'em like crime reporters. It didn't have the same reality as the other comedies, and we couldn't make it go with the same speed." *Ball of Fire* revels in its idiosyncratic array of character actors and has the quality of an urban fairy tale centered on an unlikely couple. "ONCE UPON A TIME . . . ," says the written prologue, there were these professors who were "SO WISE THEY KNEW EVERYTHING . . . BUT THERE WAS ONE THING ABOUT WHICH THEY KNEW VERY LITTLE. . . . " The basic comic innocence of the story makes it resemble a live-action variation on Disney's *Snow White and the Seven Dwarfs*, which is advertised on a theater marquee as Potts begins his expedition. Hawks characteristically claimed he thought of that parallel, but Wilder said it was his idea. Sugarpuss calls the professors "the seven dwarves." Her tally suggests Potts is not a dwarf like the others but a Prince Charming, though it is *she* who awakens *him* sexually.

An English professor and erudite film buff I know told me he dislikes *Ball of Fire* because he considers it "anti-intellectual." I disagree. Although Hawks's films tend to focus on action and behavior more than on abstract themes, he excels in conveying characters' thought processes and ingenuity in solving difficult problems. Potts's recognition of the importance of combining street research with book-learning is not anti-intellectual but a comment on the limitations of academic insularity and the importance of keeping up with reality rather than simply dwelling in an ivory tower. That theme is echoed in his relationship with Sugarpuss, who tells Potts suggestively, while still wearing her sparkling and revealing nightclub costume, "How do we start, Professor? You see, this is the first time anybody moved in on my brain." Potts starts getting overheated and orders her out of the house, admitting, "I shall regret the absence of your keen mind. Unfortunately, it is inseparable from an extremely disturbing body." She callously plays on that attraction but soon becomes sympathetic to his guileless nature and titillated by his intellect and verbal dexterity, as well as by his physical beauty: besides calling him "pretty," she says he's "a regular yum-yum type."

The way the professors in *Ball of Fire* eventually combine their historical and scientific knowledge to get the drop on the ignorant gangsters who take over their home is an ingenious piece of screenwriting and a vivid demonstration of Hawks's characteristic skill in translating thought into action. And though the professors are comical oddballs, Hawks and his writers do not mock their scholarly endeavor. As Wood points out, the film "distinguishes firmly between the absurdity of the characters and the seriousness of their work. . . . Separately, each is absurd; united in group activity, they take on dignity. . . . Sugarpuss's crude, sensual vitality stimulates the professors' capacity for spontaneous enjoyment; the professors' innocence and gentleness develop in Sugarpuss a rudimentary conscience and sensibility." And while the focus is on Potts learning not to separate his emotions and physical impulses from his intellect, "we are never invited to laugh at Bertram, only—and then uneasily—at the situation," and his "seriousness is given great weight" as he unknowingly confesses his feelings in the dark to Sugarpuss.

That core of emotional depth in the comedy struck a chord with Hawks, even though the film was something of an anomaly for him—"you had to adapt your style to it"—but unlike Leisen, he respected the screenwriters: "Brackett and Wilder were *superb* writers and they could make almost anything good."

Hawks's 1948 Technicolor musical remake of *Ball of Fire*, *A Song Is Born*, is just one of many musicals bearing Wilder's name, even though he's seldom recognized for his work in that genre; he had his own Technicolor musical in release that year, the very peculiar period piece *The Emperor Waltz*. Wilder and Thomas Monroe receive story credit on *A Song Is Born*, but it's unusual that there is no screenplay credit. A raft of other writers seriously diminished the original by stripping away most of its verbal play, since the professors in the remake are working on a history of music.

Also shot by Toland, who died prematurely shortly before its release, *A Song Is Born* has some compensatory virtues in its spectacular array of jazz and pop musicians, including Louis Armstrong, Lionel Hampton, Charlie Barnet, Mel Powell, Benny Goodman, and Tommy Dorsey. The highlight is a sublime group number on the history of jazz, drawing on Hawks's unrivaled ability to convey the camaraderie of performers working together in exuberant jam sessions. *Ball of Fire* suffers to some extent from a dragged-out finale with the tiresomely caricatured gangster characters, but in *A Song Is Born*, Hawks makes that part more compact as well as making it more entertaining by using music as a weapon.

Aside from taking pleasure in working with the musicians in the remake, however, Hawks told me he found it "an altogether horrible experience." When I asked why he did *A Song Is Born*, he said, "Because I got $25,000 a week, that's why." He said Danny Kaye, as Professor Frisbee, "was a basket case, stopping work to see a psychiatrist twice a day [actually once a day]. Now you can imagine working with that. He was about as funny as a crutch." Goldwyn cruelly made Virginia Mayo run *Ball of Fire* over and over so she could try to imitate Stanwyck. What did Hawks think of Mayo? "Pathetic." But she isn't as bad as Kaye, whose obvious discomfort is enough to sink the picture. Watching it back-to-back with *Ball of Fire* is a lesson in how much great actors and screenwriters are responsible for the qualities of a film and how much a director needs them.

A Song Is Born was only a discordant note in Wilder's career. By then he was one of Hollywood's top writer-directors, with Oscars in both categories for *The Lost Weekend* (1945), the first of six he would win. That drama about alcoholism and the classic film noir *Double Indemnity* the year before sealed his reputation as one of the most mordant and daring American filmmakers.

HOW DID WILDER DO IT?

After his unhappy initial foray into directing with *Mauvaise graine*, Wilder had used the clout he earned as a screenwriter and his complaints about Leisen mutilating his work to persuade Paramount to let him make his American directorial debut with *The Major and the Minor* in 1942. It was unusual for screenwriters to make the transition to directing in those days, but Wilder benefited from the studio's success in letting another of its top screenwriters, Preston Sturges, start directing in 1940 with *The Great McGinty*; and the year before Wilder made his Hollywood directing debut, screenwriter John Huston triumphed by directing *The Maltese Falcon* for Warner Bros.

"I made no mistakes, you know," Wilder told Crowe. "I knew they told themselves, 'Let Wilder make a small picture, he's gonna fall on his ass, then he's gonna go back to the fourth floor, he's gonna be a writer again.' I knew that, so I did a *commercial* picture, as commercial as I've ever been. Just a girl, twenty-six, pretends to be fourteen [actually twelve]. It was prematurely *Lolita.*"

Through the good graces of producer Arthur Hornblow, Jr., "who gave me my first chance," Wilder started shooting that slyly suggestive romantic comedy with Rogers and Milland on February 23, 1942. It somehow slipped below the eyes of the censors at a time when the Production Code supposedly was being strictly enforced. American naiveté and denial about pedophilia must have blinded the Breen Office and most viewers to what that seemingly innocuous comedy is actually about, just as Queen Victoria steadfastly refused to believe in the existence of lesbianism.

Although this film was an extreme case, Wilder's career as a director would be filled with examples of his cleverness in circumventing censorship to get his way in making personal films within the system. He was like Lubitsch in pushing the envelope of dealing with sexuality onscreen and outwitting the censors, but Wilder worked in gradually more permissive times as the Code bent, weakened, and finally collapsed. While leading the way in Hollywood for greater maturity in dealing with sexual themes onscreen, he restlessly pursued an eclectic, variegated career path that nevertheless followed certain obsessive preoccupations. He kept expanding on his distinctive and adventurous artistic personality in a commercial industry, an achievement that took remarkable finesse, ingenuity, and stamina.

How, then, did Wilder do it? Departing from the largely chronological approach I have been taking in studying his formative years as a writer in Europe and Hollywood, the next section of this book will trace the evolution of Wilder's characteristic themes and style while I range freely over his nearly forty years as a Hollywood writer-director. Covering that culminating period of his career becomes more insightful by following a more free-flowing, allusive, thematic method. That section will take the liberty of jumping around in time to follow themes encompassing films from different decades, tracing connections among the many disparate elements that contribute to his mature work. In bypassing the conventional approach followed by other critical studies of Wilder, I hope to tie together the threads of the evolving "figure in the carpet" (as Henry James would put it) that brought Wilder's creative vision to fruition in his twenty-five films as a Hollywood writer-director.

Wilder's first day of shooting on *The Major and the Minor* was the scene on a Paramount apartment set of jaded New York working woman Ginger Rogers giving Robert Benchley's dirty old man a "scalp massage." To celebrate the occasion, Lubitsch came to the set. Wilder's mentor brought along Sturges and several other directors for encouragement, including fellow European émigrés E. A. Dupont (whose wife, Gretl, has a small role in the film), William Dieterle, William Wyler, and Michael Curtiz, who wished him well in German. The day before, Wilder had gone to see Lubitsch to confess how anxious he was about starting his new career. He moaned about suffering from a fever and diarrhea.

Lubitsch put his arm around him and said, "I have directed fifty pictures and I'm still crapping in my pants on the first day."

6.0 (top) Barbara Stanwyck and Fred MacMurray as the furtive murderous couple in Wilder's classic film noir *Double Indemnity* (1944), which he adapted with Raymond Chandler from the novel by James M. Cain. (Paramount/Photofest.)

6.01 (bottom) Jack Lemmon and Shirley MacLaine in the film Wilder considered his best, *The Apartment* (1960). Scorned by one reviewer as a "dirty fairy tale," it shows the tenderly romantic side of Wilder contrasted with a squalid New York corporate setting. (United Artists/Photofest.)

"ISN'T IT ROMANTIC?"

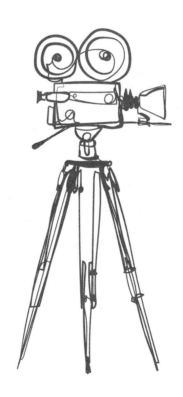

6.1 (top) Jean Arthur as a reactionary American member of Congress (*right*) getting wised up by a hard-boiled survivor (Marlene Dietrich) in the ruins of Berlin in Wilder's corrosive *A Foreign Affair* (1948). (Paramount/Photofest.)

6.2 (bottom) *Ace in the Hole* (1951), Wilder's darkest indictment of greed and cruelty, evokes imagery of the Holocaust as an unscrupulous reporter (Kirk Douglas) keeps a New Mexico spelunker (Richard Benedict) trapped in a cave. (Paramount/Photofest.)

6

DANCING ON THE EDGE

Want to buy some illusions,
Slightly used, second-hand? . . .
Some for laughs, some for tears.

—Marlene Dietrich singing a Frederick Hollander song in *A Foreign Affair*

"GOLLY!," exclaims Phoebe Frost (Jean Arthur), a member of Congress from Iowa, with quiet, all-American shock and awe as she and her colleagues fly over the ruins of Berlin at the beginning of Wilder's 1948 film *A Foreign Affair*. Through the windows of their U.S. Army Air Forces plane, we are watching aerial footage shot expressly for the film of street after street of actual bombed-out buildings. The desolate documentary images are of former dwellings gutted and pulverized and burned by American and British bombers in more than three hundred air raids on the German capital. These ruins are particularly shocking to encounter in an entertainment film, especially one taking the ostensible form of a romantic comedy. Who else but Wilder would make a romantic comedy set in the postwar ruins of Berlin?

The single word Arthur's painfully naive American lawmaker uses to react to the sight of the destroyed city is obviously inadequate to convey the devastation she is witnessing. That discrepancy and the corn-fed Americanness of the reactionary midwestern congresswoman's pious euphemism carry a dark edge of satire. But I also find her exclamation moving when heard in conjunction with Wilder's postapocalyptic images of the city where the Jewish filmmaker worked as a reporter and screenwriter before he fled Hitler.

What word could be adequate to what Congresswoman Frost sees and Wilder makes us witness? The linkage he draws between his images and her banal, understated exclamation of shock are Wilder's way of telling us, "Nothing I could write could capture this reality, only the pictures I am showing you." He conveys in one word and look the clash between innocence and experience that characterizes much of his work, the sense of innocence brutally shattered, ideals corrupted and hearts broken, illusions destroyed and replaced with a sadder but wiser view of reality.

On the level of romantic comedy, this daringly unusual film is also notably jaundiced, showing the prudish congresswoman succumbing to the bogus seduction of a corrupt Army Intelligence officer, Captain John Pringle (John Lund). While Frost is in Berlin investigating sexual carrying-on among GIs in the occupying forces, Pringle is trying to protect his ex-Nazi sympathizer German lady friend, Erika von Schlütow (Marlene Dietrich), from exposure and incarceration in a labor camp, as well as himself from being court-martialed over his involvement with her. Phoebe's political and personal comeuppance at the hands of Erika is brutal ("Now you're one of us," Erika tells her), and Wilder makes us feel the sting of Phoebe's pain sympathetically as well as Erika's generosity in springing her from arrest. But the collapse of Phoebe's puritanical hypocrisy is satisfying for Erika and salutary for Phoebe and the audience. It is this cosmopolitan filmmaker's way of persuading Americans to grow up and confront the bittersweet challenges Europe poses to their insular and deficient sense of morality. When Phoebe learns the devastating truth that Captain Pringle has been conning her romantically, he feebly apologizes and tells her, "I guess this is where the funny man says, 'Shall we dance?'" She replies with disillusionment in lines that cut to the divided heart of Wilder's personality, "You are not a funny man, Captain Pringle. But you are quite a dancer. What a waltz we had. Good night."

Despite that desperately graceful exit, the inadequacy of the congresswoman's response to seeing the ruins of Berlin and her sincerity in uttering it provide the blend of comedy and drama that Wilder learned from Ernst Lubitsch as well as from his grittier work as a reporter in Vienna and Berlin. In her *"Golly!"* we might also detect a note of revenge in Wilder's sly choice of suitably corny American heartland slang, his characteristic way of employing a joke as an "epitaph on an emotion." The flattened city Phoebe witnesses with us is the one in which the destruction of Wilder's mother and other family members and six million other Jews in the Holocaust, as well as the millions of other victims of Nazi aggression and genocide, was plotted and organized. The saturation bombings of German and Japanese cities by the Allied forces to terrorize civilians were also war crimes, but Wilder did not share that view, especially after he returned to Germany so soon after the war. A film editor who worked on *A Foreign Affair*, John M. Woodcock, recalled, "After viewing aerial shots of block after block of Berlin leveled to the ground, I remarked that I couldn't help feel sorry for the Germans. With that Billy jumped to his feet and yelled, 'To hell with those bastards! They burned most of my family in their damned ovens! I hope they burn in hell!'"

A Foreign Affair includes the caustic tour of Berlin landmarks for the members of Congress provided by Colonel Rufus J. Plummer (Millard Mitchell). It takes in the ruins of the Brandenburg Gate, the Reichstag, Hitler's bunker (where he and Eva Braun spent "a perfect honeymoon"), as well as the Adlon Hotel. The army colonel notes that the hotel was "once the heart of Europe" but now is just "another pile of stone" after "the Eighth Air Force checked in for the weekend." Part of an informal Wilder trilogy about Berlin that also encompasses *People on Sunday* and *One, Two, Three*, films that richly chronicle the downfall and transformation of a great city, *A Foreign Affair* is replete with such discordant sights and sounds. They also include Captain Pringle blithely whistling "Isn't It Romantic?" as he drives his Jeep through the pulverized streets and Dietrich's unstoppably glamorous panache as the former Nazi playgirl working in an underground cabaret, crooning a mordant Frederick Holländer ballad called "The Ruins of Berlin" as the émigré composer plays the piano. *A Foreign Affair* continues the tradition Wilder followed in both prewar UFA and his early Hollywood days of blending musical interludes with drama, but here with the sharpest kind of social commentary, as keenly as in Brecht.

Wilder's frequent use of the Rodgers and Hart tune "Isn't It Romantic?" began with Ginger Rogers's "masseuse" character approaching the apartment of a john at the start of *The Major and the Minor*. When Volker Schlöndorff asked Wilder about his recurring ironic employment of the song, Wilder tried to pass it off as a joke, saying it was just an example of cheapness, since

Paramount owned the rights to the song, which had been introduced in Rouben Mamoulian's 1932 musical *Love Me Tonight*. That was another of Wilder's characteristic denials of deeper intent, deferring a probing question with a quip. The song struck a deeper chord he preferred not to explain but that becomes clear in his films, expressing both his genuine romanticism and his skepticism about it.

The eloquent cabaret song by Holländer about the ruins of Berlin, moral as well as physical, claims with defiant optimism that "the phantoms of the past" will not return in the new Berlin—but ironically, just as Dietrich's Erika sings those words, a Nazi phantom, her former lover Hans Otto Birgel (Peter von Zerneck), does return as if from the dead. This nightmare of the rebirth of Nazism, with the fugitive Gestapo agent trying to kill Captain Pringle but being shot dead by other American soldiers, draws from the staple of a horror movie, the return of the repressed. Wilder's film constantly challenges the audience's comedic/romantic/dramatic expectations by rubbing our noses in destruction and genre confusion, while asking us to wonder how life can go on for anyone after such calamities have been visited on the world the filmmaker left behind. Wilder in his postwar European work was almost compulsive about returning to the scene of the crime that destroyed part of his family and much of the world in which he had grown to maturity. It was part of the reason he transformed himself back into a European filmmaker so often after the war.

Unlike Lubitsch, who had died in 1947 after turning his back entirely on his native Germany in 1933, Wilder boldly explored the ambivalent realities of life among the ruins of postwar Europe, juxtaposing it with the intrusions of his Ugly American characters who need wising up in that older, more sophisticated, but troubled cultural landscape. By making those pilgrimages, including by directing occasional Lubitschean romantic comedies set partly or entirely in Europe, he was seeking answers to the questions that concerned him in the contrast between the new world he had embraced and the old world he had been forced to abandon, a mixture of elegant remnants and rubble.

For a Jewish artist, confronting the aftermath of the war and the Holocaust and the realities of the ruination not only of European cities but also of the ideals of humanity was an inevitable and necessary step. Similar themes were being explored in literature, history, and art, and sometimes by other filmmakers in what was called the *Trümmerfilm* (rubble film) genre. Other

1948 films in that genre were made by both Jewish and Gentile directors: Wilder's friend and colleague from Vienna, Fred Zinnemann, made *The Search*, and the Italian neorealist Roberto Rossellini made *Germania anno zero* (*Germany Year Zero*). Concentration camp survivor Elie Wiesel wrote in his Holocaust memoir *Night* that an inmate of Auschwitz asked when a child was being hanged, *"Where is God? Where is he? . . . Where is God now?"* That question has broadly haunted postwar discourse. As Benjamin Moser writes, "In painting as in architecture, in literature as in theology, twentieth-century artists and thinkers attempted to discover some core of ultimate meaning, if such a core existed: to find the most basic forms with which to rebuild a ruined world." Other postwar writers, such as Günter Grass, Kurt Vonnegut, Joseph Heller, Graham Greene, and William Styron, would also try to make sense out of what had happened in the war and how humanity was coping with the radically changed world, as Captain Pringle, in his own compromised way, does in *A Foreign Affair*.

Juxtaposing the war's horrors and doubts about the world's future in *A Foreign Affair*—both politically and philosophically—with the almost criminal naiveté of people in government who had no excuse for their moral blindness about the meaning of the war was Wilder's way of coming to terms with this ruined world and his angry indictment of American ignorance and complacency. Ruins were a symbolic playground for his characteristic obsession with the reinvention of personality, a place to start over from scratch and transform yourself, as he had done by leaving Berlin and coming to the United States. Erika, an edgy blend of camp follower and defiantly independent woman, continually has reinvented herself according to the changing political situation and keeps doing so, calling forth a fascinatingly ambivalent mixture of disgust and sympathy from Wilder.

The deeply repressed Congresswoman Frost also manages to transform herself by leaving her fantasy world of deceptively wholesome America (aside from that "little boy in Des Moines [who] took a blowtorch to his grandmother") and falling into what she calls the "sewer" of postwar Berlin with initial horror but ultimate exhilaration. Her liberation, as the film's protagonist, is a complex affair, a mingling of disillusion, self-deception, and finally a greater, if still imperfect, self-understanding. If the balance between stark depiction of the ruins of Berlin with romantic comedy was difficult to maintain and resolve, that is part of what makes *A Foreign Affair* so central to

Wilder's work, so characteristic of his concerns, and such an intellectually and emotionally stimulating achievement.

An example of the obtuse, often factually inaccurate response to *A Foreign Affair* in the postwar era, contributing to its critical eclipse, was Herbert G. Luft's complaint about the film's point of view in a 1952 article for *Quarterly of Film, Radio, and Television*: "The camera focus on a pile of rubble was not exactly a fitting place for wholesome comedy. There are the ruins of Berlin, but not one word to explain why the city had to be utterly destroyed. . . . The Nazis are seen as double-crossers, yet drawn with much charm and noblesse, living in an atmosphere of comparative ease, with a romantic facade covering up a decade of mass murders. . . . Our occupation forces appear undisciplined and ill-behaved."

As Stephen Farber wrote in his 1971–1972 essay on Wilder:

> Twenty years later these words sound like a recommendation; one of the most daring, refreshing, and commendable things about *A Foreign Affair* is that it complicates the clearcut moral distinctions of World War II movies and presents ex-Nazis as human beings and American soldiers as corrupt opportunists. . . . By ignoring the realities of life in Berlin, it is Congresswoman Frost who seems anti-human. Wilder mocks her more than he mocks the fraternizing Americans or the world-weary Germans. For they are only trying to make the most of a bad situation. They may be cynical, corrupt, ruthless, but they have, at least, recognized the nature of their world, and they have no illusions . . . no false assumptions of moral superiority. . . . The film's criticism of American moralizing is bolder and more intelligent than in most films today.

LETTING WILDER BE WILDER

Wilder's distinctively mordant blending of romanticism with what his detractors call his "cynicism"—and what those who find that word reductive would call his sense of unblinking realism—pervades his body of work as a Hollywood writer-director. That unsettling mixture as seen in *A Foreign Affair*, with its characteristic mingling of comedy and often shocking drama, was carried on through such postwar classics as *Sunset Blvd.*, *Ace in the Hole*, *Some Like It*

Hot, and *The Apartment*. Those balancing acts helped make Wilder one of the defining American directors of the postwar period while giving his work its distinctive tone. Wilder's ambivalent looks back at Europe stem from an exile's conflicted emotions, and in his case the sadness and disgust tend to outweigh the nostalgia. His films about life in America, by contrast, are filled with both affection and social criticism, but because of his fondness for his adopted land of refuge, the balance tends to tilt in a somewhat more optimistic direction, even though the films are often caustic.

My approach to the twenty-five features Wilder wrote and directed in Hollywood will be suitably peripatetic as it draws connections among them from different periods between 1942 and 1981 and attempts to penetrate the riddles of the often enigmatic, somewhat paradoxical artistic personality lurking beneath the lucid surface of his body of work. Behind his carefully cultivated facade of a glib jokester and compulsive entertainer, beneath the rigorously lucid and gracefully crafted surface of his work, who was Billy Wilder? How are his impulses to charm his audience counterpointed and marked by the "phantoms of the past"?

True to his origins as a roving reporter, Wilder offered film audiences of the 1940s through the early 1960s trenchant cinematic exposés of contemporary social and sexual problems. After establishing his commercial bona fides as a comedy writer and director, he kept outflanking the Code while confronting audiences in that period with some of Hollywood's most daringly adult subject matter. Priding himself on his versatility, he veered from the darkest of film noir in *Double Indemnity*, to corrosive Hollywood tragedy in *Sunset Blvd.*, to light yet somewhat melancholy Lubitschean romance in *Sabrina* and *Love in the Afternoon*, to wild cross-dressing farce in *Some Like It Hot*.

After Wilder broke up his longtime writing partnership with the more genteel Charles Brackett, he worked with a variety of other cowriters before eventually settling on a more compatible partnership with I. A. L. Diamond from 1957 onward. From that point on, he was able to be more fully himself, benefiting from the audience's appetite for more adult screen fare in the 1950s. Diamond, in effect, let Wilder be Wilder. With such a simpatico partner, highly skilled with comedy, also a master craftsman and constructionist, and equally attuned to blending comedy and sentiment, Wilder was freer to exercise his talent. Despite Brackett's literate nature, novelistic sensibility, insights into character, and considerable gifts as a dramatist, he had been a somewhat inhibiting influence on his junior partner.

As time would show, not everyone was thrilled about that development in Wilder's career. But during the heady period in the 1950s and early 1960s when Wilder was acting as the bull in the china shop of American puritanism, he was a roaring success, while working with Diamond to gleefully shatter and ridicule taboos in a repressed age that barely kept the lid on an undercurrent of seething discontent.

By 1959, the classic Wilder-Diamond sex farce *Some Like It Hot* made it possible even for Middle America to enjoy cross-dressing and a flagrantly gay love story and the spectacle of a nearly naked Marilyn Monroe without feeling guilty about such pleasures. Perhaps Wilder got away with it because the film was safely stylized in a period setting and it was accepted as simply farcical, despite the serious emotional undertones and feminist themes that audiences barely seemed to register. But after Wilder's contemporary morality play *The Apartment* the following year brought him to the pinnacle of Hollywood success, winning him three Oscars (Diamond also won an Oscar for their script), and after *Irma la Douce* in 1963 became the director's biggest commercial hit, Wilder abruptly was almost run out of town when he was seen as "going too far" with his abrasive satire of small-town American sexual hypocrisy, *Kiss Me, Stupid*.

Some people already thought he had gone too far in 1951 with his corrosive exposé of the newspaper business and the heartlessness of the American public, *Ace in the Hole*, which had caused him to retreat to safer subject matter for a while, and some in Hollywood had felt the same way about having their dirty linen exposed in *Sunset Blvd.* But when *Kiss Me, Stupid* came out in December 1964, in what supposedly was a far more enlightened America, it provoked even greater mishegoss. Wilder was under the illusion that the luster of the astringent comedy-drama of *The Apartment* and the public's embrace of the elements of sexual fantasy in *Irma la Douce* would enable him to get away with another comedy about prostitution, a film that would please Hollywood, reviewers, and the public. The ill-timed Christmas season opening was coordinated with what was expected to be a triumphant celebration of his career in a retrospective at New York's Museum of Modern Art. That now seems to have been a striking display of hubris and a rare misreading of his audience's readiness to hear the bitter truth.

But this time Wilder was striking closer to home. He was too far ahead of his time with that misunderstood film and its uncomfortably realistic satire of American sexual mores. He was not dealing with New York business executives exploiting women or cartoonish Parisians indulging their sexual appetites but exposing the hypocrisy of the kind of ordinary, narrow-minded, churchgoing American small-town folk whose sensibilities had done so much to bring about the restrictions of the Production Code and the Legion of Decency. As George Bernard Shaw put it, "If you want to tell people the truth, make them laugh, otherwise they'll kill you." But the hilarity of *Kiss Me, Stupid* escaped most Americans, who were shocked at its remorseless stripping-away of their cherished illusions and their society's fraudulent facade. As Dean Martin's sleazy, sex-crazed pop singer, Dino, puts it in that film, "If you got what it takes—sooner or later somebody will take what you got. [*A beat*] Baby."

Yet when the Code was scrapped not long after that, in the waning days of the old studio system and amid the sexual and political upheavals of the late 1960s, the man who recently had outraged self-righteous guardians of conventional morality suddenly found himself regarded as old-fashioned. There was no more china shop for the old bull to shatter; the china was shattered and scattered all over the floor after the Code was abandoned in 1968 and replaced with the Motion Picture Association of America's rating system. Wilder was no longer on the cutting edge, and well before his involuntary retirement in the early 1980s, he had come to seem passé by the standards of Hollywood and its increasingly adolescent clientele. Wilder was still only in his late fifties when that began to happen, but he might have been a hundred for all the younger audience cared. I felt empathy for Wilder and other veteran directors shunted aside in the 1970s and 1980s, partly due to my own feelings of alienation as a screenwriter in an industry that was busy trashing its illustrious traditions while turning itself into a garbage dump for sequels, franchises, and spectacles of mindless juvenilia.

Rather than trying to reshape his work to pander to the new trends—as some older Hollywood directors tried to do with often embarrassing results, such as Otto Preminger, who grew up in the same period in Vienna—Wilder turned defiant. In his films after *Kiss Me, Stupid*, he did not celebrate the new creative freedom by "letting it all hang out" and simply giving freer rein to his raunchy side. In part because he was still burned by the backlash against the raw verisimilitude of that comedy, but mostly because he was forced to realize he was out of step with the changing times ("Frankly, I regard it as a compliment. Who the hell wants to be in touch with *these* times?"), he defiantly went against the curve of the new license for blatant sexuality and violence while allowing his latent romanticism to surface more overtly. For the remainder of his career, before his cameras were taken away, he reveled in his classical, "old-fashioned" status in a film world turned topsy-turvy. His response might not have been predicted by his myopic detractors who considered him cynical and misanthropic. But as our culture in general and Hollywood's output have coarsened over the years, the old criticisms of his "cynicism" have come to seem quaint.

Wilder's mellow and often mournful later period from 1970 onward, including such deeply personal works as *The Private Life of Sherlock Holmes*, *Avanti!*, and *Fedora*, was unfairly regarded as a downslide into oblivion. Predictably failing to appeal to the dominant new youth audience in what we now call "the *Easy Rider* era," they were commercial failures. Audiences stayed away in droves (as Sam Goldwyn would have put it) because these films are so unabashedly classical and Lubitschean, so at odds with the hyped-up, hyperviolent pace of film narrative in the blockbuster era and the prevailing hostility toward romanticism in the 1960s and 1970s.

Gradually, however, even Wilder's detractors came to recognize that he was actually one of the last upholders of the classical Hollywood tradition and of the mordantly romantic Lubitschean approach to film storytelling. Wilder's late style came as a rebuff toward the crudity of what passes for humor and romance in modern, post-Code Hollywood. But the most artistically successful of Wilder's several Lubitschean efforts, *Avanti!*, resoundingly flopped with the public and most reviewers in the same year (1972) that Francis Ford Coppola's classic gangster film *The Godfather* was joined on the box-office top-ten list by the hard-core porno films *Deep Throat* and *Behind the Green Door*. The graceful, emotionally generous, nostalgic *Avanti!* is an overt tribute by Wilder to the director who celebrated the romantic elegance and emotion of the times before they were born.

Like his mentor, Wilder reveled, although more often ironically, in the cultural traditions that had been destroyed in the two world wars that darkened their lives. The bitter irony of Wilder the perpetual exile being left stranded in his adopted hometown for his final two decades, with a surfeit of honors but no actual writing or directing jobs, offers unpleasant truths about the collapse of the once-great American film industry whose most audacious attributes he had once represented.

THAT WORD

"Cynical" is often used by Wilder's detractors, even today, to suggest that he somehow overreacted to the world he saw around him, that he should be taken to task for having what they regard as his overly bitter view of reality. Let's take that as a starting point to look at Wilder through the prism of his detractors and examine the validity, or lack of it, of the most frequent criticisms of his work.

I'll begin with the locus classicus of negativism toward Wilder. One of Wilder's most prominent naysayers, for a time, was the American critic Andrew Sarris. In his influential book *The American Cinema: Directors and Directions 1929–1968* (1968), he argued that "Billy Wilder is too cynical to believe even his own cynicism." Sarris had relegated Wilder to the "Less than Meets the Eye" section of that book. But within only eight years, Sarris admitted to having "grossly underrated Billy Wilder, perhaps more so than any other American director." In a *Film Comment* article entitled "Billy Wilder: Closet Romanticist," Sarris wrote that he had misjudged Wilder by not realizing that "his apparent cynicism was the only way he could make his raging romanticism palatable." When I asked Wilder in a 1978 interview about the change of heart by Sarris and some other critics, he replied, "Sarris, yeah, when he made his Hit Parade, I was in the 'Less than Meets the Eye' category. It was absolutely silly. . . . When I was very successful, they beat me over the head, now maybe some of them are a little gentler because they take pity on me. They commiserate with me. Maybe they are human, at that. They just don't feel like kicking an elderly man in the ass anymore."

As we look back over Wilder's long body of work, we can consider "cynicism" and romanticism as the twin poles of his creative personality, elements whose clash helps sharpen and define his stories and characters and his attitudes toward them. Jack Lemmon said of Wilder, "People think of him as being very ironic and very caustic. I don't think, unless you're very sensitive, that you have the ability to *see* the dark side, as Billy does—and *criticize* it, with the wicked tongue, the funny tongue, ironic humor, black humor . . . *whatever* label you want to put on it. He's a master at being able to make his points with comedy—which is tougher than making them with drama. But, if anything, Billy is a softie. And a romantic. It's very funny: he's the *opposite* of what many people perceive him to be."

Fernando Trueba, the Spanish director and former film critic, was a long-time admirer who befriended Wilder in 1988 and saw him frequently in Los Angeles over the years. Trueba recalled,

> He was always so generous, so nice. Every time I left him, I was always thinking, this guy has this reputation of being so acid, cynical, cruel, and for me, Billy Wilder is so warm and so friendly. You want to kiss him! A very curious thing—he was more interested in you to talk than him talk. I was always surprised that he was asking me what movie I was going to do next. And then he asked me to tell him the story. You have to tell him in detail. And he was suggesting things: "Why don't you do this and that?" I remember the first time I met him at his office on Brighton Way [in Beverly Hills], I was frightened about meeting him, I was nervous. And the moment door opened, I felt this man was my friend. He made me feel so comfortable from the beginning. He started reciting all the Fernandos that he knew—Fernando Valenzuela [the baseball player], Ferdinando Scarfiotti [the art director on *Avanti!*]. . . .

Whenever they chatted over lunch in years to come, after Wilder walked with him to a restaurant near his office—"like a king in his kingdom, everybody saying, 'Oh, Billy!'"—the aging master would always pump Trueba on contemporary films and insist on analyzing their strengths and structural weaknesses in fine detail. Their friendship was more than that of two professional colleagues but an enduring intellectual and emotional kinship. It also displayed the old newspaper reporter in Wilder, his interest in other people's lives and thoughts, as well as the side of him that Trueba described as "very romantic" in contrast to his largely media-generated image as a misanthrope.

A Foreign Affair seems as good a starting point as any other Wilder film to encapsulate many of the objections subsumed under the banner of Wilderian "cynicism," with its nightmarish setting, corrupt characters on both the American and German sides, sadomasochistic romance between a GI and a former Nazi sympathizer, and cruel mistreatment by the GI of a guileless woman—if only the film did not have such convincing characters in a quasi-documentary setting torn from the pages of contemporary headlines. But the utter destruction of the world from which Wilder emigrated only heightened the sense of dislocation he and other Jewish exiles from Germany felt from sentimental views of humanity and marked him as a representative twentieth-century artist of disillusionment. Dismissing Wilder out of hand as a cynical misanthrope is to treat him as a reductive caricature rather than as an artist whose films offer a probing, unblinkered view of human nature and display a rare gift for trenchant social commentary.

The complexity of Wilder's approach to human nature is what led to the frequent complaint by his detractors about his supposed cynicism. A code word for "realistic," it still holds some disparaging weight in critical circles and remains a persistent misunderstanding. "Cynicism" is a misleading term when applied to Wilder partly because it is often falsely defined or regarded with opprobrium. It may seem strange to anyone sympathetic to Wilder's work that such a charge would be leveled at an artist who lived through and survived so many cultural and political upheavals and spent much of his life as a reporter and filmmaker analyzing human nature at its worst. In a sense, he was always making journalistic exposés onscreen, probing into the hidden crevasses of human behavior and social corruption and folly. Wilder relentlessly mocked Sigmund Freud in his work, but the father of psychotherapy observed, in words that could apply to the filmmaker as well, "No one who, like me, conjures up the most evil of those half-tamed demons that inhabit the human beast, and seeks to wrestle with them, can expect to come through the struggle unscathed."

It would be useful at this point to more clearly define cynicism. Precision of language, so often lacking in critical discourse, is necessary to avoid confusion in trying to make sense of the work of a major artist. Dictionary definitions of "cynical" include "contemptuously distrustful of human nature and motives" and "based on or reflecting a belief that human conduct is motivated primarily by self-interest." To exemplify the first definition, the dictionary quotes Franklin D. Roosevelt criticizing "those cynical men who say that democracy cannot be honest and efficient." For the second definition, it cites "a cynical ploy to win votes."

As Jack Benny would put it, "*Well . . .*"

After a suitably protracted pause, we could ponder whether those examples describe the world in which we live today with some accuracy or whether they are simply figments of some curmudgeon's warped imagination. Was Wilder's portrayal of human venality in his films a product of his imagination, or is it true to what we know of human nature? To borrow a phrase from *David Copperfield*, that is what "these pages must show." Is Wilder criticized fairly or blamed unfairly for depicting the dark sides of human nature, especially in a medium such as film, which tends to be judged more unforgivingly in that regard than literature, such as, say, *King Lear* or the Book of Job? Are those works "cynical," or should Wilder be taken to task because he works in what most people consider a medium of mere entertainment?

Although FDR's point is well-taken that democracy is not *inherently* dishonest or inefficient, despite all the examples to the contrary, a key word in the dictionary's primary definition of cynicism might be "contemptuously." That in turn is defined as "manifesting, feeling, or expressing deep hatred or disapproval: feeling or showing contempt." Although Roosevelt once remarked, "I hate hate," it's hard to argue with someone showing disapproval or contempt toward social ills and injustices, as Wilder often does in his films, with his Swiftian satirical sensibility. And there is a considerable difference between hate and "deep disapproval."

Pauline Kael, in her *Film Quarterly* review of *One, Two, Three*, complained of feeling "degraded and disgusted, as if the dirt were being hurled right in my face." She described Wilder as "a clever, lively director whose work lacks feeling or passion or grace or beauty or elegance. . . . But he has never before, except perhaps in a different way in *Ace in the Hole*, exhibited such a brazen contempt for people." That judgment became a critical commonplace in the 1960s. But does Wilder harbor contempt or hatred for his characters or simply disapprove of some of them and their behavior? Does an artist have license to disapprove of his creations, or does that diminish his work? Should critics evaluate a filmmaker's work by such standards? Or are there are more complex ways of viewing both drama and human nature? Although a satirist can use broad strokes to caricature people, is it not also a dramatist's job to render human beings with a certain ambiguity rather than as simply good or bad rhetorical figures? Orson Welles remarked that "rhetoric is one of the greatest weaknesses of American artists; above all, those of my generation. [Arthur] Miller, for example, is terribly rhetorical." That is a trap into which Wilder does not fall. Welles added, "I hate rhetoric in a play, or moralizing speeches, but nonetheless the moral basis of a play is the essential thing, in my view," as it is in Wilder's films.

On some occasions Wilder does regard characters with such deep disapproval as to make their venality utterly irredeemable, such as Barbara Stanwyck's psychopathic murderess Phyllis Dietrichson in *Double Indemnity*; Fred MacMurray's Jeff Sheldrake, who callously uses the emotions of Fran Kubelik (Shirley MacLaine) for casual sex in *The Apartment*; and the heartlessly unfaithful wives played by Jan Sterling in *Ace in the Hole* and Judi West in *The Fortune Cookie*. Some of Wilder's minor characters also come in for vitriolic treatment, notably his intermittent editorial-commentary use of a "typical" American family, the Federbers (Frank Cady and Geraldine Hall), who make a holiday along with many other average Americans mindlessly participating in the spectacle of a man being killed in a New Mexico cave in *Ace in the Hole*.

In that boldly uncompromising film, Wilder's bleakest view of human venality, small-time New Mexico explorer Leo Minosa (Richard Benedict) becomes entrapped while searching for Indian artifacts. He dies because Chuck Tatum (Kirk Douglas), a ruthlessly ambitious Albuquerque newspaper reporter desperate to get back to the big time in New York, prolongs his rescue needlessly to milk a scoop. Leo is a World War II veteran married to a restless woman who despises him for being a nobody; he is a sympathetic figure but naive in trusting the unscrupulous Tatum. Tourists and other rubberneckers come to revel in the carnival environment whipped up by Tatum outside the cave. Although the film has frequent elements of black comedy, and Tatum is a diabolically compelling heel in Douglas's fierce, convincing performance, *Ace in the Hole* is so grim in its indictment of the public for its heartless enjoyment of morbid spectacle that American audiences rejected the film for holding a mirror up to them. Newspaper reviewers also predictably reacted with outrage, as the press usually does when it is criticized. Paramount desperately retitled the film *The Big Carnival* in a vain attempt to try to stir up some box office in the United States. Wilder admitted that the debacle "lost me power at the studio" and that it "changed my mind about the audience," whom he had trusted to respond to quality in a film. "But they never, at the time, they never gave it a chance. . . . I felt that I was not with it anymore." Yet he declared a few years after the film was released, "Fuck them all—it is the best picture I ever made." He made that remark to Walter Newman, who shares writing credit with Wilder and Lesser Samuels.

Wilder said that Newman, then a radio writer, proposed the idea for *Ace in the Hole* to him in 1949. It was loosely based on the 1925 entrapment and death of explorer Floyd Collins in a Kentucky cave. As Tatum mentions in the film, a newspaper reporter, William (Skeets) Miller, managed to interview Collins in the cave and won a Pulitzer Prize. The rescue efforts were widely covered by radio and newspapers and attracted thousands of spectators in a circus-like atmosphere. Another event that might have triggered Newman and Wilder's interest in the Collins case was the media hoopla in April 1949 over the entrapment and death of three-year-old Kathy Fiscus in a well near Los Angeles after a two-day rescue attempt. That event pioneered the voyeuristic appeal of live television, and the *Los Angeles Times* compared it to the Collins story. Actor and writer Victor Desny, a Yugoslavian émigré, also had the Collins story in mind around that time. Desny sued Wilder and Paramount in 1951 for $150,000 on the grounds that he written an outline of the Collins story and relayed a synopsis over the phone to Wilder's secretary, Rosella Stewart, in November 1949. Desny claimed that she had taken down his synopsis in shorthand and that his story was used without credit. Wilder denied Desny's claim of idea theft, and the Los Angeles Superior Court granted the director's motion for summary judgment against Desny in 1953. After Desny appealed, however, the case was sent back for trial in 1956 by the California Supreme Court, and the defendants settled with Desny in 1957 for $14,350. *Desny v. Wilder* became a landmark case and is a major reason film companies today are cautious about accepting unsolicited material.

As Neil Sinyard and Adrian Turner point out in their study of Wilder, *Ace* resembles Nathanael West's *The Day of the Locust* in its unsparing indictment of the public as a heartless mob, and Tatum's orchestration of events resembles the work of a movie director putting on a spectacle for a drive-in performance. Tatum exploits Leo's fear that an Indian curse has entrapped him, and the "Mountain of the Seven Vultures" where the cave is located slyly echoes the Paramount logo that displays a mountain within a circle of stars. Ironically, that element was strengthened when the studio vetoed Wilder's plan to start the film by altering the logo to eliminate the mountain, showing instead some desert sand within the traditional circle and having a rattlesnake jump and hiss at the audience, which Paramount thought would be too alarming. Tatum's crass reality show, with its steadily increasing admittance fee, is complete with a country-western singer (Bill Ramsey) warbling a song called "We're Coming, Leo" (by Jay Livingston and Ray Evans) that is hilariously obscene as well as flagrantly insensitive, while a female assistant hawks copies of the lyrics for a quarter to Al and Nellie Federber and other spectators:

> We're comin', we're comin', Leo,
> So, Leo, don't despair.
> While you are in the cave and hopin',
> We are up above you gropin',
> And we soon will make an openin',
> O Leo!

When Leo's death is finally announced, causing the merry-go-round to stop spinning (only after it keeps going for a while out of inertia), the stupid, hypocritical Mrs. Federber is shown wiping tears from her face with a handkerchief. It's telling that there are similar shots of German women in *Death Mills*, the 1945 documentary on the Holocaust Wilder helped the U.S. Army compile and write for viewing by ordinary Germans when he was involved in the de-Nazification effort at the end of the war. As American soldiers march the townspeople through a concentration camp, the narrator says with a scathing tone, "They move out as if for a Sunday walk, a pleasurable, short stroll through the wood." Then, as they are confronted with rows of bodies of inmates, the women are shown weeping crocodile tears as they wipe their faces, as Mrs. Federber will do when confronted with a man's death as part of the entertainment at an American carnival. Wilder surely kept that connection in his mind when he vented his wrath at Americans who behave with the indifference of ordinary Germans in World War II.*

But as such scenes show, however scathingly, even some of the worst behavior in Wilder's films—Tatum's murderous exploitation of the guilelessly

---

* It's not coincidental that Mr. Federber is in the insurance business, working for the same company that employed Walter Neff in *Double Indemnity*. When interviewed by a radio reporter, Federber says, "I'm in the insurance game myself. You never can tell when an accident's gonna happen. I sure hope Leo had the good sense to provide for an emergency like this. Now, you take my outfit, the Pacific All-Risk. We have a little policy that covers—." The announcer cuts off Federber's attempt to squeeze in a free commercial.

trusting Leo; songwriter Orville Spooner (Ray Walston) pimping out a prostitute disguised as his wife to sell a song in *Kiss Me, Stupid*; the elderly actress Fedora (Hildegarde Knef) destroying the life of her daughter (Marthe Keller) out of vanity in *Fedora*—is tinctured with these characters' feelings of guilt, self-disgust, or self-awareness. Other than in *Death Mills*, Wilder is not a propagandist but a dramatist exploring the complexity of human nature.

Even Tatum, Wilder's most thoroughgoing sadistic heel of a protagonist, is fully aware of how rotten he is, which helps make him so fascinatingly charismatic, as tragic figures tend to be. He draws our grudging sympathy because of his desperation to escape his own entrapment in a dead-end town and job he hates. Tatum is finally granted the kind of guilty realization of failed potential Aristotle tells us a tragic character is granted in the moments before his self-destruction, earning our pity. Tatum comes to feel anguished recognition of his crime: in close-up, we see his eyes fill with hard-won tears as a priest is heard offering final absolution to Leo off-screen. After being stabbed by Leo's widow, Lorraine, who gets away with her crimes, Tatum allows himself to die in a form of tragic self-judgment.

Fittingly, *Ace in the Hole* is Wilder's most overtly religious film, with its foregrounded themes of sin and guilt and pervasive atmosphere of the Native American sacred culture Tatum profanes as the "curse" takes on a strange reality. Maddened by the constant pounding of the drill, Leo tells Tatum, "It's enough to wake the dead." As Michael Wilmington and I wrote in our 1970 survey of Wilder's career, "There is only the merest iota of religious satire in his other work. But the religious aspects of *Ace in the Hole* are the vehicle for his deep revulsion at Tatum's actions. This, perhaps, and not *Stalag 17*, is Wilder's concentration-camp film" (we did not know then that he had worked on an actual concentration-camp film).

The symbolism of *Ace in the Hole* evokes the Holocaust in depicting a man's gratuitously cruel entrapment and death in a cave. Although Tatum differs from a German death camp guard in that he does not intend to murder the man he keeps captive, he recklessly plays with Leo's survival for selfish ends, prolonging his agony by delaying the rescue rather than using the quicker and safer method recommended by a construction foreman. Tatum even convinces Leo he is his friend and ally in order to keep him trapped in the cave, behavior that amounts to torture. Tatum gradually causes Leo's death by showing monstrous indifference to his well-being until it is too late, much as the world did not react to the Holocaust until it was too late. Tatum also offers a blasphemous parody of Old Testament iconography when he echoes Moses's speech from Mount Sinai as he rises on a crane to the top of the mountain and addresses the crowd through a loudspeaker, contemptuously telling them to go home because the rescue has failed, and Leo is dead.

Although Tatum becomes guilt-ridden as he realizes the consequences of his behavior, the film offers him no form of redemption. Sometimes Wilder goes further in his tragic empathy in giving his guilt-ridden malefactors a guarded form of redemption. In *Sunset Blvd.*, the doomed screenwriter/gigolo Joe Gillis selflessly sends away Betty Schaefer, the young woman who loves him unreservedly. At Fedora's daughter's funeral, the old actress confesses her sins to William Holden's Hollywood producer Barry Detweiler, another jaded Wilder surrogate. Those two films about the film business, starring the same actor, are narrated by their male protagonists, one a failed screenwriter who is already a dead man, a startling device for that time, and another who has had some success in Hollywood but is "dead" in the business (now that "the kids with beards" have taken over) and is desperately struggling to revive his career.

In *Sunset Blvd.*, Wilder and Brackett (and their collaborator, journalist D. M. Marshman Jr.) poignantly allow Gillis to rewrite his own life story as a film script as well as commenting sardonically on Hollywood from his vantage point face-down in a swimming pool ("The poor dope. He always wanted a pool"). Marshman, who worked for *Life* magazine, never had his name on another screenplay. As hard as it is to fathom now, Wilder and Brackett originally conceived of *Sunset Blvd.* as a comedy about an older actress and a younger man (they had Mae West and Marlon Brando in mind), and they were struggling with the project. It took on a darker tone when they told Marshman about it and he, ironically, brought it more in line with Wilder's characteristic themes. When I asked Wilder what Marshman contributed, he said casually that they gave him credit because he came up with the idea of a screenwriter becoming the kept man of the faded silent film star: in other words, the whole plot! Joe Gillis would have chuckled darkly over that one, but at least Marshman got credit and didn't wind up floating in a pool.

The unnerving device of having a corpse narrate *Sunset Blvd.* was left over from an excised opening of Gillis and other dead people in a morgue telling each other how they died. The sequence was cut after a preview audience howled with laughter at that macabre spectacle, one of the low points of Wilder's career. But as Nancy Steffen-Fluhr points out, such scenes—like another Wilder defiantly contemplated, starting *Ace in the Hole* with the dead Tatum telling us his story—involve a dead man walking. This evocation of death camps echoes the subversively ambiguous opening title of *The Major and the Minor* and the Yom Kippur (Day of Atonement) sequence in *The Lost Weekend*. The alcoholic Don Birnam desperately searches for a pawnshop to swap his typewriter for booze as he wanders through a New York landscape mysteriously empty of Jews until he is told it is a Jewish holy day. The Nazi genocide of Jews was not a subject American movie audiences wanted to contemplate with their entertainment after the war, any more than German audiences did with *Death Mills*, although what later became known as the Holocaust naturally was always on Wilder's mind. In cases when he "went too far," audiences tended to either walk out or laugh inappropriately, and the uncomfortably evocative scenes tended to be cut (although bits of the excised opening of *Sunset Blvd.* can be seen on a DVD edition).

Wilder frequently uses narration as a device to draw us into a character's confidence, and it is a form of confession. *Double Indemnity* also is framed as an extended confession, with MacMurray's Walter Neff recounting his crime to Edward G. Robinson's Keyes, first on the office Dictaphone and finally face-to-face. Neff is less brazen than Tatum; this Everyman character has the saving grace of greater self-awareness of his fatal flaws as well as, like Tatum, feeling remorse over the crime he has committed. Phyllis has coldly used her sexual wiles to lure Neff, who is eager to be corrupted, into killing her querulous, older husband (Tom Powers) to free herself from their dull middle-class existence and for the insurance money. Phyllis and Walter wind up in a literally fatal embrace, as he shoots her after she plugs him. Neff dictates to Keyes with sardonic bitterness, "Yes, I killed him. I killed him for money and for a woman. I didn't get the money and I didn't get the woman. Pretty, isn't it?" There are many other characters in Wilder films whose flaws, although serious enough, are so recognizably human and less final than murder that they engender sympathy rather than disgust. Some of them, like Jack Lemmon's C. C. (Bud) Baxter in *The Apartment*, even narrate the films they are in. Bud and the woman he loves, Fran, are lovable Everyman and Everywoman characters caught in a cesspool of corruption and struggling to free themselves from it, as they manage to do at the end of the film. It's often observed that Wilder helps his bitter pills go down by having them administered by charming actors such as Lemmon and MacLaine. Although some regard that as a weakness in his work, a sugarcoating of the themes, it is a defensible commercial defense mechanism that helped Wilder prosper and survive in the industry while dealing with such astringent subject matter.

On the rare occasions when Wilder used less-beguiling actors—notably the homely Ray Walston as the frantic small-town songwriter in *Kiss Me, Stupid*—the audience recoiled. But from the longer view of history, we can see that casting an actor who resembles the real thing is part of what makes that film so truthful, if painfully so for its contemporary audience. Peter Sellers, who was playing Orville before having a series of heart attacks, no doubt would have made the character more charming, although whether that would have been good for the movie is questionable. Wilder considered replacing him with Lemmon, and they reached out to him, but he had a scheduling conflict. The best actor of his generation, Lemmon could have made the character of Orville work on various levels, but it's bracing to see Walston's ordinary face and gawky mannerisms, symbiotic with the flaws of the character he inhabits. Cliff Osmond's Barney, the other half of the songwriting team of Millsap and Spooner, is an unrepentant schemer and amoral louse in Wilder's unfairly maligned romantic comedy. But Orville, his partner in venality, is so pathetically desperate in his second-rate ambitiousness, need to escape his life of quiet desperation, and self-defeating jealousy over being a homely guy married to "the most beautiful girl in town," Zelda (played by Felicia Farr, Lemmon's wife), that it's easy to identify with his failings while wincing over our painful self-recognition.

Wilder also is generous toward the failings of such characters as Gillis, who jokes with Betty about how he loathes himself, and Holden's self-centered Sefton in *Stalag 17*, a GI in a World War II German POW camp who is such a scheming wise guy, running constant scams, that his fellow inmates all hate him. Holden is another of those charming actors who makes you like him no matter how rotten his behavior. British actor Robert Stephens, a less familiar face to film audiences, is droll and moving as Wilder's emotionally barricaded Sherlock Holmes, who echoes Gillis when challenged by Dr. Watson (Colin Blakely) over his cocaine use: "Aren't you ashamed of yourself?" Holmes replies, "Thoroughly. This will take care of it." Holmes resorts to the needle to numb his senses again because he has uncharacteristically allowed himself to become the victim of a crushing romantic betrayal. Wilder's understanding of human foibles extends to such varied protagonists as John Lund's morally compromised Army Intelligence officer in *A Foreign Affair* (Lund is an excellent actor but not especially handsome or charismatic; he resembles a second-string Clark Gable, who would have made the character seem less real and more of a movie-star turn); Tony Curtis's glib, slick, enterprising seducer in *Some Like It Hot*, a charming rotter who gets his comeuppance (but whose way with women inspires the grudging admiration of Lemmon's nebbishy Jerry, who turns toward the camera and mutters, "Isn't he a bit of terrific?"); and Lemmon's smugly sexist American businessman Wendell Armbruster Jr., who undergoes a radical character transformation in *Avanti!*

"THE PRUSSIAN GENERAL"

One of the principal reasons Wilder acquired a reputation as a "cynic" and was blamed by his detractors for what they consider his "mean" personality was his habit of making acerbic public quips. Many of his remarks took aim at the shallowness and dishonesty of Hollywood and other social issues, but Wilder did make sarcastic comments about people. He did so especially when he was angry about colleagues he considered unprofessional or when he was retaliating against being personally attacked. Certainly Wilder was no Pollyanna, even if some of his detractors may sound like her when they bemoan his meanness. "I'm not really a cynic," Wilder protested in a 1989 interview. "Out here [in Hollywood], if you're not grinning from ear to ear all the time and you don't write pictures where the hero is some self-satisfied moron, they call you a cynic."

Sometimes Wilder's barbs could really sting. Sellers suffered his first heart attack on April 5, 1964, during the filming of *Kiss Me, Stupid* after having sex with his young wife, actress Britt Ekland, while using poppers. After eight more heart stoppages in the next two days, Sellers implicitly blamed Wilder in a *Variety* advertisement: "I didn't go to Hollywood to be ill. I went there to work, and found regrettably that the creative side in me couldn't accept the sort of conditions under which work had to be carried out. . . . The atmosphere is wrong for me." Wilder responded, "Heart attack? You have to have a heart before you can have a heart attack!" But Wilder's most caustic remarks generally, if not in that case, were redeemed by being witty, such as his comment about working with Marilyn Monroe: "She was never on time once. It is a terrible thing for an acting company, the director, the cameraman. You sit there and wait. You can't start without her. Thousands of dollars you see going into the hole. You can always figure a Monroe picture runs an extra few hundred thousand because she's coming late. It demoralizes the while company. . . . *[Sighs]* On the other hand, I have an Aunt Ida in Vienna who is always on time, but I wouldn't put her in a movie."

It has been reported that Sellers, who was fond of improvisation, chafed over Wilder's insistence on sticking to the script and found Wilder too demanding. And yet late in life Wilder surprisingly confided in his director friend Fernando Trueba that he had a much better time working with Sellers than people realized:

> Billy used to say that the best movie he had made was the four weeks he shot with Peter Sellers. He said, "That was the best work I did in my whole life." Billy told me one thing very funny: "He accused me that I was pressing him a lot. I was not very pressing. He was very friendly with me. The problem he had was that [shortly before shooting began] he had married Britt Ekland, who was twenty-one years old. And she was a sexual machine. They were fucking the whole day in the trailer. And the guy was not young anymore and he had the heart attack."

Because Wilder was such a perfectionist, or taskmaster, depending on your point of view, he has been blamed not only for what happened to Sellers but for giving other actors such a hard time that they became seriously ill. Lemmon even made a dubious joke about that history at Wilder's American Film Institute Life Achievement Award celebration in 1986, ticking off some of the instances and adding he was glad he had survived working on seven features with Wilder. Walter Matthau had a heart attack while shooting *The Fortune Cookie*; by that time, as Diamond put it, "We [had] learned our lesson" and did not replace him, and Matthau went on to win the Oscar for best supporting actor. Matthau also suffered a major back injury while sliding down a laundry chute for *Buddy Buddy*. Robert Stephens actually tried to commit suicide during the making of *Sherlock Holmes* (though Lemmon tactfully avoided mentioning that). As Stephens recalled in *Knight Errant: Memoirs of a Vagrant Actor* (1995):

> I admired Billy Wilder tremendously, still do, but that kind of obsessive perfection can make an actor feel terribly inept a lot of the time. He used to make you time the putting down of an object at the exact syllable in a word and he never stopped within a millimetre of what he wanted; he only stopped when he got *exactly* the action and the word on the beat together, and that would be one tiny thing in one scene with a million other pieces of direction going on. . . . Jack [Lemmon] said how much he adored Billy Wilder but that he drove him crazy with all that Germanic regimentation and matching of action to the slightest inflection. This was before I started, so I should have been warned. . . .
>
> In the middle of shooting, I suffered the most terrible crisis of confidence. The film was getting on top of me, and the demands Billy was making seemed to me increasingly severe. He wasn't sure how we should play Holmes; the film was meant to be an affectionate, light look at the character, but he had asked me not to try to be funny. . . . I was working with a genius who knew exactly what he wanted. Billy didn't care how much film he used, even if one little scene took thirty-five takes, it simply didn't bother him. He'd say, "Listen, I don't want very good; I want it exactly as I want it. I don't have to show the rushes to anybody. I am my own master. We can take as long as it takes." But it was too long for me.

Finally a doctor gave Stephens

> some sleeping pills, enough to kill a horse. One night, mixing them with a bottle of whisky, I was sure I had enough to kill myself. . . . They just caught me in time. I had simply had enough, although I hadn't really planned to commit suicide. I did not leave any notes or make any marks. I just drifted away from everything. . . .
>
> My crisis held up the film for two or three weeks. Billy was terribly upset and said that it was all his fault. But it wasn't, really. It was a culmination of things, and I was terribly embarrassed to return to the shoot. To their eternal credit, Billy and all the team and crew carried on as if nothing had happened, and I was immensely touched by that. He came and said that

we'd carry on and finish the picture and that we'd go a little slower and not hurry things. But of course, when I returned, it was all exactly the same!

James Cagney was another actor who suffered under the strain of working with the demanding director. Cagney decided to retire from film acting for many years after going through the grueling experience of delivering many pages of rapid-fire dialogue in *One, Two, Three*, although he does so with wonderful aplomb. Wilder and Diamond almost always strictly enforced their rule of making actors deliver the lines exactly the way they wrote them, expecting their actors to behave like professionals, not like Aunt Ida from Vienna, and they had no sympathy with Actors Studio performers who wanted to dig into their psyches to reshape their roles. Diamond told students at an AFI seminar, "If you ever listen to actors talk, you will not improvise." But even such old pros as Cagney or Matthau found it a struggle to deal with the team's need for perfection.

I watched Diamond sitting on a stool near the actors on the set of *The Front Page* in 1974, with the rare license for a screenwriter to interrupt the actors when they deviated even slightly from the text. Often Wilder would turn to him at the end of a take and ask, "Were all the lines said?" That freed Wilder to concentrate on other matters of production but did not go down well with the more casual school of modern performers who made a cult of improvisation as superior to actual writing and considered Wilder old-fashioned as a result. Some, including MacLaine and Sellers and most notably Marthe Keller in *Fedora*, had clashes with the director over their enforced line readings; the result with MacLaine, who grudgingly went along with him, was richly nuanced, but the miscast Keller's dialogue in her desperately bad performance was looped by another actress for the English version, though her voice was allowed to be heard in the French version. Even Wilder's favorite actor, Lemmon, referred to Wilder as "The Prussian General"—affectionately—when I interviewed him on the set of *The Front Page*. Wilder played on that image in *Kiss Me, Stupid* by passing out sweatshirts showing him wearing a helmet he owned from the Franco-Prussian War, a takeoff on that film's running gag of the songwriters wearing sweatshirts featuring classical composers.

Wilder and Diamond actually were somewhat more flexible, although not on the set, than actors liked to complain. As Diamond told me, once actors are cast, "You subconsciously write for them. It's really the melody you hear in your head when you write for them." In some cases they tailored roles increasingly to the actors as they watched their chemistry develop onscreen, as they did with Lemmon and MacLaine in *The Apartment*. Although it's often reported that Wilder and Diamond started filming with incomplete scripts, Paul Diamond explained,

> Everything was thought out. It's one of the misunderstood myths. People keep writing and saying, "Oh, they didn't have a full script when they started"—demonstrably untrue. You can't start shooting something unless you know exactly what you're going to shoot, where you're going to be. Everything's budgeted, everything's scheduled. You have to have the props, you have to have this, you have to have that, you have very little wiggle room. Everything has to be boarded. Everybody knows this.
>
> And so what they would do, they would leave themselves as a challenge, as a means of flexibility, knowing how the ending was going to go, knowing what the elements of that ending were going to be, they didn't necessarily have dialogue in stone. Because that way they could see if something better came up, they could get it in. There's not suddenly going to be a dream sequence on top of the Eiffel Tower in *Fortune Cookie*. It's absurd. But yes, they didn't have "Nobody's perfect" [what Joe E. Brown's millionaire tells his fiancée, Jack Lemmon, in the celebrated ending of *Some Like It Hot*] when they were approaching shooting it, that was part of the pressure of the production. But clearly, who gives you money if you don't have a script?

Some of the scripts in I. A. L. Diamond's papers at the Wisconsin Historical Society leave out the last parts, but those evidently are incomplete drafts; for example, there are three drafts of *Kiss Me, Stupid*, one that says "LAST PART TO FOLLOW," another saying, "SECOND PART TO FOLLOW," and one that is complete. When I asked Diamond's son if Wilder and Diamond would sometimes withhold the last part to outwit the front office, Paul said, "No, they weren't playing games with them. The great thing about the Mirisches [the Mirisch Company, with whom Wilder worked on eight films] was, [they knew that if] they hired good people, they would get good films, so the films would only be better if they didn't interfere, and they didn't interfere. [Wilder and Diamond] basically had a constant nonblinking green light for what they wanted to do."

Actress Hope Holiday, who memorably plays Bud's Christmas Eve bar pickup, Margie MacDougall, in *The Apartment*, complained that people keep saying that the film began shooting without a finished script:

> Shirley said it on one of the documentaries we did for *The Apartment*, "Oh, we had so many problems, we started a movie with a script that was only a third finished." And I'm thinking, How could it be a third finished when I come in toward the middle of the movie? [Margie first appears on page 78 of the shooting script.] No, it wasn't—the whole script was completely finished. They may have made changes when they were shooting. Not when I was in it; what I did was already written. So why did she say that? She's probably thinking nobody ever knew anyway, they're all dead.

MacLaine, however, was not given a complete script when filming began on *The Apartment* and didn't know how the story would end. Wilder knew she was a member of the Rat Pack, and as she recalled, "I was hangin' out with Dean and Frank [Sinatra], and they were teaching me how to play gin rummy, and Billy put that in" (for two key scenes of her playing cards with Bud, including the ending). She also remembered, "There was a wonderful scene that came in later when we were having lunch at the café at Goldwyn Studios, and I was having some kind of disastrous love affair. I said, 'Oh, why do people have to be in love with people anyway? Why can't they be in love with kangaroos or something?' And Billy said, 'That's it, that's it!' He went back and he rebuilt the set." Bemoaning her disastrous love affair in the film, Fran tells Bud, "Why do people have to love people anyway?," and he replies with a shy laugh and without her realizing his import, "I know what you mean." Wilder also drew from MacLaine Fran's memorably bitter line, "You think I would have learned by now—when you're in love with a married man, you shouldn't wear mascara." Although MacLaine sometimes chafed at Wilder's resistance to improvisation and wished he "would pay as much attention to my talent as he did to Jack's," she eventually mellowed toward the director and felt, contrary to his tyrannical image, "He was very flexible, that German-Austrian science-of-comedy person."

Wilder hardly glanced at the script throughout the day's shooting I watched on his and Diamond's version of the Hecht-MacArthur play *The Front Page*, but the care paid to following the script was punctilious. While I saw how the director's energies were devoted largely to the actors, the camera, and physical business, I studied his reliance on Diamond, who was sitting attentively near the camera, to listen for aberrations and to arbitrate dialogue squabbles. Diamond told me that his function on the set was "mainly to protect the dialogue" but also to be there in case small changes were necessary. Sometimes modifications had to be made to the dialogue "to adjust it to the camera" and for complicated action, such as in the reporters' running poker game.

Vincent Gardenia, as the apoplectic sheriff, several times said "Goddammit" when he was supposed to say "By God," and Diamond quietly corrected him until the line was delivered correctly. Once, after rehearsing the scene, Wilder paused a moment in thought and turned to Diamond, asking, "Do we have too many damns?" Diamond ran his finger down the page and said, "Yes, three damns. One should be a By God." In rare instances, they would give Lemmon and Matthau and other actors some leeway to adapt lines to their own way of speaking. During rehearsals of a scene in which Matthau was to threaten the sheriff with being thrown out of office on his "fat can," Matthau continually changed the phrase to "big fat can," and just before shooting Wilder reminded him to drop the "big." When the scene was shot, Matthau bobbled the phrase, pronouncing it "fayut can." "*Fayut?*" Wilder said incredulously, and Matthau turned to Diamond, saying almost plaintively, "Can I throw a 'big' in before 'fat'?" Diamond sniffed, "Yes, you have been doing it, and I haven't said a word." Matthau, looking a bit bemused, said to himself, "I felt guilty because I didn't say it." The scene was shot a second time, and Wilder asked sardonically, "Are all the words said? I'm going to print it."

Was Wilder an unnecessarily cruel taskmaster with his actors for making them follow the script religiously? Can he fairly be blamed for illnesses caused by longstanding medical and psychological problems experienced by actors, even if he may have caused enough stress to bring them to the point of crisis? The charge is somewhat exaggerated, although not entirely a figment of disgruntled actors or their press agents. But while I watched them filming *The Front Page*, the mood was cheerful and benign, with a stream of joking banter from Wilder and his cast, as other observers said it was throughout that shoot. But a Wilder tongue-lashing could be excruciatingly painful. His flaws of temperament, which led some screenwriters to avoid working with him, should not be the prism through which we evaluate his work. Despite the toll they could take on people, that trait stemmed from his hard-working perfectionism, a commendable trait for an artist at least in an aesthetic sense, and from impatience with mere humans who couldn't keep up with his needs and demands.

MORAL AMBIGUITY

Gleeful recounting of the filmmaker's acerbic zingers occupies too much of the space in magazine profiles and the lesser biographies, of which the locus classicus is the fittingly titled *The Bright Side of Billy Wilder, Primarily* (1970) by former publicist Tom Wood. Maurice Zolotow's biography *Billy Wilder in Hollywood* (1977) serves as a more elaborate compendium of his entertaining quips and observations (such as the one about Monroe and his mythical Aunt Ida) and sustains its generally glib tone despite being balanced by some thoughtful research and analysis. Far more thorough, in-depth biographical portraits were offered in 1998 by Ed Sikov's *On Sunset Boulevard: The Life and Times of Billy Wilder* and Andreas Hutter and Klaus Kamolz's *Billie Wilder: A European Career* (which has not been translated into English).

When I told Wilder in 1978, "You haven't had much luck with the books that have been written about you," he said, "That's absolutely right." He went on to complain about how unkind comments he did not make about people are often attributed to him, even if they were said by others. "There's no defense, you know. If it's cruel, I must have said it. And I never said anything cruel. I even have kind words for Hitler. Now how far can I go?"

Wilder was kidding about that, but he was not above making jokes about his mortal enemy, as I saw in his office, where he had a photograph of Hitler on his bulletin board skewered with the list of kosher restaurants in a Jewish enclave of Los Angeles. That was one of Wilder's black-humored ways of cauterizing his ever-present wound over the Holocaust and his inability to prevent the murders of his mother, grandmother, and stepfather, not turning away from that horrific memory but always keeping in plain sight the identity of the principal perpetrator and mocking him in the process by creating an ironic collage. Wilder's ability to make jokes even about Hitler and Nazism in his films fed into the criticism some have leveled at him as being guilty of "bad taste," but it is also an example of gallows humor, the kind often found in Jewish humor, a way of coping with the grimmest reality by transforming it into a dark joke. Audiences who have taken offense at the black humor in Lubitsch's *To Be or Not to Be* or Stanley Kubrick's *Dr. Strangelove*—two other works by great Jewish filmmakers Wilder admired—would not look favorably on Wilder's use of black humor in such films as *A Foreign Affair* or *One, Two, Three*, let alone *Ace in the Hole*.

Putting aside Wilder's penchant for jokes about Hitler and sharp quips about other people he disliked, perhaps what some people are saying when they loosely use the word "cynical" about Wilder's films is that their viewpoint is harsh (defined as "excessively critical or negative"), cruel ("devoid of human feelings"), or even nihilistic ("rejecting all religious and moral principles in the belief that life is meaningless"). Although there is no denying that his films are often severe in depicting human failings, whether that means they are excessively critical or negative depends on how one sees the world. Can it truly be argued that *The Lost Weekend* is an overstated case study of the horrors of alcoholism, *Ace in the Hole* an unbelievable portrait of the dark side of tabloid journalism, or *The Apartment* an unfair criticism of corruption and sexual exploitation in the business world?

Anyone seeking sentimentality or easy consolation from Wilder films usually will be disappointed, although it is ironic that some who claim he is too "cynical" also criticize him for sugarcoating some of his harsher situations. That is not entirely a case of "damned if you do, damned if you don't," for Wilder films often straddle a high wire between grimness and entertainment. The sentiments in his comedies and dramas alike are usually well-earned, but sometimes the films do lapse into sentimentality or schmaltzy resolutions, as is inescapable for anyone sustaining a long career in Hollywood (that issue will be studied in more detail below). As for the charge that Wilder is "cruel" toward his characters, you only have to watch his actors in such emotionally wrenching films as *Sunset Blvd.*, *The Apartment*, and *The Private Life of Sherlock Holmes* to see that the way he portrays people is far from "devoid of human feelings." Nor are films in which characters often behave cruelly toward one another—such as Wilder films in which women are cruelly misused by men—necessarily cruel films; conflating characters with their creator is usually misleading.

It would be even more foolish to argue that his films are nihilistic, since they are manifestly about moral dilemmas and principles. But Charles Higham did make that argument against the director in a vitriolic *Sight and Sound* article in 1963, "Cast a Cold Eye: The Films of Billy Wilder": "Together with Alfred Hitchcock, Billy Wilder remains the English-speaking cinema's most persistently cynical director." Higham writes that Wilder's "laughter at humanity, smartly bantering" in his 1930s scripts with Brackett, later turned "savage and wounding" and "has sounded increasingly hollow in recent years," failing to "conceal the inner nihilism, the impatience and contempt for the audience. Wilder has always savaged those unsophisticated people who make up a majority of his audience, aiming instead at a jaded and world-weary minority. One suspects that today he has ceased to care a great deal about even this section of the public." Wilder depicts the world, Higham claims, as "ugly and vicious, selfishness and cruelty are dominant in men's lives. Greed is the central impetus of the main characters . . . and the sexual relationships in his films have a peculiar insect-like quality: the matings of praying mantises. . . . As a statement against life, as destructive criticism of human beings, *Ace in the Hole* has rarely been matched in the history of commercial cinema."

And yet Higham finds room for regret in what he considers the director's decline: "Yawning one's way through the graceless crudities of, say, *The Apartment*, . . . one wonders what has happened to the Wilder of better days . . . and it may well be that, having set out to destroy our last illusions, Wilder has destroyed his own power." There is much more of this vituperation, seemingly more revealing of that critic's notoriously sour view of humanity (Higham enjoys the "pitilessly developed" *Double Indemnity* and the "cold detachment" of *The Lost Weekend*) than of the complexities of Wilder's actual artistic personality.

Despite his films' tendency toward satire and ridicule, they do not simply deride or discredit moral principles; instead they explore moral issues and deplore or mock the way principles are often violated. Anyone who comes away from a Wilder film thinking the director believes that life is meaningless is projecting on it the kind of film the spectator fears or would like to see. As cold-blooded as Wilder's characters and situations can be, as skeptical and pessimistic as he is, there is always emotion or humor in his viewpoint. When a Wilder film is "merely" funny, that is usually a temporary state, because the Wilder world represents what Honoré de Balzac called *La Comédie humaine*. Wilder is a moralist not in the sense of reflecting conventional moral judgments but in the sense that his films can be seen to some degree as morality plays. They have much in common with those medieval allegorical dramas in which the characters personify human vices or virtues. The characters of some of his most memorable films embody such traits as murderousness, greed, sexual and emotional exploitiveness, lust, betrayal, and self-destruction, to name just a few of their many human flaws. Even the characters of his lighter films are riddled with comedic weaknesses, less toxic and more ridiculous versions of those same vices.

But what makes Wilder distinctive is the depth of the gray area of moral ambiguity most of his characters inhabit and his alacrity in acknowledging that trait of human nature. "Ambiguity is the home of the artist, the great artist," writer-director Walter Hill remarks in Peter Bogdanovich's documentary *Directed by John Ford*. Despite the affinities of Wilder's films with morality plays, his characters are rarely definable as just one thing or another (e.g., as medieval "humors") but instead are conflicting blends of personality traits, flaws, and strengths. The complex tone of Wilder's films, the bittersweet nature of his moods and situations, the way they shift from comedy to drama and back again are the essence of his approach to humanity, helping us find common ground with characters who commit reprehensible actions.

Although Wilder can be a merciless satirist when the occasion demands it, far more often he views even his most flawed and complex characters—such as Neff in *Double Indemnity*, Dietrich's Erika von Schlütow in *A Foreign Affair*, Swanson's Norma Desmond in *Sunset Blvd.*, and Hildegard Knef's title character in *Fedora*—with some measure of affection, understanding, tragic pity, or even grudging admiration, despite their appalling behavior. His films recognize that human nature is inherently complex and that simply condemning people, at least in drama if not in the criminal justice system, is usually unwise. In commenting on Tatum, Erika, Hitler, or anyone else, Wilder, the inveterate skeptic about human nature, would agree with Jean Renoir's Octave in *The Rules of the Game*, "On this earth there is one thing that's terrible—it's that everyone has his reasons."

A CLOSET ROMANTIC?

Given the undeniable astringency Wilder often displays toward human nature and the pessimism usually inherent in his stories, in what sense, then, can he truly be considered a "romantic," as he and others of us have claimed? Can the worldview he expresses in his films all the way from *People on Sunday* through *Buddy Buddy*, both of which take notably jaundiced views of reality, and such dark points in between as *Double Indemnity*, *Sunset Blvd.*, and *The Apartment*, let alone more comedic films with disturbing elements, such as *The Major and the Minor*, *A Foreign Affair*, *Some Like It Hot*, and *Kiss Me, Stupid*, support a claim that Wilder is a romantic at heart?

It will not do to sidestep the argument by claiming that Wilder's films are inconsistent in their viewpoint, veering whimsically or illogically from cynicism to romanticism from film to film or even within individual films. His artistic vision is strong and easily identifiable throughout his career as a writer and a director, even though his work is remarkably diverse. Clearly his worldview is all of a piece. But his variegated approach is a sign of the breadth of his artistic personality, his way of adapting to the world around him and to the demands of the film audience, as well as to his own appetite for constant change. His creative restlessness, attraction to various genres, and blurring of lines between genres are essential to his distinctive view of the world as a riot of incongruity.

"I always have been all over the place, with an appetite for trying every species of picture," Wilder told me. "Maybe I would have been much smarter had I set out on a career like, say—and I'm mentioning a very good director—like Hitchcock. You know what a Hitchcock picture is. But it would be very boring for me to make always the same species. I make pictures of various moods. Sometimes I'm in the mood for a comedy. Sometimes I do something serious. I cannot always wear the same suit and the same tie." As peripatetic in his choice of material as he was in everyday life, Wilder went so far as to reveal, paradoxically, that he liked to make downbeat pictures when he was in a happy mood and comedies when he was depressed. Perhaps that cryptic statement is a further key to his personality—using art as an antidote or a balancing tool to stabilize his highly conflicted, racing set of obsessive thoughts and emotions. And within a Wilder film, whether it's a film noir or a romantic comedy, there are always elements of conflicting passions.

Wilder's work is uneven, especially compared with the high degree of stylistic and thematic unity and frequent perfection achieved by his idol, Ernst Lubitsch, as Wilder was the first to admit. Some of his films conspicuously fail to succeed on their own terms (to name a few: *The Emperor Waltz*, *The Seven Year Itch*, *The Spirit of St. Louis*, *The Fortune Cookie*, *Buddy Buddy*), while others are deeply flawed, such as his often sour, implausible romantic comedies with Audrey Hepburn, *Sabrina* and *Love in the Afternoon*. But I believe the elements in his work that some people have found objectionable, distasteful, or repellent can be seen from another point of view as among their foundational strengths. Wilder films that once were controversial or remain so in some circles—*A Foreign Affair*, *Sunset Blvd.*, *Some Like It Hot*, *The Apartment*, and *Kiss Me, Stupid*—I find to be among his best, partly for the same reasons other critics have considered them objectionable. To some extent that is simply a matter of taste, but we're here to dispute that distaste or at least to make a good case for explicating Wilder more clearly for those who may reject him because of misconceptions or other forms of artistic prejudice.

And I hope this study will vindicate my view that Wilder did some of his greatest work in his old age, despite its rejection by the public and many reviewers who, while claiming to look back with nostalgia at his better days, were missing out on his development of a richer, more melancholy, and more romantic vision. As the corrosive satire that established his reputation receded and the public's appetite for harsher reality made Wilder's later films seem passé, he was, as often happens to older artists, becoming more himself.

"THE AGEING . . . OF THE CINEMA"

The influential French critics and future filmmakers of *Cahiers du Cinéma* who did so much in the 1950s to rejuvenate the reputations of such American filmmakers as Orson Welles, Alfred Hitchcock, and Howard Hawks were somewhat conflicted toward Wilder. Too commercially successful in that period of his career to be perceived as an outsider in need of defense, Wilder drew some remarkably ambivalent opinions. A collective summary of his work in 1955 showed *Cahiers* at its quirkiest and least comprehensible, calling him "Dr. Jekyll and Mr. Hyde" and describing some of his most celebrated films, even *Sunset Blvd.* and *Ace in the Hole*, as "actually unviewable" because of their "vulgarity and "hand-me-down feeling."

But other Wilder films were received with more enthusiasm and clarity, including *Stalag 17* (which François Truffaut considered Wilder's best film because of its moral complexity and its portrait of a solitary, intelligent man outwitting a mob of "idiots"), *Sabrina*, and *Some Like It Hot*, which Jacques Doniol-Valcroze called "an ambiguous film, often bitter, sometimes a bit shocking, but always intelligent, subtle and, from time to time, moving." Jean-Luc Godard welcomed the less literary, more comical tone of later Wilder films and felt that with *Love in the Afternoon* and *Irma la Douce*, "he established himself as the worthy inheritor of Lubitsch in the hearts of cinephiles. For he had found once again the soul of a kid, waggishly 'Berlinish.'"

Reviewing *The Seven Year Itch* for *Arts* in 1955, Truffaut approvingly described Wilder as a "libidinous old fox" but found the enforced celibacy of Tom Ewell (due to censorship restrictions) "the most hypocritical [conclusion] in the world." Nevertheless, Truffaut enjoyed the dreamlike sexuality of the fantasy scenes involving Monroe and appreciated the film's "immense vulgarity, conscious, deliberate, meticulous, and finally very effective." By the late 1960s, having become a director himself, Truffaut declared, "Hawks and Hitchcock remain the two solid pillars of Hollywood, and also Billy Wilder, whom I like more now, especially *Kiss Me, Stupid*."

The leading theorist of the *Nouvelle Vague*, André Bazin, in his influential 1957 essay "La Politique des Auteurs" (The Policy of Authors), commenting on what Sarris later imported to the United States as the "auteur theory," approvingly quoted *Cahiers* critic and future director Eric Rohmer: "The history of art offers no example, as far as I know, of an authentic genius who has gone through a period of true decline at the end of his career; this should encourage us rather to detect, beneath what seems to be clumsy or bald, the traces of that desire for simplicity that characterises the 'last manner' of painters such as Titian, Rembrandt, Matisse, or Bonnard, composers such as Beethoven and Stravinsky." Bazin added,

What kind of absurd discrimination has decided that filmmakers alone are victims of a senility that other artists are protected from? There do remain the exceptional cases of dotage, but they are much rarer than is sometimes supposed. . . . In fact, the few exceptions one could mention only go to prove the rule. A great talent matures but does not grow old. There is no reason why this law of artistic psychology should not also be valid for the cinema. Criticism that is based implicitly on the hypothesis of senility cannot hold water. It is rather the opposite postulate that ought to be stated: we should say that when we think we can discern a decline it is our own critical sense that is at fault, since an impoverishment of inspiration is a very unlikely phenomenon.

Although Wilder's work has received more sophisticated analysis in recent years, there is still no critical consensus on his stature in film history. His films are often revived, and his American work as a director is well-represented on home video, though most of his work as a screenwriter in Germany and Hollywood is hard to see. The most popular films he directed are subjects of frequent appreciations both in print and on video, and there are numerous books about him, though not as many as on some other great directors from his era, such as Hitchcock, Welles, and Ford. In the 2012 poll of international film critics conducted by the British film magazine *Sight & Sound*, two Wilder films made the list of the top 100 films ever made —*Some Like It Hot* (#42) and *Sunset Blvd.* (#63)— while the directors' poll included three—*Some Like It Hot* (#37), *The Apartment* (#44), and *Sunset Blvd.* (#67). Polls, of course, are relatively crude and fickle indications of critical stature, but having three of his films on those lists is not a minor achievement. Yet Wilder films don't rank in the top tier headed by *Vertigo*, *Citizen Kane*, *Tokyo Story*, and *2001: A Space Odyssey*.

Perhaps because Wilder is often categorized as a comedy director, even though he made many dramas as well, he is not as widely studied in academia as some other major filmmakers, a neglect perhaps also attributable to his iconoclastic nature and the way his complex approach to gender and sexuality challenges the cult of "political correctness." The persistent belief of some of his more sentimental detractors that he is too cynical, too nasty, not humanistic enough, etc., also contributes to the sense that though he is respected and honored in many circles, he is still somehow a second-tier filmmaker. Many filmmakers and critics, however, would argue otherwise.

Even today, almost two decades after his death, it cannot be said that Wilder is fully accepted into the canon of the greatest American filmmakers.

He is not alone in being somewhat undervalued. Wilder himself told me in 1978 how he felt seeing "a questionnaire on the fifty greatest pictures ever made. And you always wind up with the same goddamn things. It's always *Citizen Kane* and *Battleship Potemkin* and *The Bicycle Thief*. But I was outraged, I must say, when I read that of the best fifty pictures, there was not one single Lubitsch picture among them." The relative neglect of Wilder's master also perhaps stems partly from the fact that Lubitsch specialized largely in comedy, which rarely gets the respect it deserves. Wilder was harder to classify and, unlike Lubitsch, determinedly elusive. But while Lubitsch has his fervent admirers, he remains, perhaps, more safely isolated in the distant, if often revered, cinematic past. For many critics and historians, Wilder and what he stood for remain all too recent, making him too contentious a figure.

As the American cinema gets coarser by the year, time has not yet caught up with, or gone back to, the virtues I and other admirers of Wilder find in his late work, nor has it managed to overcome the denigration those films received in their day (from *Kiss Me, Stupid* onward) from most reviewers and indifferent or hostile audiences. Although his final period is undeniably uneven, and he went out on what is universally considered a sadly discordant note with *Buddy Buddy* in 1981, the defiant romanticism and mordant wit of his late masterworks *The Private Life of Sherlock Holmes* and *Avanti!* have brought him some fervent support, but those films have yet to be regarded with any kind of critical consensus.

Even more controversially, Wilder's 1978 *film maudit Fedora*, his somewhat bungled but deeply personal final statement about his lifelong obsessions with the masquerade and its ultimate expression, show business, is not fully appreciated. *Fedora*'s flaws are obvious, but what it tries to do and fitfully succeeds in with such great emotional force is still a matter of considerable dispute and, I would argue, incomprehension. To fully appreciate or even understand what the film is trying to do and how it works on different levels requires a knowledge of the entirety of Wilder's career to put it into perspective. Such knowledge of a filmmaker's long and complex body of work and a late film's intricate levels of allusiveness and self-examination also is necessary for a viewer to appreciate what John Ford was doing in his final feature film, the unfairly reviled masterpiece *7 Women* (1966). Even though *Fedora* was not Wilder's last feature, like *7 Women* it was sneeringly regarded by most American reviewers as evidence of an elderly, once-celebrated filmmaker falling into dotage, although those two vale-dictory films found more admirers overseas.

And as Bazin put it, even if "one has nevertheless to accept that certain indisputable 'greats' have suffered an eclipse or a loss of their powers . . . The problem has to do with the ageing not of people but of the cinema itself: those who do not know how to age with it will be overtaken by its evolution. This is why it has been possible for there to have been a series of failures leading to complete catastrophe without it being necessary to suppose that the genius of yesterday has become an imbecile."

TRUTH AND BEAUTY

Like "cynicism," the term "romanticism" can be a source of confusion. Usually it is simply identified with a fondness for love stories. The romantic moods of classical Hollywood love stories generally traffic in "an emphasis on the imagination and emotions," and since those are essential traits in human nature, such a focus is virtually inescapable for a dramatist in any medium. But in a broader sense romanticism can refer to an idealistic view of the world and disillusionment toward its violation.

The discussion surrounding Wilder's "romanticism" rarely mentions his bedrock idealism, however. And it has little specifically to do with the romantic movement in literature, art, and philosophy, which was founded in the eighteenth century in "a reaction against neoclassicism and an emphasis on the imagination and emotions," as well as "an exaltation of the primitive and the common man" and a view of harmony between man and nature. Although Wilder did a considerable amount of location shooting, he was not into primitivism in filmmaking (unlike in his art collecting) but was mostly a city man, as such films as *The Lost Weekend, A Foreign Affair, Sunset Blvd.,* and *The Apartment* show so vividly.

The shadowy streets and menacing claustrophobia of film noir, which stemmed from German expressionism and the German *Strassenfilm* (street film), for much of his career were more his milieu than romantic views of the natural world, and it infects even his lighter films in both countries. The alienation inherent in noir's depiction of America, and particularly Los Angeles, is a symptom of the condition Sigmund Freud called *unheimlich* (creepy or uncanny); it is a place that Gerd Gemünden describes as "homely and familiar but that at the same time harbors something hidden or concealed, now pushing to come to the surface." Filmmakers with German roots were particularly adept at discerning such undercurrents in an adopted homeland whose conflicting aspects they regarded with the distancing viewpoint of exile.

And paradoxically, although Wilder often claimed to disdain Italian neo-realism, sometimes mocking it in his films and interviews as pretentious and lacking in humor, his films have elements in common with that harsh and starkly unglamorized postwar movement. While touring Europe to promote *Some Like It Hot*, he rattled off a spoof of an Italian neorealist film to colum-nist Art Buchwald, about "the plight of the sardine fishermen in the Canary Islands. . . . Because the Americans won't let the sardines lay the eggs. . . . The people live 300 to a house jammed together like a can of sardines. The can opener is the symbol of their freedom, and in the final scene the hero stabs the villain with a rusty one he finds on the dock. . . . There will be no music in the picture except for a Portuguese clavichord and naturally the picture will be out of focus as it had been filmed through a thin piece of Roquefort cheese."

But, kidding aside, he began his film career by writing movies shot exten-sively on location in Berlin, including that semidocumentary precursor of neo-realism, *People on Sunday*, as well as *The Devil's Reporter* and *Emil and the Detectives*. Other German films he helped write, *A Blonde Dream* and *Scampolo* (filmed in both Berlin and Vienna), draw meaningfully on a simi-lar urban milieu. And after becoming a Hollywood filmmaker, Wilder went so far as to shoot his unusually irreverent romantic comedy *A Foreign Affair* on the ruined streets of Berlin. Wilder's dark-comedy rubble film sometimes plays like a parody of Rossellini's unrelentingly tragic film of the same year in the same setting, *Germany Year Zero*. Wilder's next cinematic excursion to the city where he once lived resulted in *One, Two, Three*, a farce in the cha-otic location of divided Berlin, still partly in ruins but also in the process of rebuilding at the height of Cold War tension.

Wilder admittedly was a great admirer of Vittorio de Sica's *Ladri di bici-clette* (*Bicycle Thieves*, 1948), a leading example of the Italian neorealist school of filmmaking; Wilder put it tenth on his list of favorite films for a 1952 poll, and Hellmuth Karasek's 1992 biography reported that it currently was Wild-er's favorite film.* But in *Avanti!*, set on the Italian island of Ischia in the Gulf

---

* The top nine films on Wilder's 1952 list, for a poll of filmmakers by Le Comité du Festival Mondial du Film et des Beaux-Arts de Belgique, were *Potemkin*, *Greed*, *Variety*, *The Gold Rush*, *The Crowd*, *La Grande Illusion*, *The Informer*, *Ninotchka*, and *The Best Years of Our Lives*. In 1976 Wilder

of Naples, Wilder teases the earnest postwar social consciousness of neorealism with his picturesque, lyrical montage of his heroine, Juliet Mills's Pamela, touring the island, an unusually spontaneous-seeming passage in his work. The buxom Pamela thoughtlessly orders four ice cream cones in front of three hungry, winsome street urchins straight out of neorealism but walks away to eat all the cones herself. He also spoofs Italian filmmaking of another kind with the melodramatic subplot of a Sicilian hotel maid murdering a valet who seduces and abandons her, and yet there are oddly moving moments even in the midst of that parody.

Wilder displayed no special interest in or facility for exploring the beauty of primitive or rustic locations until the unexpected flowering of his late works *The Private Life of Sherlock Holmes*, set in England and Scotland, and *Avanti!* Those stories about the romantic mellowing of repressed characters are matched by a more relaxed tempo and liberal use of picturesque European locations. Wilder by then had become a largely European filmmaker again, not much wanted by Hollywood anymore but returning to his origins. Perhaps those projects reawakened the part of him that remembered how he would play as a child in the Carpathian Mountains in what may have been a more innocent time in his life, if any time of his life was truly innocent.

Godard observed of Rossellini, "With him a shot is beautiful because it is right: with most others, a shot becomes right because it is beautiful." Wilder's visual style is both right and beautiful: in collaboration with such master cinematographers as John F. Seitz, Charles Lang Jr., and Joseph LaShelle, its elegance is also functional, tending to concentrate on storytelling efficiency while eschewing flashy effects of the kind Wilder told Schlöndorff tend to give habitués of cinematheques a "constant orgasm. . . . Shoot the son of a bitch and let's go home." As Wilder's young *Front Page* cinematographer, Jordan Cronenweth, told me, he was "more into people than he is into the visual." Wilder was "very straightforward" with his style and knew "quite specifically" what he wanted: "He's probably tried every good and bad thing it is possible to do in movies." Unlike most screenplays, the ones Wilder wrote with his partners are unusually enjoyable to read, sprinkled not only with

---

told AFI fellows in a seminar that his favorite films included *The Godfather Part II, La Grande Illusion, The Best Years of Our Lives, The Bridge on the River Kwai, The Maltese Falcon, The Informer,* "and some of the old German pictures, the Murnau pictures."

character-revealing jokes—Bud in *The Apartment* "wears a Brooks Brothers type suit, which he bought somewhere on Seventh Avenue, upstairs," and the first woman we see brought to his place for a tryst is "a first baseman of a dame"—but also containing vivid, though not overly detailed, indications of how the scenes will play visually.

Even the descriptions of physical settings, usually a snooze to read in screenplays, are often amusing. Neff's narration in *Double Indemnity* tells us when he approaches the home of the tawdry Phyllis in the Hollywood Hills, a home whose cheap taste reflects her personality: "It was one of those California Spanish houses everyone was nuts about ten or fifteen years ago. This one must have cost somebody about thirty thousand bucks—that is, if he ever finished paying for it." The script by Wilder and Raymond Chandler sarcastically describes the hallway as "Spanish craperoo in style, as is the house throughout. A wrought-iron staircase curves down from the second floor. A fringed Mexican shawl hangs down over the landing. A large tapestry hangs on the wall. Downstairs, the dining room to one side, living room on the other side visible through a wide archway. All of this, architecture, furniture, decorations, etc., is genuine early Leo Carrillo period."*

Wilder told me that although it is impossible to completely visualize a scene while writing the script, when the script was finished he knew roughly how it is going to look on film. He said in his best self-deprecating manner, "I know how many words I need to get them from the bedroom to the bathroom." Still, for many years he recognized that as someone who considered himself primarily a writer, he needed help with the mechanics of filmmaking. So he relied heavily on an editorial consultant, Doane Harrison, who was always with him on the set and "taught me what celluloid was all about" (Harrison was often credited as editorial supervisor and as associate producer on Wilder films). But Wilder's visual style was sophisticated from the start of his directing career in Hollywood. He sought to be "subtle and elegant" as well as efficient in telling the story, and over time he became increasingly adventurous visually. He let loose visually in his more overtly romantic late films with some stunningly lyrical landscape work in *Sherlock Holmes*

---

* Carrillo was a flamboyant Latino actor who portrayed stereotypical characters in movies and in parades, right-wing political rallies, and other public festivities in Southern California during that period.

(cinematography by Christopher Challis) and *Avanti!* (Luigi Kuveiller), showing that he could make films that were true because they were beautiful as well as beautiful because they were true.

"THE BROKEN HEART IN WILDER"

Wilder's body of work is filled with emotion, but unlike most Hollywood films, it rarely descends into sentimentality, a crucial and often-overlooked distinction. In risking portraying unlikable or offensive characters with whom it may be hard for the audience to identify, he is using distancing techniques in drama akin to those pioneered by Bertolt Brecht, even though Wilder denied being influenced by him. Wilder had met Brecht in Berlin and knew him slightly as a fellow member of the refugee circle in Hollywood; Brecht was an unhappy sometime screenwriter until he left for Europe during the blacklist period and established his Berliner Ensemble theater company in East Berlin. What Brecht called the alienation or making-strange effect, *Verfremdungseffekt*, provides an intellectual perspective on action and drama. It gives a critical judgment on characters' misbehavior rather than employing simpler forms of audience identification with characters. Brecht explained that the main purpose of alienation effects in what he called "epic theatre" is to place staged events in their historical context and using drama to deal with "the vital forces in the sphere of politics, philosophy, science and art." He called for a "great change" from conventional dramatic theater:

> The dramatic theatre's spectator says: Yes, I have felt like that too—Just like me—It's only natural—It'll never change—The sufferings of this man appall me, because they are inescapable—That's great art; it all seems the most obvious thing in the world—I weep when they weep, I laugh when they laugh.
>
> The epic theatre's spectator says: I'd never have thought it—That's not the way—That's extraordinary, hardly believable—It's got to stop—The sufferings of this man appall me, because they are unnecessary—That's great art: nothing obvious in it—I laugh when they weep, I weep when they laugh.

Wilder does not go as far in that direction, since he works in more of a mass entertainment idiom than Brecht's plays, but he is not afraid to alienate us from characters or make us dislike them. He is frank about their vices as he goes about satirizing their misconduct and exposing the social conditions that cause it. He is not afraid to make us laugh at the most horrible things or cry at the most ridiculous things; hence the accusations of "bad taste" against his work. Many of his protagonists can be considered antiheroes or outright heels. That kind of challenge and complicating of audience involvement was rare for a Hollywood director operating in Wilder's period of greatest success. It was a trait shared mostly by his fellow German or Austrian refugees, notably Douglas Sirk and Otto Preminger, and by other directors who worked in Hollywood but with a strongly Europeanized worldview and style, such as Welles, who had a mutual admiration society with Brecht.

Sirk slyly managed to succeed commercially by making films that played on two levels, as melodramas with subversive subtexts, while Wilder and Preminger won favor from audiences in the 1940s and 1950s by enabling them to relate to characters and situations that were mostly taboo or edgy in the American film industry. Wilder found ways to deal with such themes as pedophilia—in *The Major and the Minor*—and the question of the younger man/older woman relationship in *Sunset Blvd.* Even though Gloria Swanson was only fifty at the time, eighteen years old than Holden, her character gives the illusion of being much older, because she is a relic of a lost art. Wilder also got away with (humorous) treatments of homosexuality or homoeroticism (in various films, notably *Double Indemnity*, *Some Like It Hot*, and *The Private Life of Sherlock Holmes*) and cross-dressing (*Stalag 17*, *Some Like It Hot*, and *One, Two, Three*).

Some of the heels in Wilder films engage in behavior that is vicious and shocking by the standards of any era of Hollywood filmmaking, and sometimes audiences and most reviewers in the United States punished him severely for such astringent truth-telling, as they did with *Ace in the Hole* and *Kiss Me, Stupid*, which were better received overseas.* Wilder told Schlöndorff that the reason *Ace* was rejected was that it "affronted the people who saw the picture. They don't like to be confronted with things that are true and hurt. They say,

---

* Among the memorable titles of *Kiss Me, Stupid* in other languages are *Embrasse-moi, idiot!* and *Küss mich, Dummkopf.*

'Well, I don't want to spend, now, eight dollars for a Saturday night going to see the movie and be told that I'm a son of a bitch and that we are bad people, that we are very cruel.'" Wilder added unrepentantly that when you make such a picture, "as we say in American slang, you have to give it both knees. *[And in German:]* Use both knees to kick him in the balls."

Directors who affront their audience by telling painful truths or do not encourage easy identification with their characters are often misunderstood as cold or even misanthropic, as Wilder often has been. Further misunderstanding is caused by the fact that many of his characters are cold or emotionally distant, or so disillusioned that they have trouble functioning in human relationships, and have to learn to become more compassionate or perish in the process, literally or figuratively.

Another formative trauma for Wilder, a possible "Rosebud" moment about his early disillusionment in love, was reported by his biographer Maurice Zolotow. Drawing on interviews with Wilder's brother Willie and with Billy's longtime friend Walter Reisch, Zolotow writes that the incident occurred in Vienna in 1924 when Billie was eighteen and dating a tall blonde named Ilse. She was two years older and worked as a clerk in a phonograph and record shop on the Ringstrasse. Billie and Ilse often went out and danced to the latest pop tunes; he wrote poems about her; he wanted to marry her and emigrate to America together. But as Zolotow relates, two of Wilder's friends spotted Ilse one night soliciting on the Kärntner Strasse, the city's main shopping street. He refused to believe them but went there and witnessed her plying her trade. He slapped her and called her a whore.

> He had experienced a betrayal so deep and so wounding that he was never to recover from it. . . . The shock effect of this experience reverberates throughout his life. In one sense, most of his films are an attempt to come to terms with this disillusionment. It was hard, because a shock event like this, coming at an age when one is so vulnerable, tends to narrow one's vision of other women. . . . And yet, it is precisely this romantic fantasy and the unhealed wound of Ilse's seeming betrayal that generates the emotional energy, the violence, the bitterness, the sadness and the pity as well, in Billy Wilder's greatest films, and makes even his lesser pictures . . . sometimes beautiful and sometimes disturbing.

Zolotow claims it was this experience that made Wilder drop out of the University of Vienna and become a reporter. The biographer writes that it "confirmed him in his cynical philosophy" and caused him to portray many women in his films as prostitutes or as behaving like prostitutes, willingly or under duress, with varying degrees of sympathy. Other sources say Wilder never attended the university, but he told me, "I was to have become a lawyer. You know, in most Jewish families when there are two sons, the mother is pushing the two kids in Central Park, she says, 'Hey, I would like you to meet my son the lawyer and this is my son the doctor.' So I would have been a lawyer, but the idea of it bored me, so I just dropped out and I become a newspaperman." Wilder's Austrian biographers Andreas Hutter and Klaus Kamolz report in their authoritative biography, however, that he never enrolled at the University of Vienna.

When I asked Wilder about Zolotow's psychological comments about his youth, he replied, "Garbage. Lunacy. Absolute lunacy. It was kind of on the primer level of Freudian analysis. And the conclusion of it is silly. He tried to explain why I hate women. Well, number one, I don't hate women, so there is nothing to be found." I asked whether the incident with Ilse actually happened, and he said, "No. Bullshit. Total bullshit. My God, in my youth in Vienna, sex was far less prevalent. I never slept with a hooker in my high school days (a) because I couldn't afford it and (b) because I was scared shitless. In those days, the idea of gonorrhea and the fear which it struck . . . no kid would have."

But I wrote as a footnote to Wilder's rebuttal in the interview Todd McCarthy and I conducted with him for *Film Comment*, "Wilder's denial of the story is not entirely convincing. Zolotow does not claim that Wilder knowingly slept with a prostitute; the point of the story is Wilder's disillusionment in learning that the girl he loved was moonlighting as a prostitute without his knowledge. . . . If the story is true, it is easy to see why Wilder, even today, would find it too painful to confirm." And Wilder was less innocent at age eighteen than the Ilse story would indicate; he had already sampled the wares of the prostitute "Red Fritzi" in the brothel across from his high school. He gave yet another twist on the Ilse story to biographer Kevin Lally in the 1990s, claiming unconvincingly, "I knew the girl to be a hooker. She was very pretty, and I paid her. There were hookers in my life, but I was never in love with a hooker."

Furthermore, Wilder's realization of the world's complexities undoubtedly had as much to do with other incidents in the life of a boy growing up during the collapse of the Austro-Hungarian Empire and the privations of the Great War. He lived in a household marred by his mother's penchant for beating him with a stick and his father's secret adultery and illegitimate son (information the precocious Billie discovered and kept quiet, giving him leverage over his father). Most of all, however, Zolotow's analysis of the supposed change in Wilder's view of his female characters in the 1950s onward—which he attributes, improbably, to Wilder's working with his bête noire Monroe and sympathizing with the vulnerability behind her brassy facade—is simplistic in its application to the filmmaker's work. It tends to blur the complexities and sympathies he extended to his female characters as a screenwriter from his silent days onward—Brigitte, the innocent but corrupted teenage blonde heroine of *People in Sunday*, even has the same job as the fabled Ilse, that of a clerk in a phonograph and record shop in Berlin, where Brigitte actually was working when they cast her—and that attitude toward women is what he continued to show throughout most of his work in Hollywood as a writer and director. Disillusionment with life and with both men and women was a feature of Wilder's work from the beginning, and sympathy for women was hardly a late development in his career, although it may have seemed so to observers whose outlook was clouded by the prevailing critical commentary about him in the 1960s and 1970s as a supposedly heartless cynic and misogynist.

Nevertheless, it is a highly suggestive "coincidence" that Wilder's supposed incident of romantic disillusionment is echoed provocatively in one of the flashbacks cut from his highly personal late film *The Private Life of Sherlock Holmes*. Holmes finds that the prostitute his crewmates in his final year at Oxford have bought him as a prize for winning a race against Cambridge is a woman he worshipped from afar, believing her innocent. The young prostitutes in both *Sherlock Holmes* and the Ilse story are statuesque blondes, and, furthermore, the German spy who bewitches and fools Holmes is named Ilse (although she disguises herself as a helpless Belgian woman, Gabrielle Valladon); the detective still loves the spy despite her deception. Holmes considered the prostitute "the most beautiful girl I'd ever seen—I was so madly in love with her, that I didn't even dare approach her—I kept watching her from a distance—scheming how to meet her." He tells Gabrielle, while they share a train compartment, how he watched the young blonde cavorting in the countryside and attending church with several other girls and an older woman, like characters out of Guy de Maupassant's short story "La Maison Tellier," filmed by Max Ophüls with Danielle Darrieux as one of the segments of *Le Plaisir* (1952).

We see a montage of the girl Holmes loves leaving the church with (as we come to realize) her fellow prostitutes and their madam; the girls swimming in a river; and the blonde picking daffodils (the same kind of flowers Pamela brings to her mother's body at the mortuary in *Avanti!*). Following Oxford's victory over Cambridge—with Holmes feeling that in winning the services of a prostitute, "I was betraying my beloved, whose name I didn't even know"—he encounters the girl herself, seen from behind in the boathouse, wearing a white corset and stockings. When he approaches her, she speaks in a heavy Cockney accent as she asks without turning to face him, "Unlace me, will you, ducky?" He takes a shot of whisky and starts fumbling with the back of her corset. "What's the matter?" she says. "You nervous, ducky?" When she looks back over her shoulder, as the script puts it, "HOLMES freezes when he sees her face—it is, of course, the girl of his dreams. He turns and runs like a panic-stricken deer toward the door."

As he finishes telling Gabrielle/Ilse the story in dialogue excised from the film, he explains, "It was a very small price to pay for a very valuable lesson. Any emotional involvement warps your judgment and clouds your reason." She says, "That certainly would explain all the bad poetry in the world." He replies, "I'm not against sentiment. It's all right for butchers and bakers and poets. But for anyone in my profession, it would be fatal."

This is Zolotow's argument that Wilder's films gradually transcended his early traumatized view of women:

> A growth, an evolution in his vision can be seen, I think, from the films of the middle 1950s. . . . While coming to feel the sadness of the "whore," he also came, more and more, as his relationship with Audrey Wilder [his second wife, the former chorus girl, Paramount starlet, and band singer Audrey Young, whom he married in 1949] ripened into a unity of tastes and mutual affection, to know the felicities of a life together with a woman, his woman as he was her man.
>
> It is evident that from the time he came to cowrite and create *The Apartment* he was working in himself toward what was for him a new

reconciliation of these warring elements in his character. It was to be able to see women, more and more, as persons in their own right, as individuals, as human beings, as vulnerable human beings.

But whatever the truth of the supposed incident with Ilse in Wilder's youth and his nondenial denial in our interview, it is a suggestive metaphor, at least, for his youthful disillusionment. Given the whole of Wilder's work, and the direct evocation of such an event in *Sherlock Holmes*, it is the kind of legend (if legend it is) that rings with some truth in terms of his complex view of sexuality and the relations between men and women. The feelings of emotional deadness and disillusion in Wilder characters, whatever their complex origins, are the opposite of a cynical, misanthropic attitude on the part of their creator but instead a manifestation of a deep concern with the desperate human need to make emotional connections. His satirical and transgressive attitude toward sexuality is the surface level of his preoccupation with the distinctions between love and impersonal sex and with the deeper bonds of friendship and affection shared by characters who often have to overcome a hard-bitten façade. The internal emptiness Wilder's protagonists often suffer from manifests itself in a coldness that causes them to use other people and otherwise behave in purely self-centered but also self-destructive ways before he allows them the chance to break through that barrier into emotional intimacy.

Hope Holiday, who had a relationship with Wilder for several years in the 1960s and acted in *Irma la Douce* after playing Margie in *The Apartment*, recalled, "He could be very sweet and very nice; he also could be nasty too. He had that other side. He was sweet most of the time, but sometimes he was a little insensitive. He was somebody that you never really could get that close to. He always had a wall up, he never let you get close to him. It *seemed* like you were close to him, but you weren't. He let me get just so close, and that was it."

Nowhere, perhaps, in Wilder's work as a writer-director is this emotional conflict between emotional aloofness and a character's aspiration to transcendence through romance more beautifully stated than in a heartbreaking speech he and Brackett wrote for Jean Arthur's Phoebe Frost in *A Foreign Affair*. After falling for Captain Pringle's phony romancing, she is getting tipsy at a table with him in the illicit Lorelei nightclub where Erika performs.

Phoebe doesn't realize his wooing is a scheme to con her about the behavior of army personnel in Berlin, including his risky relationship with his ex-Nazi paramour. Erika at that moment is singing, "Want to buy some illusions?," while giving Phoebe the evil eye of jealousy and looking insecure about her own future. Twice the singer in her dazzling white dress is shown in brilliantly expressive compositions in a mirror on the wall behind the couple at their table. Pringle is not only squirming under Erika's gaze but also feeling guilty over his cruel manipulation of Phoebe's feelings. His emotions are gradually beginning to be troubled, despite himself, by the sincerity of her devotion. His awareness of his own deceitfulness is heightened by the disgust he feels over learning the depths of Erika's Nazi past.

The complexity of the three characters' interactions in the narrative and Wilder's eloquent mise-en-scène are setting Phoebe up for the worst disillusionment of her life, but at this point of exhilaration the repressed, lonely congresswoman is revealing to Pringle and the audience her deepest feelings about love. The speech is played mostly in a luminous close-up of Arthur, elated, a little giddy, the fervor of her feelings visually questioned by the way the glimmer in her eyes looks a bit like madness, but it's *la folie de l'amour*, self-destructive yet pardonable:

> Oh, John, I'm so happy, I'm in heaven. Not that I was unhappy before, I was just drifting. That's it. Drifting on a gray sea all alone. It's not bad, but suddenly you get scared. You need another foresail. So you hoist up your heart. And you wait. And nobody passes by—just gray waves. Your heart gets frayed in the sun, lashed by the night winds and rain. So you haul it down, what's left of it, and you resign yourself. Then suddenly, out of nowhere, comes a boat, so unexpected, all white sails on the horizon. [She lifts a glass to toast him with Champagne] To you, my beautiful boat.

Our realization that Phoebe's yearning heart is about to be cruelly broken—as happens when she comes to her senses, finds herself under arrest in an army raid on the nightclub, and learns the truth from Erika—renders this scene of her emotional awakening all the more poignant. In the nightclub scene, Arthur's lovely voice, "an indescribable blend of huskiness and girlish vibrato," as I put it in my Frank Capra biography, conveys the fervent but tenuous nature of her devotion to Pringle and the danger of her situation. As another of her directors, George Stevens, told me, "Jean Arthur was terribly vulnerable and exposed even under the most ordinary of circumstances, even if she had to stick her hand out into traffic to make a left-hand turn." In *A Foreign Affair* these are far from ordinary circumstances when she finds herself falling in love with an American heel in a foreign land, and Wilder probably cast her for that quality of vulnerability. And for the sincerity she always conveys with her voice and face, which comes from her risking her heart so nakedly onscreen: when I asked her to define the nature of her inimitable voice, she said, "I don't know what it is, except that I mean what I say."

Screenwriter and journalist Steven Gaydos identified the crux of Wilder's work as stemming from his "broken heart." Gaydos observed in 2019, "The funny thing is that Sarris completely dismissed Wilder as fatally flawed due to a too-severe case of cynicism. Then he reevaluated Wilder later and felt he'd misjudged this. Strangely I am not troubled by Wilder's cynicism, but [Robert] Altman drives me around the bend and [Howard] Hawks seem[s] somehow deficient. Perhaps I can find the broken heart in Wilder, on brutal display in [Sam] Peckinpah, absent in Altman and Hawks." Diamond's screenwriter son Paul agreed with this view of Wilder: "He's absolutely a spoiled romantic, without question. He's a man who had his heart broken too many times, and he sees this possibility in every relationship. That drives caution."

In a provocatively paradoxical 2016 essay on Wilder's obsessive explorations of the conflicts between sex and love, Jason Carpenter argues that despite his reputation as a cinematic sexual provocateur, sex per se is not as much of a concern in his stories as his characters' need for genuine companionship. Noting the coldly transactional nature of sexual involvements Wilder often criticizes in his films, Carpenter writes that he is more concerned with "the heart—the metaphoric, moral center of human empathy—whose true yearnings go unheeded," while "sex masks the true meaning of things" for his often brokenhearted characters in their search for emotional redemption.

Crucially in the fraught relationships between troubled characters in such films as *Double Indemnity*, *The Apartment*, and *The Fortune Cookie*, the achievement of genuine emotional openness through "confession serves to clear the way for understanding, clarity of identity, forgiveness, and a hope for the future for decent characters," while cutting to "the heart of Wilder's take on friendship trumping sexual romance . . . the possibility of love enduring after all." His characters' ultimately redemptive trait "may be an ability to navigate a world increasingly enveloped by moral decay with kindness and thoughtfulness intact. . . . If, ultimately, Baxter and Fran [at the end of *The Apartment*] don't make love to justify its palpable existence, it's that they don't need to. Their emerging *trust* of one another—something imminently missing from their lives prior where sex was not—may prove more valuable and lasting."

Discussing *The Private Life of Sherlock Holmes*, Sinyard and Turner refer to how "Holmes's professional integrity and his heart have both been broken" by his involvement with the Oxford prostitute and his resulting disillusionment over women. Early in the film, Holmes criticizes his biographer, Dr. Watson, for how he has "given the reader the distinct impression that I am a misogynist. Actually, I don't dislike women—I merely distrust them. The twinkle in the eye and the arsenic in the soup." Watson's prodding on whether there have been women in his life "threatens to pierce through Holmes's defence mechanisms. . . . For all Holmes's deductive powers there seems another dark, secret side more consistent with suppressed romantic melancholia—the violin playing, the compulsive drug-taking. It is a conflict between the Romantic and the Artist in Holmes vying with the Scientist and the Logician." This "psychological split," common among Wilder's conflicted characters, "is actually a confusion of identity."

DEFENSE MECHANISMS

Wilder's films are usually about those emotionally blocked individuals having their deadness shaken up by exposure to people with more open and generous feelings. His lifelong sense of alienation as a Jew, a man who escaped the Holocaust, and a perpetual exile is also a root source of the distancing effects in his jaundiced view of society, which tempers his critical but still compassionate portraits of individuals caught up in social corruption. He repeats his obsessive concern with helplessness and detachment over and over in his films. He forces his characters into situations that test their need to remain emotionally detached. He did that with his friends and colleagues too.

Walter Matthau, middle-aged, with hangdog looks, but winningly roguish and sharply incisive, became an alter ego for Wilder onscreen when he first appeared for the director in *The Fortune Cookie* (1966) as the shyster law-yer "Whiplash Willie" Gingrich (Wilder had earlier tested him for the lead in *The Seven Year Itch* and was intrigued but thought he needed a more famil-iar screen name, so he chose Tom Ewell). The description of Matthau's char-acter in the *Fortune Cookie* script closely resembles Wilder himself: "He is a tall, loose-jointed man of 40, with a brain full of razor blades and a heart full of chutzpah." When I asked Matthau on the set of *The Front Page* if it was true that Willie was modeled on Wilder, he said, "I always play Wilder. Wilder sees me as Wilder—a lovable rogue full of razor blades." (Wilder may have picked up that description from William Holden, who once said the director had "a mind full of Gillette blue blades.") In the script for the news-paper comedy, Matthau's managing editor of Hearst's Chicago *Examiner* is described thus: "They don't make managing editors like Walter Burns any more—which is both a shame and a blessing. He operates in the great tradi-tion of Machiavelli, Rasputin and Count Dracula. No ethics, no scruples, and no private life—a fanatic, oblivious of ulcers and lack of sleep, in his con-stant pursuit of tomorrow's headlines."

Colleagues observed that Matthau, with his prickly, needling personality, tried to "test" Wilder creatively and personally when they worked together on that film. The actor told me in his dressing room, "I think I can surmount the defenses that he's erected about himself since he came here from Ger-many. He's a great fencer, but I don't think he feels like he has to fence with me." What were Wilder's defense mechanisms, I asked? Matthau shrewdly responded, "Brilliant repartee." Wilder's young protégé Rex McGee, who spent a lot of time talking with him in his later years, remembered: "He was always entertaining. He always had to leave you with a joke. That's what he was born to do—he was an entertainer. And over time I saw that as a kind of defense against intimacy. It took a *long* time to break through with him. I remember on *The Front Page*, Jack Lemmon's makeup guy, Harry Ray, said to me, 'Don't come on strong with him. Let him pull you in. If you don't push, then he will eventually pull you in.' And that's what happened."*

Although Walter Burns and Willie Gingrich are irredeemably heartless comical characters, we see Wilder's "living dead" protagonists, protected by

---

* Harry Ray also worked with Lemmon on *The Apartment*, *Irma la Douce*, and *Avanti!* In the latter he has a small role as Dr. Fleischmann, the man at the beginning who exchanges clothes with Lemmon in the airplane lavatory.

their brilliant repartee, struggling to break free of emotional entombment in such films as *Ninotchka*, *Hold Back the Dawn*, *A Foreign Affair*, *Love in the Afternoon*, *The Apartment*, *Irma la Douce*, *Sherlock Holmes*, and *Avanti!* Most of these characters are successful in doing so, at least to varying degrees, but some of their emotional escapes are temporary or qualified. Walter Neff "is already a dead man walking," as Steffen-Fluhr puts it, after he and Phyllis commit murder in *Double Indemnity*. Neff tells Keyes and the audience in voiceover, "Suddenly it came over me that everything would go wrong. It sounds crazy, Keyes, but it's true, so help me: I couldn't hear my own footsteps. It was the walk of a dead man." Steffen-Fluhr notes that Neff is also "a dead man *talking*: his self-accusing voiceover frames the film, creating a palimpsest in which past and present exist simultaneously, a German *Strassenfilm* shimmering beneath the hardboiled American plot." Other films whose protagonists fail to break free of living death include such varied works as *Ace in the Hole* and *Fedora*, as well as, in farcical form, *The Seven Year Itch*. Don Birnam barely survives his addiction to alcohol in *The Lost Weekend*. The causes for the entrapment of other Wilder characters include sexual and murderous obsession in *Double Indemnity* and the cascading con-games that continue inexorably to their tragic ends in *Ace* and *Fedora*.

In *The Seven Year Itch* (1955, written with George Axelrod from his play),* sexual repression keeps the protagonist, New York paperback book editor Richard Sherman (Tom Ewell), in a state of arrested development. Richard is trapped in his apartment while unable to act on his sexual fantasies due to guilt and a sense of boyish inadequacy. Marilyn Monroe actually lives in the apartment upstairs while his wife is on summer vacation, but she remains resolutely a fantasy figure, virtually untouchable. Wilder wanted Richard to have an actual fling with "The Girl," as she is simply called, but the censors forbade any suggestion of that, however subtle. Wilder wanted to use a Lubitsch Touch of having her hairpin found in Richard's bed, but the farthest he was allowed to go was to have the hapless protagonist give her two relatively mild kisses.

---

* Wilder throws a humorous plug for his next movie into *Sabrina* by having Bogart buy tickets for the Broadway play of *The Seven Year Itch* that he doesn't use. Instead he gives them to his prim secretary (Ellen Corby), who reports having "a very bad night" because she took her mother along.

Wilder considered the film worthless as a result, and indeed it is one of his most heavy-handed and garish works, resorting to laborious fantasy sequences and recurring scenes of Richard talking to himself, slowly spelling everything out, a surprisingly inept device that would be blue-penciled in Screenwriting 101. Richard specializes in gussying up classic literature for tawdry paperbacks with racy covers, such as *Little Women: Secrets of a Girls Dormitory*. But Axelrod's comedy about a married man having a reckless fling becomes instead an excruciating study of a middle-aged schlub with a perpetual case of blue balls. The painfully static, dead-end feeling of *The Seven Year Itch* throws a spotlight on how satisfyingly the liberation of other emotionally blocked Wilder characters plays out in his better romances.

Wilder's portraits of characters who shed their protective armor of emotional reserve, feigned indifference, or outright hostility to become more fully functioning human beings exemplify the definition of a romantic attitude as being "marked by the imaginative or emotional appeal of what is heroic, adventurous, remote, mysterious, or idealized." That form of romanticism, always present in his work, appeals to human potentiality rather than dwelling exclusively on human failure. When he deals with failure in his darkest, most pessimistic films, such as *Sunset Blvd.*, *Ace in the Hole*, and *Fedora*, the sense of thwarted potential is raised before our eyes as befits classical tragedy. The Wilder characters able to transcend their emotional deadness—striking examples include Georges in *Hold Back the Dawn*, Phoebe in *A Foreign Affair*, Fran in *The Apartment*, Sherlock Holmes, and Wendell in *Avanti!*—do so with the help of a partner who is more emotionally liberated, if not always entirely free of his or her own inhibitions or deceptiveness. With their help, Wilder's walking-dead characters are given the hope and chance of being brought back to life, achieving genuine emotional resurrection. The joyous sense of liberation in *The Apartment* and *Avanti!* marks a late flowering of more strongly romantic impulses in Wilder, as does the bittersweet nature of Holmes's willingness to drop his lifelong emotional guard. However badly it turns out for him, we feel that act of courage has made him a more human and wiser, if even sadder, man.

During Wilder's late emergence as a more overtly romantic filmmaker, Sarris brought his recanting to a climax in a 1991 *Film Comment* essay, "Why Billy Wilder Belongs in the Pantheon":

If there is a recurring theme in his most powerful films, it is that of wretched opportunists wistfully seeking redemption. . . . The gloriously redemptive romances in *Love in the Afternoon*, *The Apartment*, and *Kiss Me, Stupid* grow organically out of the base soil of shame and corruption. Redemption comes too late in *Double Indemnity*, *Sunset Boulevard*, and *Ace in the Hole*, and the result is a tragic miscalculation. The wind can blow either way, toward the lilt of Lubitsch or the savagery of Stroheim. Wilder . . . is no stranger to defeat or tragedy. Yet his instinctive perversity enables him to darken the gayest moments and brighten the gloomiest. . . . Every film Wilder has ever written and directed represents an attempt to express the complexity of his feelings that have evolved over years of eager exile. The great dramatic moments in so many of his films could not have emerged if he had not had the courage to be profoundly honest with himself.

Since Wilder's films, in relation to most other Hollywood films of his time, tend to be far more downbeat, or starkly realistic, in their depictions of people and their skeptical view of society, it's natural for filmgoers and critics to see him as someone more fascinated, both comedically and tragically, with failure than with idealistic visions of how to live a better life. But bearing Aristotle's definitions in mind—that "Comedy aims at representing men as worse, Tragedy as better than in actual life"—Wilder can be seen more clearly as a filmmaker who deals with both ways of looking at people, as ridiculous and as having the potential to be better than they usually are, even if they often fail to realize that potential. His characters struggle with those conflicts, whether in his stark tragedies or his best comedies or comedy-dramas, such as *A Foreign Affair*, *Some Like It Hot*, *The Apartment*, and *Kiss Me, Stupid*. The comedies gain much of their force from having dramatic, even dark, elements and backdrops, from a ruined city to mob violence, from corporate corruption to the sleaziest kind of show business misconduct.

WIFE FOR A NIGHT

The prostitute hired by the team of small-town songwriters in *Kiss Me, Stupid* to help them peddle a song to Dino (Dean Martin's game and gamy self-parody) is Polly the Pistol, touchingly played by Kim Novak. Though treated terribly by the men of the suitably ugly small town of Climax, Nevada (filmed partly on location in Twentynine Palms, California), Polly is adored by Wilder and Diamond. She is a sensible, tenderhearted, wisecracking woman. Although outwardly resigned to her futile and degrading life as a whore who lives and works in a house trailer, "just somebody the bartender recommends" at the Belly Button Café on the outskirts of town, Polly yearns to be a housewife, even for a night. In this mordant satire of American sexual hypocrisy, Polly's fantasy taste of home life with Ray Walston's Orville J. Spooner, the wannabe songwriter who doubles as the church organist in this hypocritical burg, finally enables her to escape her tawdry Hell on Earth. That is an unabashed fairy-tale development, pure romanticism, and yet *Kiss Me, Stupid* was flayed for its supposed obscenity.

This controversial film, the turning point of Wilder's later career, is based on a 1944 Italian play by Anna Bonacci, *L'ora della fantasia* (*The Hour of Fantasy*, or *The Dazzling Hour*). Although virtually unknown in the United States, the play has long been a major success in Europe—a situation resembling the fate of Wilder's film version. *Kiss Me, Stupid* caused an uproar in the United States on its original release but was warmly received in Europe, where its Lubitschean theme of adultery being potentially redemptive for both men and women and for marital relationships was not considered scandalous. That was the most subversive element in Lubitsch's work; he managed to get away with it in his Hollywood films partly because of his uncanny ability to create a stylized romantic world that made his sexual unorthodoxies seem acceptable even to the puritanical American audience. And the fact that almost all his American films are set in Europe enabled audiences to rationalize the characters' behavior by thinking, "Oh, those naughty Europeans!" But Wilder was pilloried for the same theme seventeen years after Lubitsch's death, partly because he transposed Bonacci's story to an American small-town setting, the kind of dead end Hollywood used to idealize, and with an insanely jealous, thoroughly obnoxious protagonist who looked as mundane as most male members of the audience (and remarkably similar to Tom Ewell in *The Seven Year Itch*).

By presenting his audience with such uninhibited, believably down-to-earth reflections of American life in 1964, Wilder made his audience recoil at seeing itself in his mirror. It did not matter to his detractors that he filmed this bawdy story with his customary visual stylishness. Wilder clearly intended the elegance and grace of the wide-screen cinematography by Joseph LaShelle (an Oscar winner for Preminger's *Laura* who also photographed *The Apartment* and Lubitsch's *Cluny Brown*) and the musical score by André Previn as counterpoint to the squalor of the setting and situation, with the visuals and music expressing the director's romantic take on the sordid goings-on. And as Glenn Erickson observed in 2015, Wilder's "adherence to the formal rules of classic farce gives all the blue humor a formal beauty."

"What we were really trying to do was a Restoration comedy in modern dress, but nobody caught on to that," Diamond said. "And like all such comedies, it was a moral and cautionary tale. A jealous husband goes to such extremes to protect his wife's virtue that she winds up losing it." He noted that the film was favorably received in London and Paris, where reviewers appreciated its satire of contemporary American mores, "But in this country, the critics were so obsessed with looking for smut that they couldn't see anything beyond that." Comparing *Kiss Me, Stupid* to another Wilder film reviled in America, *Ace in the Hole*, Diamond observed, "I think what it is, people don't like to be told they're corrupt." But he admitted, "I don't think we ever expected such a backlash of criticism. We felt we were doing a mildly suggestive comedy." Wilder declared in 1966, "Peculiarly enough, the theme of *Kiss Me, Stupid* was human dignity. It was also about the sanctity of marriage." The writing team's comments showed what a wide gulf existed between their intent and how the film was received.

"It was the biggest historic flop in my years of making pictures," Wilder told me in our 1978 interview. "They were just absolutely, totally outraged. I don't know, I never quite could understand what the scream was about." I said, "It's actually quite a romantic story," and he agreed: "I thought it was very romantic. I'd like to do it again to show them what the thing was all about. But could you imagine going and telling people that I'm going to make *Kiss Me, Stupid* again?" Alluding to a lost Lubitsch silent film, I said, "You could call it *Kiss Me Again, Stupid*." Drawing from his encyclopedic knowledge of popular songs, Wilder said, "Yeah. *Kiss Me, Stupid, Twice; Kiss Me Once and Kiss Me Twice and Kiss Me Once Again*." The uproar his film caused seems quaint in retrospect, for it appeared just before the dam broke for sexual license in American film in the late 1960s. But when Wilder was pilloried for making it, his career was drastically altered, with both negative and positive consequences.

One of the cleverest, most insightful literary works Wilder adapted, *The Dazzling Hour* is set in an English country town around 1850. It deals with a church organist named George Sedley, who is desperate to escape his surroundings and become an important opera composer. He has a loving wife, Mary, but when a sheriff with connections in the music world visits the town, George is advised that the best way to sell his opera is to let the sheriff sleep with his wife. That appalls George, so he hires a local courtesan, Geraldine Hubbes, to impersonate his wife. Geraldine admires George's music from church and is willing to go through with the charade but becomes so enthralled with the idea of being a wife for a night that she sleeps with George. The besotted composer thinks he is throwing away his chance to sell the opera but doesn't realize that Mary, who has been spending the night at the courtesan's place, is sleeping with the sheriff. Mary is invigorated emotionally and sensually by the experience, the opera is performed, and the shnook of a composer is none the wiser.

The roots of Bonacci's allegorical farce, with its theme of the mirroring of the desires of two women in very different social circumstances, have been traced back to the Latin comedies of Plautus and Terence. Such parallels and doubling are a preoccupation of the actress-turned-playwright, who has been described by director Anton Giulio Bragaglia as concentrating on the theme of "the life we never lived." The feminist implications in *The Dazzling Hour* darkly satirize the frustrations women feel in patriarchal society when they are forced into roles that either repress their sexual desires, such as Mary's as a subservient housewife, or relegate them to outcast status as sex workers, as exemplified by Geraldine despite her desire for a loving relationship within marriage. Literary critic Daniela Cavallaro notes that in most of Bonacci's work, "major and minor characters live monotonous lives of boredom and dullness, from which an unexpected event brings temporary respite, allowing them to act out and live their repressed tendencies" in the "fantasy hour."

In *The Dazzling Hour*, which Cavallaro considers Bonacci's masterpiece, the use of "the literary technique of the female double . . . construct[s] them as opposite and complementary," while liberating "Bonacci's interest towards her socially unacceptable female character," a figure both women come to represent in different ways. "The empathy in the relationship between the two female characters, in fact, is another of the conventions of the doubles . . . as representative of two halves of a complete woman." The farcical plot complications cause their roles to be interrelated and ultimately exchanged, to the benefit of both women. So it is not surprising that in some of the first productions of the play, both roles were played by the same actress.

Before Wilder's film, there was a sanitized and hence only mildly amusing and largely forgotten 1952 Italian film adaptation of the play called *Moglie per una notte* (*Wife for a Night*). Directed by Mario Camerini, the film is set in Italy in the late nineteenth century. Although Gina Lollobrigida is quite credible in her double role, *Wife for a Night* pulls its punches by contriving a happy ending that sidesteps any actual adultery by either partner. Jeanne Moreau achieved her first notable stage success in a 1953 French adaptation by Henri Jeanson, *L'heure éblouissante*, while playing both female characters in that version set in Victorian England. But the Bonacci play, for all its acclaim in Europe, never made it to Broadway, an augury of the problem Wilder's version would have in finding an audience in the United States.*

Wilder's affinities with German expressionism helped draw him to the material partly because of its mirroring of the two women's desires, despite their contrasting social circumstances. But he and Diamond opted to avoid the tempting tour de force of double casting. Paradoxically, while that decision could be seen as reflecting a male rather than female take on the material by not drawing parallels between the women as closely as Bonacci does, it also can be seen as the filmmakers not wanting to imply that all women are alike. Perhaps the stylized approach of having one actress play both parts would have made the film more palatable to American audiences, though it's harder to make a dual role work in a movie than onstage because of film's tendency toward photographic realism, the most likely reason such casting was not attempted. In any case, Wilder was going for a relatively realistic depiction of American small-town hypocrisy.

Both the play and the film have their own considerable merits while approaching the material from differing vantage points, and both reach similar conclusions while approaching the feminist theme from their divergent

---

* Oddly enough, there were a number of tangential Wilder connections in the abortive American history of the play. It was adapted in 1953 to an 1860s French setting as *The Dazzling Hour* by Ketti Frings and José Ferrer, who also served as its director. Frings was the author of *Hold Back the Dawn*, and Ferrer directed the Broadway production of *Stalag 17* before Wilder turned that play into a film; he later appeared in *Fedora*. *The Dazzling Hour* had a tryout in La Jolla, California, with *Hold Back the Dawn* star Olivia de Havilland playing the wife. Bonacci's original has continued to be revived on the European stage and was twice adapted for French television.

angles. The actresses who play Polly (Novak) and Zelda (Felicia Farr) on-screen are equally appealing in their own ways but with strikingly individu-alized personalities, as well as coming from separate social classes. As in a Lubitsch film such as *The Smiling Lieutenant* or *Trouble in Paradise*, the cast-ing choices in *Kiss Me, Stupid* do not bias the audience against one woman or the other. Wilder guides Novak in an extraordinarily sincere performance that is both funny and moving. He never condemns her profession, but he is also filled with affection for Zelda, the beautiful and tolerant wife of a boorish and unattractive loser. Zelda is so badly treated by Orville in the furtherance of his ambition that he drives her into an entirely justifiable (and enjoyable) night of prostitution in Polly's trailer living out her fantasy with the singer whose fan club she ran in high school.

These wish-fulfillment elements make the double happy ending of Wilder's film all the more poignant. After swapping roles briefly, Polly and Zelda have a warm scene together in which Zelda exchanges her $500 prostitution fee for her husband's wedding ring, which Polly wore in the masquerade. The film's por-trayal of marriage as an economic exchange like prostitution, the two women's sense of camaraderie, and Zelda's satisfying form of revenge are deeply subver-sive elements that help account for the outrage the film caused among self-appointed guardians of American morality. What the bluenoses mistook for smut are the film's sharpest pieces of social commentary. Zelda orders her clue-less husband at the end, "Kiss me, stupid," as the camera rapidly dollies into an extreme close-up of her triumphantly smiling face. She clearly has a new sense of control over her own life and an upper hand in their marriage. And Wilder reserves the closing shot for Polly's car and trailer (bought with Dino's payment to Zelda) as she drives out of Climax to newfound freedom.

Sinyard and Turner point out that, for Wilder,

a whore is not a demonic sexual siren eating at the root of respectable society, but just another human being coping as best she can with life's adversities. . . . Nevertheless, it is hardly surprising that Wilder would cause offence by presenting a local prostitute in small-town, middle-class Amer-ica who, far from being condemned, is presented as morally superior to any other character in the film. She is the only one to be singularly unimpressed by Dino's stardom, seeing his loathsomeness for what it really is. . . . Polly alone remains true to herself, clinging to her sense of identity and dignity in a mean-spirited society. Wilder grants her a true night of romance.

And how times change: Ironically, when I showed the film to a university class recently, they were not at all scandalized by a married woman becoming a prostitute, but what did scandalize them was a prostitute yearning for the life of a married woman. Some of the young viewers audibly gasped at Polly telling Zelda, "A woman without a man is like a trailer without a car—you ain't goin' nowhere—so when you find a good guy, you should stick with him."* But Polly is so bereft of love and even basic human kindness and decent treatment that we share her need for some kind of commitment, even if it is transitory and unreal and shared with a rather unlikable man such as Orville, and she craves physical and emotional release from her exploitation and suffering. The film's acute ironies about how men treat women are at issue throughout, never more so than when Orville objects to the way Dino paws at Polly. "It's a good thing you're not my wife," Orville tells her, "or I'd throw him out of the house." Suddenly realizing how insulting and unfair that is, he apologizes, a key moment in his emotional awakening about women. Those who cannot appreciate the manifold ironies and emotional subtleties of *Kiss Me, Stupid* today are as benighted as the prudish and insensitive American audiences who condemned it in 1964–1965, just before the deluge of the sexual revolution, and unfortunately for Wilder and Diamond.

When Polly tells Zelda, "You know, it was sort of fun being a wife for a night," Zelda, who is similarly good-hearted, replies, "And for one night, it was fun being Polly the Pistol." Anyone who denigrates *Kiss Me, Stupid* as a crass, cynical sex farce rather than seeing it for the satirical morality play Wilder intended is misjudging the film. The farcical developments depend on Zelda's willingness to overlook Orville's flaws as a husband and his utter lapse into venality in pursuit of ambition. That may be a tall order, but Wilder and Diamond ascribe her choice to a lack of options in a dead-end town after escaping the world's ghastliest mother, Mrs. Pettibone, played by Doro Merande, a wildly comical gargoyle Wilder first employed as the waitress in a vegetarian restaurant who proselytizes for nudism in *The Seven Year Itch*; she also plays the cleaning lady in *The Front Page*, her final film. Partly because of the scene in *Kiss Me, Stupid* in which Zelda's father refers to her mother as "Godzilla," we suspend our disbelief about Zelda being too good to be true as

---

* Polly also talks wistfully of reading a *Ladies' Home Journal* article entitled "How to Keep Your Husband Happy," a reference to Lubitsch's *Heaven Can Wait*. Gene Tierney's Martha, before her marriage, buys a book called *How to Make Your Husband Happy*; she remains loyal to her philandering husband, who is deeply touched to find the book after her death.

the allegorical film plays out, because of our sympathy for her warm but unappreciated character.

And, crucially, Zelda sticks with Orville because she senses a romantic side beneath his rough surface, as shown in his writing a genuinely touching love song for her, "Sophia." Orville finally displays some character in refusing to sell it to Dino, because it's their song, but Zelda, who is more pragmatic and wants Orville to be a success on his own merits, sells it to the crooner behind his back. She defends him to Dino by saying, "I think Orville has a lot of talent." "You know him?" Dino asks, and she replies in her hooker guise, "See him almost every night. He's one of my regulars." Orville's offenses, as deplorable as they are, finally enable Zelda to take charge of her foolish husband, allowing her to forgive him and enjoy hearing Dino sing "Sophia" on national television, despite his utter confusion.

Dino is a mordantly comical version of the unscrupulous sexual user Mac-Murray plays in *The Apartment*. Wilder adored Martin's comic abilities and had his own affinities with the wryly jaded tone of Rat Pack humor. Wilder even did some script doctoring, without credit, on the Rat Pack hit film *Ocean's 11* (1960), in which Martin appears along with Frank Sinatra, Sammy Davis Jr., Peter Lawford, Joey Bishop, and Angie Dickinson, with a cameo by MacLaine.* Martin does a sly and hilarious self-parody in *Kiss Me, Stupid*, playing Dino as an obsessed, drunken lecher. Dino would be merely repellent if it were not for the blasé cockiness and sense of nearly unshakable cool Martin brings to the role. Although the film is a scathing satire of show business presumption in the "swinging" early sixties, and Dino is a living embodiment of Hugh Hefner's "*Playboy* Philosophy," Wilder is still tougher on Middle America. Even Dino is astonished by how "civilians" desperate to break into show business to escape being nonentities can be more corrupt than people in Las Vegas or Hollywood. Dino's cynicism is a form of intelligence, but his amoral self-indulgence leads him to mistreat women, which the film does not do.

Dino's wonderment over the goings-on in Climax leads him to tell a national television audience at the end of the film how he bought a song from the team

---

of local songwriting schlubs while on a detour, when he "stayed up all night" listening to their music (though he does not mention the name of the town or that he spent the night with the composer's wife). When he cynically remarks that "sooner or later somebody will take what you got," he adds his Rat Pack coda, "Baby." The epitome of Martin's *menefreghista*—an Italian word that biographer Nick Tosches uses to define him as "one who does not give a fuck"— Dino's cynical but shrewd observation on human venality is among the funniest riffs in this Wilder-Diamond tour de force of nonstop verbal gyrations. As the sleazy lyricist of the songwriting team, Barney, who fancies himself a clever wordsmith, notes about a groan-inducing rhyme in one of their songs, "That's what makes it—the irregularity—that unexpected little twist."

The nonstop lewdness of the double entendres in *Kiss Me, Stupid* shocked people in its day but makes a more sophisticated and sympathetic modern viewer giddy with delight at the film's abandon in running rings around the censors. "It's not very big but it's clean!" Orville tells the stunned Polly while giving her a tour of his house. After Dino gets his chance to ogle Polly up close, he tells Orville, "And don't you worry about me or your wife—we won't bother you. Maybe we'll go in the garden, and she'll show me her parsley." The Legion of Decency raised objections to some of the raunchy lines and behavior before the film was shot, but Wilder, perhaps emboldened by his commercial success the year before with the bawdy *Irma la Douce*, did not accept all of them. He refused to change Orville's "not very big" line or substitute any other vegetable for parsley, as some female members of the committee demanded, since the mention of parsley conjured up particularly lewd images in their minds. Wilder's reaction: "What do they want—broccoli?"

Because of these horrified reactions from the official bluenoses and some people in the industry and reviewers who saw the film before its release, United Artists considered *Kiss Me, Stupid* so scandalous that it was dumped onto the market under the auspices of the distributor's foreign and art-house subsidiary, Lopert Pictures. Wilder was forced to reshoot Dino's seduction of Zelda for the American version to make it seem a bit ambiguous, but even then the Legion slapped a "Condemned" rating on the film, calling it "a thoroughly sordid piece of realism which is esthetically as well as morally repulsive." Wilder considered that "shabby" treatment because the Legion had promised not to condemn the film if he reshot the scene.

But though Dino falls asleep in the sanitized version, Zelda's waking nude under the bed sheet the next morning with a big smile and finding five hundred-dollar bills stuck in a liquor bottle tells us all we need to know. The price has gone up fivefold since *The Apartment*, in which MacLaine's Fran attempts suicide after the philandering Sheldrake offers her a hundred-dollar bill as a Christmas present. Or perhaps Dino is simply a bigger tipper than Sheldrake; the notoriously stingy MacMurray argued with Wilder that Sheldrake wouldn't flip a half-dollar to the shoeshine man, so Wilder changed it to a dime. The genuinely erotic and tender scene Wilder originally shot of Zelda and Dino beginning their lovemaking before the fade-out was restored to the film in the 1990s. Viewers can compare both versions on home video (in which the retake is now an extra) and appreciate the greater candor Wilder and Diamond intended. Reviewer Michael Scheinfeld observed that *Kiss Me, Stupid* now represents "A kind of cinematic litmus test that separates the casual Billy Wilder fan from the true connoisseur."

But the tenor of most of the pearl-clutching contemporary American reviews of *Kiss Me, Stupid* was encapsulated in Judith Crist's comment that "only the characters' clothes separate them from their counterparts in a stag movie" (not entirely inaccurate, but . . .). The most damaging vitriol directed at the film was Thomas Thompson's attack on Wilder in the January 15, 1965, issue of *Life* magazine for making "a titanic dirty joke, an embarrassment to audiences, the performers and the industry which produced it." The director responded, "If you like the people in the picture, then what they do does not appear dirty. What the critics call dirty in our pictures, they call lusty in foreign films."

Even though Wilder's defense is quoted in Thompson's lengthy article on how American movies are going to Hell, it carried no weight with the journalist, who wrote, "For years film director Billy Wilder has walked the shaky tightrope between sophistication and salaciousness. But with his newest film, *Kiss Me, Stupid*, he has fallen off with a resounding crash—so resounding, in fact, that he may also have pulled down whatever is left of Hollywood's decades-old system of self-censorship." Thompson reported on a Broadway preview screening: "When the picture credits began, there was a hearty burst of applause for Wilder's name. But before many minutes had passed it became painfully obvious to just about everybody that Wilder had directed with the impulse of a small boy standing at a back fence with a piece of chalk. What he put on the screen can best be compared with one of those dirty jokes that somebody tells at a sedate party, to winces of embarrassment all around."

This hysterical screed, entitled "Wilder's Dirty-Joke Film Stirs a Furor," seems strangely lubricious in retrospect. While generalizing about the Pandora's box that Wilder supposedly opened on the moviegoing audience, the article also lingers with panting relish on cataloging the film's lewdest outrages, doing so both verbally and in photographic displays. Like the scandalized bourgeois host of a "sedate party" in a hypocritical suburb, Thompson saw the film as "basically a story of adultery and its rewards—with situations and dialogue that would generate blushes in a smoker car."

It is significant that Wilder misremembered Thompson's attack as even more personally vicious than it actually was. He told me that Thompson "wrote an editorial [*sic*] in *Life* magazine after *Kiss Me, Stupid* that I should be deported—absolute lunacy!—for what I had done to the morals of my adopted country." In fact, Thompson did not call for Wilder to be deported, but that Wilder remembered it that way is a measure of how concerned and naturally sensitive the Austrian refugee from Hitler was over such an otherwise all-out and wounding assault on his artistic talents: he imagined it questioning his right to remain as a naturalized American citizen. In that sense what Thompson wrote was connected in Wilder's mind with the verbal assault Louis B. Mayer made on him for his alleged ingratitude toward his adopted hometown in *Sunset Blvd.*, which may or may not have included a reference to deportation. Clearly that threat and the attitude that underlay it was, for Wilder, what psychologists call "the point of maximum resistance."

Thompson was best known at that time for his dubious enterprise in quickly secreting Lee Harvey Oswald's wife and mother under the control of *Life* in a Dallas hotel during the weekend of the Kennedy assassination in November 1963. Thompson's profile of the murdered Oswald for the next week's issue of the magazine, and its headline, blamed the untried suspect as the president's "Assassin." Thompson's credentials in exploiting the dark underbelly of American life also included a best-selling true-crime book about sex and murder among the Texas rich, *Blood and Money* (1976). His journalistic mugging of Wilder now seems the last gasp of American puritanism before the onslaught of the sex and violence and raw language that did in fact topple the Code in 1968. By 1970 American society had changed so drastically that *Kiss Me, Stupid* seemed relatively innocent—it actually was rated GP ("All ages admitted—Parental guidance suggested")—but the damage to Wilder's career was lasting. The debacle broke the long winning streak he had enjoyed for years with audiences and reviewers. Although he had a couple of minor commercial successes after *Kiss Me, Stupid*, the other films he was able to make were mostly rejected, though without the same kind of public scandal. The "scandal" now was that he was a romantic, which had become something of a dirty word by the early 1970s.

One of the few reviewers who understood and appreciated what *Kiss Me, Stupid* was really about was the novelist Joan Didion. Her review in *Vogue* pointed toward the elements that eventually would help redeem Wilder's reputation with more sophisticated viewers. Observing that he "is not a funnyman but a moralist, a recorder of human venality," she noted that audiences who saw *Kiss Me, Stupid* on its initial release "walk out, I suspect, because they sense that Wilder means it. . . . The Wilder world is one seen at dawn through a hangover, a world of cheap double entendre and stale smoke and drinks in which the ice has melted: the true country of despair. *Kiss Me, Stupid* is, in fact, suffused with the despair of an America many of us prefer not to know."

After reading that review, Wilder wrote a note to Didion: "I read your piece in the beauty parlor while sitting under the hair dryer, and it sure did the old pornographer's heart good. Cheers. Billy Wilder."

Having Didion virtually alone on his side was, in retrospect, a major vindication of Wilder and a sign that he was ahead of the curve. Her *Vogue* review reads like a miniature version of one of her own novels, especially *Play It As It Lays* (1970, adapted as a film in 1972). Didion's caustic portraits in journalism and fiction of the collapsing American society of that period would become central to the Zeitgeist. Although Wilder managed to joke with her in his 1965 note about the scandal he had caused, he was actually dismayed by the response to the film. "Billy was spoiled lately with success, and they really let him have it," Walter Reisch, Wilder's former screenwriting collaborator, said in 1966. "He asked me not to see the picture. It is the one thing about which he has no sense of humor."

Wilder recalled the state of shock he and Diamond were in after *Kiss Me, Stupid* cast them into disgrace: "For twelve weeks we sat and stared at each other. He said we were like parents who have produced a two-headed child and don't dare to have sexual intercourse."

LOVE FOR SALE

Why was Wilder so preoccupied, throughout his career, with the theme of prostitution, in all the many variations he finds in it?

The emotional tensions to which he obsessively returns can be seen in various kinds of dramatic conflict but especially manifest themselves in situations involving sex and love, clashes between characters looking at the world either in a cold, transactional way or through the redemptive, if often disillusioning, lens of romantic idealism. From his earliest days as a screenwriter in Europe throughout his thirty-nine-year career as a Hollywood writer-director, Wilder constantly returned to situations involving sexual repression versus sexual freedom, sex without love versus sex with love, emotional withholding versus warmth and emotional commitment, cruelty versus compassion. The bittersweet nature of his films stems from the way his characters are torn in both directions. What Sarris calls Wilder's "raging romanticism" can be discerned in the emotional conflicts that beset his characters in all genres, even in a lewd sex farce that some people mistook for pornography.

Prostitution is such a pervasive theme in his work because it is the antithesis of love offered freely. Those who find Wilder's films objectionable are often horrified by his frank depiction of that facet of society, as if it does not exist, or condemning him for acknowledging its existence. But Wilder sees prostitution as an inextricable part of the human condition, afflicting the behavior of both genders, a state his characters struggle to escape, sometimes successfully, sometimes not. His fondness for mixing comedy with drama—which he does with especially brilliant seamlessness in *The Apartment*—shows that, like his protagonists, he was torn between two ways of looking at the world. They are looking for a way out of their self-protective shells, a means of resolving their warring viewpoints into a coherent way of living.

The fact that it is not only women who act as prostitutes or are kept by wealthy lovers is part of what makes Wilder's work distinctive and controversial. Many of his male characters suffer from emotional detachment, whether because they are heartless seducers, psychologically blocked, actual gigolos, or a combination of all three. Wilder's portrayals of the gigolos in *Ninotchka*, *Hold Back the Dawn*, and *Sunset Blvd.* are highly individualized, ranging from amiable romantic frivolity (Leon) to guilt-ridden venality (Georges) to a complex blend of those moods in Joe Gillis. Joe maintains a charming, devil-may-care facade around his friends and conducts a guardedly romantic courtship of Betty but can hardly cope with the rage and anguish he feels over the mutually exploitive relationship he shares with Norma, the desperately needy woman who is keeping him.

What Norma represents to Joe is Hollywood itself, the town of fatal dreams that has seduced and rejected him, the forces of decadent money and power that are rotting the place at its core without its inhabitants being able to admit the truth to themselves. Joe's failure as a screenwriter drives him into the clutches of a ghostly but still grand remnant of the glories of Hollywood's bygone past, a former silent star who is the zombielike incarnation of a "dead" art form ("We didn't need dialogue. We had *faces*"). Her mansion, a museum filled with pictures in homage to herself, and her otherwise useless wealth now are only good for buying herself a virile but prematurely dissipated younger man as a plaything and ghostwriter. While imagining she is still a great star ("I *am* big," she tells Joe; "It's the pictures that got small"), she deludes herself that their business relationship is an actual romance, not realizing he is using her as his last chance to hang on to his own illusions of success in the movie business. Just before he turns his convertible into her driveway to escape the repo men in pursuit, he is telling us despondently in voiceover, "Apparently I just didn't have what it takes, and the time had come to wrap up the whole Hollywood deal and go home. Maybe if I hocked all my junk there'd be enough for a bus ticket back to Ohio, back to that thirty-five-dollar-a-week job behind the copy desk of the *Dayton Evening Post*, if it was still open. Back to the smirking delight of the whole office. All right, you wise guys, why don't *you* go out and take a crack at Hollywood?"

Norma becomes his serendipitous meal ticket in a tawdry bargain that stirs his self-contempt for putting himself in that equally demeaning position and, gradually, when his conscience begins rebelling, for using her so cruelly. He plays on her frantic need for love, adulation, and renewed public worship from what he tries to make her realize is "the audience [that] left twenty years ago." When she visits Paramount to peddle their hopelessly anachronistic *Salomé* screenplay that he has rewritten to her old director, Cecil B. DeMille, the young assistant director callously suggests, "I can give her the brush." But the veteran who knew her from her youth in the silent days responds, "Thirty million fans have given her the brush. Isn't that enough?" That slender reed of compassion from the industry, actually only a way of humoring her, is not enough to save Norma from drowning in despondency and madness when she is finally confronted with the truth by the man who pretended to love her.

Wilder's scripts as early as *People on Sunday* often center on a jaded character sexually exploiting someone who is emotionally vulnerable, in that case the seduction and abandonment of the innocent teenage shopgirl by the older and more experienced *Eintänzer*. Wilder's most memorable female characters in other screenplays he wrote in both Germany and the United States before he became a director live out his characteristic conflict between detachment and love. The romanticism of these scripts and their sympathetic treatment of the wronged parties are so clear it seems odd that the word "cynic" is used in relation to the man who (co)wrote them.

Jou-Jou in *A Blonde Dream* toys with the two men who love and live with her while she nurses her futile yearning to escape to Hollywood like a female Joe Gillis; Elsa Strauss in *Champagne Waltz* finds herself drawn to the American jazzman rival she initially resents for trashing her culture; Ninotchka has pragmatic sexual experience but is emotionally blocked until her reserve and wariness toward capitalist luxury are thawed by the paradoxically romantic gigolo she encounters in Paris. The innocent, good-hearted, yet wise Emmy Brown in *Hold Back the Dawn* falls unwittingly into the romantic trap of the European gigolo she meets in Mexico, but her genuine feelings for Georges awaken his better instincts. The nightclub singer Sugarpuss O'Shea in *Ball of Fire* is a tough cookie, but when she finds herself falling for the shy Professor Potts because she is attracted to his innocence as well as his physical charms, she is emotionally liberated from her rough life as the moll of a brutal gangster using her as a shield from the law. Sugarpuss's transformation by love, like that of the even more hard-boiled Georges, is entirely convincing. Although Wilder to some extent indulges his wise-guy nature in these scripts for sarcastic and bitter humor, they seriously explore the psychological nature and dilemma of callous or manipulative characters, and Wilder did not resort to flippancy or irony in the romantic denouements.

After he started directing in Hollywood, Wilder became more versatile and did not specialize as much in romances or romantic comedies as he had as a screenwriter for hire, when he had to conform more to conventional studio expectations. But the underlying conflict permeates his work even in other genres: the clash between the head and the heart, between self-control and dangerously unmanageable feelings that must be addressed if his characters are to live rather than simply surviving. Some films that don't lend themselves to heterosexual romance—such as *Stalag 17*, despite its puckish gags about POWs dancing together (which stretched the tolerance of the censors), *The Spirit of St. Louis* (whose only female character of substance is the young woman who briefly appears to give Charles Lindbergh the mirror that will save his life), and *The Front Page* (like the play on which it is based, at heart a prickly bromance between reporter Hildy Johnson and managing editor Walter Burns)—still involve those deep-seated emotional issues that preoccupy him. Holden's wisecracking, acerbic Sefton in *Stalag 17* stifles his human feelings to ensure his survival in a perilous situation, despite the toll it takes on his relationships with his fellow POWs. Lindbergh is a loner who is passionate only about his airplane and fights to keep emotional and physical self-control throughout his flight. Hildy and Walter battle over whether their newspaper is more important than Hildy's impending marriage. Like other Wilder protagonists, Lindbergh and Hildy retreat from the complications of emotional involvement into their more manageable, though obsessive, occupations.

The romantic comedies Wilder directed often involve men taking cruel advantage of women, though sometimes the opposite is the case. These situations are unusually astringent for the genre, revolving around feelings versus cold calculation. In addition to Gillis's callous trading on the feelings of the distraught, abandoned Norma, Captain Pringle feigns seduction of Phoebe for his own selfish purposes in *A Foreign Affair*; Chuck Tatum (Kirk Douglas) in *Ace in the Hole* exploits the need of Lorraine Minosa (Jan Sterling) to escape New Mexico so he can enlist her in his scam against her helpless husband; the slick ladies' man played by Tony Curtis in *Some Like It Hot*, another Joe, sets out to seduce Sugar, the sweet-natured gold digger, by pretending to be a millionaire who talks like Cary Grant; and the team of Millsap and Spooner literally buy a woman as a plaything for Dino because they are afraid he won't buy their songs on their dubious merits.

Some Like It Hot's Joe has a satisfying change of heart when he scandalizes a nightclub audience and the female bandleader by kissing Sugar on the bandstand while still in full drag and pulls off his wig to reveal that he's really a man. He's the kind of heel her jaded but still hopeful character (who euphemistically regrets, "I always get the fuzzy end of the lollipop") should know better than to accept, but she does. Some of the character transformations in Wilder films, however, are less wholehearted or more incomplete. In *A Foreign Affair*,

Pringle sort of winds up with Phoebe in an unsatisfying ending we and Wilder can't really believe for that otherwise audaciously executed political and romantic satire. The last shot is ambiguous, with Wilder literally painting himself into a corner as he shows Phoebe charging after Pringle in the underground nightclub, throwing chairs out of her way, a comical echo of his pursuit of her as she yanks open cabinets of Army Intelligence files on dubious characters while he tries to distract her from finding Erika's file.

It's nearly impossible to imagine Phoebe and Pringle working it out together back in her home state of Iowa. Wilder "could not really re-build Phoebe and Pringle without rebuilding Berlin," Sinyard and Turner point out. "The war between romanticism and realism . . . finally overwhelms Wilder himself, the realist in him not quite able to believe in the positive implications of the Pringle-Phoebe relationship, the romantic in him refusing to accept 'moral malaria' [her term for the city's corruption] as the inevitable state of affairs." While the film is "an uncomfortable comedy . . . , it is also true that the discomfort arises from the film's uncompromising honesty about the way in which a war degrades the victors as well as the vanquished."

Wilder is successful, however, in resolving the conflict between realism and romanticism in *Sunset Blvd*. But the tragic price for the two parties in its morbid sham of romantic fantasies is mutual annihilation, physically in Joe's case, psychologically in Norma's. Gillis becomes overwhelmed with guilt over the way he's treated the pathetic Norma for his own selfish ends but is too weak to escape their relationship until it's too late. She can't believe the truth about her futile dreams when he tries to make her see how she's been given the brush by Hollywood. "I'm a star. . . . I'm the greatest star of them all," she tells herself, lost in her miasma of madness. When he tries to leave her, she murmurs before shooting him, "No one ever leaves a star. That's what makes someone a star." A major reason this doomed relationship resonates so deeply with the film-going audience is that it forces us to confront our own twisted involvement with the illusory dream world of motion pictures. *Sunset Blvd*. echoes the way we allow the medium to feed our need to indulge our illusions and fantasies, while the flesh-and-blood characters it depicts (ironically, as immortal shadows) coldly enact the tragedy of our warped emotional and sexual desires.

The essence of Wilder is his exploration of gray areas of character and morality, pushing boundaries and blurring lines, genres, and ambiguities of behavior, including gender fluidity, such as that exhibited by Jerry/Daphne in *Some Like It Hot*. Though some of Wilder's detractors have described him as a misogynist, that doesn't jibe with the way he portrays sex workers with such sympathy and without moralizing about their jobs. As a former *Eintän-zer*, Wilder was in no position to judge women who make their living by offering "love for sale," the phrase a group of puritanical moralists in *Kiss Me, Stupid* use for what is going on at the Belly Button Café (Orville compulsively points out that is also the title of a Cole Porter song—"a million and a half copies"). Wilder admires the way Polly the Pistol, like Irma la Douce, maintains her professionalism and good-hearted nature despite the degrading nature of her job. Those two women, like Sugar Cane in *Some Like It Hot*, aspire to transcendent love and self-respect.

Irma la Douce was based on a French stage musical by Alexandre Breffort and Marguerite Monnot that attracted interest from Jean Renoir as a film vehicle before Wilder landed the rights. He stripped away its mediocre songs other than using the bouncy "Dis-Donc" (an all-purpose exclamation) as an instrumental. The film takes a fantastical, even surreal approach to prostitution, mocking society's hypocrisy with constant irony. With its surfeit of ironic overcompensation for flouting conventional morality, *Irma* makes prostitution seem far less sordid than it actually is. Even though the characters inhabit a seedy backstreet near Les Halles, the meatpacking and produce district the film graphically calls "the stomach of Paris," the gorgeous art direction by Alexander Trauner and Technicolor and Panavision cinematography by LaShelle make the hotel neighborhood look like "Disneyland for adults," as the production crew called it. Irma is depicted as the cutest and most wholesome gal on the street, and the romantic story draws heavily on the charms of the two incongruous American leads, MacLaine and Lemmon, reteamed from their pairing in *The Apartment*.

Wilder's view of prostitution through mostly rose-colored glasses has the virtues of humor and refreshingly avoiding facile moralizing or condemnation. The viewer can glimpse the dark side around the edges, however, in the knowing portrayal of the exploitation of women by the sordid economic system of brutal pimpery and police corruption, as well as the visual symbolism of giant slabs of meat and piles of other edibles being hauled around in the neighboring market district. But the way the film makes its risqué subject more palatable by candy-coating the omnipresent corruption no doubt helped account for why it was as big a commercial success as *Kiss Me, Stupid* was a flop, for Wilder portrays the town of Climax and Polly's job and workplace as realistically squalid in black-and-white, though with elegantly stylized production design by Trauner and cinematography by LaShelle. *Irma* is often amusing and oddly poignant, but in retrospect, though the film draws from key Wilder themes—prostitution and the conflict between impersonal sex and love—it is facile and wears out its welcome with excessive length and coyness.

Despite Polly's dismal situation, Wilder does not use it to run her down. When Orville becomes jealous over the slobberingly lecherous Dino, he asks Polly, "Are you sure you want to be alone with this guy?" She replies, "Look, mister, I got a job to do, and you're in the way." The admirably matter-of-fact manner in which Wilder depicts Polly reminds me of what Barbara Stanwyck told me about the part that made her a star, the prostitute Kay Arnold in Frank Capra's *Ladies of Leisure* (1930): "Some directors don't like actors, you know, they really don't, and you can almost smell it. But he did. And he liked women—not in a lecherous way, he just liked women, period, which a lot of directors do not. He *did*. He didn't demean them in any way. If you were a hooker, you were a hooker, but you'd better be a good one. That was how you made your living."

Other than Polly's outcall to Orville's, for which she is supposed to receive twenty-five dollars (insulting and pathetic even by 1964 standards), she plies her trade in a crummy trailer behind the sleazy roadhouse. She even relates a miserable story about how she contracted poison ivy at a July 4 "bachelor barbecue" after being raffled off for eighty-three dollars and then found that the check bounced. But Polly is a warm, emotionally giving woman who blossoms while finally treated with a measure of respect by Orville when he becomes irate at Dino for trying to seduce his "wife." Orville making himself jealous while only pretending to be her husband is a gag expanded on from *Irma*, in which Lemmon's pimp, Nestor Patou, masquerades as an impotent British john he calls "Lord X." The fake aristocrat monopolizes Irma's time to keep her from other men, but Nestor becomes frenzied with jealousy over the character he has created as she tries to cure his sexual problem. *Irma* turns that joke into ridiculous surrealism, as Nestor/Lord X actually becomes impotent and one of them winds up in jail for supposedly killing the other. But the romantic pimp's dilemma is as psychologically acute as a satire on male insecurity as the more realistic *Kiss Me, Stupid*.

Wilder can separate the inherent honesty and endearing qualities of prostitutes from the lunacy and hypocrisy of how they are treated by the men in their lives. Sometimes the women in Wilder's films are not actual prostitutes but are treated like prostitutes, which he portrays as even worse, as in the nearly tragic case of Fran Kubelik. Prostitution in Wilder's films and journalism is more than just a theme; it is a metaphor for the human condition. Much of his work revolves around its examination of human fallibility and the compulsion innocence has to be corrupted. There are many forms of prostitution in his films, as many as human behavior offers, not only selling one's body (often crassly but sometimes in a mistaken attempt at love), but also selling out a friend, child, lover, or spouse for self-gratification or advancement; or selling out one's ideals. It is the interchangeability of these social conditions between the sexes that enables Wilder to treat the women with such empathy.

Wilder learned how to finesse his portraits of prostitution to slip them through the censors, but by the time he made *Irma*, the film industry had begun to relax its ban on overt depictions of what sex workers actually do behind closed doors. Wilder was still ahead of the curve, however, and the Legion gave *Irma* a B rating. *Irma* may seem tame by today's standards—or, conversely, a trigger for "politically correct" outrage in today's revisionist climate for treating a serious social problem in a romantic manner—but despite the American box-office success of the 1960 Greek import *Never on Sunday*, even as late as 1963 the topic of prostitution was still considered somewhat outré in Hollywood. The veteran producer Hal B. Wallis took time off from making his schlocky, sexually titillating Elvis Presley musicals to write Production Code chief Geoffrey Shurlock an irate letter calling *Irma* "the filthiest thing I have ever seen on screen." Wallis was an outlier in his protest against *Irma*, however, and its box-office success emboldened Wilder to become much bolder about prostitution in *Kiss Me, Stupid*, a move that backfired because reviewers and the public were not yet ready for a much rawer depiction of the trade than he had previous offered.

In the first film Wilder directed in Europe thirty years before that, *Mauvaise graine*, Danielle Darrieux's out-of-work secretary is mistaken for a prostitute because she acts as bait to distract men so her gang of thieves can steal their cars. But she does not sleep with her marks, and she eventually manages to free herself from criminality. And the first film Wilder directed in Hollywood, *The Major and the Minor*, opens with Rogers's Susan Applegate going to a Park Avenue apartment building in Manhattan to give a "scalp massage" to a slimy middle-aged man (Robert Benchley), who insists, "I can't help it! It's the vibrator." Her demeaning job, which she quickly flees out of disgust, is a coded form of being a call girl, one of the ways writers slipped their meanings through the system in those days.

The character is a disenchanted actress in the 1921 *Saturday Evening Post* story "Sunny Goes Home" by Fannie Kilbourne and the 1923 play *Connie Goes Home* by Edward Childs Carpenter on which the film was based. In the 1920s actresses were regarded as not much more respectable than call girls. But their social status had improved considerably by 1942, and making Susan an actress would have been too obvious a dramatic device for Brackett and Wilder to exploit. It would have run the risk that her scam would be exposed more easily, as happens in the play, when the twenty-year-old actress, who "looks to be a girl of about twelve" and has pulled off her masquerade briefly on a train (offstage), foolishly reveals in her very first scene what she does for a living. It takes the other characters little time to expose the sham of the "little girl." In the original short story, which more closely resembles Wilder's film, the proto-*Lolita* theme is quite blatant.* And the story mostly takes place on the train, with the actress, who is nineteen, and an adult young man openly flirting while she is pretending to be a nine-year-old girl. When they fall in love, she tells him the truth, and they promptly kiss, leaving the train to get married. The Wilder version makes the woman considerably more mature than in the two earlier versions, and while Rogers does an expertly comical turn as a child, the film invites us to laugh at nearly everyone's blindness to the obviousness of her impersonation, turning their lack of self-awareness into a key component of *The Major and the Minor*'s satirical sexual theme.

The heroine of Wilder's next feature as a Hollywood director, the French hotel maid Mouche (Anne Baxter) in *Five Graves to Cairo* (1943), behaves with nobility while being willing to prostitute herself in World War II at a hotel in the Egyptian desert. Hostile to the British because she says two of her brothers in the French Army were left on the beaches at Dunkirk by retreating British troops, she sexually toys with German officers to free another brother from a German prison camp but winds up tortured and killed. She is initially hostile to the film's supposed hero, a British Army officer, Corporal John J. Bramble (played by Franchot Tone without an accent), who has

---

* Fannie Kilbourne shows awareness of what she is getting away with by having Sunny reading *Alice's Adventures in Wonderland* on the train; in the film, the sophisticated Susan attracts unwelcome attention from the conductors by reading *Esquire*.

been spying on the enemy as a double agent in an elaborate Wilderian masquerade as a North African hotel employee named Paul Davos (named after
the Swiss town Wilder was visiting when he heard of Hitler's takeover).
Bramble cavalierly leaves Mouche to her fate as he hastens off to join his troops
to stop their legendary Field Marshal Erwin Rommel (Erich von Stroheim)
from conquering Egypt.

This semipropagandistic film tries to paper over Bramble's callous action
with unconvincing patriotic rhetoric as he gives a speech over Mouche's grave
extolling her wartime sacrifice and leaving behind a white parasol she had
desired. That smugly patriotic speech seems to dismiss the importance of her
death in the overall scheme of things, which seems all the more callous from
today's perspective. Cowriter Brackett in 1959 called the film "top-notch melodrama on which hangs a dreadful smell of propaganda." Whether Wilder
intended it or not, Bramble's abandonment of Mouche is also painfully reminiscent of Wilder's leaving his mother in 1935 Vienna to die at the hands of the
Nazis in a concentration camp, the memory that made him feel endless guilt.

Some women in Wilder films lack the kind of excuse Mouche has for using
sexual attraction coldly, even ruthlessly, since they do so not out of patriotic
idealism but simply for money or position. Among them are Phyllis in *Double Indemnity*, Erika in *A Foreign Affair*, Lorraine in *Ace in the Hole*, and Sandy
in *The Fortune Cookie*. Wilder treats only Erika among those hard-boiled
women with a degree of respect or compassion, which is remarkable under
the circumstances and the sign of a true artist, since Erika is a former Nazi
camp follower. He understands that she faces a desperate situation in the
bombed-out "cesspool" of conquered Berlin and appreciates that she shows
some humanity by rescuing Phoebe from her transgressions even after
showing such contempt for the naive and prudish American congresswoman.
By contrast, Phyllis, Lorraine, and Sandy are portrayed as reprehensible
opportunists. Do such examples among the rest make Wilder a misogynist?

Phyllis is a classic film noir temptress, one of the most memorable exem-
plars of a genre that often contains strongly misogynistic elements in its depictions of femmes fatales. Her sociopathic behavior is chillingly compelling
but so far outside the pale of ordinary human behavior that she almost seems
an abstract symbol of evil. Lorraine's villainy, matter-of-factly conveyed in
Sterling's admirable performance, is a deplorable but recognizable human failing, a combination of greed and desperation to break out of her unhappy

marriage and virtual imprisonment in a desert dump in the middle of nowhere, like her husband trapped in his cave or the songwriters trapped in Climax in *Kiss Me, Stupid*. Wilder comments visually on the twisted psychological depths of Lorraine's viciousness by dissolving from Leo telling Tatum that "she's so pretty" to a shot featuring the cheap-looking bottle-blonde standing with arms crossed and smiling with satisfaction as a carnival supply truck drives past her into the campground with these words emblazoned on its side: "THE GREAT S&M AMUSEMENT CORP." The influence of James M. Cain's brutal view of human low life is combined here with the dark sexual sensibility and perverse humor of Weimar Germany. Sandy in *The Fortune Cookie*, played by Judi West, is more gratuitously and less interestingly shown as a gold digger ruthlessly exploiting the lingering love of her deluded ex-husband, TV cameraman Harry Hinkle (Lemmon), in another insurance scam.

The last woman Wilder portrayed without a bit of sympathy is Celia Clooney (Paula Prentiss), in his final film, *Buddy Buddy*. Out of sexual frustration, she abandons her husband (Lemmon again), a puritanical network television censor, to become a lesbian. Celia is merely a caricature, and this thoroughly unfunny film wastes Prentiss's considerable comic talents as the character attaches herself to a sex clinic run by Dr. Hugo Zuckerbrot, played by the sinister German actor Klaus Kinski. Celia's paramour is the butch receptionist played by one of Wilder's favorite character actors, Joan Shawlee, Sweet Sue in *Some Like It Hot* and the "first baseman of a dame" in *The Apartment*.

Although Wilder could be said to flirt with misogyny in his portrayals of some of those female characters, they are in a small minority among his women, and if Phyllis in *Double Indemnity* is an outright monster, so is Lady Macbeth.

WILDER'S GOOD WOMEN

For each of Wilder's venal females, there are many admirable, if flawed, women played by actresses ranging from Greta Garbo and Olivia de Havilland, Ginger Rogers and Marlene Dietrich, to Jean Arthur, Nancy Olson, Marilyn Monroe, Shirley MacLaine, Geneviève Page, and Juliet Mills. They play another kind of character to which Wilder often returns and is seldom recognized, though he treats them with great affection. These are the unabash-edly good women who are not corrupted despite all the sleaze they see around them. Among them are:

- the innocent dreamer Jou-Jou in the pre-Nazi Berlin of *A Blonde Dream*
- Mouche, despite her compromised wartime position
- the proper schoolteacher Emmy Brown, who accepts Georges even after learning that he conned her into marriage in *Hold Back the Dawn*
- Helen St. James (Jane Wyman), the selfless *Time* magazine researcher who tries desperately to save Don Birnam from drinking himself to death in *The Lost Weekend* (while serving, ironically, as his well-meaning enabler, like his brother, Wick, played by Phillip Terry)
- Gloria (Doris Dowling), the tenderhearted prostitute who offers Don love and understanding but is unwisely rejected because of class snobbery
- Erika, who sells herself to successive authorities in Germany to survive but earns Wilder's grudging admiration anyway because of her ability to sur-vive (as she details in her memorable speech to Phoebe, each episode punc-tuated with "I kept going")
- Betty, the idealistic story editor and aspiring screenwriter who loves Gillis unreservedly
- the ingenuous but wised-up gamine characters Audrey Hepburn plays in *Sabrina* and *Love in the Afternoon*
- Sugar, a gold digger but a guileless one, emotionally battered and gullible yet still warmhearted and game
- the blithely above-it-all Zelda in *Kiss Me, Stupid*
- even (paradoxically) MacLaine's prostituted characters in *The Apartment* and *Irma la Douce*

Wilder's good women maintain their generosity of spirit despite inhabiting crass worlds in which women are treated with utter contempt. Betty Schae-fer, with her life in Hollywood, is a case in point.

When I lived in Wisconsin and had only a vague sense of how Hollywood actually functioned, I thought Betty was too good to be true as a Hollywood character, but after I moved there and broke into the screenwriting racket, I found that such women actually do exist in the film industry and should be cherished, as Wilder does. And in fact, they often are story editors, wise, well-educated, kindhearted, and ambitious women who work hard to prove their worth, frequently for crass male producers. Betty has a clear-eyed understanding of how Hollywood operates and yet is the character in that dark portrait of the industry with the most integrity and the least cynicism. Because she is honest, it takes her a while to recognize Gillis's duplicity or to learn that he is working as a kept man. (When I met Olson and told her I had dated several women because they reminded me of the character she plays in *Sunset Blvd.*, she said, "I'm very sorry to hear that." I am still puzzling over that remark.)

Wilder's vision of the intricate and often demoralizing world of male-female relations is generous enough to accommodate women who somehow manage to rise above the dangers of emotional involvement and offer it to troubled men. He told Karasek that Betty was modeled on his wife Audrey, who also came from a "picture family." Audrey was the daughter of a studio wardrobe woman and a used-car dealer. She lived with her parents in an unfashionable part of town east of La Brea, and when Billy started dating her in 1944 after casting her in a bit part in *The Lost Weekend*,* he made a famous quip, "I would worship the ground you walk on, Audrey, if you only lived in a better neighborhood." She attempted a mild riposte by asking him if he couldn't look upon it as "East Beverly Hills," but he soon found her repartee sharpening to match his. He realized that her experiences in show business helped give her a similarly hard-boiled attitude, enabling them to become an enduring couple. Writer George Axelrod said they resembled a sarcastic but loving couple out of a 1930s romantic comedy. "She was a pistol," said Rex McGee. She and Billy reminded him of Nick and Nora Charles in *The Thin Man*. A celebrated example of Audrey's wit worked its way into Jan Sterling's dialogue in *Ace in the Hole*. When Chuck Tatum tells her to make a show of attending a church rosary for her trapped husband, Lorraine retorts, "I don't go to church. Kneeling bags my nylons."

Billy was taken with the elegant sense of style of the chic, svelte "Aud," her gracious social skills that counterbalanced his abrasive edges, and her

---

* Nothing of Audrey's role as a hat-check girl remained in the final cut of the film, in which Wilder's then-girlfriend, Doris Dowling, has a substantial supporting role as the saucy, good-hearted hooker hopelessly devoted to the Milland character. Audrey played one more part in a Wilder film, the elegant woman Gary Cooper's character takes to a fancy-dress concert in Paris in *Love in the Afternoon*. When she goes to the ladies' room, his eyes wander to another woman in the lobby, Audrey Hepburn's Ariane.

tolerant attitude toward his foibles, including his penchant for extramarital relationships. "They were used to being with each other," McGee said, "and she was used to him having affairs. I remember Billy and Audrey took my fiancée and me out to dinner at Spago right before we got married, and I remember something Audrey said to my ex-wife, 'Listen to me, honey, it's always the woman who decides if the marriage continues.' I guess it was better to be Mrs. Billy Wilder and cheated on than not."

Wilder's longtime mistress Hope Holiday said to me of Audrey:

I think she knew that we were an item. I don't think she cared. I don't know why. I guess she liked being Mrs. Billy Wilder. And they got along well together, and she had a good sense of humor. She was a very nice lady. Audrey invited me to the memorial [for Wilder in 2002] at the Academy [of Motion Picture Arts and Sciences]. She was a character. He said he loved me, but he never was *in* love with me. He said I was the favorite of all his girlfriends. That's insulting. I said, "Thanks a lot." He said because I used to entertain him—besides whatever else [laughs].

Wilder said of Audrey, "She is a saint. And I am a shit. The saint and the shit." Like her husband, the former Tommy Dorsey band singer was fond of quoting pop songs to explain her feelings, and she quoted one to Zolotow to explain why the relationship lasted: "You might have been a headache / But you never were a bore." That was a fitting choice, since it came from "Thanks for the Memory" by Leo Robin and Ralph Rainger, a tender yet bittersweet ballad about the vagaries of romance ("The night you worked and then came home with lipstick on your tie"). Bob Hope introduced the song with Shirley Ross, including the lines quoted by Audrey, in *The Big Broadcast of 1938*, one of the films Wilder helped write without credit. McGee related, "At Westwood Village Memorial Park, where Billy is buried, she's buried there too, but her tombstone is a bench, and on the side of the bench it says, 'I'm right here, Billy.' That's her. A friend of mine who went to Billy's burial said Audrey brought a martini there, and before they closed the grave she finished off the martini and threw the glass into the grave and said, 'You may have been a pain in the ass but you never were a bore.'" The epitaph on Wilder's tombstone, a play on the celebrated ending line of *Some Like It Hot*, reads, "BILLY WILDER / I'M A WRITER / BUT THEN / NOBODY'S PERFECT." Audrey wrote that epitaph too, and both McGee and Paul Diamond said they thought Billy would have hated it. He joked about many aspects of filmmaking but never disparaged the craft of screenwriting.

Betty's fierce devotion to Gillis in full knowledge of his flaws is a trait she shares with Audrey. If a man rejects an offer of love from such a generous woman, as Gillis does after he invites Betty to see him at Norma's mansion, it can lead to his destruction. With feigned callousness but attempted gallantry, Joe throws the whole sordid situation in Betty's face, explaining, "A very simple set-up: an older woman who is well-to-do. A younger man who is not doing too well. Can you figure it out yourself?" Betty defiantly replies, "No, no! I haven't heard any of this. . . . I've never been in this house. Get your things together. Let's get out of here." We want to call out to the screen to warn Joe not to let Betty go, for she is his last hope of salvation. But he just stands there in helpless pain and watches her leave, for what he thinks is her own good, and that's the tragedy Wilder portrays. No doubt it is the kind of situation he often saw played out in his many years of rough experience dealing with the myriad twists of sex and romance.

It is paradoxical but revealing that some of the best of the good women in Wilder films are prostitutes or quasi-prostitutes or spies willing to sleep with the enemy, such as Mouche or Ilse von Hoffmanstal in *The Private Life of Sherlock Holmes* (played by the exquisite French actress Geneviève Page, the madam in Luis Buñuel's 1967 *Belle du Jour*). Paradox, as G. K. Chesterton wrote, "has been defined as 'Truth standing on her head to get attention.'" Wilder's ironic moral sense resembles Oscar Wilde's in his depiction of Mrs. Erlynne in *Lady Windermere's Fan*. A woman of the world (read: high-class prostitute or kept woman) scorned by polite society, she is more dignified and honorable than anyone else in the comedy-drama, whose subtitle is *A Play About a Good Woman*. When Lubitsch adapted the play masterfully as a silent film in 1925, he dispensed with the rather heavy-handed subtitle, but that film and Wilder's work similarly point the finger of blame at men who use women badly rather than at the women themselves.

I would argue that Wilder's view of women overall is not misogynistic but simply unsentimental, like his view of men. He depicts both men and women equally, as deeply flawed human beings. Norma, though she goes mad, is no more flawed than Gillis or her butler, her emotionally deluded former husband and silent film director, Max von Mayerling (Stroheim). While some characters of each gender are shown as villainous in Wilder films, far more often his people are portrayed as realistic mixtures of good and bad traits, with the director generally refusing to judge them harshly or at all. Wilder made most of his films in a time when Hollywood often portrayed women either sentimentally (as Madonna figures) or as hardboiled villains (such as unscrupulous whores), and not often enough as realistic mixtures of conflicting human appetites. So the candor of Wilder's more tolerant portrayals of women could appear shocking to some audience members in his day.

Before Sarris came around to appreciating Wilder, he took the director to task in his auteurist bible, *The American Cinema*: "A director who can crack jokes about suicide attempts (*Sabrina* and *The Apartment*) and thoughtlessly brutalize charming actresses like Jean Arthur (*Foreign Affair*) and Audrey Hepburn (*Sabrina*) is hardly likely to make a coherent film on the human condition." I'm at a loss to know how his affectionate portrayal of Sabrina can be said to "brutalize" Hepburn, other than showing the lovelorn girl trying to gas herself in a garage with her chauffeur father's fleet of automobiles, a scene that carries a poignant comic sympathy (even while echoing the Holocaust yet again). Wilder's depiction of Arthur's Phoebe Frost is undoubtedly severe. The puritanical congresswoman is made to wear highly unflattering outfits and hairstyles, with Dietrich's glamorous Erika making harsh remarks about her appearance, including asking if the remarkably ugly evening dress she bought on the black market is on backwards and commenting, "What a curious way to do your hair—or not to do it." As part of Phoebe's investigation of GIs chasing after German woman, in her Aryan blonde pigtails she easily impersonates a giggly German Fräulein she calls "Gretchen Gesundheit."

Arthur was brave to throw herself so vigorously into such an initially charmless role at the service of the story, and those of us who admire her find it touching to witness Phoebe's transformation through love, however misguided she is to trust Pringle. The lighting of Arthur by cinematographer Charles B. Lang Jr. often makes Phoebe's face glow as she falls in love, bringing out her offbeat beauty more and more as she lets her emotions run free.* Wilder considered her "very accurately cast." She had a nearly pathological

---

* Lang received an Oscar nomination for *A Foreign Affair* in recognition of his artistic virtuosity in combining such disparate visual elements. It was one of his seventeen nominations; he won an Oscar for Frank Borzage's 1932 *A Farewell to Arms.*

unwillingness to watch herself onscreen. Late in her life, when I made one of my visits to her home in Carmel, California, as one of the few outsiders allowed to see her, she said her actor friend Roddy McDowall had sent her videotapes of her films and insisted she watch them for the first time. She was surprised to find herself good in them, and one day she called Wilder out of the blue, without identifying herself (he recognized her distinctive voice immediately), and said, "Billy Wilder, I saw the picture." He asked what picture, and she went on, "Well, you know, that thing when I'm the congresswoman. I saw it. Somebody showed it to me, and it's wonderful. I'm so sorry that I put you through those things."

During the filming she "did not get along with me at all," Wilder recalled. One night she and her husband came to his house and angrily accused Wilder of burning a beautiful close-up of her at Dietrich's bidding to throw the film more in the German actress's direction. I asked Arthur why Wilder would do that, and she said with exasperation, "Oh, don't you understand? She was doing *dirty things* with the director!" For the record, even though Dietrich was living at Wilder's house during the filming, he denied to Cameron Crowe that he was sexually involved with her: "I do not fuck a star. That's a primary rule of mine. Because I'm so busy with the picture. Because I'm so worried about the picture. If I did have a real yen for that thing . . . then I fuck the stand-in. I go to the Valley where the stand-in lives." And he told Karasek, "I would rather have killed Audrey's dog than destroy a beautiful close-up." But he told John Lund during the filming, "What a picture. One dame who's afraid to look in a mirror, and one who won't stop."

Sinyard and Turner comment that after Phoebe suffers her disillusionment at the hands of Pringle and tells him, "What a waltz we had," she "descends the darkened staircase, in ironic contrast to her dreamy ascent of her own hotel staircase after a romantic night with Pringle some time before. The gravity of the moment is very sensitively handled and accusations of 'brutalisation' in that context would be difficult to sustain. Wilder is closest to Phoebe Frost at her moment of disillusionment: a 'brutal' director would have handled it with relish."

From today's neopuritanical perspective, some of the more censorious audience members might condemn him for misogyny for refusing to idealize the women in his films. But Wilder's affection is abundantly obvious for a sexually repressed woman treated as brutally as Phoebe as well as for such "flawed" women as Fran, Polly, Sugar, and Christine Vole (Dietrich), who disguises herself as a Cockney tart to entrap her faithless, murderous husband in *Witness for the Prosecution* (1957). The men who expect these women to behave like prostitutes or kept women and treat them as such are the true objects of Wilder's scorn. Juliet Mills's Pamela Piggott in *Avanti!*, carrying on a passionate romance in an Italian resort hotel like her late mother, is the kind of character to whom Wilder often returns and treats with great affection. These are the women who follow their emotional and sensual desires but are not corrupted despite all the sleaze they see around them.

The moment when Wilder's treatment of his complex theme of money versus love achieves a resolution comes in *Avanti!* The initially callous Wendell Armbruster Jr. has his moment of truth when he learns that Pamela's mother, Catherine, who carried on a ten-year clandestine affair with his wealthy father, worked as a manicurist at London's Savoy Hotel but never once took money from him. Wendell expresses astonishment, and Pamela responds, "You want to know whether my mother was a kept woman?" She explains that her mother never told his father what she did for a living, because "She loved him. She didn't want any tips." Wendell is left chastened and nearly speechless; he has been transformed, like Bud Baxter and Georges Iscovescu, into a mensch.

"*IN* THE WORLD AND *OF* THE WORLD"

Just as striking as the many examples of innocents or comparative innocents ill-used by men in Wilder's films are the numerous characters who are eager to give up their innocence, whether physically or emotionally or both. Some of these women, usually but not always young, have little or no romantic or sexual experience but are actively pursuing seduction, sometimes comedically and sometimes at emotional risk. Besides Pamela in *Avanti!*, they include Phoebe in *A Foreign Affair*, Fran in *The Apartment*, and, in Wilder's most farcical vein, the fantasy figure The Girl (Monroe) in *The Seven Year Itch* and the zany, airheaded southern playgirl Scarlett Hazeltine (Pamela Tiffin) in his screwball comedy *One, Two, Three*.

Some of Wilder's male characters also fit this description of the innocent eager for seduction and corruption, notably Walter in *Double Indemnity* and

Bud in *The Apartment*. And Wilder plays a raucous comic gender-fluid variation on this theme as Lemmon's Jerry/Daphne responds, swinging between reserve and abandon, to Osgood's wooing in *Some Like It Hot*. But Wilder's bittersweet view of life is at its rawest in some of these characters, and with his broken heart often openly on display, there is charm and poignancy in their yearnings. That is especially the case with the winsome yet audacious, even brazen Audrey Hepburn characters in *Sabrina* and *Love in the Afternoon*.

Class barriers prevent the enchanting Sabrina, the chauffeur's daughter on the Long Island estate of a wealthy family, from being seriously considered a figure of romance or even a love object by the playboy son of the family, David Larrabee (William Holden). Early in the film, David, on his way to a tryst, passes the lovelorn Sabrina, who has been staring at him from her perch in a tree like a wood nymph. He doesn't see her until she jumps down from the base of the tree. "Oh, it's you, Sabrina," he says casually. "Hello, David," she responds with a hopeful smile. "I thought I heard somebody," he says, walking away. In a large close-up, she tells herself sadly, "No, it's nobody." But after a two-year sojourn in Paris studying at a cooking school, the formerly tomboyish Sabrina returns as a glamorous, poised woman of the world. By this time, as Wilder subtly but clearly conveys, she has lost her sexual innocence willingly (perhaps to an elderly French baron who took care of her financially, played by Marcel Dalio).

The most poignant sequence shows Sabrina late at night writing a letter home with the lights of the Parisian landscape seen in a window behind her. Someone outside is playing "La Vie en rose" (lyrics by Edith Piaf, music by Louiguy) on an accordion. The camera tracks slowly in as Sabrina writes her father a bittersweet celebration of lost innocence:

> [The song] is the French way of saying, "I'm looking at the world through rose-colored glasses," and it says everything I feel. I have learned so many things, father—not just how to make vichyssoise or calf's head with sauce vinaigrette—but a much more important recipe: I have learned how to live—how to be *in* the world and *of* the world, and not just to stand aside and watch. And I will never, never again run away from life, or from love, either.

As a woman of the world, she is a suitable figure for David's suddenly enraptured attention. Wilder's most striking transition in this modern fairy tale (presented as such from its beginning with "Once upon a time . . .") is the shot of Sabrina back home at the Long Island train station. The camera rises to reveal her looking stunningly sophisticated in a black-and-white dress and turban, accompanied by a poodle (also named David) wearing a jeweled collar. "La Vie en rose" plays again on the soundtrack as the camera pulls back to reveal the poised young woman pacing in glorious full figure. Wilder abruptly cuts to David driving along in his convertible whistling (what else?) "Isn't It Romantic?" He doesn't recognize her until she has him drive her to the home where they both live. Wilder and his fellow writers, Samuel A. Taylor and Ernest Lehman (adapting Taylor's play *Sabrina Fair*), do not have the shallow David redeemed by love, which might have seemed too facile. Instead the plot mechanics grind to have him supplanted as her would-be lover by his older brother, Linus (Humphrey Bogart), a dour, charmless tycoon.

We can't help feeling Linus seems wrong for her, however, especially after the way she was mooning after David for so much of the story. The problem was mostly in the casting and Wilder's fabled clashes with the unhappy Bogart on the set. *Sabrina* was one of the many films for which Wilder wanted Cary Grant to play the lead. He even told Crowe he wanted Grant for "every part." And Lubitsch wanted Grant for *Ninotchka*. But Grant would never work in a Wilder film.* The plot twist that has Sabrina winding up with Linus is motivated to some extent by the character transformation she undergoes in Paris. Like Eliza Doolittle in *Pygmalion*, Sabrina has moved out of her class and no longer belongs anywhere. Her father (John Williams) says, "She's

---

* Paul Diamond said Wilder's theory was that Cary Grant "wasn't an actor really. Billy thought he was intimidated by having to work for Billy. He just found a way not ever to do with it." Wilder remained friends with Grant and didn't think the rejections were personal; at least that's how he rationalized it. Iz Diamond once remarked, "In the old studio days you would start out writing a comedy for Cary Grant, and you would wind up with Robert Hutton" (as happened to Diamond with *Love and Learn*). Grant said when he rejected *Love in the Afternoon*, "Look, I like you, Wilder, but I cannot explain it. I just . . . the wrong signals come up in me." He said on another occasion, "I'd heard he didn't like actors very much, and I'd already worked with enough of those kinds of directors to last a lifetime. Humphrey Bogart did [*Sabrina*] and he looks very unhappy all the way through." Grant said he did not like directors he found "impolite and outrageous and insensitive." The only time Wilder worked with Grant, peripherally, was when Brackett and Wilder did some uncredited rewrites on the bland comedy *The Bishop's Wife* (1947), directed by Henry Koster.

just a displaced person, I'm afraid." She has, in effect, sold out, though Wilder doesn't seem to realize it or want to go all the way in exploring that somber theme with such a charming young actress. All Sabrina is suited for now is to marry a much older businessman who looks glum as he dines and dances with her.

Linus behaves like a gigolo pretending to romance her for the sake of a business deal to woo her away from David, but like other Wilder gigolos, Linus starts feeling guilty and confesses to her. His candor is presented (unconvincingly) as the final step in making them both fall truly in love. Despite how incompatible Hepburn seems with the miscast Bogart, her character no longer feels she would be happier with Holden's David, though he is closer to her age and more free-spirited, because she has come to realize how shallow he is in contrast with his older brother. But though Sabrina may think she is choosing Linus freely, she seems a prisoner of her circumstances, a prize traded from brother to brother in a wealthy family. In the play as well, Sabrina winds up choosing Linus over David, but Linus is younger and portrayed more sympathetically than he is in the film, so it makes more sense onstage for her to choose a man who is more mature than David and has his own suavity. But *Sabrina Fair* as a play is rather pointless, downbeat, and charmless.*

The depressing denouement of Wilder's confused and conflicted film version is disguised as what it seems to think is a happy ending, even if a more bittersweet finale would have been more appropriate. A film that starts out as a fairy tale but gradually, if unconsciously, subverts it has a high road to climb and needs to maintain its footing. *Sabrina* unfortunately doesn't. Nor does Wilder's second Hepburn vehicle, *Love in the Afternoon*, released in the same year (1957) as his earlier-filmed *The Spirit of St. Louis*, another movie about a naive American being transformed into a different kind of person, but not for the better, by going to Paris.

The Spirit of St. Louis is the most uncharacteristic work in Wilder's canon, an unambiguously heroic saga of Lindbergh's epic 1927 flight across the Atlantic, a film entirely lacking in the characteristic skepticism of his worldview

---

* Margaret Sullavan was in her forties when she played Sabrina on Broadway in 1953. Her casting as a fey semi-ingénue sounds as off-kilter as having Bogart play the romantic partner who finally sweeps Hepburn off her feet.

and oddly oblivious to world-political issues. Strangely (especially for a Jewish filmmaker), it ignores the dark aspects of Lindbergh's character as a profascist, anti-Semitic Nazi appeaser while focusing intensively on his early achievement. Some people at the time of the film's release questioned that choice,* but Wilder's youthful passion for the pioneering days of aviation in the 1920s, evident in his European journalism, was detached from his own political concerns. Among the millions of others who shared the excitement over Lindbergh's flight was Brecht, who wrote a 1929 radio play with Kurt Weill and Paul Hindemith, *Der Lindberghflug* (*Lindbergh's Flight*), although Brecht revised it substantially in 1949 to denounce Lindbergh's later evolution. By failing to put the flight into similar perspective, Wilder made a film that seemed alien to his artistic as well as political sensibilities.

Wilder's expensive flop about Lindbergh was based on the aviator's Pulitzer Prize–winning 1953 memoir and was adapted with Wendell Mayes and Charles Lederer. James Stewart, who had an extensive history as a World War II bomber pilot in the U.S. Army Air Forces and was promoted to brigadier general in 1959, was considerably older than Lindbergh was at the time of the flight but gives an intense and convincing performance in the film. The shooting was slow and difficult, however, and as it went far over budget, the unhappy Wilder left the production, and parts were reshot by John Sturges, a versatile director far more adept with action. Mayes stayed on and kept track of the storyline, but the switch in directors could help account for some jarring shifts in tone. The film's abysmal box-office failure (Jack Warner called it "the most disastrous failure we ever had") has been blamed on younger audience members' unfamiliarity with Lindbergh, but it also may have been due to residual public disgust over his record in the years leading up to World War II.

Wilder later reflected that maybe he should have filmed the whole story of Lindbergh's tempestuous life. But he said later, "I committed myself to *The Spirit of St. Louis* before I learned I was absolutely forbidden from touching Lindbergh's personal life. I was even talked out of suggesting some ideas to him. He was a rather square man." Wilder admitted he felt reticent around

---

* John Kerr, who had starred in the film *Tea and Sympathy* (1956), turned down the lead role in Wilder's film because of Lindbergh's politics. Another young actor was eager to play Lindbergh but did not make a suitable impression when he met Wilder on the set of *The Seven Year Itch*. Clint Eastwood followed up with an earnest letter about his interest in the role.

the "imposing," legendary Lindbergh, to the detriment of telling his story more fully. Wilder especially wished he could have included an account some newspapermen told him of a reporter allegedly paying a young waitress to have sex with the virginal flier in his Long Island hotel room on what they thought might be his final night on Earth (a rumor denied by A. Scott Berg in his sometimes unreliable Lindbergh biography). Wilder wanted to bring the waitress back at the end waving at Lindbergh during his huge ticker-tape parade in New York (the event alluded to by Gusto Nash in his script for *Arise, My Love*), but without the aviator seeing her in the crowd, "and that would have been enough to make this a real picture." The girl with the mirror was the closest Wilder could come to that idea.*

Nevertheless, the film offers a vivid re-creation of Lindbergh's transatlantic flight and his emotional ordeal in a paradoxically claustrophobic widescreen spectacle. At least Wilder was glad he could work in scenes of Lindbergh talking with a fly that enters his cockpit, a device that not only relieved some of the film's concentration on a single character (*Cahiers du Cinéma* wryly commented, "This Bressonian adventure can be excused only as an avant-garde film") but also salved some of Wilder's long-festering indignation over Charles Boyer's refusal to talk to a cockroach in *Hold Back the Dawn*. "I didn't see the connection until you brought it up," Wilder told Zolotow, and though James Stewart had demanded that the fly accompany him only part of the way, Wilder told the biographer, "To me, the fly and Lindbergh were like two fellow aviators. Mr. Stewart does not object to talking to insects. After all, he has had to deal all his life with agents and producers."

Wilder liked to recall a quip he made during his preparation process when he and Lindbergh took a commercial plane flight to view the original *Spirit of St. Louis* at the Smithsonian Institution. When their flight ran into turbulence, Wilder leaned over and asked, "Mr. Lindbergh, would it not be embarrassing if we crashed and the headlines said, 'Lone Eagle and Jewish Friend in Plane Crash?'" Lindbergh "just smiled. He knew exactly what I

---

* Wilder told Charlotte Chandler that for the carnival atmosphere and media hoopla surrounding the cave-in in *Ace in the Hole*, he was thinking not only of the Floyd Collins story but also of the ruthless behavior of the press and public at the trial of the man accused in the kidnapping and death of Lindbergh's young son, Charles Jr. Although it is sometimes claimed that Lindbergh as a young pilot was involved in the Collins media circus in 1925 by helping fly photographs and dispatches for newspapers from the scene in Kentucky, that is unlikely, since he was stationed in Texas at the time, training in the U.S. Army Air Service.

had in my mind." After seeing *The Spirit of St. Louis*, Lindbergh wrote Wilder a letter of appreciation for the film's general authenticity in depicting his flight. Lindbergh added that though there were some minor factual discrepancies, and though he could not view the film objectively, he even liked the fly and some of the other fictional additions, such as the way his San Diego plane-building partners fry fish in their hangar. Lindbergh thought those touches were in the spirit of the adventure. Wilder responded with a letter expressing regret for the film's flaws but saying that he would always be grateful that through it he had come to know Lindbergh.

SENTIMENTAL EDUCATION

Love in the Afternoon is a considerably softened adaptation of an engrossing 1920 novel by Claude Anet, *Ariane, jeune fille russe* (*Ariane, the Young Russian Girl*). The author, whose real name was Jean Schopfer, was a journalist in Russia, a playwright, a teacher, and a champion tennis player. Wilder interviewed him in 1927, finding him "pleasant" but facetiously describing him as "very serious" about literature and very limited in his knowledge of German writers. The young reporter noted that the novel's knowingness about women seemed to be reciprocated by the fondness of many women in the author's life.

Lurid for its day, racier and more emotionally intoxicating than the Wilder film version, *Ariane* is a finely crafted ironic tale of the sentimental education of a teenage schoolgirl from the Russian provinces. She coquettishly fends off men's advances at home but after going to Moscow pretends to be sexually experienced in order to seduce a notorious international playboy named Constantin Michel. She works her elaborate ruse to provoke the jealousy of a man who claims not to believe in love but needs to be manipulated into feeling romantic. The novel is both sensual and acerbic, portraying Ariane Nicolaevna as seemingly cold-blooded and cruel in her tormenting of Constantin. She surrenders her virginity quickly and willingly but while carrying on their yearlong affair drives him to distraction with her pose of emotional indifference and sexual amorality. Although she eventually confesses her deception, and the novel ends with a romantic reconciliation, *Ariane* makes her game-playing seem almost unrelentingly harsh.

The strengths and limitations of Wilder's approach to romantic comedy at the midpoint of his filmmaking career are on view in both of his uneven films with the dazzling young Hepburn, the newly minted star of William Wyler's 1953 romantic comedy *Roman Holiday*. *Love in the Afternoon*, which followed *Sabrina* in 1957, also offers the first snapshot of Wilder's budding creative relationship with I. A. L. Diamond, perhaps the most fertile creative relationship of his career, equaling if not surpassing his work with Brackett. The novel *Ariane*, like the Wilder film version, explores the not uncommon problem a woman faces in having romantic feeling for an arrogant male and her attempts to wear down his resistance to emotional commitment. But though Ariane's pose in the novel is so strenuously maintained that it almost seems to consume her, the romantic sincerity of the film's Ariane is always clear despite her subterfuge. Skittish about possible censorship problems and evidently driven by his desire to once again showcase Hepburn's offbeat charms, Wilder portrays Ariane as sexually innocent, though flirtatious and eager for experience. She is essentially sweet-natured and coy rather than cruel in goading the older reprobate she is trying to both seduce and reform, the wealthy American playboy Frank Flannagan (Gary Cooper). Their relationship is often more disturbing than charming, however, not always as Wilder intended, and unlike the more provocative way Ariane's sexual initiation is portrayed in the novel.

Wilder had fond memories of the 1930 German film *Ariane*, an early talkie adaptation that starred Elisabeth Bergner and Rudolf Forster and was directed by Paul Czinner. At one point in that film, fairly candid for its time yet somewhat genteel, when the lovers are enjoying a tryst at an Italian inn, Bergner calls out the title of a future Wilder film, "Avanti!" The Lubitschean balance of moods Wilder captures so triumphantly in *Avanti!* was a challenge he was still struggling with in the intermittently amusing and touching but largely unsatisfying *Love in the Afternoon*. While lightening the story, Wilder moved it to Paris, where he had lived after fleeing Hitler and made *Mauvaise graine*; he also set parts of *Sabrina* and *The Spirit of St. Louis* there and later *Irma la Douce* and parts of *Fedora*. Lubitsch had set many of his films, including *Ninotchka*, in that "city of lovers."

While presenting Paris in a romanticized light, Wilder and Diamond gradually transformed the novel's man of the world from the more emotionally sensitive but fiercely defensive international businessman into one of the

Ugly American figures the director was so fond of portraying. Speaking about Flannagan to her casual boyfriend, Michel (Van Doude), Ariane says, "They're very odd people. When they're young, they've their teeth straightened, their tonsils taken out and gallons of vitamins pumped into them. Something happens to their insides. They become immunized, mechanized, air-conditioned and hydromatic. I'm not even sure whether he has a heart." Michel asks, "What is he, a creature from outer space?" She replies, "No, he's an American."

Flannagan's business enterprises include oil, construction, and Pepsi-Cola bottling plants. The Pepsi enterprise, as well as enabling some double entendre about how he "hits the spot," helps establish Flannagan as a second-rate business figure, not as original as Howard Hughes (one of their models for the character) and unlike the cocky Coca-Cola colonialist played by James Cagney with such panache in *One, Two, Three*. A thoroughly jaded aging roué who treats women like commodities, Flannagan has a notorious international reputation that has earned him the title of "Man of the Year"—not from *Time*, as we expect from teasingly being shown only the bottom part of the magazine cover, but from the sleazy gossip rag *Confidential*. His well-publicized habit of seducing women in hotel suites with a slick routine involving the aphrodisiac help of a Gypsy band should repel the initially innocent young Ariane but instead draws her into his web, arousing her excitement. The character of Flannagan has much in common with the Lothario played by Zachary Scott in a Fox film coscripted by Diamond, *Let's Make It Legal* (1951). Scott's Victor Macfarland, described as "the number-one top philanderer of the Western Hemisphere," is even sleazier and less charming than Flannagan. Another character seemingly modeled in part on Hughes, Victor is a businessman with governmental connections who woos an old flame (Claudette Colbert) while she is going through a divorce but dumps her for political expediency. The version of the international playboy Diamond wrote with Wilder is less obviously sharkish and more entertaining in his satirically portrayed shallowness yet still essentially a cad, even if he is reformed somewhat unconvincingly at the end.

The Wilder-Diamond adaptation of *Ariane* adds the key character of her father, a divorce detective, Claude Chavasse, played by frequent Lubitsch leading man Maurice Chevalier. When Ariane accuses him of being a "cynic," he readily agrees, but like Wilder, he is a disappointed romantic at heart, exposing illicit behavior while being overly protective toward his daughter. Another one of the numerous investigator characters in Wilder films, Chavasse desperately wants to keep Ariane from the sordid knowledge his profession is devoted to uncovering and feels guilty for unintentionally exposing her to such "dirt." But Ariane is something of a detective herself, rummaging eagerly in his files as she rebels against his overly strict paternalism. She throws herself at Flannagan because of, not in spite of, his unsavory reputation. That titillates and challenges her, and Wilder repeatedly shows her looking entranced to be drawn into Flannagan's orbit. The same mood is conveyed with the film's dreamy close-ups of the adorable Hepburn and by the obsessively repetitive playing of "Fascination" by Flannagan's Gypsies, reprised with genuine tenderness in Franz Waxman's score.

Hepburn was in her late twenties at the time, about half the age of Cooper, but could still pass for a somewhat naive music student. Her fey demeanor and eagerness for experience draw us toward her emotionally, but we can't help feeling a distinct unease over her risky behavior. Although she wants to be corrupted, Ariane is far removed from the coldly calculating character of the novel. An earlier version of the Wilder-Diamond screenplay, titled *Ariane*, retains the character of Constantine (as his name is spelled in the script), who is described as thirty-eight years old, which would have made him a more plausible and suitable partner than the fiftyish Flannagan. That preliminary draft makes Ariane seem more sexually brazen. But her relatively demure, if not exactly virginal, characterization in the film ironically makes her affair with Flannagan seem even gamier than in the novel, in which the two characters are more equally matched, not in experience but in attitude, since Ariane is manipulating the man in a more calculating way. Wilder compounded the problem with his dispiriting casting of Cooper, twice the age of Hepburn, rather than the actor he originally considered, Yul Brynner. That exotic, highly intelligent Russian-born star was the right age for Constantine and would have been more passionate than the tired-looking Cooper, as Hepburn's true love interest from *Sabrina*, Holden, also would have been.

The screenplay for *Love in the Afternoon* evolved into something more suitable to Wilder's own obsessions and sensibility, but watching and listening to the film is quite a different experience from reading the shooting script. Often what seems funny on the page, or bittersweet in the Lubitschean manner, seems sadder and more troubling on the screen. The acting, direction, and use of music put a stronger emphasis on Ariane's romantic yearning as she tries to wear down her unworthy lover's cynical resistance to love. She does allow herself to be seduced by Flannagan not long after they meet, but it occurs halfway through the film, after many clever narrative complications, and the off-screen sex is conveyed by Wilder with oblique but unmistakable Lubitschean touches (even if censorship evidently forced the inclusion of a line in which Flannagan tells her father, "I couldn't get to first base with her").

A year passes after the seduction before she again encounters the man who took her virginity, and like David in *Sabrina*, Flannagan fails to recognize her. It's not a sufficient excuse that Flannagan is distracted because his date for that opera gala is the soignée Audrey Wilder. The moment she leaves his sight to go to the ladies' room, he starts looking around for other women and spots Ariane. As devastating as his obliviousness probably feels to Ariane, she resumes having sex with him, somewhat perversely under the circumstances, while upping the ante on her campaign of fabrications to try to make him jealous and feel something for her. The film further departs from the novel in avoiding frank depictions of the sordid details and working mostly through suggestion.

Love in the Afternoon tries to show us that Ariane reforms the crass old Lothario, finally converting him to monogamy. Part of the problem in making this credible is that Flannagan, despite his reputation as a great ladies' man, is so utterly charmless. He is such an extreme, pathological case of male arrogance, narcissism, and entitlement, like Cooper's Michael Brandon in *Bluebeard's Eighth Wife*, that it's painful to see Ariane yearning for his affection as she throws herself at him. Wilder's penchant for caricature is so extreme here that it collides with his romantic impulses and prevents him from finding the delicate balance he seeks between comedy and drama. Even though the film fitfully tries to convince us there is some potential in their relationship, we get the sense that what Ariane feels is an attraction to romance itself more than for the unworthy object of her desires. Before the denouement, the film allows only brief opportunities for Flannagan to act halfway human.

In light of Wilder's career-long focus on the themes of love versus money and the clash between emotional commitment and prostitution, the moment with the most resonance comes on the night Flannagan departs the Hotel

Ritz after his first sexual encounter with Ariane. She waits outside to say goodbye, and it is a moment that means much more to her than to him. His ritual on leaving the hotel is to walk down a row of hotel employees, passing out tips. Wilder continues panning the unbroken shot until Flannagan turns to Ariane, still holding a bill in his hands, as if to automatically pay her off like a prostitute. But as Flannagan realizes what he is about to do, he hesitates, and Ariane says like the others, but with ironic awareness, "Merci, Monsieur Flannagan, bon voyage." He takes back the money, looking mildly ashamed, if only momentarily. He tells her, "I just wish Cartier's were open— I'd buy you something very lavish." She says, "I don't want anything from you," before changing her mind and taking a carnation from his buttonhole as a romantic souvenir.

This mordant Wilder touch is echoed later in two of the defining moments in his body of work, both in films he wrote with Diamond: Pamela telling Wendell that her mother "didn't want any tips" from his father and Sheldrake, conversely, treating Fran like a prostitute by offering her money in *The Apartment*, precipitating her suicide attempt. Fran's recognition that Bud is a different kind of man comes well before she begins to respond to his romantic feelings. She takes a carnation from her buttonhole and gives it to him out of gratitude for his gentlemanly behavior in her elevator—unlike other men who ride with her, he doesn't cop a feel but always greets her politely and takes off his hat. Her sweet gesture could also be interpreted as a sign of flirtation, or so he takes it in a hopeful spirit.

Partly at the urging of Ariane's father when his detective work uncovers the relationship, the belatedly conscience-struck Flannagan tries to flee Paris by train for what he says is a tryst with two Swedish twins. But as Ariane runs alongside, breaking down in tears, Flannagan sweeps her into his arms to take her with him. This scene is taken almost directly from the novel, where it is more satisfying, but onscreen it leaves us with a feeling of unease rather than the romantic exhilaration Wilder seems to have intended. It's a rushed, frustratingly delayed conclusion that papers over the obvious difficulties in the couple's relationship. The novel's harsher tone makes the ending a more hard-won and thus more convincing reunion of two equally combustible lovers.

The film leaves us to contemplate what kind of future Hepburn's Ariane will have now that she is doomed to spend her life with a much older and more tired version of the offensive cad Brackett and Wilder wrote for

Cooper in *Bluebeard's Eighth Wife*. The result is somewhat less disheartening than Hepburn's throwing Holden over for Bogart in *Sabrina*, but that's not saying much. *Love in the Afternoon* is a more ambitious, more urgently emotional film, but its unsatisfactory "romantic" ending is undercut by Wilder's determined attempt to avoid facing the realities of the young woman's situation.

Because the Legion of Decency threatened to give *Love in the Afternoon* a Condemned rating if Wilder let Flannagan and Ariane live out of wedlock, he and Diamond had to write a bit of suitably droll and downbeat ending narration for Chevalier in the American release version: "They are now married. Serving a life sentence in New York, state of New York, USA." Sometimes, as Howard Hawks pointed out to me, what censors would suggest in those days was actually helpful in a perverse way. When the Code office rejected the ending Hawks wanted for *The Big Sleep*, he asked them to write a new scene, "and they did, and it was a lot more violent, it was everything I wanted. I made it and was very happy about it. I said, 'I'll hire you fellows as writers.'" The cynical bit of enforced irony added to *Love in the Afternoon* by American bluenoses at least helps qualify the film's falsely euphoric conclusion, reinforcing our doubts about the future of their relationship.

Wilder blamed the film's reception not on its failings but on the audience's unwillingness to accept Cooper as a womanizer. Wilder pointed out to me in 1978 that was ironic because "he *was* the guy that I had in the picture, in real life, but he photographed like a decent, tough marshal from *High Noon*." As well as repeating Lubitsch's casting mistake with Cooper in *Bluebeard's Eighth Wife*, Wilder seemed not to recognize that by the late 1950s, the aging star had become even more hesitant and insecure in his performances than he had been even in the Capra films that solidified his image. No matter how much Wilder's film tries to persuade us that Flannagan is a great ladies' man, what we actually see is a hesitant old actor who seems unsure of himself as he makes his moves toward the young woman, often giggling and chortling as Cooper was wont to do in his later years. The audience probably felt some discomfort over that as well as over the age disparity, which the film addresses briefly. When Flannagan boasts about carrying on with the twins, Ariane asks, "Aren't you a little too old for that?" Witnessing her unshakable passion for Flannagan is the opposite of romantic; their coupling is dispiriting in contrast to the novel's emphasis on the young woman's more voraciously sexual desire to become a woman of the world. If Wilder had been allowed to pursue that theme, or indeed had wanted to do so, that might have made a better film, even if it would been hard for him to get away with it at the time.

As Todd McCarthy pointed out to Wilder in our 1978 interview, *Love in the Afternoon* resembles a less graphic version of *Last Tango in Paris*, the brutally unromantic 1972 Bernardo Bertolucci film about anonymous sex between a young French woman and a jaded older American man. Wilder seemed uncomfortable with that comparison. He said of his version of the Ariane character, "She has to hide from him that she is a virgin. That already is slightly unbelievable nowadays. And that is the whole point of the original, *Ariane*, that she's afraid to tell him. He likes to do it to them and go on, but he would never touch a virgin because it's just too involving. In fact, in *Ariane*, when they do it the first time, there is blood on the sheets and she burns the bed so that he would never find out." McCarthy said, "I assume you couldn't have done that in 1957," and Wilder replied, "I don't know, maybe I could have."

Wilder had spent his entire career finding ways to circumvent censorship and deal honestly with sexuality onscreen, never an easy task in the days before the Production Code was abolished. Although his comment on *Love in the Afternoon* perhaps reveals second thoughts in hindsight, Wilder's decision to tone down the explicit sexual content of *Ariane*, however harmful it may have been to the story, was not made out of prudery but out of his growing romantic impulses, perhaps encouraged by his professional attraction to Hepburn.

Wilder's citing both Lubitsch and Stroheim as his role models reflects the conflicting elements in his artistic personality and the way those made his work so unusual and influential, particularly in his treatment of sexuality. Stroheim's kinkiness and fascination with aberrant sexuality and other complexities of human nature rarely explored onscreen struck a kindred chord with Wilder. But as a dedicatedly commercial filmmaker, Wilder was acutely aware of how those tendencies, along with Stroheim's habitual excess in shooting, had helped destroy his directing career. Wilder's work from his days as a screenwriter in Germany through his first years in Hollywood and beyond was more influenced stylistically and emotionally by Lubitsch and his artful way of using innuendo.

But Wilder nevertheless showed his Stroheim side by pushing the envelope and getting away with it, as does in the myriad sexual gags and esoteric situations in *Some Like It Hot*; *A Foreign Affair* with its implications of rough sex in the relationship between Captain Pringle and his ex-Nazi flame (when Erika kisses him, he murmurs, "Gentle, baby, it's Mother's Day");* the hunky Holden, Norma's boy toy in *Sunset Blvd.*, getting suggestively toweled off beside the pool where he will later die at her hands (a film with Stroheim himself in the cast); and the hard-boiled sexual relationship between Walter and the dominatrix Phyllis in *Double Indemnity*.

NAVIGATING MURKY SEXUAL WATERS

Wilder and Raymond Chandler often clashed temperamentally during their collaboration on *Double Indemnity*, but Wilder admired the celebrated mystery novelist's gift for dialogue, and he said, "Chandler was more of a cynic than me, because he was more of a romantic than I ever was." The lines they wrote for Phyllis and Walter were corrosive and incandescent. The couple's relationship as they plan a supposedly perfect murder resembles the excited imaginative sparks in a creative writing partnership; many Wilder films return to that favorite pattern in teaming characters, cleverly plotting scams that blow up in their faces. In *Double Indemnity*, the transgressive couple's literally racy repartee shortly after they meet while Walter is visiting her home to sell insurance to her husband is a celebrated example of the flagrantly stylized, sardonically amusing double entendre Wilder got away with even under the straitened conditions of censorship in the 1940s:

> PHYLLIS: Mr. Neff, why don't you drop by tomorrow evening around eight-thirty? He'll be in then.
> WALTER: Who?
> PHYLLIS: My husband. You were anxious to talk to him, weren't you?
> WALTER: Yeah, I was. But I'm sort of getting over the idea, if you know what I mean.

---

* Lund, who had some writing experience (including as author of the book and lyrics for the Broadway show *New Faces of 1943*), ad-libbed that line of dialogue, which became one of Wilder's favorites. One of the goofy songs by Millsap and Spooner in *Kiss Me, Stupid*, displayed on Orville's piano, is titled "Gently, Baby, It's Mother's Day."

PHYLLIS: There's a speed limit in this state, Mr. Neff. Forty-five miles an hour.

WALTER: How fast was I going, officer?

PHYLLIS: I'd say around ninety.

WALTER: Suppose you get down off your motorcycle and give me a ticket.

PHYLLIS: Suppose I let you off with a warning this time.

WALTER: Suppose it doesn't take.

PHYLLIS: Suppose I have to whack you over the knuckles.

WALTER: Suppose I bust out crying and put my head on your shoulder.

PHYLLIS: Suppose you try putting it on my husband's shoulder.

WALTER: That tears it. Eight-thirty tomorrow evening, then. . . .

PHYLLIS: I wonder if I know what you mean.

WALTER: I wonder if you wonder.

The outrageous script revels in its flamboyant portrayal of how "rotten" the characters are in this notably unsentimental love story, such as in a sulfuric dialogue exchange when Walter returns to Phyllis. He tries to back out when he gets wind of what she wants, although he will ultimately prove too weak to resist this siren in a blonde wig with her brutal appeal to his basest instincts:

WALTER: Look, baby. You can't get away with it. You want to knock him off, don't ya?

PHYLLIS: That's a horrible thing to say.

WALTER: Who'd ya think I was, anyway? A guy that walks into a good-looking dame's front parlor and says, "Good afternoon. I sell accident insurance on husbands. You got one that's been around too long? One you'd like to turn into a little hard cash? Just give me a smile and I'll help you collect?" Huh! Boy, what a dope you must think I am!

PHYLLIS: I think you're rotten.

WALTER: I think you're swell. So long as I'm not your husband.

PHYLLIS: Get out of here.

WALTER: You bet I'll get outta here, baby. I'll get outta here but quick.

When censorship was loosened in the 1960s, partly through Wilder's influence, he took increasing advantage of the opportunities it offered for even greater frankness in dialogue and themes. Some of his situations in his later films were raunchy indeed. And though that got him into considerable trouble with *Kiss Me, Stupid*, and he dabbled in scenes involving nudity in *Irma la Douce*, *Avanti!*, and *Fedora*, he never went in for explicit coupling onscreen when he could have done so and even when the films dealt with prostitution. Those who were surprised when Wilder took a stronger turn toward romanticism in his late work, when the rest of the industry was going the other way, did not know Wilder well. They thought he was as hard-boiled as some of his most amoral characters.

Wilder explained his preferences in screen sexuality by referring fondly to a particularly delightful Lubitsch Touch, the "Breakfast Time" scene in the 1931 musical *The Smiling Lieutenant*. Wilder held it up as a model of how to slip racy content past the censors and put the salacity in the minds of the audience rather than up on the screen. Chevalier (the title character) and Colbert (a violinist in an all-girls' band) exchange double entendres in song at the breakfast table following their first (unseen) night of lovemaking. Wilder commented on this delicious scene: "Ah, but regard how they are sucking their coffee and how they are biting their toast: this leaves no doubt in anybody's mind that other appetites have been satisfied. In those days, the butter was on the toast and not the ass, but there was more eroticism in one such breakfast scene than in all of *Last Tango in Paris*." Wilder was somewhat conflating *The Smiling Lieutenant* with the lewd eating scene in *Tom Jones*, the Oscar winner for best picture of 1963. But Wilder's adherence to Lubitschean methods of conveying sexual entanglement in film obliquely rather than bluntly meant that he never would have wanted to make a film as sexually harsh as *Last Tango* or the novel *Ariane*. But since the subject matter of *Love in the Afternoon* was so essentially risqué, he misjudged his ability in 1957 to navigate such murky sexual waters at the same time as he was attempting a throwback to the subtle finesse of Lubitsch's romantic comedies of the 1930s. That was already a somewhat quixotic mission in the late 1950s and became all the more so later.

From today's perspective, *Sabrina* and *Love in the Afternoon* look even less appealing than they did at the time, when Wilder's approach to romantic comedy seemed half-hearted. Perhaps those Hepburn films were a symptom of his own middle-aged crisis (a topic he explored comedically, and stridently, when he made *The Seven Year Itch* between them), as well as of his understandable rapture over the incandescent young actress. The fact that Wilder cast Hepburn in her captivating period of early stardom opposite two aging American stars who were seriously showing their age was another depressing chapter in Hollywood's long history of sexual fantasies involving older men and much younger women. Hepburn seemed to especially inspire such fantasies, as also can be seen in her pairings with Henry Fonda in *War and Peace*, Fred Astaire in *Funny Face*, Cary Grant in *Charade*, and Rex Harrison in *My Fair Lady*.

Diamond specialized in light comedies before he began his partnership with Wilder, and as they worked together, Wilder gradually advanced his artistry blending romantic comedy and drama. *Love in the Afternoon* marked a somewhat inauspicious beginning for their long and fertile creative relationship, which would result in some of the director's greatest films. Nevertheless, the notes of my interview with Diamond in 1974 indicate that when "asked which of his films with Wilder he likes best, he said he supposed he has to follow the public's verdict and say *Some Like It Hot* and *The Apartment*, although he has a special fondness for *Love in the Afternoon* and *One, Two, Three*." Perhaps Diamond's fondness for the Hepburn film was partly a sentimental attachment to the project that made his career, just as its storyline forever changes the life of its ambitious young heroine. But Diamond's preferences among the twelve films he wrote with Wilder also demonstrate his tastes for mordant romanticism and political satire, two of the many qualities they shared.

Wilder had as much reason to be grateful when he discovered Iz Diamond. After tryouts with other potential partners to replace Brackett, Wilder had finally found the truly simpatico creative partner who had been eluding him since the start of his career in Hollywood.

7.1 (top) The team of Billy Wilder and I. A. L. Diamond began their partnership with *Love in the Afternoon* (1957). Their rare creative synergy lasted into the 1980s, beyond the end of Wilder's directing career. (Publicity photo/Photofest.)

7.2 (bottom) One of the classic movie endings, as Jerry/Daphne (Jack Lemmon) admits, "I'm a MAN!," and his/her partner in *Some Like It Hot* (1959), Osgood Fielding III (Joe E. Brown), is about to reply, "Well—nobody's perfect." (United Artists/Photofest.)

7

"NOT A FUNNYMAN
BUT A MORALIST"

FRAN (Shirley MacLaine): Why can't I ever fall in love with
   somebody nice like you?
BUD (Jack Lemmon): Yeah, well, that's the way it crumbles,
   cookie-wise.

—*The Apartment* (1960)

"**THANK YOU**, I. A. L. Diamond."

"Thank you, Billy Wilder."

They made those brief speeches after shaking hands on the way to
the podium at the Academy Awards ceremony in April 1961 when they won
their Oscars for best original screenplay with *The Apartment*. The symbiotic
nature of their partnership was never more succinctly or wittily expressed
than at that crowning moment of their careers. *The Apartment* was also honored as the best picture of 1960, and the three Oscars Wilder won that night
were unprecedented at the time for a writer-director-producer (though seven
others have since equaled that achievement). While presenting the screenwriting award, playwright and screenwriter Moss Hart grinned and said to

Wilder, "This is the moment to stop, Billy." Fortunately for us, Wilder just smiled.

From Hollywood's point of view, Hart may have been right, for Wilder and his new writing partner never again reached such a combined peak of critical and box-office success. The bawdy romantic comedy hit *Irma la Douce* marked the apogee of Wilder's rapport with the mass audience, catching the tenor of the times in 1963 with what now seems its relatively mild naughtiness in anticipation of the sexual revolution. But when I asked Wilder before giving him the LAFCA career achievement award in 1995 what he considered his best film, he told me it was *The Apartment*, because he considered it his most successful blend of comedy and drama, the mixture he said he had been working for all his life. Some would argue (as I do) that the Wilder-Diamond sex farce that preceded it, *Some Like It Hot*, is actually their masterpiece. But it is difficult, if not idle, to compare perfection with perfection.

Although both of those classics had their contemporary detractors, time has made their complaints—too raunchy, too nasty, in bad taste, etc.—seem ridiculous. But the Wilder-Diamond hat trick with *The Apartment* at the Oscars did mark the climax of their partnership, even if they gave "Climax" a different meaning in their equally brilliant but considerably more sexually provocative *film maudit Kiss Me, Stupid*, which marked the beginning of their commercial decline with its scandalous reception in 1964–1965. After that calamity, the shaken Wilder and Diamond temporized with an uncertain mixture of sourness and sentimentality in their Jack Lemmon–Walter Matthau comedy about an insurance scam, *The Fortune Cookie*. Then, while the norms Wilder had been battling against throughout his career in Hollywood were collapsing all around him, the director took his turn against the prevailing trends and deeply explored his latent romanticism in *The Private Life of Sherlock Holmes*, *Avanti!*, and *Fedora*. That marked him as old-fashioned, passé, anathema to the newer generation of filmgoers whose tastes had turned to the gritty sex and nihilistic violence of *Bonnie and Clyde*, *Easy Rider*, *The Wild Bunch*, and *Midnight Cowboy*.

Time has shown, nevertheless, that Hart was not right from Wilder's point of view or from ours, at least for those of us who value the late period of Wilder's career as highly as his earlier collaborations with Charles Brackett. That is still a somewhat unfashionable view, even if the late Wilder-Diamond collaborations have their fervent admirers. I have been arguing in favor of Wilder's late work since 1970, when Michael Wilmington and I wrote our career critique for *Film Quarterly*. We subsequently extolled in that journal the unfashionable virtues of the same year's revisionist and romantic Wilder film about the Victorian era and Sherlock Holmes. The commercial and critical failure of that film and his other later work eventually made Wilder "unbankable" in Hollywood despite his decades of success. After the lamentable dud *Buddy Buddy* in 1981, he entered into the state of forced inactivity as a director he endured for the final twenty-one years of his life.

But in his fertile late period of filmmaking that began with *Some Like It Hot* and lasted through *Fedora*, Wilder finally was freed to be fully himself. That might have happened anyway in Wilder's older years even if he had never discovered Diamond, but his new junior partner helped accelerate the process. Stravinsky once remarked that in an artist's old age, he becomes truly himself because he no longer cares what the public thinks of him. Wilder was not an avant-garde artist but a popular entertainer who had always cared what the public thought of his work. And yet when they decisively turned their backs on him, he just as decisively refused to truckle to public and critical opinion. His rejection was as cruel as the one he and Brackett had imagined for the faded silent star Norma Desmond: "Poor devil, still waving proudly to a parade which had long since passed her by."

Wilder, though, was not waving proudly at the passing parade but giving it the finger. His attitude toward the changing market, expressed in many interviews during and after the period when he was making his final films, was not self-pity but anger and bitterness toward the industry and contempt for how Hollywood too often descended into self-parody, crudity, and juvenilia. He did not go gently into that bad night. Although Wilder characteristically cloaked his feelings in biting wit—in that "brilliant repartee" his cinematic alter ego Matthau recognized as Wilder's defense mechanism—the pain he felt over that rejection was unmistakable.

Andrew Sarris's 1976 recantation of his earlier condemnation of Wilder for being "too cynical to believe even his own cynicism" marked a major stage in the ongoing critical debate over the director's later years, and not entirely coincidentally it came in the midst of the eclipse in Wilder's reputation with the public that had once embraced him. Sarris admitted in another reassessment (1991) that he had "lost my heart" to Wilder and Brackett when he saw *The Major and the*

Minor upon its release in 1942. And he confessed that "I must have seen *Sunset Boulevard* about 25 times during its first run at the Radio City Music Hall." But, "ungrateful wretch that I am," he "deserted Billy Wilder in the mid-Fifties and my late twenties" while beginning to formulate the auteurist aesthetics that led him to banish Wilder to a lesser realm of *The American Cinema.*

"Perhaps I mistrusted Wilder because I never had to work very hard to enjoy his movies," Sarris wrote. He added, "Wilder's apparently shrewd mixture of cynicism and romanticism seduced me at an early stage of my aesthetic awareness, with the result that I came to suspect him of lacking high moral seriousness." Sarris reflected on one reason Wilder was downgraded by auteurists:

> For too long he was bracketed with the very well-liked Charles Brackett, who, it was whispered in industry circles, exercised a restraining, civilizing influence on the cynical, callous, morbid tendencies of Billy Wilder. Hence, when a Wilder movie seemed particularly heartless, Wilder received all the blame; and when a Wilder movie seemed particularly compassionate, Wilder had to share the credit with Brackett. . . . Cynicism and sophistication, being relatively rare in movies at any time, tend to be seized upon as the full register of a director's personality. The passion underneath the polish is thereby overlooked.

My own locus classicus in the debate over Wilder's "cynicism" and romanticism and the changes that followed his teaming with Diamond came in a conversation I had with my editor at *Daily Variety* in Hollywood, Thomas M. Pryor, shortly after I joined the trade paper in 1974. A crusty but lovable veteran journalist who bore a distinct resemblance to James Cagney, Tom had reviewed and covered films for the *New York Times* for many years before taking over the editorship of the Hollywood publication. He was an editor with intelligence and integrity who turned *Daily Variety* into a journalistic institution that was mostly reputable in those days, a considerable achievement even if the former New York crime reporter-turned-filmmaker Samuel Fuller described it to me as "that fucking rag you love so much."

Tom Pryor knew and reported on Wilder, Brackett, and Diamond, and he had strong opinions about Wilder's career. When I was hired and asked Tom what he thought of *Avanti!,* he simply grumbled that it was "too long" to be a successful comedy. In addition to being unduly influenced by the industry's primary barometers—box-office success or failure—and by conventional wisdom about the supposed length limitations of comedy, criteria I've always disregarded as shallow, Tom went on to express his belief that Diamond had been primarily responsible for what he considered Wilder's supposed decline. Tom argued that came about because Diamond had unleashed "Billy's vulgarity." Brackett, he said, had managed to restrain that unfortunate tendency of his partner.

I tried to argue that *Avanti!* and other late Wilder-Diamond films were actually romantic as well as raunchy, and I asked what was wrong with vulgarity, anyway? I actively enjoy what others consider "vulgarity," for which "Rabelaisian" might be a better word, more acceptable at least in literary circles. But "vulgarity" is derived from the Latin word *vulgus*, meaning "the common people," and Wilder always had the common touch as an inveterate entertainer, one of his great strengths along with his tendency to *épater la bourgeoisie*. Condemning "vulgarity," especially in a comic artist, equates "good taste" with art, and Wilder often found himself accused of "bad taste," even though Picasso said, "Good taste is the enemy of creativity." But Tom just couldn't see beyond what he considered Wilder's lapses into bad taste, a bugaboo for his detractors over the years.

My editor was one of those influential film industry figures who placed a much higher value on the more "respectable" work Wilder had made with Brackett. I'd be the last person to argue that their romantic comedies and dramas, especially *Ninotchka*, *Hold Back the Dawn*, *A Foreign Affair*, and *Sunset Blvd.*, are not among Wilder's finest achievements or that his collaboration with Brackett was not greatly beneficial to both men. Brackett was primarily a literary man, a novelist and urbane wit whose graceful command of the English language and sophisticated interest in psychology and structure helped shape Wilder's developing talents and sensibility. His collaborations with Wilder (also including their much-honored, if overly one-note, adaptation of Charles Jackson's novel *The Lost Weekend*) were always impeccably crafted, as was Wilder's brilliant film version of Cain's *Double Indemnity*, which he adapted with Chandler because Brackett considered the novel too coarse. But Brackett did consult on that script from time to time, and when he went to the first sneak preview in January 1944, he found *Double Indemnity* "an absolute knockout of a picture, the most flawless bit of picture technique imaginable."

If Brackett did have something of a tempering effect on Wilder's sensibility, that was a double-edged sword, for despite their considerable achievements, their often stark differences and disagreements in taste and politics put them increasingly at odds and made Wilder feel the need to bust loose. After making their best film together, *Sunset Blvd.*—which caused Brackett some distress over Wilder's insistence on showing Norma torturing herself to get back in shape "for those cameras that would never turn"—Wilder wanted to tackle even more provocative kinds of stories and exercise his biting wit and left-liberal political viewpoint more freely. He did so decisively with his first film apart from Brackett, *Ace in the Hole*, his most caustic, uncompromising work. That profoundly disillusioned criticism of the mindless brutality of the American public reflected Wilder's darkened post-Holocaust social vision. It was the kind of all-out attack on sociopolitical and media corruption and deep dive into human vice that made Brackett uncomfortable.

The persistence of the condemnation of Wilder's later work in some circles can be seen in a 2012 article by John Patterson for the British newspaper the *Guardian*:

> Deprived of a restraining presence when he split with Brackett . . . Wilder went right overboard with his noirish journalism melodrama *Ace in the Hole*, a nihilistic howl. . . . And despite the relative wonders of *Some Like It Hot* and *The Apartment*, his late-career teaming with co-writer I. A. L. Diamond saw his movies becoming steadily less interesting visually and steadily more noisy and tin-eared. Perhaps, as antic Mitteleuropean fatalists who had both fled Europe before the catastrophe, their temperaments were too similar, too agreeable, for effective self-assessment.

I take issue with most of that and find especially baffling Patterson's view that Wilder's late films are "less interesting visually," when in fact they became increasingly rich and resplendent, like the late work of his contemporary George Cukor.

THE MEANING OF IZ

After Wilder's period of retrenchment in the wake of *Ace in the Hole* adapting safer, presold properties, he found a looser, more congenial partner whose background was less literary than cinematic. Diamond had turned from the-atrical sketch comedy to a lengthy apprenticeship in mostly light-comedy screenwriting. Like Wilder a Jewish immigrant from Eastern Europe, Diamond was more culturally compatible with the director than Brackett, the quintessential American WASP. Although Diamond was more at ease with his imagination than Brackett, and much racier in his humor, he was, if any-thing, even more punctilious in his craftsmanship, as much so as Wilder himself, who used to drive Brackett mad with his endless fine-tuning of their word choices. Diamond's widow, Barbara, said Wilder "had a near perfect ear for the rhythms of American speech and he talked the scene as he wrote to get it right. Because he took such pains, it drove him crazy when actors would substitute an approximation of the line for the actual line. One of the many pleasures for Iz working with Billy was the knowledge that was on the page would show up on the screen. And, of course, Iz was on the set every day to help Billy protect the script."

Brackett's middlebrow tastes tended to draw Wilder to more somber mate-rial, but the quietly zany Diamond helped liberate Wilder's more antic side and along with it a greater generosity toward his characters and life in gen-eral. Diamond encouraged the bawdy aspects of Wilder's personality that the more fastidious Brackett had tried, not always successfully, to tamp down. When asked whether it was his father's influence that made Wilder bawdier, his screenwriter son Paul Diamond thought the cause for that change was more "the marketplace and the culture; that's not really a personal thing." But one indication of how risqué Iz Diamond could be was quoted to me by Wilder when he talked about having to compete with the uninhibited tendency of moviemaking in the late 1970s: "Look, it has become extraordinarily diffi-cult, because as my collaborator, Mr. Diamond, said, 'Nowadays you look at the picture and under the titles, zebras are fucking women.' Now where do you go from there? I mean how do you top that?"

Nevertheless, Paul felt one reason the team's later films lean more toward romanticism was pragmatic and defensive: "I think they shied away from [bawdy material] partially because of the monetary disincentive of having another flop [after *Kiss Me, Stupid*]. It almost killed them." Traumatic though that was, it was a failure that helped liberate them further from the vagaries of the changing marketplace. If they were hoping for commercial success in the later films, they miscalculated. Although the Wilder and Diamond films tend to be funnier than the ones the director wrote with Brackett—no

American sound film is more hilarious than *Some Like It Hot*—Diamond to some extent matched, or at least helped enable, Wilder's increasingly overt romantic streak to flourish in *The Apartment, Kiss Me, Stupid, Sherlock Holmes*, and *Avanti!* Diamond recalled that what "I heard constantly for over twenty-five years was, 'Don't give me logic. Give me emotion.'"

Whether you approve or disapprove of the influence of Diamond in the second half of Wilder's directing career is a matter of taste and sensibility. And as Paul put it, "It's maybe easier to separate the contributions of Brackett and Wilder than Diamond and Wilder." That is undoubtedly the case, partly because Brackett brought to the younger Wilder a more extensive set of writing credentials and more stature in the industry than Diamond had when he joined the older Wilder, but it's also due to the extraordinarily close harmony of the later team. In my view, Diamond deserves great credit for helping Wilder realize his fullest creative potential. Those who can find nothing in *Kiss Me, Stupid* but coarseness and vulgarity, or consider even the relatively innocuous and more audience-friendly *Irma la Douce* overly racy, I consider hypocritical for failing to respond to the human emotions so strongly evident in those films and being unable to appreciate the mellower virtues of their melancholy *Private Life of Sherlock Holmes* or their autumnal romantic comedy *Avanti!*

Yet Diamond, like Wilder, was a man with a paradoxical view of human nature. Diamond's widow went so far as to say: "The person who was really cynical and really had a jaundiced view of the world was my husband. A lot of things that Billy had to apologize for were things that came rolling out of Iz's mouth. Iz was absolutely, completely honest, and absolutely, completely intolerant of all the little accommodations to truth and integrity that people make." Wilder appreciated those qualities and the complexities of Diamond's character. When they worked together and Diamond, in his more mature phase, was liberated from the constraints of studio contract screenwriting, he, like Wilder, was not merely a jokester, a funnyman, or a "cynical" flayer of sacred cows. Both found a great deal of pathos in their characters, even in the most raucous situations, and the moments of high drama and romance in their screenplays are as moving as any Wilder ever directed. Critic George Morris observed that the partners "complement each other beautifully" because "Diamond's ready wit leaves Wilder free to tap his emotional resources more fully."

With censorship relaxing and Wilder's stature in the industry allowing him greater independence (his patrons at the Mirisch Company and Mirisch Corporation and their distributor, United Artists, allowed him virtual carte blanche from 1959 onward), Wilder was able to flex his creative muscles. He was freed from all constraints other than those of his own idiosyncratic sense of taste and his need to entertain, until the audience started balking at his work. Then he began facing the even greater constraints of finding it harder and harder to find employment and to get his work before an audience. By the time Wilder and Diamond went to Europe in 1976 to make their uneven but fascinating *Fedora* (not released until 1978)—in which they revisited with considerable bitterness the subject of film industry corruption and madness Wilder had examined so acutely with Brackett in *Sunset Blvd.*—the director had lost his audience almost entirely. So there was little serious commentary of any substance at the time in the United States about his last important film except from auteurist critics such as Sarris who had come to appreciate the mordant romanticism of the late Wilder.

Yet Wilder artistically reveled in his liberation all the more when it brought him opprobrium in the place where he had chosen to live and die. His intransigent attitude and refusal to compromise, though admirable, contributed to making him *ausländisch* again for the last two decades of his life.

"QUIZZICALLY"

Wilder discovered his partner through a droll sketch Diamond wrote for the 1955 Writers Guild of America West awards show. "Quizzically" deals with a team of screenwriters struggling to write a parenthetical direction for a line of dialogue. After starting with "(quizzically)" and finding it wanting, they cycle hilariously through a wide range of alternatives before winding up back at their beginning with that word. After Diamond died, Wilder directed the sketch with Lemmon and Matthau for a WGA memorial tribute to his old collaborator in May 1988. Fittingly, it is Wilder's final piece of directing; it can be seen on the DVD *Billy Wilder Speaks.**

---

* The American DVD edition in 2006 is mostly devoted to excerpts from Wilder's interview with Schlöndorff. But the interview is longer in foreign versions of *Billy, How Did You Do It?*, and film

The "Quizzically" sketch is an affectionate and witty recognition of the symbiotic nature of a true screenwriting collaboration—the kind that works harmoniously, with the partners feeding off each other in a friendly way.

They came together on *Love in the Afternoon* after Wilder had cycled through a variety of other cowriters, not always congenially, since breaking up with Brackett in 1950. In the professorial, soft-spoken, yet assertive Diamond, Wilder found a highly skilled writing partner who was simpatico on every level, without any of the clashes he had faced with Brackett. Wilder said of Diamond in 1963, "If I ever lost this guy, I'd feel like Abercrombie without Fitch."

Diamond had been born Itec Domnici in 1920 in Ungheni, Romania, to a family of Russian heritage. He spoke Yiddish and Russian at home and Romanian at school. He emigrated to the United States with his mother and sister in 1929 to join his father and grandfather, who had changed their name to Diamond. Itec had his first name Anglicized as Isidore by the principal on his first day of grammar school in Brooklyn, at a time when "he had never heard a word of English spoken," as the *New York Times* reported in a 1937 profile. Gerd Gemünden notes in his critical study of Wilder that "the films scripted with Diamond, a Central European Jew like Wilder, are more Yiddish [than those Wilder wrote with Brackett] and often reminiscent of boulevard sex comedies and farce," as well as of the plays of Arthur Schnitzler, a connection made by Diamond himself.

Isidore scored the highest grades in the history of Boys High School in Brooklyn (99.4 percent) while editing six school publications. His distinctive initials, I. A. L., were part of the Americanized nom de plume he adopted as a freshman at Columbia University. "I wanted a *goyische* handle," he later explained. He was majoring in mathematics and physics at Columbia, planning a career in engineering, until his talent for writing humor turned him to show business. Because he was a math whiz, the legend that has appeared in print over the years is that the initials I. A. L. were derived from a competition he won as a high school student with the Interscholastic Algebraic League. Even Wilder did not know the true story. But in an unpublished memoir, "A Definite Maybe," Diamond recalled that when he had his first

---

clips were removed for the American version, as well as the invaluable section in which Wilder comments on his influence by Lubitsch.

piece printed in Columbia's humor magazine, the *Jester*, he found that his byline was changed to Ian Diamond. Confronting the managing editor, Eugene Williams, he said, "What's this?" Williams explained, "We have too many Jewish names on the masthead," and they figured they would give him something less ethnic (Williams himself was Jewish, as was the editor of the magazine, Ralph de Toledano). Diamond objected and went home, briefly playing around with takeoffs on "Ian" and thinking he needed some initials. "I chose the nearest euphonious combination" of letters, I. A. L.: "If I was going to make up initials, I figured I might as well go all out. That may be the best piece of writing I've ever done." (Some *Times* articles during his college years, however, listed his name as a hybrid, Isidore A. L. Diamond.) His son said that someone later asked his father if he took his name after the Algebraic League, and from then on he would not dispute it but would agree with "a little twinkle" in his eyes. Paul noted that he "pretty much had to" have a sense of humor about his name. Wilder and other friends always called him "Iz." Paul said that only people who didn't know his father well called him "Izzy," since he didn't like that nickname and tolerated it only from Jack Lemmon.

At Columbia, Diamond edited the campus newspaper, the *Columbia Spectator*, and wrote the books and lyrics for an unprecedented four annual varsity shows in a row (the all-male shows included some students in drag, giving the playwright some early practice for *Some Like It Hot*). He not only had his shows reviewed in the *Times* (following the illustrious path of such former Columbia students as Oscar Hammerstein II, Richard Rodgers, and Lorenz Hart) but earned the honor of a profile. The paper highlighted the seventeen-year-old Romanian immigrant's spectacular scholastic achievements and his winning the competition as a freshman for his musical comedy script *You've Got Something There*, "a satire that manages to encompass the motion picture industry, fascism, and communism. It deals with a Hollywood film company, which, harassed for choosing its villains from foreign countries, offers to buy a government for convenience" and manages to "convert Hitler, Mussolini and Stalin to democracy."

Diamond's sophomore show in 1939, *Fair Enough*, "involved the reappearance of the nine framers of the Constitution in the twentieth century . . . to redraft the document under modern conditions . . . [while] getting a cigarette manufacturer to sponsor a constitutional convention at the New York World's

Fair." The show also lampooned the Dies Committee (the newly formed House Committee on Un-American Activities), *Gone With the Wind*, and the British royal family. Diamond's blend of liberalism and raucous penchant for political satire skewering all sides (later evident in his collaboration with Wilder on *One, Two, Three*) was already on view in *Life Begins in '40*, his junior show that year, "chiefly at Republican expense" while depicting "an unsuccessful G.O.P. revolution and a third-term victory for President Roosevelt, followed by dictatorship and the secession of all the States."

Diamond wrote comedy routines during the summers at a hotel in the Berkshires before heading to Hollywood after graduation in 1941. A Paramount staffer had recruited him after noticing one of the articles in the *Times* about his writing prowess at the university. By then Diamond was already a skilled professional, but while he developed his craft in movies, he found himself stuck mostly collaborating on formulaic comedies, several of them so-so musicals, virtually plotless, with sketch-comedy interludes reminiscent of his college work. With only intermittent exceptions, the films are forgettable and resolutely lighthearted and inconsequential, conspicuously lacking the depth of the films he later wrote with Wilder.

Diamond noted that Lewis Carroll (Charles L. Dodgson) was one of the few other mathematicians who became a writer. That bedrock of logic and precision may help account for the penchant the screenwriter shared with the author of *Alice's Adventures in Wonderland* for surreal fantasy and humor, with the jokes carefully laid out in a contrapuntally methodical, deadpan fashion. And while working under the expert influence of Wilder, Diamond learned how to integrate his humor more smoothly with the storylines, a skill he had not been able to hone fully in his apprentice film work on vehicles over which he had little control, since he was part of a studio factory conveyor-belt writing system. Not until his final film before his collaboration with Wilder began, *That Certain Feeling* (1956), an unusually dramatic Bob Hope romantic comedy costarring Eva Marie Saint, did Diamond manage to combine those elements successfully. That film is the most like his work with Wilder.

Diamond broke in with a rackety Universal B movie, a zany old-dark-house spoof called *Murder in the Blue Room* (1944) that centers on a funny girls' singing group called The Three Jazzybelles, precursors of the all-girls' band in *Some Like It Hot*. He then found a niche on several Warner Bros. programmers featuring the amiable team of Dennis Morgan and Jack Carson, including their popular buddy-buddy comedy *Two Guys from Milwaukee* (1946). The mildly handsome Morgan improbably plays a Balkan playboy prince visiting New York, a fan of American movies whose dream is to meet Lauren Bacall, a goal he finally achieves on a flight to Milwaukee before Humphrey Bogart commandeers his seat. The prince yearns to be a regular guy like Carson, whose clownish Brooklyn cabbie becomes a celebrity with an off-the-cuff Capraesque radio speech extolling the virtues of American democracy.

Romance on the High Seas (1948), a featherweight but lively Michael Curtiz-Busby Berkeley Technicolor musical, is also sketchlike but somewhat more substantial. Principally written by the twin brothers Julius and Philip Epstein, with Diamond contributing additional dialogue, it nominally stars Carson as a private eye trailing a wandering wife on a cruise to the Caribbean. That less-than-scintillating story hook morphed into a star-making showcase for the debuting Doris Day in an incandescent role echoing her own life as a struggling band singer.

Diamond didn't manage to capitalize much on his sporadic successes at Warners, perhaps because he often shared credit on formulaic vehicles with generic titles featuring character actors and newcomers, some more promising than others. After moving to Twentieth Century–Fox, he spent several years foundering under contract there. His only enduring work at the studio was a third-position screenwriting credit on Howard Hawks's 1952 screwball comedy about rejuvenation, *Monkey Business*. Diamond was unhappy that his work on what was originally titled *Darling, I Am Growing Younger* was rewritten by the seasoned pros Ben Hecht and Charles Lederer from a story by Harry Segall. The film is a well-crafted but grimly unrelenting fable about a chemist and his wife (Cary Grant and Ginger Rogers) who drink a youth potion mixed by a chimpanzee. They revert to childhood, a state portrayed unsentimentally as pure savagery. In the sheltered intellectual milieu of the absent-minded scientist and his subconsciously lecherous but actually innocent dalliance with Marilyn Monroe (his boss's secretary), there are echoes of the Hawks-Wilder collaboration *Ball of Fire*, but *Monkey Business* lacks its warmth and falls short of its witty virtuosity.

Otherwise, Diamond's films at both Warners and Fox mostly were the kind of formula fluff that soon would be rendered obsolete by television sitcoms and variety shows. The most pointless of these programmers is *Love and Learn* (1947), a vapid comedy about a team of struggling songwriters (Carson and Robert Hutton) that lacks the bite of *Kiss Me, Stupid*. Although Diamond's work developed a high degree of polish, the characterizations and stories in these vehicles only rarely touched on anything beyond light banter and fooling around, mostly lacking the gravitas that underpinned his later work with Wilder in both comedy and drama. Occasionally the pat setups of the plots Diamond was handed in his apprentice period allowed for some modest growth in his dramatic range, such as in the affecting performance by Colbert in *Let's Make It Legal* as the middle-aged Los Angeles woman going through a divorce. Her expert, believable characterization in that marital reconciliation comedy stands out among Diamond's early work with a more three-dimensional feeling than he usually managed in these light comedies.

A more typical early Diamond assignment is *Love Nest* (1951), whose misleadingly racy title acts as cover for an intimate domestic story of a returning World War II veteran (William Lundigan) and his wife (June Haver) trying to establish a foothold as landlords of a rickety old New York building. The endless, disheartening problems of this ordinary couple (who bear a passing resemblance to Bud and Fran in *The Apartment*) seldom carry much emotional weight. *Love Nest* constantly skirts the edgier elements of its storyline, such as when an old army acquaintance of the husband in Paris who is looking for a room turns out to be a model played by Marilyn Monroe.

The roles Diamond wrote for Monroe (including a similarly decorative turn as another model in *Let's Make It Legal*) allowed him to try out some aspects of her developing star persona. That process ultimately would enhance his ability to help Wilder create a three-dimensional characterization for her as the wistful, sadly manhandled band singer in *Some Like It Hot*. But the way she was used in the sanitized Fox comedies to which Diamond contributed in her buildup to stardom amounts to a prolonged exercise in cinematic prick-teasing, even if that flaw cannot entirely be blamed on the studio contract writer. *Chinatown* screenwriter Robert Towne aptly defined Monroe's paradoxical appeal as that of "the child-woman," a quality of innocent sexuality Fox took a while to understand how to deal with before Hawks and Wilder developed her screen personality most fully. Hawks shrewdly employs Monroe as the saucy, scatterbrained secretary, Miss Laurel, in *Monkey Business*, but there she is strictly a fantasy figure untouchable by the gentlemanly

Grant's hands, much like the role she would play three years later in Wilder's sour comedy of sexual frustration, *The Seven Year Itch*.

Sometimes the sex comedy in the early Diamond films without Wilder is crudely witless, especially in *The Girl from Jones Beach* (1949). A leering comedy starring Ronald Reagan, of all people, as a pinup artist who literally sees women as "just a bunch of disconnected parts," it's a Frank Tashlin kind of subject lacking the cartoonishly satirical Tashlin touch. The most intriguing element, to modern eyes, is Reagan's impersonation of a Czech immigrant (with an awful accent, supposedly for comedy) to woo a teacher of European refugees. She is played by Virginia Mayo, whose casting as an intellectual is as convincing as Reagan playing a rake. With his own immigrant background, Diamond could have brought more substance to the schoolroom scenes, but it's amusing to see Reagan display an abysmal ignorance of American history, even if it proves feigned as he reveals his hidden familiarity with the subject, including reciting a litany of presidents.

Errol Flynn plays a pinup artist more seriously than Reagan in *Never Say Goodbye* (1946). But Diamond's limitations with dramatic writing in his apprentice period are evident in this schmaltzy, would-be-Leo McCareyish comedy-drama about remarriage. Flynn and Eleanor Parker are a divorced New York couple who fall back in love as she tries to reform his philandering ways and they juggle their responsibilities toward their small daughter (Patti Brady). She shuttles between them and is sometimes sentimentalized but often ignored by the filmmakers. *Never Say Goodbye* coasts on its glamorous cast while failing to find much of the emotion latent in its situation, remaining tiresomely cute and superficial. There is one sharp exchange when Phil and a pal, Jack (Tom D'Andrea) are getting soused on Christmas Eve, like Bud in *The Apartment*. The elderly European immigrant restaurateur (S. Z. Sakall) tells Jack that a little girl being separated from both parents at Christmas "could never happen in the old country." "What old country?" Jack asks. The old man replies, "*Any* old country."

Generally Diamond was most comfortable in larky, easygoing comedy with meta showbiz aspects, such as *It's a Great Feeling* (1949), with Carson and Morgan playing spoofs of themselves as second-rate Warner Bros. actors. While they try to advance their status by making a star out of a waitress in the studio commissary (Day in another vivacious showcase), the film sometimes turns realistically acerbic like one of Wilder's films, such as when

Carson observes, "Nobody's happy in Hollywood—you get knifed in the back by your best friend." The twist is that this small-town girl proves too smart and sensible to stay in Hollywood. She goes back home to marry her supposedly dull old flame—a jolly cameo by none other than Flynn.

Diamond admitted he was embarrassed by seeing some of his early movies on television, and when asked why they were of inferior quality to his work with Wilder, he said that asking such a question is "like asking a man about the girls he knew before he was married." He added that the films he wrote under studio contract were often spoiled by producers and studio executives after being turned out in the assembly-line process: "It was not uncommon to have three, four, even six writers on a screenplay. You were assigned to various stages. Either an early treatment, or a last-minute doctoring job, or something in between. . . . I don't think it was a good system. . . . Whatever picture had just finished, you were immediately assigned to write a sequel. If Bob Hope had just done an Army picture, you were assigned to write a Bob Hope Navy picture."

The Hope vehicle Diamond cowrote at Paramount just before teaming with Wilder, *That Certain Feeling*, draws a performance considerably more subdued and heartfelt than his usual comic turn. This adaptation of the play *The King of Hearts* by Jean Kerr and Eleanor Brooke adroitly blends the various elements Diamond had been playing with for years: romance, comedy, drama, and music. He was one of four screenwriters, also including the film's producer-director team of Melvin Frank and Norman Panama as well as TV writer William Altman. Hope plays a neurotic, impecunious, self-sabotaging cartoonist, Francis X. (Dig) Dignan. He gets a job as the well-paid ghost for an insufferably pompous, far more successful, but coldhearted cartoonist played by George Sanders (a situation resembling Wilder's cowritten 1940 comedy about a couple of songwriting ghosts, *Rhythm on the River*). Dig finds the job especially humiliating because it comes by courtesy of his ex-wife, Ethel (Eva Marie Saint), now his employer's secretary and fiancée.

Dig is a lovable shnook whose typically Hope-ish cowardliness is given some emotional weight here, linked with having taken refuge in art and humor as what he calls "a defense mechanism" against childhood bullying (after illness made him bald, the kids taunted him as "Erich von Stroheim"). Although Ethel finds Dig's inability to stand up for himself exasperating, they are akin to Fran and Bud as exploited losers in Manhattan who eventually find the backbone to rebel. Like Bud, Dig rehearses a defiant speech to his boss about the woman he loves but fails to deliver it; *The Apartment* adds a clever twist by having Bud's boss preempt him with the same lines he was planning to use. Dig fittingly defies Larry in his art instead and during an uproarious spoof of an Edward R. Murrow *Person to Person* live television broadcast.

What helps win back Dig's former wife is his genuine kindness toward an orphan Larry is adopting as a public relations prop (Jerry Mathers). Diamond and his cowriters effectively counterbalance potential sentimentality by making the boy's loneliness palpable and portraying Dig as intermittently "cynical" (as Larry calls him) and emotionally sincere, a Wilderian conflict. Although *That Certain Feeling* is little-known, its blend of emotional pain and romantic comedy, evocative contrasts of wealth and marginal living in New York City, exploration of identity issues, satire of the media, and sophisticated use of narration (by Pearl Bailey, droll as Larry's feisty maid) demonstrate some of the qualities Diamond would bring to *The Apartment* and his other work with Wilder.

Diamond's limitations continued to be apparent, however, in the rare work he did away from Wilder after their teaming. With veteran screenwriter Isobel Lennart, Diamond adapted *Merry Andrew* (1958), an elaborately produced but laboriously unfunny, unmelodious musical with Danny Kaye as a shy British archaeologist turned circus clown; Diamond was recycling *Monkey Business* antics to less advantage. He also adapted an Abe Burrows version of a French play into the clumsy, gabby *Cactus Flower* (1969). That lugubrious romantic comedy could not have surmounted the miscasting of Walter Matthau as a playboy dentist whose supposedly dowdy nurse (Ingrid Bergman) harbors a secret flame for him while masquerading as his wife to fool his young mistress. Bergman naturally proves radiant once she cuts loose, but the role was reduced from its importance in the play to cater to the younger nature of the movie audience, as Diamond admitted. The film is noteworthy only for giving a career boost to the zany TV comedian Goldie Hawn, just as Diamond had played a part in helping Doris Day to stardom. Hawn won a supporting-actress Oscar for playing a hippie with more nuanced sexual ethics than her philandering middle-aged lover. But *Cactus Flower* now plays as one of those painfully square attempts by old-school Hollywood hands to seem "with-it" as the studio system collapsed around them.

The film's shallowness and crassness make it resemble a remake of *The Apartment* from the viewpoint of the sleazy executive Jeff Sheldrake. *Cactus Flower* even starts with Hawn's character trying to commit suicide over Matthau's Dr. Winston by gassing herself; the scene recalls Fran's suicide attempt in the earlier film, but there it was placed well after we came to know and care for her. The differences between the two films throw into sharp contrast *The Apartment*'s far more intelligent and morally acute treatment of an exploitive sexual relationship between a mendacious, repellently self-centered older man and a vulnerable young woman in New York City. Diamond may have been hired because he helped write *The Apartment*, but *Cactus Flower* not only is deficient in believability, sensitivity, and compassion but is directed by Gene Saks like a TV movie on garish, over-lit sets.

Wilder brought out the best in Diamond's creative personality and helped him escape the missteps that played into his shallower side. It's fortunate that Wilder discovered Diamond's latent creative talents in the 1950s, or the junior writer probably would have wound up writing TV sitcoms and movies of the week, without much opportunity to develop the wit and eye for psychological observation that peeks through his early outings from time to time. As Paul Diamond put it, becoming Wilder's collaborator "just snapped his father up from a midlevel journeyman writer into the stratosphere." What Diamond brought to Wilder was his well-honed professionalism, a keen knowledge of how to write gags and tailor them to actors' personalities, and a shared interest in several areas of cinematic storytelling that perhaps trace back to their common pasts as émigrés. As Wilder did throughout his career, Diamond from the very opening scene of *Murder in the Blue Room* loved to play around with the comic potential of masquerades and reinventions, meta plot twists, and movie jokes while satirizing genres and characters who exhibit a high degree of self-awareness or a comical lack of awareness. Wilder was in synch with Diamond's mordant sensibility and lack of sentimentality, qualities that help *That Certain Feeling* shine but are also evident in the younger writer's awkward inability to pull off schmaltzy situations in some of his earlier films.

Most of Diamond's films before Wilder show his appreciation for feisty, independent women and an understanding of the struggles of people stuck in the urban rat race, qualities that would become more evident in *The Apartment*, *Avanti!*, and their other films together. Diamond's extensive work in musicals, like Wilder's in that genre, would come in handy when they collaborated on films that use music extensively for plot purposes as well as entertainment, notably *Some Like It Hot* and *Kiss Me, Stupid*. One way the team complemented each other was that, as Paul Diamond observed of his father, "The characters he wrote on his own are usually a bit more positive than Billy's stuff. He was a lighter-weight writer on his own than Billy. Dad was able to adapt to the tone Billy wanted. I don't think Dad worked on a drama per se until *Fedora* [although that leaves out *The Apartment*, a comedy-drama with more emphasis on drama]. I think he would have been happy as a clam writing musical comedy. He was more influenced by Broadway, less so by cinema." But even though Iz did not exhibit much affinity for drama before teaming with Wilder, as he matured and was given more creative latitude and better material, he proved equal to the challenge Wilder gave him on seriocomic films as an invaluable sounding board and skillful, synergistic collaborator.

Wilder's more varied and combative life experience as a European vagabond and adult refugee from Hitler helped bring the needed gravitas to Diamond's work, and Wilder's acerbic, bittersweet nature was balanced by Diamond's quietly merry yet still often barbed disposition. Their rising to the challenge of effortlessly intermingling comedy and drama in such films as *Some Like It Hot*, *The Apartment*, and *The Private Life of Sherlock Holmes* brought out the deepest instincts in both men, and Wilder's unrivaled sense of screenplay construction helped channel Diamond's talents more fruitfully, removing their scattered feeling and making him also into a master of structure. William Goldman, in his book *Adventures in the Screen Trade*, emphasized "what I believe to be the single most important lesson to be learned about writing for films. . . . SCREENPLAYS ARE STRUCTURE. Yes, nifty dialog helps one hell of a lot; sure, it's nice if you can bring your characters to life. But you can have terrific characters spouting just swell talk to each other, and if the structure is unsound, forget it."

"Today movies that are constructed are something from the past," Fernando Trueba, Wilder's Spanish screenwriter-director-critic friend, commented in 2020.

Not only do people not know how to do them anymore or write them, but they despise them, like [they are] old-fashioned. But for me, all I know, if I know something about writing stories, I learn from Billy Wilder. Because for me, I always thought to discuss who is the best director ever is stupid. You say John Ford, you are right. You say Lubitsch, you are right. You say Renoir, you are right too. Buster Keaton also. You are right. All of them are the best director ever. But if you say, Who is the best screenwriter ever? And then I say there's no doubt, it's Billy Wilder, and then the world. I can prove that in a jury, in front of the judge. It's not an opinion. It's not a judgment of taste. It's a scientific truth.

While working more harmoniously with Wilder than Brackett had, Wilder's new writing partner had much more in him than "just swell talk." Diamond shared with Wilder a shrewd knowledge of human nature and an expertly honed sense of craftsmanship developed in often trying and stifling studio conditions. Their work for the Mirisches liberated them both to be more independent and daring. Diamond found collaborating with Wilder nirvana in contrast to his frustrating time as a studio hired hand. Now it was just the two of them in a room for months, creating their world for Wilder to execute onscreen. As Diamond said, "This way, with Billy, once we decide, nobody changes a word."

Diamond grew up without a European accent and was more confident in his English, a trait Wilder relied on in his collaborators. Paul said, "Billy's English never, ever got to be completely fluent. They say that if you become immersed in another language by the time you're nine, you can become fluent and accent-free. Billy was not here until he was in his late twenties and never lost his Austrian accent. . . . He was the most *clever* person in the English language, but he needed a second pair of ears to make sure that things were going well, and he trusted Dad. He wanted Dad near him on the set."

Like Brackett, Iz Diamond did the typing when they worked in the office while Wilder paced around and made notes on a yellow pad. Their relationship, though friendly, was strictly professional, which Wilder appreciated. They seldom exchanged personal stories and did not socialize outside work. When the team were asked at an American Film Institute seminar in the late 1970s how they worked together, Wilder said,

I'm already very gratified if anybody asks that question, because most people think the actors make up the words. In our case it's very prosaic. We meet at nine-thirty in the morning and open shop like bank tellers [he varied that line to me, describing themselves as "*farkakte* bank tellers," using the Yiddish word for "shitty"]. We read *Hollywood Reporter* and *Variety*, exchange the trades, and then we just stare at each other.* Sometimes nothing happens. Sometimes it just goes on until twelve-thirty, and then I'll ask him, "How about a drink?" And he nods, and we have a drink and go to lunch. Or sometimes we come full of ideas. This is not the muses coming through the window and kissing our brows; it's very hard work, and having done both, I tell you that directing is a pleasure and writing is a drag.

Directing is a pleasure because you have something to work with: you can put the camera here or there; you can interpret the scene this way or that way. But writing is just an empty page; you start with nothing, absolutely nothing, and, as a rule, writers are vastly underrated and underpaid. It is totally impossible to make a great picture out of a lousy script; it is impossible, on the other hand, for a mediocre director to screw up a great script altogether.

Wilder felt that "It was wonderful to talk about dialogue, or about structure" with Diamond, "whom I liked very much, like a younger brother." In their office sessions, "There was no arm-twisting, no pulling the rank, no shouting, no screams of ecstasy because one came up with an idea that was maybe not too bad. The highest accolade that you could get out of Iz was, 'Why not?'" Wilder was grateful to have a writing collaborator who, unlike Brackett, was not emotionally needy and moody. Wilder tellingly described Diamond as "taciturn," in contrast with Brackett; Wilder liked to be the loquacious and extroverted one. He was sometimes moody as well, but more often with Brackett than with Diamond.

That is not to say Wilder as the senior partner did not have the ultimate authority in that relationship, unlike in his tense junior collaboration with Brackett. Wilder was a leading Hollywood filmmaker by the time he started working with Diamond in 1957, and that gave Wilder more confidence to exercise his creative autonomy, although he always took pains to give ample

---

* Sometimes while reading the trades, they would mutter to each other, "God damn that Irwin Allen." Allen was a bête noire of theirs because he was the leading producer of the all-star disaster film extravaganzas, such as *The Poseidon Adventure* and *The Towering Inferno*, that were helping make the more intimate Wilder-Diamond films obsolete in the 1970s.

credit to his writing partners. He initiated the projects he wrote with Diamond. He made more money on the films they did together and was always the producer as well as the director. On their later films Diamond had an associate producer credit; Wilder once quipped that an associate producer is "The only guy who will associate with a producer." Yet Wilder valued Diamond's precision and perfectionism both in the office and on the set, and they worked closely together from the beginning to the end of each project, not only privately in their office but in all the more public phases of casting and location scouting and on other production and postproduction details.

Their screenplays, most of which have been published, are a pleasure to read, unlike most film scripts, and are as perfectly constructed as a fine watch. Their smooth operation, intricacy, subtlety, wit, psychological depth, and durability are a product of an unusually harmonious and respectful working relationship, rare in any art form but even rarer in Hollywood.

Occasionally Wilder flirted with other writers, including on the film he made immediately after *Love in the Afternoon*, *Witness for the Prosecution* (based on the play by Agatha Christie, adapted with Harry Kurnitz and Larry Marcus), and on some projects temporarily when Diamond was otherwise occupied. Other writers worked for a time on *Sherlock Holmes* and *Avanti!* before Wilder turned back to Diamond with the security that those projects would turn out right with him; they spent much of a ten-year period working on *Holmes*, the most ambitious of all their projects. Away from Wilder, as well as working on *Cactus Flower*, Diamond wrote an unproduced 1975 screenplay about Hollywood with the clichéd title *Tinseltown* (based on Oscar Wilde's comical mystery story "Lord Arthur Savile's Crime"), which was far below the standard of *Sunset Blvd.* or even *Fedora*. Those projects and Diamond's pre-Wilder scripts show how crucial was the zing and wit and narrative energy Wilder brought to their collaborations. But aside from their occasional separate excursions, by and large, through their final film in 1981 and until their partnership ended with Diamond's untimely death at age sixty-seven, Wilder and Diamond were virtually symbiotic.

Although Wilder felt that his many elements of personal disharmony with Brackett helped their partnership creatively—at least he rationalized their problems that way—his calm relationship with Diamond demonstrated that in his later years he no longer felt he needed or wanted that kind of creative friction. That does not mean Wilder and Diamond did not have creative disagreements or frustrations, but they were private, and by all accounts the two never threw anything at each other. "It was all very very peaceful," Wilder recalled. ". . . Sometimes I would leave the office in an angry mood, but in the morning, it's all forgotten. Or I knew when he said, 'I'm going to go to the library'—when Diamond was upset he went to the Beverly Hills library. He was a fine man, an absolute jewel. He was a gentleman."

When Wilder and Diamond could not agree on something, they would move on to another way to do it. That was the method they evolved for their mutually beneficial collaboration. And they did not let the usual Hollywood curse of egotism and credit-grabbing get in the way of their work. They had a discreet pact never to discuss publicly who did what, who wrote what line, who had what idea—idle questions anyway, for the most part, in a successful writing partnership, especially in the film industry. But though Diamond, as far as can be determined, never broke that rule, it was a measure of Wilder's respect for Iz that he credited him not only with coming up with the title of *Some Like It Hot* but also with urging on him the need for the crucial element that made the film's cross-dressing plot work (more later on what they called the "hammerlock") *and* with contributing the immortal ending line, "Well—nobody's perfect." Higher compliments could not be bestowed by one partner on another.

Diamond's impeccable craftsmanship was perfectly in synch with Wilder's; their strengths complemented each other. Walter Mirisch, who began a long-term alliance with Wilder while supervising the production of *Love in the Afternoon* for Allied Artists before forming his own company with his brothers Marvin and Harold, writes in his autobiography of the Wilder-Diamond partnership: "Iz was a man of strong opinions, and Billy had great respect for him. Iz also sat on the set with Billy during the shooting of all their pictures. Billy listened to his comments, and they discussed problems while Billy was shooting, or they might make some changes that they would both agree upon. In terms of the writing, they were exceedingly collaborative, with a great deal of respect on both sides."

Wilder said he valued Diamond's "discretion," and that quality of his personality was never more evident than at the very end of their working relationship. One day in 1988, Diamond surprised Wilder by calling him to his house and saying, "Shit! I'm dying." Diamond said he had an advanced state of multiple myeloma, a secret he had been keeping for four years. Wilder was bereft when death ended their partnership four weeks later. He told the audience at the WGA memorial, "Well, it's lonely now in that office of ours. I look at that empty chair and I miss him so much. On his birthdays maybe I should put a red rose there, like DiMaggio for Marilyn."

WALKING AROUND IN WOMEN'S SHOES

The oddly unbalanced romantic situations that made some of Wilder's work in the 1950s so unsatisfying (*Sabrina, The Seven Year Itch, Love in the Afternoon*) were partly a function of misjudged casting and partly due to his forced attempts to do Lubitsch. Wilder was trying to emulate a style that was not entirely compatible with his own, at least in that period; he did not manage to make more truly Lubitschean films until his latent romanticism fully flowered when his career was in its final stages.

With *Some Like It Hot*, however, Wilder began to transcend the dysfunctional kinds of romances he had been making and became more confident in his own idiosyncratic romantic approach. Paradoxically, that greater ease in dealing with the delicate subject of love came with a screwball comedy about cross-dressing, a comedy-drama about sexual exploitation (*The Apartment*), and romances involving prostitution (*Irma la Douce, Kiss Me, Stupid*). As Wilder aged, he intermittently found a measure of hard-won optimism that men and women can escape their emotional and social traps and find some common ground emotionally. Having dug down to the depths with *Sunset Blvd.* and *Ace in the Hole*, and after foundering somewhat in the 1950s with more safely commercial but uneven fare until he found his way again with *Some Like It Hot*, Wilder gradually worked through his obsessive dilemmas. His fruitful collaboration with Diamond was a major factor in that development.

"*Some Like It Hot* is the one picture that both of them said they wouldn't change a line if they had to do it over," Barbara Diamond reported. "And this was from two men who second-guessed themselves for years after a picture was out of their hands." The film is a compendium and culmination of key themes that had been building up throughout Wilder's career. It all came together in one of the few films that can be regarded as absolutely perfect, like *Citizen Kane, Casablanca, Tokyo Story*, or *Trouble in Paradise*.

The masquerade theme that permeates Wilder's work reaches its apogee in *Some Like It Hot*, the story of two male musicians, Tony Curtis's Joe and Jack Lemmon's Jerry, who have to go in drag with a girls' band after witnessing the infamous St. Valentine's Day Massacre in 1929 Chicago. That Wilderian scam enables him to play with every nuance of sexual behavior and gender fluidity and to go wild with lewd double entendre like never before. The serious underpinning of this farce is the gradual transformation of Joe the lady-killer saxophone player from a cad into a more sensitive lover. He comes to appreciate Monroe's band singer Sugar Cane, formerly Sugar Kowalczyk, as a human being, not merely a blonde bombshell. This is among the most satisfying treatments of the pervasive theme of sexual detachment versus love in Wilder's work. The alcoholic Sugar's vulnerabilities are expressed in her desperation to escape the clutches of men who want her only for her body. Like other such women in Wilder films, she pines for genuine love and marriage, but her solution is to go after a millionaire who can take care of her, a sign of her low self-esteem as well as her survival instincts. But she tells Joe she actually prefers men who wear glasses because it makes them seem "gentle and sweet and helpless," and in the end she accepts this flawed man, an impecunious phony who reveals he's been conning her but who truly loves her, despite his duplicity. She accepts Joe with full knowledge of his dual nature, as Jerry's ultimate partner will do in accepting him.

Most of *Some Like It Hot* takes place on a train and in a gaudy Florida resort hotel, the kind of transient, louche environments Wilder knew best from his early years. The girls' band, Sweet Sue's Society Syncopators,* is drawn in part from Wilder's early encounters as a reporter with the Tiller Girls, who came to Vienna by train with a hard-boiled female supervisor and on another visit were falsely reported as kidnapped by gangsters. But an equal influence on Wilder was the Lubitsch film he held up as a model of sexual innuendo, *The Smiling Lieutenant*, and its all-girls' band with the suggestive name of The Viennese Swallows. The more high-toned name and supposedly strictly enforced moral code of Sweet Sue's girls' band barely paper over the salacious activities behind the scenes. One of the film's wittiest double entendres is the

---

* The band's name may stem partly from the Weintraub Syncopators, a jazz dance band in Berlin during Wilder's time there, in which his friend and longtime collaborator Franz Waxman (formerly Wachsmann) was a pianist and arranger.

sign-off to their act by Joan Shawlee's Sweet Sue, "reminding all you daddies out there—every girl in my band is a virtuoso—and I intend to keep it that way!"

Filled with the "hot" American jazz standards the director loved from his time in 1926 as a publicist in Berlin for Paul Whiteman, *Some Like It Hot* is another in the long line of semimusical "revue" films Wilder worked on in Germany and Hollywood. He always had encyclopedic and impeccable taste in popular music, and he lovingly and nostalgically showcases hits of the Roaring Twenties in *Some Like It Hot*, from the jaunty "Runnin' Wild," "Sweet Georgia Brown," and "Down Among the Sheltering Palms" to the more soulful "I Wanna Be Loved by You" and "I'm Thru with Love." Wilder significantly considered "I'm Thru with Love" his favorite song:

> I've locked my heart
> I'll keep my feelings there
> I've stocked my heart
> With icy, frigid air

He uses that disillusioned romantic lament as the emotional climax of the movie, when Sugar sings it to express her pain over Joe's deception before he reveals the truth behind his disguise.*

The film has some new elements Wilder was able to introduce in a time of waning censorship, none more provocative than the transformation of Jerry from a gawky male into an even more awkward but flamboyantly campy woman. When he and Joe, broke and desperate for work, learn about the openings in a girls' band headed for Florida, Jerry is the first to impulsively suggest that they might consider going with it and to "call ourselves Josephine and Geraldine." That appalls Joe, the inveterate ladies' man, until they witness the St. Valentine's Day Massacre later that day, and he realizes it's their only way of saving themselves from being shot full of holes by the natty mobster Spats Colombo. Spats is iconically played by George Raft, who had

---

* Wilder's old friend Matty Malneck, whom he met when Malneck was a jazz violinist and violist with Whiteman, collaborated on that 1931 ballad with Fud Livingston and Gus Kahn. After Malneck contributed to *Love in the Afternoon* and wrote the score for *Witness for the Prosecution*, Wilder brought him in to supervise the songs for *Some Like It Hot*, with Adolph Deutsch composing the rest of the score.

been a gangster himself but turned to dancing and acting and made his first film splash in Hawks's *Scarface*. *Some Like It Hot* takes its wildest leap into gay abandon when the two musicians arrive at the train station in drag. Hobbling in high heels, Jerry is moaning about his uncomfortable and humiliating disguise until he spots Sugar undulating down the train platform with her suitcase and ukulele ("Look at *that*—look how she moves—it's like Jello on springs. . . . I tell you it's a whole different sex"). The train joins in, blowing two puffs of steam at her derrière. When Wilder came up with that gag on the spot, he remarked, "She's so sexy, even the train had to goose her."

Jerry drops his vestigial panic over masquerading as a woman when he hears a newspaper vendor hawking a headline about the massacre. Reporting at the train to Sweet Sue, Jerry, who had been planning to introduce himself as Geraldine, unexpectedly blurts out, "I'm Daphne!" That is the most revealing moment in *Some Like It Hot*, its epiphany, the time when Jerry's subconscious (and the film's) pops boldly into view. His drag act works a radical transformation by liberating his inner female. What is most remarkable, and one of the principal reasons *Some Like It Hot* endures as a revered classic of American cinema, is that it is such a feminist work. That might seem surprising or counterintuitive for people who persist in regarding Wilder as a misogynist. Even Wilder seemed a bit surprised when my wife, Dr. Ruth O'Hara, a psychologist, met him in 1992 and complimented him on making this feminist film. He said, "Not that many people tell me that." For all its farcical elements, *Some Like It Hot* literally is about how men learn to respect the opposite sex by walking around in women's shoes. Wilder emphasizes their shoes from the first time we see Joe and Jerry in drag. He shows them from behind in a tracking shot focused on their legs and rumps as they prance along the platform toward the train. Jerry is complaining, "How *do* they walk in these things, huh? How do they keep their balance? . . . And it is so drafty. They must be catching cold all the time, huh? . . . I feel naked. I feel like everybody's starin' at me." Joe retorts, "With those legs? Are you crazy?"

Throughout their escapades with the girls' band, Jerry revels in his womanly disguise, while Joe endures his more stoically as he concentrates on conning Sugar into the sack. The two men couldn't be more different as women, Josephine acting all hifalutin' (Curtis modeled his "rather aloof and stylish" behavior on the ladylike actresses Dolores Costello and Grace Kelly and his mother) and Jerry camping it up with utter, infectious delight

(Lemmon modeled Daphne on *his* mother). Clumsy Jerry is not as ladylike as Joe manages to be while playing the poised Josephine, so Lemmon's female voice did not have to be as convincing. But Curtis's fluting ladylike tones were not high-pitched enough and had to be dubbed by the versatile voice actor Paul Frees. "You didn't want them both doing the same shtick," Lemmon recalled, "and Tony was much more successful at the imitation. I was clumsy, I was an asshole, the shoes were killing me, my ankles were turning. But Tony could carry it off with a great aloofness; he just put his head up in the air and parted his lips. His Josephine was fearless about it, but my Daphne was scared shitless." Color photos taken during the production reveal how garish their women's makeup actually looked, and Wilder decided to make the film in black-and-white mostly for that reason. He also realized that the stylization of the period setting and the black-and-white cinematography by Charles Lang helped sell the idea that the men could pass as women, since all the costumes and other trappings of the 1920s looked exotic and funny to the 1959 audience.*

Less clever than Joe and more emotionally open, Jerry proves to be more at home emotionally as a woman, having a ball with feminine mannerisms and locutions. Despite his initial resistance to the disguise, the first indication of fundamental change comes as he boards the train with the girls' band under the skeptical eye of Sweet Sue. The need to survive makes "Daphne" quickly adjust to being a woman. She alarms even the butch female bandleader by declaring vehemently, "We wouldn't be caught dead with men. Rough, hairy beasts with eight hands. And they all just want one thing from a girl." Daphne has a ball gossiping and partying with the other dames in the band, to the point of worrying the smarter, more pragmatic Joe, who is afraid Jerry will blow their disguise.

Wilder and Diamond counterpoint Joe's caution with a lot of comic mileage from Daphne's male nature repeatedly breaking through with lustful reactions to the voluptuous Sugar. Joe, meanwhile, is methodically plotting to seduce her by adopting yet another disguise, as "Junior," a millionaire heir to the Shell Oil Company. And with impeccable farcical logic, Jerry/Daphne's

---

* Lang (billed as Charles Lang Jr. for most of his career) worked with Lubitsch on *Angel* and shot two films Wilder cowrote but did not direct, *Midnight* and *Arise, My Love*, as well as *A Foreign Affair*, *Ace in the Hole*, *Sabrina*, and *Some Like It Hot*.

gender confusion spirals out of control as their masquerade becomes more and more overwhelming. While ogling fellow band members parading around the train's sleeper compartment in their skimpy pajamas, Daphne repeatedly tries to assure herself, "I'm a girl! I'm a girl! I'm a girl!" But after Joe E. Brown's zany millionaire mama's boy Osgood Fielding III proposes marriage at the Florida resort, she changes her mantra to a desperate, almost poetic incantation: "I'm a boy, I'm a boy, I'm a . . . I wish I were dead. I'm a boy. Boy, oh boy, am I a boy."

The dual pattern the film follows—Jerry's acceptance of his inner Daphne, and Joe's reformation into a mensch—is both comedic and seriously dramatic, an exquisite balance. The film starts out as hard-boiled farce but gradually takes a more somber turn when Joe, who has unscrupulously weaseled out of Sugar her deepest vulnerabilities and uses them to seduce her by trickery, becomes ashamed of his callous deceit. He risks his life to pull off his wig and openly express his love for her by kissing her on the bandstand during a show at the hotel. This scandalizes Sweet Sue, who may be a lesbian herself but can't abide Josephine seemingly being open about her desires. Wilder intercuts the moving romantic story line of Joe's transformation with the comical business of Daphne succumbing to the infatuation of "her" lascivious millionaire. *Some Like It Hot* shows how deeply Wilder internalized the influence of Lubitsch, whose films at their heart are morality plays about how men should treat women and vice versa, although the films of both directors also are in opposition to conventional morality.

Wilder had frequently explored the theme of the heartless cad getting his emotional comeuppance by falling genuinely in love. *Some Like It Hot* is among the most poignant such stories he ever told. He wheedled an extraordinarily touching performance out of Monroe, a notoriously difficult task, the subject of many funny/sad anecdotes. Like many Wilder films, *Some Like It Hot* is a meta-film, a postmodernist work that reflects on itself. Here he deconstructs the elements that made Monroe a sex symbol in his own *Seven Year Itch* and other films—her creamy-soft skin and improbably curvy body, draped in flamboyantly lewd dresses by Orry-Kelly, coupled with a dizzy, childlike manner and a seemingly dim mind ("I'm not very bright, I guess," she says of her miserable love life) that intermittently reveals itself as surprisingly shrewd. Although she doesn't realize "Josephine" is a male or that his Cary Grant imitation as an impotent millionaire is a ploy to seduce her (his leg slowly rising in the background of the shot as he lies supine on a couch in Osgood's yacht and she smothers him with kisses is one of Wilder's slyest double entendres), she is realistic about the perfidy of men. She has learned enough from her bitter experience as a woman whose heart has been broken repeatedly by her "thing about saxophone players." Sugar is Monroe at her most complex, at once her sexiest and most sensitive performance, the epitome of her persona and a bittersweet commentary on it, a triumphantly iconic characterization.

How did Wilder and Diamond get away with the openly gay innuendos between Joe E. Brown and Jack Lemmon, so truly outrageous in the context of 1959 Eisenhower America? Wilder described *Some Like It Hot* as *"Scarface* meets *Charley's Aunt." Charley's Aunt* is a venerable 1892 play by Brandon Thomas about cross-dressing that was a popular farce for many years and was made into numerous films, including a 1941 version starring Jack Benny. Cross-dressing is an ancient device in the theater going back to the Greek dramatists Euripides and Aristophanes, and it was frequently employed by Shakespeare, partly because men played women's parts in the Elizabethan theater, enabling the playwright to work clever twists on gender roles. In a similar vein, Lubitsch made a delightful silent romantic comedy precursor to *Some Like It Hot* in 1918, *Ich Möchte Kein Mann sein (I Don't Want to Be a Man)*. The saucy comedian Ossi Oswalda plays a young woman rebelling against her stifling gender role to go out on the town in male drag. The ironic twist is that Ossi realizes men also have to endure many indignities, so she goes back to being a woman, a more liberated one, but not until Lubitsch has flirted with gay humor by having her necking with her male guardian at a nightclub.

Wilder lived through the Weimar era when cross-dressing and all varieties of sexual expression were inescapably overt in the Berlin theater, cabarets, nightclubs, and bars. During that period he had written his ladies' advice column in *Tempo* under the guise of a woman; and after coming to American, he learned that his nickname of Billie was the female spelling. The lesbian drama *Mädchen in Uniform* was one of the three films that most influenced him in those early days. Even in the United States during the years of the strictest censorship, cross-dressing was widely accepted as a comedic device that didn't threaten audiences unduly, and it was popular on TV with Milton Berle and Jerry Lewis in the period immediately before *Some Like It Hot*.

But when an American filmmaker occasionally tried to use drag to make a challengingly incisive and witty commentary on gender fluidity, such as in George Cukor's fascinating film *Sylvia Scarlett* (1935) with Katharine Hepburn masquerading as a boy, the audience was not amused. Drag seemed more threatening to the public in the days of the Hollywood studio system when a woman was doing the gender switch and a handsome romantic lover (Brian Aherne) found himself attracted to a "boy."

Wilder was treading a delicate line by pivoting from farce to romance in *Some Like It Hot*. But by smuggling in his feminist and gay themes under the exotic guise of period comedy, he was enabling the American mass audience to enjoy it all as a "gay romp" in the other sense of that word. Although there are numerous instances of overtly and covertly gay subject matter scattered throughout Wilder's career, which reach their apogee in *Some Like It Hot* and continue throughout his later career, the motivations of Joe and Jerry to wear women's clothes are not kinky, at least initially. Nor did Wilder and Diamond set out to foreground the subject of cross-dressing for its own sake.

Wilder explained:

> Very early in the structure of that picture my friend Mr. Diamond very rightly said, "We have to find the hammerlock. We have to find the iron-clad thing so that these guys trapped in women's clothes cannot just take the wigs off and say, 'Look, I'm a guy.' It has to be a question of life and death." And that's where the idea for the St. Valentine's Day murder came. If they got out of the women's clothes they would be killed by the Al Capone gang. That was the important invention. . . . That's what made the picture. The two men were on the spot, and we kept them on the spot until the very end.

As Wilmington and I wrote of the film in 1970, the gangster backdrop pays other dividends as well: "The psychotic intensity of the backdrop throws the boisterous vulgarity of the blue humor into a kind of limbo between innocence and depravity."

The strengths of *Some Like It Hot* are highlighted in contrast to the German film Wilder was remaking. If few people realize that *Some Like It Hot* was a remake, that was intentional. The credits simply state that it is suggested by a story by two writers who seem to lack first names, R. Thoeren and M.

Logan (Robert and Michael).* No mention is made of the two previous films made from their story. The first was the French film *Fanfare d'amour* (*Fanfare of Love*, 1935), and the second was the German version, *Fanfaren der Liebe* (*Fanfares of Love*, 1951). The working titles of *Some Like It Hot* were *Fanfares of Love* and *Not Tonight, Josephine!*[†]

The successful German version of *Fanfares of Love* was directed by Kurt Hoffmann, who was assistant director to writer-director Reinhold Schünzel on *Viktor und Viktoria* (*Victor and Victoria*), a 1933 German comedy about a woman who takes the place of a man working as a female impersonator.[‡] Of the first two versions of the Thoeren-Logan story on which Wilder based his film, only *Fanfares of Love* is available for study today, but it is so obscure that I had to go to Berlin to view it on an editing machine in the national film archive. Although Wilder minimized the connection and disparaged the German film, it does bear some strong similarities to *Some Like It Hot*, although their differences are just as important as the points in common. Other writers had screenplay credits on the two European versions, with Thoeren and Logan relegated to story credits; Heinz Pauck wrote the screenplay for *Fanfares of Love*.

Wilder reportedly knew Thoeren in Berlin and was persuaded by him to watch *Fanfares of Love* in 1957. The director disparaged it too harshly to Cameron Crowe as "a very low-budget, very third-class German picture . . . absolutely terrible. Deliriously bad." Wilder also incorrectly referred to it as an early 1930s German UFA film, which had the effect, intentional or not, of erasing the memory of the French original, which starred Fernand Gravey and Julien Carette as members of the "Tulips from Holland" band and was directed by Richard Pottier. Wilder and his producing partners, the Mirisches, and United Artists, the distributor, seemed to go out of their way to avoid

---

* Robert Thoeren was a Moravian immigrant who left Germany for France in 1933 and had a fairly successful career in Hollywood, working on such films as *Hotel Imperial, Summer Storm, Mrs. Parkington, Singapore, The Fighting O'Flynn*, and *The Prowler* before dying in 1957 after a car crash in Munich. Michael Logan's only other notable screen credit came as the author of the source novel for the French crime film *Carré de dames pour un as* (*An Ace and Four Queens*, 1966).

† The latter from the title of a 1911 ditty by Will A. Heelan and Seymour Furth, "Not To-night, Josephine," inspired by Napoleon's alleged, probably apocryphal way of turning down sex with his empress, whom he divorced after a childless marriage. Lemmon's character speaks the line in the film.

‡ That film was remade by Blake Edwards in 1982 as *Victor/Victoria*, with Julie Andrews in the title role(s).

letting people know *Some Like It Hot* was not an original. This is an unfortunately typical example of the frequent failure to give due recognition to writers who come up with original ideas for films.

Although Wilder claimed that aside from the men going into drag to play in a girls' band in *Fanfares of Love*, "there was not one other thing that came from this terrible picture," that is not the case, even if the German film is far inferior to the American remake. Like the French original, *Fanfares of Love* deals with struggling musicians whose desperation after trying other gigs causes them to join a girls' band, the "Violets of the Alps." Neither of the European versions is in a period setting or involves gangster violence. But the male buddies in *Fanfares of Love* are not dissimilar to Curtis and Lemmon: there's a tall, good-looking seducer named Hans (Dieter Borsche) and a shorter, funny-looking sidekick named Peter (Georg Thomalla, an actor who went on to dub Lemmon's voice into German in *Some Like It Hot* and subsequent films). After the musicians disguise themselves as Hansi and Petra and travel from Munich with the band to the Bavarian alpine resort town of Neuhaus, Hansi falls for the beautiful blonde band singer, Gaby (Inge Egger). He sets out to seduce her by using his knowledge of her romantic predilections, as Joe does with Sugar at the remake's Florida resort. Meanwhile, the middle-aged hotel manager has the hots for Petra, as the considerably older Osgood does for Jerry. The German film also has a somewhat similar train sequence, a strict female bandleader, and even gags with maracas.

Hans and Peter join the girls' band not out of any life-or-death compulsion, however, but because they need work. Dressing as women is just an expedient, however comical, and they don't view it as particularly humiliating after all they've been through. Before putting on drag, they try busking and take disguised gigs in a Gypsy band and even in blackface. Their agent's secretary calls the latter *neger*, or "nigger," roles; as Wilder said of *Fanfares of Love*, "We could do that in Germany," which was also an allusion to how he had been labeled with that derogatory term while working as a screenwriting ghost in his early days. The lower stakes for the masquerade in the German film in contrast with *Some Like It Hot* reduce the men's motivations for disguise and, as a result, the tension of the storytelling. Gaby is much smarter than Sugar, and while Hans is trying to seduce her, she figures out rather quickly that the men are in disguise, which takes away most of the remaining suspense. Hans's undisguised eagerness to seduce her also works against the storyline, since he doesn't resort to the elaborate subterfuge Joe has to use in *Some Like It Hot*, a gift to Wilder and Diamond from the game-playing of Hollywood under the Code. Hans and Peter even risk blowing the whole game by showing up at a nightclub in their men's attire. Despite Diamond's claim that *Fanfares of Love* is "heavy-handed and Germanic. . . . It was all rather *Mädchen in Uniform*," the gay subtext so strongly and subversively present in his and Wilder's film actually is only an inconsequential comic riff in *Fanfares of Love*, which is more staunchly heterosexual. It led to a sequel called *Fanfaren der Ehe* (*Fanfares of Marriage*, 1953), in which the two men are married to female musicians and go into drag to join their wives on a cruise ship.

Most crucially, however, *Fanfares of Love* does not contain the serious spine of the Wilder film, its dramatic examination of a callous man's comeuppance and character transformation when confronted with the emotional devastation caused by his exploitation of a vulnerable woman. The closest the German film comes to *Some Like It Hot*'s feminist understanding of what it's like to be a woman is a fleeting suggestion (evidently picked up by Wilder and Diamond) when Petra is painfully laced into a corset and exclaims, "The poor ladies, what they have to suffer!" Despite some amusing and insightful moments, *Fanfares of Love* overall is not only utterly implausible but clumsy in its execution, lacking the grace and verve of the Wilder-Diamond remake as well as its highly sophisticated way of transforming a far-fetched farcical premise into something both persuasive and captivating.

Turning Sugar into a dumb blonde who gives out with some surprisingly savvy remarks is as crucial to the success of *Some Like It Hot* as adding the 1920s gangster backdrop. The story works better because Sugar's innocent obliviousness enables the men to maintain their scam. The viewer of *Fanfares of Love* wonders why Gaby doesn't just blow the whistle on the whole game. Seeing the men switch back and forth between women's garb and their male street clothes undercuts the premise of the German film, but the elaborate switch on this gag in *Some Like It Hot* more daringly depends on Joe's risky ability to pull off his "Cary Grant" disguise. This is among Wilder's anachronistic movie jokes in the film, including parodies of gangster movies.[*]

---

[*] The gangster genre parodies include an homage to James Cagney's grapefruit-in-the-kisser gag in his 1931 film *The Public Enemy*, a celebrated bit Wilder also evokes in *One, Two, Three* (with Cagney himself) and *Kiss Me, Stupid*.

Curtis claimed credit for suggesting that Joe do a sort of half-assed Grant imitation as the faux millionaire, even though Cary Grant was not Cary Grant in 1929 (Jerry objects, "Nobody talks like *that*!"). Archibald Leach did not assume that name until his film debut in 1932 and did not develop his familiar screen character until he made *Sylvia Scarlett* and *The Awful Truth* (1937). Curtis's imitation most closely resembles Grant's girl-shy paleontologist with round glasses who is pursued by Katharine Hepburn in Hawks's *Bringing Up Baby*. Wilder claimed that Grant enjoyed their spoofing him, but Curtis reported that Grant told Wilder, "I never talked like that." In any event, it was a sly way for Wilder to get Grant, his perennial choice for a leading man, into one of his movies, after a long series of turndowns.*

THAT IMMORTAL ENDING LINE

The ending with Osgood and Jerry riding off into the sunrise and uncharted sexual waters on the feckless old millionaire's motorboat has always elicited screams of laughter from audiences, because it is so beautifully calibrated, with escalating double-entendre dialogue—including even a reference to genital amputation. Jerry finally admits he's a man, and there's a blackout on his speechlessly muttering to himself after Osgood calmly assures him, "Well— nobody's perfect." Contemporary viewers go to pieces when they hear what is considered one of the greatest ending lines in film history, but the first preview audience in the Pacific Palisades reacted as viewers often do when they are confronted with a new kind of film. They sat mostly in stony silence, apart from the TV personality Steve Allen, whose wonderful laugh was audible throughout the film. Early on there had been some horrified walkouts by mothers dragging children up the aisles when Joe and Jerry are revealed in drag. Refusing to panic, unlike nervous studio executives who huddled in the lobby afterward, Wilder didn't change his film but, as he said, changed his audience.

Making only one minor trim, he held another preview a few days later in Westwood, a more sophisticated venue near the UCLA campus, and the

---

* In a less showy way, Wilder had Jay Lawrence do a Grant imitation as one of the POWs in *Stalag 17*.

reaction was uproarious. The film went on to gross more than $8 million in the United States, the year's third-biggest box-office hit (after *Ben-Hur* and *Operation Petticoat*), and despite a few grouchy or pearl-clutching reviewers, it was generally recognized as an instant comedy classic. The edgy elements that audiences accepted helped point the way toward the greater sexual freedom eventually allowed by Hollywood within less than ten years. And those elements are a large part of what makes the film seem so sophisticated and modern today. If many people even now don't especially focus on its romantic aspects but more on the raunchy burlesque elements, that demonstrates Wilder's skill at tunneling under the surface and working on different levels at once.

Wilder's unusual public acknowledgment of the crucial elements of Diamond's contributions to this masterpiece demonstrated his recognition that his second major writing collaboration was a marriage made in heaven, unlike his stormy first creative marriage with the conservative and often prudish Brackett, who would never have countenanced a film such as *Some Like It Hot*. Wilder's grateful admission about the final scene offers a rare window to examine just what Diamond contributed to their work together, with his expert sense of comic timing and understanding of human psychology. But it's intriguing that, as with any creative partnership, there are conflicting versions of how the scene came together.

Daphne and Osgood are isolated in the motorboat in the final two-shot, filmed before a process screen at the Goldwyn Studios. In an oft-repeated tale, Wilder and Diamond remembered having to write the scene the night before shooting it, toward the end of the production schedule. Supposedly that frantic writing job was caused by Monroe's lack of availability because of one of the illnesses she suffered during the shoot (including an overdose of sleeping pills).* But they managed to shoot around her with the simple expedient of having her and Joe, while kissing passionately, sink below the frame line in the back seat of the motorboat. Most of the closing dialogue between Jerry and Osgood already appears in the first draft of the screenplay, dated May 2, 1958—with the exception of the closing line. The filming began on August 11, and the ending was shot in late October. So other than a few minor variations in the dialogue onscreen, that was all they belatedly

---

* When Sugar comes back from her sexual encounter with Joe on the yacht, she flops on a bed at the hotel and says, "It was suicidally beautiful."

added to the scene, but it was a stroke of genius. This is how the scene is written in the shooting script dated November 12:

Up front, Osgood is blithely steering the boat, keeping his eyes straight ahead. Jerry is looking over his shoulder at the activities in the back seat.

OSGOOD: I called Mama—she was so happy she cried—she wants you to have her wedding gown—it's white lace.

JERRY (steeling himself): Osgood—I can't get married in your mother's dress. She and I—we're not built the same way.

OSGOOD: We can have it altered.

JERRY (firmly): Oh, no you don't! Look, Osgood—I'm going to level with you. We can't get married at all.

OSGOOD: Why not?

JERRY: Well, to begin with, I'm not a natural blonde.

OSGOOD (tolerantly): It doesn't matter.

JERRY: And I smoke. I smoke all the time.

OSGOOD: I don't care.

JERRY: And I have a terrible past. For three years now, I've been living with a saxophone player.

OSGOOD: I forgive you.

JERRY (with growing desperation): And I can never have children.

OSGOOD: We'll adopt some.

JERRY: But you don't understand! (he rips off his wig; in a male voice) I'm a MAN!

OSGOOD (oblivious): Well—nobody's perfect!

Jerry looks at Osgood, who is grinning from ear to ear, claps his hand to his forehead. How is her [sic] going to get himself out of this?

But that's another story—and we're not quite sure the public is ready for it.

FADE OUT

THE END

In 1972 Diamond offered William Froug, a television writer-producer who interviewed him for a book called *The Screenwriter Looks at the Screenwriter*, an account of how the ending was written: "That was sort of desperation time.

We had not yet written the ending when Monroe took sick, and we suddenly found ourselves having to shoot around her, and there was very little in that picture that we could do without her. And so we found ourselves having to write that tag." They already had a big laugh when Osgood says, "We can have it altered," and Jerry shrieks, "Oh, no you don't!" A line about a sex-change operation in a 1959 Hollywood movie! But they still needed the top-per from Osgood when Jerry pulls off his wig and admits he's a man. At that point, Diamond recalled, "I mentioned a line I'd considered using at some earlier point. And Billy said, 'Do you think it's strong enough for the tag of the picture?' And I said, 'I don't know.'"

The line had been written for the hilarious scene that follows Jerry's riot-ous tango sequence with Osgood. They dance to the strains of "La Cumpar-sita," the same music Wilder used in *Sunset Blvd.* for Norma's New Year's Eve tango with Gillis. Jerry breaks the news to Joe in their hotel room that Osgood has proposed. Giddy with booze and romance, Jerry is lying on a bed shak-ing a pair of maracas, which Wilder handed Lemmon to punctuate each line with and leave room for the laughter. Joe tries to bring his pal back to earth by saying, "But you're not a girl. You're a guy!" Jerry was to tell him, "Well—nobody's perfect." But Diamond worried that laugh line would detract from the next exchange: Joe asks, "And why would a guy want to marry another guy?," and Jerry responds, with some confusion, "Security?!" That was the big laugh for that scene (and a line that gets even more audience appreciation today). So Diamond dropped "Well—nobody's perfect" from the hotel room and eventually suggested recycling the line as the film's topper, with an added exclamation point.

As Wilder recalled the process at the memorial for Diamond, "We needed a final line, a final, final line, a spleen-shattering belly laugh. And Iz came up with 'Nobody's perfect.' We were not crazy about it, but it was late at night, and we were pooped. So we decided, 'Let's put it on paper so they can mim-eograph it,' fully expecting to find something *really* funny when the time came to shoot this scene. That just goes to show you how little we know."

Barbara Diamond remembered with more specificity:

One of the results of the way they worked is that it was impossible for them to separate one person's work from the other. They honestly didn't know who had written particular scenes or individual lines, and truthfully, they didn't much care. The one line that they did know about turned out to be the one that everyone asks about, "Nobody's perfect." When asked, Billy always said that it was a throwaway line of Mr. Diamond's and they had hoped that overnight they would think of something better, and Iz never contradicted him.

However, I have a different version of it. Iz wrote the scene the day before it was shot and left a copy here with me while he took it over to Billy. When he came back and asked me what I thought, I told him it was a great scene but the last line was weak. He said, "That's what Billy thinks and you're both wrong," and proceeded to tell me why. First of all, audiences love being able to anticipate a joke. The dimmest members of the audience know that Jack's last line is going to be "I'm a man," and they are bracing themselves for the explosive reaction. Therefore the only way to surprise them is to have no explosion, and the flatter the line the better. The laugh comes from the structure of the scene, not the particular line. . . . One reason Billy always called it a throwaway was because it had briefly been in the scene where Tony is explaining to Jack why he can't marry Osgood and it was taken out because it stepped on another joke. . . . Iz loved that [final] scene.

Paul Diamond added:

In the [original] maracas scene, after Jack's engaged, "Nobody's perfect" is one of the responses. The maracas are there to give the audience time to laugh before the next line comes. So "Nobody's perfect" goes out. "We'll find another place for it," Billy says. And at the point where they now have to finalize the last line, a couple of weeks later or something, Dad pitches "Nobody's perfect" for the last line, and Billy goes, "It's not strong enough" as an ending line. Dad insisted and said, "Yeah, it is, we should use it." And I am told that my father came home pissed off as hell and said to my mother he fought with Billy. And I'll tell you something else that changes the history a little bit. He said, "We're not going to find anything better. It's much stronger than he thinks it is. And I'm going to go in there tomorrow and basically I will kill him if he doesn't put it in." Eventually [they reached] the compromise of "We'll put it there temporarily," and then [Wilder] shot it. There's no alternate, so he apparently he had come around to that way of thinking. It was the only time I was ever told that Dad was ready to fight, that he was ready to go to the wall to get something in. He was that insistent.

"It was actually a rhythm joke," Iz Diamond explained to Froug. "The lines Brown had just before that were 'It doesn't matter,' 'I don't care,' 'I forgive you.' They all fell into the same pattern, which lulled the audience and set them up for the topper."

Note how technical all that sounds, and how expert in its craftsmanship, how accurate in its complex and subtle reading and playing of audience reactions. What's missing from that discussion is the line's subversive meaning and impact: Osgood's free-spirited acceptance of Jerry as a sexual partner, leaving Jerry speechlessly quizzing himself (but not clapping his hand to his forehead as in the script, which would have been too broadly signaling) while the audience roars with delight at the fade-out. The gift of Diamond's writing—passed on to his collaborator and to the actors—was to make the audience accept Osgood's attitude by using flawless comic logic, expressed through mathematically precise timing and rhythm. The psychological setup makes the line seem inevitable and therefore acceptable even to an American audience at the end of the Eisenhower era. That's how artistry evolves out of craftsmanship and the two become indistinguishable.

And yet Diamond could not resist complaining about how some people analyzed their masterpiece. In doing so, he gave the critics the last laugh.

Froug, who rails in his book against auteurist film critics with a "deep-rooted sense of moral outrage," put this question to Diamond: "There's sometimes a tendency among film critics or film journalists to read into a film all sorts of bizarre, hidden meanings that were never intended in the first place. . . . Can you give me any particular examples where you found something read into a film that was never intended and never there?"

Diamond replied, "Well, I don't remember who the critic was . . . it was a lady writing in *Film Quarterly*, or maybe *Films in Review*. Anyway, there was a review of *Some Like It Hot*, and she made a list of phallic symbols in the picture—everything from the saxophone to the machine gun to references to the Graf Zeppelin and a squeezed-out tube of toothpaste. Now, of course, I just marvel at this. It reveals a lot more about the critic's mind than the writer's."

Diamond seems to have conflated a couple of commentaries. He may have been partly referring to the 1970 essay on Wilder that Wilmington and I wrote for *Film Quarterly*. We refer fondly to the film's "filthy stream of *double-entendre*" and discuss the way "Joe exploits women's dress to heterosexual advantage, but Jerry camps up his role, giggling and shrieking like a slapstick drag queen. Their sexual dissonance may have been suggested to Wilder by the tensions in the Martin and Lewis comedy act; there is even a little joking innuendo in their musical instruments. Joe plays a tenor sax and Jerry thumps along on a big, maternal bass fiddle whose case is riddled with bullets."

We forgot to mention the Graf Zeppelin or the tube of toothpaste. But it is hard for me to understand how anyone over the age of eleven (my age when I first saw the film) could hear Marilyn Monroe complaining about a saxophone player dumping her and "All that's left is a pair of old socks and a tube of toothpaste all squeezed out" and not finding that a hilarious and poignant double entendre.

THE KEY TO *THE APARTMENT*

Upon its release in June 1960, *The Apartment* was slammed by one influential reviewer as "a dirty fairy tale, with a shnook for a hero, and a sad little elevator operator (Shirley MacLaine) for a fairy princess." The author of that insult was Hollis Alpert, then in his square period on the *Saturday Review*. He was condescending to movies in a pseudo-intellectual, moralizing way before he belatedly discovered the sexual revolution and wrote the prurient "Sex in the Cinema" series for *Playboy* with Arthur Knight. Alpert's evolution from hypocrite to voyeuristic wannabe libertine is the kind of irony Wilder might have turned into a satire of film reviewers if he thought it worth the bother.

Alpert's clueless review of *The Apartment* complained of what he found to be the film's "muddledness. . . . Sometimes it's funny, and sometimes it isn't funny at all." He was confused by the mixture of "pathos" with "a streak of meanness and cynicism," along with an ending he considered "sickeningly sweet." Mystifyingly, Alpert thought that the film, while portraying Lemmon's Bud Baxter as sympathetic, seemed to condone his letting married executives use his apartment as a trysting place and that "the quickest way up the ladder is through pimping. . . . As for the girl, she obtains purification through an attempt at suicide in the apartment, accompanied by some sick and sick-making jokes." Alpert was not alone in his incomprehension of films that dared to mix moods, as was becoming more prevalent as the classical Hollywood cinema began to shatter and, along with its audiences, increasingly reflected fracturing social attitudes as the 1950s drew to an end. The influence of the French Nouvelle Vague spurred that advance, and Bosley Crowther of the *New York Times* had a similarly befuddled reaction in 1962 to François Truffaut's film *Tirez sur le pianiste* (*Shoot the Piano Player*, 1960), asking, "Why does he scramble his satire with a madly melodramatic plot and have the little piano player kill a man in defense of a girl? It looks, from where we are sitting, as though M. Truffaut went haywire in this film." More sophisticated audience members were able to go along for the ride in films that captured the topsy-turvy nature of real life, and the artistry of Wilder and Diamond was able to guide them along with *The Apartment*.

Wilder at first resented Alpert's "dirty fairy tale" description, but the more he thought about it, he came to embrace it. *The Apartment* led the way for the 1960s with a more candid look at everyday American sexual mores than most Hollywood films had previously allowed. Although the film has a gamy realism with its setting in a low-rent Manhattan apartment and an antiseptic office skyscraper dominated by sleazy male executives, and though its two romantic leads are ordinary people representing the disenchanted contemporary working class, *The Apartment* in some ways is as much a fairy tale as *Sabrina*. But it does not require the fantasy trappings of a Long Island mansion and a hard-boiled executive turning unexpectedly softhearted to bring a couple together romantically. *The Apartment*'s story of two people working as drones in the anonymity of a large corporation is grounded in the noisy desperation and grit of metropolitan daily life. What makes it a far more satisfying romance than *Sabrina* is that it more candidly depicts the "dirty" (read: morally complex) doings of its easily relatable characters before they reject their lives of corrupt compromise under the thrall of a predatory system that conflates sex and money and are able to recognize each other's emotional sincerity.

As Wilder said late in life, "Something is only funny when it's essentially true. If it's totally fantastic and impossible, it isn't funny. It's only funny when people say, 'Yes, that's the way it is.'" He added,

People have called my pictures dirty or immoral. It's not true. In *The Apart-ment* I tried desperately to show how the Jack Lemmon character fell into a trap and wanted to disentangle himself. But it was too late because his future with the company had become so dependent on letting his bosses use his apartment as a love nest. And Shirley MacLaine's character was in the eternal trap of the "other woman."

In the end, though, they found in each other the strength to free them-selves. Every picture I make involves people making moral choices. How can I show that without showing the seamy side of the world these char-acters are choosing against?

MacLaine's winsome charm counterpoints her character's degradation, coex-isting with a profound sadness that makes her a victim both of male exploi-tation and her own moral confusion; that unsentimental, very human mixture makes her perhaps Wilder's most touching character. And as for Lemmon's lovable shnook, despite his own willing degradation, film critic Molly Haskell observed, "There's something deeply honorable about him that you feel all along, so the casting has a lot to do with the redemptiveness that the film has."

Set in late 1959, *The Apartment* draws its imagery and some of its social themes from the critiques that proliferated in the 1950s about the "organiza-tion man" and other representatives of a national culture seen as soulless in its dull conformism. Bud is a clerk in the giant insurance company, Wilder's favorite metaphor for a heartless capitalistic enterprise. But now the director's protagonist is even lower in the chain than Walter Neff in *Double Indemnity*, who at least gets out of the office to peddle policies to blonde sirens. And though MacLaine's elevator operator gets around, that's part of her problem, since she's literally a cog in a machine, the symbolic enabler of the upward mobility to which Bud aspires, and the prey of men from various levels of the building who sexually harass her.

Not for nothing does Alexander Trauner's memorable art direction for *The Apartment*, with its almost surreal expanses of desks behind Baxter's cramped work space, visually emulate King Vidor's *The Crowd*, the heartrending late-silent classic about an ordinary working man. The increasingly desperate tra-vails of Vidor's office functionary anticipate later cultural critiques on the dehumanization of "the lonely crowd." Vidor's visual metaphors are echoed in the pathos of Bud's bachelor life in the hectic office and his modest apartment. As he tells us in his opening narration, "I have this little problem with my apartment." Wilder doesn't make any direct reference to the dead-end emptiness of that other great Middle European modernist Franz Kafka, but Orson Welles used the endless rows of desks in the Vidor and Wilder films as models for his modern take on *The Trial* two years later. When an uncomprehending interviewer told Wilder that *The Apartment* was "a little too sentimental," the director said bluntly, "It was made so as not to be sentimental. . . . We have a prefabricated loneliness in America—TV dinners and everything. With this loneliness goes the urge to better oneself and rise from the masses. . . . I portray Americans as beasts. . . . I never considered *The Apartment* to be a comedy."

The story for *The Apartment* came from a blend of sources only Wilder could have thought to put together. He became fixated on a minor character in the British romantic drama *Brief Encounter* (1945), directed by David Lean from a Noël Coward one-act play, *Still Life*. The outwardly sedate but passionate couple (Celia Johnson and Trevor Howard) who meet in a suburban railroad station are borrowing a friend's apartment for a planned adulterous affair but are prevented from consummating it by the friend's inopportune return. Wilder couldn't help thinking about that fellow (played by Valentine Dyall), who is only briefly seen and snidely refers to how "disappointed" he is by the undignified nature of the married woman's escape. As Wilder reimagined the story in even more sordid terms, the friend "climbs into the warm bed the lovers just left, this man who has no mistress of his own," and is stuck cleaning the soiled sheets and emptying the ashtrays. Wilder's mental rewrite of Coward and Lean is revealing, since the hapless couple never made it into bed, and the actual scene with the sneering friend cuts to a tracking shot of Johnson running down a street in the rain, similar to a memorable shot of Shirley MacLaine near the end of *The Apartment*.

Although Wilder claimed to consider *Brief Encounter* a "very fine picture by David Lean," he couldn't help mocking it in his films. He seemed to consider its moving but repressed middle-class romance overly earnest and genteel and the film on the pretentious side. In *The Seven Year Itch*, Tom Ewell tries to seduce Marilyn Monroe in one of his fantasies by flamboyantly playing Rachmaninoff's Second Piano Concerto, the passionate theme music of the British film's solemn love story. There's also a comical reference to the key suburban setting of *Brief Encounter* in *The Private Life of Sherlock Holmes*. When Dr. Watson becomes frantic about insinuations that he and Holmes are a homosexual couple, insisting they move apart for appearance's sake, Holmes dryly replies, "Of course, we can still see each other clandestinely—on remote benches in Hyde Park, and in the waiting room of suburban railroad stations."

After his creative joy working with Lemmon in *Some Like It Hot*, Wilder wanted an encore, and when he remembered the old idea he had jotted down, the passing character from *Brief Encounter* metamorphosed into Bud Baxter. But to make that happen, Wilder and Diamond still needed a plot. Fittingly for the links Wilder saw between the corruption and whoring of Hollywood and the insurance business, they drew their plot hook from a notorious Hollywood incident, the 1951 shooting of agent Jennings Lang by producer Walter Wanger.

Lang represented Wanger's wife, actress Joan Bennett, and they were having an affair. Wanger shot Lang in the parking lot at the MCA talent agency in Beverly Hills. The Hollywood gossip was that Lang was shot in the testicles and lost one or both of them, and the shooting became a subject of morbid merriment in the industry for many years. But according to Lang's son, Rocky, who became a producer-director, when he heard the story from schoolmates long after the event, he asked his mother if it was true that his father had been shot in the balls. That night, his father took him into his home office, dropped his pants, and pointed to a small scar on his upper thigh. He told his son, "The guy was a lousy shot and hit me in the leg. But Hollywood is Hollywood, and getting shot in the balls is a better story than getting shot in the leg." So much for the legend; and as Rocky quipped, "I'm living proof."

What Wilder and Diamond took from this incident was that Lang had been using the apartment of a young mailroom employee, Jay Kanter, to carry on the affair. Kanter went on to become a well-known agent and producer. Lang became a producer and one of the top executives at MCA/Universal. Wilder said, "We did not go to this gentleman to produce the picture." But they were friendly, and Lang, as executive producer of *The Front Page*, suggested Wilder as its director.*

---

* There's also a delicious inside gag about MCA in *Some Like It Hot*: in 1929 it's a humble one-room office in the building where Joe and Jerry open doors looking vainly for a job. As they open the door reading "MUSIC CORPORATION OF AMERICA, JULES STEIN, *President*" and ask "Anything today?," the secretary, drinking from a bottle, replies, "Nothing."

In *The Apartment*, Bud, a likable young go-getter, tries to rise from his lowly perch at a desk in Consolidated Life of New York by lending his apartment to executives for their sexual assignations. Bud's lonely bachelor existence is made more miserable by his knowledge that his apartment is being used as a bordello while he has to kill time working late at the office or, on one particularly painful occasion, sleeping on a park bench on a freezing night. He carries an unrequited torch for Fran, his cheery, sweet, and seemingly wholesome coworker, without realizing why she keeps turning him down for dates even while coyly putting the carnation she wears into his buttonhole, grateful for his unusually gentlemanly behavior.

The film carefully balances its often-light tone with escalating drama until it reaches a devastating emotional climax. As the couple-to-be fight their way through the jungle of corporate sleaze, MacLaine's transformation from a sexually misused, suicidal young woman into a revivified partner for the genuinely romantic but depressed and morally compromised Bud is entirely compelling. They are among the long line of couples in Wilder's work whose romance has to overcome bitter betrayal and disillusionment as well as his characteristic situation of deception by a more cynical character of a more gullible one. In the engaging modesty of the performances by Lemmon and MacLaine, Bud and Fran closely resemble the average members of the audience in the way they have to cope with the emotional upheavals and humiliations of American working-class serfdom. That, along with the film's consummate craftsmanship and their ultimate escape from the system, is what makes *The Apartment* so memorable and beloved for moviegoers, even more so in some ways than *Some Like It Hot* with its more exotic world and outré characters.

Fran is sexually exploited by Bud's loathsome boss, the epitome of the callously sexist American male of the 1950s, who leads her on with phony promises of marriage. Fred MacMurray's Jeff Sheldrake cynically confides to Baxter, "You know, you see a girl a couple of times a week, just for laughs, and right away they think you're going to divorce your wife. I ask you, is that fair?" Bud can't help replying, "No sir, it's very unfair—especially to your wife." "Yeah," says Sheldrake, obliviously. And no scene in Wilder's work more succinctly or movingly tells a story visually, or with such great compression and eloquence, than the one when Bud discovers that Fran is the woman his boss has been taking to his apartment. The philandering

Sheldrake is played to chilling perfection by MacMurray, in another surprisingly harsh characterization the director had to coax him to play, as he had with *Double Indemnity,* again seeing the dark underpinnings of his superficial wise-guy charm.

Bud learns the bitter truth during his encounter with Fran in his new private office during a raucous Christmas Eve celebration. The sexually uninhibited partying and holiday music all around them serve as ironic counterpoint to their deeply painful situation, rubbing salt into their wounds. Fran has just been hit with the truth about Sheldrake's cynical routine with women—seduce them: promise marriage: abandon them for others in the office—by Sheldrake's drunken, vindictive secretary, Miss Olsen (Edie Adams), one of those former playmates. Bud innocently takes the stunned Fran into his office to ask her opinion of his new bowler hat, a symbol of the junior-executive status he has gained through his corruption. Bud jauntily tilts the hat on the side of his head, looking ridiculous, like the singing and dancing Michigan J. Frog in Chuck Jones's classic 1955 cartoon *One Froggy Evening.*

Going for the laugh at Bud's expense makes the film's subsequent mood change all the more devastating. Bud adores Fran and wants her to share his admiration for his new hat, but when he poses in it, she responds with a blank, numb look and hands over her compact so he can inspect himself. As Bud looks at his image, saying with a defensive laugh that "after all, this is a conservative firm—I don't want people to think I'm an entertainer," his face drops as he sees that the compact has a shattered mirror. Earlier, when he had returned the compact to Sheldrake after finding it in his apartment, the executive smirkingly told him that his female conquest threw it at the wall during a postcoital argument. Now Bud realizes with a horrified grimace that Fran is the woman Sheldrake has been bringing to the apartment. This masterfully compressed way of telling the story in the screenplay and direction simultaneously conveys Bud's shattered feelings about Fran and her similar image of herself. When he says with difficulty, with light from the mirror reflected in his eyes, "The mirror—it's broken," she replies flatly, "Yes, I know—I like it that way—makes me look the way I feel."

Although the use of the mirror here is effortlessly naturalistic, the revelation of Fran's bleak situation harks back to the way German expressionist films during Wilder's formative years used mirrors to reveal the inner lives of characters; exterior reflections of psychological truths are the essence of expressionism. And as a supreme example of Wilder's narrative economy, "That's about a dozen pages of dialogue saved," as Lemmon put it. Wilder told Crowe, "When Baxter sees himself in the mirror . . . he adds up two and two. Better than a third person telling him about the affair—that we did not want to do. This gave us everything, in one shot."

The mirror shot is, in effect, a brilliant Lubitsch Touch, an example of the lesson Wilder learned from his master about letting "the audience add up two and two. They'll love you forever." Conversely, Fran's statement that the mirror "makes me look the way I feel" to some extent contradicts that lesson by verbalizing the point already made visually. That can be viewed as an illustration of what Brackett called "Billy's terrifying neurosis that everything isn't crystal clear to the audience." But in this case Fran's acutely aware verbalization works powerfully by allowing her to express her tragic recognition of her self-loathing. Her admission to this man who has made clear his fondness for her only to have it shaken is a link in the dramatic chain of events through which Wilder allows them to transcend their squalid circumstances through the affirmative power of love.

Bud's utter disillusionment with the woman he thought he loved is intensified by what follows. The revelation in the mirror scene helps lead to Fran's suicide attempt the same night in the apartment. And that eventually leads to the loving rapprochement between Bud and Fran. But before that, Fran confronts Sheldrake with her knowledge of his deceit and tries to kill herself, and the writers daringly intersperse a wildly comical skit at a bar in which the drunken Bud is picked up by the wacky Margie MacDougall. Hilariously and touchingly played by Hope Holiday,* Margie babbles about her jockey husband being put in a Cuban jail by Fidel Castro; a jukebox is playing, in a mischievous double entendre, "Adeste Fideles (O Come, All Ye Faithful)." Bud sloppily brings his equally soused new companion to the apartment to find his record player stuck on a recording of Charles Williams's "Jealous

---

* Hope Holiday also has a role in *Irma la Douce* as a feisty prostitute named Lolita, wearing the same kind of heart-shaped glasses Sue Lyon wears in the iconic publicity photos by Bert Stern for the 1962 Stanley Kubrick film version of the Vladimir Nabokov novel *Lolita*. Wilder earlier used the name Margie sarcastically when Neff in *Double Indemnity* is talking on the phone with Phyllis about their murder plot but evasively calls her Margie, prompting Keyes to exclaim, "Margie! I bet she drinks from the bottle. Why don't you settle down and get married, Walter?"

Lover." That is the film's theme music, heard repeatedly at the Chinese restaurant where Sheldrake takes Fran to warm her up for their trysts.

Bud's discovery of the record is preceded by the most devastating scene in the film. Fran gives Sheldrake the album by the restaurant's piano player as a romantic Christmas present. But Sheldrake tells her they had better keep it in the apartment. Since he has neglected to buy her a present, he peels a hundred-dollar bill from his money clip and tells her to buy an alligator bag at Bergdorf's.* Sheldrake shows not the slightest compunction or awareness of what a grave insult he is inflicting. Fran gives him a look to kill. It is also the drained look of a dead woman. She doesn't take the money, so he sticks the bill in her purse (a production still shows the money sticking out of a liquor bottle in front of her, but that is not how it appears in the film; her purse is a more suitably symbolic receptacle for his grimy offering). In response, Fran takes off one of her gloves, stands, drops her coat, and says flatly, "OK. I just thought, as long as it was paid for. . . ." This ultimate humiliation is what drives her to attempt suicide, with the prompting of another mirror (she spots Bud's sleeping pills reflected in it), but also leads, after her painful recovery, to her resurrection through Bud's loving ministrations.

Wilder makes this redemption theme most explicit in the person of Dr. Dreyfuss (Jack Kruschen), who lives next door to Bud. It comes out explicitly when Dr. Dreyfuss berates Bud for supposedly causing Fran's suicide attempt. The irony is that the doctor thinks Bud is a heartless playboy, constantly partying with different woman, instead of the lonely bachelor and romantic shnook he really is. The protracted, grueling sequence of Dreyfuss narrowly reviving Fran from her overdose attracts criticism from some naive modern viewers who feel Wilder is abusing his actress and that this is a sign of his supposed "misogyny." After the doctor pours coffee into the prostrate,

---

* Holiday told me that one Christmas during her relationship with Wilder, "I bought him a beautiful black Wedgwood tea set. And he gave me an electric back scratcher. I started to cry, the tears were streaming down my face, I was so hurt. I thought that was so insensitive and insulting. About five or six days later, he called me and said, 'Can I come by?' He came by my apartment, and he sat down, and I made him a drink. He said, 'Here. I'm sorry about Christmas. Here's a hundred dollars. Why don't you buy yourself an alligator bag?' I said, 'That's interesting—that's a line from the movie I was in. Don't you have any original dialogue? You insulted me again. I'm not a whore, and you make me feel like I am. Take back your hundred dollars. I don't need it. I come from a good family.'" Wilder "was apologizing all over the place," she recalled. "I don't think he did it purposely, using the line from the film. It just came out of him. It hurt my feelings. That's why I used to get headaches. If he would do something like that to me, I'd get a splitting headache."

nearly comatose Fran and makes her throw up (just off-camera), he repeatedly slaps her as he administers smelling salts and marches her up and down the floor, with the passing time conveyed in a series of dissolves. As Wilder pointed out to his critics, he had medical advice on the set and actually portrayed the treatment in a relatively mild manner.* Those who object to such astringent honesty are showing their blindness toward reality and missing the acutely painful, viscerally moving nature of the drama of the good doctor bringing the young woman back to life. And by extension, Fran's revival is also her rebirth as a woman with self-respect and feelings that are taken seriously by another man, Bud, who metaphorically comes back to life in these moments as well.

After that harrowing sequence, the doctor chastises Bud, "Why don't you grow up, Baxter? Be a mensch! You know what that means?" Bud says, "I'm not sure." Dreyfuss tells him, "A mensch—a human being!" Although Dreyfuss is referring to Bud's false image as a womanizer, Bud recognizes the criticism in a deeper sense, ashamed of his complicity in the mistreatment of Fran and other women by Sheldrake and their fellow executives. The WASPish Bud uses the Yiddish word himself at the end of the film when he returns the key to the apartment to Sheldrake, telling him, "Just following doctor's orders. I've decided to become a mensch. You know what that means? A human being."

Given Wilder's ethnic and cultural background, it is significant that he gives the voice of conscience in what he considered his best film to a Jewish character, Dr. Dreyfuss, a healer with a wise sense of humor who shares a similar name with one of the most prominent victims of anti-Semitism and employs a Yiddish word to express the film's central theme. Wilder's explicit, and unusual for his work, depiction of the doctor as Jewish, the man who brings life and teaches Bud to be a "mensch," is an indication of how deeply felt and deeply personal *The Apartment* was to him. In his critical study *A Foreign Affair*, Gerd Gemünden, who writes insightfully of the influence of exile on Wilder's worldview, observes that *The Apartment* "offers a rare and conscious recasting of the experience of exile, portraying nonbelonging and alienation as a predicament for which Jews, commonly associated with

---

* From my own experience around hospitals and suicides (including the girlfriend whose death I wrote about in *The Broken Places: A Memoir*, 2015), I know that this sequence, even with its restraint, is utterly realistic.

diasporic or nomadic identities, can offer a remedy. That they do so by using a German and Yiddish word—mensch—underscores not only their appeal to a common humanity but also that the German language, considered by many Holocaust survivors *non grata,* can still provide a universally accepted terminology." The philosophical point about being a mensch is believably integrated into this Wilder-Diamond masterpiece of screenwriting—elegant, elaborately painstaking, with covertly intricate but deceptively straightforward construction.

C. C. (for Calvin Clifford) (Bud) Baxter, an Anglo-Saxon Gentile,* is conspicuously out of place in the Big City but determined to assimilate at all costs to his health, sanity, and morality. It is no accident that Bud is an exile from the largely German Midwestern city of Cincinnati, a place where many Jewish refugees settled and the birthplace of Reform Judaism. Fran Kubelik is of Czechoslovakian heritage, although her hometown is not identified (she perhaps is named after the celebrated Czech violinist and composer Jan Kubelík). The two alienated young exiles adrift in the often hostile or indifferent metropolis find happiness and finally become a couple partly through the kind ministrations of the Jewish couple who are Bud's neighbors.

As Gemünden notes, the fellow dwellers of Bud's apartment building represent the *haimish* qualities of New York City as an American immigrant haven: Dr. and Mildred Dreyfuss (Naomi Stevens), along with Bud's kvetching Jewish landlady, Mrs. Lieberman (Frances Weintraub Lax),

> are the only true New Yorkers in a cast of bland middle Americans, providing the local color which the rest of the characters and the locations programmatically lack. In Mildred Dreyfuss, Wilder created, to my knowledge, the only character specifically drawn on his upbringing, modeling her after a woman who lived in the same building in Vienna where he grew up: "She used to visit my mother. . . . I could hear her voice in my head, like it was yesterday. . . . She was a plump muse, always cooking. . . . She spoke German in the Viennese way, and I tried to put that into English." Naomi Stevens's Jewish mama certainly radiates warmth and concern, and enjoys with her husband (who "tells [her] everything") the kind

---

* Named after Wilder's and Frank Capra's longtime assistant director and sometime B-movie director Charles Clifford "Buddy" or "Bud" Coleman Jr., whom Wilder considered efficient but "an idiot." Coleman did not work on *The Apartment* but did work with Wilder again on *Kiss Me, Stupid.*

of honesty and respect that models a valid relationship for Bud and Fran. As Ed Sikov has astutely remarked, in this film "home is where the Jews are."

It's ironic that some viewers have seen Mildred Dreyfuss as stereotypical, when in fact she is so true, a symbolic equivalent of his own mother, and presented by Wilder with such affection. Wilder responded, "She was *under-done*. I ask, did *they* know my neighbor?"

Diamond recalled how tricky he and Wilder found it "to combine a basically serious story with jokes," especially in the complex setup of the suicide sequence:

[Lemmon] was playing a comedy seduction with one girl [Margie, whom he drunkenly brings back to the apartment] while another girl was dying, and when he discovers MacLaine, he tries to get rid of this girl. There was a delicate balance there between drama and comedy, and we were afraid that if we got a laugh in the wrong place, the whole picture would go out the window. When we sat through the preview, when they accepted that, when they laughed at the right places and took the rest seriously, then I think we knew we were in, because that was the really tricky part. It's [Aldous] Huxley's *Point Counter Point*—while Smith is pushing the pram, Jones is murdering his wife. I mean, this shuttling back and forth between tragedy and comedy. On that occasion it worked for us.

There are numerous suicides or suicide attempts by major and minor characters in Wilder films, including Bud's comical account of having shot himself in the knee when he was in love with the wife of his best friend. But it was Diamond who came up with the idea of Fran's attempt when Sheldrake treats her like a prostitute. As his son, Paul, recalled, "My father, when he was living in Hollywood early in his career, he'd had another friend, another writer, who'd broken up with his girlfriend and come home to find this girlfriend dead in his bathtub, having committed suicide. . . . And this was the kind of thing that stayed with my father as an intriguing situation, so it went into the picture. It's a risk to throw a suicide attempt into a comedy. But the suicide comes about an hour-plus into the picture. If you're believing in these characters, this is just another turn."* And, like the shooting of Jennings Lang, the amoral behavior of the executives, and the way they treat women as commodities, the suicide attempt is a further macabre connection between the plot of *The Apartment* and life in Hollywood, its violence an echo of the star shooting her screenwriter/gigolo when he walks out on her in *Sunset Blvd.*

Most screenwriters would have been content to create the stirringly dramatic scene of Bud discovering the nearly comatose Fran in his apartment. But only Wilder and Diamond would have dared to intercut it with comedy, "the irregularity—that unexpected little twist," as Barney puts it in *Kiss Me, Stupid.* Although the shuttling back and forth between those modes shocked some dull-witted reviewers, the public in this case was wiser than the reviewers. The contemporary audience who embraced *The Apartment* recognized its candor about the highs and lows of human emotions, its generous and sophisticated refusal to condemn Fran or Bud for their human flaws, and its accuracy in depicting a contemporary couple whose dilemmas as functionaries in a heartless corporation make them representative of modern life. The reason "a basically serious story with jokes" is more powerful than the film would have been without "jokes" is that Wilder and Diamond were going for the full richness of human emotions, the unexpected complexity of life and death in ordinary situations. As John Lennon put it in a song line that encapsulates the challenge a screenwriter has in bringing a sense of real life to the screen, "Life is what happens to you while you're busy making other plans."

Wilder's identification with these urban apartment-dwelling characters was solidified when he chose to spend his later years not in a lavish Beverly Hills or Bel-Air home like many of his successful contemporaries but in an apartment, albeit a posh condominium in a high-rise overlooking Wilshire

---

* In addition to Goldie Hawn's suicide attempt in the opening of Diamond's *Cactus Flower* script, there's a failed precursor of the blending of suicide with comedy in one of his early, pre-Wilder scripts, *The Girl from Jones Beach.* A New York talent agent (Eddie Bracken) constantly tells women he is planning to kill himself in the hope that they will rescue him and fall in love with him. Not only is the running gag unfunny, but the women oddly find that pathetic shnook's self-pitying act appealing. When Bud confesses to Fran that he once tried to kill himself, he and the script do not milk the story to gain sympathy, an example of the lack of sentimentality Wilder brought to his collaboration with Diamond. Another suicide gag in a Diamond script has Bob Hope's cartoonist rebelling against his employer in *That Certain Feeling* by having a child character point a gun at his own head, with the caption, "THIS IS THE END!!"

Boulevard in Westwood, a dwelling more suited to his lifelong sense of transience.* In that sense it is fitting that a film about life in a big-city hotel, *Grand Hotel*, is what the miserable apartment-dweller Bud becomes so frustrated trying to watch on TV while it is constantly delayed by commercial breaks.[†]

The Apartment is as much a mordant "city film" as *People on Sunday*, another daring Wilder work grounded in the mundane lives of ordinary people caught up in moral dilemmas common to impersonal cosmopolitan environments. His German film similarly shows the deadening daily routine of working-class characters and examines with a magnifying glass the romantic problems of an ordinary young woman. In both films a casually indifferent male user takes advantage of the woman's guileless giving of love and sex. The romantic disillusionment both Fran and Bud in *The Apartment* experience, in different ways, when they are wised up about the callousness of big-city life makes the depiction of their ultimate coming-together believable and satisfying to an audience, while the somewhat tentative conclusion expresses the doubts we may have about their chances for happiness. The sense of battered innocence MacLaine and Lemmon radiate as performers not only helps make their characters so relatable and their sordid situation more palatable to audiences, it conveys a guarded sense of hope and optimism. In that rests the final proof of Wilder's romantic sensibility—not one that denies reality for a comforting fantasy but a realistic sense of how the world works, a depiction of how troubled people navigate the pitfalls of love and how they somehow can overcome and survive those dangers.

---

* The Wilders' condo at 10375 Wilshire Boulevard, with a spacious living room filled with art works, two bedrooms, and a den and spectacular views of the ocean and the mountains, was on the twelfth floor of the Wilshire Terrace building. It sold for $1.385 million after Audrey Wilder died in 2012.

[†] Referring to MGM's all-star extravaganza *Grand Hotel*, set in Weimar Berlin, is the director's nostalgic homage to Berlin's Adlon Hotel. But my only reservation about *The Apartment* is that Bud keeps switching channels irritably whenever John Ford's classic *Stagecoach* appears on his TV. The screenplay calls it simply "a Western—Cockamamie Indians are attacking a stagecoach. That's not for Bud. . . . [And] the U.S. Cavalry is riding to the rescue. Will they get there in time? Bud doesn't wait to find out." Rather than using that as an indication of poor taste on Bud's part, Wilder implicitly ratifies his protagonist's disdain. Zolotow notes, "Wilder detests Westerns." Paul Diamond, however, argues that the clips were randomly chosen to represent a Western cliché and did not reflect Wilder and Diamond's feelings about *Stagecoach*, because his father considered Dudley Nichols's screenplay his favorite script, and Wilder also praised it.

Wilder said *The Apartment* has "as fairy-tale a third act as anything by Capra." There is no more beautiful or moving shot in Wilder's work than the close-up of Fran in the Chinese restaurant near the end as it gradually dawns on her that she loves Baxter. The realization comes after Sheldrake, who has tried to con her once too often, reveals that Bud lost his job because he gave back the key to the apartment: he wouldn't let her be taken there for yet another night of impersonal sex. While "Auld Lang Syne" plays as a New Year's celebration breaks out at the restaurant, Fran's face goes through a series of subtle emotional changes as the reason for Bud's action sinks in, her defenses melt away, and she breaks into a radiant smile. After a life of being beaten around and not expecting tenderness or compassion, she accepts Bud's honestly offered love into her heart. Sheldrake turns around from the celebration to find her seat at the restaurant empty—and Wilder dissolves to the rapturous tracking shot of Fran running along a street to find Bud.

When she rushes up the stairs to his apartment, Wilder characteristically flips the mood with a heart-stopping suicide gag borrowed from his German scripts *The Man Who Searched for His Own Murderer* and *The False Husband* (and from a more jocular twist in *Ninotchka*): Fran mistakes a popping Champagne cork for a gunshot. But *The Apartment*, despite its frequently somber tone, concludes with the heartfelt, if conditional, happy ending we want to see, a loving card game with the characters enjoying each other's company. Wilder and Diamond avoid the clichéd romantic clinch. They further balance the temptation to schmaltz by having Fran respond sardonically to Bud's expression of love with only a friendly smile as she quips, "Shut up and deal." Detractors of the director consider even that guardedly happy ending a sugarcoating of an often painful story, or the director trying to have it both ways, but it seems true to life in its mixed moods, its undertone of anxiety and tentative optimism.

8.1 (top) *Kiss Me, Stupid* (1964) provoked the most notorious scandal of Wilder's career, but he considered this satire of small-town American sexual hypocrisy "very romantic." Dean Martin's lecherous singer reacts to Ray Walston as a wannabe songwriter wooing a prostitute played by Kim Novak. (United Artists–Lopert Pictures / Photofest.)

8.2 (bottom) Jack Lemmon's stuffy right-wing American businessman is liberated in an Italian resort hotel by a free-spirited young Englishwoman (Juliet Mills) in *Avanti!* (1972), the most artistically successful of Wilder's attempts to emulate Lubitsch. (United Artists.)

8

"I AM NO LONGER AFRAID"

MOLLIE MALLOY (Carol Burnett): Well, if it's in the papers,
it must be true. They wouldn't print a lie.

—*The Front Page* (1974)

A MAJOR reason *Some Like It Hot* and *The Apartment* were so successful
was that they marked a triumphant return by Wilder to the audacious social
commentary that had characterized his best work in his earlier days as a Hollywood director. He had been running for cover since the commercial and
critical rejection in 1951 of *Ace in the Hole*, his most corrosively political film,
and throughout the 1950s tended to play it safe with pretested material, often
drawn from the stage. His films either were determinedly unengaged and
even evasive about sociopolitical issues or, at most, commented obliquely on
contemporary issues, as was the case with the theme of informing in the
World War II comedy-drama *Stalag 17* (1953). The political chill that descended
over Hollywood in the postwar blacklist era caused most filmmakers to
disguise or express their sociopolitical views in microcosmic human dramas
carefully divorced from hot-button "big" issues. As a result of Wilder's
uncharacteristic caution, the period between *Ace* and *Some Like It Hot* was the
weakest of his Hollywood directorial career, a time of relatively impersonal,
tentative, and muted filmmaking. But when he regained his fully distinctive

personal voice with I. A. L. Diamond's help, Wilder resumed his role as the American cinema's most caustic social critic.

As the 1950s turned into the '60s, Wilder showed what he had meant in 1947 when he told Charles Brackett that he wanted to end their partnership so he could do "more politically daring" films: "I am no longer afraid." In the later stages of Wilder's career, he often found graceful and meaningful ways of integrating human drama and comedy with social issues. It was not coincidental that Wilder was at the peak of his popular appeal in the repressed era of the late fifties and early sixties. His iconoclasm, candid view of sexuality, harsh critiques of American materialism and corruption, and unusually mordant view of the world were bracing. Those qualities appealed to audiences long frustrated with censorship and other forms of repression but hardly knowing what to do about it. His sociopolitical satire in those films frequently was bold and incisive, even if by inclination he still tended to express his viewpoint by burrowing into intimate, allegorical stories with far-reaching social implications rather than taking the sweeping, outside-in route with the kind of grandiose historical topics favored by such colleagues as Stanley Kramer, George Stevens, and Fred Zinnemann.

But *One, Two, Three* (1961), the farce Wilder chose as a change of pace after *The Apartment*, was an exception to that rule, his most politically topical film since *A Foreign Affair*. A satire about the Cold War ideological divide between capitalism and communism before the building of the Berlin Wall, *One, Two, Three* takes a broadly caricaturish approach to world events, making it resemble a series of editorial cartoons. That helps explain why this unfortunately timed, only intermittently funny comedy, which flopped at the box office, was also something of a dud artistically, as both Wilder and Diamond admitted in retrospect. Diamond nevertheless confessed to me a particular fondness for this raucous lampoon, perhaps because more than any other film he wrote with Wilder it seems in the anarchic spirit of the Columbia University varsity shows that gave him his start. For Wilder, the film was a throwback as well, a frantic follow-up of sorts to his 1948 film *A Foreign Affair* and his final cinematic foray into his old reportorial haunt. But though *One, Two, Three*, thanks to its nonstop irreverence, has its champions, it lacks the depth and sting of the earlier film about corruption in postwar Berlin. And it is a far cry from *Ninotchka*, another, more nuanced political satire he wrote with Brackett, his principal collaborator on *A Foreign Affair*.

An updated adaptation of the Ferenc Molnár play *One, Two, Three* from 1929, Wilder's film began shooting on location in June 1961 and was in production when the Wall was erected in August. The communist German Democratic Republic built it to keep people from East Berlin from escaping to West Berlin. Originally the film was set in July 1960 and was to start with footage of Winston Churchill, Joseph Stalin, and Franklin Roosevelt at the 1945 Yalta Conference in which the city was divided. A *March of Time*–type narrator would have declared, "Subsequent events have proved that this decision was—to put it diplomatically—a boo-boo." Then it would have shown life in the "city with a split personality": East Berlin border police suspiciously checking people passing through the Brandenburg Gate, an anti-Yankee parade in the eastern sector, and the Coca-Cola headquarters in West Berlin (sarcastically referred to as "an outpost of freedom—a showcase of democracy in action").

After the wall went up, Wilder and Diamond quickly had to rejigger the story with narration and a flashback structure to set it before the crisis, in June 1960, an awkward process, with narration by James Cagney's Coke executive C. R. MacNamara about the Wall. Wilder moved the shooting to the Bavaria Studios in Munich for interiors earlier than planned and had a partial replica of the Brandenburg Gate and the Tempelhof airport built there. The great Alexander Trauner was art director, as he was on *The Apartment* and *Irma la Douce*; he also was production designer on *Kiss Me, Stupid, Sherlock Holmes*, and *Fedora*.

By the time *One, Two, Three* was released in December 1961, the drastic change in the divided city and the world tension resulting from the standoff between the nuclear powers of the United States and the Soviet Union had dampened the public's mood for a comedy set in that hot spot. The problem was compounded by Wilder's stubborn decision to keep the body of the story as he had conceived it before the building of the wall. That gave the film the unfortunate impression of blithely ignoring the existence of the crisis. *One, Two, Three* is a scattershot frolic that seems all over the map, literally, in mocking both capitalism and communism. To Wilder, that was the point: when the French critic Michel Ciment noted that the film was attacked by both left and right, the director replied as he lit a cigar, "Ain't that nice? I love it, you know, to irritate everybody. Ultimately, naturally, they're going to put me up against a cellophane wall and shoot me from both sides—the

Communists, the capitalists—I love it." Glib and wisecracking in the extreme, *One, Two, Three* is occasionally hilarious and incisive but more often grating in its simplistic, heavy-handed attempts at humor. What could have been a biting send-up of political hypocrisy on both extremes of the ideological divide instead devolved into a wearisome parade of toothless gags aiming at easy targets on both sides.

The indiscriminate flippancy of *One, Two, Three* can be cited to validate the conventional view of Wilder as merely a nihilistic cynic about humanity and social issues. But is this failed attempt at a political satire on clashing modern political systems merely an anomaly in his career, a divergence from the social acuity of such films as *Ninotchka*, *A Foreign Affair*, and *Ace in the Hole*? How seriously can Wilder be taken as a political satirist in those and his other films? And what *were* his political principles?

For answers to those questions, we need to examine the sociopolitical underpinnings of his career from its beginning in the late 1920s until its conclusion in 1981, to study his evolution as an émigré artist who keenly observed and often criticized his adopted country and contrasted it with the Europe he had fled but never entirely abandoned psychologically. Wilder's political history and his response to his times explain how he came to be "no longer afraid" in his years with Diamond. When Wilder burst forth as fully himself, his transgressive filmmaking gleefully broke taboos, crossing and blurring political and sexual boundaries with greater daring and freedom than he had ever shown before, while (somewhat paradoxically) allowing his latent romanticism full vent. He continued on that defiant path even though he often caused outrage or bafflement eventually while finding himself out of step with volatile social change.

WILDER'S POLITICAL BEDROCK

Wilder's political views are often misunderstood, sometimes to the detriment of his artistic reputation. The fact that he worked successfully with two longtime collaborators who had diametrically opposite political views—the conservative Brackett and the liberal Diamond—heightens the confusion about where Wilder stood and how his films should be interpreted. After his contentious, somewhat stifling, but still creative working relationship with Brackett,

Wilder's more congenial collaboration with Diamond allowed the director greater freedom in his later years to explore his wide-ranging bent for political satire, but the earlier films with Brackett retain their special power to illuminate sociopolitical issues dramatically and comedically.

Wilder's films, dramatic or satirical or both, often deal overtly with political and historical issues, both European and American. A satirist often invites confusion in people who misunderstand irony and prefer more earnest and literal proselytizing, which is not the realm of the artist but of the polemicist. And though Wilder, despite his allegiance to America, rarely indulged in polemics or propaganda, his films, whether written with Brackett or Diamond or others, are replete with sharp, eclectic jabs and observations about the communist, capitalist, and fascist systems. And not only in his overtly "political" films: Wilder's microcosmic skewering of American small-town sexual hypocrisy in *Kiss Me, Stupid* is as acidulous as his frontal attack on the corruption of the news media in *Ace in the Hole* and his devastating take on urban alienation and conformity in *The Apartment*. As his late work progressed, Wilder's satire continued to be topically pointed even in films that seem detached in other ways from the contemporary scene. He works satire of Nixonian conservatism into both a romantic comedy (*Avanti!*) and a 1920s newspaper comedy (*The Front Page*). In *The Private Life of Sherlock Holmes*, the most ambitious film of his later period, Wilder manages to gracefully combine an intense romantic drama with political elements dealing with some of his deepest historical concerns involving Victorianism and German militarism.

The differences between the unrestrained buffoonery of *One, Two, Three* and Wilder's films with Brackett—although *A Foreign Affair* and *Sunset Blvd.* are more sedate in tone, they are much more acute social satires—give some credence to the idea that having Brackett as a partially restraining force to bounce ideas against was not entirely detrimental to Wilder's career. Nevertheless, I would argue that Diamond's liberating influence helped lead to Wilder's triumphs with provocative sociopolitical material in the films that may seem deceptively limited in political scope but successfully take aim at their targets with varying degrees of romantic drama and acerbic satire. The criticisms and controversies *Some Like It Hot*, *The Apartment*, and *Kiss Me, Stupid* provoked in their time helped define the qualities admirers of those films value today. Those stories tapped as profoundly into Wilder's personal conflicts as the best of his more overtly political films and certainly more deeply than the weaker ones. As Yeats put it, "We make out of the quarrel with others, rhetoric, but of the quarrel with ourselves, poetry." Wilder's late films reflect the director's bedrock political values in their trenchant social criticism, as did his work with Brackett.

As a lifelong liberal and antifascist, a Jew dealing with anti-Semitism in Europe, and with his experiences living through and reporting on times of social turmoil, Wilder was always highly aware and sophisticated politically. As an American immigrant who fervently believed in the Constitution, he remained strongly committed to freedom of speech and association and other rights that were under attack in the blacklist years and beyond. But he tended to keep a low political profile after the blacklist was imposed, as many former liberal activists did, including those who, like Wilder, had been vocal opponents of the imposition of the Screen Directors Guild loyalty oath in 1950.

But Wilder, unlike some of his colleagues, did not abandon his liberal convictions during the blacklist era, even though some of his comments on the blacklist caused controversy. Despite his films' tendency to avoid overt political engagement in that period, sometimes to the point of evasive contortions, Wilder's work in the 1950s still reflected his sardonic, irreverent social perspective. That characteristic became more pointed as he was newly emboldened, sometimes in the face of fierce opposition, by the changing political climate in the United States as the 1960s approached and censorship in Hollywood began loosening. Anthony Heilbut observes in *Exiled in Paradise* that Wilder and other émigrés were often critics of the American political system because "they knew too much to trust in it completely or to abandon their commitment to intellectual nonconformity." They "also tried to goad Americans into leading a more responsible public life, encouraging them to act upon political principles that the natives might have forgotten but that émigrés had learned as background for their citizenship examinations."

"THE DEATH HE CHOSE NOT TO DIE"

David Walsh, the incisive film critic of the *World Socialist Web Site*, while interviewing me in 2019 about the political satire in *Ninotchka*, made a comment that is also a criticism of Wilder as a screenwriter:

Personally, I don't think you watch a Lubitsch film to discover the secrets of the social and historical process in the 20th century. *Ninotchka* [1939] has its amusing sides and its reactionary sides, but if you want to understand the Russian Revolution and the character of Stalinism, that is not the work I would rush to. That's not Lubitsch's strength, he's often over his head in relation to these big questions. His strength, I think, is his tolerance and his sophisticated insight into certain forms of human behavior, his amused and amusing grasp of human foibles and problems. This is a part of life, although it's not the only part of life.

Walsh and I agree to disagree on how effective the satirical point of view *Ninotchka* is in dealing with both communism and capitalism. I believe that as a satire, it is insightful and fair-minded and witty in mocking the flaws of both systems. Although it is clearly made from the viewpoint of a director and writers in the capitalist camp, Wilder and Ernst Lubitsch were not ideologues but satirists and are often acutely critical of the capitalist way of life. But how much does Walsh's criticism, by extrapolation, apply to the political approach of Wilder's work in general, as a screenwriter and as a director?

Lubitsch and Wilder shared a disdain for authority and convention, and both were antitotalitarian. Their satirical perspective benefited from being, to varying degrees, skeptical and iconoclastic Jewish outsiders throughout their lives. Lubitsch's appalled reaction to Stalinism when the director, who had grown up as a Russian citizen, visited the USSR in 1936 had a strong influence on *Ninotchka*. Wilder's political acumen and theoretical hostility toward Stalinism helped make the film a biting as well as knowledgeable critique of the humorless inhumanity of the central character. When she softens under the influence of the essentially worthless but charming gigolo in Paris, that development is a combination of the best and most characteristic elements of both Lubitsch and Wilder. It's the kind of romantic situation with social overtones Wilder would replicate in many of his other films as writer and director.

Maurice Zolotow's 1977 biography defines Wilder's politics when he was working on the screenplay of *Ninotchka*:

Billy's political feelings at this time were on the radical side. He thought of himself as a "social democrat" in the European sense. He had vague sympathies for socialism and was almost a fellow traveler. Egon Erwin Kisch [the leftist political journalist and author who was a friend and mentor of Wilder in Berlin] had made him see the promise of socialism and Kisch believed that, in the long run, the Soviet Union would become a free, democratic society. Billy was for the Spanish Loyalists and he was of course a passionate anti-Nazi. However, he did not like to join organizations. He did not like meetings. He was, however, on friendly terms with many Communist and left-leaning writers. He recalls now that several of them ceased talking politics to him after *Ninotchka*. He thinks that Communists, by and large, lack a sense of humor. It was sacrilege to poke fun at them.

The Brackett-Wilder screenplay *Arise, My Love* is politically committed but shallow in its depiction of the issues surrounding fascism and the Spanish Civil War. Its flag-waving speechifying about those issues and the coming of World War II, which makes its political aspects seem trite and overwrought today, was de rigueur for a Hollywood film that took a rare venture into the still-controversial subject matter of Spain in that period. The political rhetoric of their war drama *Five Graves to Cairo*, one of the first films Wilder directed, indulges in a similar kind of rote flag-waving, although relatively limited for a war film of that period. Wilder usually found that approach antithetical to his creative interests, as he told the U.S. Army before making *A Foreign Affair* in the aftermath of the war. Although committed to American democratic values, he usually reserved his right to criticize their violation, and his general resistance to waving the flag was inherent in the skeptical personality he had developed over his peripatetic lifetime.

Aside from its disturbingly propagandistic ending, *Five Graves* mostly is a wryly ironic drama about the British officer spying on the Germans while in disguise as one of the enemy; it offers a sophisticated portrayal of low-key heroism. And Erich von Stroheim's portrait of the suave, canny Field Marshal Rommel, the one German military commander whose brilliance as a strategist attracted admiration from the Allies, is unusually complex for a Hollywood film in wartime (although Rommel's giving away of the intelligence secret of the story by boasting within earshot of the spy is a flaw in the film, uncharacteristically imprudent for Rommel as well as dramatically too convenient). *Five Graves to Cairo* represented the kind of contribution to the war effort through entertainment that was expected from a Hollywood director not in uniform. It and Wilder's partnership with Brackett probably helped protect him during the postwar Hollywood Red Scare. And even *Arise, My Love* did not get Wilder in trouble with the witch-hunters. It backs the Allied cause so vociferously and was released well enough into World War II for its support of the defeated Republican cause in Spain not to brand Brackett and Wilder as "premature antifascists," in the Orwellian language of the blacklist era.

Five Graves also was partly Wilder's attempt to pay his dues as a newly minted American citizen who was not eager to get into uniform. His reluctance to enlist during a period when his Hollywood directing career was being launched could be regarded as opportunistic. That he felt some guilt over not serving is evident in the reports in Brackett's diaries of Wilder unfairly blaming his collaborator for keeping him out of uniform. Although Brackett thought Wilder could have more influence making films in Hollywood than serving in a token role in the army, Brackett snidely commented that "to tell the truth[,] enlistment as a soldier would have been unsure considering Billy's neuroses."

Serving belatedly with the U.S. Army in Germany and Austria at the end of the war, albeit as a civilian, may have helped assuage whatever guilt Wilder may have felt for not being a combatant. But it's hard to stand in retrospective judgment of a Jewish filmmaker who had tried and failed to persuade his mother to leave Austria before she was killed by the Nazis. Indeed, one of Wilder's main goals in going to conquered Europe in 1945 was to try to learn what had happened to her, an effort largely in vain, since he never knew for certain where she had died, thinking it may have been in the Kraków ghetto or Auschwitz or Terezin and not knowing the evidence that she actually died in the Plaszów camp. In any event, Wilder had to live with the feeling that "I could have maybe saved my mother—but I didn't dare because then there would have been one more."

As Nancy Steffen-Fluhr puts it, Wilder buries beneath the haunted surface of his body of work obsessive "images of the death he chose not to die, of the escape that was forever fettered to abandonment. Over and over, he does the moral calculus. . . . 'I didn't dare because then there would have been one more [dead Jew].' . . . Wilder's World War II–era films are palimpsests, located in the present and the past—America and Europe—simultaneously."

"ONE MORE BLACKLISTEE"

The confusion over where Wilder stood politically was intensified by his widely reported quips to the media about sociopolitical subjects, which tended to treat such topics with sarcasm and iconoclastic mockery, often with biting insight but sometimes making his viewpoint seem more flippant than serious. People often tend to read too much into artists' work from what they say about it or their own personalities, but especially in the case of a celebrated wit such as Wilder, it's tempting to let his witticisms take the place of a more nuanced analysis.

In particular, a couple of notorious quips Wilder made about the Hollywood blacklist have caused considerable confusion and doubt, since they deal with the most serious political crisis in the history of Hollywood. Asked what he thought of the Hollywood Ten—the first victims of the blacklist, who were called "unfriendly" witnesses and sent to prison for contempt of Congress because they refused to cooperate with HUAC's postwar anticommunist investigation—Wilder said, "Two of them have talent. The rest are just unfriendly." That was how Zolotow recorded the remark in his biography of Wilder. Reminding the reader of Wilder's principled opposition to HUAC and blacklisting and his supporting the Committee for the First Amendment in defending the Hollywood Ten, Zolotow writes, "But he just couldn't keep a civil, or civil rights, tongue in his head." A similar version of Wilder's quip was reported by Ezra Goodman, whose 1961 book, *The Fifty-Year Decline and Fall of Hollywood*, quotes him as adding, "Blacklist, schmacklist, as long as they're all working" (he was referring to how some blacklisted writers had been working through fronts).

Those remarks, which Wilder never disavowed, were so glibly insulting that some people have assumed he was in favor of the blacklist or at least irresponsibly indifferent toward it. In fact, he was strongly and openly opposed to the blacklist, which the studios instituted in November 1947 following the sensational Washington hearings conducted by HUAC from October 20 to 30. Wilder took stands during the postwar Red Scare that required unusual courage, particularly since he was an immigrant. So why did he make those callous wisecracks about the Hollywood Ten? Wilder of course was known for his caustic remarks on a wide variety of subjects, and as a noted wit he was not prone to censor his characteristic irreverence no matter what the subject, even Adolf Hitler. But his jokes about the incendiary issue of the blacklist seemed to raise and demand serious questions and analysis. The blacklist deeply affected all of Hollywood in the 1940s and 1950s, including Wilder himself by inhibiting his ability to deal frankly with political subject matter, and the fear it engendered has had a lasting effect on American film-making. It continues to affect Hollywood by helping discourage the treatment of serious adult material in a market now aimed primarily at juveniles.

When I proposed in 1994 to our Los Angeles Film Critics Association that we give Wilder our career achievement award, a veteran member of the group, Dorothy Rochmis, objected in correspondence with me, angrily denouncing him for those remarks. In her view, he was not being sufficiently committed on that issue while he remained prolific during the blacklist period, which made him doubly culpable in her eyes. Nor did she appreciate Wilder's work, which I thought she tended to see through the prism of that issue while she quoted critic David Thomson's description of Wilder in his *Biographical Dictionary of Film* as "a heartless exploiter of public taste who manipulates situation in the name of satire. He prefers dialogue to character, sniping to structure." I researched the matter and answered Rochmis with a lengthy letter summarizing Wilder's political positions and viewpoint, but even though our group ultimately gave him our award in January 1995, I was not able to convince my colleague that Wilder actually was a fervent opponent of the blacklist or that his later flippant remarks about it, though regrettable, did not define where he stood politically throughout his life.

The belated publication of an edited version of Brackett's diaries in 2015 revealed just how bitter the political conflict over HUAC and the blacklist was between the writing partners and how central it was to causing their final breakup in 1950. The diaries record personal friction between them almost from the beginning of their work together in 1936, and ongoing strife that often prompted Brackett to swear (privately) he would not work with Wilder anymore, along with Brackett's expressions of anti-Semitism and other evidence of contempt toward Wilder. But after all this, it was the onset of the 1947 HUAC investigation that marked the true beginning of the end for them.

Although they had never seen eye-to-eye on most political issues, since Brackett was an old-line Republican and Wilder a fervent liberal, they had been united on one important political cause, the formation of the Screen Writers Guild in the late 1930s, a deeply divisive issue when Hollywood labor was organizing during the Great Depression. In the successful effort to achieve certification to represent screenwriters in bargaining with the studios, Brackett and Wilder and the other militant early members of the SWG had to overcome fierce opposition from the studios, who were supporting a rival company union set up by MGM executive Irving Thalberg, the Screen Playwrights. Brackett was SWG vice-president in 1937–1938 and president in 1938–1939, and Wilder was an active supporter of the fledgling organization. But like many others in the guild, Brackett failed to be sympathetic to the left-wing screenwriters later targeted by HUAC.

Wilder and Brackett vehemently disagreed over whether HUAC had the right to investigate the political beliefs of screenwriters and others in Hollywood. As an immigrant who cherished his liberties under the Constitution, Wilder was outraged by the committee's infringement of freedom of speech and expression, but Brackett, with his conservative views that sometimes tended toward the reactionary, defended the committee, infuriating his writing partner. Brackett argued in his diary in October 1947 that the HUAC hearings were not violating the Bill of Rights in demanding expressions of political allegiance: "It doesn't seem to me that to have to state things is a denial of freedom. That there are certain instances where you can't say 'None of your damned business.' I developed a thesis that the right of free speech also carries a complementary duty of expression." Furthermore, the anticommunist Brackett seemed willing to accept the blacklisting of those accused of communist sympathies who were unwilling or unable to "clear" themselves by naming names of colleagues and cooperating with the committee in what Victor S. Navasky, in his 1980 book *Naming Names*, describes as its "degradation ceremonies."

As the political climate heated up in Hollywood in early 1947, Wilder predicted to Brackett that they would have more violent political arguments than ever before, since the project they were working on was *A Foreign Affair*. That film began shooting on location in Berlin in August and September, but work on the script continued, as well as the shooting at Paramount. Sure enough, during filming in December, Brackett recorded to his horror, "Suddenly I find my own picture doing the very kind of things the Unfriendly Witnesses were hauled up before Congress for." Evidently he was alluding to the film's satire of the prudish right-wing member of Congress from Iowa, Phoebe Frost (Jean Arthur), its mockery of her shock over what she considers morally dubious activities among GIs occupying Germany, and its complex critique of the muddled American efforts to reform postwar Germany. Brackett felt that Wilder, whom he called "that ill-mannered, egotistical, vital, slightly mad creature," by February 1947 already was "pushing me out of his life." Their arguments reached the point of crisis when the public HUAC hearings began in October, following secret testimony in Los Angeles that May by members of the militantly anticommunist Motion Picture Alliance for the Preservation of American Ideals and others who provided HUAC with names of alleged motion picture industry communists.

Nineteen Hollywood figures were subpoenaed in September to testify as what became known as "unfriendly" witnesses, although only eleven were called to testify (the one member of that group who avoided going to prison for contempt of Congress was Bertolt Brecht, who immediately left for Europe after testifying and settled in East Germany). Along with such other prominent liberal directors as John Huston, William Wyler, and George Stevens, Wilder worked behind the scenes to give advice and encouragement to their subpoenaed colleagues about how to deal with HUAC. That kind of activity Brackett characterized as "saving the world for the Politburo." Wilder was a member of the Committee for the First Amendment, a group spearheaded by screenwriter Philip Dunne, Wyler, and Huston to combat the hearings and the influence of the Motion Picture Alliance. Wilder's activities on behalf of the Hollywood Nineteen—and the eventual Hollywood Ten—were brave in that climate.

Another courageous move by Wilder was his defiance of the 1950 attempt by Cecil B. DeMille and a group of other right-wing directors to impose a loyalty oath on the members of the SDG and recall guild president Joseph L. Mankiewicz, who opposed the oath. That was part of a drive by the Motion Picture Alliance to require a noncommunist oath from everyone in the film industry. Wilder signed a petition of twenty-five SDG members needed to call for a general meeting in opposition to that move. The signatures were gathered, with some difficulty, by Mankiewicz allies headed by Huston. Wilder's fellow immigrant colleagues who signed the petition were Wyler, Fred Zinnemann, Walter Reisch, Jean Negulesco, Charles Vidor, Andrew Marton, Peter Ballbusch, and Otto Lang.* Ironically, the petition contained

---

* The other petitioners were Huston, H. C. Potter, Michael Gordon, George Seaton, Maxwell Shane, Mark Robson, Richard Brooks, John Sturges, Felix Feist, Robert Wise, Robert Parrish, Richard Fleischer, Joseph Losey, Nicholas Ray, Don Hartman, and John Farrow.

a loyalty oath they all took in order to be considered in good standing with the guild. Under the circumstances, with the blacklist in effect and the Korean War underway, it was a major career risk for foreign-born directors such as Wilder and the others to oppose blacklisting over the issue of a loyalty oath, when they knew that nativist reactionaries such as DeMille would call into question their loyalty as naturalized American citizens.

The membership meeting on October 22 resulted in a tumultuous debate, with discrediting attacks on DeMille by George Stevens, Huston, Wyler, John Ford, and others, but did not prevent the imposition of the oath soon thereafter. At the meeting, DeMille read a list of alleged Communist front groups with which he said some of the petitioners had been affiliated. Then, "to accentuate the fact that we weren't born in this country," as Zinnemann put it, DeMille mocked the accents of foreign-born directors at the meeting in reading the names of the petitioners, calling them "Vilder," "Vyler," "Tzinnemann," et al., which Mankiewicz and others interpreted as a display of anti-Semitism. Rouben Mamoulian, a founder of the guild who had emigrated from Russian Georgia to England and the United States, told me in 1985, "It was the first time anybody had ever mentioned my accent. That man sat there with his red face—it was a terrible moment, and it has haunted me all this time. DeMille said we should be governed by real Americans, that there were too many accents, and I said I was a better American than he was, because he was just born here and I *chose* the place."

The audience "booed [DeMille] until he sat down," Mankiewicz remembered. "When DeMille heard those boos, he knew the meeting had turned against him. He was beat." On a motion by Ford, the board of directors resigned, and a newly elected board soon took their place. The twenty-five signers of the petition supporting Mankiewicz—the men DeMille had vilified—were given a vote of confidence at the general membership meeting. Mankiewicz remained president, but in an act of capitulation he never adequately explained, he recommended four days later that the guild members sign the loyalty oath "as a voluntary act." It was ratified by the membership in May 1951, remaining part of the bylaws until 1966, when the U.S. Supreme Court upheld a lower court's ruling that the guild could not deny membership to directors who refused to sign it.

Wilder's casting of DeMille as himself in 1950's *Sunset Blvd.* is strangely generous under the circumstances. DeMille plays an avuncular old pro who bears little resemblance to the vengeful reactionary and leading proponent of the blacklist he actually was. His moving and nuanced performance as a longtime colleague who tries to humor Norma Desmond may have been another attempt at protective coloration on Wilder's part, like his long professional partnership with the conservative Brackett, which continued despite their friction over HUAC. It was a time when blacklist opponents, however courageous, were facing potential ruination of their lives, and some were taking various forms of self-defensive action. If that was what Wilder was trying to do, those moves helped insulate him from blacklisting.

Wilder's passionate commitment to American constitutional protections of freedom of speech and political association as an immigrant who loved and felt grateful to his adopted country was something the blue-blooded, reactionary Brackett appeared unable to comprehend. The vehemence and intemperance, the even hateful nature of Brackett's attitudes toward his writing partner and the witnesses being persecuted in the HUAC hearings is disheartening to witness in his diaries. On October 27, 1947, Brackett and Wilder had a bitter argument over whether screenwriter Dalton Trumbo (the most prominent member of the Ten) had the right not to cooperate while testifying before HUAC, as he defiantly did the following day. Brackett wrote, "I voiced my opinion that the congressional committee had a right to ask him whether he was a communist, whereupon Billy had a complete tantrum, saying that if that was so, this wasn't the country he'd been lead [*sic*] to believe it was, and he'd prefer to go back home. We lunched together somewhat silently." On November 2, while they were discussing the Committee for the First Amendment's recent "Hollywood Fights Back" radio broadcast defending the Bill of Rights, "Billy informed me that he wasn't a communist but he gave considerably to the left, which makes him a Fellow Traveler I should think."

Small wonder it was two days later that Wilder told Brackett, "This is the last picture we will do together [*A Foreign Affair*; as it happened, they went on to do *Sunset Blvd.* after that]. I want to do things more politically daring than you would permit. . . . I am no longer afraid." Brackett "heard this with a mixture of consternation and relief, for the stress of laboring on this picture has been hellish. We resumed writing." Brackett was recording that Wilder showed "great coldness" toward him and that working together again was "a prospect that makes my innards curl. All fun has gone out of the relationship." On November 23 Brackett found "Billy in a very belligerent (pro-Communist) mood" as a result of learning that the motion picture companies were planning to institute a blacklist, which they decided on and announced November 25 as the Waldorf Statement following their two-day meeting at New York's Waldorf-Astoria Hotel. On the day of the announcement, Brackett wrote, "Billy seemed to have convinced himself during the night that I was Congressman Rankin"—the racist, anti-Semitic congressman John Rankin (D-Mississippi) was a leading figure in the establishment of HUAC as a standing committee of Congress—"and it was a day of bitter storms, in which he [Wilder] said, among other things, 'I spit upon the Congress of the United States.'"

The vehemence of that remark is shocking for an émigré who valued his newfound freedoms in the United States but understandable because he saw them under such threat. As Gerd Gemünden writes in *Continental Strangers*, "The experience of the Red Scare shook many exiles' faith in the democratic foundations of the United States, a country they had eagerly made their home during the 1930s. Many of them considered a permanent return to Germany, because they no longer felt at home in their adopted country." But Wilder, for all his unhappiness over what was happening in the United States, was not one of those who after the war considered returning to live in Germany. America was his home, for better or worse, and though he was willing to work in Germany, he could not re-embrace the country that had carried out the Holocaust.

The fact that Wilder, after *A Foreign Affair*, continued working with the politically hostile Brackett on yet another film under such conditions is remarkable. Probably he did so for a combination of reasons. One was that from October 1946 onward they were planning to write that pet project, the film about Hollywood that would become *Sunset Blvd.*, their final work together. Collaborations have ways of keeping themselves going even when they are acrimonious yet still creative, as Gilbert and Sullivan and many other teams have demonstrated. And remaining in partnership with Brackett, however distasteful it may have been for Wilder, was prudent in a time of peril when he otherwise might have been scrutinized by Congress and the studios as what Brackett called a "Fellow Traveler."

Many Hollywood liberals shamed themselves in the blacklist period, trying to protect their careers by betraying their friends, writing contrite letters to studios, or otherwise trying to clear their names of suspect associations. When I asked the great blacklisted writer-director Abraham Lincoln Polonsky how liberals behaved during that period, he said, "The liberals were the worst." There is no evidence of Wilder taking any such craven actions during the blacklist era, but his stated desire in 1947 to make "more politically daring" films, at least about the contemporary political scene, faltered due to the commercial and critical failure of his first film apart from his old partner, *Ace in the Hole*.

That darkly comical drama about an unscrupulous newspaper reporter, Chuck Tatum (Kirk Douglas), who causes a man's death by creating a media circus, is Wilder's boldest and most ferocious film. "I can handle big news and little news," Tatum boasts while applying to the editor for the job. "If there's no news, I'll go out and bite a dog. . . . I'm a pretty good liar. Done a lot of lying in my time." *Ace* is a blistering, uncompromising exposé of corruption in the media, law enforcement, and the American public at large, three major targets indeed. Wilder hits all of them squarely and hard, at a time when the blacklist was intensifying in Hollywood with a new round of HUAC hearings in 1951. David Walsh observed in his obituary of Douglas for the *World Socialist Web Site* in 2020 that *Ace in the Hole* was "influenced, one would assume, by the media's foul role in generating the [Red Scare] hysteria of the late 1940s and early 1950s, although it approaches the issue of deceitfully manipulating public opinion only by way of allegory." While *Ace* is one of Wilder's best films, and one of his personal favorites, its fierce rejection by the American public (unlike its favorable reception in Europe) made him wary of overly controversial political subject matter.

Did Wilder, after taking a strong and courageous public stand against the blacklist while the issue was being debated in 1947–1950, when even his writing partner considered him subversive, retreat into allegory (in *Ace in the Hole* and *Stalag 17*, which is about informing) and public silence (accompanied with defensive bursts of sarcasm) about the political situation in Hollywood when the blacklist took firm hold on the industry? Yes. Could he have done more than he did overtly to combat the blacklist? It can be argued that the only truly honorable course for any employable person in Hollywood during that era would have been to refuse to work there while others were denied work. Like others who continued working during that period, he could not openly defy the blacklist or he would have had to be blacklisted himself or quit the business. Wilder stopped fighting it directly. Nor, as far as is known, did he work with any blacklisted writers under the table or through fronts. And his work suffered in the 1950s from his generally less than noble acquiescence to the corrupt status quo of safe, relatively uncontroversial filmmaking. To paraphrase what Steffen-Fluhr wrote about Wilder's futile attempt to save his mother, he may have felt that to defy the blacklist any further would mean only "one more blacklistee."

"AN EPITAPH ON AN EMOTION"

Perhaps Wilder may have resorted to a wisecrack or two on the subject several years later as part of his characteristic way of masking his true feelings about a painful subject and/or as a way of dealing with such pain. Michael Wilmington and I noted in 1970 that in *One, Two, Three*,

> Wilder makes nihilistic sport of every political and moral idea and ideal held by each of the conflicting characters, and his gags about Nazis are surprisingly flippant for an Austrian Jew who lost members of his family in Auschwitz [he and we then thought they had died there]. Wilder's profusion of gags seems to mask a desperation—a fear, perhaps of telling the truth about his own emotions. If everything is foolish, then nothing is unbearable. (We recall Nietzsche's words, "A joke is an epitaph on an emotion.") Only in the superb, unjustly slighted *Ace in the Hole* does Wilder give full vent to the disgust buried deep beneath his blasé exterior.

I now believe that some of the gags about ex-Nazis in *One, Two, Three* are actually quite caustic and that Wilder was able to give vent to his deepest feelings in his postwar films more often than I realized at that early stage in my study of his work; furthermore, the article was written before the release of *The Private Life of Sherlock Holmes* and other profoundly moving later Wilder films. Wilder used satire and other forms of humor throughout his career as his way of dealing with the otherwise unbearable. Although he sometimes appeared overly flippant in his films or public comments, that tendency toward anesthetizing pain through sharp wit did not preclude his films from finding powerfully moving drama even in the midst of comedy.

Wilder's ability and determination to find comedy in the bleakest of circumstances is perhaps most striking in *A Foreign Affair*, a film that has acquired a greater reputation in recent years after having been largely overlooked. Wilder's daringly irreverent and idiosyncratic approach distinguishes it from other examples of the postwar *Trümmerfilm* (rubble film) genre that tend to treat the subject with unrelentingly grimness. It is especially remarkable that a Jewish director could make such an iconoclastic mixture of comedy and drama while returning to the bombed-out city where he lived before fleeing Hitler. Released in June 1948, the political satire was neglected by Paramount because it was such a hot potato. It evoked displeasure from the U.S. Congress and the army for its irreverent view of both institutions, including its scathing mockery of the right-wing Iowa congresswoman and its frank depiction of GI corruption in the ruins of Berlin. The film's complex view of Germans and Nazism and its unflinching look at the effects of Allied bombing of civilian areas also made some people uneasy, as Wilder intended.

A Foreign Affair has found a new audience for its bracingly honest, black-humored approach to its subject matter. Wilder's experiences in Berlin both before and after the war allowed him an unusually enlightened and unflinching perspective on a wide range of American political attitudes in dealing with the conquered enemy. And in dealing with the Germans themselves, Wilder's artistry, as usual, prevents him from simply expressing the rage he felt personally but enables him to create a complex portrait of people trying to survive amid the rubble while making further moral compromises.

Wilder's own experience in the army enabled him to create a generally sympathetic portrait of the realistically unpuritanical commanding officer. Millard Mitchell's mature and worldly Colonel Plummer takes a tolerant view of his men's sex lives with German women, at odds with pious military propaganda. Yet he cold-bloodedly uses the compromised Army Intelligence officer (John Lund) as a cat's-paw to snare a fugitive ex-Nazi, Hans Otto Birgel (Peter von Zerneck), who was also the lover of Marlene Dietrich's Erika von Schlütow. *A Foreign Affair* seems astonishing today in its bracing lack of the usual American sentimentality, political cant, and hypocrisy about the war and postwar politics. Knowing of Brackett's behind-the-scenes political feuding with Wilder in that period, and Brackett's outrage over Wilder's graphic bluntness in depicting the sadomasochistic sexual relationship between Lund and Dietrich's former Nazi sympathizer, it is tempting to consider the satire of the straitlaced Republican congresswoman Phoebe Frost partly as Wilder getting back at Brackett.

A Foreign Affair and other Brackett-Wilder scripts dealing overtly with political themes are mostly exceptions in their canon, however. *The Emperor Waltz* (a film Brackett could not understand Wilder's reasons for making) deals with matters of state in the Austro-Hungarian Empire in a more purely comedic, but crushingly unfunny, manner, seemingly because Wilder, subconsciously or not, had other concerns on his mind (i.e., the Holocaust). But mostly the Wilder films of his 1942–1950 period are political in the sense that such later films as *The Apartment* and *Kiss Me, Stupid* are, as acute examinations of sociopolitical ills seen through the prism of individual lives. Filmmaking that dramatizes the moral issues surrounding how people should treat each other, particularly in male-female relationships (as in Lubitsch's work), is profoundly political, because it deals with society at its root level, exploring such human situations as class barriers, greed, jealousy, sexual betrayals, and other kinds of deception.

Double Indemnity and *Sunset Blvd.* paint deeply insightful portraits of the seamy side of Los Angeles culture from the dual perspectives of protagonists ensnared in the corruption of the insurance business and the film industry. Wilder draws visual and moral parallels between the two businesses in those films and *The Apartment*, making them examples of capitalism heartlessly preying on human weakness (the parallel extends to Wilder making the offices of the Pacific All-Risk Insurance Company in *Double Indemnity* a sly replica of Paramount's corporate headquarters in New York). Hitting the jackpot in an insurance scam, as Walter and Phyllis try to do, is not dissimilar to the corrupt dreams of big money that many people have when they come to Hollywood. As another European émigré director, Fritz Lang, acidulously commented in the 1960s, the American Dream "today is not what it once was" but had degenerated into the pursuit of wealth, "Or, to be very crude—but I'm afraid there is something in it—'How to commit the perfect crime and not get caught.'"

On the other hand, the 1945 Brackett and Wilder adaptation of *The Lost Weekend*, while digging deeply into the physical and psychological torment of an alcoholic, seems oddly distanced from other social issues. It avoids the war by keeping the story set around 1937, a year later than the time period of the Charles Jackson novel.* Viewers can be excused for missing the period of Wilder's film version, since the only date shown is in a flashback with a poster outside the Metropolitan Opera for the 1934–1935 season, and the events of Don Birnam's weekend take place in hermetic settings mostly unrelated to the greater world surrounding him.

THE "BASENESS OF THE CROWD"

The riskiness of overt social criticism in the blacklist era turned not only Wilder but many other writers for the screen and the stage more inward, toward dramas exploring complex psychological themes, as seen most notably in the work of Tennessee Williams, whose landmark plays help define the American artistic landscape of the late 1940s and the 1950s. Steering largely clear of topical material in that period had a mixed effect on Wilder's career, for while he tended to find his subject matter after the calamitous reception of *Ace in the Hole* in stage or literary successes, he dealt more adventurously than before with sexual and romantic themes, sometimes with a focus on class issues, as in his Audrey Hepburn films drawn from a successful play and a popular novel. Although *Sabrina* and *Love in the Afternoon* are not among his best work, going in that direction at least helped Wilder develop, however fitfully, toward the more artistically successful romantic comedies and dramas he made with Diamond in later years.

One partial exception to Wilder's avoidance of hot-button political themes in "The Time of the Toad," as Trumbo called the blacklist years, was the film with which the director followed *Ace in the Hole*, *Stalag 17*, based on the play by Donald Bevan and Edmund Trzcinski. Nazis were relatively safe targets of satire by that time, and the German characters are portrayed in a mostly comical vein that is intensified in the play adaptation by Wilder and Edwin Blum. The Germans include Wilder's strutting colleague and fellow Jewish Viennese refugee Otto Preminger as the camp commandant, Colonel von Scherbach, and Sig Ruman as a sergeant named Johann Sebastian Schulz who

---

* Similarly, *Double Indemnity*, although released during the war, is set in 1936; the novel was written in 1936.

pretends to be chummy with the Americans while helping the informer among their ranks betray them. Casting Preminger and Ruman involves movie jokes: Preminger deliciously satirizes his infamous reputation as a sadistic director, and Ruman, while playing "Concentration Camp" Ehrhardt in Lubitsch's *To Be or Not to Be*, shouts "Schultz!" repeatedly, calling haplessly for his aide, most hilariously after failing in a suicide attempt. The sneering anti-Semitism of Preminger's colonel is displayed early in *Stalag 17*, in one of the wittier references the screenwriters added to the play: "Nasty weather we are having? And I so much hoped we could give you a white Christmas, just like the ones you used to know. Aren't those the words that clever little man wrote, the one who stole his name from our capital, that something or other Berlin?"

Stalag 17 is overly broad in its farcical aspects, especially with its grossly unfunny indulgence of Robert Strauss's aptly named buffoon, "Animal," a role (considerably expanded from his stage part) that brought him an Oscar nomination for supporting actor. The film later probably helped inspire the TV sitcom *Hogan's Heroes*, although a lawsuit by the playwrights for plagiarism was unsuccessful. But though Wilder's film is not nearly as trenchant in its depiction of the Nazis as *To Be or Not to Be*, its actual raison d'être for the director seems to have been to comment (without being too obvious) on the political situation closer to home, the blacklist. The drama revolves around the men's attempt to uncover the identity of the informer in their midst. Hollywood was rife with informers in that period, and many American films of the 1950s, while unable to deal directly with the political corruption of their own industry, nevertheless concentrate on themes of betrayal and informing in one form or another, usually in interpersonal relationships. Wilder borrowed these themes from a period piece that had already been popular on Broadway. Utilizing a "safe," pretested property has always been a traditional way of making difficult or unusual themes acceptable in Hollywood. And even in a time of such general repressiveness, treating social issues in the disguise of other genres, especially period pieces such as the war film or the Western, provided a further level of safety and plausible deniability. Such strategies enabled a director opposed to blacklisting to convey his disgust and dramatize its damaging effect on the human psyche.

The central character in *Stalag 17*, Sefton (William Holden in an Oscar-winning performance), is a cynic who makes no attempt to befriend any of his fellow POWs other than a stammering young stooge named Cookie (future sportscaster Gil Stratton Jr.), a hero-worshipper who narrates the story. Cookie is so ignorant that he complains in his opening narration, "I don't know about you, but it always makes me sore when I see those war pictures. . . . What gets me is that there never was a movie about POWs— about prisoners of war." That line is apparently not intended ironically but is a rather dismaying bit of American cultural chauvinism. François Truffaut, reviewing *Stalag 17* in 1954, wrote sarcastically of two POWs who attempt to break out by digging a tunnel that they "have not seen *Grande Illusion*." Wilder obviously had seen Jean Renoir's film, however, since Preminger's Colonel von Scherbach is a sly and often hilarious parody of Stroheim's Captain von Rauffenstein in the 1937 French classic.

Sefton is a hard case from a Boston working-class background with a major chip on his shoulder—he despises on sight the upper-crust Boston airman thrown into their midst, Lt. James Dunbar, played by Don Taylor—and a talent for running various kinds of rackets and con games with his fellow inmates so he can barter for food with the enemy. That earns Sefton their contempt and results in their unjust suspicion that he is the informer, which leads to a savage group beating similar to that in Stanley Kubrick's *Full Metal Jacket* (1987), one of Wilder's favorite modern films. It is telling that in Wilder's interview book with Crowe, when asked which of his characters he felt closest to, the director replied, "I liked Holden in *Stalag 17*. . . . I loved Holden in *Stalag 17*. . . . My love will always be with Mr. Holden." And Wilder once joked when Holden asked his advice about whether he should buy a painting, "If I were you—and I am. . . ."

Although Sefton on first glance may appear to be little more than a louse, like Wilder he is a realist, unsentimental, uninterested in currying favor with people he despises. Sefton is much cooler and more sardonic than he is in the play, in which he indulges in some violent outbursts. In the film he plays his emotional cards close to his vest and enjoys fleecing his foolish comrades with his elaborate scams, which the film amplifies considerably. Sefton bids them a sardonic farewell as he escapes at the end, telling them, "If I ever run into any of you bums on a street corner, just let's pretend we never met before. Understand?" He disappears into the tunnel but pops up again to give them a cheery little salute. This could be considered the final irony or, as Andrew Sarris complained, the ultimate proof that Wilder is "too cynical to believe even his own cynicism." Holden chafed at playing the role, finding Sefton in the play too unlikable, "just a con man without any motivation for the deals he's pulling"—an especially ironic example of how little actors often understand the quality of their parts. He also asked Wilder, "Couldn't I have a line or two that would show Sefton really hates the Germans?" Wilder didn't go that far but may have indulged Holden's unease a bit at the end, although that depends on how you interpret Sefton's parting gesture: Crowe finds it "a great 'I love you,'" and Wilder agrees, but Ed Sikov calls it "a sarcastic little salute, a final *screw you*." What makes it so memorable, like the best of Wilder, is that it's both simultaneously—it's ambivalent.

Truffaut, as a young reviewer in France, appreciated the film's implicit as well as explicit political themes and admired "the haughty skeptic" Sefton. He considered *Stalag 17* "a harsh and uncompromising film" that examines the role of the solitary intelligent man in a world of "idiots . . . his simpleminded companions. Sefton is not vulgar, and that seems fishy; he's intelligent, and that makes him unusual; he's a loner, and that's disturbing. . . . For the first time in films the philosophy of the solitary man is elaborated; this film is an apologia for individualism." While noting that Wilder dramatizes the "baseness of the crowd" that leads to lynchings, Truffaut admired his departure from the conventional viewpoint portraying the leaders of such mobs as "contemptible." He pointed out how Wilder focuses on the kinds of characters the audience traditionally finds sympathetic (prisoners) to serve as the lynch mob and on Sefton's desire "to get away from the companions whom he despises. . . . What can be more dreadful than good folk who take justice into their own hands? What is worse than this moral superiority born of a clear conscience and a certainty of total innocence? . . . The depravity of the group versus the individual's moral solitude, is this not a large theme?"

Sefton is willing to endure the contempt of his comrades, though he reacts by conducting his own investigation to reveal the actual informer played by Peter Graves, a German-born POW who had lived in Cleveland and masquerades as a fellow American airman named Price. When the men realize how unjust they have been to Sefton, they barely apologize, and he doesn't care anyway. Instead he arranges to help Dunbar escape while they use Price as a decoy and as a bonus let the German spy be mown down by his own men, who mistake him for an escaping American. Unlike in the play, Wilder and Blum show no compunction about that action. In the play the men argue over the morality of what Hoffy (the level-headed barracks leader) considers "cold-blooded murder," telling the others, "Let's not act like Krauts!" But he changes his mind when reminded that he's been wrong all along about Price. In the film, the only concern Wilder shows over the morality of their action is to have Hoffy (Richard Erdman) hesitate briefly while the men remind him of Price's treachery. Then he tells them, "It's all yours."

Wilder regards their verdict as similar to the ruination of the Nazi capital, Berlin, by the American and British air forces and Sherlock Holmes's equally ruthless dispatching of the squad of seven German spies at the end of *The Private Life of Sherlock Holmes* (but the detective is shattered when he learns of the execution of the spy he loved, even though she betrayed him). Wilder's political viewpoint as an American immigrant Jew who lost members of his family in the Holocaust manifests itself in his unsentimental lack of sympathy for the lives of German combatants and even (in *A Foreign Affair*) his lack of outrage over the killing of civilians. That an informer pays the ultimate price for his betrayal in *Stalag 17* is also a sign of Wilder's contempt for those who betrayed his and their comrades in Hollywood.

Stalag 17 marked a turning point in Wilder's career, with his refusal to accede to a shameful political demand by Paramount. It led to a rupture with the studio where he had been working for seventeen years. As Zolotow relates, the director received a note from George Weltner, president of Paramount International, the studio's foreign sales division:

> Weltner wanted to make a special dubbed version of *Stalag 17* for German release. Germany was now a rich market for Hollywood pictures. Weltner suggested that Wilder change the Nazi spy into a *Polish prisoner of war who has sold out to the Nazis!*
>
> Wilder dictated a letter in white heat [with copies to Paramount's president, Barney Balaban, and vice-president in charge of production, Y. Frank Freeman]. He told about his own background in Galicia, and about what the Nazis had done to the Jews. [Wilder recalled that he also wrote that "the Nazis killed my mother, my grandmother, and my stepfather in Auschwitz, and I was not ready to betray my film for the possibility of a few shabby dollars in Germany."] He was proud of the Jewish resistance in Warsaw. Not only would he not make this change but unless he received an apology he would sever his connection with Paramount.

He got no apology [or any other response]. He walked out on the best contract a writer-director ever had. . . . His honor had been impugned.

And so after twenty years, he drove his Jaguar . . . through the Bronson Gate, never to return.

As Volker Schlöndorff put it, "That's the true Billy Wilder. No cynic, but a moralist with an uncompromising sense of decency." For the rest of his career, Wilder was a freelance director. It is satisfying to report that his principled decision made him both happier and freer.

After making films for Fox and Warners, Wilder found a more congenial home than Paramount when he began working with the Mirisch brothers when they were executives at Allied Artists (AA). Joining such a small company was a sign of Wilder's boldness and desire for independence following his bitter experience with his longtime studio. AA had begun as the B-movie company Monogram and was branching out into more expensive, more ambitious pictures, signing not only Wilder but also William Wyler and John Huston, although Huston did not wind up making a film for AA. But *Love in the Afternoon* and Wyler's *Friendly Persuasion* (1956), both starring Gary Cooper, were box-office flops, and Walter Mirisch and his brothers Harold and Marvin left AA to form their Mirisch Company to release films through United Artists. The Mirisches made eight of the director's late films with UA, everything from *Some Like It Hot* through *Avanti!* Working mostly with Walter, Wilder enjoyed his rare degree of creative freedom in that period (aside from the drastic recutting of *The Private Life of Sherlock Holmes*) due to the Mirisches' faith in him and his clout in the industry, which had helped the producers establish their fledgling company.

"THE CHILDREN OF MARX AND COCA-COLA"

But that freedom could be a double-edged sword. The problem was demonstrated by the uninhibited approach that made Wilder's most overt political satire of his later years misfire. So what essentially went wrong with *One, Two, Three?* He kept the spine of the Molnár farce but drastically reshaped its social context. In updating the play from 1920s Paris to Cold War Berlin, Wilder and Diamond turned the banker into the politically conservative, morally slippery manager of the West Berlin Coca-Cola bottling plant, Cagney's MacNamara, who does a lightning renovation job on an angry young Communist. Otto Ludwig Piffl (Horst Buchholz) is transformed like a male Ninotchka, but in a farcical vein, frantically overeager, since Piffl is forced to make his radical change under pressure of time and expediency.

MacNamara engineers the fraud to further his own career, and deception is second-nature to this cynical businessman. He flagrantly cheats on his long-suffering wife, Phyllis (Arlene Francis), with his curvaceous German secretary, Fräulein Ingeborg (Lilo Pulver), and makes her accept it as his male prerogative. Phyllis calls him "Mein Führer." Cagney gives a spectacular performance as he pulls off MacNamara's brash manhandling of the pompous, slogan-spouting Marxist. MacNamara has to make Piffl a suitable marriage partner for an airheaded southern belle, the witlessly named Scarlett Hazeltine (Pamela Tiffin), the visiting daughter of MacNamara's boss (Howard St. John) from the home office in Atlanta. This farce revels in Cagney's lengthy monologue about the fancy clothing, jewelry, fake aristocratic title, and other trappings of capitalism he imposes on Piffl. The veteran star's machine-gun patter, while reminiscent of the gangsters he played at Warner Bros. in the 1930s, draws directly on Wilder's memories of the virtuosic stage star Max Pallenberg playing the role in the Molnár play in Berlin. The *One, Two, Three* screenplay indicates, "THIS PIECE MUST BE PLAYED MOLTO FURIOSO—AT A RAPID-FIRE, BREAKNECK TEMPO, SUGGESTED SPEED: 100 MILES AN HOUR—ON THE CURVES—140 MILES AN HOUR ON THE STRAIGHTAWAY." Cagney is fully up to the challenge, even more energetically charismatic than usual onscreen, but he found the experience so exhausting and aggravating that he did not play another film role for twenty years.

Diamond called *One, Two, Three* "an attempt to go back and do the kind of fast-paced comedy they were doing in the thirties. What we were really trying to do was *Front Page*. We wanted something with that kind of momentum. And, I don't know, maybe it was too much for an audience to absorb. That's a wearing picture, because it never stops. It just keeps moving for two hours. There are no quiet spots in it. And maybe that hurt it." The script has MacNamara do a riff on the famous last line of *The Front Page*, "The son of a bitch stole my watch!" MacNamara tells one of the Russians why Piffl is being held by the Stasi, "The son of a gun stole my cuckoo clock."

One, Two, Three is a comical illustration of Henry David Thoreau's maxim, "I say, beware of all enterprises that require new clothes, and not rather a new wearer of clothes." After Piffl puts up a fierce initial resistance to his make-over (he tells Scarlett, "I am a worker, not a gigolo! I will not take any money from you. . . . I will not be turned into a capitalist!"), the increasingly fren-zied young Communist becomes gung-ho in adopting his phony new iden-tity. That is part of the film's satirical perspective on what it portrays as the shallowness of both political systems. But while reserving its most pointed jabs toward communism and the lingering influence of Nazism in postwar Germany, it tends to treat capitalist corruption with engaging indulgence. *One, Two, Three* is a distillation of Wilder's career-long obsession with the masquerade and reinvention of character, the raison d'être of its farcical plot. Molnár's one-act, one-note play is clever but without the subtlety of *The Guardsman*, his romantic comedy about impersonation that Wilder acknowl-edged as one of his greatest influences.

One, Two, Three lacks the acidulous satirical insight of *A Foreign Affair* into the tangle of postwar politics, let alone that film's rare achievement of mixing inflammatory political humor with potent romantic drama, but Wild-er's farce pokes fun at what has been called "Coca-Cola colonialism" through Cagney's outrageously crass but engagingly roguish Ugly American. Jean-Luc Godard might have been thinking of this film when he referred to "The Chil-dren of Marx and Coca-Cola" in his 1966 *Masculin féminin*. Wilder broadly lampoons die-hard communism with such gags as a parade lifted from *Ninotchka* with marching throngs carrying banners, including "NIKITA UBER ALLES" over a picture of Soviet Premier Nikita Khrushchev. Showing Com-munists equating their own ideology with Nazism is the kind of cheap, dumb joke that backfires on the film. On the other hand, the banner "WAS IST LOS IN LITTLE ROCK?" makes a savvy reference to how Communists exploited America's racial unrest and the way that festering problem undercut Ameri-can propaganda about democratic values. And sometimes the film was so sophisticated politically that it became prescient. When Leon Askin's Perip-etchikoff offers MacNamara a Havana cigar, the Soviet commissar explains, "We have trade agreement with Cuba. They send us cigars—we send them rockets." MacNamara tries the cigar with distaste and tells him, "You know something? You guys got cheated. This is a pretty crummy cigar." The Soviet replies slyly, "Do not worry. We sent them pretty crummy rockets." Although

Wilder's film never reached the sustained satirical level of Stanley Kubrick's masterful 1964 black comedy *Dr. Strangelove*, it did predict 1962's Cuban Missile Crisis.

The gags about Cagney's German subordinate, Schlemmer (Hanns Lothar), most consistently hit the mark, showing how at home Wilder was with mocking Nazis. Schlemmer is an ex-SS man who exasperates MacNamara with his habitual heel-clicking but tries to pretend he didn't know anything about Hitler because he was only working in "the Underground"—by which he means the U-Bahn, or subway. MacNamara also blackmails a prying newspaper reporter from the *Berliner Tageblatt*, Untermeier (Til Kiwe), by threatening to expose his past as Schlemmer's commanding officer (the actual *Tageblatt* had been an anti-Nazi paper before it was taken over by the government in 1933 and eventually shut down in 1939). Another bright spot amidst the chaos of *One, Two, Three* is the zany black comedy of the East German Stasi torturing Piffl, whom they suspect of being an American spy for the CIA, into screaming in German that he is "paid by Wall Street" and "a secret agent of [CIA Director] Allen Dulles." The Stasi's method of eliciting that bogus confession is to repeatedly play the maddening novelty song "Itsy Bitsy Teenie Weenie Yellow Polka-Dot Bikini."*

But despite the engagingly comical performances by Cagney, Buchholz, Lothar, Pulver, and others, *One, Two, Three* is marred by dismayingly "cute" supporting performances by Tiffin, Francis, and St. John that telegraph their broad domestic comedy as if in a TV sitcom. *One, Two, Three* also borrows the three trade commissars from *Ninotchka*—this time played by Leon Askin, Ralf Wolter, and Karl Lieffen—but makes them mere buffoons rather than the earlier film's memorably human and evolving characters. The portrayal of political opposites through nuanced characters in *Ninotchka* and *A Foreign Affair* is more illuminating not only dramatically but also politically.

President John F. Kennedy was worried enough about how Wilder might exacerbate the world crisis with *One, Two, Three* that before the film went before the cameras, he invited the director to Peter Lawford's Santa Monica beach house to ask for a copy of the script. In a gutsy act especially remarkable for an immigrant filmmaker who was also a liberal Democrat, Wilder

---

* The film also sports a German rendition of "Yes! We Have No Bananas," a song previously used in *Sabrina*.

politely refused. He and JFK also talked about sports and beautiful actresses and "about power," as Wilder recalled, while Audrey nonchalantly sat nearby doing the *New York Times* crossword puzzle.

Kennedy need not have been worried by the final product, however. When *One, Two, Three* was released, the essential silliness of Wilder's approach went over like a lead "Yankee, Go Home!" balloon with audiences on both sides of the ocean. The *Berliner Zeitung* complained, "What breaks our heart, Billy Wilder finds funny." Bosley Crowther of the *New York Times* enjoyed Cagney's "wildly ingenious and glib" character and the film's "impudence toward foreign crises" but began his review by lamenting, "It is too bad the present Berlin crisis isn't so funny and harmless as the one Billy Wilder and I. A. L. Diamond have whipped up. . . . And it is too bad it can't be settled as briskly and pro-Americanly as James Cagney settles the one in this picture . . . a typical American farce." It took until 1985 for audiences in the reunited Germany, when the film was reissued there, to appreciate it as a lighthearted nostalgia piece. Today the film's relentlessly glib topicality not only misses the bigger historical targets but also makes it seem unhelpfully mired in trivial, once-contemporary allusions; it requires the gloss of an audio commentary to be fully intelligible now, as was provided by film historian Michael Schlesinger for the 2017 Kino Lorber Blu-ray edition, but that inadvertently emphasizes the film's ephemeral nature.

The test of time often enables us to read films quite differently from their contemporary reception. *A Foreign Affair* remains a more enduring kind of time capsule, because its topical references, while equally specific, are less rhetorical and more seriously grounded, more troubling and not as merely jokey. And *One, Two, Three* feels like a yellowing newspaper compared with *The Apartment* and *Kiss Me, Stupid*, those seemingly "apolitical" but more biting and universal social satires. They were not as directly "ripped from the pages of today's headlines" but are recognizably about ordinary people in the America of their period, and so their social commentary cuts closer to the nerve. As Elia Kazan observed, "The deepest conflicts of our society are through the violent, intimate acts that are on page 4 of that awful daily newspaper, those acts where the pressure of society forces individuals to do things that are violent and final."

Although the audience and most reviewers of 1960 embraced Wilder's social commentary about the corrupted lives of two working people in *The*

Apartment, the reaction to *Kiss Me, Stupid* in 1964 was overwhelmingly virulent in its hostility, since it did not try to be as endearing in the midst of its seamy situations. Even if Polly the Pistol is one of Wilder's most sympathetic characters, the film's contempt toward the sexual hypocrisy of small-town America is as venomous as the disgust Wilder displayed toward the callous gullibility of the American public in *Ace in the Hole*. In both of those cases, the American audience and reviewers returned the insult in kind, though with *One, Two, Three*, the audience mostly just shrugged. As Sam Goldwyn once put it, "If people don't want to go to the picture, nobody can stop them."

SHELLSHOCK

The shell-shocked Wilder and Diamond, after their nearly comatose inaction in the wake of the *Kiss Me, Stupid* debacle, regrouped for one of their weaker efforts in 1966 with *The Fortune Cookie*. Only mildly successful at the box office but enough so to reestablish their viability, this comedy-drama about an insurance scam is rather depressingly one-note in its satire, characterizations, and plot machinations. The sole bright spot is the gleeful villainy of Walter Matthau's glibly cynical shyster lawyer, Whiplash Willie Gingrich, who tears into that ruthless character with such relish that he won the Oscar for best supporting actor and helped establish himself belatedly as an unlikely movie star, following his stage success in the 1965 Neil Simon play *The Odd Couple*.

Wilder's penchant for depicting the insurance racket as a metaphorical playground for American economic corruption, exercised so tellingly in *Double Indemnity* and *The Apartment*, is more programmatic in *The Fortune Cookie*. The director and Diamond seem to be going through the motions, shuffling a worn old deck of cards. Lemmon plays a TV cameraman, Harry Hinkle, who suffers a minor injury while covering a Cleveland Browns football game but reluctantly allows it to be inflated by his brother-in-law, Whiplash Willie, into a fake case of paralysis. Harry is a sad sack pining for his worthless slut of an ex-wife, Sandy (Judi West); he hopes he can win her back by scoring a major settlement. But he becomes guilt-ridden over scapegoating the football player who caused his injury, Luther (Boom Boom) Jackson (Ron Rich), especially when the distraught Boom Boom descends into alcoholism.

Making the athlete a sweet, guileless victim who is also African American was a rare sentimental misstep for Wilder and Diamond. In their anxious efforts after *Kiss Me, Stupid* to demonstrate that they were not heartless misanthropes, they seemed to be going out of their way in that racially charged time to portray a saintly Black character as Harry's savior. Boom Boom is the kind of character Spike Lee would later dub a "Magical Negro," an allegorical contrivance to salve the conscience of white people by redeeming and forgiving their flaws. It's a move by Wilder and Diamond that comes off not only as surprising for such usually astringent social commentators but as condescending and insulting under the circumstances, especially since Boom Boom is victimized by Harry and Willie. In the uncharacteristically schmaltzy ending, Harry, having reformed and blown the scam, tosses a football back and forth with Boom Boom at night in the empty Cleveland stadium to celebrate their newfound palship.

That's straight out of the Leslie Fiedler playbook as the tendency the critic saw in American literature of two interracial buddies running away from women into the wilderness to share a seemingly sexless but covertly homoerotic kinship. Fiedler first propagated his theory with a then-controversial 1948 essay, "Come Back to the Raft Ag'in, Huck Honey," about the relationship between Huckleberry Finn and Jim, the slave he helps escape in Mark Twain's *Adventures of Huckleberry Finn*. Fiedler expanded the essay into his insightful and sharply witty book *Love and Death in the American Novel* (1960), the kind of work Wilder might have written if he had gone into literary criticism instead of film directing.

The Fortune Cookie's belated, straight-faced, and corny use of this anachronistic interracial trope during the time of riots in the streets was a sign that Wilder and Diamond, falling back on old-fashioned liberalism and sentimentality, were beginning to slip out of touch with the contemporary audience. In a film that shares the misogynistic nature and suggestive but evasive homoeroticism of other Hollywood buddy-buddy films in the 1960s and beyond, the love story of Harry and Boom Boom seemed a disheartening run for cover, a misjudged attempt by Wilder and Diamond to pander for audience sympathy by showing they weren't really such nasty cynics. Diamond, in his 1972 interview with Froug, demonstrated his awareness of Fiedler's theory while seeming especially touchy about this line of criticism, complaining, "To think that the ending of *The Fortune Cookie* gave aid and comfort to

Leslie Fiedler. I think more crap is being written about films today than was ever written about Abstract Expressionism. I wish they weren't so solemn about it."*

PRIVATE LIVES

Wilder's prematurely jaded upbringing in the louche atmosphere of hotel life and his early prurient interests—having his passion for art stimulated by an Egon Schiele drawing, and saving up for a tumble with the prostitute "Red Fritzi"—help explain his career-long obsession as a filmmaker with every kind of sexual relationships. Throughout his life, Wilder retained his keen interest in erotica, often of the most exotic European variety, which he would indulge by buying books and nude paintings in Paris and elsewhere, part of his extensive and eventually celebrated art collection. His stated interest (possibly facetious) late in life of filming the 1906 German sex novel *Josephine Mutzenbacher* was a not unnatural outgrowth of such obsessions, for the word "pornography" comes from the Greek word *pornografia*, meaning "writing about prostitutes."

Prostitution was Wilder's principal metaphor for the social transaction and the corruption of loving relationships, the conflict that preoccupies much of his work. When Hepburn's wistful young Ariane, yearning to lose her troublesome innocence, says in *Love in the Afternoon*, "If people loved each other more, they'd shoot each other less," the philandering American tycoon played by Gary Cooper, who treats his women like prostitutes, replies with alarm, "Are you a religious fanatic or something?" After Lubitsch liberated the American cinema from Victorianism, Wilder, the sexual connoisseur, followed his example by leading Hollywood, sometimes kicking and screaming, into the post–World War II era. His sophisticated, increasingly frank

---

* The *Film Quarterly* essay Wilmington and I wrote that seemed to irritate Diamond in his interview with Froug with its analysis of sexual symbols in *Some Like It Hot* also made reference to Fiedler, in what today seems to me a jejune criticism: "Wilder's flippancy toward plot and characterization in *Some Like It Hot*, droll as it is, only underscores the fact that he shares what Leslie Fiedler diagnosed as the shortcomings of many American story-tellers: a proclivity for edgy sex and violence and an inability to deal maturely with love and death." We also referred to "the memorably boyish ending scene of *The Fortune Cookie*."

perspective exposed the erotic lives, fantasies, and brutalities of both ordinary and unusual people.

Weimar Berlin, where Wilder worked as a reporter and began his screenwriting career, was rife with sexual experimentation. Gay and bisexual life was open and relatively accepted in the world Wilder inhabited as a young man, flourishing in theaters, cabarets, nightclubs, and bars. Given his fascination with sexual esoterica and his more open-minded European point of view, it's hardly surprising that situations verging on homoeroticism frequently show up in his work from the 1950s onward, sometimes openly though sometimes covertly, and that they were touched on occasionally in his films even before that, including in the first film he codirected, *Mauvaise graine*. A subplot involves the romantic devotion of the boyish Jean-la-Cravate (nicknamed after his phallic fetish for stealing neckties and played by Raymond Galle) to the protagonist, Henri (Pierre Mingand). Although Henri has only a friendly interest in Jean and is escaping their gang of car thieves with the young man's sister and preparing to go into exile, he makes a risky journey from Marseilles back to Paris in a failed attempt to save Jean, who refuses to leave and is killed in a police raid. (This now seems like a premonition of Wilder's failed 1935 trip to Vienna to persuade his mother to leave for a safe haven overseas. Such anxieties were "in the air" in 1933 Europe.)

The openness of this gay subplot in Wilder's directorial debut reflects the comparative freedom of European cinema and the influence of Weimar culture on the émigré filmmaker. The gradual loosening of the Hollywood Production Code in the postwar era helped liberate Wilder's willingness to explore sexuality more adventurously and to include a deeper concentration on various forms of male bonding even while homosexuality was still widely considered a sexual aberration. David Ehrenstein, one of the major chroniclers of gay themes in Hollywood, noted "just how deeply [Wilder] had dared to cut, particularly in the 1960s when he broke free of studio control, became an independent producer and threw caution to the winds—especially in the arena of sexual politics. Never was this more apparent than in the case of *Kiss Me, Stupid*, a sex farce . . . that opened in 1964 to the sort of hostile reviews that had greeted Michael Powell's *Peeping Tom* three years before and would welcome Pier Paolo Pasolini's *Salo* 10 years later." Ehrenstein cited Joan Didion's *Vogue* review of Wilder's film for an explanation of why audiences walked out on it: "Because they sense that Wilder means it."

Wilder's brazen, explosively successful dive into cross-dressing themes and flirtation with depicting an actual gay relationship in the gender-bending frolic of *Some Like It Hot* inaugurated the intensified focus in his emotionally freer later work on complex nuances of male friendship, collaboration, and rivalry. Sometimes these situations are platonic, but occasionally they go somewhat beyond that. Homoerotic themes may appear subtextually in the treatment of key relationships in his late films, such as in *The Fortune Cookie* and *The Front Page*, but other times they are right out in the open, especially in his most ambitious late film, *The Private Life of Sherlock Holmes*, which probes into the ambiguities of the celebrated detective's sexuality. Wilder even considered making a gay love story a key element in *Avanti!* before having cautious second thoughts. That skittishness about going all the way with such a ticklish subject was indicated in his anxious and unconvincing denial that Daphne's liaison with Osgood as they ride off into the sunrise in his speedboat at the end of *Some Like It Hot* would turn into anything physical. Despite all appearances to the contrary, Wilder insisted of Daphne, "But when he forgot himself it was not a homosexual relationship. It was just the idea of being engaged to a millionaire. It's very appealing. You don't have to be a homosexual. It's security."

Perhaps the key tip-off in that disclaimer is the phrase "when he forgot himself," which suggests that Daphne's subconscious was at play in his/her relationship with the fond, lecherous millionaire so blithely unconcerned over Daphne's declaration, "I'm a MAN!" Occasional homophobic jokes in Wilder's later films, including *The Front Page*, indicate a lingering discomfort with such themes, yet his exploration of such ambiguities in male sexuality is still remarkable for a director of his generation. Wilder's expanded focus on homoerotic tendencies and the complexities of modern gender politics coincided with the increasingly bold emphasis in his late work on transgressive sociopolitical themes in general. Both preoccupations intensified his career-long dramatic and satirical examination of the crossing and blurring of boundaries in social relationships.

Exploring various forms of sexual ambivalence and gender fluidity in matters of love and companionship is one of the elements that makes Wilder's later work so intriguing today, even if those tendencies sometimes worked against him with audiences of his time, including the public that delivered his most crushing rejection with the release of *Sherlock Holmes* in 1970. But its box-office failure was mostly due to the fact that it was seen as stylistically and narratively old-fashioned in a period dominated by trendy, fast-paced, showily photographed youth pictures. Wilder went out of his way in his film's original prologue in a London bank to explicitly position Holmes's more civilized methods of deduction as a riposte to the brutal James Bond model of modern spy films, and though that part of the film was eliminated before its release, the implicit point was clear enough to audiences at the time. The favorable review Wilmington and I wrote at the time, which focused on the unusual intensity of Wilder's exploration of Holmes's sexual ambiguity, noted that "Wilder's tone is unusually subdued, even elegiac, perhaps because the film is set in a simpler, more gentlemanly era far from the barbarism of James Bond and Pussy Galore." But that overlooks the more "gentlemanly" form of Victorian era barbarism practiced in the film by Holmes's brother Mycroft and Sherlock's own cold-blooded dispatching of a submarine full of German spies.

Delving into the elusive question of the sexual nature of a protagonist who reflects many aspects of the director's own personality makes *Sherlock Holmes* a self-analysis of both Wilder's attitudes toward male sexuality and his complex views about women. Wilder and Diamond made the question of the possible homosexuality of the great detective created by Sir Arthur Conan Doyle a centerpiece of their exploration of the mystery of Holmes's diffidence toward women. Their revisionist look at the legend of a beloved literary character was fairly audacious even for that tumultuous period in filmmaking and society in general, and it helped account for the film's rejection by audiences and most reviewers and for the unhappiness of some Holmes purists. On the reactionary end of the critical spectrum, *Films in Review* was thrown into a fit: "Some of [the film's] sequences have no purpose other than to suggest Holmes was a sex pervert and his use of narcotics a legitimate relief from boredom. The deliberate utilization of a fictional character of world-wide popularity to promote or condone those two vices is reprehensible." The negative backlash against the film for tampering with Holmes's image might seem predictable for its unorthodox treatment of such a beloved, even sacrosanct character but for the fact that other revisionist Holmes films and books that followed would find a more open-minded and successful reception. Wilder once again was a few years ahead of his time with what he unusually described as "a very personal film. . . . He's always fascinated me. Holmes. And his relation to Watson. Ever since I was a boy."

While exploring Wilder's familiar themes of prostitution and sexual deceit, as well as the detective's need for the comfort of live-in male companionship, *Sherlock Holmes* directly confronts the vexing question raised by some of Wilder's critics, i.e., that he was a misogynist. In a sense the film may have been partly a response to his detractors. But examining the sexual ambiguities latent in male friendship, as the film does mostly comedically while examining the other dimensions of Holmes's enigmatic personality, was not entirely a departure for Wilder. Not only did he get away with some of the most audaciously transgressive treatments of sexuality in the American cinema in *Some Like It Hot*, but even when the Code was more strongly in effect, he memorably managed to explore a coded but now unmistakable emotional bonding in *Double Indemnity* between the corrupt insurance salesman, Walter Neff, and his mentor, Barton Keyes, the father figure whose love and trust Walter betrays. The fumbled treatment of homoeroticism in *The Fortune Cookie* showed that Wilder and Diamond, off their game, felt temporarily uncertain about how to proceed with outré stories about love and sexuality until they confronted the subject of homosexuality openly and extensively in *Sherlock Holmes*, released two years after the Code was abandoned. Undoubtedly they expected a more sympathetic reception for their film in the same year that an X-rated film dealing with male hustling and an intense male love story, *Midnight Cowboy*, had been honored with the Academy Award for best picture.

Although biographers have reported no homosexual experimentation or relationships in Wilder's active love life, Sarris noted that he was "married to two different women and two different screenwriters." Wilder and Diamond used similar language, Paul Diamond said: "They were very close. They described it as a marriage, and it was in many ways like a marriage. They blew hot and cold with each other, they wouldn't speak for a while, and then the rest of the time they were in a room together forty hours a week without fighting. But I don't know how they got so *wonderful*. There was a magic in there between only two of them in the room that I haven't seen replicated much, if anywhere, in the business." The other of Wilder's platonic "marriages" was to a screenwriting partner who may have been a closeted homosexual, Charles Brackett. Despite Wilder's own occasional homophobic wisecracks, it does not appear that he had a prejudice or concern about Brackett for that reason— their battles were over many other subjects, including Brackett's prudish distaste for Wilder's tendency toward lewdness—or that Wilder harbored any genuine aversion to homosexuals. The nastiest recorded remarks Wilder made about a gay person came while he was attacking the flamboyant homosexuality of Mitchell Leisen in his litany of complaints about that director, calling him "too goddam fey . . . a stupid fairy." Those were low blows, but it is possible to regard them and other jibes Wilder made about gayness in his interviews and his film work as further evidence of a tellingly defensive anxiety stemming from a fascination that was not entirely latent.

Hollywood has a long tradition of what Howard Hawks liked to call "a love story between two men," a tale of male bonding and men without women, the kind that dominated Hawks's career and is seen in the films of many other supposed he-man directors in Wilder's generation and beyond. The perennially popular "buddy-buddy" movies reflect deep, sometimes clearly homoerotic feelings, often more intensely than men in Hollywood films have been allowed to express toward women without such tenderness being stigmatized as "unmanly" by the rigid standards of American heteronormative culture. The reason the male buddy genre became so rampant in the 1970s, as François Truffaut observed to me in that period, was that it was a refuge for Hollywood filmmakers who had no idea how to deal with the uncomfortable demands of the women's liberation movement, so they solved the problem by largely eliminating women's roles from their stories. It is not surprising that buddy films have often been seen as expressing covert or even overt misogyny as well as homosexual impulses. Wilder unfortunately squandered an opportunity for sharp satire of the genre when he feebly mocked it in his final, dispiritingly sour and unfunny film, *Buddy Buddy*.

Depiction of an overtly gay character or relationship (other than as a figure of ridicule, affectionate or not, such as with the "sissy" characters engagingly played by Franklin Pangborn) was a major taboo under the Production Code, although Hawks and other filmmakers sometimes found clever ways to suggest such subversive content. The *absence* of a gay theme in one of the major Wilder films of that era can be striking in itself and, ironically, an indication of the filmmaker's unusual sophistication. Brackett and Wilder excised the gay element from Charles Jackson's 1944 novel *The Lost Weekend* when they adapted it to the screen in 1945. Their decision to eliminate Don Birnam's feeling of shame over a homosexual episode in college and lingering torment over his sexual insecurity, problems Jackson portrays as causing him to descend into alcoholism, was inevitable given Hollywood censorship of the time. But though the dropping of that theme has predictably been criticized, it actually strengthens the film.

Wilder does not attempt to offer a psychological explanation for the severely alcoholic state of Birnam (Ray Milland), portraying it in more enlightened modern terms as a physical disease. The screenwriters do not rely on Jackson's trite, defensive pseudo-explanation of why Don drinks, which reads today as the kind of tragic self-deception, stemming in part from self-hatred, that a gay novelist (or a gay man of any other profession) could fall into during that benighted period of persecution. *The Lost Weekend* is one of many examples of Wilder's obsession with masquerading and the secrets of people's hidden lives. His film replaces the self-protective lying of a closeted gay life with the perpetual denial that characterizes an alcoholic's desperate existence. Rather than the hiding of lovers, the film shows the hiding of bottles. Brackett and Wilder emphasize a different kind of anguished psychological secret, Don's crippling insecurity that manifests itself as writer's block. Their depiction of him as a hopelessly mediocre talent who believes he drinks to palliate his creative anxiety contributes powerfully to their portrait of addictive torment. Brackett's first wife was an alcoholic; that intimate knowledge and his friendships with numerous alcoholic writers, including F. Scott Fitzgerald, helped give the film its unusual and harrowing authenticity.

The only overt trace of a gay theme that made it into the film is the secondary but compellingly creepy character of Bim (Frank Faylen), the effeminate, smirkingly oleaginous orderly who taunts Don when he hits bottom in the Bellevue ward for patients with d.t.'s. Bim's malice makes him something of a negative gay stereotype, but however sadistic he seems, at least he is offering Don some hard truths about his condition that other people unhelpfully shy away from giving him (such as his fiancée and his brother, sympathetic figures who also are his enablers). In his brutal honesty and ability to see through cant, Bim is not unlike Wilder himself. Another character who talks bluntly to Don but does it with more compassion is the bartender, Nat (Howard Da Silva), who by profession is an enabler yet cares enough about his customer to try to talk him into sobriety, a nearly impossible balancing act. Nat functions as Don's conscience and is the quasi-angelic figure who appears at the end, as if in a miracle, to hand him back his lost typewriter with a beatific smile and the film's lovely poetic concluding line of hopeful dialogue, "How are all them lilacs in Ohio?"

"CLOSER THAN THAT"

The year before *The Lost Weekend*, Wilder had memorably explored one of the most moving male relationships in the American cinema in *Double Indemnity*. With suggestive complexity straddling both confession and denial, he described that prototypical film noir as "a love story between the two men and a sexual involvement with the woman." Although the close relationship between Fred MacMurray's Neff and Edward G. Robinson's Keyes is not sexual, at least on their conscious level, it is deeply emotional and complex, unlike the simply lustful relationship Neff enjoys, or suffers, with the violently sociopathic femme fatale Phyllis Dietrichson (Barbara Stanwyck).* "Much has been said about Keyes's possible homosexual attraction for Neff," Phillip Sipiora notes in a 2011 essay on the film. He adds, "A 'love' story can, of course, have many meanings, including a father-son type of relationship of love and respect, which clearly is part of the Keyes-Neff relationship."

Keyes is the paternal friend and conscience who supervises and trains Neff in the art of insurance investigation. The Sherlock Holmes character in this mystery story, Keyes is the ace claims adjustor who supervises his covertly treacherous younger salesman in the insurance company. Like Holmes in Wilder's film about the detective, Keyes has been soured on the opposite sex by discovering the truth about a woman he loved; he ran an investigation on his fiancée that revealed an unsavory background. Neff's symbolically named mentor offers him a chance for salvation by dangling a job before him as a fellow claims adjustor, a form of semidomestic settling-down with him in the safely homey confines of the office. "The job I'm talking about takes brains

---

*   Phyllis Dietrichson's surname in the novel is Nirdlinger. The change to Dietrichson is one of the film's allusions to the sadomasochistic relationships between Marlene Dietrich's characters and the weakly submissive men in Josef von Sternberg's films, especially *The Blue Angel*, in which Dietrich plays the cabaret temptress Lola Lola, who destroys the besotted professor played by Emil Jannings. Phyllis's stepdaughter (Jean Heather), who turns against her while having a romance of sorts with Neff, is named Lola.

and integrity," says Keyes. "It takes more guts than there is in fifty salesmen." But Neff foolishly prefers to remain only a salesman, partly because he can't control his libidinous impulses toward female clients out in the field and also perhaps because he realizes the limitations of his brains and integrity. "You don't want to work with your brains," Keyes says. "All you want to work with is your finger on a doorbell. For a few bucks more a week." He adds with disgust, "There's a dame on your phone."

Keyes is emotionally as well as professionally betrayed and abandoned when Neff, despite (and because of) his admiration and fondness for the older man, tries to outwit him by conspiring with Phyllis to murder her husband. There are enough coded bits of business in this classic film noir to support a contention that the relationship between Keyes and Neff to some extent is subconsciously homoerotic for both men. Especially symbolic is the running motif of Neff lighting Keyes's cigar by striking a match with his thumbnail. Keyes never carries matches in his pocket because of the odd fear they might "explode"; perhaps that is a covert Wilder reference to his mentor, Lubitsch, who often forgot where he put the matches to light his cigars. Collaborators, friends, or partners need both a match *and* a cigar or cigarette to function together, as Wilder conveyed in using the metaphor of striking matches for his rocky relationship with Brackett.

That motif climaxes with Keyes compassionately reciprocating with a light as the younger man lies dying on the floor outside his office, a cigarette dangling from his mouth. Neff says as he dies, "You know why you couldn't figure this one, Keyes? I'll tell ya. 'Cause the guy you were looking for was too close. Right across the desk from ya." Keyes answers sadly, "Closer than that, Walter." The film's last words, from Neff, are, "I love you too." These words are echoed in *The Private Life of Sherlock Holmes* when the female German spy who deceives Holmes and rouses his dormant romantic passion tells him after she is unmasked, "I couldn't resist the challenge of coming up against the best. I'm sorry I didn't give you a closer game." Holmes replies in a melancholy tone, "Close enough."

Wilder omitted a coda he had shot for the ending of *Double Indemnity* of Keyes watching Neff going to his execution in the gas chamber at San Quentin. Although that would have been another echo of the Holocaust in Wilder's work, and an especially direct one, as a finale it would have seemed anticlimactic after the emotionally powerful ending the film now has with the two men and the cigarette bit. *Double Indemnity* lingers in our memory as both a twisted story about the lethal sexual involvement of Neff and Phyllis and a tender story intimately focused on the two men and the tragic destruction of their loving friendship.

Even taking into account Wilder's adventurous late work in *Some Like It Hot* and *Sherlock Holmes*, the betrayed friendship between Neff and Keyes in *Double Indemnity* remains his most memorable male relationship. He explored it with great subtlety within the shoals of the rigorous censorship of the 1940s; perhaps the censors were distracted by the more sensational heterosexual coupling and murderous aspects of Cain's source novel and the screenplay Wilder wrote with Chandler. As much as any of Wilder's male-female relationships, the betrayal of love between Neff and Keyes exemplifies the filmmaker's romantic vision of human potentiality and how painfully it can be thwarted. The corrupted Everyman character, Neff, considers himself a sharpie in the insurance racket but is naive enough to be duped by a lethal woman. Neff mistakes the sexual heat Phyllis generates for honest emotional involvement while not realizing she is manipulating him for her own murderous ends. But more agonizing for the viewer, as well as for Neff in his dying moments, is his betrayal of the trust and even fully admitted love he shares with Keyes.

Parker Tyler, a critic who displayed a famously provocative penchant for teasing out intricately hidden sexual meanings in films, made the fullest case for a homoerotic reading of the Keyes-Neff relationship. Disagreeing with the comment attributed to Freud that "sometimes a cigar is just a cigar," Tyler wrote in his chapter on *Double Indemnity* for his 1947 book, *Magic and Myth of the Movies*:

> On the surface [Neff repeatedly lighting Keyes's cigar] is an empty form, and it may be as a mere symbolic form that Keyes accepts it—just as a lady secretly in love with the doorman of her hotel may derive a subtle, withal empty, satisfaction from his touch as he hands her into a cab. . . . [But] Neff is demonstrating to Keyes his successful sexual "spark" and *symbolically* communicating this capacity, which Keyes lacks and of which he is envious no less than suspicious. . . . It seems to me that the presence of the little ritual between Neff and Keyes is no accident and that its graphic nature is highly suggestive. Keyes has reason to be envious of Neff in those very

sexual relations at which he scoffs, for Keyes is short and homely, and Neff is tall, younger, attractive, and obviously lusty. . . .

Neff's personality has undoubtedly been doped out by the friendly psychologist Keyes as sexually promiscuous, uncomfortably so, entailing the sort of irresponsibility and lack of serious intention that makes a man drink too much, carouse too hard, and eventually fall down on his job. Therefore Keyes's offer of another job seems an effort to reorientate Neff psychologically to a position where he does not have to make himself so persuasive with people. . . . Subtly envious of Neff's success with women and having an incoherent affection for him, Keyes aims basically with the job offer at a specific reorientation of Neff's attitude toward women—a curbing of sexual promiscuity by the suggestion of the curbed promiscuity of his sales personality. . . . [But] when Neff first meets Phyllis and hears her daring, scarcely veiled suggestion, he may grasp at the deed as a way of finally ridding himself of Keyes, *who presides over his life as the hidden judge of his sexual claims as well as the insurance claims of his clients.* [Emphasis in original]

Although homoerotic references of such significance had necessarily been rare or deeply buried in Wilder films when the Code was fully in force, his World War II prison camp comedy-drama *Stalag 17* caused the censors some anxiety in 1953 because it was more overt. Its cross-dressing gags among the POWs and lighthearted references to gay behavior are actually less prevalent than in the play, but they foreshadow the far more extensive, uninhibited romp Wilder and Diamond make of *Some Like It Hot*. Some of the men in the barracks dance together in *Stalag 17*, and Robert Strauss's "Animal" becomes sexually turned on while dancing with his fellow clown, Harry Shapiro (Harvey Lembeck). Animal's basic heterosexuality is conveyed through a running gag about his obsession with Betty Grable, the favorite GI pinup girl of World War II. But he fantasizes so much about her that it leads to a fantasy vision of his buddy Shapiro dressed as Grable in a dress and blonde wig, which causes the fellow soldier to become alarmed.

That vein of humor, however mild, is Wilder's way of acknowledging that men confined without women in a wartime barracks for more than a year would naturally develop some homosexual impulses, whether or not they entertained them before. Wilder managed to get away with these gags partly because the censors usually gave filmmakers more leeway in dealing with material that came from the stage (although the neutering of the adultery theme of the Wilder-Axelrod adaptation of the playwright's *Seven Year Itch* was one of the director's major disappointments during that period). Without some reference to homosexuality, *Stalag 17* would seem unreal, but as was usual then, it had to be done with oblique humor. In so doing, it did not have to be taken seriously but was only a safe flirtation before the deluge of *Some Like It Hot*.

A pseudonymous blogger called QSCRIBE wrote an article in 2009 provocatively entitled "Billy Wilder: My Gay Icon." It argues that of the great Hollywood directors, Wilder was

> the one whose films were most consistently not just gay-friendly but quite actively gay-positive. He laughed with us, not at us, and in film after film he managed to get an astonishing amount of queer content past the censors. . . . It's not entirely clear why the abundantly heterosexual Wilder should have been drawn to queer subject matter time and again . . . [but] what we frequently think of as a "queer sensibility" is really pretty much an outsider sensibility, something Wilder shared. As a Jewish immigrant . . . Wilder early developed a sharp, sympathetic sense of the ways American society deals with outsiders . . . That and his ongoing fight with the moralists are connected with his fascination with hypocrisy and disguise. Film after film—probably more than three quarters of his total output—turns on a character pretending to be someone or something he isn't. . . . I'd go so far as to say hypocrisy was Wilder's great theme.

Wilder's obsessions with disguise and hypocrisy are indeed central to his worldview as a perennial outsider, so it is not surprising that when censorship was loosened, as well as intensifying his focus on deception and repression in straight relationships, he would turn his largely sympathetic sights on the effects of such role-playing and repression on gay relationships, which for so many years had to be masked, both in Hollywood films and throughout American society. His career-long concern with the conflict between emotional detachment and love was broad and generous enough to encompass studies of intimate male bonding as well as male-female love.

"WATERGATE MAKES ME COME"

Unlike the uninhibited romp *Some Like It Hot* and the searching investigation of sexuality in *Sherlock Holmes*, some of Wilder's other late treatments of male relationships are intermingled with defensive reactions. A ploy Hollywood has often used as a safety valve is to deflect accusations of homosexual overtones in a central male relationship by treating secondary characters as targets of homophobic jokes, which usually come off today as painfully unfunny and/or offensive.

The Front Page (1974) is a sadomasochistic male love story of sorts between the emotionally needy Hildy Johnson and the domineering Walter Burns. That was the third film version of the funniest American play. The first was directed by Lewis Milestone in 1931; Hawks, despite his specialty in male love stories, reversed Hildy's gender when he made the screwball comedy *His Girl Friday* (1940). Although that film is the most popular version today, Wilder told me he thought it was more akin to Leo McCarthy's 1937 screwball comedy of divorce starring Cary Grant, *The Awful Truth*, than to the original Ben Hecht-Charles MacArthur stage version. Wilder's film about Chicago newspapermen, though deviating in some important respects from the source material, adapts the play more faithfully than the Hawks film did.

Wilder benefited from greater screen freedom, including the ability to finally use the play's celebrated curtain line, "The son of a bitch stole my watch!" The line previously had been rendered unusable for filmmakers because of the Production Code. One of the journalists visiting the set of Wilder's film, Jack Smith of the *Los Angeles Times*, had been inspired to go into the newspaper business by the 1931 version. He asked Wilder if he planned to keep the ending line. Wilder replied, "Are you crazy? That's the whole picture! I couldn't change it. It's sacred." Paul Diamond said his father told him they wanted to do *The Front Page* mostly so they could put that line onscreen and to bring back Allen Jenkins, the old Warner Bros. character actor who had appeared in the original production of the play. Jenkins had appeared as the hipster garbage man in *Ball of Fire* and plays his final film role as the telegrapher to whom Burns dictates the ending line of *The Front Page*.

Iz Diamond told me that when they wrote the script, "We started with the first scene in the newspaper office between Walter and Jack," because they felt it crucial to establish the "essential relationship" between the men around which the film revolves. It's a significant improvement over the play that they introduce Burns much earlier; the play keeps this key character offstage until the end of the second act. Diamond admitted to me that they took the liberty of making many changes in the material, rewriting about 60 percent of the dialogue (including some famous lines), as well as elaborating considerably on the edgy but oddly affectionate relationship between Burns and his restless reporter and moving parts of the play with cinematic free rein to locations other than the city hall press room. Yet Wilder's collaborator claimed somewhat misleadingly that the adaptation was "really mechanics, most of it; really logistics." Perhaps he made that statement on the set to an actual newspaper reporter because he didn't want the public to know how much he and Wilder had tampered with a newspaper classic while transforming it into their own sardonic, less indulgent, and necessarily less comedic view of the journalism racket.

One reason the film is less funny is that the pacing is somewhat slower than that of the original play, in which the actors often overlapped their dialogue, and not as fast as Hawks's *His Girl Friday*, partly because, as Lemmon put it, "I'll tell you what I miss . . . I think the idea of overlapping is repugnant to Billy, because you're going to lose some of the dialogue. And he *really* stopped us from overlapping." Wilder and Diamond also may have been reacting against what they considered the overly frenetic pace of *One, Two, Three*, which had been partly inspired by *The Front Page*.

Despite Wilder's fondness for the play and the pleasure he took in re-creating the ratty pressroom milieu, the old Vienna and Berlin reporter from the Roaring Twenties did not look back on that trade with the rosy-eyed nostalgia that was fashionable in Hollywood period films of the 1970s. Instead he viewed the amoral callousness of the reporters with a sharply critical eye, even while taking characteristically dark amusement in much of their ruthless, virtually criminal behavior. As Neil Sinyard and Adrian Turner observe, "Those critics, like Pauline Kael, who complain about the film's raucousness, coarseness and relentlessness—the general air of bedlam—might care to consider that the air of Bedlam is very much what Wilder is striving to create."

There's a real bite in Hildy's telling off his fellow members of the press, as Wilder moves in ruthlessly for a close-up of his scornful face, by giving the reasons he is quitting that profession to go into the advertising business. "Journalists!" he says. "Bunch of crazy buttinskis, with dandruff on their shoulders and holes in their pants. Peeking through keyholes. . . . Stealing pictures off old ladies of their daughters that get raped in Oak Park. And for what? So a million shop girls and motormen's wives can get their jollies. And the next day somebody wraps the front page around a dead mackerel. [With disgust] *Ahhh!*" One of the other reporters, stung by his contempt, accuses Hildy of being "a gigolo" since his fiancée's uncle owns the advertising agency, and another demands, "Where's your pride? Where's your integrity?" Hildy chastens them into silence as the hard truth sinks in by snapping, "What's the newspaper business ever done for me? See, I don't want to end up the way like you guys will—on a copy desk—gray-haired, humpbacked, half-blind—bummin' cigarettes from office boys."

Although Wilder and Diamond transformed the comedic play to some extent into their own, more serious vision of the seamy aspects of journalism, one stumbling block they couldn't get around was the discordant nature of one of the two important female characters, the prostitute Mollie Malloy. In what may be a nostalgic throwback to "Red Fritzi" of Wilder's youth, she sports curly red hair and red headband, necklace, and bracelet. She is played by the brilliant comedian Carol Burnett, who was miscast (as Wilder admitted to me) in a shrill, off-kilter performance that acutely embarrassed the actress. She declared, "I stank," and while traveling on a plane showing the film, borrowed a microphone to apologize for her performance to the passengers who had just watched it. After doing so, she said, "I felt cleansed." For once a Wilder film dealing with prostitution doesn't know how to handle the subject. Mollie implausibly and jarringly jumps out a window in the pressroom to distract the reporters from her fugitive boyfriend, the meek, stammering "Red" agitator Earl Williams (Austin Pendleton), who is hidden inside a rolltop desk.* "I will admit in no version I've ever seen could I figure out why she jumped," Diamond told me on the set. "We've tried to prop it up in various ways," such as having a phone ring inside the desk where Earl is hiding. "We couldn't eliminate it; it's too important."

The screenwriters intensify the reporters' cruelly taunting Mollie and turning on her as a mob before she jumps, and after they appear momentarily stunned, one says, "What'd you expect? All whores are a little goofy." The

---

* As Sinyard and Turner point out, Earl's entrapment is a black-comical version of Leo's fatal imprisonment in the cave by another newspaperman in *Ace in the Hole*, part of a macabre streak that runs throughout Wilder's work, including his frequent imagery of coffins or surrogate coffins. The situations of entrapment in his films, literally or metaphorically, are perhaps an outgrowth of his fear of confinement in Europe in the period leading up to the Holocaust.

men's crude and crass remarks are suitably revolting, which gives some weight to what nevertheless stubbornly remains a misconceived scene. Wilder is struggling against the general tone of the play in attempting to counter the reporters' cynicism by having Mollie attack them for "crackin' jokes" while Earl is facing death. Although Hellmuth Karasek argues that Mollie is the "heroine" of the story, "the only selfless person in the piece," Wilder's indictment through her of the callousness of the press (whom Mollie calls "bums . . . bastards . . . lousy punks . . . Shame on you! Shame!") is diminished by the overwrought writing and direction of that confrontation. It seems an overcompensation for the clichéd and implausible dramatic device the good-hearted prostitute represents.

There is a haunting moment of genuine poignancy and pain in Burnett's performance, and it is played in a more subdued, more thoughtful tone. Earl, who absurdly shot a policeman while grabbing his gun in a panic, asks Mollie if it is true, as the papers reported, that she was willing to marry him on the gallows. She has angrily denounced the story to the press as false. But she replies to Earl, "Well, if it's in the papers, it must be true," and as she does so, she is making an accusing look at Hildy. He shakes his head, and she adds uneasily, "They wouldn't print a lie." That is the film's most cutting denunciation of the amorality of the press. As in the play, Wilder and Diamond let Mollie improbably survive the suicide attempt, which only compounds the overall problem with tone. The film's epilogue about the fates of the various characters, a spoof of a similar device in the hit 1973 youth film *American Graffiti*, frivolously has Mollie and Earl marrying after his release from prison and running a health food store in Evanston, Illinois.

In a further instance of confusion and conflict over the material, as if to distract reflexively from the emotional bonding of Hildy and Walter, Wilder and Diamond went out of their way to compound the play's homophobic jokes. They added a painfully naive cub reporter named Rudy Keppler (Jon Korkes), who is seduced by a character from the play, the flamboyantly foppish older reporter Bensinger (David Wayne). The epilogue tells us that Bensinger and Keppler moved to Cape Cod and opened an antique shop. Although that couple at least are given a happy ending (however stereotypical), *The Front Page* has only the thinly veiled excuse that the gay-baiting jokes at their expense demonstrate the general crudity of the play's newspapermen in that period, even if it sometimes sounds as if

Wilder and Diamond are reveling in it. "Never, *never* get caught in the can with Bensinger," Hildy warns Rudy. And when Hildy tells Walter he is quitting to become an advertising copywriter, Burns snarls, "Jesus, Hildy, you're a newspaperman, not some faggot writing poetry about brassieres and laxatives." But though Wilder and Diamond found those jokes amusing and acceptable, they did take pains to remove the racist remarks by reporters in the play, some of which actually are sharply satirical and quite funny in sending up the blatant bigotry of the 1920s. Nevertheless, it says something about the difference in sensitivities toward certain kinds of humor in 1974 that Diamond told me he felt those racist lines were "extraneous" to the story: "We aren't using the word 'niggers'—we're not opening up those wounds particularly. There's no reason for it."

The Front Page, with its debunking of official corruption and equally corrupt, heartless journalists, has been interpreted as a disquieting fable about Watergate. When I read the script of *Buddy Buddy* before seeing that film, I laughed out loud only once, and that line is not even in the finished film. In a group therapy session at the sex clinic devoted to the topic of how to avoid premature ejaculation, one man says he thinks about Watergate, but another says, "Watergate makes me come." That mischievous quip intermingling sex and politics, so characteristic of the late Wilder, is a mysterious and regrettable omission from the finished film; the sex clinic scenes noticeably suffer from ragged editing due to Wilder's problems dealing with Klaus Kinski, the erratic German actor who plays the clinic's deranged director.

A similarly jaded but less biting successor to Wilder's broadside against the press in *Ace in the Hole*, *The Front Page* presents his skeptical view of the overly romantic idolizing of the press that was fashionable in 1974 because of the stardom of *Washington Post* Watergate reporters Bob Woodward and Carl Bernstein. While Wilder was shooting the film that spring and summer, those reporters were working with their covert sources in U.S. intelligence who helped topple President Richard Nixon that August. The president was a former member of HUAC, the red-baiting committee that made Wilder so angry he wanted to "spit upon the Congress of the United States." While casting an unfashionably dim eye on the venal behavior of corruptly self-aggrandizing reporters—a move that didn't enhance the box-office prospects of the film, which was released that December, after Nixon was toppled— Wilder also characteristically transformed the anger he felt against Nixon into vitriolic humor against both the press and political figures in *The Front Page*, an indictment of the whole rotten system.

Matthau's facial and bodily resemblance to Nixon, as well as their similarly cynical demeanor, imbued the actor's crooked lawyer Willie Gingrich in *The Fortune Cookie* with an added zing, and Wilder further exploited that affinity by casting Matthau as the amoral Walter Burns in *The Front Page*. There are jokes in that film explicitly evoking the behavior of Nixon's men in the Watergate scandal—Burns tells Hildy to describe the executed man's body as "twisting slowly, slowly in the wind"—as well as contemporary-seeming gags about Nixonian red-baiting, including a police raid on a supposed front group called the Friends of American Liberty. Democrats come in for their share of satire, thanks to the malefactions of a sputtering Chicago sheriff (Vincent Gardenia) who bears a distinct resemblance to Mayor Richard J. Daley. The mayor in the film (Harold Gould) is a thoroughly corrupt and kinky habitué of a local brothel.

Diamond told me he thought people would see their version of *The Front Page* as modern because "it's quite similar to Watergate. Nobody's going to believe that some of those things are in the play. And this kind of newspaper work is coming back into [vogue] today. They've started to get individual initiative in stories again. What's kept the play alive is a certain irreverence on the part of these guys—they don't revere anything."

Despite some felicitous writing and performing in *The Front Page*, and a graceful sense of choreography in enclosed spaces, the film to some extent lacks the zany, often farcical qualities that make the play so entertaining. But it is fundamentally a darker, more serious work, which compensates for some of the loss of humor. While capturing the profane sarcasm of the original, it heightens it with what *New York Times* reviewer Vincent Canby called "a giddy bitterness that is rare in any films except those of Mr. Wilder." Diamond thought the difference in tone was that "1928 was an optimistic time; 1974 isn't. I suppose it's as simple as that. But I can only quote what Hecht and MacArthur wrote: 'We set out to do an exposé; we wound up writing a valentine.'" While that may have been the screenwriters' intent, it was not the result, since Wilder's insider's view of the press was so thoroughly jaundiced and his sociopolitical outlook by that point in his career so acerbic. Although Hecht and MacArthur revel in the ruthless amorality of their reporters, Wilder's retrospective look at the yellow-press underbelly of journalism makes his reporters seem even sleazier and often viciously unfunny.

When I asked him on the set if the film was going to reflect any of his experiences as a reporter in the 1920s in Vienna and Berlin, he said with an ironically raised eyebrow, "Hardly. It would be very censorable even today."

Gay-baiting also makes a brief, uneasy, strangely gratuitous appearance in *Fedora* (1978), the dark Wilder-Diamond film about the movie business. The male lead, Barry Detweiler (Stephen Collins) in his youthful days (1947) as an assistant director, acts extremely blasé upon seeing the bare breasts of the legendary actress Fedora (Marthe Keller) on a film set. Stung by his indifference, she harshly demands to know if he is "a queer—a faggot." Barry replies with smug defensiveness, "Boy, have you got the wrong guy, lady," boasting about his casual sexual conquests. He sets out to prove his heterosexuality by having sex with her that night on the beach. In an odd ellipsis, we don't see their lovemaking, only their waking at dawn fully clothed in his convertible. What actually happens between them, and why don't we see any of it? It's one of the film's peculiar ellipses; it might seem to indicate that Barry's braggadocio was more talk than action. But Fedora fondly remembers that night many years later, to Barry's immense satisfaction, since it shores up his now-shaky sexual and professional self-esteem.

And there is the curious case of Wilder's lovely romantic comedy *Avanti!* (1972). Before the credits it has an extended gay joke in pantomime when the brash American businessman Wendell Armbruster Jr., not properly attired for picking up his late father's body in Italy, exchanges his golf clothes with the outfit of a conventionally dressed older man in the bathroom of an airplane. The rest of the passengers, including a fat and sweaty Italian priest puffing a cigarette, watch with leering fascination as the two men sheepishly emerge from the toilet in each other's clothing. That gag is lighthearted, but what makes the film so revealing of Wilder's inclinations and disinclinations toward sexual material is his claim that he had a different kind of plotline in mind. When he told me in 1978 that *Avanti!* was "too gentle" to succeed with modern audiences, he went on, "In other words, the way the picture would have aroused interest or made them talk about it is that the son of the chairman of that enormous corporation goes to claim the body of the father and finds out that the father and a naked bellhop have been found dead in that car. The father was a fag. But it's just a young girl. So who cares? So he got laid. So big fuckin' deal, right? It needs that added element."

I thought Wilder was joking about the idea of turning *Avanti!* into a gay love story, but he told Crowe that he actually proposed that to the Mirisch

Corporation and "they talked me out of it." When Crowe pressed him about why he couldn't do it, given his cachet with the Mirisches, Wilder admitted, "I myself was not so sure" and that the idea was "not so safe." Although it is hard to imagine Wilder's most perfectly crafted romantic comedy being improved by undergoing any kind of change, we will never know how he would have dealt with such a radical element in that story. The abandoned notion shows his daring impulses as well as his limitations, and it's one of the unanswered questions that hang over his somewhat frustrated and ultimately truncated late career.

Buddy Buddy mocks its own title and the vogue for the skewed sexual politics of that Hollywood genre. This failed farce revolves around acute male sexual frustration in the midst of that period's rampant sexual liberation and the protagonist's resulting hysterical emotional attachment to another man; it also touches on lesbianism. The central character is Victor Clooney (Lemmon), a neurotic CBS-TV network censor. Wilder vents his ridicule on censors by making Victor so ridiculously prudish that his wife, Celia (Paula Prentiss), has left him to live at Klaus Kinski's outlandish sex clinic in the Southern California desert. That humiliation to Victor's masculine ego causes him to attempt suicide at a nearby hotel. Celia is studying techniques of Chinese foreplay at the "Institute for Sexual Fulfillment." She is the sexual partner of the sinister-looking guru played by Kinski, Dr. Hugo Zuckerbrot (whose name is German for "sugar bread"), the last in the long line of quack doctors and psychotherapists Wilder enjoyed ridiculing in possible revenge for Dr. Freud's ordering him out of his apartment in 1925. Celia eventually runs off with the clinic's receptionist, played by Wilder favorite Joan Shawlee (Sweet Sue from *Some Like It Hot*, Amazon Annie in *Irma la Douce*, and the formidable dame Sylvia in *The Apartment*).

The despondent Victor clings to Matthau's dour hit man, Trabucco, who despises him but keeps him around out of expediency. Trabucco is in the same hotel preparing a sniper hit on a mob witness at the courthouse across the street. Victor keeps getting in the way and has to be subdued repeatedly. He's a much more frantic version of Lemmon's already manic Felix Ungar from *The Odd Couple*, who also becomes suicidal after a marital breakup. Wilder, Lemmon, and Matthau had wanted to work together on the 1968 film version of that classic Neil Simon play. Even though Simon considered Wilder the greatest of all Hollywood directors, the playwright was proprietary about his writing and didn't need Wilder trying to improve on it. Furthermore, Paramount didn't think they needed Wilder, who was pricey as well as creative, so the journeyman director Gene Saks was hired instead to transfer the play and Simon's own adaptation unimaginatively to the screen.

Buddy Buddy, even more than *The Emperor Waltz*, is ostensibly a comedy but is not funny in the slightest. It is mostly set in a place whose grimness rivals Wilder's fictional Climax, Nevada, the terminally dismal city of Riverside, California, fifty miles from Los Angeles, a former resort that had been rendered a wasteland by smog.* *Buddy Buddy* is so bleak that, with its constant bickering between two existential clowns, it resembles a work of Samuel Beckett. But if Wilder made his 1948 Viennese musical to covertly address the Holocaust, perhaps he used *Buddy Buddy* subconsciously to vent his distaste on what passed for a bankably crass Hollywood project in 1981, a slapdash remake of a 1973 French film that wasn't very funny in the first place. *Buddy Buddy* exemplifies Diamond's observation to me, "Present-day comedy is really the comedy of frustration."

This thoroughly sour, sad botch is based on *L'emmerdeur*, directed by Édouard Molinaro from a play by Francis Veber, who adapted it to the screen. The French film's title is literally translated *The Shithead*, but it was released in the United States as the doubly euphemistic *A Pain in the A—*. Thanks in part to the more believable casting of Lino Ventura as the hit man opposite Jacques Brel as the suicidal loser, it is more watchable than *Buddy Buddy* but still a basically pointless exercise in black comedy. Matthau's casting as the surly, one-note gunman, as Wilder belatedly recognized, was all wrong, and the kind of roguish sarcasm the actor so engagingly displays as Whiplash Willie in *The Fortune Cookie* is not utilized here. His character simply acts as a soulless mechanic endlessly packing and unpacking his rifle from a briefcase with a look of blank frustration while trying to pull off the hit if he can only get rid of the sniveling Victor. The audience keeps expecting laughs from Matthau that never come. As Wilder noted, the film would have been funnier if a more authentic tough-guy star such as Clint Eastwood or Charles Bronson had been cast to play it straight opposite the characteristically

---

* I paid penance for going to Hollywood by working for a year as a reporter on the *Riverside Press-Enterprise* before joining the staff of *Daily Variety*. While in Riverside I was an extra in James Ivory's 1920s Hollywood film, *The Wild Party*, filmed at the historic Mission Inn, where Douglas Sirk had made his 1951 religious drama, *The First Legion*.

agitated Lemmon. "I didn't want to say no to being in a Billy Wilder picture," Matthau later reflected. "But this wasn't a Billy Wilder picture."

I think it's likely that Wilder could have made the film somewhat funny if he had wanted to but simply was too angry at his treatment by Hollywood to bother trying anymore. He had already turned *The Front Page* into a bleaker, less funny reflection of the play, which hurt it with most reviewers. As usual with films criticizing the press, that kind of reception was predictable, and Wilder's harsh treatment should have been expected from the man who had skewered the "Gentlemen of the press" so unrelentingly in *Ace in the Hole*. Wilder's similarly jaded railing at the film industry in his later interviews and in his penultimate film, *Fedora*, was the product of a man stung by rejection by both the audience and by his peers. Wilder was not one to go quietly into that bad night. His surprisingly inept, visually ugly final film seems like a dispirited throwaway. Reviewer Dennis Cozzalio in 2016 called *Buddy Buddy* "an aging director's defiant 'fuck you' to a system he could sense was about to toss him to the curb, a last blast of venom disguised as a tired formula comedy." The film lacks any of Wilder's characteristic wit or style; any director of TV movies could have done a better job. Reviewers of *Buddy Buddy*, like Hollywood in general, concluded from this leaden fiasco, which includes an embarrassingly out-of-touch and corny song interlude about a hippie couple having a baby, that Wilder had simply lost his comic touch. That effectively ended his and Diamond's careers.

Paul Diamond was so disconcerted by *Buddy Buddy* that he admitted he was "not unhappy" his father and Wilder didn't make another film after that, because he felt

it wouldn't be any good. The times changed, and Billy didn't. Their age was showing. The references [in the script] were so dated, and Lemmon and Matthau were too old. I was thirty and I knew what I was talking about. I went to my father and said, "You shouldn't do this. And in fact, if you do it, you should have somebody else write it besides you two. Even me. *I'd* make it better. And I'm not the greatest writer in the world. Let me go through it and take out and fix the dated stuff. A little young blood." And it took a lot of balls to walk up to my father and say that, because it's disrespectful and unpleasant. . . . It was dead serious, but my father just brushed me off. He knew this wasn't good. He didn't receive it badly, but he just sort of shook his head; he was along for the ride.

And that was again not a happy set. . . . That picture again—horrible—
nobody wanted to see it. Lemmon is tired. Matthau is tired. And it's very,
very overlong. Age was showing on all kinds of things. For instance, on
location, when Matthau was arguing over a line, they let me talk him out
of it. They just sent me out, because they were too tired to deal with shit.

"HE IS YOUR GLASS OF TEA?"

Wilder's most overt and serious exploration of sexual ambiguity came at the
start of the late phase in his career, in his 1970 film *The Private Life of Sherlock
Holmes.* Its depiction of the sexually elusive detective, his suggestive friendship with Dr. Watson, and his deep distrust of women—indeed, his professional suspicion of the human race in general—makes overt Wilder's covert
investigation of the relationship between Keyes and Neff in *Double Indemnity.* Holmes and Keyes are the kind of characters who repeatedly material-
ize in Wilder's work, detective figures of rare intelligence and sensibility but
flawed as investigators because of their susceptibility to emotion. Although
Wilder ruthlessly mocks psychoanalysts, he treats his investigator characters
with greater empathy. Despite their cautious pose of professional detachment
in probing the vagaries of human nature, they do so with less pretension and
more passion. Like Holmes, Keyes has learned to avoid emotional commitment with women because of lack of trust (Keyes almost married once before
he unfortunately had the woman investigated) but nevertheless falls victim
to his fatal flaw, his inability to deny his human feelings. It is Keyes's fondness for Neff that causes him to fail at his job, as well as leaving him emotionally devastated when Neff betrays his trust after the older man acts, in
effect, as his conscience.

We see the same conflict between intellect and emotion and the same flaw
(if you want to consider it a flaw) in such figures as Phoebe Frost (the uptight
congressional investigator who comes from the opposite end of the political
spectrum from Ninotchka but still needs a similar thawing); the editor
Mr. Boot in *Ace in the Hole* (who, like Keyes, is overly trusting, which turns
Boot into Tatum's enabler despite also being his conscience); and a Holmes-
like figure of legendary skills as an investigator, Charles Laughton's British
barrister Sir Wilfrid Roberts in Wilder's film of Agatha Christie's *Witness
for the Prosecution.* Both Holmes and Sir Wilfrid are fooled by women in

disguise, and Sir Wilfrid is also gulled by his own client despite his instinctive distrust of the glibly charming murderer Leonard Vole (Tyrone Power).

Sherlock's case is more serious dramatically, however, because unlike the confirmed bachelor Sir Wilfrid, he warily succumbs to love for the first time since his disastrous experience long ago at Oxford. As a result, he finds himself betrayed by the German spy Ilse von Hoffmanstal (Geneviève Page), masquerading as the Belgian Gabrielle. Holmes's skills as an investigator temporarily desert him because of that lapse from cool rationality into emotional blindness. Clearly, like Keyes, who was also deceived by the woman he loved, the reason Holmes became an investigator in the first place was to shield himself from the danger of such emotional involvement. Sir Wilfrid's feeling of betrayal is more a blow to his professional vanity, which makes *Witness for the Prosecution* a less emotionally involving film, if still highly entertaining.

A more comic, charming variation on the Wilder "investigator" is Carlo Carlucci (Clive Revill), the all-wise, endlessly efficient, droll Italian resort hotel director in *Avanti!* Carlucci shows no sign of intimately personal sexual or emotional attachment to anyone outside the hotel but exhibits a professional warmth and sympathy that transcends selfish concerns. He is never fooled by the people he helps to carry out clandestine affairs under his roof but is complicit with their schemes in a benign way. Carlucci's cheerful amorality helps account for the more free-spirited tone that characterizes Wilder's depiction of the happiest romantic affair in any of his films. *Avanti!* lyrically depicts the liberation of Wendell, the uptight "swinger," from his emotionless marriage and empty affairs when he falls into the loving embrace of Mills's sensual Pamela Piggott. Carlucci's professional detachment is something of an illusion, since he is so fond of the lovers under his care, but he maintains the pose impeccably nonetheless. He does not let his personal feelings interfere with his work, as Keyes and Holmes do, but is able to maintain a sensible and empathetic balance between his intellect and his emotions. That enables Carlucci to help Wendell and Pamela realize their romantic goals, just as he did with their parents, even if it involves creatively bending some rules.

The flawed investigators in Wilder's films, on the other hand, are those who let their emotions overwhelm their intellects or their intellects close off their emotions. These all-too-human investigator characters in Wilder's films have much of Wilder in them and serve as subjects of auto-critiques, as much, perhaps, as any of his people, although parts of him are also present in his innocent dupes, scheming con men, callous gigolos, heartless reporters, jaded roués, ingénues yearning for seduction, guilt-ridden seducers, and disappointed idealists. The whole gallery of Wilder rogues—lovable or not—and outright heels are people he carried within him from his rough days on the streets of Vienna and Berlin to the cutthroat world of Hollywood. He can summon up empathy for the feelings of most of them so vividly he usually can forgive if not overlook their foibles or actual crimes. The characters for whom he cannot summon up sympathy are those whose use of other people for their own ends is so heartless (Sheldrake) or even sociopathic (Phyllis) that they have no hope of redemption, no empathy, no humanity. If depicting such characters makes Wilder a cynic, then we all could be called cynics, for we see such people far more often in real life than we do in his films.

Those who find his films objectionable are often horrified by his frank depiction of the darker aspects of society, as if they do not exist, or condemn him for acknowledging its existence. That Pollyanna attitude is a ludicrous distortion of film criticism that is hardly worth answering. Wilder regards prostitution, to name the most common vice in his films, as a pervasive part of the human condition, afflicting the behavior of both genders. It is a state his characters struggle to escape, sometimes successfully, sometimes not, and his view of prostitution is tolerant toward sex workers because they are professionals, unlike amateur "prostitutes," toward whom he can be scathing.

Rather than being misogynous, Wilder's view of women is often ambivalent, as is his view of men, and that is a principal reason he devotes much of his work to exploring how men treat women. Wilder directly confronts his issues with the conflict between "cynicism" and romanticism in *The Private Life of Sherlock Holmes*. His film about the bachelor detective, an ambitious work ten years in the writing and three years in production, not only questions whether Holmes might be homosexual but frankly explores the issue of "What indeed *was* his attitude toward women?," as Dr. Watson puts it. "Was there some secret he was holding back—or was he just a thinking machine, incapable of any emotion?" The same question has been asked by those who have disparaged Wilder. He clearly made the film because he identified with the celebrated character's emotional reserve, felt the need to examine its roots, and dramatized Holmes's dilemma about women to satisfy his own curiosity about himself. Wilder's teasing portrayal of Holmes never gives us a definitive answer to whether the detective actually has gay tendencies, even if the characterization by Robert Stephens, who wears eye shadow and other makeup, seems distinctively effete in an Oscar Wildean way. Early in the film, Colin Blakely's Watson asks, "Holmes, I hope I'm not being presumptuous, but there *have* been women in your life, haven't there?" Holmes replies, "The answer is yes. You're being presumptuous. Good night." The film is mostly concerned with exploring Holmes's traumatized dealings with women. His taking refuge in male companionship by living with a comical foil is not portrayed by the director as a consciously gay desire, even if the bluff and somewhat unimaginative Watson appears overly defensive on that score.

The suspicions voiced about the resolute bachelor Holmes's homosexuality by other characters and Holmes himself allow Wilder and Diamond to poke fun at the alarm they cause in Watson, his resolutely straight roommate and devoted biographer. In the wittiest sequence, a Russian ballet impresario, Rogozhin (Clive Revill), fails to interest Holmes in fathering a child with his diva, Madame Petrova (Tamara Toumanova), after striking out with Tolstoy ("Too old"), Nietzsche ("Too German") and Tchaikovsky ("Women are not his glass of tea"). The angular-faced, rather mad Madame Petrova, who stares into three mirrors while sitting at her vanity table, bears a distinct resemblance to Norma Desmond. Holmes wiggles out of the situation by blaming "a cruel caprice of Mother Nature." Rogozhin is a blasé man of the world but can't help asking with surprise, "You mean, you and Dr. Watson— *he* is your glass of tea?" Rogozhin goes backstage to assure Watson, "Come now, no need to be bashful. We are not bourgeois. Maybe with doctors and detectives, this is unusual—but in ballet, is very usual."

Wilder follows that exchange with an uproariously funny, gracefully staged sequence of a line of chorus girls dancing with Dr. Watson before they are gradually replaced by a line of gay chorus boys. Holmes says afterward, "Watson, you have my most abject apologies. But have you ever been cornered by a madwoman? It seemed like the only way to get out of it without hurting her feelings." To which Watson sputters, "And what about my feelings and my reputation? You realize the gravity of what you've done, the possible repercussions?" Holmes replies lightly, "So there'll be a little gossip about you in St. Petersburg." Watson is so worried that he even suggests they get married. "Then they'd *really* talk," Holmes responds dryly. As Wilmington and I wrote in our review, "Colin Blakely's Watson is constantly on the verge of hysteria—alternately, hysterical admiration and hysterical jealousy. The sexual tensions in his character have more to do with Jack Lemmon's characterizations in earlier Wilder films than with Doyle's sedate, dignified Watson, who acquired a wife early in the series."

The answer to whether Holmes is "incapable of any emotion" comes when he uncharacteristically succumbs to love for the first time since Oxford. The man considered all but infallible in detecting criminal behavior is conned by the alluring Ilse/Gabrielle, who shows up on his doorstep at 221B Baker Street one foggy night in 1887, disheveled and seemingly suffering from amnesia and identified by a luggage tag as a Belgian. Against his better judgment, Holmes finds himself increasingly attracted to her, only to find to his dismay that she has been spying on him on behalf of (who else?) the German government, to uncover British plans for a submarine to use in the impending Great War. Holmes's brother Mycroft (Christopher Lee), a sinister figure who resents his brother's interference, is involved with those plans on behalf of the Foreign Office. But Queen Victoria (Mollie Maureen) scuttles the British submarine on the grounds that a sneak attack is unsporting. Victoria gets to utter her famous line "We are not amused." The diminutive monarch, who lent her name to the era of strict morality against which Wilder spent his lifetime rebelling, is portrayed with surprisingly indulgent affection, as a man might portray his own grandmother. Wilder's directorial credit even appears over a *Citizen Kane*–like glass ball of Victoria with snow shaken inside it, as if to acknowledge that, after all, he cannot fully escape the lifelong effects of the social attitudes she represents.

When Holmes and "Gabrielle" are sharing adjoining berths in a train compartment en route to the submarine base in Scotland while masquerading as Mr. and Mrs. Ashdown (even the submarine is masquerading as something it is not: the Loch Ness Monster), Gabrielle is reading one of Watson's stories, in which Holmes is quoted as saying, "Women are never to be trusted entirely—not the best of them." Although Holmes protests, "The good doctor is constantly putting words into [my] mouth," he refuses to deny the sentiment, telling her in an understatement, "I am not a whole-hearted admirer of womankind." She responds, "I'm not very fond of them myself." In the film as released, he goes on to discuss the women he has encountered in his work—"kleptomaniacs, nymphomaniacs, pyromaniacs"—as well as the fiancée who died of influenza twenty-four hours before their wedding. "It just proves my contention that women are unreliable and not to be trusted."

That near-miss recalls the blunder Keyes almost made in *Double Indemnity*, but with an even more darkly comical twist. The scene on the train is the one that was to be interrupted by the flashback in which Holmes recalls the incident at Oxford with the prostitute. After Gabrielle says she is not very fond of women, Holmes was to say, "It is a philosophy I acquired at Oxford." He relates the story of "the most beautiful girl I'd ever seen" and his subsequent disillusionment when he belatedly recognizes the face of "the girl of his dreams," realizes her profession, and darts out the door of the boathouse, heartbroken.

The excision of this scene, the culmination of so many conflicts between men and women in Wilder films, so much ambivalence about the failure of emotional detachment and the need for love, is the most tragic loss in Wilder's career. *The Private Life of Sherlock Holmes* was planned as a roadshow running three hours and twenty minutes, including a modern-day prologue about the opening of a safe-deposit box including the manuscript of Watson's unpublished stories involving "personal matters of a delicate and sometimes scandalous nature" that "will shortly become apparent to the reader." There also were two comical episodes preceding what is now the dramatic heart of the film, which would have begun after an intermission. But as Diamond told me, "The motion picture business changed in the three years it took to make this picture." By then, roadshows and period films were doing poorly, and there were walkouts at a dismal preview in Long Beach after each episode. The Mirisches and United Artists made the decision, against Wilder's wishes but with his reluctant compliance, to have editor Ernest Walter cut the film down to a standard two hours. In a rare admission, Wilder told Crowe, "I had tears in my eyes as I looked at that thing. . . . But it was a very, very well-done picture. It was the most elegant picture I've ever shot."

The unfashionably romantic and sedate-looking period film still did poorly at the box office when it was released in October 1970. Although the loss of the negative of the complete version is greatly to be regretted, some of the excised material can be partially accessed as extras in home video versions. One episode exists without sound ("The Dreadful Business of the Naked Honeymooners," shown with subtitles) and the other without film footage ("The Curious Case of the Upside-Down Room," shown with still photographs). Diamond felt that with the excisions of those early comical episodes, "most of the fun part of the picture went out the window."

All that remains of the tragic flashback with the prostitute are some tantalizing color photographs of the Oxford crew race and Holmes being confronted with the ravishing young blonde (Jenny Hanley).* Even from a purely narrative point of view, it was foolish to lose that relatively short episode, which would have helped "explain" Holmes's view of his ambivalence toward women, if not fully clarifying why he remained that way. Wilder was shocked that the Oxford flashback was cut along with the other parts of the film, although he can be faulted for not keeping closer control on the editing and not exercising his contractual rights, even under duress. It may be heretical to suggest that the other missing parts, with the exception of the scene with the prostitute, were expendable, but they seem relatively slight by comparison, and the film as it exists, in focusing on the emotional core of the story, is a deeply moving yet often hilarious masterwork, even without the crucial flashback.

The exquisite production design by Trauner and cinematography by Christopher Challis balance the tragic aspects by making the film a charmingly nostalgic time capsule (visually at least) of Victorian England and Scotland. Miklós Rósza's music, including the adaptation of his haunting 1953–1954 composition "Concerto for Violin and Orchestra Opus 24," pervades it with voluptuous melancholia.† The period settings and decor are lovingly detailed, and the camerawork is some of Wilder's most elegant and graceful. Wilder and Diamond steeped themselves in Doyle's stories and books about the author, his work, and the Victorian era, taking delight in alluding with arcane erudition in their screenplay to various Holmes stories. More obviously, the character of Ilse/Gabrielle is derived from the American opera singer Irene Adler of the first Holmes story, the often-dramatized "A Scandal in Bohemia," of whom Doyle's Watson writes, "To Sherlock Holmes she is always *the* woman. . . . In his eyes she eclipses and predominates the whole of her sex." Adler is one of the few people who outwits Holmes, as Ilse does for a time, and despite the evidence of his fascination

---

*   Hanley is an actress-model who attracted attention as a "Bond girl" in *On Her Majesty's Secret Service* (1969).

†   Rósza also appears in the film, conducting the Russian ballet company's orchestra in Tchaikovsky's *Swan Lake*.

with Irene, it is perhaps for that reason that Watson writes enigmatically, "It was not that he felt any emotion akin to love for Irene Adler."

Wilder and Diamond comment wittily and often in a meta way on Holmes's image and his self-conscious frustration with Watson's chronicling of his exploits in *Strand* magazine. After a new issue arrives, Holmes says, "I'm sure I'll find out all sorts of fascinating things about the case that I never knew before. . . . Oh, come now, Watson, you must admit that you have a tendency to over-romanticize. You have taken my simple exercises in logic and embellished them, embroidered them, exaggerated them—." Watson defends his writing as "a bit of poetic license," but Holmes continues, "You have saddled me with this improbable costume, which the public now expects me to wear."

There were some complaints that the release version, in focusing mostly on a failure by Holmes caused by his uncharacteristically allowing his feelings to overtake his reason, underplayed his celebrated skills in deduction, perhaps the foremost pleasure readers draw from Doyle's stories. But that vulnerability in Holmes also exists in "A Scandal in Bohemia," and if the complaint about the film has any validity, it is partly because Wilder and Diamond take Holmes's genius partly on assumption. They show some examples of his methodology, however parodistically, and his deductive skills were to have been more elaborately demonstrated in a cleverly fanciful missing scene following the prologue that was removed from the original version. A disheveled Italian singing teacher bursts into the two men's train compartment while they are returning from solving the case of the mysterious death of Admiral Abernetty in Yorkshire. The Italian falls asleep, whereupon Holmes amusingly deduces the story of the man's escape from a sexual scandal purely through the details of his appearance. When Watson sensibly enough protests, "Holmes, I'm afraid for once you're letting your vaunted imagination run away with you," Holmes concedes, "It's only a theory, of course." There's no doubt that Wilder was gently sending up the Holmes myth, but his affectionate way of doing so here and in the tragic denouement shows his respect for the character and his desire to restore some hidden human dimensions to a seemingly superhuman figure of legend. In any case, we will never know how it all would have played in its original version, and the partial ruination of Wilder's pet project, on which he and Diamond had labored so long and lovingly, was a severe setback for the director personally and for his career. A sense of "melancholy" pervaded the two men after the failure of that "dream" project, Paul Diamond recalled. "They never felt the drive quite as strongly after that, I think. They knew that there was a train coming through the tunnel. The light was visible."

Holmes is devastated when he is informed at the end that Fräulein von Hoffmanstal was executed by a Japanese firing squad for spying on naval installations in that country, where she had been living under the name of Mrs. Ashdown. That sentimental gesture on her part is not lost on the newly romantic detective, but his response is to deaden his senses with cocaine. The last time she saw Holmes, she said farewell by signaling in Morse code with a white parasol, "*Auf Wiedersehn*." Wilder borrowed the device of the parasol from another doomed romance in one of his earlier films. The Frenchwoman Mouche in *Five Graves to Cairo* told Corporal Bramble she wanted a white parasol, a small and somewhat pathetic token of femininity in the midst of war. So when the British conquer Egypt, he brings a parasol from Cairo, only to find that she has been executed by the Germans. He can only leave it on her grave in an inadequate gesture of tribute. Ilse and Mouche act as spies and, in effect, as prostitutes, but to Wilder they are heroines. He is able to appreciate the gallantry of both women even though they act for opposing sides in world wars in which his family suffered. And this is a director whom some regard as a misogynist.

The culmination of Wilder's career-long process of trying to understand his own ambivalent feelings about women, *The Private Life of Sherlock Holmes* is not only an auto-critique but also a witty yet melancholy riposte to his critics, who wondered just what was *his* attitude toward women. As a great artist does, Wilder inhabits his own ambivalence and does not shy away from it. In his long and varied body of work, he confronts the issues that he or any other man, artist or not, might have toward sexuality, women, and emotional involvement with the opposite sex. The answers are never simple in this artist's work; they are often profound.

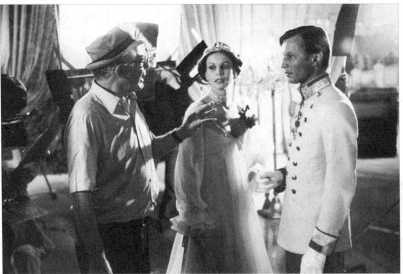

9.1 (top) Robert Stephens and Jenny Hanley as the prostitute the young Sherlock Holmes wins in an Oxford crew race in a crucial flashback scene lost when *The Private Life of Sherlock Holmes* (1970) was severely truncated. (United Artists / From the Collections of the Margaret Herrick Library, Academy of Motion Picture Arts and Sciences.)

9.2 (bottom) Wilder directing Marthe Keller and Michael York on the Vienna Schönbrunn Palace set of a romantic film-within-the film in the troubled yet haunting drama *Fedora* (1978). (United Artists / Photofest.)

9

"TAP-DANCING ON THE GRAVE OF HOLLYWOOD"

Endings are very important. That's what people remember—the last exit, the final close-up.

—Fedora (Hildegarde Knef) in *Fedora* (1978)

BY CONTRAST with Wilder's timid, unsatisfactory attempts to do Lubitsch in *The Emperor Waltz*, *Sabrina*, and *Love in the Afternoon*, he finally succeeded triumphantly in *Avanti!* (1972). Wilder's most fully achieved and most perfectly crafted romantic comedy was adapted with I. A. L. Diamond from a mediocre play by Samuel Taylor, also the author of *Sabrina Fair*. The droll Italian screenwriter Luciano Vincenzoni, who also worked with directors Pietro Germi and Sergio Leone, made uncredited contributions to the script. Wilder's visually ravishing film, shot on location on the Italian island of Ischia in the Gulf of Naples, captures the spirit of his master by having its lovers exist simultaneously in the present and the past, i.e., the past of Lubitsch movies.

Jack Lemmon's middle-aged American industrialist, Wendell Armbruster Jr., and Juliet Mills's Pamela Piggott, who works in a London boutique, have a macabre "meet-cute" while picking up their parents' bodies on the island. The elderly pair, secret lovers, were killed in an auto accident while staying at a health resort hotel catering to a mostly geriatric clientele. The uptight, reactionary Wendell, who is planning to eulogize his father back in

Baltimore as "a tireless crusader for all that is decent," is outraged by what he learns about the old man's cavorting abroad but gradually becomes a mensch through the good graces of the dead woman's daughter. The free-spirited, sensible Pamela convincingly represents the youthful generation's view of sexual freedom yet also reveres the past. She manages to persuade the reluctant Wendell to reenact the kind of clandestine romance their parents enjoyed each summer for ten years.

Wilder and Diamond play on the double entendre of the title, Italian for "Come in!," using it for knocks on the door of Wendell's hotel suite and for Pamela's response to his eventual romantic overture. It comes after he has been angrily resisting her but finally accepts her tenderness and passion. The sexual connotations of the title are not lubricious but gently applied: Pamela agrees to kiss him after he asks twice, "Permesso?"; she softly replies, "Avanti." Their love affair is redemptive, as adultery tends to be in the Lubitsch films to which Wilder pays homage. But by 1972, in a supposedly more "liberated" time, what was once considered entertainingly risqué and provocative in movies was thought to be old-fashioned, and the positive way the more romantic past is treated in *Avanti!* accounted for the film's box-office and critical rejection. The film's flop demonstrated Wilder's rueful observation that Lubitsch himself "would have had big problems in this market."

Today *Avanti!* seems thoroughly delightful as a relaxed throwback to the classic era of romantic comedy in movies, as well as one of Wilder's most thoughtful satirical contrasts of American puritanism and European sophistication. Like *Sherlock Holmes* and the later *Fedora*, *Avanti!* represents the late trend in Wilder's career to return to his European cultural roots, his partial transformation back into a European filmmaker, partly out of a need for comfort and nostalgia in his advancing years, when he was finding American culture too abrasive and coarse for his tastes, and partly because he was turning his back on the Hollywood that was rejecting him. But though *Avanti!* is in some ways a thoroughly European film, it also revolves around an American while examining the cultural conflicts Wilder so often explored before. This time, his focus is on the liberation of Wendell's sensibility in an age when the "free love" attitude he hypocritically endorses has exacerbated the tension always present in Wilder's work between romantic love and impersonal sex. When viewed in retrospect, the film's sharpness in capturing the changing sexual mores of its unsettled times makes *Avanti!*

one of the liveliest and most socially engaged of his comedy-dramas. Wilder's subsequent films, especially his morbid drama *Fedora*, have a haunting
resonance, but they are distinguished by their dissonant tones, their stubbornly defiant removal from the Zeitgeist. *Avanti!* is the gem of Wilder's
later work, his final fully achieved artistic success, the last time he was operating at the peak of his form.

Although Wendell shares some of the same arrogant, obnoxious traits of
the Ugly American businessmen Wilder had trouble resolving in his previous Lubitschean homages, Lemmon's portrayal gradually becomes genuinely
appealing and emotionally vulnerable beneath his brusque surface. The role
was tailored for the actor, who asked to play it after reading the first half of
a script draft. At that point, as in Taylor's play, the character was younger, a
bland St. Louis businessman. Taylor's character lacked the outrageous attributes Wilder and Diamond gradually added as they reworked him to sharpen
the satire with Lemmon in mind and his skill in playing a neurotic middle-
aged character. The 1968 Broadway failure was titled *Avanti! or a Very Uncomplicated Girl*, and Taylor revised the play without appreciable improvement in
1975 into *A Touch of Spring* for a London production starring Mills's sister,
Hayley. Both are feeble romantic comedies set in Rome, tritely written and
dramatically conventional, lacking the witty dialogue, acerbic social satire,
and richly layered themes of the film adaptation.

"The confrontation between the values of America and those of Europe is
arguably Wilder's most insistent preoccupation," Neil Sinyard and Adrian
Turner write of *Avanti!*:

> Clearly, his fascination with innocence and experience . . . derives partic-
> ularly from this cultural conflict. . . . Wilder's interest in America's inter-
> national role, in films like *A Foreign Affair* and *One, Two, Three*, reflects
> not only his concern with coming to terms with the ideology and cultural
> identity of the country of his adoption; it is, implicitly, an attempt to come
> to terms with his own identity as a European in America. It is perhaps sig-
> nificant that in the last decade [the 1970s], Wilder's films, having become
> increasingly reflective, mellow and *personal*, have also become increasingly
> obsessed with Europe and the past. . . . In Wilder, the conflicting values
> of America and Europe are most thoroughly examined in *Avanti!* . . . One
> feels that in the romantic reconciliation and the commitment between

Wendell and Pamela, Wilder has finally found himself able to reconcile his own ambivalence towards America and Europe, love and greed.

Wendell's defiant abrasiveness and emotional complexity are lacking in the play's Sandy Claiborne, who is initially conservative and unimaginative and falls in love too easily with the free-spirited London actress Alison Ames, not in the fierce, grudging way Wendell resists his deeper emotional liberation in the film. The crucial seduction in the play takes place offstage, while the film's romantic dinner and postprandial nude swim are its incandescent comical and romantic centerpiece. The onstage romance is further dampened by having Sandy's imperious wife repeatedly intruding on the action; Wilder and Diamond keep the wife as a distant telephone audience for Wendell's increasingly elaborate lies about his developing romance. Wilder and Diamond greatly enhanced the farcical complications about Italian bureaucracy impeding the export licenses for the coffins of the couple's dead parents. While driving Wendell to distraction, those practical obstacles, and the theft of the bodies by a local mob family, enable the romance to develop more gradually, helping provide the barriers to sex that modern romantic comedy often lacks to its detriment, and those allow his romance with Pamela sufficient time to blossom. The screenplay transformed a silly bisexual Italian factotum into the richly three-dimensional character of Clive Revill's hotel manager Carlo Carlucci, who serves as the warmhearted master of ceremonies managing the couple's romance and masquerade. And the screenwriters comically prolonged the hypocritically "swinging" male lead's shocked discovery of his father's secret adultery.

The essential difference between the play and the film is that the film is more genuinely romantic. The play is more about exploiting the free-love trendiness of the period through its depiction of Alison as a relatively unsentimental sexual pragmatist who shakes up Sandy's complacent and shallow existence. Alison would have been content with a one-night stand before entering into the spirit of her dead mother's annual romantic interlude with Sandy's father. A predictable, "uncomplicated," and thus uninteresting product of her times, she protests, "I'm not my mother's daughter," while Sandy defensively mocks himself as "a romantic fool." Both are opened up emotionally by their willingness to take that step, a development that occurs belatedly and somewhat unconvincingly. But in the film, the characters' reenactment of their late parents' romance is far more serious and consequential to their lives. The effect of the role-playing is Wilder's heartfelt way of contrasting the shallowness of the present day with the deeper emotional spirit Wendell and Pamela find in the past. And that's what made the 1972 audience reject it. When the couple have their dinner on the hotel terrace, Wendell steps into his late father's elegant, sporty clothing and symbolically assumes his identity, which releases his innate sense of warmth and humor. Pamela is wearing her mother's dress, and this celebratory event is one of the most satisfying, poignant, and amusing of the many masquerades in Wilder films. *Avanti!* is simultaneously an old writer-director's bittersweet reflection on mortality and a joyous affirmation of rebirth.

The young woman engineers a replay of the old couple's favorite romantic Italian music at the outdoor restaurant of the Grand Hotel Excelsior as she and Wendell share their parents' menu and she dances rapturously at dawn with the band to "Senza Fine" (Without End). Then she leads the hesitant Wendell in a nostalgic romp of skinny-dipping in the Bay of Naples. This was not Wilder's first plunge into the brave new world of screen nudity, but it's his most extensive and sensual. He had flirted with nudity in *Irma la Douce*; Geneviève Page appears discreetly nude in *Sherlock Holmes*; and one of the sequences cut from that film was a comical flashback entitled "The Dreadful Business of the Naked Honeymooners." That episode is partly restored on home video versions, but the woman's bare breasts, seen on the 1994 laserdisc, are obscured on the subsequent DVD and Blu-ray editions released in this neopuritanical age.

Avanti! takes unabashed delight in displaying Pamela's *zaftig* figure, while Wilder characteristically mixes the mood by poking fun at Lemmon's prune-like rear end and the black socks he has failed to remove. Hollywood was reveling in its newfound prurience, but Wilder, while happily taking advantage of that freedom, couldn't help poking fun at it as well. The sight of Lemmon's ass in what otherwise is a transcendentally sensual scene removes the undue, embarrassed solemnity that often marred nude scenes in those days. The capper comes when the bare-breasted Pamela gaily waves to a boatload of excited fishermen, and Wendell frantically tries to cover her nipples with his soggy socks. Another comical nude scene with Lemmon ensues in the hotel bathroom, and there is some additional, fleeting nudity with Mills in the bedroom. The couple's lovemaking is not shown but implied, so their romantic communion outdoors is the most purely erotic passage in Wilder's work, in a film whose hotel setting provides many opportunities for Lubitschean doorway shots as sexual ellipses (an explicit scene of lovemaking in the script did not make it into the film).

Such frolics were not enough to make *Avanti!* palatable for the younger audience of its day who could have cared less about the reenactment of a dead old couple's romantic rituals. Those are Wilder's way of paying tribute to the faded Lubitschean past as well as rebuking the sexually liberated modern world for its lack of genuine romanticism. As Pamela and Wendell explore their new relationship in homage to their departed yet romantically adventurous parents, the emphasis, as always in Wilder, is more toward love than toward impersonal sex. Juliet Mills, in her exquisite performance, liberates Lemmon's Wendell from his hypocritical, emotionally blocked existence, much as Leon melts the reserve of Ninotchka, Emmy Brown heals Georges, and Sugar turns Joe into a man of genuine feeling. Wendell's flowering under Pamela's influence and the charm of the two lead performances give *Avanti!* a delicacy and sweetness of tone unlike any other Wilder film.

An aspect of *Avanti!* that has caused criticism even among some of its admirers, however, is the film's emphasis on the luscious Pamela as being, supposedly, overweight. I plead guilty to faulting Wilder in my 1973 *Film Heritage* review, "The Importance of Being Ernst," for having his Rubenesque heroine "constantly harp on her weight problem." Under the influence of the prevailing critical opinion (a hangover from his scathing depiction of Sandy in *The Fortune Cookie*), I wrote that Wilder was something of a misogynist. But the script describes Pamela as "lovely, touching, warm, and let's face it, overweight. Pity, that." Wilder asked Mills to gain twenty pounds to play the young woman who, he said, "is teased for her weight and who is nonetheless adorable, touching, and in the end erotic." Mills was 5'2", and Pamela actually weighs only 133 pounds; in the script, she says she weighs 140, but Mills could not add that much, even though she tried. Some of Wilder's other comments on his and Diamond's decision to give Pamela a weight problem, and their choice of giving her the caricaturish last name of Piggott, can be said to reflect a strain of sexual ambivalence on their part, like the prudery that makes Wendell disparage her appearance. Wilder told Cameron Crowe that originally he "wanted her to be real fat, so that you don't feel sorry for him because he goes back to his wife. . . . She had to have some defect."

The theme as it plays out onscreen is actually much different from that misogynistic comment; the film is far more psychologically complex than some of Wilder's stated intentions. As D. H. Lawrence put it, "Never trust the artist. Trust the tale. The proper function of a critic is to save the tale from the artist who created it." The nude-swimming sequence is a lyrical interlude with the director exulting in the lush, voluptuous shape of Mills's magnificent body. The absurd blindness Wendell initially conveys toward Pamela's figure and the sensual approach to life it eventually represents to him redoubles our feeling for her and heightens our sense of the limitations he has to overcome. As I wrote in my review,

> Wendell's initial contempt for Pamela is partly sexual incompetence, partly moral outrage, and largely a reaction against the tainting of his father's upstanding middle-class image, the justification of everything Wendell has lived for. . . . Even before she meets him, Pamela realizes that Wendell is a latent romantic; she knows it because she knows so much more about his father than he does. Lemmon's subtle seriocomic performance balances his two sides and makes his transformation believable. The hotel staff collaborate in Wendell's rejuvenation process by continually telling him, "You're exactly like your father."

Sorry for Wendell is the opposite of what we feel at the end of *Avanti!* as he realizes he loves Pamela and will continue their life-giving affair, having shaken free of his repressed, sexist, reactionary attitudes. And the screenplay, direction, and acting all make Pamela deeply sympathetic. She is one of the most warmhearted and emotionally open Wilder heroines, akin to Emmy Brown in *Hold Back the Dawn*, who may be virginal but displays a similar sensuality while splashing on the Mexican beach and undoing her long hair as she prepares to make love on her wedding night.

Pamela's disproportionate anxiety about her weight and struggle not to eat are part of the film's examination of the neuroticism about sexuality that persisted for both men and women even in that age of sexual "liberation" and continues today. Despite her essentially sensual nature, Pamela has internalized the ludicrous and offensive modern hang-up that women should be rail-thin, an antifeminist neurosis that has even led some people to describe Marilyn Monroe as having been "fat" (I thought they were joking when I first heard that). Pamela's neurosis about her body, which has her under the treatment of a psychiatrist, conflicts with her consciously liberated attitude, just as Wendell's hypocritical sexual hang-ups contrast with his pathetic belief that he is a real 1970s "swinger" (because he has "a thing, you know, with a secretary or with an airline stewardess" and eats lunch at "a topless joint" while on business trips to Los Angeles). *Avanti!* can be seen as something of a sequel to *The Apartment*, showing what would have happened to Bud Baxter if he hadn't given back the key to the executive washroom but had turned into another Sheldrake, a sexual user.

Lemmon allows Wendell's sensitive side to flow in a lovely way when he interacts with Pamela's engagingly spontaneous sexual candor. Her sensible and frankly erotic nature convincingly represents a more open generation's view of sexual freedom, daringly mixed by Wilder with the old-fashioned values of romantic comedies past. But Wendell, who like Bud becomes a mensch, is not the only character liberated in *Avanti!*, which triumphantly chronicles Pamela's process of self-acceptance and emergence from her shell of repression. At the end, when they make plans to see each other every following summer and she says with tears in her eyes, "I promise you, I'll be *so thin*," Wendell tells her lovingly, "Miss Piggott, you lose one pound—just one pound—and it's all over between us."

To measure how far Wendell has grown, the most jarring moment earlier in their relationship was his telling Carlucci, "Ask fat-ass if she wants a ride." That remark comes, ironically, at the very end of one of the most moving scenes in all of Wilder's work, the visit of the couple to the municipal morgue to identify their parents' bodies. Set at a hillside church, the seventeenth-century Santa Maria del Soccorso, with mostly natural light streaming through the windows (softly photographed by Luigi Kuveiller),* the scene has a sacramental feeling and represents the first significant softening of Wendell's unsentimental attitude. Wilder movingly holds on Pamela for a long time in close-up as she lifts a sheet to look at her mother's off-screen body, with a tear falling from her eye, while Wendell appears behind her, out of focus. His look of wonderment and admiration is the turning point in his character.

---

* Kuveiller had been camera operator on numerous films, including Michelangelo Antonioni's *L'avventura*, before becoming a director of photography. Wilder chose him after admiring his work on Elio Petri's *Un tranquillo posto di campagna* (*A Quiet Place in the Country*, 1968). Working with an Italian cinematographer helped give *Avanti!* its authentic feeling of place.

The use of focus tells us Wendell knows he is intruding on a private grief he does not quite belong with and reinforces the shy tenderness in his movement toward Pamela. She is holding a bouquet of daffodils that provides the only bright color in the composition, and the soundtrack is quietly playing the old couple's love theme, "La Luna" (The Moon) by Don Backy and Detto Mariano. Although Wendell earlier sheepishly revealed, like a small boy, that he didn't even know what daffodils were, he thanks her with newfound gentleness when she splits the bouquet and puts half of the flowers on his father's body. The mood is one of discreet respect, with subtle overtones of a wedding ceremony between the younger couple when both raise their hands and swear "I do" to identify the bodies; the setting and tone are similar to the visit to the Mexican church that helps bring Emmy and Georges emotionally closer in a quasi-marriage sacrament. Although Wendell has been guilty of a series of crude assaults on Pamela's sensibilities, he is appalled when the coroner (Pippo Franco) breaks the spell in the morgue/church by elaborately stamping the triplicate death certificate in a coolly practiced routine.

That gag is hilarious, serving as counterpoint to the emotional impact of the sequence; here is the true Lubitschean mixture of sadness and gaiety. Wendell's harsh remark to Pamela that further jars the mood is his response to her suggestion that they simply bury the old couple in Ischia, which he finds unthinkable (but by the end agrees to do). After he stomps out, and we see her hurt reaction in close-up, there is a long shot of Pamela alone in the mortuary, opening a window to let the air and sunlight into the room. It is the most beautiful and quietly symbolic moment in a film that represents the summit of Wilder's romantic sensibility.

"THE REEVALUATION OF OUR VALUES"

Although *Avanti!* was criticized by impatient 1972 audiences for being "slow," and reviewers often scolded Wilder for letting it run two hours and twenty-four minutes (even Lemmon told me, "I did feel it is long"), the pacing is part of Wilder's point. He defiantly luxuriates in relaxed pacing to demonstrate the leisurely rhythms of life on the Italian island in contrast to Wendell's frenzied American personality and inability to appreciate the finer aspects of life. Although Wendell's rude remark at the end of the morgue scene breaks the mood in an expressive way, signaling the crass and impatient nature from which he has yet to be released, Pamela gives him the cold shoulder until he persuades her to reenact their parents' favorite dinner on the terrace of the charming old hotel. He has an ulterior motive, thinking she has abducted the bodies, which are actually being held for ransom by a local mob family, so he is behaving like one of Wilder's gigolo characters in pretending to romance her before he succumbs to the spell of the romantic past and her erotic charms. His play-acting gradually turns into genuine affection as he is transformed into a better man.

The pacing is also Wilder's rebuke to the frantically accelerated tempo of early 1970s filmmaking. "I was very fond of that picture," Diamond told me. "We are firm believers in doing in comedy what Mr. Hitchcock believes in doing in suspense: let the audience into something and let them enjoy it." Citing the prolonged suspenseful sequence in *Sabotage* leading up to a bomb exploding, Diamond said *Avanti!* was "so constructed that you knew long before Lemmon did that his father had had an affair—maybe we extended that too long" (actually it takes only half an hour before Carlucci admits, "They were making it"). I wouldn't want to lose a minute of *Avanti!*, whose screenplay, constructed with the painstaking care Wilder and Diamond always brought to their work, also takes its time orchestrating the farcical intricacies of Wendell and Carlucci trying to deal with Italian bureaucracy, the subplot about the murdered valet, and other jokes contrasting Italian and American attitudes. If the Mirisch Corporation had taken cutting shears to *Avanti!* as they did to *Sherlock Holmes*, those elements would have been tightened to the detriment of the film, along with the film's luxuriating in the romantic-comedy misunderstandings between Wendell and Pamela that are its heart. *Avanti!* has the intricate texture of a good novel, which helps make it, in my view, one of Wilder's three best films, along with *The Apartment* and the perfectly crafted farce *Some Like It Hot*, which remains perhaps the funniest American sound film.

Although the nude swimming scene in *Avanti!* escaped trimming, it surprisingly came in for criticism from some prudish and humorless reviewers. For those who have misunderstood Wilder's attitude toward the female body, it was made explicitly clear in an engaging 1993 French television documentary by Annie Tresgot about his lifelong passion as an art connoisseur. *Billy Wilder, artiste (ou: Ne réveillez pas le cinéaste qui dort)* (*Billy Wilder, Artist: or, Don't Wake the Sleeping Filmmaker*) shows him proudly displaying some of

the many nude paintings by European artists he had collected since the 1920s.*
Wilder comments engagingly on many pieces in his collection while thumbing through the lavishly published catalogue from the 1989 auction he held
at Christie's in New York. One is a Botero, a painting of a *zaftig* woman in a
bathtub with her back to the camera, peering at herself in a mirror, her behind
looming large toward the spectator. Wilder says, "I wake up in the morning,
and I see her behind, and I feel good. Then I come to the studio, and I feel
very depressed—nobody has a behind like this." His erotic affection for such
a painting by an artist known for his well-rounded women helps explain the
genuine delectation Wilder takes in Pamela's *zaftig* figure. The documentary
demonstrates that he emphatically does not share the modern obsession with
thinness, although that should be abundantly clear from *Avanti!* As the
screenplay puts it while describing the nude swimming scene, "Maybe she is
a little overweight, but in the early morning light, she glistens quite
appetizingly—that's if you prefer Rubens to Giacometti."

The kind of Ugly American Wendell represents—akin to the crass businessmen Gary Cooper plays in *Bluebeard's Eighth Wife* and *Love in the
Afternoon*—allows *Avanti!* elements of sharp political satire that go well
beyond the mild social commentary of those films. The political themes
mostly were unappreciated in the general dismissal of *Avanti!* but seem even
savvier in hindsight. And perhaps Wilder's barbed, more specific anti-
American jibes helped contribute to the film's dismissal, as previously happened when he blended political satire with romantic comedy in *A Foreign
Affair*. When Pamela (mistakenly) thinks Wendell has moved her into his
suite without asking, she unloads about the roots of his arrogant behavior in
a speech that reflects the refugee filmmaker's disillusionment late in life about
his adopted land:

> Not that I expected any subtlety from you. After all, you're American—
> you're accustomed to having everything your own way—you see something
> you want, and you just grab it. London Bridge, for instance—you simply
> took it apart, stone by stone, and shipped it off to some place in the Wild

---

* Tresgot earlier directed a 1980 documentary entitled *Portrait d'un homme "à 60% parfait"* (*Portrait
of a "60 Percent Perfect Man": Billy Wilder*), featuring critic Michel Ciment interviewing Wilder in his
apartment, office, and modest Malibu beach weekend retreat.

West. Or the *Queen Mary*—with all that tradition—sitting there off the coast of California—reduced to a floating cafeteria. Ah, such conceit. Such arrogance. You act as though you owned the world. Playing golf on the Moon! Now, really! And then you wonder why people don't like you, though you're like spoiled children. No manners, no consideration.

She adds a critique of sexual presumption, Wilder's comment on the loss of the Lubitschean sensibility in the modern world: "It's not that I'm Women's Lib or anything—I don't mind being treated as a sex object. But it's like any other game—you have to play according to the rules—or it takes all the fun out of it."

The screenplay describes Wendell (at his originally intended age of thirty-two) as "a Young Republican, he occasionally plays a game of squash with S. Agnew.* To him, W. Cronkite is a Maoist and R. Nader is a pain in the ass. He thinks J. E. Hoover should do *something* about J. Fonda and bell-bottoms." A staunch Nixon supporter, Wendell has lined up Henry Kissinger to appear at his father's funeral in Baltimore; all 216,000 employees of Armbruster Industries will watch it live on closed-circuit color television, "except for Puerto Rico—they get it in black-and-white." En route to the island, Wendell dictates his eulogy into a tape recorder, claiming that his father was "an old-fashioned man—I mean that in the noblest sense of the word," and he is horrified when he discovers that his father was actually "a dirty old man. . . . You mean all the time that we thought he was over here getting cured he was getting *laid*? . . . Why, that gray-haired, self-righteous son of a bitch!"

Wilder, as a boy, had made a similar discovery about his own father having an illegitimate son, which he used as leverage against him; clearly Wendell envies his father the fun he has never allowed himself to have. But by wearing his clothes, adopting his romantic rituals, and having a romance with the daughter of his father's mistress, Wendell in effect is transformed into his father, assuming the identity of a man who lives by the more generous, sexually freer standards of Lubitsch's world. After he and Pamela return from

---

* The draft copy in Diamond's papers has age "42" handwritten over "32." Lemmon was forty-seven when he made the film.

their nude swim, the couple tenderly address each other by their parents' nick-names: "Good night, Willie.—Good night, Kate."

By the end the newly sensitized Wendell is repelled by the cynical behav-ior of an old family friend from the State Department, J. J. "Jojo" Blodgett (Edward Andrews, in a role written for Walter Matthau, who had a sched-uling conflict). Blodgett tells Wendell, "Mind you, I don't object to foreign-ers speaking a foreign language—I just wish they'd all speak the *same* foreign language." Blodgett bamboozles the Italian customs authorities to hustle the body of Wendell's father out of Ischia under diplomatic cover, saying to Wen-dell with a smirk, "Someday I'll tell you how we got Batista out of Cuba." One of the Italians Blodgett orders around gives him the fascist salute after invoking the name of Mussolini, another of Wilder's sly digs at Nixonian pol-itics. Blodgett is so right-wing he tells Carlucci that Benjamin Franklin, a much earlier honored guest of the hotel, couldn't get a security clearance in modern America. But the diplomat does offer the hotelier, who is thinking of relocating, a precise (and prescient) overview of the Middle Eastern polit-ical situation, even referring to the taboo topic of Israel having a first-strike nuclear capability. When asked if there will be a war in the Middle East, Blodgett first says huffily, "We don't give out that kind of information," but goes on to offer it anyway on a confidential basis (the film was released about ten months before the Yom Kippur War).

Such jokes may seem incidental (indeed, I made the mistake in my con-temporary essay on the film of regarding them that way), but, like Pamela's speech about Americans, they help put Wendell's arrogance into a sociopo-litical context. In doing so, they bring up topics rarely discussed in Holly-wood films, like Wilder's savvy and equally eclectic satirical zingers in *A Foreign Affair* and *One, Two, Three*. Trudy Bolter, in a 2007 essay on *Avanti!*, makes a compelling case that this line of humor is no mere diversion from the love story but part of what makes the film a potent political satire of American arrogance and the colonialist mentality in the disastrous latter stages of the Vietnam War. Wendell and Blodgett epitomize blundering, clueless Ugly Americans contemptuously trying to boss around and domi-nate the inhabitants of a foreign country. But Blodgett is so joyously reac-tionary that when he appears near the end he throws into relief Wendell's newfound (though not total) enlightenment.

And since nothing is unmotivated in a Wilder-Diamond screenplay, the unusually frank discussion of realpolitik between Carlucci and Blodgett is unobtrusively raised as a stalling device by the hotel director to prevent the diplomat from discovering Pamela in Wendell's suite: adultery is more of a state secret than impending war. As a counterpoint to its theme of sexual liberation, *Avanti!* pokes further fun at the pompous, portly Blodgett by suggesting that he is impotent. Blodgett is also deceived by Wendell into running a double Wilderian scam without his knowledge: Wendell by now has decided to bury his father on the island with Pamela's mother. He has substituted another body to put in the U.S. Navy helicopter—a criminal, the murdered valet who, like Wilder himself, always wanted to become an American. The expatriate Bruno (Gianfranco Barra) was deported from New York for pulling a pistol on Vietnam War protesters who were burning the American flag on the Fourth of July. And when Wendell sneers at "Italian justice," the usually jovial Carlucci replies simply, "What about Sacco and Vanzetti?"

Even though only the opening of *Avanti!* takes place in the United States, the film's jokes about right-wing politics and misguided patriotism help round out the film's satirical portrait of the national mindset in the Nixon era. In an interview before its release with the French film magazine *Positif,* Wilder told Michel Ciment that what he intended with *Avanti!* was "the reevaluation of our values. . . . It's at its heart a story of love between a son and his father. He starts to understand a father about whom he never thought. . . . He's closer to his dead father than to his living father. It's a reevaluation of Americans, of their mistakes, of that which matters and that which doesn't." Reflecting on his increasing tendency to shoot in Europe in his later years, Wilder first called it "unconscious" but then admitted, "Maybe it comes from a deep desire to return here from time to time—to change my eating habits, to see the place I come from."

Bolter's essay argues that the film's basic subject is "a retreat into the past by an adulterous couple gripped by a 'crisis of modernity,' unable to find a creative solution to the jumbled world left behind by the onward advance of the 1960's." Although that emphasis on the aesthetic superiority of the past helps account for *Avanti!* being considered old-fashioned in its day, I disagree with Bolter that reenacting their dead parents' romance in a "ghost play" makes Wendell and Pamela "reactionaries . . . lost and uncreative people obsessed with the past and unable to move on." On the contrary, fortunately for Wendell, the exposure to another, more truly liberated, even if older, culture, and the influence of the modern younger generation represented by Pamela, makes him a mensch. I regard the recurrence of that theme as Wilder's defiant view of the values he prefers to the crassly unromantic, emotionally exploitive, politically and culturally callous world of 1972 and particularly in the United States. Bolter more accurately points out that the film's political satire could have been perceived (on whatever level of audience consciousness) as "anti-American" in the waning days of the American defeat in Vietnam, and the year of the Watergate break-in, since Nixon was on Wilder's mind in this film as well as in *The Front Page*. Although Wilder seemed out of step with its times, he actually was *opposed* to his times, a crucial distinction. It was not the first occasion in his long and iconoclastic career when he was regarded as out of step, but being mistaken as a reactionary damaged his career.

As Lubitschean as *Avanti!* is, if Lubitsch had lived to make a romantic comedy in 1972, would he have shown a couple swimming naked? Probably not, since his style was more discreet than Wilder's, but Wilder was not simply trying to bend to the changing times by being more au courant. He was genuinely enjoying his newfound freedom as a filmmaker to express his full feelings about romance and sexuality. So when the audience that was flocking to *Deep Throat* and *Behind the Green Door* rejected his buoyantly alive, lyrically romantic frolic as old-fashioned, no wonder Wilder was offended: "So he got laid. So big fuckin' deal, right?"

Wilder pretended he didn't think much of his supposed failures, telling me in 1978, "*Avanti!*, I wiped that off too. That was fine, but, you see, too soft." But he acknowledged that as a filmmaker trying to keep working in the New Hollywood that had replaced the old studio system, he had become passé and had lost his audience:

> If you are a decent human being, and if you are, let us say, a composer of dance tunes, and if all you can do are the polka and the waltz, and you keep composing those and the dance floor is empty, they don't come out to dance, then you say, "Well, screw that, if they want rock 'n' roll or disco, I can do that." But *I* can't do it. I cannot even *pretend* that I can do it, because if I did it, that would be real suicide. They still would know it is a phony, and they would not come out to dance. It just is that they don't want this kind of picture nowadays.

Or as Diamond put it at the American Film Institute Life Achievement Award tribute to Wilder in 1986, "Tonight we've been looking at clips from a lot of old pictures. This business has come a long way since then. But why should I depress you?"

Wilder publicly tended to brush off the pain he felt over his career problems by maintaining what Matthau shrewdly described as his facade of "brilliant repartee." When an AFI fellow asked Wilder and Diamond at a seminar in the late 1970s what they were working on, Wilder replied, "We very probably will retire, like Secretariat, to stud. No, we'll do something, but . . . you get a little scared. Is it pertinent enough? Is it new enough? Is it big enough? Who are we going to have in there? Just another picture—that doesn't interest us. You hope that the game will go into an extra inning, because you feel you've still got a few hits left. And if that does not work, I'm just going to sign up with a Japanese team and sit on the bench and wait for Kurosawa to break his leg."

Shortly after *Avanti!* came out and flopped, Wilder's deepest feelings were more privately revealed. They echoed the premonitory anxiety, the "Filmterror," he had publicly expressed in 1927, before entering the film business. When Rex McGee was a University of Southern California film student, he wrote a letter of appreciation for *Avanti!* Expressing dismay at the audience reception, McGee asked if there was anything he could do to help. To his surprise, Wilder called him at his dormitory and asked him to visit his office at the Goldwyn Studios.

McGee recalled, "Billy might have needed somebody to talk to at that point and to kind of lay out his concerns. I remember just sitting there in that chair in that Goldwyn office where he had written his great films. He was pacing and pacing back and forth incredibly, with that walking stick he always carried: 'What should I do? Should I stop making movies? Should I write plays? Should I play the horses at Hollywood Park?' And I was just sinking in my chair. It was an amazing moment, because I was twenty-one at that time, two years out of small-town Texas." His youthful admirer found it "pretty bizarre" to find his hero confessing his doubts about his viability after more than four decades in the film industry. "I was just scared—what am I doing here?" But he felt Wilder was reassured that in "the young audience, there's somebody out there who likes what I'm doing." That led to a long friendship with McGee, who observed all the filming on *The Front Page* and

Fedora and worked as an unofficial assistant on the latter film, as well as taking dictation for Wilder on speeches and other writing after Diamond died.*

But even if Wilder still had some admirers in the early 1970s, he realized that with *Avanti!*, in which he had expressed himself so freely only to be rebuffed by the general public, he had reaching a turning point in his career and was coming to the finale. As the script describes the cemetery scene at the end of the film, "If you've got to be buried, this is the place: it's lovely, peaceful and wildly romantic."

"I WENT TO A MASQUERADE, DARLING"

In the 1993 French documentary about Wilder's lifelong obsession with art collecting, the camera pans across a row of leather-bound volumes of his screenplays on a shelf in his office. They range from his early Hollywood collaborations with Brackett through almost every film he wrote and directed after that. But the shot ends with the screenplay of *Fedora*. *Buddy Buddy* is not represented on Wilder's shelf. That is a clear indication of what he considered the real end of his filmmaking career. And so it is fitting that this critical study of Wilder will concentrate its final sustained attention on *Fedora* and what that 1978 film reveals about him.

Despite its uneven and flawed nature, its troubled status as a *film maudit*, *Fedora,* the story of a retired movie queen who persuades—and eventually compels—her daughter to impersonate her, is eloquent and sometimes overwhelmingly moving. Perhaps more deeply than any other in his canon, it encapsulates Wilder's major themes of disguise and masquerade, the illusions and corruption of show business, and the problem of identity and how it is constructed.

This brings us to fully resolving a question that baffled me when I began this study. Why is it that so many of Wilder's films involve masquerades? The

---

* McGee was an AFI intern on *The Front Page* and kept a journal of the shooting. He also chronicled *Fedora* for the Directors Guild of America (Lemmon contributed funding to that project). McGee appears in *Fedora* as the photographer in the scene of the impromptu Academy Award presentation to the faux Fedora by Henry Fonda as the Academy president. In his own career as a screenwriter and screenwriting teacher, McGee says he thinks every day of lessons Wilder taught him.

more I studied him, that obsession seemed the key to uncoding his work. His characters use disguises and false names, they adopt false identities, they fool each other endlessly. They reinvent themselves, successfully or otherwise. They try to outwit society and circumvent laws and customs by pretending to be what they are not. They are exposed or expose themselves, whether happily or tragically. And even when actual impersonation is not involved, scams and con-games proliferate, elaborate deceptions abound. Indeed, society in Wilder films seems to be built largely around deception. The many tongue-in-cheek movie jokes in his work and his self-conscious playing with the audience about their awareness of movie conventions stem from his foregrounding of the deceptiveness inherent in storytelling, especially Hollywood storytelling, with its many forbidden areas he learned to navigate.

Besides the *loci classici* of this pattern in Wilder's work—*Some Like It Hot, One, Two, Three, Kiss Me, Stupid, Avanti!*—the numerous other Wilder movies that involve elaborate physical masquerades are *The Major and the Minor*; *Five Graves to Cairo* and *Sherlock Holmes* (with characters who are spies); *Love in the Afternoon* (a virginal student pretending to be a sexually experienced woman of the world); *Witness for the Prosecution* (Dietrich's character impersonating a Cockney slattern); and *Irma la Douce* (Nestor the policeman-turned-pimp passing himself off as "Lord X" to keep other men from having sex with Irma). Even the American POWs in *Stalag 17* at one point imitate Hitler en masse to mock their German guards.

Then there all the scams and frauds, some of them criminal, in such films as *Mauvaise graine, Double Indemnity, Ace in the Hole, The Fortune Cookie*, and *The Front Page. The Apartment* is perhaps the most intricate case in Wilder's work of moral deception revolving around a fraud, while characters in *A Foreign Affair, Sunset Blvd.*, and *Sabrina* also deceive others or are transformed into something they previously were not. *The Lost Weekend* is about a man constantly deceiving himself and everyone around him by trying to hide his addiction.

Although some of the transformations in Wilder films are beneficial to the characters, when the changes are self-deceptive they tend not to be salutary. As Thoreau adds in *Walden* after his warning about enterprises requiring new clothes, "If there is not a new man, how can the new clothes be made to fit?" The new old clothes Wendell wears in *Avanti!* fit because in the process he does become a new man, letting his latent romanticism surface.

There are exceptions to the destructive quality of self-deception in Wilder films—the complexities of Lindbergh's character may seem to be outside of the limited scope of *The Spirit of St. Louis*, yet we could say that the character, based on what we know of his later life, is deceptively heroic. The flight that transforms his life—an Icarus-like act of hubris—will have destructive consequences of which the character is not aware. If there is any overriding moral to all these stories, perhaps it is the one Kurt Vonnegut draws in his novel *Mother Night* about an American agent who pretends to be a Nazi propagandist and finds he can't shake the disguise: "We are what we pretend to be, so we must be careful about what we pretend to be."

That's the ultimate horror involved in a masquerade—the loss of one's identity, a fear to which exiles and immigrants are particularly susceptible. It's the fate that befalls the false "Fedora" and causes her to commit suicide in the opening scene. Other Wilder characters suffer from this dilemma to varying degrees, but in his lighter works actual loss of identity is not the issue, only a feigned transformation. When Ginger Rogers's Susan Applegate in the first Hollywood film Wilder directed, *The Major and the Minor*, pretends to be a child, the joke is on (almost) everyone else in the film. "Su-Su" is never in danger of forgetting who she really is or being tempted to let her false identity take over her life. She can't wait to escape it and be herself.

When Susan explains at the end to her inquisitive mother, "I went to a masquerade, darling," Mrs. Applegate wonders, "For three days?" Susan responds, "Not now, mother. Don't ask any more questions, please."* At various points in the intricately absurd plot, Susan impersonates her mother and the fiancée of Ray Milland's character as well as her own childish persona. By the end she's metamorphosed from woman to child to mother and back to grown woman again, sexily decked out in traveling attire at the hometown train station, ready to wed her unlikely, somewhat unwholesome semiadult partner in this queasily funny fairy tale.

Making a precursor to *Lolita*, as Wilder boasted in later years, was an astonishing achievement to slip past the censors in 1942. Wilder got away with the satire of that sexual taboo right at the start of his Hollywood directing

---

* In a further twist, Mrs. Applegate is played by Rogers's own mother, Lela, a leading Hollywood reactionary who became a blacklist ringleader. Her casting may have been another factor that protected Wilder during the postwar Red Scare.

career by hiding his darker concerns behind a facade of frivolity. The innuendo about subconscious sexual urges is barely masked, at least from our more knowing viewpoint today, but how much the public discerned that playfully subversive theme at the time is unclear. The trailer winked at the theme by proclaiming the film "A BEDROOM STORY FOR GROWNUP CHILDREN." And an ad for the film asked, "Is she a kid . . . or is SHE KIDDING?"

Wilder approached the opportunity with canny calculation. As Ed Sikov puts it, "An adroit bridge player, Billy understood the concept of vulnerability: because he'd been scoring extremely well as a screenwriter, the penalties for losing the next round were much greater. By agreeing to direct something as apparently inconsequential as a light romantic comedy, Wilder reduced the chances of catastrophe enormously. The executives would still be watching his every move, but they would be doing so under lights that were much less glaring." Wilder recalled thinking, "I'm going to make a picture that is going to be very popular, and they're not going to send me back now to the typewriter." He told Crowe, "And I kind of forced myself, you know, to not make a deep picture, but to be pretty close to the surface. . . . I built from there." Nevertheless, his thematic intentions beneath the surface were as deviously deceptive as his commercialism in working from such a seemingly innocuous and silly plotline.

Susan retreats sexually into her protective little-girl disguise as "Su-Su" not only because she can't afford the adult fare to return home from New York but also to protect herself from predatory men. Her disguise is so comically obvious that the film becomes a Brechtian demonstration of the alienation effect, revealing the blindness and moral denial of nearly everyone she meets. But in trying to flee, she outwits herself, because while on the train, Su-Su becomes the love object of Milland's thoroughly obtuse U.S. Army Major Philip Kirby. They share a train compartment en route to his military academy in Wisconsin, but he fails for the longest time to recognize that she is a grown woman. She tells him accurately, "You are a strange gentleman." And when he tells her, "You know, Su-Su, you're a very precocious child," she replies with a smirk, "You *bet* I am." The film "explains" Major Kirby's subconscious proclivity only by giving him a bum eye and making him squint curiously while he says such things as, "You look almost grownup . . . not a child anymore . . . Su-Su, you're a knockout!"

The point of the most bizarre scene from today's perspective further reveals the absurdity of the attitudes toward sexuality in America of the early 1940s. After Philip arrives at the academy with Susan, his bitchy fiancée, Pamela (Rita Johnson), and the school's board members initially are shocked to find that Susan traveled in his train compartment. But Philip assures them it was fine, because she is only twelve. They are vastly relieved, and the chaplain even says, "What a happy solution!" Rather than having Philip arrested, as might happen today, they all breathe a huge sigh of relief, even Pamela. Wilder's wickedly knowing satire of the obliviousness of American puritanical society is surpassed only by his thoroughly corrosive portrayal of the hypocrisy of the rancid small town of Climax, Nevada, in *Kiss Me, Stupid*.

Wilder is exposing, for those who can recognize it, how dumb and hypocritical the system of censorship was. Su-Su's masquerade is so transparent that it exposes and ridicules the other characters for not seeing through it. Aside from a couple of professionally skeptical train conductors, the only other exception, fittingly enough, is an actual teenage girl, Lucy Hill (Diana Lynn). A sarcastic budding scientist with a keen eye and mind, Lynn virtually steals the show. Despite her often facetious tone, Lucy is sincere in her sisterly bond with Su-Su, helping her maintain her disguise and navigate the intricate social waters of the military academy, its dubious adult ranks and squad of horny cadets. Lucy's precociously wised-up prodigy is Wilder's alter ego onscreen.

The censors apparently were as oblivious as Paramount to what he actually had in mind, and this devious but thorough satirical treatment of the forbidden subject of pedophilia is part of the covert satirical point of the film. Its masquerade theme demonstrates the blindness of the self-appointed moral guardians of society and modern American society's inability to see what is happening before its eyes. What James Agee wrote about Preston Sturges's outrageously cheeky parody of the Virgin Birth following the gang bang of a drunkenly oblivious small-town woman in *The Miracle of Morgan's Creek* (1944) is also true of Wilder's Hollywood directing debut: "In proportion to the inanity and repressiveness of the age you live in, play the age as comedy if you want to get away with murder. . . . The wildly factitious story makes comic virtues of every censor-dodging necessity. Thanks to these devices the Hays office has been either hypnotized into a liberality for which it should be thanked, or has been raped in its sleep."

"I *AM* BIG. IT'S THE PICTURES THAT GOT SMALL"

After the faded silent-movie goddess Norma Desmond kills Joe Gillis and descends into utter madness in *Sunset Blvd.*, she murmurs to herself, "The stars are ageless." The legendary old Polish-born movie star in *Fedora* (Hildegard Knef) never entirely loses touch with reality, even if she behaves in some mad ways, including trying to circumvent and deny the aging process. Fedora's torment in her disfigured, isolated old age is to be fully conscious of the harm she has done to herself and others through her vanity and ambition. *Fedora* is Wilder's mournful testament film about show business as the terminal form of the masquerade, symbolized by its annihilating effects on a great star's personality. As Cecil B. DeMille says of Norma, "A dozen press agents working overtime can do terrible things to the human spirit." The harsh realities of obsolescence, aging, mortality, and, worst of all, loss of identity conspire to make Fedora's life a hellish demonstration of how even the stars are not, in fact, ageless.

Nor is the film medium portrayed as immortal: Fedora's career in classic films is shown as largely forgotten, like Norma's career in silent films. Wilder's farewell to his art form in *Fedora* as something obsolete, a distant memory, is almost unrelievedly bitter. Yet it is laced with some of his characteristic dark humor as well as poignant regret about the lost possibilities of the film medium, as represented by his re-creations of the style of Golden Age Hollywood in flashbacks to the making of a 1940s Fedora vehicle and a more recent period film in the bygone vein. That most moving evocation of the past in *Fedora* carries overwhelming symbolic significance in Wilder's career. He shows us a modern London (emphatically not Hollywood) soundstage where, with eloquent and defiant improbability, a nostalgic musical in the Lubitschean style is being filmed. Against a painted backdrop of Vienna's Schönbrunn Palace, the summer residence of the Hapsburg royal family, characters dance to the grand accompaniment of a Miklós Rósza composition entitled "The Last Waltz." As a camera on a crane follows the dancers, Wilder's camera tracking gracefully along with them, it is a thrilling cinematic moment encapsulating the elegant artifice of a lost art form and the era of Wilder's youth. And he can't help having the director of the film-within-the-film call for a retake to improve on the vision.

Although *Fedora* is severely damaged by casting and other problems, as a supreme example of an artist's late style, it has the eloquent simplicity and compression, and the obsessive nature, of a valedictory work. And it has the occasional awkwardness, incoherence, and disregard for the audience and current fashion that often accompany such works of final abandon. Made with a gracefully restrained visual approach (with the help of production designer Alexandre Trauner and cinematographer Gerry Fisher), *Fedora* has the overwhelming sense of regret that is often characteristic of an artist's farewell. As a melancholy survey of Wilder's worldview, it abounds with references to his earlier films and becomes a culmination of his themes. And like its heroine(s) and the director himself by this stage in his imperiled career, it is something of a grand ruin, a disaster with elements of faded glory.

A funereal tone pervades *Fedora*. The framing device surrounding the flashbacks that reveal the mystery of Fedora to the viewer of the film, though not to the general public as they appear onscreen, is the ghoulish display of the reconstructed corpse of the fabled star's daughter lying in state in their Paris mansion. The younger woman known as "Fedora," whose actual name was Antonia (Marthe Keller plays that double-faceted role), has killed herself after secretly impersonating her mother (known as "The Countess") onscreen for years, ultimately to the destruction of her own personality. The false Fedora is displayed for her fans, many of whom are casually dressed, to ogle. Like the hoopla at the cave disaster in *Ace in the Hole*, it's a morbidly voyeuristic media event, televised "like it was some goddam premiere," as William Holden's producer character, Barry Detweiler, contemptuously puts it in his narration. But he admits that "at least she was going out in style."

The music played at the grotesque memorial spectacle, which in effect is Wilder's funeral for Hollywood and the movies, is Sibelius's "Valse Triste" (Sad Waltz). *Fedora* itself is Wilder's eloquent elegy for the cinema. He laments how it has been destroyed, in part by large, impersonal forces beyond the control of himself and his characters, by changing times and fashions and economic conditions, but also by the human failings common to weak, spoiled, narcissistic creatures who are victims of the system but collude with it to obliterate the more gracious traditions of filmmaking he cherished.

This alarmingly dark film about what Irving Thalberg, in a profound phrase, called "the business of creating illusions" predictably caused consternation and derision from the Hollywood studios, most reviewers, and the public of the late 1970s. Those who did show up to see it often were aghast at Wilder's final pulling-back of the curtain to reveal the ugly reality behind the carefully cultivated facade of the movie business. Wilder's equivalent of Ingmar Bergman's meta-film *Persona* was his cri de coeur as his career approached its soon-to-be-enforced ending. He anticipated that his camera would soon be taken away, for, like Fedora herself and the kind of classical filmmaking she embodied, he was regarded as fit only to be shipped off into exile and oblivion. It was twenty-eight years since Joe Gillis had called Norma Desmond a "poor devil, still waving proudly to a parade which had long since passed her by," a line that inspired the title of Kevin Brownlow's classic 1968 history of silent films, *The Parade's Gone By . . . .* And now the line applied to Wilder himself. He also clearly identified with Barry, a has-been producer struggling to keep viable in a radically changed business. "Countess, I'm gonna level with you," he finally tells her about the comeback project he has been pitching. "I've got nothing—zilch. It's a whole different business now—the kids with beards have taken over. They don't need scripts—just give 'em a hand-held camera with a zoom lens."

Although you can clearly hear the cranky voice of Wilder behind that old man's complaint—and of Diamond, "quite vociferously," his son said—it doesn't entirely reflect Wilder's own more complex attitude toward the state of the film business in the 1970s. By the time he made *Fedora*, the challenge and promise of the New Hollywood—the time when the kids with beards briefly ran the show—already had largely evaporated, with the resilient power of the commercial system reasserting itself as the formulaic blockbuster mentality took over. Wilder was keenly aware that he had grown out of touch with filmmaking trends. "I could never do a picture like *American Graffiti*, good as it was," he said when *Buddy Buddy* was released. "I don't know those kids, and if I tried to do it they would sense that I'm not one of them. To keep your sanity and your self-respect, you must believe that there will be an audience for what you want to do. It may not be the blockbuster of all time, but what is wrong with a modest success?"

But he also admitted uncertainty about how to proceed with his own ideas in a market increasingly dominated by special-effects extravaganzas and other films designed for the youth market. While stubbornly continuing to cast his favorite aging stars, such as Lemmon, Matthau, and Holden, Wilder told me a few months before the long-delayed *Fedora* opened with little success in the United States:

> Unless you are riding on an enormous hit, unless you have a deal with Travolta, unless you are willing to do *Damien III*, it is very difficult. You have to go to the money people, the Bank of America, you say, "Hey listen, I've got this great story. I think it would make an absolutely marvelous picture. I need $4,000,000." They say, "Who is in it?" You say, "Wouldn't you like to hear the story first? Because it's real, kind of brand-new, it's got great scenes, it's got excitement." "*Who is in it?*" "I don't know yet." "Sorry."
>
> Another guy comes and he's got a brown bag. He says, "I want to make a picture out of this. I have Newman and I have Redford and I have Jane Fonda." "How much?" "I need $12,000,000." "Here it is." And on the way out the guy from the bank says, "What is in that brown bag?" He says, "Horseshit!" "It doesn't matter. You have those three people, go and do it." That's the way it goes."

But despite Wilder's angry disdain for the generally unimaginative and sleazy level to which Hollywood had sunk, he was capable of appreciating the rare good work when he saw it. He expressed great admiration for some films made in that decade and beyond. Talking with fellows of the AFI, he described a film by one of those "kids with beards," Francis Ford Coppola's *The Godfather Part II* (1974), as "certainly among the five best American pictures ever made. In execution, in perception, I thought it was an absolute masterpiece." Wilder admired numerous other films made in his old age, such as his longtime friend Fred Zinnemann's *Julia*; Woody Allen's *Annie Hall*; Steven Spielberg's *Close Encounters of the Third Kind*; Volker Schlöndorff and Margarethe von Trotta's *The Lost Honor of Katharina Blum*; *Quiz Show*; *The Full Monty*; *American Beauty*; the German World War II saga *Das Boot*; the Japanese romantic comedy *Shall We Dance?*; and (incongruously) Robert Zemeckis's schmaltzy right-wing fantasy *Forrest Gump* (Wilder called it "a picture about America that could have only been made in America"). Wilder also admired directors Hal Ashby, Martin Scorsese, Barry Levinson, and Bernardo Bertolucci.

And Wilder said to Crowe of Stanley Kubrick's harrowing Vietnam War film *Full Metal Jacket* (1987), "The first half of *Full Metal Jacket* was the best picture I ever saw. Where the guy sits on the toilet and blows his head off? Terrific. Then he lost himself with the girl guerrilla. The second half, down a little. It's still a wonderful picture." Wilder even more passionately admired Spielberg's Holocaust film, *Schindler's List* (1993), a project he had wanted to film himself. But the American studio films he admired were unconventional exceptions pushed through the system by major filmmakers who had earned the clout to circumvent the limitations most directors labored under, including himself.

What made Wilder despondent about his medium by the time he made *Fedora* was that the system was mostly mired in endless sequelitis, too often cranking out a parade of incompetent trash, stupidly violent or smarmy material, and mindless juvenilia. He told me that while watching cable television, "I get to see those lunatic kinds of pictures that obviously have been compiled by a computer that says what works, what doesn't work. I saw a thing of Clint Eastwood's called *The Gauntlet*. It is unbelievable. It takes everything that has worked in a picture, kind of piled up and superimposed. The whole thing is like a mad goulash." Paul Diamond recalled that before Wilder found the source material for *Fedora*, one of the projects he and Iz were discussing making was a film dealing with the New Hollywood, a companion piece to *Sunset Blvd.* reflecting on the changes that had taken place in the industry in the interim. Like other veteran directors who had come through the studio system, Wilder was used to being fully financed and mostly left alone to do his job without having to scramble for funding and take notes from young executives who didn't know much about the art and craft of picture-making, and he was foundering in the 1970s, especially because his commercial position had weakened as the industry radically changed. As Paul put it, when Wilder and his father made *Fedora* and had to cope with the new ways of working, "They were victims of the New Hollywood."

That's the problem Barry Detweiler, like Wilder, is forced to confront. They were prescient in their warnings of the ruinous danger to the art of film, like canaries in a coal mine. If anything, the situation has become much worse in subsequent years, driving most stories about characters and genuinely adult subject matter to cable or streaming. Even long before the COVID-19 pandemic that upended the theatrical market, with rare exceptions it had become largely a playground for the adolescent male sensibility, rather than the broadly encompassing habit audience it was in Wilder's heyday. That market allowed distinctive filmmakers ways to flourish more often, if they were clever in out-witting the system. Wilder quickly recognized the changes when they were beginning to happen in the 1970s, and while mourning the loss of the once-fertile art form and industry of his adopted country, he despaired of turning around its inevitable outcome, especially in his own career, at his advancing age and with his faltering commercial and critical track record.

So Wilder identified unusually closely with Barry in *Fedora*, just as he had with his earlier alter ego Joe Gillis, also played by Holden. The changes Wilder and Diamond made in Barry's character from the source material make it a much more personal work for Wilder. *Fedora* is based on a novella of the same title by Thomas Tryon, the former actor who turned to writing after becoming disillusioned with acting partly because of the abuse he suffered from director Otto Preminger while playing the title role in *The Cardinal* (1963). As a writer, Tryon was best known for the horror novel *The Other* (1971), which he adapted into a film. *Fedora* is part of his collection *Crowned Heads* (1976), a collection of tales about the film business. Tryon was a film buff with a savvy affection for Hollywood despite its often-sinister failings, and *Fedora* shows the extent to which the author had been influenced by *Sunset Blvd.*

Paul Diamond said of the novella, "My father was not enthusiastic about this book. He thought it was a very small anecdote. He felt that comparisons would be made, inevitably, to *Sunset Blvd.*, and they would probably not be flattering. And my father basically went along for the ride." He said his father had no say over the choice of material when he worked with Wilder, but "Billy had done many dramas of this nature. My father had always been a comedy writer and was perhaps not as comfortable doing this as he might have been. But, that being said, they were proud of the work. They thought they'd done a good picture. They knew that it might be a difficult sell, but they knew they had something good. The fact that it was a little melodramatic, they *liked* that. That was what Hollywood was about in the old days. And to do it in a new frame, it pleased them."

Their adaptation of the novella is one of their most elegant screenplays, with one of the most complex and gracefully executed flashback structures of any Wilder film. The script often reads better than it plays, although *Fedora* on the screen has a haunting, lyrical quality that makes it a powerful, if disconcerting and deeply flawed, emotional experience. As was typical of the impeccable Wilder-Diamond craftsmanship, the adaptation cleans up some narrative weaknesses in the source material. The comically sinister Dr. Vando (José Ferrer), the disgraced specialist in rejuvenation, is alive instead of dead, and the film shows in grisly detail how his outlandish treatments and surgery failed disastrously with Fedora in 1962. But most important, *Fedora* makes major alterations in the Barry Detweiler character. It changes him from a Norman Mailerish journalist and author who has scored a rare interview with the reclusive Fedora to a second-rate, faded Hollywood producer desperately trying to persuade her to make another comeback—or as Norma would put it, "I hate that word! It's '*return*'! A return to the millions of people who have never forgiven me for deserting the screen."

Fedora, with her enigmatic life as an iconic star going by an androgynous single name, is modeled partly on Greta Garbo, but elements are drawn from other actresses, notably Corinne Griffith (1894–1979). She testified in court late in life that she was not Corinne Griffith but her much younger sister; she claimed she had replaced the dead Corinne on the screen. As Tryon makes a point of mentioning ("Fedora's story isn't dissimilar"), Griffith also made a silent film, Frank Lloyd's *Black Oxen* (1923), in which she plays a fifty-eight-year-old Austrian countess made to look much younger through treatments resembling Dr. Vando's.

In Tryon's novella, Barry has written an as-yet-unpublished book, *The Last Fedora*, solving her mystery, which she rather implausibly revealed to him at length. He tells the story in turn to a friend who is a television personality, but on the frustrating condition that she cannot use it. That character is modeled on the pioneering TV anchorwoman Barbara Walters, for whom Wilder and Diamond wrote the role of the reporter who announces Fedora's suicide and refers to her "enigma," but the part went to Arlene Francis, a cast member of *One, Two, Three* who was best known as a TV personality. The film more dynamically shows Barry acting as an amateur sleuth while pursuing the film project to rescue his career and in the process solving a mystery he can never reveal other than by confiding it to us through his voice-over narration, a favorite Wilder device used by the dead Holden in *Sunset Blvd.* Barry is another walking dead man and another of Wilder's flawed investigator figures, someone who fails to penetrate and understand the riddle staring him in the face until it is too late.

Barry has to dun his ex-wife for money to journey to Fedora's private island in Greece so he can persuade her to star in *The Snows of Yesteryear*, an independent adaptation of Tolstoy's *Anna Karenina*. In one of the film's many grim ironies, the script he is peddling seems to give Fedora's deranged, drug-addicted daughter the idea of throwing herself under a train, as Anna famously does in the novel (which was twice filmed with Garbo starring). "I love that ending," Antonia says. "It's touching—and so inevitable." When Barry confesses to the Countess, under duress, that he is struggling to pull together the funding for the Tolstoy adaptation, he says, "For two years I've sweated blood to get this project off the ground. Now I finally found me some tax shelter guys. They're willing to finance it, but only if I can deliver Fedora. Without her there's no picture."

This is one of the many meta aspects of *Fedora*, since Barry is describing what had to be done after Universal, much to Wilder's dismay and outrage, passed on the project after buying the rights to Tryon's book and commissioning the script under option. Part of the reason the studio, led by Sidney Sheinberg, its president and chief operating officer, rejected the Wilder-Diamond script was that a wave of films about the movie business, activated because of the early-1970s nostalgia trend, had tanked. Wilder's shaky recent track record and the perception that a story about an old-time star was itself hopelessly old-fashioned also worked against *Fedora*. The other Hollywood studios passed in turn, so Wilder was pounding the pavement again as he had as a tyro in the 1930s. Universal wanted to retain the right of first refusal on any distribution deal, but Wilder defiantly repaid his own fee to prevent that. Bringing Wilder back full circle to his roots as a fledgling screenwriter in Germany, tax-shelter funding in that country eventually was arranged by the Hollywood émigré agent Paul Kohner, who in 1929 had helped make Wilder's first filmed screenplay, *The Devil's Reporter*.

It was somewhat humiliating yet strangely fitting for Wilder, after having been snubbed by Hollywood, to have to go back to Germany for financing. The Geria production was based at Bavaria Studios in Munich, the same lot where Wilder had filmed *One, Two, Three* for the Mirisches and United Artists. Lorimar, a second-tier American company, became involved in the production of *Fedora* and had a deal for a U.S. release by Allied Artists, but AA dropped the film after bad previews. Wilder had tried to "improve" *Fedora* by cutting thirteen minutes by April 1978 after a charity preview in New York and a screening for Lorimar executives, but many of his elisions misguidedly came from brief comical bits he thought prompted the audience to laugh at the serious scenes.* A May preview at a Santa Barbara theater—before an audience that had come to see *House Calls*, a contemporary comedy-drama with Matthau and Glenda Jackson—went poorly. Audience members booed and laughed derisively at parts of *Fedora*, including the scenes of Barry stripping away wallpaper in Antonia's bedroom to reveal her collage of photos of Michael York, the young actor she fruitlessly adores, and of York appearing at her memorial service. McGee said of that preview, "It was torturous." But Wilder refused to make any more cuts before the world premiere at the Cannes Film Festival on May 30. Consideration was even given to dumping *Fedora* straight to television, but United Artists eventually gave it a perfunctory release in the United States.

"It was an ordeal," Wilder told Todd McCarthy and me when we interviewed him about the production history of *Fedora* in October 1978, after it had played in Germany and France but months before its American opening the following April. "It just sapped all my strength."

When we asked why he changed Barry to a producer, Wilder said, "I could write *four* pictures about that character. Yeah, sure. That guy that's dragging his ass along Hollywood Boulevard." *Fedora* spotlights Barry's precarious and humiliating financial status, of which he is constantly but gently reminded by the manager of his shabby hotel on Corfu (Mario Adorf in a charming characterization reminiscent of Tamiroff's in *Five Graves to Cairo* and Revill's in *Avanti!*). But the struggling, superannuated producer is also a stubborn, resourceful, dignified, and carefully (if somewhat unstylishly) dressed man whose sense of pride never deserts him. Barry is ultimately a futile figure, though, an exile stranded in a world he no longer understands or accepts and in a business where he no longer belongs and that treats him as insignificant. Although Barry's wry, civilized manner does him little good anymore, he maintains his style and character. He even manages to be gracious when the Countess rejects his film project and apologizes with, "I'm sorry you came all this way for nothing." Kissing her hand, he tells her wryly, "Well, as Sam Goldwyn said, in life you have to take the bitter with the sour."

---

* Cut material can be seen as extras on the 2016 British Blu-ray/DVD edition from Eureka!/Masters of Cinema, which includes a 2013 restoration of the release version. McGee donated a print (now faded) of a preview version, eight minutes longer than the release version, to the Academy of Motion Picture Arts and Sciences' Film Archive, along with outtakes and sound recordings.

Some of the best Hollywood films and novels, such as *Sunset Blvd.* and Nathanael West's *The Day of the Locust* and George Cukor's version of *A Star Is Born*, are about failures and fringe characters, who, after all, make up most of Hollywood. The veteran *Variety* reviewer Art Murphy once observed to me that films about Hollywood characters who wind up being destroyed, whether by themselves, the industry, or both, often are successful with audiences because they display the glamour of Hollywood while simultaneously allowing spectators to feel relief that their lives are not as hopeless as the ones going down in flames onscreen. But that successful formula did not apply to *Fedora*, which harshly undercuts the illusion of Hollywood glamour every step of the way, showing it to be a hideous sham.

It's sadly fitting that Wilder, at this late stage in his illustrious career, has to make his screen surrogate an aging has-been producer who tries to maintain his aplomb but is having such a hard time getting a film off the ground. Earlier Wilder had expressed his jaundiced feelings about Hollywood through the handsome yet troubled face of the younger Holden, impersonating the struggling screenwriter Wilder had been in the 1930s. Now he projects himself through the ruined face of the once-beautiful but much older-looking Holden, whose appearance is integral to the deep truthfulness of his performance. The actor was fifty-nine when he made *Fedora* in the summer of 1977, but he was prematurely aged by his struggles with alcohol, making him look haggard, faded, and drawn. Howard Hawks told me that when he watched Sam Peckinpah's *The Wild Bunch* in 1969, he didn't realize Holden was playing the lead role until someone informed him afterward, and he replied incredulously, "That old man?" But much of the meaning of *Fedora* is conveyed poetically through the close-ups of the ravaged face of Holden, sadder but wiser in his disillusionment, sardonically accepting the tragic absurdity of a life in show business.

"My only problem was, I knew Bill was going to bring the ghosts of *Sunset Blvd.* along with him," Wilder said, but as Diamond recognized, those were inevitable anyway. Both films revolve around an enigmatic, unwillingly retired star existing in a restless, ghostlike state of living death in an isolated Gothic mansion. As Gillis tells us of Norma's house, "It was like that old woman in *Great Expectations*—that Miss Havisham in her rotting wedding dress and her torn veil, taking it out on the world because she'd been given the go-by" (Miss Havisham in the Charles Dickens novel is in her mid-thirties but prematurely aged; she usually is portrayed as elderly on-screen). But there are major differences between the two Wilder films, both in narrative approach and in historical context. Norma left the screen because the coming of talking pictures left her obsolete, but Fedora went into seclusion because the hideous accident in Dr. Vando's antiaging process left her so disfigured that she resorted to having her daughter impersonate her before the public. That makes *Fedora* even more centrally concerned with the process of aging and mortality than *Sunset Blvd.*, in which Norma is "old" only by sexist contrast with the youth of her gigolo and in cruel Hollywood terms as a discarded actress and survivor of the lost art form of silent pictures. As Joe tells her, "Norma, grow up. You're a woman of fifty. There's nothing tragic about being fifty—not unless you try to be twenty-five." Fedora, however, is a wizened woman in her late sixties hiding her ruined face behind a black veil, a painful contrast with her vital-looking, if decadent, daughter.

Contrary to Wilder and Diamond's qualms, the audience's mental intercutting between the 1950 and 1978 films—between the moral and financial compromises of the younger Holden and the desperate attempts of the almost terminally disenchanted older Holden to keep viable in the industry; between Norma's "We had *faces*" and Fedora's disfigurement—only strengthens *Fedora* artistically. The casting of Holden as the surrogate figure of both director and audience helped guarantee the project would not appeal to the predominantly youthful market of its time, but *Fedora* is a quintessential old man's film, viewing the industry and its history from a long, regretful perspective.

"I couldn't make *Fedora* without him," Wilder admitted. "You couldn't get somebody *like* Bill Holden because nobody was like him. He had a seriousness, a presence, a maturity, an inner strength which made him absolutely indispensable. He made it look easy." And there was the eloquent aesthetic value of his aged face to consider, for as Wilder said, "When he made *Fedora*, Bill was just about the only actor of his age who had not had any cosmetic surgery. That in itself is remarkable in a town where the leftover scraps of flesh from the face-lifts of just one star could be sewn together to make half a dozen stars."

That macabre joke is echoed in *Fedora*'s ghastly scenes in the French clinic of Dr. Vando, the quack "rejuvenator" who resembles a mad doctor in a Universal horror movie of the 1930s. The backfiring of his exotic schemes to keep Fedora looking ageless turns Wilder's film itself into a gothic horror movie with lacings of black comedy, like a work by James Whale. The disaster in Dr. Vando's clinic and the rest of *Fedora* amplify the montage of Norma undergoing various forms of self-torturing bodywork to prepare for her imagined return to the screen, described by Gillis as "a merciless series of treatments. . . . She was determined to be ready—ready for those cameras that would never turn." Those images were a major bone of contention Wilder and the more fastidious Brackett, who objected to such grotesque debunking of the heartless process of movie stardom.

For Wilder, that was the point of both films. He portrays the quest for and maintenance of stardom as a pathology, an extreme form of narcissism that literally eats up the mad dreamer who wants to maintain her fabricated image beyond its cruelly limited shelf life. Both films are explicitly as well as implicitly critical of Hollywood for its mistreatment of actresses in exerting such enormous pressure to maintain their seemingly eternal youth and beauty and for ruthlessly discarding them when those qualities are gone. "You see," the wild-eyed Norma confides to the newsreel cameramen before being taken away, presumably to a mental institution, "this is my life." Fedora's attempt to desperately avoid the inevitable fate of an actress leads to her own tragic self-destruction and, worse, that of her daughter.

"ALMOST UNCASTABLE"

When Henry Fonda, as the Academy president, presents "Fedora" with an honorary Oscar, he asks what it would take to lure her back to the screen. In her Fedora guise, Antonia says, "They don't make women's pictures anymore."

Fonda replies, "Because they don't make women like you anymore."

The casting of the lead female roles backfired in *Fedora*, to the grave detriment of the picture. As had happened with Crosby on *The Emperor Waltz*, Wilder lost control of a picture because of serious problems with a star. He was so sensitive about what happened that when he and I did a question-and-answer session about *Fedora* at the Los Angeles County Museum of Art and I asked about Marthe Keller's voice being dubbed, he quickly asked me not to discuss it. And he became angry over his acolyte McGee's frank account in a 1979 article for *American Film* magazine of the problems with the shooting and postproduction—especially his revelations about the casting issues, as detailed below with reports from McGee and other sources.

"He was very upset with me," McGee recalled of Wilder's reaction to the article.

> I thought it was going to be the end of our friendship. And I remember showing the story to Diamond when I finished it, and Diamond said, "This is just fine." And when it finally came out, I went to Billy's office, and he was very upset with me. I think I blocked it, but I think it was something about "You're finished." I was *extremely* upset—I think I had tears in my eyes with him on that day. I thought I was just telling the truth as best I had seen it. Maybe he thought of it as a betrayal or something, I don't know, and I could see how he might. Because he didn't go into it thinking it was going to be a disaster, as it was. That's one of the worst moments in my friendship with him.

But they patched it up, McGee watched some of *Buddy Buddy* being shot, and they remained friends until Wilder's death in 2002.

During the period when Universal was mulling whether to make *Fedora*, the studio proposed having Katharine Hepburn and Audrey Hepburn as the mother and daughter. They might have worked because of their physical similarities and star power, but Wilder did not think they were right for the parts, a decision he may have regretted after the project was put into turnaround. He thought of casting his old friend Marlene Dietrich as the Countess and Faye Dunaway as Antonia, but they both turned him down, Dietrich with indignation, thinking it was a reflection on her own life. Then Wilder went the route of using a lesser-known star, perhaps feeling it would make the character transformation more plausible. He cast Keller, a young Swiss actress, on the recommendation of Sydney Pollack, who had directed her opposite Al Pacino in a film about European car racing, *Bobby Deerfield* (1977).

Wilder's judgment must have deserted him when he watched a rough cut of that terminally dull love story, in which the actors have no chemistry even though they became romantically involved off-screen. At least in retrospect, it's glaringly easy to spot the problems with Keller in *Bobby Deerfield* that Wilder should have recognized. She plays a dying woman with a masklike face, awkward movements and gestures, and German-inflected English line readings (her character is supposed to be Italian) that are so opaque Pacino often has to ask her onscreen what she is saying. He tells her, "You know, you're a very difficult person to have a conversation with." She admits, "I'm sorry if I make you uncomfortable." As Vincent Canby commented in his *New York Times* review, her character's "manic behavior is supposed to indicate a love of life but suggests rather more strongly that she's in desperate need of a Valium."

Nevertheless, Wilder initially considered having Keller play both demanding parts in *Fedora*. But as he recalled, "Keller is difficult if she is only playing the one part. Naturally, if I had had a young Garbo, it would have been marvelous." He also pondered and rejected the idea of having an "unknown" actress play the Countess, with Keller providing that voice as well as playing Antonia. Keller unfortunately proved disastrous as only Antonia, while the Countess was more expertly, but still problematically, played by Knef, the veteran German actress and singer. She had also had a Hollywood career and played Garbo's former role in the 1955 Broadway musical version of *Ninotchka*, *Silk Stockings*. Even the dialogue of *Fedora* acknowledges the casting problem. When Barry "wryly" admits at the end that Fedora's true story "would make a much better picture than the script I brought you," she says before pulling a veil over her face, "Yes. But who would you get to play it?" McGee notes that Wilder "was left with second-rate movie stars. He couldn't make them seem like The Star. I think he had never been turned down by a major studio before to do one of his films. I think he was going to make that film come hell or high water. That problem had something to do with him trudging on. By God, he was really going to make this goddam film."

Wilder admitted in retrospect to McCarthy and me that *Fedora*

was almost uncastable and maybe it should never have been done, because there are certain things that read very well but you cannot photograph them. It's extremely difficult. Actually the same person should play both parts; there's no question about it. But if you have Dietrich playing the old countess, from the first shot you know, "Shit, this is Fedora, don't fool around with me." But if I had Dietrich and, say, Faye Dunaway—some similarity, of course—they would say, "That's Dietrich, or that's Gloria Swanson, or that's Bette Davis. . . ." Or you fake it and you have it shot from the back or in the shadows, then they get suspicious. Certain things are unphotographable. *Equus*: unphotographable. The moment it's a real horse—even if you had a Secretariat or Seattle Slew—it would not work.

It's the mere fact that it's stylized that made it work in a book or on the stage.

The problems with Keller began, according to Wilder, when they tested the makeup she would have worn to play the Countess. He said Keller had a bad cut from an automobile accident, and "the nerve ends are such that when you try heavy makeup, with rubber and stuff like that, she could not tolerate the pain when they took it off." McGee, who saw that test, said he did not recall hearing of any problem with her makeup, but she "didn't look very good" as the older Fedora. In any case, after Wilder made the test shortly after his arrival in Munich, he should have recast the lead role right there, but he failed to do what was needed in that critical moment. As he recalled to Hellmuth Karasek, "That was the time when I could have said, 'Too bad! It would have been wonderful! It was not meant to be!' And separate myself from her. That's it. But I did not do it." Soon after the shooting began, Wilder confided to actor Mario Adorf, "It's not going to work. I've made a mistake." Adorf asked, "What kind of mistake?" Wilder told him, "I can't say right now. It was to do with the casting." Wilder would not elaborate, but Adorf "had a hunch" it had to do with Keller. When Crowe asked why he did not replace her, Wilder admitted, "We were already in Munich, and I'm a company man. I try to protect [the investment in a production]. Which was wrong in this case. . . . I wanted to stop the whole thing after we were shooting for a week or so, [but] I couldn't. . . . I mean, I could, but it would have been a loss of income, so I just finished it."

That mistake, the kind he would not have made earlier, was a sign of how desperate Wilder was not to jeopardize the production of a film at that point in his career, even with a dubious star, and an indication of how he was losing his ability to cope with the changing film business. So *Fedora* went on in a state of "pending doom," said Paul Diamond, who watched it filming. Although production coordinator Harold Nebenzal recalled that the shooting otherwise went smoothly, McGee said Wilder did not follow his usual routine of making jokes throughout the shoot, partly because the German and French crews didn't understand them.* Wilder also was unable or

---

* Nebenzal is the son of Seymour Nebenzal, who produced *People on Sunday* with Moriz Seeler.

unwilling to rescue Keller when she proved inadequate to the film's central role. "I think people on the crew felt sorry for her," McGee recalled.

> You could see she was struggling, she desperately needed to talk to him and consult with him, and he just wouldn't have it. He was not helping her at all. He ignored her. He didn't want to sit down and talk about the character with her. She had just come from working on *Bobby Deerfield* with Pacino and Pollack; they would have done that. But Billy just said, "I hire the best people I know. I'm not a drama school, not an acting school." He didn't say it to *her*. And I remember Audrey saying one time to me, "He didn't help her at all." And Audrey even said that he treated Marilyn that way too. He never helped her with anything. She was so messed up, he just didn't have the fatherly [attitude], or the whatever, to ease her mind. He just put up with it. Marilyn was worth it. He knew he had gold on his hands there. Marthe was just miscast.

Jean Renoir once said a director should always change the script to fit the actor, and not the other way around, but Wilder and Diamond were less inclined to take such drastic action, although they did try to modify some of Keller's scenes. But this was not simply a case of Charles Boyer refusing to do a single scene in a Wilder screenplay, or even Monroe being out of control during the shooting of *Some Like It Hot*, a problem the director in his prime was able to finesse because of her incomparable, if sometimes unreliable, talent. This was the crucial role in the film played by someone out of her league. As Frank Capra put it, "A film faces the audience with a single thin front line—the actors. If that front line collapses, the show is over. A bad performance can kill the finest story."

Keller's original line readings were monotonous, erratic, and unconvincing. They can be heard on a recording of the rough cut (without music) supplied to me by McGee. Her physical gestures onscreen are clumsy and inauthentic; she has no idea what to do with her hands, and she lurches around waving her arms amateurishly, jutting her jaw forward as she talks, her head bobbing back and forth uncertainly. In a word, the performance looks frantic, even if Antonia, in the period before her suicide, is supposed to be a speed freak. As Sikov puts it, Keller not only doesn't communicate the stature of a legendary movie star but acts "like a clumsy drag queen."

To make matters worse, the young actress chafed at Wilder's characteristically stubborn insistence that she deliver the lines as he wrote them rather than allowing her to improvise; like Shirley MacLaine and some other modern "Method" actors, she considered him autocratic in that regard. Keller complained that she felt like a mere "object" and that in one scene, Wilder would not even let her brush her hair back from her face because it wasn't in the script. Although that may have been an example of his exasperation with her inability to execute his wishes, she told Holden, "I can't work with a director like that! He treats me just like a puppet!" Unlike a more skilled and truly flexible actor, such as Lemmon, Keller could not adapt to the disciplined working habits of the man Lemmon teasingly called "The Prussian General." She felt that "times had changed. But he didn't."

Wilder reacted to her problems with disdain: "Keller had just done *Bobby Deerfield* and she came on the set with her nose high in the air and said, 'With Sydney Pollack, we rehearsed, and rehearsed, and rehearsed.'" Wilder responded to her complaint by saying, "Okay, then let us rehearse now," and she told him, "Not now." Wilder went on, "Okay, then we won't have to rehearse anymore. Let's do the scene." But Keller recalled with frustration, "I just had to do as he said. I said, 'Can I try it this way?' He said, 'Of course, but I'll cut it out later.' . . . I must trust him totally. When he says I must do this or that, I do it. I bite my tongue, but I do it. I'm not accustomed to working this way. I'm a fighter. I ask, I challenge, I discuss. But this is the way of my generation, not Wilder's, not Fedora's. . . . In the end I went a bit crazy and had to see a doctor. . . . I didn't recognize myself in the mirror."

For one scene shot ten days into production on Madouri Island, the location for Fedora's Villa Calypso, Keller in her Fedora persona had to play what the script calls "an outré parody of yesterday's screen sirens," a scene from a 1956 Fedora vehicle entitled *East of Suez*. She was to sing "C'est si bon" and dance gaily over to Dr. Vando while telling him, "Cheer up, Reverend. Let's gin some and sin some. East of Suez, there are no Ten Commandments."*

---

* This last line of dialogue is borrowed from Rudyard Kipling's poem "Mandalay": "Ship me somewheres east of Suez, where the best is like the worst, / Where there aren't no Ten Commandments an' a man can raise a thirst." The title of Fedora's film also alludes to a lost silent film starring Pola Negri and directed by Raoul Walsh, *East of Suez* (1925), a story about a half-caste woman based on the play of that title by W. Somerset Maugham. And the dialogue evokes the story of *Rain*. When I asked Wilder in 1978 about the "closet romantic" characters in his films, including Ninotchka, Sherlock Holmes, and Wendell, whose "coolness and rigidity" are "gradually dissolved

But in the rehearsal, McGee reported, "Keller was having difficulty with some unusual English words." Following Wilder's usual convivial practice, the exterior location was crowded with onlookers, reporters, and photographers, which she found distracting. "Apart from her problems with English," McGee wrote, "she was very tense, which had the effect of making her physically awkward." She demanded that the photographers stop shooting but also was upset because she thought Wilder, while running the dialogue, was trying to give her line readings, which is anathema to most actors. "Keller begged him, 'Please don't tell me any more.' By now she was so nervous and self-conscious that it was impossible for her to give the scene what it needed—an air of zany abandon. Her English deteriorated with each take." Cinematographer Gerry Fisher's need for her to adjust a sun reflector to avoid glare "further restricted her movements and made her even more nervous," McGee observed. "She delivered the 'East of Suez' line, and I. A. L. Diamond sighed and said, 'I know what it says, and *I* didn't understand it.'"

Wilder's "spirits went down after that," McGee recalls. "I think he knew he had a problem, a big one." McGee was in a room with Wilder and Diamond when they rewrote the scene to shoot it later in the interior set of Fedora's bedroom at the Munich studio to make the atmosphere less hectic and more playable for the actress. "I sat with him and Diamond when they watched a rough cut of the scene, and they were both just going, 'Oh, my God, Oh, my God, we can't . . .' And I think they forgot I was in the room as they started to rewrite the scene, one of my treasured moments. I remember Diamond said, 'She can't move, she can't dance, what shall we do with her?' And Wilder said, 'Put her in a chair.' Then in the scene as it was finally produced, she's playing backgammon with José Ferrer, and the old Fedora is in bed behind them." But it still didn't work well. Keller's singing and slower delivery of the intricate, tongue-in-cheek dialogue from Fedora's old movie

---

by [their] romantic adventures with a European," he said, "Yeah, that's the Reverend Henderson in *Rain*. It's predictable now, maybe." He meant the Reverend Alfred Davidson in the 1922 play *Rain* by John Colton and Clemence Randolph from a 1921 short story by Maugham. Davidson is a fanatical minister in the South Pacific who falls in love with a prostitute and winds up committing suicide. The first of four film versions of the play, Walsh's *Sadie Thompson* (1928), stars Swanson, with Lionel Barrymore as the minister; in the iconic 1932 MGM version directed by Lewis Milestone, the minister is played by Walter Huston, opposite Joan Crawford as Sadie.

again were rendered awkward by her heavy accent. So her second attempt at that part of the scene had to be excised.*

When Wilder and Diamond heard the entire soundtrack after the film was assembled, they realized Keller's voice was unacceptable. Wilder decided to redub both her and Knef (for consistency) with the same young German actress, Inga Bunsch, who had to loop more than four hundred lines. Bunsch did little to improve the zigzagging quality of Keller's line readings, and Bunsch's own voicing is also dully monotonous. Even worse, the looping seriously damaged the performance of Knef, whose face had already been so hideously masked with rubber makeup that she looks bizarrely unreal. The original soundtrack recordings demonstrate that Knef gave a remarkably rich vocal performance on the set. Her voice is strong, passionate, bitterly sarcastic, sometimes desperately anguished, and subtle. Bunsch's line readings for Knef are unsubtle and gratingly coarse. Knef complained about Wilder, "First he destroys my face, now he takes my voice. What is left?" Editor Fritz Steinkamp told Diamond, "You've lost a whole performance. Knef's is *the* performance of the picture." Diamond and Wilder agreed but felt legally powerless to fix the problem. So an uneasy, unsatisfactory compromise was reached in which Keller did Antonia's final scenes in her own voice and dubbed both parts in French, while Knef dubbed both parts in German.

None of this chaotic process did anything to make the film succeed. And yet there is something strangely fitting and expressive about Keller's awful performance. She is so out of place and inept among the older, sophisticated, more accomplished actors that she becomes an object of pity, like Antonia herself when, to her dismay, she is forced to play a role in life and onscreen that she cannot handle. Keller's very inadequacy in *Fedora* is a touching expression of her character's horrifying situation. Watching her is like seeing yourself in a bad dream, one of those nightmares in which you are somewhere you don't belong and are unable to function. That may seem a far-fetched rationalization for what is simply a poor performance mishandled by a director who made a regrettable casting choice, but it is how I experience Keller's characterization in *Fedora* after many viewings. Would I prefer that a more accomplished actress had played the part? Of course. Does this problem make

---

* It is one of the bits that can be seen as an extra on the British Blu-ray/DVD edition.

the film even more ineffably sad than it otherwise is, and a somewhat sorry swan song for Wilder's career? Yes.

Such a glaring flaw was symptomatic of Wilder's own inability to come to terms with the New Hollywood he is attacking. But when you watch a film, which unlike a play cannot be recast, you have to approach it as it is, not as you wish it might have been. And within those peculiar confines, Keller's desperate, amateurish flailing around, helplessly and angrily, sort of works for the film emotionally.

THE DILEMMA OF IDENTITY

The actress's feeling that she "didn't recognize myself in the mirror" echoes Antonia's desperation over losing her identity as the elaborate sham intensifies. The once-narcissistic Fedora has ordered all sixty-three mirrors removed from her home so she won't have to look at herself anymore, saying, "More and more I began to see myself in Antonia—*she* had become my mirror." At first Antonia regards taking over her screen roles as a lark and a way of getting closer to her mother, who coldly neglected her in her childhood (think Joan and Christina Crawford). But since a mirror underscores the sinister Germanic theme of the *doppelgänger*—a double or apparition of a living person—we see the role eventually subsuming the performer, becoming a terrible trap. *Fedora* comments not only on the actor's dilemma of losing herself in her screen persona but even more painfully on Antonia's sense that she is losing herself in *someone else's* persona. When Barry breaks into her bedroom, he finds a long row of notebooks pitifully filled with the handwritten mantra, "I am Fedora." As a revelation of mental collapse, it resembles the wife's horrified discovery of her husband's novel manuscript two years later in Kubrick's *The Shining*, consisting entirely of the repetitively typed line "All work and no play makes Jack a dull boy."

The scene in Antonia's bedroom contains the most notorious "bad laugh" in *Fedora*, when Barry rips away some wallpaper and finds that she has created the collage of photographs of Michael York.* She has developed a crush

---

* This moment was anticipated in Wilder's German silent film *People on Sunday* in the collage of photos of film stars, notably Garbo and Gilbert, on the wall of the shabby Berlin apartment where

on the handsome young actor (who plays himself); when she threatens to tell him the truth about the masquerade, that is so threatening to her keepers they forbid her to do so, shutting down the film she is making with York, having Dr. Vando impersonate his voice on the telephone, and terminating her career after she makes a failed suicide attempt. I have always found the revelation of the collage and her fixation on York a moving frisson, a visual demonstration of Antonia's thwarted, hidden romantic obsession and need to strike out on her own. And I have always failed to understand why audiences found it funny that Antonia is enamored of York, except perhaps because he was only a second-level star at the time (even if he had starred in *Cabaret*), and her dottiness about him is so extreme. But that makes her passion all the more touching, an *amour fou*. York almost seems a figure materializing out of her fantasy when he makes his poignant appearance at her coffin near the end. Today at least the reference to York, since it is no longer contemporary, doesn't provide the same excuse for foolish derision.

What finally precipitates Antonia's suicide is a direct confrontation over her identity with Miss Balfour (Frances Sternhagen), her mother's stern British factotum, who controls her life. Strung out on drugs, Fedora is a horror-movie apparition as she dashes toward the train in close-up (as she does at the beginning of the film) while Balfour screams her name in futile admonition. Among other things, *Fedora* is another of Wilder's portraits of an addict surrounded by enablers. The classic example is Don Birnam in *The Lost Weekend*, but some Wilder characters are workaholics with correspondingly diminished emotional lives: Phoebe in *A Foreign Affair*; Linus in *Sabrina*; MacNamara in *One, Two, Three*; Nestor in *Irma la Douce*; and both Walter and Hildy in *The Front Page*. Dino in *Kiss Me, Stupid* is a sex addict who admits, "It's a habit with me, like breathing. . . . Well, it's not that I like to. You see, I have to, because if I skip one night, I wake up the next morning with *such a headache*." Addiction is another form of mask to hide one's feelings and true inner life, and if Antonia is addicted to drugs, Fedora herself, like Norma Desmond, is addicted to fame.

Antonia's enablers are not as well-meaning as most of Don's or Norma's. At the studio where Antonia is making *The Last Waltz*, when Balfour refuses

---

Annie and Erwin live. The mordant scene of the young couple destroying some of each other's favorite pictures of filmic fantasy figures contrasts Hollywood glamour with their unhappy love life.

to let her tell York the truth about the masquerade, Antonia says, "You mean it's going to go on like this until the day she dies?" Balfour says chillingly, "No. Until Fedora dies. And you are now Fedora." That announces the dead end of Wilderian masquerades. None is more tragic than this one. Antonia's secret father, Count Sobryanski (Hans Jaray, a former actor for Lubitsch's mentor, Max Reinhardt) tells Fedora, "You took away her identity—you, you took away her youth!" While waiting for York at the train station, Antonia realizes that they never sent him her love letters. She becomes hysterical and tells Balfour, "I'm not Fedora. I'm not, I'm not. I'm Antonia!" Balfour says flatly, "There is no Antonia."

Antonia/Fedora's conflicting declarations of her identity are tragic versions of the comical dilemma Lemmon's character faces about his/her identity in *Some Like It Hot,* alternately declaring "I'm a girl! I'm a girl!" and then repeatedly insisting "I'm a boy" while adding "I wish I were dead." Antonia *literally* wishes she were dead. As Balfour forces her to stare, panic-stricken, into the cracked and cloudy mirror of a vending machine, a warped and tawdry facsimile of screen-star imagery, her keeper orders, "Look at yourself. Ask a million people, 'Who does that face belong to?'" "It's a lie!," insists Antonia, but Balfour replies, "You can't escape from it—ever." And yet she does, by throwing herself under the approaching train after shouting, "I hate this face! I hate it! Hate it!" That is the point when we hear the whistle of the fatal train approaching. The film has returned full circle to the opening shot, expressing the fateful nature of the dilemma of entrapment within a constructed persona. As Gillis tells the audience while his body floats in the pool being photographed and the police prepare to fish it out, "Well, this is where you came in."

The Countess has suffered a grievous loss of identity similar to her daughter's with the ruination of her face and career. Since she was so narcissistic, she had nothing else to live for, like Norma when she murmurs, "No one ever leaves a star. That's what makes one a star. . . . The stars are ageless—aren't they?" Like so many other Wilder characters, Fedora is torn between the refuge of delusion and the compulsion toward revelation. At the memorial ceremonies when Barry confronts her with the charge of killing Fedora, the old lady lifts her veil to show who she really is (the script says "it's like the curtain going up on an Ibsen drama"). Barry asks, "You are Fedora?" She replies grimly, "I *was* Fedora." By trying to re-create herself in her daughter, she has destroyed both herself *and* her daughter.

For Barry, the dilemma of identity is less a matter of life and death but still a matter of considerable urgency. As it was for Wilder at that late point in his career, Barry's viability in his profession is at stake in his all-out attempt to make one more film and score the coup of bringing the legendary Fedora back to the screen. But he's so obscure that Balfour mistakes his name as "Getweiler"—perhaps a pun by Wilder on how he and his colleague William Wyler were often confused with each other in a comical loss of identity ("Don't get Wilder, get Wyler"), even though his name somewhat echoes that of Wilder himself. But even more important to Barry's sense of self-worth is his need to make Fedora remember him. He is bewildered and hurt that she does not remember "Dutch" Detweiler, the lowly but cocky assistant director at MGM in 1947 (he is played as a young man by Stephen Collins) who spent a night making love with her on the beach in Santa Monica (or so he recalls; the scene is visually ambiguous on that score). When the older Dutch first encounters Antonia, he says vainly, "Madame Fedora? Hi. I'm Barry Det-weiler. Remember me? . . . They called me Dutch. I had a crewcut then. . . . Don't you remember? The beach—in Santa Monica—in my roadster?"

For "Fedora," as he thinks she is, not to remember him is crushing to his pride, consigning him personally to the oblivion where he has been sliding professionally. But Antonia's obliviousness is also a significant clue he fails to grasp, and eventually the aged Fedora lets the truth slip by referring to him as "Dutch," with a certain residual fondness lingering in her hoarse voice that touches him deeply. He says, "Then you *do* remember." Here is another affinity between Barry and the aging, similarly discarded director, an anxiety about being forgotten in Hollywood and elsewhere and a longing to be remembered and cherished. That the reclusive Fedora, lost to the world, actually remembers Barry seems to make him feel his otherwise futile existence has been validated.

"THE BUSINESS OF CREATING ILLUSIONS"

Probably Wilder was right that he should not have attempted to film Tryon's novella because of all the problems inherent in making such a strange story seem believable onscreen. Something that reads well does not necessarily play well in a photographic medium, even if *Fedora* does not especially try to be "realistic." Its outlandish story resembles grand opera, with its over-the-top acting and flamboyantly romantic score by Miklós Rósza; Wilder recognized the operatic dimensions of his similar diva in *Sunset Blvd.* Andrew Lloyd Webber adapted that film for the musical stage in 1993, but Wilder, not enchanted by the transformation, had earlier told another aspirant, Stephen Sondheim, that such a story *must* be an opera because it is about a "dethroned queen."

When Fedora, at her lavish self-memorial, reminds Barry about the importance of endings, she says fiercely, "The legend must go on." He remarks—sardonically, the script notes—"Magic time." Wilder is borrowing the phrase Jack Lemmon used before each take. As Wilder explained, "That means—we're going to enter into this character, we are going to make the public enter his make-believe world." With the problems the "almost uncastable" *Fedora* encountered and its uncertain tone, the film's many quieter virtues were overlooked by people unsympathetic to Wilder's late mode of romantic storytelling. The resulting *film maudit* was resoundingly rejected by audiences and many reviewers in the United States, other than those who knew Wilder's work well, respected him and what he was trying to do, and were able to see the film in context as his artistic testament. *Fedora* was received sympathetically in France, and the German distributor pointedly ran quotes from French reviews side-by-side in ads with hostile German reviews.

The derisive laughter that greeted *Fedora* at some New York screenings was decried by Wilder's belated defender Andrew Sarris: "There is nothing quite so hideously heartless as the idiot cackle of the in-crowd when it senses that a career may be on the skids." That reception reminded me of what I heard another Hollywood old master, George Cukor, say in that era while reprimanding members of an audience at the Academy of Motion Picture Arts and Sciences Theater who hooted at his masterful 1933 film *Little Women*: he called their reaction "a bum's laugh." McGee reports that the Santa Barbara preview audience for *Fedora* "laughed hysterically" at York placing a red rose on the breast of Antonia/Fedora in her coffin—a touch Wilder remembered from the funeral of the Emperor Franz Josef I, when his mistress, actress Katharina Schratt, laid white flowers on his chest. You can imagine how Wilder felt while hearing such a response from the ignorant hyenas in the modern audience. It's worth recalling that a preview audience was in hysterics during the original opening sequence of *Sunset Blvd.*—set in a mortuary—that

Wilder cut before the film's release, a foreshadowing of *Fedora*'s grisly take on the film industry and depiction of its characters as among the living dead.

"It nearly killed my father," Paul Diamond said of the *Fedora* experience. "I watched my father sink into depression which really lasted the rest of his life, during this film. That's why I find it hard to watch." Paul remembered his father "bent over in pain" for most of the shoot. He was suffering not only from an agonizing attack of shingles that kept him up nights, "but from the sheer not-feeling-it on this picture. And it was something that had to succeed—it had to bring them back from what became financially a disaster with *Sherlock Holmes*—and it didn't. And the sadness just pours off the DVD box when I look at it."

Sarris wrote in his *Village Voice* review of *Fedora*, "Even Wilder's comedies—*The Apartment*, *Sabrina*, *Avanti!*, most notably—have been shadowed by death and self-destruction. But in *Fedora* the cinema itself ends up in a coffin of Wilder's own design. And one can hardly expect 1979 screening audiences to join Wilder at the wake." Perhaps a bit patronizingly, yet with sympathy and accuracy, Janet Maslin's review in the *New York Times* called *Fedora*

> a fabulous relic, a grand old villa fallen slightly into disrepair. And if it seems outmoded, well, that is very much Mr. Wilder's intention. *Fedora* is old-fashioned with a vengeance, a proud, passionate remembrance of the way movies used to be, and a bitter smile at what they have become. It is rich, majestic, very close to ridiculous, and also a little bit mad. It seems exactly what Mr. Wilder wants it to be, perfectly self-contained and filled with the echoes of a lifetime; no one could mistake this for the work of a young man. Indeed, it has the resonance of an epitaph.

Dave Kehr, not always an admirer of Wilder, thought the commercial failure of *Fedora* "might be the surest sign of its artistic success." Reviewing the film for the *Chicago Reader*, Kehr found it haunting and even frightening, not so much for its flimsy storyline but as a self-portrait of the filmmaker split into the characters of Fedora and Barry Detweiler. Calling it "a deliberate anachronism, a movie meant to seem out of its time . . . a personal summation, an emotional autobiography," Kehr felt Wilder was talking to his colleagues from the past, sharing made-up memories of how things were or should have been. And he is also addressing some indefinite audience of the future, putting down some of his deepest thoughts and intuitions for a time when they might seem more meaningful and more important. *Fedora* is Billy Wilder's last will and testament (although there is no reason why it should be his last film). It doesn't belong in a movie theater, but in a bank vault. . . . The film is full of anger, regret, self-pity, and flashes of terror; it's the work of an old man who won't lie down, who won't accept what has happened to him and his world. . . . By imagining himself in the place of his heroine, Wilder has executed a sublime, madly romantic explosion of ego, one of the most extreme in film history. . . . Wilder's vision of his death is a violent one. He must be pushed out, just as he and his art have been pushed out of Hollywood.

Bill Krohn, the Hollywood correspondent for *Cahiers du Cinéma*, aptly described *Fedora* to me as "Billy Wilder tap-dancing on the grave of Hollywood."

"THIS WRETCHED MASQUERADE!"

If Wilder had thought more carefully about making *Fedora* and decided that the better part of valor would be not to attempt it, he would have been spared this critical and commercial failure, which helped hasten the end of his long career. But we would have been deprived of so much that is moving and meaningful in this somber valedictory meditation on some of his central preoccupations. For all its grievous flaws, *Fedora* is a Wilder film that has stood the test of time. The masquerade at its center is as extravagant and doomed as any in a 1920s German expressionist film. No other film more thoroughly examines his lifelong fascination with that theme or more urgently faces the dilemma human beings encounter when they attempt a false transformation. Even though sometimes in Wilder films masquerading works beneficial change and even helps characters survive, sometimes it obliterates them and others, when the masks take over the people.

Twenty-four centuries ago, Aristotle discussed the function of "the mask" in the best screenwriting manual ever written, his *Poetics*: "As for Comedy, it is (as has been observed) an imitation of men worse than the average; worse, however, not as regards any and every sort of fault, but only as regards one particular kind, the Ridiculous, which is a species of the Ugly. The Ridiculous may be defined as a mistake or deformity not productive of pain or harm to others; the mask, for instance, that excites laughter, is something ugly and distorted without causing pain." But in *Fedora*, though its situation verges on the ridiculous and is often the cause of sardonic comedy, the mask is primarily tragic and causes pain.

Fedora in Tryon's novella recalls her pleasure in training her daughter to impersonate her onscreen: "It was as if we were getting her ready for a giant masquerade party." But the joy of such play-acting is transitory. At the dubious price of worldly success, people who wear masks in their daily lives run the painful risk of utter inauthenticity. In their failure to be who they are and to connect with other people with emotional honesty, they face disastrous, even fatal, consequences when exposed as frauds. So it's ironic when Tryon's Fedora gives Barry a quotation from Colette: "Rien d'ailleurs ne rassure autant qu'un masque" (Nothing is as reassuring as a mask). But after Fedora demands of Barry in the film, "What would *you* give to be reborn? To have a second chance?," Count Sobryanski tells him, "I was against this whole scheme, right from the beginning. This wretched masquerade!"

Fedora is an almost abstract, ultimate distillation of that theme that runs throughout Wilder's work. Artists' late works often tend toward such levels of abstraction or allegory and introspection as their themes are laid bare and foregrounded, not infrequently at the expense of verisimilitude; that is a value older artists tend to find incidental to their concentration on ideas. In John Ford's testament film, *The Man Who Shot Liberty Valance* (1962), the stripping-away of the romantic trappings of the Western genre he helped create resulted in another striking example of a film of ideas that appears unabashedly artificial. Both it and *Fedora*, while thoughtfully reflecting on the process of Hollywood mythmaking, revolve around charades that consume the lives of their characters ("When the legend becomes fact, print the legend"). These two late works contain unusually explicit discussions of that process: they analyze themselves; they are films of ideas. Similarly obsessed with obsolescence, aging, and mortality, *Fedora*, like *Liberty Valance*, implicates the media and how they distort reality to maintain social illusions deemed necessary by characters and their enablers. Ford, like Wilder, played audacious games with casting his allegory, and the way the two principal characters in *Liberty Valance* don't seem to change much as they age caused some reviewers to find that film's lack of realism absurd. But because of the inherent stylization of the Western genre, John Wayne and James Stewart were more compatible collaborators in the process of mythic role-playing and interrogation than the relatively unfamiliar female stars Wilder employed to play with such awkwardness against the iconic William Holden.

In some of Wilder's many complex variations on the theme of the masquerade, which range from farce to tragedy, role-playing is a matter of life or death, such as with Corporal Bramble in *Five Graves to Cairo* or the two men successfully impersonating women to avoid being rubbed out by the mob in *Some Like It Hot*. Other characters find masquerading an escape into a better existence, a positive form of rebirth, in such films as *The Major and the Minor*, *Sabrina*, *Love in the Afternoon*, *Kiss Me, Stupid*, and *Avanti!* Wilder leaves it an open question whether Otto Ludwig Piffl will find his life improved by being turned from a communist into a capitalist by the masquerading that's the entire elaborate plot of *One, Two, Three*. But those ruined by such deceit and character transformation include Joe Gillis and Antonia in Wilder's conjoined films exposing the deceitful, soul-destroying underpinnings of the film industry. Both *Sunset Blvd.* and *Fedora* explore how the industry promotes empty dreams of success and rebirth (perhaps that's why Norma so hates the word "comeback"). The scam and con artists who populate other fields of human endeavor in Wilder films were already central to his directorial debut, *Mauvaise graine*, with its unhappy middle-class young man slumming in a gang of car thieves who transform stolen vehicles for a living. The most memorable criminals in Wilder films are those whose scams blow up in their faces after initially managing to deceive even wiseacres who should know better, Neff in *Double Indemnity* and Tatum in *Ace in the Hole*.

Yet in some cases—such as with Georges Iscovescu in *Hold Back the Dawn* and Bud Baxter in *The Apartment*—Wilder characters are rescued from self-destruction by a change of heart brought about through another person's devotion and sincerity. But others are not so fortunate. Sherlock Holmes has his broken heart shattered all over again when he falls in love with the German spy who deceives him. Antonia's descent into madness by losing her identity in taking her mother's place onscreen is prefigured comically in *Irma la Douce* by Nestor's adoption of the false identity that causes him to become irrationally jealous of *himself.* That absurdist comic twist also enmeshes Orville J. Spooner in the masquerade plot of *Kiss Me, Stupid,* which manages to be both funnier and more emotionally intense.

Underlying Wilder's intricately worked-out and highly varied lifelong obsession is the fundamental conflict he sees in human nature between self-protective scheming and genuine emotional commitment. The emotional duplicity involved explains his fascination with all varieties of prostitution (including role-playing by gigolos) as well as with nonpro forms of sexual, financial, and emotional exploitation. The so-called cynical side of Wilder is his realistic recognition of how central these flaws are in human nature; his romantic side represents his hope that such failings, such coldness and deceit, can be overcome by love and compassion. Since his emphasis sometimes tends toward destruction and other times toward redemption, this is the principal reason his work divides so unusually between comedies and dramas (or mixtures thereof).

Although the elaborate deception in *Fedora* has elements of farce and what Aristotle calls "The Ridiculous," it is one of Wilder's bleakest works, an old man's cry of despair like those uttered by Ford in *7 Women,* Carl Theodor Dreyer in *Gertrud,* or Orson Welles in *The Other Side of the Wind.* Although Wilder had explored his dark side extensively before *Fedora,* it is not accidental that he found this mood so overwhelming in a story dealing with his conviction that the industry he loved for decades had fallen into terminal decay. Although *Sunset Blvd.* is a much livelier and more assured film than *Fedora,* reflecting Wilder's greater confidence in his professional stature in 1950, *Fedora's* kinship with Norma as female stars ruined by the demands and vicissitudes of the film industry underscores Wilder's characteristically harsh critique of show business as a colorful and entertaining yet ultimately rapacious state of existence. Ironically, *Fedora* itself brought his place in showbiz crashing down on himself. We can almost see a ghostly image of the old *Eintänzer* dancing toward the camera in the mansion of his art—yet remaining lucid, not going out of focus—while offering his last testament to "those wonderful people out there in the dark."

The horror-film qualities of *Fedora* were anticipated back in Germany by the naive dreamer Jou-Jou's nightmare of her trip to Hollywood in Wilder's 1932 screenplay *A Blonde Dream.* That fantasy experience results in utter humiliation, derision, and a literal stripping-away of her personality, especially by men who degrade her as a woman trying to succeed in the film business, a fate that awaits Norma and Fedora. Since *A Blonde Dream* is a comedy, Jou-Jou manages to escape that fate in actuality, but the nightmare teaches her what another character says, "Film, that's no profession for adults," the unusually admonitory line from a writer who had not even made it yet to the illusory vistas of Sunset Blvd.

Although the young Wilder yearned to spend his life in Hollywood, even back in Germany he realized that "the business of creating illusions" could be self-annihilating ("Filmterror") if one is not careful to preserve a clear sense of identity and integrity. His later films about filmmaking are cautionary tales that show how the dream of stardom can be the ultimate illusory refuge for someone with no personality of her own, and how the achievement of that dream becomes a prison for a person whose career is her sole raison d'être. Tryon has Fedora tell Barry in her younger days, stabbing his chest with her finger, "Heart or art. You cannot have them both, you know—eventually you must choose." The older actress's loveless, narcissistic existence, shown in the way she destroys her daughter, reveals a void of character that is the worst cause and effect of treating life as a masquerade. These dilemmas in Wilder's work do not only affect women; although he recognizes how women especially are victimized by Hollywood, the creation of illusions is an integral part of what this canny perpetual exile sees as the danger involved in the human condition.

Wilder's preoccupation with show business, the meta nature of his work, and the constant stream of movie jokes and references he incorporated from his earliest days as a screenwriter in Germany show how central such role-playing is to his worldview, a serious form of having fun with his chosen medium. Although *Sunset Blvd.* and *Fedora* have more than even the expected number of movie references, those films' ultimate expressions of his themes of masquerading expose Wilder's most closely guarded feelings about the dangers involved in succumbing to illusions. As a Hollywood writer and director dependent on actors to bring his scripts to life, Wilder could see even more clearly that being an actor mirrors the archetypal role of an exile. His harrowing black-comic explorations of the lives of movie stars and their courtiers encapsulate the complexities and contradictions of identity and character transformation. In Gillis's desperate transformation from failed screenwriter to gigolo, Wilder was recalling his own struggles as a newcomer to Hollywood, and in Fedora's remaking of herself into a youthful facsimile to hold onto her stardom, Wilder was projecting his anxieties as an increasingly out-of-vogue elderly filmmaker, with the same actor naturally playing both of his *doppelgängers*.

Fedora's mad scheme to arrest time—the epigraph on the screenplay is a quote from Kipling, "YOUTH HAD BEEN A HABIT OF HERS FOR SO LONG, THAT SHE COULD NOT PART WITH IT"*—represented Wilder's covert wish, which he realized was mostly an illusion, that he could be reborn in the late 1970s as the successful filmmaker he had been in his prime. The canny exile who had already been "reborn" several times knew more than anyone else the allure of continual self-reinvention but also its limitations. His awareness that you always remain who you essentially are, however peripatetic your existence in trains, hotels, apartments, or studios, informs the tragic dilemma he confronts in the life of the self-exiled Hollywood star living in deathlike oblivion on a foreign island in *Fedora* and that film's exploration of the dangers of losing one's identity.

No matter how successful, or unsuccessful, Wilder's earlier characters had been in trying to carry off their masquerades and con-games, *Fedora* represented the final stop on the train, a dead end, an Edvard Munch–like final scream on the way to the grave. For Wilder, as much as for his futile but gallant characters Fedora, Antonia, and Dutch Detweiler, the business of creating illusions finally reveals itself as a devastating trap. That is what makes this flawed but eloquent film such a melancholy comment on his métier by an aging master, a reflection on the strengths and limitations of his art and his life. In *Fedora*, Wilder sums up and defines his own identity and destiny as an artist.

"THE BITTER WITH THE SOUR"

When Wilder accepted the AFI Life Achievement Award in 1986, more than four years after his career was involuntarily ended, he began by amplifying on the Goldwynism he had Barry Detweiler quote in *Fedora*:

—

* From his story "Venus Annodomini" (1888) about an Anglo-Indian woman deity who appears blessed with perpetual youth and attracts the devotion at different times of a father and son who are both in the British army. She introduces a young woman who seems older than her as her daughter.

Many years ago I worked on the Goldwyn lot, and I was taking a little walk between the stages, and I heard my name. And I turned around, and there was Sam Goldwyn standing in the window. And he says, "Wilder! What's the matter with you? You look depressed." And I said, "I *am* depressed, Mr. Goldwyn, because my last picture—[makes gesture with whistling sound] down the tubes." And he says, "Wilder, when are you gonna learn? In life you have to take the bitter with the sour."[*]

Wilder defined Goldwyn's unconscious wit as "an idiotic sort of illiteracy and yet it makes some sense." It was characteristic of Wilder to deploy a sardonic joke at his moment of coronation by an industry that had given him a safe harbor to live and work but now had passed him by. The pain he felt over his rejection was unmistakable yet cloaked as usual in the "brilliant repartee" that served as his defense mechanism. The industry figures listening to Wilder's speech in the Beverly Hilton Hotel knew firsthand how his career had gone "down the tubes" and could not help realizing that many of them had participated in that process.[†]

Wilder badly wanted to keep working, at least for a while. After *Buddy Buddy* flopped, he still went to the office every day for seven years to brainstorm film projects with Diamond. "I was retired, but I didn't know it, because I was too busy and working too hard," Wilder later said to biographer Charlotte Chandler. "If someone had told me I wasn't going to get another picture through, I would've said they were crazy. . . . Iz and I had so many ideas, we'd work on one for four weeks, and then we'd start another. We'd been burned; we chose wrong with *Buddy Buddy*, and we didn't want to make another mistake. We'd had some failures, so our confidence wasn't as good. . . . [But we] had a good time, Iz and me. Even though we weren't going to sell

---

[*]   Goldwyn must have said that to Wilder in the late 1940s about *The Emperor Waltz*, because in an excised moment from the screenplay of *Sunset Blvd.*, Artie Green, the assistant director played by Jack Webb, was to have said to Betty, "Babe, it's like that producer says: in life, you've got to take the bitter with the sour."

[†]   Although Wilder continued making features sporadically until the relatively old age of seventy-five, he was not the only veteran Hollywood director who found it hard to get work. Most of Wilder's peers from Hollywood's Golden Age, such as John Ford, Howard Hawks, and King Vidor, found themselves unemployed in their later years. There were rare exceptions, however. In the same year *Buddy Buddy* was released, George Cukor set a record for a Hollywood studio director by making a film at age eighty-one, *Rich and Famous*; and John Huston continued making features until 1987, when he died at eighty-one with *The Dead* awaiting release, although its funding came mostly from overseas. Clint Eastwood's long directing career is a more recent anomaly.

anything, we didn't know it, so it gave us both something to get up for in the morning."

That lasted until the day in 1988 when Diamond notified him that he was dying. That came as a complete surprise to Wilder, because Diamond had always been such a private man. Diamond lived only four more weeks. Wilder fitfully tried to work on his own after that but recognized it was futile. He had always needed a collaborator to parry ideas with and to serve as a sounding board and critic, a helper with the intricacies of the English language, a friend and ally. Wilder told Crowe that even though he had wanted to quit when he was eighty, "I quit when I was eighty-two." That was in the year of Diamond's death, when he finally came to "feel like Abercrombie without Fitch." There is no doubt that the loss of Diamond's partnership hit Wilder terribly hard. Coupled with his advancing age, that made it next to impossible for him to function at anywhere near his previous creative strength. He could not start over with a new collaborator or hope to find another as simpatico as Diamond.

Earlier Wilder had told biographer Maurice Zolotow, "I'll never retire. They'll have to take my camera away before I'll stop making pictures. I'll die making pictures." Wilder's pride did not allow him to announce his retirement, and part of him never fully accepted the situation, although he maintained a chipper enough facade in his many print and video interviews as he skewered the contemporary Hollywood scene and revisited his past. At the end of an interview in 1995, he said, "I'm late already and I have an appointment before I have to get back to finish a script. You see, I do still enjoy writing the scripts, it's just the producers who won't let me do what I want with them." Wilder kept up that constant but unproductive, futile activity as he continued going into his office. A German critic who wrote a 1988 book on Wilder, Claudius Seidl, observed in a 2017 documentary, "In this radical denial of reality, he simply didn't want to be a contented pensioner who plays golf and who is already sipping his first cocktail by late morning. He went to work. He pretended that he still was an in-demand director and screenwriter, just as Gloria Swanson in *Sunset Blvd.* deludes herself that she is still an in-demand actress and diva as she was decades earlier. He had basically turned into a character from one of his films."

Part of Wilder never gave up on wanting to make another film, but after a while at least, another part of him came to accept his forced inactivity. Fernando Trueba, who knew him in the years after Diamond's death, reported:

In Spain—I don't know in America—but in Spain, for years the critics and cinema journalists were always saying, "Ah, Billy Wilder, because the Hollywood system is so cruel, he can't do any more movies, because he's old and the insurance companies don't insure him." Always when they mentioned Billy Wilder, they were complaining about the system. But I remember Billy Wilder saying to me, "These guys are idiots. They are always writing that I can't do any more movies because the system is cruel, and Hollywood is very bad. No. Hollywood has been wonderful to me. I'm very grateful. And I don't *want* to make more movies. What I would like is to have made six movies *less*." I asked him, "Six movies less? You are talking in general? Or you are referring to some precise six movies?" He said, "Want to hear them? *Buddy Buddy. Fedora. Seven Year Itch. Spirit of St. Louis. Emperor Waltz.* And *The Front Page*." I told him, "Well, I understand perfectly, but *The Front Page* and *Fedora* are very good movies." He said, "They are unnecessary. I did *Sunset Blvd.*, and Howard Hawks did *His Girl Friday*."

Wilder remained, as always, a caustic commentator on Hollywood, a fertile source for fellow reporters, an unquenchable fount of wit and wisdom, if increasingly jaundiced as time went by. He found time for the 1999 book-length interview with Cameron Crowe and various filmed interviews and profiles. From 1986 onward, Wilder was involved with Hellmuth Karasek, a professor, screenwriter, and critic, on *Billy Wilder: A Close-up*, the biography published in Germany in 1992; they worked so closely that when Wilder gave me a copy, he called it "a book I wrote" with Karasek. Wilder qualified that by claiming he wrote parts of it, and that his biographer wrote "things I'd be embarrassed to say." Nevertheless, when Karasek showed him the lengthy manuscript, Wilder responded, "Is that all? . . . And we have not even scratched the surface of my present personality. . . . Do not forget: God is not finished with me yet." Wilder in truth was disappointed in the published result, even unfairly calling it "stupid." Karasek's breezy prose, enlivened by interspersing the fresh comments provided by the subject, gives a tour of his life that is entertaining and often vivid but not substantially deeper than the earlier biography by Zolotow and less thoroughly documented than the first-rate biographies by Ed Sikov and Andreas Hutter and Klaus Kamolz.

There was talk of a Wilder autobiography that never came to pass. A veteran book editor, Herman Gollob, collaborated briefly with him after its announcement by Doubleday in 1988. Wilder told the *New York Times* that the book would be called *Who I Was, How I Became What I Am, and Who the Hell Am I?* But it's doubtful Wilder wanted to allow such access to his closely guarded inner life. In his interviews he gave out only as much as he cared to provide the public, while reserving his deepest emotions and humor for his films. After his death, Audrey said to McGee, "They will never get Billy on paper. They will never get him." Wilder told me in 1995 he had been working on a final chapter ("the third act") to add to Karasek's book for a possible English version. But he admitted that he was having problems doing so and concluded that he would just live out his third act instead.*

Any sensible Hollywood screenwriter who wants to avoid the dirtiest secret of Hollywood—idea theft—is cautious about protecting his or her material, and Wilder kept most of his late film ideas or projects close to the vest. There was talk from time to time of remaking some of his earlier films. He and Diamond showed interest in revisiting *Love in the Afternoon* with more suitable casting, a project that fell through when *Buddy Buddy* tanked, and Wilder even entertained the idea of producing a remake of *One, Two, Three* set in China, with Jackie Mason starring and Arthur Hiller directing. Wilder was emphatically displeased with the 1995 Paramount remake of *Sabrina* directed by Sydney Pollack and starring Harrison Ford and Julia Ormond. Wilder had suggested Paramount skip the remake and just reissue the original, the kind of suggestion that does not go over well in modern Hollywood. And he was irked because a good suggestion he had for updating the story—to give Sabrina competition from the daughter of a Japanese businessman during negotiations to seal a merger with the bankrupt Larrabee company—was rejected. And perhaps Wilder also was angry at Pollack for urging Marthe Keller on him.

One friend of Wilder's who was genuinely upset that the great filmmaker was being slighted by Hollywood was the veteran producer David Brown. But when Brown offered him a comedy script to direct, Wilder was not interested in what he considered lackluster material; he did not want to repeat the mistake he had made with *Buddy Buddy*. Another prominent producer, former MCA agent Jerry Weintraub, after becoming chairman and chief executive officer of United Artists, persuaded Wilder in January 1986 to take a job as his special assistant. Wilder was tasked with reviewing scripts and films to

---

* Unlike Wilder's journalism collected in Germany and Austria in 1996 and 2006, Karasek's book has not yet seen publication in English.

give his expert advice. But he quickly found the job unappealing; he and the crass Reagan-era Hollywood were a distinct mismatch. When Weintraub showed him a rough cut of Brian De Palma's mob comedy *Wise Guys*, Wilder responded, "This picture is a big pile of shit. Perhaps I could tell you how to make it into a smaller pile, but it will still be shit." He barely endured his consultancy for about three months until Weintraub was forced out.

And while McCarthy and I were interviewing Wilder in his office at the Writers and Artists Building in Beverly Hills in 1978, he briefly took a phone call, simply saying "No" repeatedly and with increasing emphasis. When he hung up, he told us that Samuel Goldwyn Jr. had asked him to do a remake of *Ball of Fire*. Wilder's disdain for what could have been a "go" project is not hard to understand. The film had already been remade once poorly by Hawks himself, and Goldwyn Jr., as I knew from my own dealings with him, was untrustworthy and a dim reflection of his father's eminence as a producer. Robert Towne had warned me against working with the junior Goldwyn, and Wilder surely knew of his reputation. But the veteran director, who felt so out of touch with modern Hollywood, probably also felt unable or unwilling to grapple with the world of contemporary slang, as would have been required in remaking the brilliantly witty 1941 film he wrote for Hawks with Charles Brackett. Time had caught up with the Racing Reporter.

I harbored my own fantasies of working with Wilder. I once suggested that Evelyn Waugh's *Scoop* seemed like a perfect subject for him. Naturally I hoped we could collaborate on the script. The wickedly satirical 1938 novel deals with a bunch of bored British foreign correspondents killing time in an East African colonial hotel by filing dispatches inflating minor local conflicts into a major international crisis. Christopher Hitchens, describing *Scoop*'s "world of callousness and vulgarity and philistinism," called it "a novel of pitiless realism; the mirror of satire held up to catch the Caliban of the press corps, as no other narrative has ever done save Ben Hecht and Charles MacArthur's *The Front Page*." Since Wilder's adaptation of that play similarly skewers the reckless amorality of the press with an insider's acerbity, as he does in *Ace in the Hole* and other films, I thought the subject would appeal to the former reporter whose films often revolve around elaborate scams and con-jobs.

I assumed that Wilder was familiar with *Scoop*, because he and Waugh shared affinities as caustic social critics, and the editor with (imperfect) integrity played by Porter Hall in *Ace in the Hole* is named Mr. Boot. The central character in *Scoop* is William Boot, a meek birdwatching columnist for

London's *Daily Beast* who through mistaken identity finds himself in the fictional African country of Ishmaelia. While the other correspondents are playing their journalistic con-games, the naive, inept Boot inadvertently comes away with a genuine scoop. But when I mentioned *Scoop* as a film idea to Wilder in the 1990s, he surprised me by saying he had never heard of the novel: "I'm afraid you overrate my erudition, Mr. McBride." I gathered that one of the other screenwriters of *Ace in the Hole* must have suggested the character's name. I took a copy of the novel to Wilder's office anyway and left it on his doorstep with a note but never heard back about it.*

Some of the late projects Wilder did mention to me and others seemed as if they might be facetious. A couple were so outrageous that he may have been pulling the leg of Hollywood or sneering at the industry by pretending to give it the crude kind of stuff it liked to crank out. One of his publicly announced projects was the German sex novel *Josephine Mutzenbacher* by Felix Salten, an unrelentingly lewd look at an adolescent girl's descent into the netherworld of sexual abuse and prostitution. Although the novel was filmed four times in Europe between 1976 and 1987, it seems inconceivable that Wilder actually would have tried to adapt it, at least with any semblance of fidelity to the hardcore material, given his preference for dealing discreetly, although honestly, with sex onscreen and his disdain for the opening of the floodgates to unimaginative lewdness after the collapse of the Production Code.

When asked by the AFI fellows in 1976 how the relaxation of censorship affected his work, Wilder replied:

> Well, one can tackle more daring themes, and one can write dialogue without that straitjacket. . . . But I don't think we would ever write an out-and-out porno picture. . . . *Shampoo* [1975, written by Towne and Warren Beatty, directed by Hal Ashby] had an absolutely marvelous idea, the ambulatory hairdresser with the penis hairdryer under his belt, chugging around Beverly Hills, and it had those couple of dirty lines, you know [including Julie Christie saying of Beatty, "I want to suck his cock"]. But I personally would be embarrassed to go to Julie Christie and say, "Here's the dialogue for tomorrow." . . . But I do respect a director such as William Friedkin, who suddenly is confronted with a scene in *The Exorcist* such as a party going on

---

* *Scoop* had been adapted for a BBC limited series in 1972 and was made as a British television movie in 1987.

and the eight-year-old girl joins the party and pees on the carpet. That's just
a day's work, right? Where do you put the camera? It is not easy. . . . But it
is this kind of never-seen-before that makes for enormous box office.

Wilder's perception that a grabber of an opening and risqué elements were
de rigueur for a modern audience was evident in a project entitled *Naked in a
Volkswagen*. He mentioned it to McGee, who recalled, "The picture started
with this woman driving a Volkswagen stark naked, leaving her boyfriend or
husband of many years with what she had on her back when she met him. She
wanted nothing to do with everything he had given for her or bought for her.
That's as much as I ever heard." That notion, McGee thought, probably only
went as far as the notes stage, like most of Wilder's late film ideas. He kept
voluminous files of notes in a drawer, but after his early days, he was not one to
write a complete screenplay on spec. Another of his ideas was set in an old
actors' home, with a Shirley Temple–like former child star moving in because
her career is prematurely finished. In a black-comic twist on *Sunset Blvd.*, she
proves so obnoxious that the other residents decide to kill her. And for a long
time Wilder nursed a witty opening for a project he thought might finally lure
one of his favorite actors to work with him: Paris in the Middle Ages, at the
time of the Crusades. Knights lock their women in metal chastity belts and
ride off to the Holy Land. As they depart, the camera swings over to a locksmith's shop, and out the front door steps the locksmith, Cary Grant. Wilder
told Karasek he was pitching that idea to Universal when Grant died in 1986,
and the studio asked, "Can you see Sylvester Stallone in the part?"

And there was Wilder's announced intent to film the story of Le Pétomane. That pseudonymous performer, whose real name was Joseph Pujol, was
a celebrated French music hall star of the late nineteenth and early twentieth
centuries whose act consisted of creative variations on farting, including playing "O Sole Mio" and "La Marseillaise" through his ass. Wilder did have an
illustrious precedent for his project: Thomas Edison made a brief film of Le
Pétomane farting (silently, accompanied with elegant hand gestures) into a
large megaphone in 1900, *Le Pétomane du Moulin Rouge*. But how Wilder
intended to show such antics, with full sound effects, and stretch out the
biopic to two hours is hard to fathom. Part of the comedy would have come
from Le Pétomane not telling his family what he did for a living each night.
Wilder also mentioned what could have been a cockeyed romantic scene of
Le Pétomane's difficulty in explaining his profession to the parents of a woman

he wanted to marry. As Trueba noted, this bizarre project at least would have taken place in Wilder's favorite city, Paris, and a period he loved, the Belle Époque. But Trueba thought Wilder might have been only playing around with the notion.

One reason I also wonder that was Wilder's comment about how he and Diamond reacted to the hilarious (and notorious) farting scene in Mel Brooks's *Blazing Saddles*: "We come from a whole different school. The idea that people can sit around a campfire and break wind and people scream for fifteen minutes—that is very strange to us."* Perhaps Wilder's desire to tell the story of Le Pétomane onscreen sprang from the same angry impulse that led him to make *Buddy Buddy* so violently unfunny: if Hollywood wanted fart jokes, by God, he would give them the ultimate fart joke. When Trueba asked if he was serious, Wilder said, "No, I abandoned it—can you imagine the headline, 'The Last Fart of Billy Wilder'?" McGee, however, thought Wilder *was* serious about it, because he talked about the project a lot and liked to joke that the headline in *Variety* announcing the production would read, "Wilder Breaks Wind."

That may have been a nod to a fake *Variety* headline, "Critics Break Wind," displayed in Blake Edwards's acerbic comedy about Hollywood, *S. O. B.* (1981), referring to a disastrous flop directed by the William Holden character, *Night Wind*. That was Holden's final film before his death that November by hitting his head in an accidental fall in his Santa Monica apartment caused by his alcoholism. Wilder told the *New York Times*, "I really loved Bill, but it turned out I just didn't know him. If somebody had said to me, 'Holden's dead,' I would have assumed that he had been gored by a water buffalo in Kenya, that he had died in a plane crash approaching Hong Kong, that a crazed jealous woman had shot him and he drowned in a swimming pool. But to be killed by a bottle of vodka and a night table—what a lousy fadeout for a great guy."

Oliver Stone and his producing partner Ed Pressman came to Wilder to pitch a project they wanted him to direct, an adaptation of attorney Alan Dershowitz's 1986 book, *Reversal of Fortune: Inside the von Bülow Case*. It told the story of the trial and eventual acquittal of the European-born aristocrat Claus von Bülow, who was accused of attempting to murder his wealthy American

---

* Brooks pays homage to the French flatulist by playing Governor William J. Le Petomaine.

wife, Sunny. The film of *Reversal of Fortune* was directed in 1990 by Barbet
Schroeder, with Jeremy Irons winning an Oscar as von Bulow. Stone recalls
in his memoir *Chasing the Light* (2020):

> After meeting with the charming Old World agent Paul Kohner, we
> decided to ask his client Billy Wilder, then eighty and retired, but with the
> mental vigor of fifty, to direct. In person, Wilder was sardonic and tart.
> He . . . completely demolished the von Bülow tale we were offering him,
> saying it had no old-time story essentials, "twists, turns, conflicts, emotional
> involvement. . . . Every script they bring me is a beautiful woman, but if I
> don't get an erection, there's nothing I can do." He shared stories of Europe
> in the 1920s with Kohner, and then told us what he really wanted to do . . . if
> we truly believed he could still direct a great film. Of course we believed!
> From his shelf he pulled out a coffee table book on Le Pétomane, an 1890s
> Frenchman infamous for his musical farting on stage. Wilder, thankfully,
> would never make that movie.

Another showbiz project Wilder worked on, one with considerable satiric
potential, was about Hollywood in the silent days. It would have dealt with
the actor H. B. Warner, who played Jesus in DeMille's *The King of Kings* (1927)
and had a small part in *Sunset Blvd.* as one of the silent-film "waxworks" playing bridge with Norma. While impersonating Jesus, Warner had a drinking
problem and caroused with prostitutes. So DeMille insisted that during the
shooting of the Bible epic, Jesus could not engage in such scandalous activities, at least around Hollywood. Instead they let Warner travel to and from
Mexico on weekends to get his kicks in dives and brothels. McGee said
Wilder wanted to cast Matthau as the studio publicist who has to cope with
Warner's problems during shooting on Catalina Island. Such a situation
offered Wilder an opportunity for a genuinely biting and entertaining comedy about the film industry, a deliciously irreverent take on religious pictures
and Hollywood hypocrisy, taking jabs at the popular blend of sanctimony and
sensationalism practiced by DeMille, with whom he had worked amiably
enough in *Sunset Blvd.* When I asked Wilder about this project, he put forth
a jocular title and description that may have been tongue-in-cheek but captured the ribald nature of his mockery: "I wanted to call it *The Foreskin Saga.*
It's about the Mayer family. *Roots.*" Note Wilder's mischievous glee in

getting back at Louis B. Mayer for berating him over shaming the industry with *Sunset Blvd.* It's too bad Wilder never managed to progress even to the script stage on that idea about Hollywood in the silent days; he and Diamond put that project aside to work on *Fedora.*

In the late 1980s, after Diamond's death, Wilder tried to revive *The Foreskin Saga* with the novelist and screenwriter John Gregory Dunne. Dunne's work included the novel *True Confessions* and, in collaboration with his wife, Joan Didion, the screenplays for the 1981 film adaptation, the searing 1971 drama *The Panic in Needle Park,* and the cheesy 1976 version of the venerable showbiz saga *A Star Is Born.* Dunne recalled that Wilder

> asked me to do a screenplay with him for an idea he had, about a silent movie star playing Christ in a biblical epic. The twist was that the movie star was a dissolute drunk who was screwing everybody on the set, including the actress playing the Virgin Mary, while the actress playing Mary Magdalene spurned him, another twist. Billy wanted him to repent at the end of the picture, and actually walk on water—a gag he would set up throughout the picture, and then pay off at fade-out. Nothing came of the idea, but we had some funny meetings, because Billy has perfect pitch for truly hilarious bad taste.*

They never wrote the script, Dunne added vaguely, because he had to finish a novel, "and the time did not work out."

The project of Wilder's later years that he most regretted not being able to make, and that his admirers wish he could have made, was *Schindler's List.* But Spielberg had the rights to the 1982 Thomas Keneally book and, after agonizing over facing such a challenge, ironically had his resolve tested by Wilder's desire to make the film. A Wilder version of *Schindler's List,* different as it would have been from Spielberg's and its semidocumentary feeling—a quality Wilder greatly admired, saying he forgot the "technical stuff" and watched it "like a newsreel from the period . . . so authentic it makes you shiver"— and as excruciating as it would have been for Wilder to make as it was for Spielberg, would not have been a stretch for the older filmmaker who

---

* Perhaps Wilder was inspired by the ending of Hal Ashby's 1979 film version of Jerzy Kosinski's novel *Being There,* with the simpleminded pundit played by Peter Sellers walking on water.

had survived the rise of Hitler. Wilder never lost his guilt feelings—"fury, tears, reproaches," as he confessed to the *New York Times* in 1996—about leaving his mother behind with his stepfather when she refused his entreaties to escape from Vienna.

Oskar Schindler was the kind of man Wilder knew inside and out. He was a charming con-man and hedonist who pulled off a colossal scam against the Nazis in the midst of a world war. The story would have encapsulated Wilder's characteristic themes about con games, masquerades, corrupt and often criminal schemes in which his characters become enmeshed, making them face the moral dilemma of extricating or destroying themselves. The Gentile businessman and Nazi Party member born in Moravia (then part of the Austro-Hungarian Empire) used the fortune he made as a war profiteer to bribe and cajole a corrupt Nazi officer in order to save eleven hundred Jews from Auschwitz. And in the process of doing so he became a mensch. Schindler was a quintessential Billy Wilder character.

Wilder's *Schindler's List*, if made under the right conditions, would have called forth his deepest passions, feelings he usually expressed more obliquely onscreen, and could have made a crowning and perhaps somewhat cathartic end to his career. But whether he would have been physically up to the demands of such a difficult location shoot in wintry conditions in his native Poland—a punishing ordeal even for the much younger Spielberg—is an unanswered question. Wilder might have able for that challenge in the first half of the 1980s, but by the early 1990s he was becoming frail. He had begun to come to terms with the fact that, like it or not, he was retired from the craft he had practiced for most of his life.

But Wilder's attitude toward his forced retirement was not simple; he was in conflict over it. As Sikov puts it, Wilder in those later years was "gracious one minute and bitter and rude the next." Sometimes a certain tinge of mellowing could be detected. He told Charlotte Chandler, "People still ask me about *The Apartment*. They ask, 'Did Fran and Bud live happily ever after?' I always used to say the cards were stacked against it. I've changed my mind. Maybe my marriage to Audrey made me more of a romantic. Now I think it worked out for them. The marriage lasted, and they got a better apartment." But at other times, the mask of mellowness dropped, and the rage festering below his surface at how he was treated by Hollywood burst forth.

When I presented Wilder our LAFCA career achievement award on January 17, 1995, at the Bel Age Hotel in West Hollywood, I could tell how desperately part of him still wanted to work. Although he initially was cordial as we sat with Lemmon during lunch and the ceremony, Wilder became increasingly anxious as the acceptance speeches droned on and the event ran well over schedule. He began muttering profanities during the bloviating acceptance speech by *Pulp Fiction* producer Lawrence Bender, calling him a "son of a bitch." Although I tried my best to keep Wilder pacified, I did not know why he was so agitated. Finally the time came for my presentation. I linked Wilder with Lubitsch as filmmakers who transformed Hollywood with what Renoir called the "Berlin style," corrected the record on the supposed cynicism of a filmmaker who was actually a "closet romantic," and berated the industry for neglecting Wilder in his later years:

> It's our loss that a man of Billy Wilder's artistic accomplishment and influence wasn't given the opportunity to write and direct a film for the last twenty-one years of his life. In the late 1970s, I was having lunch with a producer in the Universal commissary. She was preparing to make a romantic comedy and complained that she couldn't find a director who was up to the challenge of directing one. "What about Billy Wilder?" I suggested. She reacted with surprise: "Billy Wilder? But he's not bankable." The indignation I sputtered did not suffice to overcome that idiocy.

I told the audience that "those mellow late-Wilder masterpieces *The Private Life of Sherlock Holmes*, *Avanti!*, and, yes, *Kiss Me, Stupid* demonstrate that he carried on Lubitsch's elegantly romantic legacy and infused it with his own distinctive blend of trenchant wit and corrosive social criticism."*

Then came Wilder's acceptance speech. I found it disappointingly brief. He did little more than make a joke he was fond of telling in his later years about a man who goes to his doctor to complain that he has trouble peeing.

---

* When Wilder died, I wrote an article based on that speech for the Writers Guild of America magazine *Written By*, and the guild showed its high esteem for him by placing his portrait on the cover.

The doctor tells him, "You've peed enough." I had hoped for a more eloquent career summation, but Wilder was honored so often throughout the world in those later years when he was not allowed to work that he clearly felt his listeners deserved little more than a rude kiss-off.

As I escorted Wilder from the ballroom, he finally revealed that he was anxious because he had a four o'clock appointment with a man he hoped might finance a film project. Our show had gone on so long that he was worried he might miss his appointment. As I parted our way with difficulty through the spectators in the packed hotel lobby, a mob of fans and photographers pursued us, but their attitude was excited and affectionate, not threatening as Hollywood paparazzi often can be. Nevertheless, when one photographer became too persistent, Wilder suddenly wheeled around and snapped at him viciously, ordering him to back off. The photographer and the rest of the crowd fell back in silent shock.

I was aghast as well as saddened and, to the extent I still could be in Hollywood, disillusioned. By that stage in my own career as a reporter and chronicler of filmmakers, I was almost entirely inured to idols displaying feet of clay, and the nasty side of Wilder had been well-documented over the years, yet it was painful to witness at such close range the full extent of his public rage at someone who only meant well. It was like watching the final scene of *Sunset Blvd.* with Norma making her way through the corridor of photographers not in dreamy madness but in helpless fury over her mistreatment by Hollywood. I realized that I was being given a sobering glimpse into how all the awards and other acclaim Wilder received in his final years in the United States and abroad, as flattering as he sometimes may have found them, could not fill the gap in his existence of not being allowed to practice his craft as a filmmaker. Even though his career had been over for almost fourteen years, he was still racing to try to make one more movie.

As Schlöndorff put it in a 2017 German documentary about Wilder, "The real tragedy of Billy Wilder was that he hardly worked in his last twenty years, when he was still very much in form. The revolution in Hollywood, the end of the studio system, was so radical that someone like him wasn't in demand anymore." Despite Wilder's tendency to make sarcastic remarks about Hollywood, its fixation on youth, and his inability to fit in anymore, Schlöndorff said, "They are jokes, but it wasn't amusing. And you noticed it, when he told them. He was extremely bitter in the last fifteen years. He realized: I still have the energy. I have the ideas. But I'm not given the chance."

When Wilder was coaxed into appearing in a 1999 documentary called *The Shoe Store*, made by a filmmaker named Steve Proto who sold shoes in a shop near his office in Beverly Hills, he said on camera, "I've always been depressed, even to the point of suicide. . . . My chums that I used to hang around with, most of them, are dead. . . . I wait for things to happen."

FIRE SALE

Yet the part of Wilder that came to accept the reality of retirement, however grudgingly, became evident as he made a creative shift to art collecting and art making. It was an obvious substitute for filmmaking but a drive he could more easily control, pleasing himself while not having to answer to anyone. It was not just a hobby but another obsession, a quieter and saner one than going to film studios and dealing with actors and crews and the front office and censors and critics. When Lemmon dropped into his Beverly Hills office one day to ask how he was doing, Wilder said, "I'm happy. I'm working. . . . I'm an artist now." And by turning to art, he was, in a sense, turning back to his past outside the world of filmmaking.

In his boyhood, Wilder had collected buttons, stamps, coins, posters, the usual found objects. Then in Berlin during the artistic ferment of the Weimar era, he became more serious about collecting paintings and Bauhaus furniture. But when he fled to Paris, he had to sell everything he had. He was too impoverished in the year he spent there to do more than look longingly at paintings. But he started collecting anew when he began making good money as a Hollywood picture-maker. Over the years, wherever he went in the world to work or vacation, he bought more artworks. With his discerning and idiosyncratic tastes, Wilder was prescient about discovering work that only much later would be highly valued by others.

A 1921 pastel by Picasso, *Tête de femme* ("Head of a Woman"), which Wilder had bought for about $5,000, sold for $4,840,000 on November 13, 1989, when he parted with his most valuable items at Christie's auction house in New York. "It was less nerve-wracking than a film preview," Wilder told the press. The auction brought in $32,641,400, more than he had made from all his films (though he could not help noting that he paid about $14 million in taxes and commissions).* Wilder still kept many of his paintings and other objects and "fell off the wagon" shortly after the auction when he could not help collecting again.

His addiction was not limited to paintings and sculptures but encompassed all kinds of other *objets trouvés* (found objects) in "Wilder's flea market," as he called his collection. The holdings of his dizzyingly eclectic miniature Xanadu spilled through every nook and cranny of his and Audrey's Westwood apartment, and there were many other objects he kept in a storage facility for occasional visits. His tastes were as whimsical and unconventional as could be imagined, from modern to primitive, portraits and abstract paintings, sketches and watercolors, sculptures and pre-Columbian art and African masks. Not surprisingly, given his often taboo-breaking film work, Wilder collected a wide array of erotic art, including nudes of all shapes and ages, from young girls to middle-aged women, ranging from thin to voluptuous and points between. He collected some American artists, such as his friend Saul Steinberg, Ellsworth Kelly, and Frank Stella, but primarily Europeans, among them Picasso, Miró, Dufy, Klee, Renoir, Matisse, Klimt, Giacometti, and his scandalous boyhood favorite, Egon Schiele.

And in a throwback to his youth, Wilder collected more humble tchotchkes, such as his beloved back scratchers, clocks, and a Prussian helmet as well as other objects reminiscent of his days in Europe, to stay in touch emotionally with the furnishings and world he had to leave behind. He kept a roomful of furniture collected on his travels and preserved from his movies, including the bed in which Fran recovers from her suicide attempt in *The Apartment* with the ministrations of Mrs. Dreyfuss. He also had a couch designed for his office by his friend Charles Eames, "very thin, very very narrow. . . . If you got a girlfriend built like a Giacometti, you got it made."

With his lifelong penchant for artistic collaboration, Wilder in his old age discovered at an exhibition a new collaborator, an eccentric middle-aged Palm Springs artist named Bruce Houston. In Annie Tresgot's charming documentary on Wilder's art collection, he affectionately calls Houston

---

* After Billy's death in 2002, Audrey donated $5 million to the Hammer Museum in Westwood, which created a Billy Wilder Theater, and following her death in 2012, the Wilders' estate bestowed $11 million on Children's Hospital Los Angeles for its neurosurgery programs.

"the strangest guy I ever met." They worked closely together in the 1990s on various objects, notably a whimsical series of small statues, acrylic painted plaster forms called *Variations on the Theme of Queen Nefertete I.* "I don't pick up a brush," Wilder said of that collaboration. "I'm kind of an idea man." Nefertete as an archetype of female beauty fascinated Wilder with the many ways he could reimagine and adorn her like an eternal mistress in different modernist guises. Those he chose not to sell. When I visited Wilder's apartment in 1995, he proudly showed me those statues lined up in a row like the six Oscars he had on display. The statues depicted the ancient Egyptian queen as if she had been imagined by such varied artists as Modigliani, Miró, Botero, Stella, Jackson Pollock, Christo, and Andy Warhol (with a Campbell's Tomato Soup can for a crown); there was even a Groucho Nefertete complete with cigar.

A piece of pop art Wilder created on his own was *Stallone's Typewriter,* an old Underwood manual machine he found and festooned with bullet holes, toy soldiers, and other patriotic gizmos, his way of mocking what Hollywood had turned into while it was rejecting his more civilized form of entertainment. That kind of activity gave him some consolation while he was gratifying his unquenchable artistic impulses. Unlike Schlöndorff, or my own glimpses of the part of Wilder that felt rage and frustration, McGee did not find Wilder particularly bitter in his old age, because, he said, "After *Fedora,* and I think after *Buddy Buddy* too, he threw himself into these art works you saw in the documentary—[such as] *Stallone's Typewriter.* He got totally involved in art and in being the legend, too. And that's what I remember. So I don't remember him being depressed at all. I never saw him in that mood. He seemed to be very busy."

Perhaps surprisingly for a popular Hollywood filmmaker, but befitting such an unconventional and cosmopolitan man who had lived through the most fertile years of artistic experimentation in Europe, Wilder's tastes in art ran more toward the abstract than the realistic. He was more a modernist than a classicist in his drive for collecting. As a filmmaker, the elegance of his visual style, his sense of balance and grace, was informed by his deep knowledge of painting and sculpture, but when he let his imagination roam free of commercial constraints, he found himself gravitating toward the avant-garde, toward artists he called "very daring . . . very challenging and very original." He found abstraction a tonic for his mind, soothing in its distancing effect and stimulating in its sense of formal play: "I prefer to look at abstract works when I work, rather than landscapes, portraits, or still lifes. You look around a lot when you write a script, when you try to resolve a narrative problem or find a good reply, and if you fix on a landscape or a cup of fruit, it quickly becomes annoying. But an abstract canvas can signify different things at different times. It can become a portrait or a still life. It stimulates my imagination and lets me invent my own story." He also loved pop art, and many of his acquisitions were works that amused him, acquired and appreciated in a playful spirit.

When Wilder took the momentous step of parting with much of his collection at Christie's, he explained that he was running out of room in the apartment and starting to bump into paintings leaning on the floor against the walls. But beyond that practicality, there was the psychological release involved in yet another break with the past, a starting over from scratch. That was a condition Wilder was familiar with from his departures from one country or another, especially from Germany. When he finishes thumbing through the Christie's catalogue in Tresgot's documentary, Wilder confesses that he had another reason for his lucrative fire sale:

> All right, this is where I end my song and fold my book, with a tear in my eye. I miss all these paintings that I sold. But in any case this constituted many, many, many millions of dollars. And they're gone. And sure, I miss them, but it's better to have that money in the bank and not have to work on a picture that you intensely dislike. Not to do something that they would like you to make, and you know it's not your dish, it's not anything that you can get excited about, but you have to get the money. But now I'm independently wealthy. I'm not as rich as the people who own the studios, but I'm wealthy enough not to look for a job.

That sounded like a rationalization, but it was genuine as well. Ever the survivor, Wilder was experiencing another of the numerous rebirths he had undergone in his lifetime. By divesting himself of prized possessions he had been schlepping around for decades, many of them found in Europe and brought home to Hollywood, he was transforming his anger and humiliation into another positive, forward-looking survival mechanism. "I just wanted to write my own third act," he said. But what life dictated to him violated some of the principles he laid down to Crowe in his "Tips for Writers":

> 6. If you have a problem with the third act, the real problem is in the first act. . . .
>
> 10. The third act must build, build, build in tempo and action until the last event, and then—
>
> 11.—that's it. Don't hang around.

When he had sold his furniture and car and other possessions in Germany in 1933, that was the kind of escape familiar to Jewish refugees throughout the ages who had to flee to safety with only the clothes on their backs, the hats on their heads, and the wits in their heads. Since Hollywood had turned its back on Wilder in his old age, by becoming more financially independent he was rejecting the industry he had once loved and its now-advanced state of philistinism for complete freedom from any further obligations or servitude. He had said what he wanted to say and made so many important films that he realized he had no need to make any more, even if from time to time he still felt an urge to keep creating, as any artist cannot help doing.

THE RECKONING

As Wilder aged, he eventually came to face the fact that his time had truly passed and he could find a certain peace and nobility in retirement. He was retiring on his own terms, playing with his art collection and dabbling with new objects while accepting the endless series of awards, grudgingly or not. No matter how prestigious (along with the AFI Life Achievement Award, he received the Kennedy Center Honor, the Lincoln Center Award, the National Medal of the Arts, and even tributes from countries he had left, Poland and Austria), he could not help viewing those belated trophies and ceremonies with a jaundiced eye as feeble substitutes for actual work. They were the consolation prizes an artist is awarded when he is being safely confined to history rather than accepted as part of the troublesome present. Of the AFI award, Wilder grumbled, "I'm getting it because Lubitsch is dead." And he said on another occasion, "Medals, they're like hemorrhoids. Sooner or later every asshole gets one." While playing that game of not-always-gracious elder statesman, what he was avoiding was a worse fate: knocking on doors and serving as a slavish director-for-hire on movies and TV shows, as some of his contemporaries had been willing to do. But he was also avoiding, as he told me, "the obligatory working on the jury of the Teheran Film Festival. That's *Sunset Blvd.* That's sort of the wind-up, you know. But I refuse to do it."

And even if much of the moviegoing audience had deserted him, Wilder could take well-deserved pride in his artistic legacy and accept the praise of those who appreciated it. But he could not resist quipping, "Yes, I have a very small cult of admirers. One of these days I will take them to Guyana." It is more than a small cult. Wilder's stature has grown over the years as a keen observer of the human condition, an artist scrutinizing the foibles, compromises, and aspirations of people and society with unsparing candor and honesty. His personal style is a mordant blending of unflinching reality with wry humor, a supremely graceful visual style, and what Diamond defined as his "disappointed romanticism"—his broken heart and his fitful attempt to heal it onscreen. The contrast between the low, adolescent humor of much contemporary American filmmaking and Wilder's sophisticated, caustic wit makes his rich and diverse body of work more highly valued to those who can appreciate it. Aspects of his work that once were condemned in some circles as his "vulgarity" can now be valued as a refreshingly adult shattering of taboos, as Wilder's more perceptive critics did regard it in his heyday.

His raucously irreverent *Some Like It Hot* is widely considered one of the greatest sound comedies, if not the greatest. His masterpiece still seems daring today; its openness to gender fluidity makes it seem all the more modern and avant-garde. Other Wilder classics such as *Double Indemnity*, *Sunset Blvd.*, and *The Apartment* are often revived, written about, and suitably honored. And some Wilder films that were undervalued or even considered disasters in their time—*A Foreign Affair*, *Ace in the Hole*, *Kiss Me, Stupid*, *The Private Life of Sherlock Holmes*—have developed impassioned followings. Screenplays by Brackett and Wilder and Wilder and Diamond continue to find publication, unlike most scripts that, if published at all, quickly vanish. The best films Wilder wrote with Brackett before becoming a Hollywood director, *Ninotchka*, *Hold Back the Dawn*, and *Ball of Fire*, live on, as does Wilder's work on the German silent classic *People on Sunday*.

If pockets of resistance remain among some critics and academics who find Wilder too acerbic or (that word again) unacceptably "cynical," that only shows how an artist with an iconoclastic social viewpoint inevitably provokes dissension and pushback. And if, compared with some other directors of his era, Wilder still is not studied as much or as deeply as he should be, considering his rare acuity in dissecting the American character and serving as a bridge between his adopted country and the Europe he left behind, that is the reason a critical study such as this one exists.

But perhaps what counts most in the legacy of Billy Wilder is the esteem in which many of his fellow filmmakers have held him. The immigrant who followed Lubitsch in reshaping the American film industry in his cosmopolitan image has had a great influence on many other screenwriters and directors throughout the world. After seeing *The Apartment* in 1960, Alfred Hitchcock wrote Wilder, "I cannot tell you how much I enjoyed it, and how beautifully made. I felt this so much that I was impelled to drop you this note." Orson Welles, in a televised interview on the last night of his life in 1985, referred simply to "wonderful Billy Wilder." Steven Spielberg called Wilder "the greatest writer-director who ever existed." Spanish director Pedro Almodóvar said, "I feel very close to the films of Billy Wilder. . . . [When] people say, 'Which Billy Wilder, the drama or the comedy?' I like both." He instructed his actress Carmen Maura to model her performances on the blend of comedy and poignancy MacLaine achieved in *The Apartment*. But when they met, Wilder warned the younger director, "Don't come to Hollywood, no matter what," and Almodóvar could see in his eyes "memories of compromises, failures, and misunderstandings."

Robert Towne, who captured 1930s Los Angeles so memorably in *Chinatown*, said of Wilder's equally mordant portrait of the city in *Sunset Blvd.*, "That was Billy's particular gift, is to take Lubitsch to the nether world. . . . and wed that to his own particular vision of people who are avaricious, greedy, do anything for a buck, whatever it is, but he's so cute about it [laughs] that he makes you *like* it. I think that selling out is something that he saw every day of his life and worried about it himself even as he did whatever he could to avoid it. I think it's true of all our lives, I think that's the thing that we're always worried about, is negotiating away ourselves."

Spike Lee, who sought out and befriended Wilder in his later years, especially appreciated the way he dealt with "the choices people make and the consequences of those choices. . . . The final shot of [*Ace in the Hole*] in my opinion is one of the greatest final shots in cinema. . . . And for me this film really is [about] the beginning of where we're starting to see things change in America, how the media control people. And also it's about morals, scruples, values, and how people will pray at the altar of the Almighty Dollar . . . and then there comes that reckoning moment, like, 'My God, why did I do this?'"

Woody Allen called *Double Indemnity*

Billy Wilder's best movie—but practically anyone's best movie. . . . even though he's often thought of as a comic director. . . . It's photographed simply and correctly: just a good story well-told, like that good American writing you find in Mark Twain or Ernest Hemingway. No frills. The script is sensational. . . . There's not a shred of sentimentality in it. It's hard-nosed, no-nonsense and entertaining from the first to the last—as always in Wilder's films, it's got a beautiful blackout at the end. It reeks of everything American. Wilder came from a tradition that was more artistic than the American one and brought that to bear on Hollywood filmmaking, with its higher budgets, better technology and wonderful movie stars. He became a genuinely American filmmaker, without any question, but his roots were always European.

Perhaps fittingly, then, it was Wilder's longtime European filmmaker friend Fernando Trueba who offered the most memorable tribute. It came in 1994 when Trueba brought Spain the best foreign language film Academy Award for his comedy-drama set in the days before the Spanish Civil War, *Belle Epoque*. When he accepted the Oscar, he said, "I would like to believe in God in order to thank him, but I just believe in Billy Wilder. So thank you, Mr. Wilder."

Wilder was mixing a martini when he heard that tribute on television at the apartment. Audrey screamed. Billy dropped the gin bottle. The next day he called Trueba at his hotel and announced,

"Fernando, it's God."

10.1 Wilder rehearsing his Lubitschean fairy-tale romance *Sabrina* (1954) with one of his favorite actresses, Audrey Hepburn. (Paramount/From the Collections of the Margaret Herrick Library, Academy of Motion Picture Arts and Sciences.)

FILMOGRAPHY

BILLY WILDER'S film credits in Europe and the United States as a screenwriter, director, and producer are drawn from a variety of sources. They include the films themselves; Steve Seidman's book *The Film Career of Billy Wilder* (1977); and other books about his life and career, notably Ed Sikov's biography *On Sunset Boulevard: The Life and Times of Billy Wilder* (1998), as well as the Internet Movie DataBase (IMDB), which provide many further cast and crew credits. Key personnel are listed below, including the three major cast members for each film. Note that Wilder's screen credit was "Billie" until *Champagne Waltz* in 1937.

Original distributors are listed but not foreign or subsidiary rights distributors. English translations are included for the original foreign-language titles of Wilder's European films. Production companies (sometimes several for a given film) are not all listed, with the major exception of the Mirisch Company or the Mirisch Corporation, which produced or coproduced eight of Wilder's later films; the Mirisch name is listed after the distributor of those films, United Artists (or its art-house subsidiary, Lopert Pictures, which released *Kiss Me, Stupid* in the United States).

Wilder's uncredited contributions to films are not listed except in the cases of these important films in his career: *Der Kampf mit dem Drachen oder: Die Tragödie des Untermieters* (*The Fight with the Dragon or: The Tenants' Tragedy*) (short); *Was Frauen träumen* (*What Women Dream*) (BW's writing credit was removed by the Nazi regime before the premiere); *That Certain Age*; *Die Todesmühlen* (*Death Mills*) (documentary); and *A Song Is Born*; other uncredited contributions are noted in the text of this book and in Charles Brackett's diaries of their collaboration (see listings for books in notes on sources). Previous versions of films and remakes are listed in this filmography; BW is credited on some but not all the remakes. Documentaries in which Wilder appears are not all listed here, but some are listed in the notes on sources; others are listed on IMDB.

Other writers who contributed to Wilder's films without credit are not listed (some are noted in the text). Despite being uncredited on *The Spirit of St. Louis* for his major contributions as director on reshoots, John Sturges is listed with Wilder for that film.

FILMOGRAPHY KEY

BW   Billy Wilder
CB   Charles Brackett
DIST   Distributor
ID   I. A. L. Diamond
JL   Jack Lemmon
P   Producer
D   Director
S   Screenwriter and source material
C   Principal cast members
UA   United Artists
UFA   Universum Film AG

GERMAN SILENT PERIOD AS SCREENWRITER (1929–1930)

1929

Der Teufelsreporter: Im Nebel der Grosstadt (*The Devil's Reporter: In the Fog of the Big City/The Daredevil Reporter/A Hell of a Reporter*). DIST: Deutsche Universal-Film; P: Joe Pasternak; D: Ernst Laemmle; S: BW; C: Eddie Polo, Gritta Ley, Fred Grosser. With BW in uncredited cameo as a reporter.

1930

Menschen am Sonntag, ein Film ohne Schauspieler (*People on Sunday, a Film Without Actors*). DIST: Film Studio 1929, Filmstudio Berlin; P: Seymour Nebenzal, Moriz Seeler; D: Robert Siodmak, Edgar G. Ulmer; S: BW, based on a reportage by Kurt Siodmak; C: Erwin Splettstösser, Brigitte Borchert, Wolfgang von Waltershausen.

GERMAN SOUND PERIOD AS SCREENWRITER (1930–1933)

1930

Der Kampf mit dem Drachen oder: Die Tragödie des Untermieters (*The Fight with the Dragon or: The Tenants' Tragedy*). DIST: Universum Film (UFA); D: Robert Siodmak; S: Kurt Siodmak, Robert Siodmak, BW [uncredited]; C: Hedwig Wangel, Felix Bressart. A short subject.

Ein Burschenlied aus Heidelberg (*A Student's Song of Heidelberg*). DIST: Universum Film (UFA); P: Günther Stapenhorst; D: Karl Hartl; S: Hans Wilhelm, BW, Ernst Neubach, from an idea by Neubach and Wilhelm; C: Hans Brausewetter, Betty Bird, Willi Forst.

1931

Der Mann, der seinen Mörder sucht aka *Jim, Der Mann mit der Narbe* (*The Man Who Searched for His Own Murderer* aka *Jim, The Man with the Scar*). DIST: UFA; P: Erich Pommer; D: Robert Siodmak; S: Kurt Siodmak, BW, based on the play by Ludwig Hirschfeld and Ernst Neubach; C: Heinz Rühmann, Lien Deyers, Hermann Speelmans.

   Ihre Hoheit befiehlt (*Her Highness Commands* (*Her Grace Commands*). DIST: UFA; D: Hanns Schwarz; S: Paul Frank, Robert Liebmann, BW; C: Käthe von Nagy, Willy Fritsch, Reinhold Schünzel. Also made in French as *Princesse, à vos ordres!* (*Princess, at Your Command!*, 1931). Remade in English as *Adorable* (1933).

   Seitensprünge (*Affairs*). DIST: Deutsche Universal-Film; D: Stephan Székely; S: Lajos Biró, Bobby E. Lüthge, Károly Nóti, from an idea by BW; C: Gerda Maurus, Oskar Sima, Paul Vincenti.

   Der falsche Ehemann (*The Wrong Husband*). DIST: UFA; P; Bruno Duday; D: Johannes Guter; S: Paul Frank, BW; C: Johannes Riemann, Maria Paudler, Gustav Waldau.

   Emil und die Detektive (*Emil and the Detectives*). DIST: UFA; P: Günther Stapenhorst; D: Gerhard Lamprecht; S: BW, based on the novel by Erich Kästner; C: Rolf Wenkhaus, Käthe Haack, Inge Landgut. Remade in English version in UK as *Emil and the Detectives* (1935), in West Germany as *Emil und die Detektive* (1954), in Japan as *Chiisana tantei tachi* (1956), by Disney in Germany as *Emil and the Detectives* (1964), and in Germany as *Emil und die Detektive* (2001).

1932

Liebe ist Liebe (*Love Is Love*) aka *Der Sieger* (*The Winner*). DIST: UFA; P: Erich Pommer, Eberhard Klagemann; D: Hans Hinrich, Paul Martin; S: Leonhard Frank, Robert Liebmann, Martin, and BW; C: Hans Albers, Käthe von Nagy, Julius Falkenstein. Also made in French version as *Le vainqueur* (*The Winner*, 1932).

   Es war einmal ein Walzer (*Once There Was a Waltz*). DIST: Aafa-Film; P: Gabriel Levy; D: Viktor Janson; S: BW; C: Mártha Eggerth, Rolf von Goth, Paul Hörbiger. Also made in English version as *Where Is This Lady?* (1932).

   Ein blonder Traum (*A Blonde Dream*). DIST: UFA; P: Erich Pommer; D: Paul Martin; S: Walter Reisch, BW; C: Lilian Harvey, Willy Fritsch, Willi Forst. Also made in 1932 in French version as *Un rêve blond* (*A Blonde Dream*) and in English version as *A Blonde Dream* aka *Happy Ever After*.

Scampolo, ein knd der strasse (*Scampolo, A Girl of the Street*) aka *Ein Mädel der Strasse* (*A Girl of the Streets*) and *Um einen Groschen liebe* (*Love for a Penny*). DIST: Bayerische Filmgesellschaft; P: Lothar Stark; D: Hans Steinhoff; S: Max Kolpé, Felix Salten, BW, based on the play *Scampolo* by Giuseppe Adami; C: Dolly Haas, Karl Ludwig Diehl, Oskar Sima. Remake of 1917 and 1928 film versions, both entitled *Scampolo*. Also made in French version, *Un peu d'amour* (*A Little Love*, 1932), on which BW shares screenplay credit with Kolpé, Salten, and Paul Nivoix. Remade in 1941 (Italy) and 1958 (Italy) as *Scampolo* and in 1953 (Portugal) as *Scampolo 53*.

Das Blaue vom Himmel (*The Blue from the Sky*). DIST-P: Aafa-Film AG; D: Viktor Janson; S: Max Kolpé, BW; C: Mártha Eggerth, Hermann Thimig, Fritz Kampers.

1933

Madame wünscht keine Kinder (*Madame Wants No Children*). DIST: Europa-Film-Verleih AG; P: Anatol Potock; D: Hans Steinhoff; S: Fritz Rotter, adaptation by Max Kolpé and BW, based on the novel by Clément Vautel; C: Liane Haid, Georg Alexander, Lucie Mannheim. Remake of *Madame wünscht keine Kinder* (1926). Also made in French version as *Madame ne veut pas d'enfant* (*No Children Wanted*, 1933).

Was Frauen träumen (*What Women Dream*). DIST: Europa-Film-Verleih AG; P: Julius Haimann; D: Géza von Bolváry; S: Franz Schulz, BW, based on the novel by Emil Hosler [BW credit removed after the Nazi takeover before the film's premiere]; C: Nora Gregor, Gustav Fröhlich, Peter Lorre. Remade in Hollywood as *One Exciting Adventure* (1934).

FRENCH SOUND PERIOD AS SCREENWRITER-DIRECTOR (1934)

1934

Mauvaise graine (*Bad Seed*). DIST: Pathé; P: Georges Bernier; D: Alexandre Esway and BW; S: Jan Lustig, BW, Max Kolpé, with the collaboration of Claude-André Puget; C: Danielle Darrieux, Pierre Mingand, Raymond Galle. Remade in France as *La voyageuse inattendue* (*The Unexpected Voyager*, 1950).

AMERICAN SOUND PERIOD AS SCREENWRITER ONLY (1933–1948)

1933

Adorable. DIST: Fox; D: Wilhelm (William) Dieterle; S: George Marion Jr. and Jane Storm, based on the story by Paul Frank and BW; C: Janet Gaynor, Henry (Henri) Garat, C. Aubrey Smith. A remake of *Ihre Hoheit befiehlt*.

1934

One Exciting Adventure. DIST: Universal; D: Ernst L. Frank; S: William Hurlbut, William B. Jutte, Samuel Ornitz, based on a story by Franz Schulz and BW; C: Binnie Barnes, Neil Hamilton, Paul Cavanagh. A remake of *Was Frauen träumen.*

Music in the Air. DIST: Fox; P: Erich Pommer; D: Joe May; S: Robert Liebmann, Howard I. Young, and BW, based on the play by Oscar Hammerstein II (lyrics and book) and Jerome Kern (music); C: Gloria Swanson, John Boles, Douglass Montgomery.

1935

Lottery Lover. DIST: Fox; P: Al Rockett; D: William Thiele; S: Franz Schulz, BW, from a story by Siegfried M. Herzig and Maurice Hanline, dialogue by Sam Hellman; C: Lew Ayres, Pat Paterson, Peggy Fears.

1937

Champagne Waltz. DIST: Paramount; P: Harlan Thompson; D: A. Edward Sutherland; S: Don Hartman and Frank Butler, from a story by BW and H. S. Kraft; C: Gladys Swarthout, Fred MacMurray, Jack Oakie.

1938

Bluebeard's Eighth Wife. DIST: Paramount; P-D: Ernst Lubitsch; S: CB-BW, based on the play *La huitième femme de Barbe-bleue/Bluebeard's Eighth Wife* by Alfred Savoir; C: Claudette Colbert, Gary Cooper, Edward Everett Horton. Remake of 1923 film.

That Certain Age. DIST: Universal; P: Joe Pasternak; D: Edward Ludwig; S: Bruce Manning [and CB-BW, uncredited], from a story by F. Hugh Herbert; C: Deanna Durbin, Melvyn Douglas, Jackie Cooper.

1939

Midnight. DIST: Paramount; P: Arthur Hornblow Jr.; D: Mitchell Leisen; S: CB-BW, based on a story by Edwin Justis Mayer and Franz Schulz; C: Claudette Colbert, Don Ameche, John Barrymore. Remade as *Masquerade in Mexico* (1946).

What a Life. DIST: Paramount; P-D: Jay Theodore Reed; S: CB-BW, based on the play by Clifford Goldsmith; C: Jackie Cooper, Betty Field, John Howard.

Ninotchka. DIST: MGM; P-D: Ernst Lubitsch; S: CB, BW, Walter Reisch, based on a story by Melchior Lengyel; C: Greta Garbo, Melvyn Douglas, Ina Claire. Remade as *Silk Stockings* (1957) and for television in 1960 (United States) and 1965 (West Germany) as *Ninotchka.*

1940

Rhythm on the River. DIST: Paramount; P: William LeBaron; D: Victor Schertzinger; S: Dwight Taylor, from a story by Jacques Théry and BW; C: Bing Crosby, Mary Martin, Basil Rathbone.

Arise, My Love. DIST: Paramount; P: Arthur Hornblow Jr.; D: Mitchell Leisen; S: CB-BW, adapted by Jacques Théry, based on a story by Benjamin Glazer and John S. Toldy (Hans Székely); C: Claudette Colbert, Ray Milland, Dennis O'Keefe.

1941

Hold Back the Dawn. DIST: Paramount; P: Arthur Hornblow, Jr.; D: Mitchell Leisen; S: CB-BW, based on the story "Memo to a Movie Producer" by Ketti Frings; C: Charles Boyer, Olivia de Havilland, Paulette Goddard.

Ball of Fire. DIST: RKO; P: Samuel Goldwyn; D: Howard Hawks; S: CB and BW, based on the story "From A to Z" by BW and Thomas Monroe; C: Gary Cooper, Barbara Stanwyck, Oskar Homolka. Remade as the musical *A Song Is Born* (1948) by Hawks and Goldwyn for RKO, without credit to BW.

AMERICAN SOUND PERIOD AS SCREENWRITER-DIRECTOR (1942–1988)

1942

The Major and the Minor. DIST: Paramount; P: Arthur Hornblow Jr.; D: BW; S: CB-BW, based on the play *Connie Goes Home* by Edward Childs Carpenter and the short story "Sunny Goes Home" by Fannie Kilbourne; C: Ginger Rogers, Ray Milland, Rita Johnson. Remade as *You're Never Too Young* (1955).

1943

Five Graves to Cairo. DIST: Paramount; P: CB; D: BW; S: CB-BW, based on the play *Hotel Imperial* by Lajos Biró [uncredited]; C: Franchot Tone, Anne Baxter, Erich von Stroheim. Remake of *Hotel Imperial* (1927 and 1939).

1944

Double Indemnity. DIST: Paramount; P: Joseph Sistrom; D: BW; S: BW and Raymond Chandler, based on the novel by James M. Cain; C: Fred MacMurray, Barbara Stanwyck, Edward G. Robinson. Remade for television in 1973, with Steven Bocho receiving teleplay credit and CB and BW credited for their earlier screenplay.

1945

The Lost Weekend. DIST: Paramount; P: CB; D: BW; S: CB-BW, based on the novel by Charles R. Jackson; C: Ray Milland, Jane Wyman, Phillip Terry.

Die Todesmühlen (*Death Mills*). DIST: U.S. Office of Military Government in Germany/U.S. Army Signal Corps/U.S. War Department; D: Hans Burger; S: Burger, Oskar Seidlin [and BW, uncredited for contributions to Seidlin's narration text and to film editing]. A documentary short about the Holocaust. Segments appear in Orson Welles's feature *The Stranger* (1946).

1948

The Emperor Waltz. DIST: Paramount; P: CB; D: BW; S: CB-BW; C: Bing Crosby, Joan Fontaine, Roland Culver.

A Foreign Affair. DIST: Paramount; P: CB; D: BW; S: CB, BW, and Richard L. Breen, adaptation by Robert Harari from a story by David Shaw; C: Jean Arthur, Marlene Dietrich, John Lund.

1950

Sunset Blvd. (aka *Sunset Boulevard*). DIST: Paramount; P: CB; D: BW; S: CB-BW and D. M. Marshman, Jr.; C: William Holden, Gloria Swanson, Erich von Stroheim.

1951

Ace in the Hole. DIST: Paramount; P-D: BW; S: BW, Lesser Samuels, Walter Newman; C: Kirk Douglas, Jan Sterling, Robert Arthur. Retitled *The Big Carnival.*

1953

Stalag 17. DIST: Paramount; P-D: BW; S: BW and Edwin Blum, based on the play by Donald Bevan and Edmund Trzcinski; C: William Holden, Don Taylor, Otto Preminger.

1954

Sabrina. DIST: Paramount; P-D: BW; S: BW, Samuel Taylor, Ernest Lehman, based on Taylor's play *Sabrina Fair*; C: Humphrey Bogart, Audrey Hepburn, William Holden. Remade by Paramount in 1995 as *Sabrina*, directed by Sydney Pollack, with BW receiving one of the screenplay credits for cowriting the earlier film.

1955

The Seven Year Itch. DIST: Twentieth Century-Fox; P: Charles K. Feldman, BW; D: BW; S: BW and George Axelrod, based on Axelrod's play; C: Marilyn Monroe, Tommy (Tom) Ewell, Evelyn Keyes.

1957

The Spirit of St. Louis. DIST: Warner Bros.; P: Leland Hayward; D: BW [and John Sturges, uncredited]; S: BW and Wendell Mayes, adapted by Charles Lederer, based on the book by Charles A. Lindbergh; C: James Stewart, Murray Hamilton, Patricia Smith.

Love in the Afternoon. DIST: Allied Artists; P-D: BW; S: BW-ID, based on the novel *Ariane, jeune fille russe* (*Ariane, the Young Russian Girl*) by Claude Anet; C: Gary Cooper, Audrey Hepburn, Maurice Chevalier. Previously made by director Paul Czinner in three languages: German, as *Ariane* (1931); English, as *The Loves of Ariane* (1931); and French, as *Ariane, jeune fille russe* (1932).

Witness for the Prosecution. DIST: UA; P: Arthur Hornblow Jr.; D: BW; S: BW and Harry Kurnitz, adaptation by Larry Marcus, based on the play and novel by Agatha Christie; C: Tyrone Power, Marlene Dietrich, Charles Laughton. Remade for television in 1982.

1959

Some Like It Hot. DIST: UA/Mirisch; P-D: BW; S: BW-ID, based on a story by R. (Robert) Thoeren and M. (Michael) Logan; C: Marilyn Monroe, Tony Curtis, JL. Remake of the French *Fanfare d'amour* (*Fanfare of Love*, 1935) and the German *Fanfaren der Liebe* (*Fanfares of Love*, 1951).

1960

The Apartment. DIST: UA/Mirisch; P-D: BW; S: BW-ID; C: JL, Shirley MacLaine, Fred MacMurray. Remade in France for television as *La Garçonnière* (*The Bachelor Pad*, 2018).

1961

One, Two, Three. DIST: UA/Mirisch; P-D: BW; S: BW-ID, based on the play *Egy, kettö, három* (*One, Two, Three*) by Ferenc Molnár; C: James Cagney, Horst Buchholz, Pamela Tiffin.

1963

Irma la Douce. DIST: UA/Mirisch; P-D: BW; S: BW-ID, based on the musical play by Alexandre Breffort and Marguerite Monnot; C: JL, Shirley MacLaine, Lou Jacobi. Remade for television in France (1972) and in Italy as *Irma la dolce* (1980).

1964

Kiss Me, Stupid. DIST: Lopert Pictures [UA subsidiary]/Mirisch; P-D: BW: S: BW-ID, based on the play *L'Ora della Fantasia* (*The Dazzling Hour*) by Anna Bonacci; C: Dean Martin, Kim Novak, Ray Walston. Play previously filmed in Italy as *Moglie per una notte* (*Wife for a Night*, 1952).

1966

The Fortune Cookie. DIST: UA/Mirisch; P-D: BW; S: BW-ID; C: JL, Walter Matthau, Ron Rich.

1970

The Private Life of Sherlock Holmes. DIST: UA/Mirisch; P: BW; D: BW; S: BW-ID, based on characters created by Arthur Conan Doyle; C: Robert Stephens, Colin Blakely, Geneviève Page. Home video versions contain extra footage and audio cut from the film's theatrical release.

1972

Avanti! DIST: UA/Mirisch; P-D: BW; S: BW-ID, based on the play *Avanti! or a Very Uncomplicated Girl* by Samuel Taylor; C: JL, Juliet Mills, Clive Revill.

1974

The Front Page. DIST: Universal; P: Paul Monash; D: BW; S: BW-ID, based on the play by Ben Hecht and Charles MacArthur; C: JL, Walter Matthau, Susan Sarandon. Play previously filmed as *The Front Page* (1931) and *His Girl Friday* (1940) and adapted for television in 1945, 1948, and 1970, as a TV series in 1949–50, and remade as *Switching Channels* (1988).

1978

Fedora. DIST: Cinema Service/UA (Bavaria/Geria/Lorimar); P: BW; D: BW; S: BW-ID, based on the novella *Fedora* in the collection *Crowned Heads* by Thomas Tryon; C: William Holden, Marthe Keller, Hildegard Knef.

1981

Buddy Buddy. DIST: MGM/UA; P: Jay Weston; D: BW; S: BW-ID, based on the Francis Veber play *Le contrat* (*The Contract*); C: JL, Walter Matthau, Paula Prentiss. Remake of *L'emmerdeur* (*The Shithead/A Pain in the A—/A Pain in the Ass/The Troublemaker*, 1973). Remade in Hungary as *Bas belasi* (*Pest Head*, 1982) and in France as *L'emmerdeur* (2008).

1988

Quizzically. D: BW; S: ID; C: JL, Walter Matthau, BW. BW directed ID's short sketch for the 1988 Writers Guild of America West memorial to his collaborator. A videotape is included on the DVD of the Volker Schlöndorff–Gisela Grischow documentary *Billy Wilder Speaks* (Kino International, 2006).

11.1 (top) Exasperated but still in control, Wilder directs the discombobulated Marilyn Monroe in this hotel scene requiring dozens of takes for *Some Like It Hot* (1959). (United Artists/Photofest.)

11.2 (bottom) The New Year's Eve climax of *The Apartment* (1960) as Shirley MacLaine's Fran realizes from her married lover, Jeff Sheldrake (Fred MacMurray), that she should go to the man who truly loves her, Jack Lemmon's Bud Baxter. (United Artists/Photofest.)

NOTES ON SOURCES

SOME OF the biographical data on Billy Wilder and information on his film career were provided by the books cited in full in this section (including some not yet published in English): the most thorough Wilder biography to date, Ed Sikov's *On Sunset Boulevard: The Life and Times of Billy Wilder*; the revealing and authoritative *Billy Wilder: A European Career* by Andreas Hutter and Klaus Kamolz; and others, including Hellmuth Karasek's *Billy Wilder: A Close-up* and Maurice Zolotow's *Billy Wilder in Hollywood*, both of which contain extensive comments by Wilder; Kevin Lally's *Wilder Times: The Life of Billy Wilder*; Gene D. Phillips's *Some Like It Wilder: The Life and Controversial Films of Billy Wilder*; and Charlotte Chandler's *Nobody's Perfect: A Personal Biography*. Key items specific to individual books are cited by chapter. Other biographical information and quotes about his work also are listed in these notes. Seidman's *The Film Career of Billy Wilder* provides bibliographical information and a filmography through 1977, and other books contain useful bibliographies.

Conversations with Wilder by Cameron Crowe and the collection *Billy Wilder: Interviews*, edited by Robert Horton (including two of my interviews), are the closest we have to a Wilder autobiography. Numerous documentaries on Wilder and his work have been made, including some with extensive interview material; the most notable documentaries are listed in this section. Two invaluable collections of Wilder's reporting in Vienna and Berlin are *"Billie": Billy Wilder's Viennese Journalism* and *The Prince of Wales Is Going on Vacation: Berlin Reports, Features and Reviews of the Twenties*; a collection in English translation drawn from articles he wrote in both cities is *Billy Wilder on Assignment: Dispatches from Weimar Berlin and Interwar Vienna* (2021).

Books on individual films were also helpful for research. Particularly insightful critical studies include Neil Sinyard and Adrian Turner's *Journey Down Sunset Boulevard: The Films of Billy Wilder*, Gerd Gemünden's *A Foreign Affair: Billy Wilder's American Films*, and the collections edited by Karen McNally, *Billy Wilder Movie-Maker: Critical Essays on the Films,* and Georges-Claude Guilbert, *Literary Readings of Billy Wilder.* Charles Brackett's diaries, edited by Anthony Slide as *"It's the Pictures That Got Small": Charles Brackett on Billy Wilder and Hollywood's Golden Age,* provide a detailed firsthand perspective on their work together between 1936 and 1950. Various books on the histories of the Austro-Hungarian Empire and Germany, German cinema, and exile cinema and culture were resources to provide context for Wilder's life and work.

Many other sources in books, periodicals, and document collections were consulted for this book. Some Wilder screenplays (written with Brackett or I. A. L. Diamond) have been published, and many are in the collections of the Writers Guild of America West, Los Angeles (to which Wilder's scripts were donated by his widow, Audrey, for its Billy Wilder Collection; the Writers Guild Foundation Shavelson-Webb Library has a Billy Wilder Reading Room), and the Wisconsin Historical Society, Madison (to which Diamond donated his scripts).

ABBREVIATIONS

AFI American Film Institute

AMPAS Academy of Motion Picture Arts and Sciences' Margaret Herrick Library, Beverly Hills

AP Associated Press

BBC *Berliner Börsen Courier* (*Berlin Stock Exchange Courier*) (Berlin newspaper)

BW Billy Wilder

CB Charles Brackett

DGA Directors Guild of America

DV Daily Variety

EL Ernst Lubitsch

FT François Truffaut

HH Howard Hawks

HR Hollywood Reporter

ID I. A. L. Diamond

JL Jack Lemmon

JM Joseph McBride

KMS Kiss Me, Stupid

LAFCA Los Angeles Film Critics Association

LAT Los Angeles Times

MPAA Motion Picture Association of America

MW Michael Wilmington

NYT New York Times

PCA Production Code Administration

PD Paul Diamond

RM Rex McGee

TM Todd McCarthy
WGA Writers Guild of America

SELECTED BOOKS

Armstrong, Richard. *Billy Wilder, American Film Realist.* Jefferson, N.C.: McFarland, 2000.

Bahr, Ehrhard. *Weimar on the Pacific: German Exile Culture in Los Angeles and the Crisis of Modernism.* Berkeley: University of California Press, 2007.

Brackett, Charles. *"It's the Pictures That Got Small": Charles Brackett on Billy Wilder and Hollywood's Golden Age.* Ed. Anthony Slide. New York: Columbia University Press, 2015. CB's diaries from 1932 to 1949.

Castle, Alison, ed., with interviews by Dan Aulier. *Billy Wilder's "Some Like It Hot": The Funniest Film Ever Made: The Complete Book.* Cologne: Taschen, 2001.

Ceplair, Larry, and Steven Englund. *The Inquisition in Hollywood: Politics in the Film Community, 1930–1960.* Garden City, N.Y.: Anchor Press/Doubleday, 1980.

Chandler, Charlotte. *Nobody's Perfect: Billy Wilder: A Personal Biography.* New York: Simon & Schuster, 2002.

Crowe, Cameron. *Conversations with Wilder.* New York: Knopf, 1999.

Curtis, Tony, with Mark A. Vieira. *The Making of "Some Like It Hot": My Memories of Marilyn Monroe and the Classic American Movie.* Hoboken, N.J.: Wiley, 2009.

Dick, Bernard F. *Billy Wilder.* Boston: Twayne, 1980.

Gemünden, Gerd. *Continental Strangers: German Exile Cinema 1933–1951.* New York: Columbia University Press, 2014.

——. *A Foreign Affair: Billy Wilder's American Films.* New York: Berghahn Books, 2008.

Guilbert, Georges-Claude, ed. *Literary Readings of Billy Wilder.* Newcastle, UK: Cambridge Scholars, 2007.

Harvey, James. *Romantic Comedy in Hollywood: From Lubitsch to Sturges.* New York: Knopf, 1987.

Heilbut, Anthony. *Exiled in Paradise: German Refugee Artists and Intellectuals in America from the 1930's to the Present.* New York: Viking, 1983.

Henry, Nora. *Ethics and Social Criticism in the Hollywood Films of Erich von Stroheim, Ernst Lubitsch, and Billy Wilder.* Westport, Conn.: Praeger, 2001.

Hopp, Glenn. *Billy Wilder: The Cinema of Wit 1906–2002.* Cologne: Taschen, 2003.

Horowitz, Joseph. *Artists in Exile: How Refugees from Twentieth-Century War and Revolution Transformed the American Performing Arts.* New York: HarperCollins, 2008.

Horton, Robert, ed. *Billy Wilder: Interviews.* Jackson: University Press of Mississippi, 2002. Includes JM, "Shooting *The Front Page:* Two Damns and One By God," *Real Paper* (Boston), July 31, 1974; and JM-TM, "Going for Extra Innings: Billy Wilder Interviewed," *Film Comment* (January–February 1979.)

Hutter, Andreas, "Vom Tages Zum Filmschrifsteller, Der Junge Billy Wilder als Reporter und Drehbuchautor im Wien und Berlin der Zwischenkriegszeit, 1925–1933" (Filmwriter from Day to Day, the Young Billy Wilder as a Reporter and Screenwriter in Vienna and Berlin Between the Wars, 1925–1933). Master's thesis, University of Vienna, 1991.

Hutter, Andreas, and Klaus Kamolz. *Billie Wilder: Eine europäische Karriere* (*Billie Wilder: A European Career*).Vienna: Böhlau Verlag, 1998.

Kaes, Anton, Martin Jay, and Edward Dimendberg, eds. *The Weimar Republic Scrapbook*. Berkeley: University of California Press, 1994.

Karasek, Hellmuth. *Billy Wilder: Eine Nahaufnahme* (*Billy Wilder: A Close-up*). Hamburg: Hoffmann und Campe, 1992.

Kracauer, Siegfried. *From Caligari to Hitler: A Psychological History of the German Film*. Ed. Leonardo Quaresima. Rev. and exp. ed. Princeton, N.J.: Princeton University Press, 2004. First published 1947.

Kreimeier, Klaus. *The UFA Story: A History of Germany's Greatest Film Company, 1918–1945*. Trans. Robert Kimber and Rita Kimber. New York: Hill and Wang, 1996. Originally published as *Die Ufa-Story: Geschichte eines Filmkonzerns*. Munich: Carl Hanser, 1992.

Lally, Kevin. *Wilder Times: The Life of Billy Wilder*. New York: Holt, 1996.

Lane, Jeffrey, and Douglas Borton, eds. *Billy Wilder*. AFI Life Achievement Award program book. Los Angeles: AFI, 1986.

Lewis, Jon. *Hollywood v. Hard Core: How the Struggle Over Censorship Saved the Modern Film Industry*. New York: New York University Press, 2000.

MacLean, Rory. *Berlin: Portrait of a City Through the Centuries*. New York: St. Martin's, 2014. Originally published as *Berlin: Imagine a City*. London: Weidenfeld & Nicolson, 2014.

Madsen, Axel. *Billy Wilder*. BFI Cinema One series. London: Secker & Warburg, 1968; Bloomington: Indiana University Press, 1969.

Maslon, Laurence. *"Some Like It Hot": The Official 50th Anniversary Companion*. New York: HarperCollins, 2009.

McBride, Joseph. *How Did Lubitsch Do It?* New York: Columbia University Press, 2018.

——. *Two Cheers for Hollywood: Joseph McBride on Movies*. Berkeley: California, Hightower Press, 2017. Includes JM, "Shooting *The Front Page*: Two Damns and One By God," and JM-TM, "Going for Extra Innings: Billy Wilder Interviewed."

McNally, Karen, ed. *Billy Wilder, Movie-Maker: Critical Essays on the Films*. Jefferson, N.C.: McFarland, 2011.

Mirisch, Walter. *I Thought We Were Making Movies, Not History*. Madison: University of Wisconsin Press, 2008.

Petrie, Graham. *Hollywood Destinies: European Directors in America, 1922–1931*. Rev. ed. Detroit: Wayne State University Press, 2002. Originally published in London by Routledge & Kegan Paul, 1985.

Phillips, Gene D. *Some Like It Wilder: The Life and Controversial Films of Billy Wilder*. Lexington: University Press of Kentucky, 2009.

Sarris, Andrew. *The American Cinema: Directors and Directions 1929–1968*. New York: Dutton, 1968.

Saunders, Thomas J. *Hollywood in Berlin: American Cinema and Weimar Germany*. Berkeley: University of California Press, 1994.

Savino, Fábio, and João Candido Zacharias, eds. *Billy Wilder*. São Paolo, Brazil: SESC—Serviço Social do Comércio, 2013. Includes JM-TM, "Going for Extra Innings: Billy Wilder Interviewed," trans. Ismar Tirelli Neto.

Schickel, Richard. *Double Indemnity*. BFI Film Classics. London: British Film Institute, 1992.

Seidl, Claudius. *Billy Wilder*. Munich: Heyne, 1988.

Seidman, Steve. *The Film Career of Billy Wilder*. Boston: Hall, 1977.

Sikov, Ed. *On Sunset Boulevard: The Life and Times of Billy Wilder*. New York: Hyperion, 1998.

Simsolo, Noël. *Masters of Cinema: Billy Wilder*. London: Phaidon, 2011.

Sinyard, Neil, and Adrian Turner. *Journey Down Sunset Boulevard: The Films of Billy Wilder*. Ryde, UK: BCW, 1979.

Smedley, Nick. *A Divided World: Hollywood Cinema and Emigré Directors in the Era of Roosevelt and Hitler, 1933–1948*. Bristol, UK: Intellect, 2001.

Staggs, Sam. *Close-up on Sunset Boulevard: Billy Wilder, Norma Desmond, and the Dark Hollywood Dream*. New York: St. Martin's, 2002.

Taylor, John Russell. *Strangers in Paradise: The Hollywood Emigres 1933–1950*. New York: Holt, Rinehart & Winston, 1983.

Weinberg, Herman G. *The Lubitsch Touch: A Critical Study*. New York: Dutton, 1968. Rev. ed., 1971; 3rd rev. and enl. ed., New York: Dover, 1977.

Weitz, Eric D. *Weimar Germany: Promise and Tragedy*. New and exp. ed. Princeton, N.J.: Princeton University Press, 2013. First published 2007.

Wilder, Billy. *Billy Wilder on Assignment: Dispatches from Weimar Berlin and Interwar Vienna*. Ed. Noah Isenberg, trans. Shelley Frisch. Princeton, N.J.: Princeton University Press, 2021. English translations of BW articles from Vienna and Berlin publications.

———. *"Billie": Billy Wilders Wiener journalistische Arbeiten* (*"Billie": Billy Wilder's Viennese Journalism*). Ed. Aurich, Rolf, Andreas Hutter, Wolfgang Jacobsen, and Günter Krenn. Vienna: Verlag Filmarchiva Austria, 2006. BW's reporting for the Vienna publications *Die Bühne* (*The Stage*) and *Die Stunde* (*The Hour*).

———. *Der Prinz von Wales geht auf Urlaub: Berliner Reportagen, Feuilletons und Kritiken der zwanzinger Jahre* (*The Prince of Wales Is Going on Vacation: Berlin Reports, Features and Reviews of the Twenties*). Collected by Klaus Siebenhaar. Berlin: Fannei & Walz Verlag, 1996. BW's reporting in Berlin for various publications.

Wood, Tom. *The Bright Side of Billy Wilder, Primarily*. Garden City, N.Y.: Doubleday, 1970.

Zolotow, Maurice. *Billy Wilder in Hollywood*. New York: Putnam, 1977.

PUBLISHED SCREENPLAYS (IN CHRONOLOGICAL ORDER OF FILM RELEASE)

BW. *Emil und die Detektive* (*Emil and the Detectives*). Based on Erich Kästner's novel. Munich: Edition Text + Kritik, 1998.

CB, BW, and Walter Reisch. *Ninotchka*. Based on a story by Melchior Lengyel. Condensed in *The Best Pictures 1939–1940 and the Yearbook of Motion Pictures in America*, ed. Jerry Wald and Richard Macauley. New York: Dodd, Mead, 1940. "Excerpts from the Screenplay of *Ninotchka*" in Weinberg. Complete screenplay in MGM Library of Film Scripts, New York: Viking Press, 1972. Also published in a photobook with dialogue and frame enlargements, ed. Richard Anobile. New York: Universe Books, 1975.

BW and Raymond Chandler. *Double Indemnity*. *The Best Film Plays of 1945*, ed. John Gassner and Dudley Nichols. New York: Crown, 1946. Separate edition of script, intro. Jeffrey Meyers. Berkeley: University of California Press, 2000.

CB-BW. *The Lost Weekend*, based on the novel by Charles Jackson. In *Best Film Plays, 1943–44*, ed. John Gassner and Dudley Nichols. New York: Crown, 1943. Separate edition of script, intro. Jeffrey Meyers. Berkeley: University of California Press, 2000.

CB-BW and D. M. Marshman, Jr. *Sunset Blvd.*, intro. Jeffrey Meyers. Berkeley: University of California Press, 1999.

BW and Edwin Blum. *Stalag 17*. Based on play by Donald Bevan and Edmund Trzcinski, intro. Jeffrey Meyers. Berkeley: University of California Press, 1999.

BW-ID. *Some Like It Hot*. New York: New American Library of World Literature, 1959. Screenplay also published in the book on the film edited by Alison Castle for Taschen, with a reproduction of the May 2, 1958, first draft and other material.

——. *The Apartment & The Fortune Cookie: Two Screenplays*. London: Studio Vista, 1971.

——. *The Apartment*. In *Classic Screenplays: Film Scripts Three* (with *The Misfits* and *Charade*), ed. George P. Garrett, O. B. Hardison, Jr., and Jane R. Gelfman. New York: Appleton-Century-Crofts, 1972.

——. *The Apartment:* London: Faber & Faber, 1998.

——. *Irma la Douce*. Based on play by Alexandre Breffort. New York: Midwood-Tower Books, 1963.

SELECTED DOCUMENTARY FILMS (IN CHRONOLOGICAL ORDER OF RELEASE)

Kerr, Charlotte. *Regie: Billy Wilder* (*Direction: Billy Wilder*). Munich: Bayerischer Rundfunk, 1978.

Tresgot, Annie, and Michel Ciment. *Portrait d'un homme "à 60% parfait": Billy Wilder* (*Portrait of a "60% Perfect Man": Billy Wilder*). Paris: Agat Films et Cie, 1980.

Schlöndorff, Volker, and Gisela Grischow. *Billy Wilder, wie haben Sie's gemacht? (Billy, How Did You Do It?)*. BW in conversation with Schlöndorff, Bioskop Film (Munich)/Hessischen Rundfunk/Westdeutschen Rundfunk/Bayerischer Rundfunk, 1992. Shown on BBC-TV (UK) as *Billy, How Did You Do It?*, 1992; released in United States on DVD edition (condensed) as *Billy Wilder Speaks*. Kino International, 2006.

Marconil, Michael, and Annie Tresgot. *Billy Wilder, artiste (ou: Ne réveillez pas le cinéaste qui dort) (Billy Wilder, Artist (or: Don't Wake the Sleeping Filmmaker))*. Paris: Agat Films et Cie/La Sept-Arte, 1993.

Shavelson, Melville. *An Informal Conversation with Billy Wilder*. Writers Guild Foundation, associated with the Writers Guild of America, West, narrated by JL, 1995.

Stuart, Mel. *Billy Wilder: The Human Comedy*. PBS *American Masters*, 1998.

Koll, Gerald. *Weekend am Wannsee (Weekend at the Wannsee)*. ARTE/KirchMedia/Perraudin/Zweites Deutsches Fernsehen, 2000. On the making of *Menschen am Sonntag (People on Sunday)*.

Kerr, Paul. *Nobody's Perfect: The Making of "Some Like It Hot."* London: October Films and BBC, 2001.

Inside "The Apartment." Fox Home video documentary, 2007, DVD and Blu-ray eds.

Thomas, Karen. *Cinema's Exiles: From Hitler to Hollywood*. Deutsche Kinemathek für Film und Fernsehen/Film Odyssey/Institut National de l'Audiovisuel/Thirteen-WNET/Turner Entertainment, PBS (German-French-American coproduction), 2009.

Fischer, Robert. *Swan Song: The Story of Billy Wilder's "Fedora."* Germany: Fiction FACTory Filmproduktion and Paris: Carlotta Films, 2014.

Kuperberg, Clara, and Julia Kuperberg. *Billy Wilder, la Perfection holllywoodienne (Nobody's Perfect)*. Paris: Wichita Films, 2016. With JM.

Hannover, Jascha, and André Schäfer. *Du sollst nicht langweilen: Billy Wilder (Never Be Boring: Billy Wilder)*. Germany: Florianfilm, 2017.

EPIGRAPH

BW on waterfall: Richard Gehman, *"Playboy* Interview: Billy Wilder," *Playboy* (June 1963), reprinted in Stephen Randall and the editors of *Playboy*, eds., *The Playboy Interviews: The Directors* (Milwaukie, Ore.: M Press, 2006), in which the interviewer is mistakenly listed as Robert Gehman.

CHAPTER 1: AUSLÄNDISCH

Books

Friedrich Nietzsche, "A joke": *Menschliches, Allzumenschliches, Anhang: Vermischte Meinungen und Sprüche (Human, All Too Human, A Supplement: Miscellaneous Maxims and Opinions)* (Chemnitz, Ger.: Schmeitzner, 1879), ed. and trans. R. J. Hollingdale as *Human, All*

Too Human: A Book for Free Spirits (Cambridge: Cambridge University Press, 1996). Collections of BW's reporting: *"Billie," Prince of Wales*, and *Billy Wilder on Assignment*. "Der rasende Reporter" (The Racing Reporter") and BW caricature: reprinted on cover of *"Billie": The Stage*, February 18, 1926; BW's biographers Andreas Hutter and Klaus Kamolz suspect he drew the portrait himself. "Der rasende Reporter" (The Racing Reporter") nickname for BW: see *The Prince of Wales Is Going on Vacation*, Hutter-Kamolz, and notes for chap. 2 on Egon Erwin Kisch. BW, "never could stand still": Chandler. BW, "I'm an old man" and Hans Lovage hiring him: Karasek. Joseph Stein (book), Jerry Bock (music), Sheldon Harnick (lyrics), based on Shololm Aleichem's stories, *Fiddler on the Roof* (New York: Crown, 1965). EL played character called Wilder: Robert Carringer and Barry Sabath, *Ernst Lubitsch: A Guide to References and Resources* (Boston: Hall, 1978).

BW, "Oh, we love Vienna": "Bei den Wiener Optimisten" (With the Vienna Optimists), *BBC*, November 8, 1927, reprinted in *Prince of Wales*. Sarris, "a curdled Lubitsch": *The American Cinema*. JL, BW "was a live wire": Castle. BW questioned Max Ophüls's return to Germany: Chandler. BW, "We wondered": Sikov. EL background: JM, *How Did Lubitsch Do It?* BW on his brother Wilhelm (aka Willie, W. Lee, William), "a dull son of a bitch": "Dialogue on Film: Billy Wilder and I. A. L. Diamond," *American Film* (July–August 1976). BW, mother's "hotel mentality" and "The town where": Chandler; BW, "I got a Rosebud": Crowe; "A large hotel": Zolotow.

History and culture of the Austro-Hungarian Empire: Barbara W. Tuchman, *The Proud Tower: A Portrait of the World Before the War: 1890–1914* (New York: Macmillan, 1966); Peter Gay, *Schnitzler's Century: The Making of Middle-Class Culture, 1815–1914* (New York: Norton, 2002). BW, "I remember the attitudes": Lally. Nancy Steffen-Fluhr, "Wilder was *ausländisch*"; and on BW, Nazism, Holocaust, and *The Emperor Waltz*: "Palimpsest: The Double Vision of Exile" in McNally. Genocide theme in *The Major and the Minor*: Gemünden, *A Foreign Affair*. Austrian rejection of Hersch Mendel (Max) Wilder application for citizenship: Sikov, citing document found by Hutter. BW thought his mother a "shrew": CB diaries, May 24, 1946.

BW, Egon Schiele, and "Red Fritzi": Sikov. BW, "iron discipline" in Vienna schools: Hutter-Kamolz. "Red Fritzi": Karasek; Sikov. BW said to have stolen a motorcycle and cars: Zolotow; Sikov; Hutter-Kamolz. Eugenia Dittler Wilder had remarried to Bernard Siedlisker: Karasek. Thomas Keneally, *Schindler's Ark / Schindler's List* (London: Hodder & Stoughton; New York: Simon & Schuster, 1982). *Schindler's List* film (1993): JM, *Steven Spielberg: A Biography* (New York: Simon & Schuster, 1997); BW telling Crowe *Schindler's List* would have been his most personal film and calling Spielberg "a gentleman." *Die Todesmühlen* (*Death Mills*): Karasek; Sikov. CB, "I don't suppose": Matthew Dessem, "Charles Brackett, Billy Wilder, and the Rise and Fall of Hollywood's Happiest Couple," *Dissolve*, June 26, 2014. BW on *Emperor Waltz*, "I was not up to": Crowe; "The picture didn't": Chandler. EL objection to *The Emperor Waltz*: Scott Eyman, *Ernst Lubitsch: Laughter in Paradise* (New York: Simon & Schuster, 1993). William J. Lederer and Eugene Burdick novel, *The Ugly American* (New York: Norton, 1958).

BW on Mayerling tragedy, Bert Prelutsky, "An Interview with Billy Wilder," in *The Movies: Texts, Receptions, Exposures*, ed. Laurence Goldstein and Ira Konigsberg (Ann Arbor: University of Michigan Press, 1996); Hutter-Kamolz. BW's unfilmed screenplay *The Austrian Mystery*: Hutter-Kamolz. BW watching emperor's funeral and on Otto von Habsburg, "He wanted": Karasek. BW on anti-Semitism in Austria: Lally, Steffen-Fluhr. Fred Zinnemann's memories of Austria: *Fred Zinnemann: An Autobiography* (London: Trafalgar Square, and New York: Scribner, 1992). BW, "I watched . . . pockets" and "The next day": Sikov, with "I made a move" from Lally. BW saw Adolf Hitler as "ridiculous figure": Hutter-Kamolz; BW at premiere with Hitler and "We believed": Karasek. BW taunted as "the Polack" by fellow schoolboys: Sikov. BW and law school: JM-TM; Chandler. BW leaving Berlin: Karasek and other biographies. Fritz Lang story of departure: Patrick McGilligan, *Fritz Lang: The Nature of the Beast* (New York: St. Martin's, 1997).

Articles

ID, "Billy is too restless": Murray Schumach, "Bright Diamond," *NYT*, May 26, 1963. BW, "If I look back": Vanessa Brown, "Broadcast to Kuala Lumpur," *Action* (November–December 1970), reprinted in Horton. BW on EL sign in office: Michael Blowen, "The Art of Billy Wilder," *Boston Globe*, October 22, 1989, reprinted in Horton. BW, "Oh, if": his contribution to "A Tribute to Lubitsch 1892–1947," *Action*, DGA (November–December 1967), reprinted in Weinberg; "Ernst Lubitsch, who": BW in Jon Bradshaw, " 'You Used to be Very Big.' 'I Am Big. It's the Pictures That Got Small,' " *New York*, November 24, 1975, reprinted in Horton.

BW, "fury": Michelle Kakutani, "Culture Zone: Ready for His Close-Up," *NYT Magazine*, July 28, 1996. Hutter and Heinz Peters, "Gitla stand nicht auf Schindlers Liste" (Gitla Was Not on Schindler's List), *Neue Zürcher Zeitung* (*New Zurich Newspaper*), June 10, 2011. BW and *Schindler's List*: BW, "as a memorial . . . absolutely perfection": Army Archerd column, *DV*, December 20, 1993; and Spielberg, "He made me look": Diane K. Shah, "Steven Spielberg, Seriously," *LAT*, December 19, 1993; BW, "best movie ever": Hutter-Kamolz; BW article "Man sah überall nur Taschentücher" (Everywhere Around You Could Only See Tissues), *Süddeutsche Zeitung Magazin* (*South German Newspaper Magazine*), December 18, 1994, quoted in Sikov.

BW had photograph of Hitler in office: JM-TM. Otto Preminger on Austrians: JM, "O'Toole Ascending: Peter O'Toole Interviewed," *Film Comment*, March-April 1981. BW on Basil Zaharoff: "Wie ich Zaharoff anpumpte" (How I Scrounged Money from Zaharoff), *Der Querschnitt* (*The Cross-Section*), March 3, 1933, reprinted in *Prince of Wales*; Sikov on BW and Monte Carlo. JM to BW exchange on "cynical" description: JM-TM.

Other Sources

Fritz Lang told his tale of leaving Berlin to JM's International Film Directors class at Sherwood Oaks Experimental College, Hollywood, 1974. BW's EL sign by Saul

Steinberg in office: seen in European versions of Schlöndorff-Grischow; and EL "one of the talented ones" (British version of documentary but not American); the documentary erroneously discusses BW's nickname. BW on the Schiele nude at grammar school: Paul Kalstrom (with Louis Stern), "Oral History interview with Billy Wilder, 1995 February 14," Smithsonian Archives of American Art. Schlöndorff on BW romanticizing Paris: *Never Be Boring*. BW's apartment: JM visited while working on his LAFCA tribute to BW. PD, "sharks don't sleep": JM interview. Audrey Wilder deplored BW taking uppers while shooting films: JM interview with RM.

Renoir, "He invented": quoted in Peter Bogdanovich, video on *Trouble in Paradise*, DVD, Criterion Collection, 2003, EL U.S. citizenship: certificate of U.S. citizenship issued January 24, 1936, by U.S. District Court, Los Angeles. BW (Samuel Wilder) U.S. citizenship records, National Archives and Records Administration, Washington, D.C., and Riverside, Calif., from U.S. Southern District of California, Los Angeles: Declaration of Intention, January 10, 1935, following arrival in U.S. at Calexico, Calif., from Mexicali, Mexico, November 10, 1934; Petition for Naturalization, U.S. May 1, 1940, witnessed by Charles Brackett and Don Hartman; naturalization certificate as an American citizen ("WILDER, Billy [formerly Samuel Wilder]"), August 9, 1940. BW lists his citizenship in 1935 as Polish: Hutter-Kamolz. Wilhelm (William) Wilder: California Death Index, 1940–1997, lists his birth in Poland, August 22, 1904, and death in Los Angeles, February 14, 1982; U.S. immigration records from the National Archives and Record Administration list him as arriving in New York in both 1923 and 1924. Eugenia Wilder and other family genealogy: geni.com and Yad Vashem, Jerusalem, Israel: Wilder family page and page of Testimony on Eugenia Wildar [*sic*: Eugenia Ditler Wilder Siedlisker] filed by her half-brother Mikhael (Michael) Baldinger, May 12, 1957, along with three other Shoah memorial sheets for members of his family. BW told Fernando Trueba he thought his relatives may have died in Terezin: JM interview with Trueba. Orson Welles's admiration for BW: interview with Merv Griffin, *The Merv Griffin Show*, taped October 9, 1985, broadcast in syndication October 15.

CHAPTER 2: "A KEEN OBSERVER"

Books

Eugenia Wilder, "Get up!": Hutter-Kamolz, also including the story of how BW broke into journalism and discussing his crossword puzzles; BW compared her to Scheherazade: Chandler. Other key sources on his reporting in Vienna and Berlin: the two German collections of his journalism, *The Prince of Wales Is Going on Vacation* and *"Billie"; Billy Wilder on Assignment: Dispatches from Weimar Berlin and Interwar Vienna*; and Hutter-Kamolz; Karasek; Sikov. BW posing as female advice columnist for Berlin publication *Tempo*: Hutter-Kamolz. BW, "I myself started": American Film Institute seminar, January 7, 1976, in Horton (this seminar was also incorporated with BW's December 13, 1978, AFI seminar in JM, ed., *Filmmakers on Filmmaking, Volume One: The American Film*

Institute Seminars on Motion Pictures and Television [Los Angeles: Tarcher, 1983]). Berlin life during Weimar Republic: Kaes, Jay, and Dimenberg; MacLean; Weitz. Ben Hecht and Charles MacArthur, *The Front Page* (New York: Covici Friede, 1928). BW supposedly interviewing Freud, Alfred Adler, Richard Strauss, and Arthur Schnitzler for *The Hour*, 1925: Zolotow; Hutter-Kalmolz; also JM interview with BW. BW card as reporter for *The Hour*: reproduced in *"Billie."* Freud, *Der Witz und seine Beziehung zum Unbewussten (Wit and Its Relation to the Unconscious)* (Leipizig: Franz Deuticke, 1905), trans. and ed. James Strachey, as *Jokes and Their Relation to the Unconscious* (New York: Norton, 1960, 1989), with biographical introduction by Peter Gay, "Sigmund Freud: A Brief Life." Kracauer, *From Caligari to Hitler.* Edward Kennedy (Duke) Ellington on Paul Whiteman: *Music Is My Mistress* (Garden City, N.Y.: Doubleday, 1973).

Ferenc Molnár, *A Testör (The Guardsman),* 1910: acting edition by Philip Moeller, trans. Grace I. Colbron and Hans Bartsch (New York: Boni & Liveright, 1924); BW on play: Crowe. Molnár's play *Egy, kettö, három (One, Two, Three)* (Budapest: Franklin Társulat, 1929): trans. Sidney Howard as *President,* in *Romantic Comedies: Eight Plays by Ferenc Molnár* (New York: Crown, 1952). BW watching Max Pallenberg and on "What I hate most": Karasek. BW "remaking the Holocaust" in *The Emperor Waltz:* Steffen-Fluhr; BW, "waltzes, Tyrolean hats": Chandler. Hans Sohl on BW: Sikov. UFA: Kreimeier, *The UFA Story.*

BW, "Some of this": Chandler. James M. Cain, *Double Indemnity,* in *Three of a Kind: Three Short Novels* (New York: Knopf, 1943, and separately by New York: Avon, 1943); first appeared in eight issues of *Liberty,* February 15–April 5, 1936. Berlin journalism scene: Hutter-Kamolz. BW's friend and role model Egon Erwin Kisch ("Der rasende Reporter/The Racing Reporter" or "The Raging Reporter"): *The Prince of Wales Is Going on Vacation;* Hutter-Kamolz; Sikov. Renoir, "To maintain": July 22, 1967, letter to Weinberg, *The Lubitsch Touch. Berliner Schnauze* ("Berlin lip"): Heilbut. BW's youthful "world-weariness": Zolotow. BW reportedly contributed to *The Fight with the Dragon or: The Tenants' Tragedy:* Hutter-Kamolz; Sikov. BW, "I think it is all the result": Zolotow. Christopher Isherwood, *Goodbye to Berlin* (London: Hogarth Press, 1939). Vicki Baum, *Menschen im Hotel (People in a Hotel)* (Berlin: Ullstein, 1929), trans. Basil Creighton as *Grand Hotel* (London: Geoffrey Bles, 1931). BW as *Eintänzer:* Karasek; Sikov; Hutter-Kalmolz; and BW articles cited below. George Bernard Shaw play *Pygmalion,* in *Androcles and the Lion, Overruled, Pygmalion* (London: Constable, 1916). BW on Stroheim: Zolotow; Crowe. BW infatuation with Tiller Girl: Karasek. BW female impersonation as *Tempo* columnist: Hutter-Kamolz. BW connections in becoming screenwriter and his claimed ghostwriting: Sikov. Eddie Polo: Sikov; Chandler. Sugar Cane: screenplay of *Some Like It Hot*: published versions cited above, including May 2, 1958, mimeographed first draft in Castle. A book whose title BW alluded to in his series on being an *Eintänzer*: Joseph Frieherr von Eichendorff's novella, *Aus dem Leben eines Taugenichts* (Berlin: Vereinsbuchhandlung, 1826), title rendered in English as *Memoirs of a Good-for-Nothing,* trans. Charles Godfrey Leland (New York: Leypoldt & Holt, 1866).

Articles

BW articles written in Vienna and Berlin are reprinted in the two collections of his journalism, cited above. BW (as Billie S. Wilder) article in *The Stage*, "Antonia—die Fedák in Wien/ Antonia—the Fedák in Vienna," January 22, 1925, profile of Sári Fedák. Imré Békessy: Hutter-Kamolz, Sikov. BW and Tiller Girls (1926): "Die Tiller-Girls sind da! Sie sind heute Vormittag auf dem Westbahnhof angekommen" (The Tiller Girls Are Here! They Arrived at Westbahnhof This Morning), *The Hour*, April 3, and "Pensionat Tiller im Prater" (A Boarding House Named Tiller at the Prater), *The Stage*, April 15. BW, "Hier kam Christoph Columbus zur Alten Welt" (Here Christopher Columbus Came to the Old World)," *BBC*, April 3, 1927; "Asta Nielsens theatralische Sendung. Ein Interview" (Asta Nielsen's Theatrical Program. An Interview)," *The Stage*, February 4, 1926; "'Hallo, Herr Menjou?' Er spricht ein reizendes Deutsch—Seine Mutter stammt aus Leipzig" ("Hello, Mr. Menjou?" He Speaks Delightful German—His Mother Is from Leipzig), *Tempo*, August 5, 1929; "Zehn Minuten mit Schaljapin" (Ten Minutes with Chaliapin) *BBC*, November 12, 1927.

BW on Paul Whiteman (1926), including "People's voice" and "Necessary blood renewal" in his article "Paul Whiteman, sein Schnurrbart, der Cobenzl und der Heurige. Ein Nachmittag mit Amerikas zweitberühmtestem Mann" (Paul Whiteman, His Mustache, the Cobenzl and Taverns. An Afternoon with America's Second Most Famous Man), *The Hour*, June 13, 1926, and "Whiteman feiert in Berlin Triumphe. Viertausend Zuhörer bei der Premiere im Grossen Schauspielhaus. Spezialbericht der *Stunde* (Whiteman Celebrates Triumphs in Berlin. Audience of Four Thousand Witnesses the Opening at the Great Theater: Special Report of *Die Stunde* [*The Hour*]), June 29 (filed from Berlin). BW journalistic ethics: Sikov, citing article by Hutter and Kamolz, "Billie und Barkassy [Békessy]," *Profil*, September 28, 1991, and Hutter's thesis, *Vom Tages Zum Filmschrifsteller* (*Filmwriter from Day to Day*), as well as a letter from BW to Hutter, May 25, 1990.

BW's *Eintänzer* series: January 19–24, 1927, in *B. Z. am Mittag*, as "'Herr Ober, bitte einen Tänzer!' Aus dem Leben eines Eintänzers" (Waiter, Bring Me a Dancer! From the Life of an *Eintänzer*), and in *The Stage*, June 9, as "Herr Ober, bitte einen Tänzer! Erlebnisse eines Eintänzer" (Waiter, Bring Me a Dancer! Experiences of an Eintänzer). BW on series causing "scandal": Michel Ciment, "Billy Wilder urbi et orbi," *Positif* (July–August 1983); Mihaela Petrescu, "Billy Wilder's Work as *Eintänzer* in Weimar Berlin," *New German Critique*, no. 120, From Weimar Cinema to Postmillennial Urban Culture (Fall 2013). BW to JM on being *Eintänzer*: JM-TM and on another occasion; see also the series for his explanation of why he took that job. BW, "I danced": Gehman. BW tribute to Alfred Henschke (aka Klabund) and claim about Zinnemann being dead: BW, "Vor einem Jahr starb Klabund. Der Dichter und der Eintänzer" (A Year Ago Klabund Died. The Poet and the Gigolo), *Tempo*, August 12, 1929.

Other BW articles: on Wotan Wotawa: "Passende Weihnachtsgeschenke für 12-bis 14 jährige Knaben" (Suitable Christmas Gifts for Boys 12 to 14 Years), *The Hour*, December 16, 1925; "Helene Odilons Rückkehr nach Wien" (Helene Odilon Returns to Vienna),

The Hour, February 28, 1926; "How I Scrounged Money from Zaharoff"; interview in Berlin with Cornelius Vanderbilt IV, not Jr., as the article has it: "Ich interviewe Mr. Vanderbilt. Ein Gespräch mit dem amerikanischen Multimillionär—Er trägt nur 250 Mark bei sich—Auch hat er keine Zeit, einen Zahnarzt zu konsultieren" (I Interview Mr. Vanderbilt—A Conversation with the American Millionaire—He Only Carries 250 Marks with Him—He Also Has No Time to Consult a Dentist), *The Hour*, July 10, 1926; "Der Prinz von Wales geht auf Urlaub" (The Prince of Wales Is Going on Vacation), *BBC*, August 31, 1927. "Stroheim, der Mann, den man gern hasst" (Stroheim, the Man You Love to Hate), *Cross-Section*, April 4, 1929.

H. L. Mencken, "Valentino," *Baltimore Evening Sun*, August 30, 1926, reprinted in *A Mencken Chrestomathy* (New York: Knopf, 1949). ID re BW and "an old Viennese tradition": Kakutani, "Billy Wilder Honored at Lincoln Center Gala," *NYT*, May 4, 1982, quoted in JM, "Thank You, Mr. Wilder: Billy Wilder, 1906–2002," *Written By*, May 2002, based on JM speech honoring BW with Los Angeles Film Critics Association career achievement award, January 17, 1995: reprinted in *Two Cheers for Hollywood*. BW, "Hardly": JM, "Shooting *The Front Page*."

BW tribute to Alfred Henschke (aka Klabund): "Vor einem Jahr starb Klabund: Der Dichter und der Eintänzer" (Klabund Died a Year Ago: The Poet and the Eintänzer), *Tempo*, August 12, 1929. JL on BW taste in music: MW, "Saint Jack." BW and Tiller Girls: see his articles cited in notes for chap. 2; also Kracauer on Tiller Girls: "Ornament der Masse" (The Mass Ornament), first published in *Frankfurter Zeitung*, July 9 and 10, 1927, English trans. in *New German Critique*, no. 5 (Spring 1975); also in his book *Das Ornament der Masse* (*The Mass Ornament*) (Frankfurt am Main: Suhrkamp, 1963), and as *The Mass Ornament: Weimar Essays*, ed. and trans. Thomas Y. Levin (Cambridge, Mass.: Harvard University Press, 1995); see also Weitz.

BW watching filming of *Der Rosenkavalier* (*The Knight of the Rose*), "Der Rosenkavalier am Rosenhügel" (*Der Rosenkavalier* at Rose Hill in Vienna), *The Hour*, August 1, 1925. BW, "Die Requisiten des amerikanischen Films" (The Props of the American Film), *The Stage*, February 25, 1926. BW on *Greed* and Stroheim: "*Gier nach Geld. In der kamera*" (Lust for Gold. In the Camera) (review of *Greed*), *B.Z. am Mittag*, July 6, 1928, and "Stroheim, der Mann, den man gern hasst" (Stroheim, the Man You Like to Hate), *Cross-Section*, April 1929; JM-MW on BW and Stroheim: JM-MW, "The Private Life of Billy Wilder," *Film Quarterly* (Summer 1970). BW on EL: "Lubitsch entdeckt" (Lubitsch Discovered), *The Stage*, February 18, 1926. BW, "Filmterror," *BBC*, September 1, 1927. BW on Eddie Polo: JM-TM. Charles Williams's 1949 "Jealous Lover" used in *The Apartment*: Phillips; "*The Apartment*," FSM online liner notes, *filmscoremonthly.com*. BW as sports fan: JM-TM; JM-MW, "Private Life."

Other Sources

BW on Eden Hotel and Zinnemann at reception at home of the Los Angeles consul general of Germany, September 23, 1992, presentation of Order of Merit from Federal

Republic of Germany to Curt Siodmak: JM was covering the event for *DV.* BW told JM his story about Freud ordering him out of his apartment. BW guest appearance on *The Jack Benny Program* (CBS-TV): "Jack Goes Back into Pictures," April 1, 1962, directed by Frederick de Cordova.

CHAPTER 3: "FILM, THAT'S NO PROFESSION FOR ADULTS"

Books

Epigraph: BW, "Back then": Heinz-Gerd Rasner and Reinhard Wulf, "Gespräch mit Billy Wilder: 'Ich nehm das alles nicht so ernst . . .'" (A Conversation with Billy Wilder: "I Don't Take It All So Seriously . . ."), in *Billy Wilders Filme* (*Billy Wilder's Films*) (Berlin: Verlag Volker Speiss, 1980). Lally, trans. Robert Sheff. EL, "That's finished:" Bella Fromm. *Blood and Banquets: A Berlin Social Diary* (London: Geoffrey Bles, 1943, and New York: Garden City, 1944). EL refused to allow German be spoken in home: Nicola Lubitsch to JM: *How Did Lubitsch Do It?* BW work as civilian with U.S. Army in de-Nazification effort: see notes for chap. 5. Sikov on *Ein blonder Traum* (*A Blonde Dream*). BW on Pommer and UFA: Karasek, Lally; Walter Reisch on BW. UFA and Alfred Hugenberg: Kreimeier, quotes Willi Münzenberg, "Film und Propaganda," *Film und Volk* 2, no. 1:5. Kracauer, "a culture of distraction": *Die Angestellten: Aus dem neuesten Deutschland* (*The Salaried Masses: From the Newest Germany*) (Frankfurt am Main: Frankfurter Societäts-Druckerei, 1930). Peter Watson, *The German Genius: Europe's Third Renaissance, the Second Scientific Revolution, and the Twentieth Century* (New York: HarperCollins, 2010). Noah Isenberg, *Edgar G. Ulmer: A Filmmaker at the Margins* (Berkeley: University of California Press, 2014).

BW, three films that influenced career choice, *Battleship Potemkin, Sous let toits de Paris* (*Under the Roofs of Paris*), and *Mädchen in Uniform* (*Girls in Uniform*): Karasek. The 1928 kidnapping stunt involving a Vienna visit by the Tiller Girls as inspiration for *Daredevil Reporter* screenplay: Hutter-Kamolz. Eddie Polo: Lally; BW in JM-TM; BW romance with Olive Victoria: Hutter-Kamolz; Crowe; Chandler. Kracauer on German escapist films: *From Caligari to Hitler.* BW, "Writers are not": Chandler. Nazis disrupting Berlin opening of *All Quiet on the Western Front*: Lally; BW, "And so we had." Erich Kästner novel *Emil und die Detektive* (*Emil and the Detectives*) (Berlin: Williams, 1929; London: Jonathan Cape, 1931); and published screenplay. Kästner criticism of BW: Sikov; Kevin Macdonald, *Emeric Pressburger: The Life and Death of a Screenwriter* (London: Faber and Faber, 1994). Douglas Sirk on the "happy ending": Jon Halliday, *Sirk on Sirk* (London: Secker & Warburg and British Film Institute, 1971, and exp. ed., London: Faber and Faber, 1997). BW, "Occasionally": Eyman, *Ernst Lubitsch: Laughter in Paradise.* Josef von Sternberg borrowing shots from EL's *The Patriot* for *The Scarlet Empress*: Weinberg.

BW on Hans Steinhoff: Karasek; Joe Hembus and Christa Bandmann, *Klassiker des deutschen Tonfilms, 1930–1960* (Munich: Goldmann, 1980). Felix Salten (anon.), *Josefine Mutzenbacher oder Die Geschichte einer Wienerischen Dirne von ihr selbst erzählt* (*Josephine Mutzenbacher or The Story of a Viennese Whore, as Told by Herself*) (Vienna: Private printing, 1906); *The Memoirs of Josephine Mutzenbacher*, trans. Rudolf Schleifer, intro. Hilary E. Holt (North Hollywood, Calif.: Brandon House, 1967). BW read the book frequently: Karasek; BW wanting to film it: *Times* (London), June 7, 1994. BW conversation with German actor about allegedly hiding Jews: Sikov. BW credit removed from *Was Frauen träumen* (*What Women Dream*): Karasek.

BW's forced departure in 1933–1934 from Germany to United States via Paris on Austrian passport: Karasek; Zolotow. Paris's "cold and repellent atmosphere": Karasek; Holländer on Hotel Ansonia in Sikov and Hutter-Kamolz, from Holländer, *From Head to Toe: My Life with Lyrics and Music* (Munich, 1965); BW made *Mauvaise graine* (*Bad Seed*) "out of sheer necessity" and "I cannot say": Karasek; Hays Office killed plans for remake in English: Sikov. BW to Chandler, with quote from Danielle Darrieux; similarity with BW background: Sikov; Hutter-Kamolz; Max Kolpé letter to Marlene Dietrich, November 2, 1933: Hutter-Kamolz. Steffen-Fluhr, "this liminal figure." Sarris on *Mauvaise graine*, quoted in Lally. BW on Parisian exile: "It was sad": Crowe.

BW departure on *Aquitania* for United States, January 22, 1934. BW sale of "Pam-Pam" treatment to Columbia and Joe May: Sikov, Karasek; Kolpé turned it into a 1937 stage musical: Hutter-Kamolz. BW travel to United States to stay with brother Willie in January 1934: Karasek; Sikov. BW having to leave Los Angeles for Mexico and living in hotel in Calexico: biographies. U.S. immigration laws in that period: various sources, including Donna Rifkind, *The Sun and Her Stars: Salka Viertel and Hitler's Exiles in the Golden Age of Hollywood* (New York: Other Press, 2020). BW living at Chateau Marmont, Los Angeles: see notes for chap. 4. BW becoming U.S. citizen described by Zolotow as "one of the shining days." BW teaming with CB: see notes for chap. 5.

Articles

BW on return to Germany for *Fedora*: JM-TM. BW promotional articles on *People on Sunday*: "Wir von Filmstudio 1929" (We at the Film Studio in 1929), *Tempo*, July 23, 1929, and "Wie wir unseren Studio-Film drehten" (As We Made Our Studio Film), *Der Montag Morgen* (*Monday Morning*) February 10, 1930 (and comment to Crowe on length of script). Cost of *People on Sunday*: Isenberg, *"People on Sunday*: Young People Like Us," June 27, 2011, criterion.com; quotes Eugen Szatmari review, *Berliner Tageblatt*. Curt Siodmak claimed he helped finance the film: Gundolf S. Freyermuth, "Despite His Fate, He Found His Fortune," *LAT*, September 14, 1997; see also Sikov. BW, "Filmterror." BW interview with Claude Anet: "Claude Anet in Berlin," *BBC*, November 25, 1927. Unidentified Paris reviewer on *Mauvaise graine*: Hutter-Kamolz.

Other Sources

"Irgendwo auf der Welt gibt's ein kleines bisschen Glück" (Somewhere in the World There's a Little Bit of Happiness) (lyrics by Robert Gilbert and Werner R. Heymann, music by Heymann) from *A Blonde Dream*: sheet music provided by Elisabeth

Trautwein-Heymann, daughter of the composer, who told JM in 2019–2020 that he regarded the song as his favorite work. "Film, that's no profession for adults": Willy II (Willi Forst) from subtitles of *A Blonde Dream*. Ulmer on BW: audiotape of interview with Peter Bogdanovich, 1970, in documentary by Michael Palm, *Edgar G. Ulmer: The Man Off-Screen* (2004). Brigitte Borchert on *People on Sunday: Weekend at the Wannsee*; JM interview with Curt Siodmak on *People on Sunday*: 1992, see notes for chap. 2. BW acceptance speech for Irving G. Thalberg Memorial Award from Academy of Motion Picture Arts and Sciences, April 11, 1988: YouTube. Willys A. Myers: Karasek writes that BW was told name of American consulate official was Meyer, but his name was listed as Willys A. Myers in "Index to Politicians," Political Graveyard.com; he was U.S. vice consul in Veracruz, 1924–1929, and Mexicali, 1932–1938; amateur magician: his collection of material about magic, 1900–1960, at UCLA Library Special Collections, Charles E. Young Research Library, OAC: Online Archive of California, www .oac.cdlib.org.

CHAPTER 4: "I WAS NOT IN THE RIGHT COUNTRY"

Books

Bertolt Brecht poems on exile and Hollywood quoted: "Sonnet in Emigration," "Hollywood," and "Hollywood Elegies" in *Poems, 1913–1956*, ed. John Willett and Ralph Manheim (London: Methuen, 1976, rev. ed. 1987). Bahr and other books cited subsequently on German exiles in Hollywood; Brecht considered himself an "exile": Heilbut. BW, "the low point": Otto Friedrich, *City of Nets: A Portrait of Hollywood in the 1940's* (New York: Harper, 1986). BW at Chateau Marmont: Karasek; Sikov; Raymond R. Sarlot and Fred E. Basten, *Life at the Marmont* (Roundtable, 1987, with new afterword by Basten, New York: Penguin, 2013), including quotes from manager Ann Little and desk clerk and information about BW's cars in Berlin and Hollywood; Shawn Levy, *The Castle on Sunset: Life, Death, Love, Art, and Scandal at Hollywood's Chateau Marmont* (New York: Doubleday, 2019); BW, "Women were coming in . . . worried. . . . This Christmas," "I had the feeling": Zolotow. Nathanael West's novel *The Day of the Locust* (New York: Random House, 1939).

BW scripts with Oliver H. P. Garrett: Zolotow; Rifkind. BW going to see mother in Vienna: Zolotow; Karasek; Hutter-Kamolz. "I dragged": Herbert G. Luft, "A Matter of Decadence," published with CB's "A Matter of Humor," as "Two Views of a Director— Billy Wilder," *Hollywood Quarterly* 7, no. 1 (Fall 1952), reprinted in *Hollywood Quarterly: Film Culture in Postwar America, 1945–1957*, ed. Eric Smoodin and Ann Martin (Berkeley: University of California Press, 2002). BW teaming with CB and collaborating with EL: see notes for chap. 5. CB on *Music in the Air*: note added to diary entry for August 18, 1936; CB on BW reaction to *Champagne Waltz*: November 18, 1936. Joe Eszterhas on multiple writers on scripts: *The Devil's Guide to Hollywood: The Screenwriter as God!* (New York: St. Martin's, 2006). The making of *Lottery Lover*: Sikov; *The AFI Catalog of Feature*

Films, aficatalog.afi.com. EL, "Paris, Paramount": to Garson Kanin, quoted in Bogdanovich, *Who the Devil Made It* (New York: Knopf, 1997). BW on *Under Pressure*: Karasek. Menahem Mandel (Manny) Wolfe teamed BW and CB: see notes for chap. 5. BW told mother he had changed name to Thornton Wilder: Lemon.

German colony in Hollywood: Salka Viertel, *The Kindness of Strangers: A Theatrical Life: Vienna, Berlin, Hollywood* (New York: Holt, 1969); Rifkind; Bahr; Gay; Gemünden, *Continental Strangers*; Heilbut; Horowitz; Petrie; Saunders; Smedley; Weitz; Taylor. "Weimar on the Pacific": Bahr. Theodor Adorno, "For a man": *Minima Moralia: Reflexionen aus dem beschädigten Leben* (*Minima Moralia: Reflections from Damaged Life*) (Frankfurt: Suhrkamp, 1951), trans. E. F. N. Jephcott (London: Verso, 1978). Bahr cites Jan-Christopher Horak, *Fluchtpunkt Hollywood* (1986), a compilation of filmographies of more than eight hundred anti-Nazi refugees in Southern California. European Film Fund: Heilbut; Rifkind. Gemünden on exile cinema and allegory and BW, EL: *Continental Strangers*; "The loss": *A Foreign Affair*; Joel Fineman, "The Structure of Allegorical Desire," in *Allegory and Representation*, ed. Stephen Greenblatt (Baltimore: Johns Hopkins University Press, 1981). Heilbut, exiles as "professional explainers."

Hollywood Anti-Nazi League: Ceplair-Englund; Victor S. Navasky, *Naming Names* (New York: Viking, 1980); Nancy Lynn Schwartz, completed by Sheila Schwartz, *The Hollywood Writers' Wars* (New York: Knopf, 1982); Viertel; Rifkind. Screen Writers Guild (SWG): Ceplair-Englund; Navasky; Schwartz. Bill Krohn, "Hollywood and the Shoah, 1933–1945," in *Cinema and the Shoah: An Art Confronts the Tragedy of the Twentieth Century*, ed. Jean-Michel Frodon, trans. Anna Harrison and Tom Mes (Albany: State University of New York Press, 2010), originally published as *Le cinéma et la Shoah: Un art à l'épreuve de la tragédie du 20e siècle* (Paris: Cahiers du Cinéma, 2007). Sulzberger family and *NYT* coverage of Holocaust: Laurel Leff, *Buried by the Times: The Holocaust and America's Most Important Newspaper* (New York: Cambridge University Press, 2005). Hollywood interventionist films and backlash: Ceplair-Englund. Bernard F. Dick on *Arise, My Love: The Star-Spangled Screen: The American World War II Film* (Lexington: University Press of Kentucky, 1985); see also David Chierichetti on that film and the CB-BW screenplay project *La Polonaise*: *Mitchell Leisen: Hollywood Director* (Los Angeles: Photoventures Press, 1995), rev. from original publication as *Hollywood Director* (New York: Curtis Books, 1973).

West, *The Day of the Locust.* EL refusal to allow German spoken in home: JM, *How Did Lubitsch Do It?*; Lang would not read or write German: Friedrich. Julia M. Sloane, "the land": *The Smiling Hill-Top and Other California Sketches* (New York: Scribner, 1919). Thomas Mann, "Here in this young land": "Address on Heinrich Mann's Seventieth Birthday," in *Letters of Heinrich and Thomas Mann, 1900–1949*, ed. Hans Wysling, trans. Don Reneau, additional trans. Richard and Clara Winston (Berkeley: University of California Press, 1998), originally published as *Thomas Mann and Heinrich Mann, Briefwechsel 1900–1949*, ed. Wysling (Frankfurt am Main: Fischer, 1968). Viertel, "when I attempted": *The Kindness of Strangers.* BW self-conscious about accent: Zolotow. BW confrontation with Louis B. Mayer, 1950: his accounts in biographies and BW interview by Richard Brown, *Reflections on the Silver Screen*, American Movie Classics, 1993, quoted by Phillips.

Hollywood blacklist: Ceplair-Englund; Navasky; Schwartz. Screen Directors Guild (SDG) controversy over loyalty oath and Cecil B. DeMille campaign to remove Joseph L. Mankiewicz as SDG president, opposed by BW et al.: Kenneth L. Geist, *Pictures Will Talk: The Life and Films of Joseph L. Mankiewicz* (New York: Scribner, 1978); JM, *Frank Capra: The Catastrophe of Success* (New York: Simon & Schuster, 1992; rev. ed. New York: St. Martin's, 2000); JM, *Searching for John Ford* (New York: St. Martin's, 2001). BW praying at synagogue: Zolotow. Anthony Burgess on James Joyce: *ReJoyce* (New York: Norton, 1965). Graham Greene, "Innocence": *The Quiet American* (London: Heinemann, 1955).

Articles

BW on brother Willie's films, "They weren't anything": Chandler; Glenn Erickson on BW and Willie: review of *Phantom from Space* and other films, *DVD Savant*, October 17, 2014; also see Jim Knipfel, "Happy Birthday, W. Lee Wilder," *Den of Geek*, August 24, 2013. BW, "were films that," "Those of us," and "We who had": Gene D. Phillips, "Billy Wilder" (interview), *Literature/Film Quarterly* (Winter 1976), reprinted in Horton. BW, "I had no confidence": Burt Prelutsky, "An Interview with Billy Wilder," *Michigan Quarterly Review* (Winter 1996), reprinted in Horton. BW writing down words he didn't know, learning twenty a day, and "Most of the refugees": Aljean Harmetz, "Seven Years Without Directing, and Billy Wilder Is Feeling Itchy," *NYT*, October 3, 1988. On Brecht: Isenberg, "The Poet of Ill Tidings," *Nation*, December 4–11, 2017. BW article on *Schindler's List*: see notes for chap. 3. W. Lee Wilder: BW comments, see notes for chap. 1. Chateau Marmont and BW, "I would rather": Jean Nathan, "What's Up in the Old Hotel?," *NYT*, August 1, 1993.

Hollywood interventionist films and backlash: John E. Moser, "'Gigantic Engines of Propaganda': The 1941 Senate Investigation of Hollywood," *Historian* (Summer 2001); Senator Gerald Nye on war propaganda: Jennifer Frost, "Dissent and Consent in the 'Good War': Hedda Hopper, Hollywood Gossip, and World War II Isolationism," *Film History: An International Journal* 22, no. 2 (2010). Farber on BW, Americans, and Europeans: "The Films of Billy Wilder," *Film Comment* (Winter 1971–1972). Jonathan Robbins, "Billy Wilder in *Billy, How Did You Do It?*," *Film Comment* blog, October 2, 2012. BW, "mad goulash": JM-TM (on *The Gauntlet*). Frank S. Nugent review of *Champagne Waltz*, *NYT*, February 4, 1937. BW, "There was a certain nobility": Stephen Farber, "A Cynic Ahead of His Time," *NYT*, December 6, 1981, reprinted in Horton.

Other Sources

BW return from visiting his mother in Vienna: BW arrival in New York from Southampton, England, on ship *Champlain*, December 18, 1935: Passenger Lists of Vessels Arriving at New York, New York, 1897–1957, U.S. Customs Service, National Archives, Washington, D.C.; departure from Southampton, December 11: List or Manifest of Alien Passengers for the United States, UK and Ireland, Outward Passenger Lists, 1890–1960. Martin Sauter, "Liesl Frank, Charlotte Dieterle and the European Film Fund," Ph.D. diss., University of Warwick, UK, 2010. BW putting "Cum Deo" on scripts: Zolotow; e.g., BW-ID scripts *The Private Life of Sherlock Holmes*, *Avanti!*, and *Buddy Buddy*; BW, "I got that": Chris Columbus, "Wilder Times," *American Film* (March 1986). PD on Myles Wilder: JM interview. Claudette Colbert on "high comedy": JM interview; Colbert on *It Happened One Night: The American Film Institute Salute to Frank Capra*, CBS-TV, 1982 (written by George Stevens Jr. and JM). FT to JM about foreign directors in Hollywood: 1970s conversation. BW, "You know, when": *Portrait of a "60% Perfect Man*," 1980, quoted in Sikov. BW on CB in AFI acceptance speech: *The American Film Institute Salute to Billy Wilder*, NBC-TV, 1986. BW speaking German in Schlöndorff-Grischow; and release delayed; Karasek reports BW was dissatisfied with it and did not want it released; also JM interview with RM.

CHAPTER 5: "BRACKETTANDWILDER . . . AND LUBITSCH"

Books

Information on films BW helped write without credit and production background on films he was credited for with CB and other writers is from BW biographies and CB diaries. Manny Wolfe teaming BW and CB: CB diaries, August 17, 1936, including CB's description of BW as "a young Austrian" and comment that EL knew of BW's work in Germany. Wolfe's background and later career: slide appendix to CB diaries, "Leading Names and Subjects." CB on EL, "I don't really know": July 6, 1936; meeting of CB, Frank Partos, and EL: July 7, 1936; BW "shouted indignantly": September 19, 1936. BW on EL, "Actually he wanted to have Brackett," "a rabid," a very loquacious," "difficult": Crowe, including EL, "They'll love you": "Wilder's Tips for Writers." BW, "[Brackett] spoke excellent English": Lally. Jacques Théry work on CB-BW scripts: various entries in CB diaries.

CB background: slide introduction to diaries; BW biographies; slide discusses whether CB was gay or bisexual. Zolotow on CB-BW collaboration. CB anti-Semitic comments in diaries: "Was never so impressed," May 24, 1941; "I wonder if a Jew," March 10, 1949; "the most insultingly," July 14, 1938. Comments by CB on BW in diaries: "a jaunty young foreigner," "a slim young fellow," "I was enormously," "paces constantly," "blasé quality," "some place in Poland," "just about the education," "a dancer for hire," "a delightful," and "One great advantage" in note by CB added later to entry for August 18, 1936; "My little Manic Depressive," March 31, 1941; "He is a hard," September 7, 1936; "almost driven mad," September 11, 1936; "to suggest," under November 7, 1936, but note says comment was added later; "If I do more," November 10, 1936; "Billy playing," December 29, 1937; "Arrived at the office," February 20, 1939; "delighted at a respite," September 15, 1938;

"Violent quarrel," July 27, 1939; "I've long felt," August 30, 1944; "Billy's terrifying neuro-sis," March 21, 1941; "somewhat infuriated," May 6, 1944; and "The Rebel," October 4, 1946. BW found demeanor of ID refreshing contrast to CB's: Crowe; Barbara Diamond on ID, "He is withdrawn": Schumach. BW on his "ridiculous" English in early years in United States: Lally. BW on CB, "We fought a lot": David Freeman, "Sunset Boule-vard Revisited: Annals of Hollywood," *New Yorker*, June 21, 1993. BW, CB "didn't think like I did": foreword to Macdonald, *Emeric Pressburger*. BW, "I found that if I had," "I liked," and "Twelve years": Linville; his other comments on CB: Lally; Chandler. BW defense of CB in 1962 in telegram to Darryl F. Zanuck: Wood, *The Bright Side of Billy Wilder, Primarily*.

EL background, films in Germany and United States, and dealings with censorship: JM, *How Did Lubitsch Do It?* David Niven on EL: *The Lubitsch Touch*, which also quotes the 1967 Renoir letter to Weinberg and Samson Raphaelson on EL. JM on EL's "Paris, Paramount": see notes for chap. 4. *Bluebeard's Eighth Wife* is based loosely on the play by Alfred Savoir, *La huitième femme de Barbe-bleue*, published in *Abonnement Annuel (Annual Subscription)*, Paris, March 26, 1921, and on that same year's English adaptation by Charlton Andrews, *Bluebeard's 8th Wife*. BW's "meet-cute" for *Bluebeard's Eighth Wife*: Crowe; "AMERICAN UNDERSTOOD": Crowe; Eyman. BW on EL "Superjoke" and "never blunt" and EL, "Go ahead": Crowe. John Belton on screwball comedies and 1950s sex comedies: review of Sikov, *Screwball: Hollywood's Madcap Romantic Comedies* (New York: Crown, 1989), *Film Quarterly*, Spring 1991. CB on *Bluebeard*, "It is terrible!," December 20, 1943. JM and Pauline Kael on Gary Cooper; JM, *Frank Capra: The Catastrophe of Success*; Kael, *Deeper Into Movies* (Boston: Little, Brown, 1973).

Leisen on BW and John Barrymore: Chierichetti. BW on Leisen: Zolotow; BW, "All of that is gone": JM-TM. BW on Claudette Colbert: Crowe. Dick on anti-isolationist films and scenes for *Arise, My Love* shot in two versions: *The Star-Spangled Screen*; also Ceplair-Englund. SS *Athenia* sinking with Nicola Lubitsch aboard; Weinberg; Eyman; death toll, Ben Farmer, "SS Athenia, First British Ship Lost in WW2, 'Found Off Irish Coast,'" *Telegraph* (UK), October 3, 2017. Chierichetti on *Arise, My Love*; film's title from *Song of Solomon*, Old Testament, 2:13, *American Standard Version Bible* (New York: Thomas Nelson & Sons, 1901). CB arguments about BW not enlisting in U.S. Army early in World War II: October 9 and 23, 1947. Sikov discusses BW's civilian army service and the writ-ing credits.

CB, *Blossoms on Broadway* "terrible": September 8, 1937. Leisen's secretary, Eleanor Broder, blamed W. C. Fields for director's first heart attack: Chierichetti, which also quotes Leisen calling *The Big Broadcast of 1938* "embarrassing." CB argument with BW about HUAC and Dalton Trumbo: October 27, 1947; "Billy informed me": November 2, 1947; arguments over political issues made BW realize he had to write with other part-ners: see notes for chap. 8. CB, BW, and Reisch petitioned SWG to let EL share *Ninotchka* writing credit: Sikov; BW on EL as writing collaborator: Sikov; Eyman, "If the truth." CB on BW mood swings: diaries, passim. Judith Coppicus [Balken] and BW marriage and other information on her and her family: Zolotow. CB-BW screenplay *The Lost Weekend*, based on novel by Charles Jackson (New York: Farrar & Rinehart, 1944). CB novels: *The Counsel of the Ungodly* (New York: D. Appleton, 1920) and *Entirely Surrounded* (New York: Knopf, 1934).

JM on *Ninotchka: How Did Lubitsch Do It?* Screenwriting and production process on *Ninotchka:* CB diaries. George Cukor's firing from *Gone With the Wind* and switch from *Ninotchka* to *The Women:* Patrick McGilligan, *George Cukor: A Double Life* (New York: St. Martin's, 1991). EL financed preproduction on *The Shop Around the Corner:* Sabath; JM, *How Did Lubitsch Do It?* CB on EL having no studio commitment: June 3, 1938. Reisch interview in *The Lubitsch Touch.* EL, "You can photograph": Sikov. BW on Garbo's face: Zolotow. EL resigning from Hollywood Anti-Nazi League: Viertel, *The Kindness of Strangers.* EL and European Film Fund: see notes for chap. 4.

EL as writer on *Ninotchka:* CB to Joan Franklin and Robert C. Franklin, Oral History Project/Columbia University, 1959, quoted in Karen Swenson, *Greta Garbo: A Life Apart* (New York: Scribner, 1997). Ninotchka character reportedly based partly on Ingeborg von Wangenheim: Eyman; Hanisch, *Ernst Lubitsch (1892–1947): Von der Berliner Schönhauser Allee nach Hollywood (Ernst Lubitsch (1892–1947): From Berlin's Schönhauser Allee to Hollywood)* (Judische Miniaturen) [Jewish Miniatures] (Berlin: Hentrich & Hentrich, Centrum Jüdaicum, 2003), quoting Wangenheim's book *Die tickende Bratpfanne (The Ticking Skillet)* (Germany: Rudolstadt, 1974). EL troubled by postwar Red Scare and infuriated by HUAC hearings: Weinberg. William Paul on *Ninotchka: Ernst Lubitsch's American Comedy* (New York: Columbia University Press, 1983). Fromm on Hitler's fondness for Felix Bressart: *Blood and Banquets.* Aaron Schuster on EL's political films: "Comedy in Times of Austerity," in *Lubitsch Can't Wait: A Theoretical Examination,* ed. Ivana Novak, Jela Krecic, and Mladen Dolar (Ljubljana: Slovenian Cinematheque; New York, Columbia University Press, 2014). BW on EL's reaction after Long Beach preview: Crowe; wording on card: Eyman. *Silk Stockings:* JM, *How Did Lubitsch Do It?*

Ketti Frings, *Hold Back the Dawn* (New York: Triangle, 1941); her film treatment, "Memo to a Movie Producer," and involvement with Kurt Frings: CB diaries, March 6, 1941; AFI Catalog. Pressures put on *Hold Back the Dawn* production by Kurt and Mexican government, and BW and CB changing credit to "Written by": Zolotow. BW on narration: "Wilder's Tips for Writers" in Crowe. Leisen on film *Hold Back the Dawn:* Chierichetti, which also notes ending clinch was filmed but not used. Molly Haskell, Melanie's "moral majesty" in *Gone With the Wind: Frankly, My Dear: "Gone With the Wind" Revisited* (New Haven, Conn.: Yale University Press, 2009). Katharine Hepburn on immigrants: JM, *Frank Capra: The Catastrophe of Success,* which also reports on Capra wanting de Havilland for *You Can't Take It with You, Meet John Doe,* and *It's a Wonderful Life.* Steffen-Fluhr comments, including on "living deadman." Colonel Charles E. Stanton, U.S. Army, "Lafayette": John J. Pershing, *My Experiences in the World War* (New York: Stokes, 1931). BW desire to direct in Hollywood prompted by experiences with Leisen and cockroach excerpt from script of *Hold Back the Dawn*: Sikov. BW, "I'll kill him": Zolotow, and details of story from Zolotow and CB diaries, March 6 and 7, 1941; CB on seeing rough cut with BW: May 14, 1941. BW as "The Terror": quoted in Lane and Borton. CB, "Billy's terrifying neurosis": March 21, 1941, cited earlier.

Background of writing *Ball of Fire*: Zolotow, Sikov. BW on HH: JM-TM. Sarris on HH's personality: *The American Cinema*. Robin Wood on *Ball of Fire: Howard Hawks*, BFI Cinema One series (Garden City, N.Y.: Doubleday, 1968); HH on *Ball of Fire* and *A Song Is Born: Hawks on Hawks*; see also TM, *Howard Hawks: The Grey Fox of Hollywood* (New York: Grove Press, 1997). Lucille Ball wanted Sugarpuss role: CB diaries, June 5, 1941. Shaw, *Pygmalion*. Henry James's short story "The Figure in the Carpet," first published in *Cosmopolis* (January–February 1896) and in his collection *Embarrassments* (London: Heinemann, 1896). William J. Lederer and Eugene Burdick novel *The Ugly American* (New York: Norton, 1958).

Articles

"Charlie Brackett, meet Billy Wilder"; "Brackettandwilder" term; CB background; comments on BW-CB working relationship; BW's "meet-cute" in *Bluebeard*; and BW, "Oh, well": Lincoln Barnett, "The Happiest Couple in Hollywood," December 11, 1944, reprinted in Horton (also reports a producer suggested "Bracketandwilder" as their credit). BW, "simply met" EL, "I found," "I liked," and "meet-cute": James Linville, "Billy Wilder: The Art of Screenwriting," *Paris Review* (Spring 1996), reprinted in *The Paris Review Interviews, I* (New York: Picador, 2006). CB obituary: "Charles Brackett Dies at 77; Made Oscar-Winning Movies," *NYT*, March 10, 1969. Tom Allen, "Bracketting Wilder," *Film Comment* (May–June 1982). BW on CB, "We fought a lot": David Freeman, "Sunset Boulevard Revisited: Annals of Hollywood," *New Yorker*, June 21, 1993. Schumach profile of ID. Sarris on screwball comedy: "The Sex Comedy Without Sex," *American Film* (March 1978). EL, "Subtlety, ha?": Idwal Jones, "Touching Upon Lubitsch," *NYT*, March 20, 1938. Nugent review of *Bluebeard*: *NYT*, March 24, 1938.

CB-BW, "terrifying statement": their contribution to "Ernst Lubitsch: A Symposium," *Screen Writer*, January 1948, reprinted in Weinberg. FT, "Lubitsch était un prince" (Lubitsch Was a Prince), *Cahiers du Cinéma* (February 1968), reprinted in his book *The Films in My Life* (Paris: Flammarion, 1975), trans. Leonard Mayhew (New York: Simon & Schuster, 1978). EL, "We can't": 1939 interview with *New York Sun*, quoted in Eyman, *Ernst Lubitsch*. Lengyel's pitch of *Ninotchka*: Fred Stanley, "How Garbo Laughed: Writer of 'Ninotchka' Tells of His Feat," *NYT*, January 4, 1948. EL 1936 visit to USSR: *World-Telegram* (New York), May 23, 1936, quoted in Sabath. BW on EL as writing collaborator: Columbus; "We worked weeks" and EL as a "plastic artist": Jean Domarchi and Jean Douchet, "Entretien avec Billy Wilder" (Interview with Billy Wilder), *Cahiers du Cinéma* (August 1962); EL, "Boys, I've got it" and BW, "she has fallen," "It's funny," and "I guess now": Linville. EL, "What exactly": Mollie Merrick, "25 Years of the 'Lubitsch Touch' in Hollywood," *American Cinematographer* (July 1947).

Garbo, "tired of period pictures": interview with Hettie Grimstead, *Screenland*, April 1938, quoted in Barry Paris, *Garbo* (New York: Knopf, 1994). EL on Garbo, "most inhibited": "Garbo, as Seen by Her Director," *NYT*, October 22, 1939; EL on Garbo's "fine sense of humor": "Sex, Gangster Films Upheld by Lubitsch," United Press, March 25, 1932. Mercedes de Acosta on Garbo: *Here Lies the Heart* (New York: Reynal, 1960). BW hanging out on set to watch Garbo: Clive Hirschorn, "The Billy Wilder Way with Women," *Sunday Express* (UK), September 14, 1969. *Ninotchka* censored in some countries: Carringer and Sabath. *New York Daily Mirror* on *Ninotchka*, November 19, 1939; Otis Ferguson review, *New Republic*, November 1, 1939. BW discomfort over film's anti-Soviet satire: Barnett; CB noting EL wrote "mass trials" lines: "A Matter of Taste," *Quarterly of Film, Radio, and Television* 7, no. 1 (Autumn 1952) (Sikov misattributes "mass trials" lines to BW, and Zolotow writes that "almost all of the anti-Soviet jibes" came from BW).

Carrie Fisher on *Hold Back the Dawn*: "Guilty Pleasures," *Film Comment* (November–December 2011). "Ketti Frings, Stage and Film Writer" (obituary), *NYT*, February 13, 1981; Wikipedia entry on Kurt Frings. De Havilland on playing character who is good: Anita Gates, "The Good Girl Gets the Last Word," *NYT*, November 7, 2004. BW, "Anyone who knows me": Paul Rosenfield, "Billy Wilder's 50-Year Itch in Hollywood," *LAT*, March 2, 1986. Jacques Rivette on HH's comedies: "Genie de Howard Hawks" (The Genius of Howard Hawks), *Cahiers du Cinéma* (May 1953), trans. Russell Campbell and Marvin Pister [JM], adapted from trans. by Adrian Brine that appeared in *Movie* (December 1962), in *Focus on Howard Hawks*, ed. JM (Englewood Cliffs, NJ: Prentice-Hall, 1972), which also includes Peter John Dyer on *Ball of Fire* as "piquant variation" from "Sling the Lamps Low," *Sight and Sound* (Summer 1962). BW on *The Major and the Minor*: Crowe; EL visit with fellow directors and "I have directed": Zolotow; Heilbut. Elaine Lennon, "Billy Wilder's Berlin Women: *A Foreign Affair* (1948), offscreen.com 19, no. 3 (March 2015). Branch Rickey, "Luck": *Sporting News*, February 21, 1946. Obituaries of Francis C. Coppicus (June 9, 1966): "Francis Coppicus: Stars' Agent, Dies," *NYT*; "Francis Coppicus," *San Rafael Daily Independent-Journal*.

Other Sources

BW-Judith Coppicus Balken marriage license application, Superior Court of Arizona for Yuma County, Yuma, December 20, 1936; their twin children, Vincent and Victoria, born December 21, 1939: California Birth Index, 1905–1995; Vincent's death on March 31, 1940: California Death Index 1940–1997; other governmental records pertaining to Judith and her other family members from ancestry.com. Paul Iribe: biography on collections. glasgowmuseums. Published screenplay of *Ninotchka*, including Anobile comment in photobook. EL, "As to satire": letter to Weinberg, July 10, 1947, in Weinberg, "A Tribute to Lubitsch, with a Letter in Which Lubitsch Appraises His Own Career," *Films in Review*

(August–September 1951); reproduced in *Film Culture* (Summer 1962), reprinted in *The Lubitsch Touch*. BW defining the Touch as "a different way of thinking" and describing "key scene": Schlöndorff-Grischow ("key scene" in British version but not American). BW opposed to Soviet-Nazi Pact: Anthony Slide lecture "Billy Wilder and Hollywood's Golden Age," Hillsdale College, Michigan, 2018, YouTube. Raphaelson busy on other projects when *Bluebeard* written: Sabath, "Ernst Lubitsch and Samson Raphaelson: A Study in Collaboration," Ph.D. diss., New York University, 1979. BW, "Make subtlety obvious" and plaque at Mr. Chow: JM interview with RM.

JM interview with PD on ID. Robert Mitchum on Lillian Gish: *The American Film Institute Salute to Lillian Gish* (CBS-TV, 1984, written by George Stevens Jr. and JM). Emma Lazarus poem on plaque inside pedestal of Statue of Liberty: "The New Colossus," 1883. Sarris on HH's personality: *The American Cinema*. BW on Arthur Hornblow Jr.: AFI award speech. BW memo, "Propaganda Through Entertainment," to Davidson Taylor, assistant to Col. William Paley, supervisor of Postwar Information Control Division, U.S. Forces European Theater, August 16, 1945.

CHAPTER 6: DANCING ON THE EDGE

Books

Elie Wiesel, trans. Stella Rodway, *Night* (New York: Hill and Wang, 1960; first published as *La Nuit*, Paris: Les Editions de Minuit, 1958). Benjamin Moser on "a ruined world": *Sontag: Her Life and Work* (New York: HarperCollins, 2019). *Desny v. Wilder* and *Ace in the Hole*: Sikov. Information on ID: see notes for chap. 7. George Bernard Shaw, "If you want": widely attributed to Shaw. Andrew Sarris on BW "too cynical": *The American Cinema*. Welles's opposition to rhetoric in plays: Mark W. Estrin, ed., *Orson Welles: Interviews* (Jackson: University Press of Mississippi, 2002): "rhetoric is": Juan Cobos, Miguel Rubio, and J. A. Pruneda, "A Trip to Don Quixoteland: Conversations with Orson Welles," 1964 interview trans. Rose Kaplin, *Cahiers du Cinéma in English*, no. 5 (1966); "I hate rhetoric": André Bazin, Charles Bitsch, and Jean Domarchi, "Interview with Orson Welles," *Cahiers du Cinéma* (1958), trans. Alisa Hartz and Peter Wollen for Estrin. CB in 1959 on *Five Graves to Cairo*: Sinyard-Turner. BW, *Ace in the Hole* "lost me," "Fuck them all": Zolotow. Aristotle's discussion of comedy: *Poetics: On the Art of Poetry*, trans. Ingram Bywater (Oxford: Clarendon Press, 1920).

Renoir interest in filming *Irma la Douce*: Pascal Mérigeau, trans. Bruce Benderson, *Jean Renoir: A Biography* (Burbank: California: Ratpac Press, 2016, originally published as *Jean Renoir*, Paris: Flammarion, 2012). Hal B. Wallis on *Irma*: letter to Shurlock in MPAA file on film, AMPAS, quoted in Sikov. *KMS* "Condemned": Sikov. Peter Sellers's heart attack during making of *KMS*, heart stoppages, and his and BW's responses: Zolotow; Sikov, *Mr. Strangelove: A Biography of Peter Sellers* (New York: Hyperion, 2002). CB, "Billy's terrifying neurosis": see notes for chap. 3. Robert Stephens on BW: *Knight*

Errant: Memoirs of a Vagrant Actor (London: Hodder & Stoughton, 1995). Shirley MacLaine, "wished he would": *My Lucky Stars: A Hollywood Memoir* (New York: Bantam Books, 1995). Film noir and *unheimlich/creepy* or *uncanny:* Gemünden, *Continental Strangers*; Freud's use of that term: his 1919 essay "Das Unheimliche," trans. James Strachey in collaboration with Anna Freud, *The Standard Edition of the Complete Psychological Works of Sigmund Freud*, vol. 12 (1917–1919): *An Infantile Neurosis and Other Works* (London: Hogarth Press and Institute of Psycho-Analysis, 1925). Italian word *menefreghista* as applied to Dean Martin: Nick Tosches, *Dino: Living High in the Dirty Business of Dreams* (New York: Doubleday, 1992). Legion of Decency, *KMS* "thoroughly sordid": quoted in Sikov; BW complaint about "shabby" treatment by Legion: Crowe. Sigmund Freud, "No one who": *Dora: An Analysis of a Case of Hysteria*, 1905.

Published screenplays: *Double Indemnity*, *The Apartment*, and *The Fortune Cookie*; unpublished screenplay *The Front Page* (Revised Final, quoted in JM, "Shooting *The Front Page*," and Phillips). BW on Raymond Chandler, "more of a cynic than me": interview with Robert Porfirio in *Film Noir Reader 3: Interviews with Filmmakers of the Classic Noir Period*, ed. Porfirio, Alain Silver, James Ursini (New York: Limelight Editions, 2002). ID, "If you ever": AFI 1976 seminar. Brecht, "Verfremdungseffekte in der chinesischen Schauspielkunst" (Alienation Effects in Chinese Acting), first published in trans. by Eric W. White as "The Fourth Wall of China: An Essay on the Effect of Disillusion in the Chinese Theater," *Life and Letters*, 1936, and in John Willett, ed., *Brecht on Theatre* (New York: Hill and Wang, 1964); also the source of Brecht's quotes on "epic theatre . . . I weep when they laugh": from his essay "Theatre for Pleasure or Theatre for Instruction" (c. 1936). Wilder's acquaintance with Brecht and denial of influence: Sikov. Zolotow on BW and Ilse; as Zololotw also claims, BW said he dropped out of University of Vienna; JM-TM; see also his retort to Zolotow's story about Ilse in JM-TM, and the interviewers' comment in footnote; BW to Lally on Ilse and prostitutes; Hutter and Kamolz report that BW never enrolled at the University of Vienna. William Holden, BW "a mind": Ezra Goodman, *The Fifty-Year Decline and Fall of Hollywood* (New York: Simon and Schuster, 1961). George Axelrod play *The Seven Year Itch* (New York: Random House, 1953).

Anna Bonacci's 1944 play *L'ora della fantasia* (*The Fantasy Hour*), in Daniela Cavallaro, trans. and intro., *Italian Women's Theatre, 1930–1960: An Anthology of Plays* (Chicago: University of Chicago Press, 2011), with Cavallaro's notes on Bonacci and the play, quotation from Anton Giulio Bragaglia, and information about stage productions. Stanwyck on playing a prostitute for Capra: JM interview for *Frank Capra: The Catastrophe of Success*. Production Code abolished in 1968: Lewis, *Hollywood v. Hard Core*.

Edward Childs Carpenter's play *Connie Goes Home*, 1923 (New York: Samuel French, 1934), based on the Fannie Kilbourne short story "Sunny Goes Home," *Saturday Evening Post*, May 7, 1921. BW, Betty in *Sunset Blvd.* modeled on second wife, the former Audrey Young: Karasek. Background on Audrey: Zolotow (and JM's meeting with her in 1995); "I don't go to church" her line: Chandler. G. K. Chesterton on paradox: "When Doctors Agree," in *The Paradoxes of Mr. Pond* (London: Cassell, 1937). Oscar Wilde, *Lady*

Windermere's Fan: A Play About a Good Woman (London: Elkin Mathews & John Lane, 1893). Sarris on BW's treatment of actresses and the auteur theory: *The American Cinema*. BW and Jean Arthur: Crowe; Karasek; Sinyard-Turner; BW, "What a picture": Steven Bach, *Marlene Dietrich: Life and Legend* (New York: Morrow, 1992). BW on Dietrich and not being sexually involved with stars: Crowe; BW, "I would rather": Karasek. Comments by Arthur on her screen personality: interviews with JM, including for *Frank Capra: The Catastrophe of Success*; George Stevens on Arthur: from a 1974 interview by JM and McGilligan, which appeared as "A Piece of the Rock: George Stevens," *Bright Lights*, no. 8 (1979), reprinted in McGilligan, *Film Crazy: Interviews with Hollywood Legends* (New York: St. Martin's, 2000), and JM, *Two Cheers for Hollywood*.

ID, "In the old studio days": 1976 AFI seminar. Shaw, *Pygmalion*. Samuel Taylor play *Sabrina Fair; or, a Woman of the World, A Romantic Comedy* (New York: Random House, 1954). Charles A. Lindbergh, *The Spirit of St. Louis* (New York: Scribner, 1953). Story about Lindbergh allegedly having sex with waitress: Zolotow, with BW quote on James Stewart and the fly in the film of *The Spirit of St. Louis*; Crowe; A. Scott Berg, *Lindbergh* (New York: Putnam, 1998), which also discusses Stewart's complaint about the fly and Lindbergh's time in Texas training with U.S. Army Air Service.

Anet novel *Ariane, jeune fille russe (Ariane, the Young Russian Girl)* (Paris: Les Editions G. Crès, 1924, and New York: Knopf, 1927, reprinted in movie tie-in edition (New York: Signet, 1957) as *Love in the Afternoon*. BW interview with Anet: "Claude Anet in Berlin." Earlier version of screenplay, *Ariane*: ID papers. *Love in the Afternoon* ending enforced by Legion of Decency: *Variety*, July 10, 1957; HH on censors rewriting *The Big Sleep*: *Hawks on Hawks*. BW on reception of *Love in the Afternoon* and Cooper's actual personality: Karasek. BW on Lubitsch Touch in *The Smiling Lieutenant*: Zolotow. ID on *KMS*, "What we were really," "But in this country," "I think what it is," and "I don't think we ever": William Froug, *The Screenwriter Looks at the Screenwriter* (New York: Macmillan, 1972). Production Code replaced by Motion Picture Association of America rating system in 1968: Lewis, *Hollywood v. Hard Core*. *KMS* eventually (1970) given GP rating: Mirisch, *I Thought We Were Making Movies, Not History*. Cary Grant on not working with BW: discussed in Scott Eyman, *Cary Grant: A Brilliant Disguise* (New York: Simon & Schuster, 2020); Grant quotes from James Bawden and Ron Miller, *Conversations with Classic Film Stars* (Lexington: University Press of Kentucky, 2016). BW considered Walter Matthau for *The Seven Year Itch*: Sikov.

Articles

John M. Woodcock on BW's feelings about the bombing of Berlin: "The Name Dropper," *American Cinemeditor* (Winter 1989/90). *Desny v. Wilder* and *Ace in the Hole*: Jay Handlin, "How the Battle Over Ideas Began," *Variety*, November 18, 2003; and Eric Hoyt, "Writer in the Hole: *Desny v. Wilder*, Copyright Law, and the Battle Over Ideas," *Cinema Journal* 50, no. 2 (Winter 2011), which cites BW's statement in the case that Walter Newman proposed the idea for the film to him. Kathy Fiscus entrapment and death: "Kathy's Plight Recalls 1925 Tragedy of Floyd Collins," *LAT*, April 10, 1949.

Sight & Sound polls of international film critics and directors on the hundred best films ever made: bfi.org.uk., 2012 (JM participated and put *Some Like It Hot* on his alphabetical top-ten list); BW outraged no EL film made another list of the best fifty films: JM-TM. BW, "Frankly, I regard": RM, "The Life and Hard Times of *Fedora*," *American Film* (February 1979), quoting *New York* magazine. Sarris, "Billy Wilder: Closet Romanticist," *Film Comment* (July–August 1976); Sarris, "recent critical resurrection" and redemption theme in BW's work: "Why Billy Wilder Belongs in the Pantheon," *Film Comment* (July–August 1991). BW response to Sarris and "It was the biggest": JM-TM, "Going for Extra Innings: Billy Wilder Interviewed," *Film Comment* (January–February 1979), reprinted in Horton and *Two Cheers for Hollywood*. Kael, review of *One, Two, Three*: *Film Quarterly* (Spring 1962). JM-MW, "The Private Life of Billy Wilder." Farber, "The Films of Billy Wilder"; Herbert G. Luft on *A Foreign Affair*: "A Matter of Decadence," *Quarterly of Film, Radio, and Television* (Fall 1952). BW, "I'm not really a cynic": Michael Blowen, "The Art of Billy Wilder," *Boston Globe*, October 22, 1989, reprinted in Horton. JL, "People think of him": MW, "Saint Jack: Jack Lemmon Interviewed by Michael Wilmington," *Film Comment* (March–April 1993). BW, "I know how many words," and Walter Matthau, "I always play Wilder": JM, "Shooting *The Front Page*." BW, "as subtle" and discussion of books about him and comments allegedly made by him: JM-TM. Charles Higham, "Cast a Cold Eye: The Films of Billy Wilder," *Sight and Sound* (Spring 1963). Mae West and Marlon Brando for film that became *Sunset*: Linville. Didion review of *KMS*.

André Bazin, "La Politique des Auteurs" (The Policy of Authors), *Cahiers du Cinéma*, no. 70 (April 1957). Eric Rohmer quoted by Bazin: [as Maurice Scherer], "Renoir Américain" (The American Renoir), *Cahiers*, no. 8 (January 1952). Sarris on "auteur theory": "Notes on the Auteur Theory in 1962," *Film Culture* (Winter 1962–1963). *Cahiers du Cinéma* on BW: J. D. Copp, "Billy Wilder and the *Cahiers du Cinéma* 'Young Turks,'" *my gleanings*, jdcopp.blogspot.com, January 13, 2007, including dictionary of American directors in Christmas 1955 issue; Jacques Doniol-Valcroze review of *Some Like It Hot*, November 1959; Jean-Luc Godard, December 1963–January 1964. FT review of *The Seven Year Itch*, *Arts*, March 7–13, 1956, reprinted in *Chroniques d'Arts-Spectacles* (1954–1958), ed. Bernard Bastide (Paris: Gallimard, 2019); FT on BW and *KMS* in late 1960s: *Truffaut on Cinema*, comp. Anne Gillian, trans. Alistair Fox (Bloomington: Indiana University Press, 2017, originally published as *Le Cinéma selon François Truffaut*, textes réunis par Anne Gillain [Paris: Flammarion, 1988]); see also *Les Films de ma vie* (*The Films in My Life*) (Paris: Flammarion, 1975, and New York: Simon & Schuster, 1978, trans. Leonard Mayhew), for FT reviews of *Stalag 17*, 1954, and *Seven Year Itch*. Anon., review of *Spirit*, *Cahiers du Cinéma* (July 1957).

"Disneyland for adults": Kristin Hunt, "Hollywood Codebreakers: 'Irma la Douce' Pushes Prostitution Into the Mainstream," *Medium*, November 2, 2018. "I committed myself": John McDonough, "For 44 Years, Billy Wilder's Given Movies New Direction," *Chicago Tribune*, April 20, 1986. Lindbergh alleged to have been involved in media circus surrounding entrapment of Floyd Collins: Casey Bukro, "Folk Hero's Burial Ends 3 Generations of Anguish," *Chicago Tribune*, March 26, 1989. Steven Gaydos, BW "broken heart": *Hollywood Elsewhere* blog post, August 29, 2019. Sex and love in BW films: Jason Carpenter, "Some Like It Not: The Key to Successful Relationships in the Films of Billy Wilder," *Bright Lights*, February 29, 2016. *Last Tango in Paris* compared with *Love in the Afternoon* and BW citing EL and Stroheim as role models: JM-TM (which also discusses Cooper in the BW film). JM, "Shooting *The Front Page:* Two Damns and One By God," *Real Paper* (Boston), July 31, 1974, also published in shortened form in *Sight and Sound* (Autumn 1974), as "*The Front Page*," reprinted in Horton and JM, *Two Cheers for Hollywood*.

BW and *Bicycle Thieves*: Karasek and poll of filmmakers, Le Comité du Festival Mondial du Film et des Beaux-Arts de Belgique, cited in Gavin Lambert, "As You Like It," *Sight and Sound* (July–September 1952); *Bicycle Thieves* remained BW favorite: Karasek; BW list for 1976 AFI seminar. Jean-Luc Godard on Roberto Rossellini: 1962 interview with *Cahiers du Cinéma*. BW spoof of neorealist film: Art Buchwald, "How to Make a Festival Movie," *LAT*, June 4, 1959. Joan Didion review, "*Kiss Me Stupid*, 'Minority Report,'" *Vogue*, March 1, 1965; BW letter to Didion: JM, "Thank You, Mr. Wilder." Glenn Erickson on *KMS*: review of Olive Films Blu-ray edition, *DVD Talk*, February 9, 2015. BW, "Peculiarly enough" and "For twelve weeks," and Reisch on BW upset over reaction to the film: Richard Lemon, "The Message in Billy Wilder's Fortune Cookie: 'Well, Nobody's Perfect . . . ,'" *Saturday Evening Post*, December 17, 1966, reprinted in Horton. Michael Scheinfeld on *KMS* as "cinematic litmus test": tvguide.com, n.d. Thomas Thompson attack on *KMS* and BW, "Wilder's Dirty-Joke Film Stirs a Furor," *Life*, January 15, 1965, including response from BW; BW to JM re Thompson, JM-TM; Thompson and the Oswalds: "Assassin: The Man Held—and Killed—for Murder," *Life*, November 29, 1963; *Blood and Money* (New York: Doubleday, 1976). *KMS* GP rating: JM-MW review, *The Private Life of Sherlock Holmes*. Sarris on BW's "raging romanticism": "Billy Wilder: Closet Romanticist." Jordan Cronenweth, "more into people": JM, "Shooting *The Front Page*." Heart-shaped sunglasses worn by Hope Holiday in *Irma la Douce*: "Extraordinary Publicity Photos of Sue Lyon as Stanley Kubrick's Iconic 'Lolita,' Photographed by Bert Stern," designyoutrust.com, January 3, 2020.

Other Sources

D. M. Marshman Jr. involvement in *Sunset Blvd.*: BW to JM. BW on his fondness for "Isn't It Romantic?": Schlöndorff-Grischow. *Desny v. Wilder:* Judge Stanley Mosk, summary judgment granted to Wilder and Paramount by Los Angeles Superior Court, December 16, 1953; *Victor Desny v. Billy Wilder, Paramount Pictures Corporation and Paramount Film Distributing Corporation*, District Court of Appeal, Second District, Division 3,

California, July 15, 1955; *Victor Desny v. Billy Wilder et al.*, Supreme Court of California, 46 Cal. 2d 715, 726 (Cal. 1956), June 28, 1956.

Legion of Decency changes demanded in *KMS*: letters in ID papers, including Robert S. Benjamin, chairman of the board, United Artists, to BW, November 9, 1964, with list of suggested dialogue and visual changes. Original uncut roadshow screenplay of *The Private Life of Sherlock Holmes*, August 25, 1969: part of *The Special Edition*, Image Entertainment 1994 laserdisc, along with cut scenes from the film (video and audio). JL, "The Prussian General": JM interview notes. MacLaine contributions to *The Apartment*, dialogue and gin rummy: *Inside "The Apartment"* and "Shirley MacLaine Discusses Billy Wilder & *The Apartment*," Hudson Union Society, November 30, 2013, YouTube. JL joking about actors' misfortunes while in BW films: *The American Film Institute Salute to Billy Wilder*, 1986; BW in acceptance speech on Doane Harrison. BW on working with Sellers in *Kiss Me, Stupid*: JM interview with Trueba. JM interviews with ID, BW, JL, Matthau, Jordan Cronenweth: JM interview notes on set of *The Front Page*. PD on ID and BW: JM interview. Scripts for BW-ID films in ID papers at Wisconsin Historical Society. Walter Hill on ambiguity: *Directed by John Ford*, d. Bogdanovich, 2006 revised ed. BW, "constant orgasm" and why *Ace* rejected in United States: Schlöndorff-Grischow. JM interview with RM on BW "defense against intimacy." JM discussion with Nancy Olson about her character in *Sunset Blvd.* Arthur to JM on *A Foreign Affair*. Franklin D. Roosevelt, "I hate hate" quoted by Katharine Hepburn in World War II war bond short. BW, Audrey, and Hope Holiday: JM interviews with RM and Holiday.

CHAPTER 7: "NOT A FUNNYMAN BUT A MORALIST"

Books

Moss Hart, "This is the moment": Sikov. CB refusing to collaborate on *Double Indemnity*: Sikov; but CB diary entries on consulting on script, August 6 and 18, September 16, November 1, 4, and 5, 1943, and finding film an "absolute knockout," January 28, 1944. ID background: Froug; Barbara Diamond on ID and dialogue and BW-ID view of *Some Like It Hot*: Castle, and on "the person who was really cynical": Lally. ID, Gemünden on ID influence on BW: *A Foreign Affair*. Robert Towne on Monroe: "On Moving Pictures," introduction to *"Chinatown" and "The Last Detail": Two Screenplays* (New York: Grove Press, 1997). ID on contract system: Froug. William Goldman on screenplays: *Adventures in the Screen Trade: A Personal View of Hollywood and Screenwriting* (New York: Warner Books, 1983). BW on how he worked with ID and "Very early": 1976 AFI seminar; BW, ID "taciturn," "it was wonderful," and "It was all" and CB "loquacious": Crowe. BW definition of associate producer: Zolotow. Published BW-ID screenplays: see earlier listings. Walter Mirisch and Mirisch Company/Mirisch Corporation: *I Thought We Were Making Movies, Not History*.

ID background and working methods: Sikov; Crowe; AFI seminars in *Filmmakers on Filmmaking*, vol. 1. Comparisons of *Some Like It Hot* and *Fanfares of Love*: Maslon; Gemünden, *A Foreign Affair*, which also discusses the German film's sequel, *Fanfaren der Ehe* (*Fanfares of Marriage*). More information on *Fanfares of Love* and its writers and director: Terri Ginsberg and Andrea Mensch, eds., *A Companion to German Cinema* (Malden, Mass.: Wiley-Blackwell, 2012); BW on the film: Crowe. Paul Frees dubbed Tony Curtis's voice as woman; JL on his and Curtis's female impersonations: Maslon; Curtis, *The Making of "Some Like It Hot"*; Maslon. BW, "*Scarface* meets *Charley's Aunt*": Phillips; Brandon Thomas play, *Charley's Aunt*, 1892. BW fondness for *Mädchen in Uniform*: see notes for chap. 3. Working title of *Some Like It Hot* was *Not Tonight, Josephine!*: Maslon; from 1911 song "Not to-night, Josephine" by Will A. Heelan and Seymour Furth. BW, "We could do": Castle; use of "neger" in Germany for ghost screenwriter: Karasek. Curtis claimed credit for suggesting Cary Grant impersonation: *The Making of "Some Like it Hot"*; Grant telling BW, "I never": Castle. Reactions of preview audiences: Sikov and books on the film.

Some Like It Hot ending line: not in first draft of screenplay, May 2, 1958, but in November 12 shooting script (quoted): Castle; ID in Froug. ID, "to combine": Froug, which also includes ID about film critics and ID's response, as probable partial reference to JM-MW, "The Private Life of Billy Wilder." "The organization man": title of book by William H. Whyte Jr. (New York: Simon & Schuster, 1956). Screenplay of *The Apartment*; and discussion of mirror scene: JL: Chandler; BW: Crowe. Charles Williams's "Jealous Lover": see notes for chap. 2. JM on suicide: *The Broken Places*. Gemünden on *The Apartment* and Jews: *A Foreign Affair*; BW on Mildred Dreyfuss from Chandler. Genesis of *The Apartment* in *Brief Encounter*: biographies; BW, "a very fine": Crowe. Jennings Lang-Walter Wanger incident: BW-ID, *Filmmakers on Filmmaking*, vol. 1; Rocky Lang, *Growing Up Hollywood: Tales from the Son of a Hollywood Mogul* (Los Angeles: Harbor Lights Productions, 2014); Sikov; Chandler.

Articles

ID's writing at Columbia University: *NYT* articles: "Freshman Is Author of Columbia Show; Films, Fascism and Communism Lampooned," December 19, 1937; "Varsity Show This Week," March 27, 1938; "'Pony Ballet' Back in Columbia Show," April 1, 1938; "Varsity Show Cast Picked at Columbia," February 26, 1939; "Columbia Players Open 'Fair Enough,'" March 31, 1939; "Columbia Players Offer Burlesque," April 5, 1940; "Three Honor Groups Elect at Columbia," September 27, 1940; and "U.S. in War by 1946, Students Predict," January 8, 1941 (ID chosen school's "best writer" in yearbook as senior); and "I. A. L. Diamond Is Dead at 67; Won Oscar for 'The Apartment,'" April 22, 1988. BW, "If I ever lost this guy" and ID on embarrassed watching early movies, "like asking," and "This way": Schumach, who tells part of the story about ID's name; ID, "I wanted a *goyische* handle": Howard Rodman, "I. A. L.," *Village Voice*, June 14, 1988. "Look, it has become":

JM-TM. BW female advice column under woman's name in *Tempo*: see notes to chap. 2. JM-MW on *Some Like It Hot* and other BW films, "The Private Life of Billy Wilder." ID, "heavy-handed": "The Day Marilyn Needed 47 Takes to Remember to Say, 'Where's the Bourbon?,'" *California* (December 1985). Sarris on his changing views of BW: see his previously cited articles. Pablo Picasso on good taste: widely attributed to Picasso. John Patterson, "Deprived": "Billy Wilder, Still Less than Meets the Eye," *Guardian* (UK), June 8, 2012. BW and ID "complement": George Morris, "The Private Films of Billy Wilder," *Film Comment* (January/February 1979). ID, "Middle European": Kakutani, 1982. JM-MW, review of *The Private Life of Sherlock Holmes*, *Film Quarterly* (Spring 1971).

Hollis Alpert, *The Apartment* "a dirty fairy tale": "The Unquiet Bed," *Saturday Review*, June 11, 1960; Crowther, "Scrambled Satire: Truffaut's 'Shoot the Piano Player' Opens," *NYT*, July 24, 1962. BW response to interviewer calling *The Apartment* "a little too sentimental": quoted from *Cinema* magazine by Sinyard-Turner. BW, "People have called my pictures dirty": John McDonough, "For 44 Years, Billy Wilder's Given Movies New Direction," *Chicago Tribune*, April 20, 1986. Lang-Wanger incident: Rocky Lang, "I'm living proof" and Jay Kanter apartment connection: Stephen Galloway, "Which Producer Shot an Agent in the Groin Over a 'Little Women' Star?," *HR*, November 18, 2019; Jennings Lang suggested BW for *The Front Page*: Paul Monash in JM, "Shooting *The Front Page*." Wilders' Wilshire Blvd. condominium: "Audrey Young Dies; Actress and Widow of Billy Wilder," *HR*, June 7, 2012 (sale price in 2013: listing on redfin.com). BW, "as fairy-tale": Kakutani.

Other Sources

"I'm Thru with Love" (1931) by Fud Livingston, Matty Malneck, and Gus Kahn as BW's favorite song: Maslon. Academy Awards acceptance speeches by BW and ID: April 17, 1961, video on oscars.org, with statistics about Oscar winners. ID background: PD interview (including information from ID's unpublished memoir, "A Definite Maybe"); biography with I. A. L. Diamond Papers, 1941–1981, Wisconsin Historical Society; ID on Lewis Carroll: Internet Movie Database. ID, "Quizzically": 1955 sketch directed by BW in 1988 for WGA memorial tribute to ID, and BW's eulogy of ID: *Billy Wilder Speaks*. JM interviews with ID and PD. PD, "They were very close": on BBC Radio 3 *Arts & Ideas* program, "Billy Wilder," November 5, 2020. Ending line of *Some Like It Hot*: BW at ID WGA memorial, May 1988, *Billy Wilder Speaks*; PD: JM interview; Barbara Diamond in *Nobody's Perfect: The Making of "Some Like It Hot."* ID, "I heard constantly": *American Film Institute Salute to Billy Wilder*. ID unproduced screenplay *Tinseltown,* based on Oscar Wilde's short story "Lord Arthur Savile's Crime": ID papers, Wisconsin Historical Society.

BW on train gag in *Some Like It Hot*: reported by publicist Dick Guttman in the documentary *Never Be Boring*, which also includes BW, "Something is only funny." BW-ID on Irwin Allen: JM interview with RM. BW to Ruth O'Hara at 1992 reception honoring Curt Siodmak. Molly Haskell on Bud and PD on ID contributing suicide attempt: *Inside "The Apartment."* PD to JM on his father's and BW's regard for Dudley Nichols's

Stagecoach screenplay (1939, based on short story "Stage to Lordsburg" by Ernest Haycox) and, uncredited, Guy de Maupassant's story "Boule de Suif" (Ball of Fat). John Lennon, "Life is what happens": "Beautiful Boy (Darling Boy)" song on album with Yoko Ono, *Double Fantasy*, 1980. BW calling *The Apartment* his best film: to JM at LAFCA tribute luncheon, 1995.

CHAPTER 8: "I AM NO LONGER AFRAID"

Books

BW, "more politically daring" and "I am no longer afraid": CB diaries, November 4, 1947. Molnár play basis of *One, Two, Three*: see notes for chap. 2; previous draft of screenplay: ID papers, Wisconsin Historical Society. Differing political views of BW and CB: CB diaries, passim. Zolotow on "Billy's political feelings." Emigrés as critics of American political system: Heilbut. Donald Bevan and Edmund Trzcinski play *Stalag 17* (New York: Dramatists Play Service, 1951). CB, "to tell the truth": October 9, 1947. BW, "I could have maybe saved": Lally; what BW learned about his mother's death: Sikov (see later reference to Plaszów); Steffen-Fluhr, "images of the death." BW, "Two of them have talent": Zolotow; "Blacklist, schmacklist": Goodman. HUAC and its October 1947 hearings, Committee for the First Amendment (CFA), and imposition of blacklist by the motion picture companies on November 25, 1947: Ceplair-Englund; Navasky. SDG signers of petition calling for general meeting of membership in 1950 and other information and quotes on the meeting: JM, *Frank Capra: The Catastrophe of Success*; see also JM, *Searching for John Ford*. David Thomson, BW "a heartless exploiter": *The New Biographical Dictionary of Film*, 5th ed. (New York: Knopf, 2010).

CB entries in diaries: "It doesn't seem," October 25, 1947; "Suddenly I find," December 3, 1947; "that ill-mannered," October 16, 1946; and in 1947: BW "saving the world": October 24, and advising the Hollywood Nineteen, October 23; "I voiced," October 27; "Billy informed me," November 2; "This is the last picture" and "heard this," November 4; "great coldness," November 17; "a prospect," November 5; "Billy in a very," November 23; "Billy seemed" and BW, "I spit upon the Congress," November 25; BW predicted they would have more violent political arguments, January 18; CB, "pushing me out," February 4.

"SDG loyalty oath controversy: see notes for chap. 4. Gemünden, "The experience of the Red Scare" and postwar *"Trümmerfilm"* ("rubblefilm"): *Continental Strangers*. CB and BW plans to write film about Hollywood: diaries, October 18, 1946ff. Abraham Polonsky, "The liberals" to JM: "'A Pavane for an Early American': Abraham Polonsky Discusses *Tell Them Willie Boy Is Here*," with JM and audience at Los Angeles International Film Exposition (Filmex), 1980, in Andrew Dickos, ed., *Abraham Polonsky: Interviews* (Jackson: University Press of Mississippi, 2011); and JM, *Two Cheers for Hollywood*. Lang on the American Dream: Bogdanovich, *Fritz Lang in America* (London: Studio Vista, 1967; New York: Praeger, 1969). BW on Holden and Sefton: Crowe; Holden about

Sefton, question to BW about the character, and BW, "If I were you": Bob Thomas, *Golden Boy: The Untold Story of William Holden* (New York: St. Martin's, 1983). BW leaving Paramount over *Stalag 17*: Zolotow; George Weltner obituary, *NYT*, November 19, 1985; BW, "the Nazis killed," Karasek.

Jackson, *The Lost Weekend*; Blake Bailey, *Farther and Wilder: The Lost Weekends and Literary Dreams of Charles Jackson* (New York: Vintage, 2013); CB-BW screenplay. Lindbergh, *The Spirit of St. Louis*; BW-Wendell Mayes screenplay, adaptation by Charles Lederer. John Kerr turning down lead in film version and other problems with production: Karasek; Zolotow; Sikov; reshoots directed by John Sturges: Sikov; Jack Warner, "The most disastrous": *My First Hundred Years in Hollywood* (New York: Random House, 1965). BW, "imposing" and "Jewish friend" story: Zolotow; Berg.

Dalton Trumbo, *The Time of the Toad: A Study of Inquisition in America* (Hollywood: The Hollywood Ten, 1949). Larry Ceplair and Christopher Trumbo, *Dalton Trumbo: Blacklisted Hollywood Radical* (Lexington: University Press of Kentucky, 2015). Lawsuit involving *Hogan's Heroes* and *Stalag 17*: Brenda Scott Royce, *Hogan's Heroes: Behind the Scenes at Stalag 13* (Los Angeles: Renaissance, 1998). *Full Metal Jacket* one of BW's favorite films: Crowe. FT on *Stalag 17*: see notes for chap. 6; Sarris on that film's ending: *The American Cinema*. BW on influence by Molnár's *The Guardsman*: see notes for chap. 2. ID on *One, Two, Three*, "an attempt": Froug; President Kennedy asking BW for copy of screenplay: Sikov; more on that meeting: Karasek (with photo) and Crowe. Elia Kazan, "The deepest conflicts": Michel Ciment, *Kazan on Kazan*, British Film Institute Cinema One series (London: Secker & Warburg, 1973, and New York: Viking, 1974). Samuel Goldwyn, "If people don't want": widely attributed to Goldwyn. Leslie Fiedler, *Love and Death in the American Novel* (New York: Criterion, 1960); ID, "To think": Froug. Hecht and MacArthur, *The Front Page*.

BW interest in filming *Josephine Mutzenbacher*: see notes for chap. 3. Phillip Sipiora on Keyes and Neff: "Phenomenological Masking: Complications of Identity in *Double Indemnity*" in McNally. BW, "But when he forgot": 1976 AFI seminar. BW, "very personal": Karasek. Silde on CB's sexuality. BW, Leisen, "too goddam fey": Zolotow. HH, "a love story between two men": Bogdanovich, "Howard Hawks Interview," *Movie* (November 1962), reprinted in Scott Breivold, ed., *Howard Hawks: Interviews* (Jackson: University Press of Mississippi, 2006); see also JM, *Hawks on Hawks*, and TM, *Howard Hawks: The Grey Fox of Hollywood*. Parker Tyler and *Double Indemnity*: "Magic-Lantern Metamorphoses III: Double Into Quadruple Indemnity," in *Magic and Myth of the Movies* (New York: Holt, 1947). Freud, "Sometimes a cigar": attributed to Freud.

Samuel Taylor play *Avanti!, or A Very Uncomplicated Girl*, Dramatists Play Service, New York, 1968, revised as *A Touch of Spring*, 1975. Truncating of *Sherlock Holmes*: biographies; Mirisch; BW, "I had tears": Crowe. Arthur Conan Doyle, "A Scandal in Bohemia": *Strand Magazine* (July 1891), collected in *The Adventures of Sherlock Holmes* (London: George Newnes, 1892). BW on needing Clint Eastwood in *Buddy Buddy* and

Matthau on the film: Chandler. BW interest in directing the film of Neil Simon's *The Odd Couple:* Sikov; Simon on BW in his *Rewrites: A Memoir* (New York: Simon & Schuster, 1996). Alternate views of Watergate: Jim Hougan, *Secret Agenda: Watergate, Deep Throat, and the CIA* (New York: Random House, 1984); Len Colodny and Robert Gettlin, *Silent Coup: The Removal of a President* (New York: St. Martin's, 1991), and Colodny paperback ed. (Walterville, Ore.: Trine Day, 2015). William Butler Yeats, "We make": *Per Amica Silentia Lunae* (New York: Macmillan, 1918).

Articles

Fiedler, "Come Back to the Raft Ag'in, Huck Honey," *Partisan Review* (June 1948); JM-MW, "The Private Life of Billy Wilder." David Ehrenstein on BW sexual themes: "Born to Be Wilder," review of Lally, *LAT*, June 16, 1996, including quote from Didion review of *KMS*. BW description of *Double Indemnity* as "a love story between the two men": John Allyn, *"Double Indemnity:* A Policy That Paid Off," *Literature/Film Quarterly* (Spring 1978); Sarris, "Why Billy Wilder Belongs in the Pantheon"; see also Hugh S. Manon, "Some Like It Cold: Fetishism in Billy Wilder's 'Double Indemnity,'" *Cinema Journal* (Summer 2005). JM articles on *The Front Page*; BW comparison of *His Girl Friday* to *The Awful Truth* and considering gay theme in *Avanti!*: JM-TM. JL on BW's version of *The Front Page* and absence of overlapping dialogue: MW, "Saint Jack"; BW on ending line of play put on film: Jack Smith articles, "Oh, for the Hard-Bitten Cynicism of Days Gone By," *LAT*, March 7, 1990, and "'The Front Page': A Picture Worth a Thousand Words," *LAT*, November 23, 1992. David Walsh on *Ninotchka* and political satire: *"How Did Lubitsch Do It?* Joseph McBride's Engaging Study of Filmmaker Ernst Lubitsch," *World Socialist Web Site*, wsws.org, April 24, 2019; Walsh, "American Film Actor Kirk Douglas (1916–2020)," wsws.org, February 10, 2020. BW, "I never": JM-TM. The Waldorf Statement appears as "Johnson Gives Industry Policy on Commie Jobs," *DV*, November 26, 1947, along with "Drum Cited 10 Out of Pix." FT review of *Stalag 17*: see notes for chap. 6.

Reviews of *One, Two, Three*, *Berliner Zeitung*: Karasek; Bosley Crowther, *NYT*, December 22, 1961. Spike Lee coined "Magical Negro" term in 2001: Matt Zoller Seitz, "The Offensive Movie Cliché That Won't Die," *Salon*, September 14, 2010. QSCRIBE, "Billy Wilder: My Gay Icon," shadowproof.com, March 27, 2009. Vincent Canby review of BW's *Front Page*, *NYT*, December 19, 1974. Dennis Cozzalio, "The Strange Case of Billy Wilder's *Buddy Buddy*," trailersfromhell.com, February 20, 2016. JM-MW review, *The Private Life of Sherlock Holmes*, including BW, "He's always fascinated me" and quote from *Films in Review*.

Other Sources

Bertolt Brecht radio play *Der Lindberghflug* (*Lindbergh's Flight*), with music by Kurt Weill and Paul Hindemith, 1929. Wendell Mayes kept track of *Spirit of St. Louis* story line after

BW left: JM interview with RM. Clint Eastwood interest in playing Lindbergh: East-wood to BW, October 26, 1954, and Arthur Lubin to BW, October 20, 1954; and Lind-bergh-BW 1957 correspondence about the film: Lindbergh to BW, April 9; BW to Lindbergh, April 23, Heritage Auctions website, entertainment.ha. Eugenia Wilder death in Plaszów camp: see notes to chap. 1. BW leaving Paramount: Schlöndorff in *Never Be Boring.*

First version of *One, Two, Three* screenplay and subsequent drafts (quoted in Sikov): ID papers, Wisconsin Historical Society. BW, "Ain't that nice?" *Portrait of a "60% Per-fect Man."* Exchange (1994) on BW quips about blacklist: JM to members of Los Angeles Film Critics Association proposing BW for career achievement award, November 23, 1994; Dorothy H. Rochmis to JM, November 24; JM to Rochmis, November 30; Roch-mis to JM, December 4; the award was presented by JM on behalf of LAFCA on Janu-ary 17, 1995, and an adapted version of his speech published in *Written By* as "Thank You, Mr. Wilder." Secret testimony before HUAC in Los Angeles, May 1947: researched by JM in previously sealed files released in 2001, National Archives, Washington, D.C. "Hollywood Fights Back" radio broadcast, ABC, November 26, 1947. Michael Schlesinger audio commentary for *One, Two, Three*: Kino Lorber Blu-ray edition, 2017.

Uncut screenplay, *The Private Life of Sherlock Holmes*, and video and audio extras on *Sherlock Holmes* homevideo versions; ID and BW to JM on the cutting. PD, "melan-choly," BBC Radio 3 "Billy Wilder" program. "Watergate makes me come": BW-ID, *Buddy Buddy* screenplay, August 8, 1980, final draft with revisions on January 12, 1981. FT to JM in 1970s about male buddy genre in Hollywood. Carol Burnett embarrassment over *The Front Page*: interview with Conan O'Brien on *Conan*, TBS, May 21, 2018, You-Tube. ID and PD on *The Front Page* and ID on "Present-day comedy": interviews with JM. PD on *Buddy Buddy*: JM interview and in *Never Be Boring.*

CHAPTER 9: "TAP-DANCING ON THE GRAVE OF HOLLYWOOD"

Books

Goldwyn line about "the bitter with the sour": excised from CB-BW-Marshman screen-play for *Sunset Blvd.* BW-ID screenplay for *Avanti!* revised April 18, 1972, quoted from Trudy Bolter with her comments, "Going Backwards with Billy Wilder: *Avanti!*, A Ghost Play," in Guilbert. Taylor play *Avanti!*: see notes for chap. 9. Luciano Vincenzoni worked on *Avanti!*: Sikov. BW wanting Pamela "to be real fat": Crowe; Karasek. D. H. Law-rence, "Never trust the artist": *Studies in Classic American Literature* (New York: Thomas Seltzer, 1923). Catalogue for *The Billy Wilder Collection* (New York: Christie's, Novem-ber 13, 1989). BW, "We very" and comments on Hal Ashby and Bernardo Bertolucci: *Film-makers on Filmmaking*, vol. 1. Thoreau, *Walden*. Kurt Vonnegut novel, *Mother Night*

(New York: Harper & Row, 1966). Lela Rogers's role in blacklisting: Ceplair-Englund; Navasky. Thalberg, "the business of creating illusions": Mark A. Viera, *Irving Thalberg: Boy Wonder to Producer Prince* (Berkeley: University of California Press, 2009). Kevin Brownlow, *The Parade's Gone By . . .* (New York: Knopf, 1968). BW's admiration for various films made by other directors in his old age: Karasek; Crowe; 1976 AFI seminar (also see sources below); on *Schindler's List*: see notes for chap. 3.

Thomas Tryon novella *Fedora* in his collection *Crowned Heads* (New York: Knopf, 1976. Problems making *Fedora*: JM-TM; Crowe; biographies and other sources listed below. BW on casting Holden in *Fedora*: Chandler. Marthe Keller complaints about BW: Thomas, *Golden Boy*; and other sources below. Renoir, director should change script, not actor: JM, *What Ever Happened to Orson Welles?: A Portrait of an Independent Career* (Lexington: University Press of Kentucky, 2006). BW remembering Katharina Schratt gesture: Chandler. Rudyard Kiping's poem "Mandalay" (published in the *Scots Observer*, June 21, 1890) was first collected in his book *Barrack-Room Ballads, and Other Verses* (London: Methuen, 1892); Kipling, "YOUTH HAD BEEN": "Venus Annodomini," *Plain Tales from the Hills* (London: Thacker, Spink, 1888), quoted in BW-ID, *Fedora* screenplay. W. Somerset Maugham play, *East of Suez* (New York: George Doran, 1922); BW on influence of *Rain*: the 1922 play by John Colton and Clemence Randolph (New York: Boni and Liveright, 1923), from a short story by Maugham, "Miss Thompson," *The Smart Set*, April 1921. Aristotle on the mask in his *Poetics*.

Holden's death: Thomas, *Golden Boy*. BW, "I was retired": Chandler; ID telling BW he was dying: biographies; BW, "I quit" and "Wilder's Tips for Writers": Crowe. BW to Stephen Sondheim on idea for musical version of *Sunset Blvd.*: Sondheim letter to Sikov, July 21, 1997; Sikov on Andrew Lloyd Webber version. Evelyn Waugh's novel *Scoop* (London: Chapman and Hall, 1938); and Christopher Hitchens's introduction to 2000 ed. (London: Penguin Classics).

BW on explicit cinema: "Well, one" and farting: 1976 AFI seminar. BW late projects: *One, Two, Three* set in China: Sikov; comedy about a Parisian locksmith: Zolotow, Karasek; *Josephine Mutzenbacher:* see notes for chap. 3. *Schindler's List*: see notes for previous chapters. David Brown offered script: Chandler. Oliver Stone offered BW *Reversal of Fortune*: Stone, *Chasing the Light: Writing, Directing, and Surviving* Platoon, Midnight Express, Scarface, Salvador, *and the Movie Game* (Boston: Houghton Mifflin Harcourt, 2020). BW job with Jerry Weintraub at UA and on Brian De Palma's *Wise Guys:* Sikov; Lally; Peter Bart, *Fade Out: The Calamitous Final Days of MGM* (New York: Anchor, 1991). Audrey Wilder, "They will never": McGee to JM. BW worked on autobiography with Herman Gollob: Sikov (misspells name as Gollub). BW on ending of *The Apartment* and "I just wanted": Chandler. BW, "Is that all?": Karasek. Woody Allen, "Billy Wilder's best movie": Eric Lax, *Woody Allen: A Biography* (New York: Knopf, 1991). BW, "I'll never retire": Zolotow. Fernando Trueba Academy Award tribute to BW, March 21, 1994: Karasek.

Articles

JM review of *Avanti!,* "The Importance of Being Ernst," *Film Heritage,* Summer 1973. BW, "the reevaluation," returning to Europe, and comment on JL mantra, "Magic time!": Michel Ciment, "Nouvel Entretien avec Billy Wilder (sur *Avanti!*)," *Positif* (January 1974). BW, *"Avanti!,* I wiped," "Unless you are," "I get to see," "the obligatory," and on Gold-wynisms: JM-TM. W, EL "would have had": Bradshaw. BW, "I could never": Farber, "A Cynic Ahead of His Time." James Agee review, *The Miracle of Morgan's Creek, Nation,* February 5, 1944. Problems making *Fedora:* RM, "The Life and Hard Times of *Fedora*"; JM-TM. Vincent Canby review of *Bobby Deerfield, NYT,* September 30, 1977. Keller complaints: Roderick Mann, "Wilder Tips His Hat to 'Fedora's' Keller," *LAT,* March 16, 1979; "I didn't recognize": Pamela Andriotakis, *People,* November 28, 1977. Reviews of *Fedora* (1979): Janet Maslin; *NYT,* April 15, 1979; Sarris, *Village Voice,* April 16; Dave Kehr, *Chicago Reader,* June 22, 1979; French reviews: Gemünden, *A Foreign Affair.*

BW late projects and "internal exile": Geoffrey Macnab, "Billy Wilder: Reconsidering the final chapter of Hollywood's most revered and overlooked director," *Independent* (UK), July 28, 2016 (JM interview). BW's admiration for various films by other directors: JM-TM; Kakutani, 1996; Crowe, "Billy, How Did You Do It?," *Sight & Sound* (December 2005). BW on Holden's death: Stephen Farber, "Wilder: A Cynic Ahead of His Time," *NYT,* December 6, 1981. Penguin Random House website on Herman Gollob; autobiography project title: Aljean Harmetz, "Seven Years Without Directing, and Billy Wilder Is Feeling Itchy," *NYT,* October 3, 1988. Consulting at UA: Bart, "Running Wilder: H'w'd Needs a Dose of the Master," *DV,* April 22, 1996, quoting BW; Geraldine Fabrikant, "Chief Is Out at UA," *NYT,* April 15, 1986 (on Weintraub's ousting). BW, "I don't pick up" and "fell off": Meg Sullivan, "For Billy Wilder, the Pictures Keep Getting Bigger," *Los Angeles Daily News,* February 1, 1994. BW, "I'm late": Pat Kirkham, "Saul Bass and Billy Wilder: In Conversation," *Sight & Sound* (June 1995), reprinted in Horton.

JM speech honoring BW with LAFCA career award: "Thank You, Mr. Wilder" (lunch with producer: JM conversation with Renee Missel). BW, "Medals": *Los Angeles,* June 1982. BW, "Yes, I have": Farber, "Magnificent Obsession," *New West,* May 7, 1979. "Auction of Billy Wilder's Art Fetches \$32.6 Million," *LAT,* November 14, 1989. Audrey Wilder gift to museum and Wilder estate bequest to hospital: Gary Baum, "Billy Wilder Estate Gives \$11 Million to Children's Hospital Los Angeles," *HR,* December 19, 2012. *The Foreskin Saga*: JM-TM; John Gregory Dunne in George Plimpton, "The *Paris Review* Interview," *Paris Review* (Spring 1996), reprinted in Dunne, *Regards: The Selected Nonfiction of John Gregory Dunne* (New York: Thunder's Mouth, 2006). Allen, "even though he's": Sheila Johnston, "Film-makers on film: Woody Allen," *Telegraph* (UK), March 21, 2005. Trueba Oscar tribute to BW: Kevin Thomas, "A Director on Heroes and a Hopeful 'Epoque,'" *LAT,* March 28, 1994; Kirkham.

Other Sources

BW-ID, *Avanti!* screenplay (including draft with annotations in ID's papers at the Wisconsin Historical Society). Cut sequence in *The Private Life of Sherlock Holmes:* see notes for chap. 6. JL and ID on *Avanti!*: JM interview notes. JM interviews with Vincenzoni on his work on *Avanti!* and with Matthau, "Brilliant repartee." ID, "Tonight" and BW quoting Samuel Goldwyn: *The American Film Institute to Billy Wilder.* JM interview with RM on his relationship with BW; BW on rejection of *Avanti!*; problems with *Fedora*; BW's late projects, including the one on Le Pétomane; and Audrey Wilder, "They will never." Le Pétomane and project about old actors' home: JM interview with Trueba.

BW-ID, *Fedora* screenplay. JM interview with PD: BW-ID discussing project about New Hollywood before *Fedora*; PD on ID's view of the film, "They were victims," "Billy's English," and Universal proposing Katharine Hepburn and Audrey Hepburn: *Swan Song*, which also includes Harold Nebenzal on the filming. HH on Holden: JM interview. *Fedora* cut scenes (including "C'est ci bon") as extras on 2016 British Blu-ray and DVD eds., Eureka!/Masters of Cinema, which include a 2013 restoration of the film. Problems between BW and Keller: JM interview with RM; Keller in *Swan Song*; Mario Adorf in *Never Be Boring*. French and German reviews in German advertisements: *Swan Song*. Frank Capra, "A film faces the audience": speech he wrote for *The American Film Institute Salute to James Stewart*, CBS-TV, 1980. Audio recordings of original undubbed *Fedora* soundtrack: provided by RM to JM. Bill Krohn, "Billy Wilder tap-dancing": to JM. BW's cuts in *Fedora:* RM interview; inventory of materials donated to Academy Film Archive by RM: letter from Michael Friend, archive director, to RM, December 11, 1996; Robert Fischer's inventory of cuts, "FEDORA/Full version viewing report," Los Angeles, January 2013; anon., "FEDORA—Final Changes After Answer Print—April, 1978."

PD, "quite vociferously," "pending doom," and "It nearly killed my father": BBC Radio 3 "Billy Wilder" program. BW on ID telling him he was dying: WGA memorial to ID, in *Billy Wilder Speaks*; also JM interview with Trueba. BW's admiration for various films made in his old age: to JM; Schlöndorff-Grischow. Marconi-Tresgot documentary with BW quotes and other information on his art collecting and collaboration with Bruce Houston, and comment to JL, "I'm happy": also, JM interview with artist Judy Schavrien. Claudius Seidl and Schlöndorff on BW's forced retirement: *Never Be Boring*. BW to JM on Karasek biography. BW refusing Samuel Goldwyn Jr. offer to remake *Ball of Fire*, 1978: witnessed by JM in BW's office and discussed with BW. BW joke about trouble peeing: LAFCA acceptance speech; JM witnessed BW's tongue-lashing of photographer after LAFCA event, 1995. Audrey Wilder donating BW's scripts to WGA: *Written By* editor Richard Stayton to JM.

Alfred Hitchcock letter to BW, June 29, 1960. Spielberg on BW, "the greatest writer-director": "Billy Wilder Celebrates His Birthday with Hollywood's Elite Directors," accessed on YouTube, posted September 30, 2015, from *Meet Me at the Club*, d. Stewart Maclennan, at Beverly Hills Country Club party. Pedro Almodóvar on BW: "Almodóvar

Looks to Films of Wilder," *Chicago Tribune*, March 2, 1989; D. T. Max, "The Evolution of Pedro Almodóvar," *New Yorker*, November 28, 2016. Robert Towne, "Writer Robert Towne on Billy Wilder's *Sunset Blvd.*," AFI video, 2011, accessed on YouTube. Orson Welles, "wonderful Billy Wilder": *The Merv Griffin Show*, taped October 9, 1985, broadcast October 15. Spike Lee on *Ace in the Hole*: introducing the film with Robert Osborne on TCM, 2012, accessed on YouTube. Trueba Oscar acceptance speech and BW: JM interview with Trueba; Oscar acceptance speech text, 1994, oscars.org, and video on YouTube.

ACKNOWLEDGMENTS AND INFLUENCES

Articles

"To Aristophanes & Back," *Time*, May 14, 1956, cover profile of Marilyn Monroe (written by Brad Darrach from reporting by Ezra Goodman et al.). Legion of Decency warning on *Some Like It Hot*: David Eldridge, "*Some Like It Hot*," Library of Congress, n.d., loc.gov/static/programs/national-film-preservation-board; Clarissa Saunders, "Nothing but praise for it as a hilariously funny movie," April 2, 2017, *Stars and Letters* (blog), including March 5, 1959, letter from Rev. Thomas F. Little of Legion of Decency to Geoffrey Shurlock of PCA. Father Raymond Parr on *KMS*: *Variety*, December 23, 1964. BW on *Sunset Blvd.*, "valentine": JM-TM.

12.1 (top) Wilder being interviewed by young reporter Joseph McBride on the set of *The Front Page* in 1974. (Universal.)

12.2 (bottom) Wilder talking with the author in 1995 at a West Hollywood hotel before receiving the career achievement award from the Los Angeles Film Critics Association. (Courtesy of Sam Robbins.)

ACKNOWLEDGMENTS
AND INFLUENCES

I SUPPOSE it all began with Marilyn Monroe. At the lowest point of my life, in the spring of 1956, *Time* magazine published a cover story on Marilyn. It opened with "Sin, sin. sin," an imprecation often thrown at her in childhood, and her account of dreaming about "standing up in church without any clothes on, and all the people there were lying at my feet on the floor of the church, and I walked naked, with a sense of freedom." The cover was adorned with a golden-hued painting of the reigning screen love goddess smiling gently with bright cherry-red lips. The profile is remarkably insightful into her life and image, though I hardly realized that at the time, since I was only eight years old.

As a deeply repressed Catholic boy living in a suburb of Milwaukee, Wisconsin, I was just discovering my sexual impulses. And I was physically and psychologically abused in those days at home and at school. That spring I was in a state of anguish over the abuse and my guilt feelings over the rules of the church, which I found maddeningly illogical and impossible to follow. In the midst of this mishegoss, the hope of salvation arrived in the form of *Time* and Marilyn Monroe. Her air of unbridled libertinism seemed an alluring promise of a better way to live. Though I was a regular moviegoer from childhood, I had not seen a Monroe movie by that time. I didn't know who Billy Wilder was, and I had not seen *The Seven Year Itch*, his 1955 comedy with Marilyn virtually playing herself as a sexual fantasy figure. I had no idea how central Wilder's films were in lampooning, attacking, and eroding our repressed, puritanical American mindset in the 1950s. But like me, the nation was subconsciously eager for change, yearning for liberation that would finally come in the following decade when the old sociopolitical norms exploded in the midst of national turmoil.

Now we dissolve to 1959, and I am watching *Some Like It Hot* at my neighborhood theater in Wauwatosa, the Tosa Theatre (today more felicitously known as the Rosebud Cinema). Somehow I made it to Wilder's bawdy sex farce despite the Legion of

Decency's slapping the film with a B rating ("Morally Objectionable in Part for All"). The cultural watchdogs of our church warned that "the dialogue was not only 'double entendre' but outright smut," and with its suggestive costuming and "clear inferences of homosexuality and lesbianism," the film was "seriously offensive to Christian and traditional standards of morality and decency." Although *Some Like It Hot* actually upholds a higher sense of morality in dealing in an unorthodox, enlightened way with how men should treat women, I was less cognizant of that at the time than of how *Some Like It Hot* illuminated realms of sexuality I had never dreamed existed. I was transfixed by the lubricious spectacle of Marilyn's breasts virtually exposed onscreen in a milky, semitransparent dress by Orry-Kelly and by the transgressive behavior of two men camping it up in women's makeup and dresses.

Billy Wilder was becoming my sex education teacher. The film that marked one of the key turning points in exorcising my Catholic guilt was *Irma la Douce*. It was playing at one of the more prestigious downtown Milwaukee theaters in 1963. *Irma* advanced my liberation when I was sixteen not only with its ample, lewdly displayed female flesh but also with Wilder's frank, unabashed, come-hither sense of erotic comedy. I enjoyed the quirky relationship between the winsome Shirley MacLaine as a good-hearted, matter-of-fact Parisian hooker and Jack Lemmon as an uptight but romantic policeman, and I identified with the sexual mania Lemmon exuded after his precipitous fall from puritanism.

The impact *Irma la Douce* had on me can be measured by the comical difficulty I had sitting through it. I was so scandalized I kept stalking out before it was over and going back to see it again. The first time I left indignantly in the middle, flushed with guilt and shame. The second time I made it almost to the end but dashed out in alarm when Irma is about to give birth in a church shortly after her shotgun wedding to her pimp, which I found outrageously sacrilegious. The third time, though, I managed to make it all the way. My best friend in boyhood, Bob Kidera, who left Milwaukee in our youth and eventually became an acclaimed mystery writer, reminded me recently that we saw a double bill of *Irma* and *Some Like It Hot* downtown when he returned to our hometown for a visit in 1964. He said I "insisted" we see those two Wilder films.

I may not have fully realized it, but I was on my way to an open-eyed engagement with the adult sexuality shown by Wilder in his tolerant and compassionate manner. I am not sure how much I recognized that *Irma* is a romance, even a sentimental romance, beneath its superficial trappings of depravity. But I was affected by Wilder's flair for pushing the envelope of censorship, his acerbic social criticism, and his unflinching candor about human flaws. And in time I would come to appreciate and champion his undervalued, still inadequately recognized romanticism, which came to dominate his later work.

Thanks in large part to Wilder, my first overt act toward rebellion against my religious upbringing involved the movies. While home from the University of Wisconsin, Madison, in the winter of 1965, I refused to stand for the annual church pledge to support the Legion of Decency. My father was furious. At college I was already in the process of choosing movies as my new religion. I was rebelling against the repressive organization that had slapped a "Condemned" rating on Wilder's corrosive morality play *Kiss Me, Stupid* the year before. I was not able to see that film on its first run because the Milwaukee director of the Legion of Decency, Father Raymond Parr, pressured a local theater to cancel it as a 1964 Christmas attraction. Sounding like the minister in the movie, the priest told the press, "I said that I considered it offensive, though I haven't seen it." It would take me a few years to catch up with *Kiss Me, Stupid*, *Sunset Blvd.*, *The Apartment*, *Ace in the Hole*, and other major Wilder works when I was a student film buff in Madison, where I started writing about him.

My first attempt was "The Private Life of Billy Wilder," the career profile written with Michael Wilmington and published in *Film Quarterly* in 1970. We followed that essay by reviewing for the same publication Wilder's neglected, revealingly personal and moving *Private Life of Sherlock Holmes*. And I wrote an essay for *Film Heritage*, "The Importance of Being Ernst," on Wilder's captivating, seriously undervalued 1972 romantic comedy *Avanti!* After moving to California, I spent a delightful and revelatory day in 1974 observing Wilder at work on his newspaper comedy *The Front Page* at Universal, taking time off from my job as a reporter at the Riverside *Press-Enterprise,* fifty miles from Hollywood. I interviewed Wilder, I. A. L. Diamond, producer Paul Monash, Lemmon and Walter Matthau, and cinematographer Jordan Cronenweth. I wrote about that invaluable experience for Boston's *Real Paper* and the British film magazine *Sight and Sound* and saved the unedited notes of those interviews for future use. As a fellow reporter, I felt an immediate rapport with Wilder, much as I did when I met another veteran writer-director who also began as a reporter, Samuel Fuller; we all talked the same language.

When I moved to Hollywood later that summer to try my hand as a screenwriter—failing to heed the scathing cautionary tale of *Sunset Blvd.*—I found myself renting, by sheer chance (or was it?), a cockroach-infested apartment in the same neighborhood as the dump where the down-and-out Joe Gillis lived, his Alto Nido Apartment House "above Franklin and Ivar." My new digs were also near the seedy apartment hotel on Ivar Street where Nathanael West wrote *The Day of the Locust* (set in its fictional equivalent, the San Bernardino Arms). When West wrote his nightmarish novel, Ivar was called "Lysol Alley" because the buildings reeked of disinfectant, and when I complained about the cockroaches in my apartment, the manager left a spray can of Raid outside my door. It's not for nothing that every Hollywood screenwriter identifies with Joe Gillis, but when I mentioned to Wilder in 1978 that after following in his character's footsteps, I found *Sunset Blvd.* a virtual documentary about Hollywood, he told me with a philosophical shrug, "It's a valentine."

While working as a screenwriter in 1978, I had a lively two-day interview with Wilder, mostly about what I consider his unjustly maligned and neglected later work, with Todd McCarthy for *Film Comment*. It and the article I wrote on *The Front Page* for the *Real Paper* are reprinted in a collection edited by Robert Horton, *Billy Wilder: Interviews* (2002), and in my collection *Two Cheers for Hollywood: Joseph McBride on Movies* (2017); the interview was reprinted in 2013 in translation in a Brazilian anthology on Wilder. When he died in 2002, I published a tribute as the cover story in the Writers Guild of America magazine *Written By*, "Thank You, Mr. Wilder: Billy Wilder, 1906–2002," based on the speech I had given while presenting him with the Los Angeles Film Critics (LAFCA) career achievement award in 1995.

Although I was fortunate to watch Wilder at work and to have numerous opportunities to speak with him over the years, experiences that have contributed greatly to my understanding of his films, like most people I found it difficult to get to know him closely on a personal basis, since he held his emotions so close. Although he was always an enthusiastic, kaleidoscopically witty interviewee, skewering changes in the industry with acerbic sarcasm, and though he did open up candidly with me about his films, he was more evasive about his personal life, parrying such questions with obfuscation or dismissing the probing with quips. Some of the weaker books about Wilder fail to delve beneath the surface of his wit, consisting mostly of collections of his most familiar bons mots and droll anecdotes, although even those books cannot help be entertaining.

In writing this critical study, I have often felt like Dr. Watson in *The Private Life of Sherlock Holmes*, trying to probe the firmly barricaded personality of a legendary man who gratified the press's need for a colorful and amusing character but remained a somewhat enigmatic figure because of his emotional aloofness. Following up on the affinities Wilder shares with Ernst Lubitsch, I began writing what I planned as a joint study of the master and his most celebrated acolyte in 2009. I thought it was a clever idea to study them together. I pursued that concept for a while and researched their common roots in Berlin. But I realized what an impractical approach it was to write a joint critical study of these directors, both for length considerations but, more important, because I came to understand how different they actually are. I came to realize that Wilder's sporadic aspirations to emulate Lubitsch and the passionate sense of kinship he felt toward his mentor reflect only a part of Wilder's artistic personality and not always the most characteristic or fertile part. But my extensive research on their shared backgrounds benefited this book, as it did the critical study that became *How Did Lubitsch Do It?*, published in 2018 by Columbia University Press.

Most, though not all, of the many books on Wilder are sketchy about his work in Europe as a journalist and screenwriter and concentrate on the films he cowrote and directed in Hollywood (after he made his directorial debut in France). And much of the discussion of Wilder concentrates on several films generally acclaimed as classics, while other major films, less frequently revived, and films regarded (accurately or not) as minor works or failures have tended to be brushed over. While admiring his recognized classics, I also consider some of those lesser-known or disregarded films as among his best work, including a few of the films he wrote for other directors.

How Billy Wilder became Billy Wilder before he became a director—his apprenticeship as a journalist and screenwriter—is a large part of this book, an area of research and analysis that makes even his most widely known films as a writer-director more intelligible. Biographical insights are valuable in understanding his work, but the answers to the fundamental questions about his enigmatic, somewhat paradoxical artistic personality are mostly to be found in the work, more than in his public persona, as is usually true with an artist.

Since this book is drawn from more than fifty years of thinking, talking, reading, teaching, and writing about Billy Wilder, while watching his films over and over with great pleasure, I have many debts to people who have helped me along the way. And since this is a critical study, not a biography, among the people whose influence has been most valuable are the authors whose work on Wilder helped establish a factual groundwork for study of his life and work and those who have offered insightful commentaries on the films. I have acknowledged them along the way in the text of this book, but here I express my special thanks again to the authoritative biographies by Ed Sikov and by Andreas Hutter and Klaus Kamolz, in particular, with their diligent, groundbreaking research and indefatigable effort in telling the story of Wilder's life and helping trace the themes and sources of his work.

I also benefited from the research and writing of other biographers, notably Maurice Zolotow, Hellmuth Karasek, Kevin Lally, and Charlotte Chandler; Cameron Crowe's interview book; Horton's collection of Wilder interviews; and the critical studies by Neil Sinyard and Adrian Turner, Gerd Gemünden, and others, including the contributors to the anthologies of criticism edited by Karen McNally and Georges-Claude Guilbert. Nancy Steffen-Fluhr's essay in the McNally book, "Palimpsest: The Double Vision of Exile," was especially helpful in unlocking certain mysteries beneath the surface of Wilder's work. Charles Brackett's diaries, edited for publication by Anthony Slide, offered many insights, although often skewed, into Brackett's long collaboration with Wilder and Wilder's personality. Several books on the making of individual films provided valuable information.

We are fortunate that numerous Wilder screenplays (written with Brackett and Diamond and others) have been published. Other scripts that have not been published have been made available by websites, collectors, and archives. The two German-language collections of Wilder's journalism in Vienna and Berlin—edited by Rolf Aurich, Hutter, Wolfgang Jacobsen, and Günter Krenn, *"Billie": Billy Wilder's Viennese Journalism*, and Klaus Siebenaar, *The Prince of Wales Is Going on Vacation: Berlin Reports, Features and Reviews of the Twenties*, are fascinating and provided a basis for my study of his previously underexamined formative work in that field. For expert help with translations of German printed material and films, I thank Christiane Buchner, Eszter Tompa, and Mason Kamana Allred.

Many writers have written insightfully about the European exile community in Hollywood, of which Wilder was an important part, and about its members' profound influence on American culture. I have benefited from the cultural and historical contextualization these studies provide, as well as from numerous books on the history and culture of the Austro-Hungarian and Wilhelmine empires, in which Wilder grew up, and the Weimar Republic era, during which he worked as a journalist and screenwriter before fleeing the Nazi takeover in 1933. Scholarly studies of German cinema and exile cinema have also been useful, notably those by Gemünden and Klaus Kreimeier and the anthology on the Weimar Republic edited by Anton Kaes, Martin Jay, and Edward Dimendberg. All these books and other published sources listed here are fully credited in the Notes on Sources.

Many journalists interviewed and covered Wilder over the years and had the pleasure, as I did, of talking with that former Racing Reporter and following his acerbic and insightful observations on the film business and his life and art. Critical commentaries on Wilder and reviews of his films by Andrew Sarris, François Truffaut, Joan Didion, and numerous other writers in journals and newspapers in both English and other languages contributed to my understanding.

For facilitating my own writings about Wilder and interviews with the director in periodicals, I am especially grateful to my collaborators Michael Wilmington and Todd McCarthy; my editors Ernest Callenbach (*Film Quarterly*), Anthony Macklin (*Film Heritage*), Stuart Byron (*Real Paper*, Boston), Penelope Houston and David Wilson (*Sight and Sound*), Thomas M. Pryor (*Daily Variety*), Richard Corliss (*Film Comment*), Elif Cercel (*Directors World / Creative Planet*), and Richard Stayton (*Written By*); and *Daily Variety* publisher Michael Silverman.

I am grateful to Frank Tarzi and Bret Wood of Kino Lorber for asking me to record audio commentaries for the Wilder films *Irma la Douce*, *A Foreign Affair*, *Five Graves to Cairo*, *The Lost Weekend*, *The Fortune Cookie*, and *The Emperor Waltz*, and to the expert technician I worked with in a Berkeley recording studio, Alberto Hernandez.

Documentary filmmakers who have made portraits of Wilder have provided intimate and wide-ranging views of him and his work. Foremost among these are Volker Schlöndorff and Gisela Grischow, for their lengthy interview, conducted in German with the help of biographer Karasek; and Annie Tresgot, for her documentary portrait of Wilder (with the French critic Michel Ciment) and her essay film on his art collecting (with Michael Marconil). Robert Fischer's probing documentary on Wilder's late feature *Fedora* is an unusually valuable record of an individual film. I am grateful to Clara and Julia Kuperberg for including me in their documentary *Billy Wilder: Nobody's Perfect* (2016) and several other documentaries over the years on Hollywood history.

Archives with important collections of material on Wilder films and/or copies of his films include the Margaret Herrick Library of the Academy of Motion Picture Arts and Sciences, Beverly Hills; the Writers Guild Foundation Shavelson-Webb Library, Writers Guild of America West, Los Angeles (Wilder's collection of scripts); the Wisconsin Historical Society, Madison (Diamond's collection of scripts); the Deutsch Kinemathek (German Cinematheque), with thanks to Julia Riedel; Das Bundesarchiv's Abteiling Filmarchiv (Federal Film Archive), Berlin, with thanks to Carola Okrug; the Filmmuseum im Müncher Stadtmuseum (Munich Film Museum), with thanks to Stefan Drössler; and the Osterreichisches Filmmuseum (Austrian Film Museum), Vienna, with thanks to Regina Schlagnitweit. Eszter Tompa translated for me in Berlin while I researched Wilder and Lubitsch at those institutions, and Fischer was also helpful in Berlin. I had translation assistance in Hebrew from Dror Izhar in Israel. Elmar Kruithoff in Denmark generously helped with my film research, and artist Judy Schavrien in Berkeley with her analysis of Wilder's taste in art.

I thank the late curator of film programming at the Los Angeles County Museum of Art, Ronald Haver, for inviting me to conduct a question-and-answer session with Wilder at the time of the release of *Fedora*. Thanks to Sam Robbins for taking photographs of me talking with Wilder at the LAFCA event. I spoke on *The Apartment* at both the University of California, Los Angeles, and the Christopher B. Smith Raphael Film Center, San Rafael (through the invitation of Richard Peterson). My appearances with Nicola Lubitsch at the Lubitsch festival honoring her father in 2018 in the Billy Wilder Theater of the UCLA Film and Television Archive, curated by Jan-Christopher Horak, were memorable occasions. I am grateful to hosts of several podcasts who have had me on their shows talking about films and politics.

I thank my students and teaching assistants (especially Pauline Lampert) in the School of Cinema at San Francisco State University for participating in courses I taught on Romantic Comedy: Lubitsch and Wilder, Women in the Films of Billy Wilder, and Auteur Cinema: Lubitsch and Wilder, and for giving me many insights as I tested my ideas with them. My colleagues in the School of Cinema have also been supportive of my research during the writing of this book, especially Chairs Celine Parreñas Shimizu, Britta Sjogren, Stephen Ujlaki, and Daniel Bernardi, as well as Steven Kovacs and Dean Andrew Harris.

In addition to Wilder and Diamond and their colleagues on *The Front Page*, I thank other key people who gave me thoughtful and revealing interviews about Wilder and his work: Paul Diamond (the screenwriter son of I. A. L. Diamond); Rex McGee (screenwriter, teacher, and Wilder protégé); writer-director Fernando Trueba (thanks to Nat Chediak); actress Hope Holiday; and writer Curt Siodmak. I had the pleasure of meeting Audrey Wilder, the filmmaker's second wife, at their apartment in 1995. She not only invited me to his memorial tribute at the Academy of Motion Picture Arts and Sciences in 2002 but also donated his script collection to the WGA Library because she appreciated my tribute to him in *Written By*. McGee generously provided me with valuable research materials on the making and postproduction of *Fedora*. Elisabeth Trautwein-Heymann, daughter of the late film composer Werner R. Heymann, sent me copies of her father's songs from the German film *A Blonde Dream*.

Many friends over the years have shared their thoughts about Wilder with me, including Wilmington, Truffaut, Kidera, McCarthy, Errol Morris, Bill Krohn, Sam Hamm, James Naremore, Patrick McGilligan, Fischer, Kaes, the Kuperbergs, David Bordwell and Kristin Thompson, Laura Truffaut and Stephen Wong, Marilyn Fabe and Griffin (Grif) Dix, David and Pamela Benson, Selise Eiseman, Dorothy Rochmis, Kirk Honeycutt, Sam Robbins, David Walsh, Ray Kelly, Julia Sweeney, Nick Redman, and Julie

Kirgo, and my family members Jessica McBride, Anne Bucher, Ruth O'Hara, and John McBride.

John Belton, who edited my book on Lubitsch for Columbia University Press, gave me extraordinary help with this book as well. John offered his expertise and wise judgment in reading the manuscript and making valuable suggestions that substantially improved it. His knowledge of film history is wide and his insights into critical analysis deeply helpful. I am grateful to have such a distinguished and sensitive and generous editor on my books. I also benefited considerably from the skillful and perceptive copyediting of this book by Anita O'Brien. Silvia Benvenuto carefully and creatively indexed the book. My other expert and valued collaborators at Columbia included the book designer, Lisa Hamm; the production editor, Susan Pensak; and senior editor Philip Leventhal, who acquired the book with John and gave it his enthusiastic, indefatigable, and wise support. It was a great pleasure working again with Columbia after we did our book on Wilder's mentor Ernst Lubitsch.

Ann Weiser Cornell, my beloved partner of more than two decades, has been a source of rich insight and witty commentary on Billy Wilder. We have shared many lively screenings and discussions of his films, and she applied her sharp eye and critical sense to helping edit my manuscript. Ann is a writer and teacher of keen psychological insight into human nature in all its parts, and she helped me understand the nuances of such a variegated artist. She has taught me much about life during our many years together. Her influence is profound on all my work, and her support, encouragement, and compassionate nature make our lives together a constant source of joy.

Joseph McBride
Berkeley, California
2009–2021

INDEX

FILM AND CULTURE

A series of Columbia University Press

Edited by John Belton